D1709536

This is the first introductory survey of twentieth-century music in the West to address popular music, art music and jazz on equal terms. It treats those forms as inextricably intertwined and sets them in a wide variety of social and critical contexts. The book comprises four sections – Histories, Techniques and Technologies, Mediation, Identities – with sixteen thematic chapters. Each of these explores a musical or cultural topic as it developed over many years, and as it appeared across a diversity of musical practices. In this way, the text introduces both key musical repertoire and critical-musicological approaches to that work. It historicises music and musical thinking, opening up debate in the present rather than offering a new but closed narrative of the past. In each chapter, an overview of the topic's chronology and main issues is illustrated by two detailed case studies.

TOM PERCHARD works on the history and historiography of jazz and popular music. He is the author of *After Django: Making Jazz in Postwar France* (2015) and *Lee Morgan: His Life, Music and Culture* (2006). He is the recipient of a Leverhulme Major Research Fellowship for a project on popular music in the postwar British home.

STEPHEN GRAHAM is the author of *Sounds of the Underground: A Cultural, Political and Aesthetic Mapping of Underground and Fringe Music* (2016). He has written articles on late style, fringe music writing and popular modernism. He is working on a book about noise music.

TIM RUTHERFORD-JOHNSON is a contemporary music journalist and musicologist. He is the author of *Music after the Fall: Modern Composition and Culture since 1989* (2017) and *The Music of Liza Lim* (forthcoming) and is editor of the sixth edition of the *Oxford Dictionary of Music* (2012).

HOLLY ROGERS works on experimental audiovisual culture and is author of *Sounding the Gallery: Video and the Rise of Art-Music* (2013). She has edited books on documentary film sound, experimental film soundtracks, transmedia, cybermedia and YouTube, and edits a book series for Bloomsbury on music and media as well as the journal *Sonic Scope*.

Twentieth-Century Music in the West

An Introduction

TOM PERCHARD
Goldsmiths, University of London

STEPHEN GRAHAM
Goldsmiths, University of London

TIM RUTHERFORD-JOHNSON
Independent Music Critic and Editor

HOLLY ROGERS
Goldsmiths, University of London

CAMBRIDGE
UNIVERSITY PRESS

CAMBRIDGE
UNIVERSITY PRESS

University Printing House, Cambridge CB2 8BS, United Kingdom

One Liberty Plaza, 20th Floor, New York, NY 10006, USA

477 Williamstown Road, Port Melbourne, VIC 3207, Australia

314–321, 3rd Floor, Plot 3, Splendor Forum, Jasola District Centre,
New Delhi – 110025, India

103 Penang Road, #05–06/07, Visioncrest Commercial, Singapore 238467

Cambridge University Press is part of the University of Cambridge.

It furthers the University's mission by disseminating knowledge in the pursuit of
education, learning, and research at the highest international levels of excellence.

www.cambridge.org
Information on this title: www.cambridge.org/9781108481984
DOI: 10.1017/9781108680899

First published 2022

Printed in the United Kingdom by TJ Books Limited, Padstow Cornwall

A catalogue record for this publication is available from the British Library.

Library of Congress Cataloging-in-Publication Data
Names: Perchard, Tom, author. | Graham, Stephen, author. |
Rutherford-Johnson, Tim, author. | Rogers, Holly, author.
Title: Twentieth-century music in the West : an introduction / Tom Perchard, Stephen
Graham, Tim Rutherford-Johnson, Holly Rogers.
Other titles: 20th-century music in the West
Description: [1.] | Cambridge, United Kingdom ; New York : Cambridge University Press,
2022. | Includes bibliographical references and index.
Identifiers: LCCN 2021059608 (print) | LCCN 2021059609 (ebook) | ISBN 9781108481984
(hardback) | ISBN 9781108680899 (ebook)
Subjects: LCSH: Music – 20th century – History and criticism. | Music – 20th century –
Analysis, appreciation. | Music trade – History – 20th century. | Music – Social aspects –
History – 20th century.
Classification: LCC ML197 .T98 2022 (print) | LCC ML197 (ebook) | DDC 780.9/04–dc23
LC record available at https://lccn.loc.gov/2021059608
LC ebook record available at https://lccn.loc.gov/2021059609

ISBN 978-1-108-48198-4 Hardback
ISBN 978-1-108-74173-6 Paperback

Contents

Figures

Tables

Acknowledgements

This book is based on a course that we have been teaching at Goldsmiths since 2008. One or two fragments of the present text date from the course's first outing, but the rest was developed over a decade as we tried to work out how to open up twentieth-century music to students of classical, jazz and popular music alike. First and foremost, then, we would like to thank those classmates – more than 1,000 of them at the time of writing – whose responses, insights and ideas have contributed so much to this project.

It has been a pleasure to work with our publisher, Kate Brett, and senior editorial assistant, Hal Churchman. Their enthusiasm, good humour and, above all, faith in the book have been unwavering, and are deeply appreciated. Thanks are also due to Frances Tye for her insightful and forensic copy-editing.

Many thanks to Tamsin Alexander for various literature suggestions, to Laura Moeckli, Fiamma Mozzetta and Regan Bowering for feedback on draft versions of the text – Regan also provided valuable editorial assistance – and to Leonel Segovia for his setting of the musical examples.

Thanks to those who generously granted permission to reprint copyright materials: Nam June Paik Estate, Museum moderner Kunst Stiftung Ludwig Wien (MUMOK), J. K. Miloszewski, Fiona Corbett-Clark (Edition Peters), Tom Farncombe (Hal Leonard Europe), Rebecca Smith (Williams Research Center, New Orleans) and the family of Ruth Crawford Seeger.

Finally, thanks to our families for their constant support: Coline and Stella (TP), Isobel, Lena and Ronnie (SG), Daisy, Jigs, Polly and John (HR) and Elizabeth, Miriam and Conor (TRJ).

Introduction

Steve Reich pitched up in San Francisco in September 1961. He was a young musician, one who had been taken by the early-century work of the Hungarian composer and folklorist Béla Bartók, and he had journeyed west from New York in the hope of studying with Leon Kirchner, a composer in the rough-lyric Bartók tradition who had been teaching at Mills College. But Kirchner had just left for Harvard, so Reich ended up working at Mills under Luciano Berio. Over the course of the previous decade, Berio had become identified as a figurehead of the European postwar avant-garde: his ultramodern serialist work was quite a different proposition to Kirchner's own.

As well as doyens of the contemporary music world like Berio, San Francisco was home to unique forms of counterculture and experimentalism. One collection of composers and artists, working in a building they called the San Francisco Tape Music Center, was making strides in the development of electro-acoustic music. The works Pauline Oliveros, Morton Subotnick and Ramon Sender were constructing using tape – still a very new medium – were radical not just in how they were made, but also in how this performer-less music was to be experienced. Reich came under those composers' influence in 1962 and soon began experimenting with tape himself, at first producing collages of looped and overdubbed samples. (His first tape player was shared with another Mills student, Phil Lesh, soon to become the bassist for the Grateful Dead.) In 1964 he played in the first performance of Terry Riley's *In C* at the Center, and in the same year in San Francisco's Union Square he made the recording of the Pentecostal preacher Brother Walter that would supply material for his first major tape work, realised at the Center: *It's Gonna Rain* (1965) (Bernstein 2008).

But Reich was not only interested in classical and experimental music. He also loved jazz, and had studied drumming as a teenager and at weekends played for dance bands. Around the time that Reich arrived on the West Coast, John Coltrane, one of the leading jazz musicians of the time, was playing a run of gigs at San Francisco's Jazz Workshop. The young composer watched Coltrane play many times during the early 1960s, and very probably went to some of these September shows (Potter 2000: 158). He had struck lucky. With his core sidemen of Eric Dolphy (alto sax, flute), Elvin Jones (drums), McCoy Tyner (piano) and Jimmy Garrison (bass), Coltrane at this time was assimilating influences from Africa, South Asia and Latin America to construct new principles for jazz form and harmony and an *oeuvre* that would become one of the century's most influential.

That September, Coltrane's band were still riding the wave from their first two albums in this outward-looking style, *Africa/Brass* (recorded for Atlantic on 23 May and 7 June 1961) and *Olé Coltrane* (recorded 25 May). The audience at the Jazz Workshop had been able to see the group just weeks before these sessions, where they played a run from 25 April to 7 May. It was now that the saxophonist started to introduce elements from West African music into his group's style. In an interview conducted on 2 May, right in the middle of his San Francisco shows, Coltrane explained something of what he was up to:

I have an African record at home, and they're singing these rhythms, some of their native rhythms, so I took part of it and gave it to the bass, and Elvin plays a part and McCoy managed to find something to play, some kind of chords. ... Still no melody, though. [laughs] I had to make the melody as I went along. But at least I'm trying to think of a melody; I'm not referring to the chords to get the melody. (Porter 1999: 213)

Coincidentally, Reich had been listening to similar records – newly issued LPs of West African, particularly Ghanaian, drumming. When Reich bought a copy of A. M. Jones' 1959 book *Studies in African Music* in 1962, he formed a better idea of how that music was constructed. Reich had been led to the book by a talk given by Gunther Schuller at the Ojai Festival, an event to which he had been taken by Berio. Models of form, harmony and gesture common to Euro-American art music composition would begin to seem problematic to the younger composer; at the same time, West African music – via Jones' transcriptions and Coltrane's jazz – became imprinted on his imagination (Reich 2002: 55–70). Over the coming years, all these influences would seep into the texture of Reich's music, helping develop a style that would later become known as 'minimalism'. By the century's end, that music would have become popular enough to make Reich one of the world's most admired and recognised composers.

Reich's story, in which musical success is born of cross-generational, cross-continental and cross-cultural encounter and immersion, is not unique. A glance at the biographies of the other names mentioned in the story above – Bartók, Berio, Coltrane, Oliveros, Lesh, Riley, Schuller – indicates the extent to which worlds of art, popular and folk music had become intertwined. In fact, it would be truer to say that music in the twentieth century was listened to, received and created like this more often than not: here was a newly small, newly connected world in which difference was confronted and synthesised as a matter of necessity, and as a matter of course. The examples are endless. George Gershwin listening to Igor Stravinsky; Stravinsky listening to Duke Ellington; Ella Fitzgerald listening to the Beatles; the Beatles listening to Karlheinz Stockhausen; Stockhausen listening to – if not much liking – Aphex Twin; and Aphex Twin listening to and being performed alongside Reich. As the century progressed, such meetings and reactions only increased, with artists as varied as Diamanda Galás, Outkast and Liza Lim all exploring styles of music from well outside their immediate generic contexts. Reich himself was listened to and referenced by many outside the fold of Western art music, including Brian Eno, Kraftwerk, Andrea Parker and Radiohead.

But despite the extent of such musical intermingling in the twentieth century, we still make strong distinctions between the territories these artists notionally inhabited; these distinctions are usually described by way of genre labels ('classical', 'pop', 'jazz', 'folk'), or else in terms which sort and segment what were diverse theories and practices into singular historical schools, or – a particular characteristic of the period – into 'isms' (like the minimalism we have already encountered). We imagine even the most cosmopolitan and mobile musicians speaking through interpreters at frontier checkpoints, rather than as stateless multilinguists going where they please. Why?

Music 'High' and 'Low'

A common understanding that Western music was comprised of discrete genres, styles and practices held sway throughout the century. And not all musics were seen as being created equal. However these styles were heard and felt by their followers, variously vested interests – institutional, academic, journalistic – worked to maintain a discursive separation of musical cultures, this most obviously embodied in the often-cited 'high/low', or highbrow/lowbrow, binary; here, 'high' forms, such as classical music, were granted the status of timeless art and 'low' forms, such as popular music, were seen as transient, commercial trivia.

In a study of this phenomenon made at one end of the century, Charles Hamm (1995) examines a book written at the other, Nathaniel I. Rubinkam's *Masterpieces of Melody and the Musical Art* (1906). Rubinkam's is a relatively obscure and unremarkable piece of music commentary, but almost for that reason it offers a good illustration of some of the commonplace assumptions about music and value that existed at the end of the Victorian era. Rubinkam writes that

'Classical Music', like Classical Literature, is that which has been recognized by the ages as of the best and highest class. Thus, in common acceptance, 'classical' is the antithesis of 'popular'. In a stricter sense, a classical production is one that has stood the test of time, and has come to be acknowledged by scholars and teachers of the art as a model of purity of style and form, and most worthy of emulation … because of [its] purity of style and form, universality of idea and permanent value to musical art.

In general terms that music is popular which makes an easy appeal to the masses. There can be no definition of popular music that will apply equally to the music of all nationalities, for the reason that standards of taste differ in the various countries. Less civilized peoples, even the wildest tribes of Africa or fiercest islanders of the South Seas, have a 'music', and rude musical instruments which are their own. They have their battle songs, and their funeral dirges.

Feasts, weddings, even cannibal orgies, are accompanied with some sort of a succession of sounds chanted with accompaniments pounded from rude instruments. The more civilized the people, the nearer to some form or rhythm and the more intelligible their music. (Quoted in Hamm 1995: 3–4)

These kinds of arguments found their basis in a racist, and indeed classist, assumption of the superiority of bourgeois European culture. Yet, as Hamm writes, they had come 'to dominate Western attitudes towards music throughout the modern era, enabling musicologists and critics to ignore all music lying outside the Western classical repertory' (Hamm 1995: 4).

Rubinkam's screed was a popularising product of the German Idealist tradition that stretched back to the eighteenth century (Hamilton 2007: 40–94), and the philosophical work by thinkers like Schopenhauer and Kant that gave rise to the related Romantic concepts of autonomous and absolute music. Autonomous music was that which did not have a purpose or function, for instance to act as the accompaniment for ritual or dance; absolute music was that which did not try to represent stories or scenes, as opera or programme music did. Instead, this music – almost always instrumental – aimed to lead the attentive listener towards something mystical, spiritual: a 'truth' beyond language and, most importantly, beyond body, time and place. The earthly and passing pleasures of bodily excitement were identified with coarse, simple and 'popular' leisure activities: communal song and dance, or feasting and sex – hence, presumably, Rubinkam's drum-backed cannibal orgies. 'Art' was something of much higher purpose and worth.

The alleged transcendence of absolute music was closely linked to its customary tonal and structural complexity. Most valued were music's organic integration (whereby all the many parts of the musical whole were derived from a few kernels of material) and its teleology or goal-direction (whereby those parts, in their development, grew a long and large-scale musical form to its climactic fruition). These methods were enabled by musical notation (Solie 1980; Tomlinson 2003); the lack of such technical complexity in non-notated popular and folk musics supposedly demonstrated their spiritual and historical triviality.

Rather than a thing of technique and artifice, such complexity and scale was often seen as an expression of that higher, natural musical law. This was something that could only be glimpsed and caught by the composer genius, one of the most important figures in Romantic discourse (Cook 1998: 32–3). Heinrich Schenker, one of the most influential music theorists of the late nineteenth and early twentieth centuries, argued that while the everyday composer wrote what he wanted to write, the genius was inhabited by a force beyond himself (and, as we will see later, it was always a 'he' that was intended).

The greatest European instrumental works were abstracted and collected into the Western art music 'canon', that is, an imaginary museum of musical works (Goehr 1992). These works and their composers were laid end to end, from Palestrina to Bach to Beethoven, each work or practice seen as the inevitable development of the last. This was an expression of historical positivism, an important intellectual trend of the later decades of the nineteenth century (Tomlinson 1984). While non-notated musics were doomed to pass into (deserved) obscurity, the essence of these great works, their truth and spirit, would forever remain accessible through the study of authoritative scores. The task of the performer – in theory if not always in practice – was to give listeners access to this 'superior force' of truth by playing the music in the manner most faithful to the genius composer's vision (see Monsaingeon 2001: 153).

The mystical ambiance that surrounded nineteenth-century Romantic arguments about art music's autonomy would dissipate in the next, more sceptical century, and the rather extreme ideological positions sketched out above were subject to much qualification. But many of the foundational distinctions between the artistic and the popular endured in updated from. While popular culture and music were routinely positioned as the regressive, anaesthetising products of the new 'culture industries', art music was now often staged as uniquely 'critical' of this debased reality (Greenberg 1989; Adorno 1991a/1938; 1991b), this a Marxian spin on the old Romantic vision of music's transcendence of earthly bonds.

Beyond these theoretical perspectives, the high/low dichotomy remained pervasive both in everyday cultural attitudes to different musical forms and in the persistence of stark social distinctions. Across the West, the practitioners and audiences of classical and popular musics were strongly associated with, respectively, higher- and lower-class positions, educational levels and income (Bourdieu 1984/1979). These distinctions were restated and reproduced in school and university curricula and, as a result, in academic music studies. Certainly, ethnomusicology – at first also known as 'comparative musicology', and devoted at first to the study of non-Western musics – and later, popular music studies, emerged in a small number of universities from mid-century. But these projects were outliers, and their scholars, methods and moral support often came from anthropology and sociology rather than music departments, the majority of which remained dedicated to the Western art music tradition.

Musicology and Music Historiography in the Late Twentieth Century

In the latter decades of the twentieth century, a number of disciplinary initiatives encouraged a gradual decline in this rigid, 'Eurocentric' ideology. Kaplan (1972), Brantlinger (1983) and Novitz (1992) offered critiques of the high/low distinction in general terms; Gracyk (1996), Griffiths (2011), Clarke (2007) and Taruskin (2007) offered critiques anchored in debates on music. These examples are taken from a whole range of texts and movements that attempted to complicate the kinds of cultural divisions – in which assumptions about the relative values of arts, 'races' and classes were all interwoven – that are sketched above (see Fisher 2005 for an overview).

For many of these writers the attempt to sort cultural groups and activities into hierarchies of worth, in which bourgeois European culture was always given supremacy, was abhorrent. Moreover, it entailed the imposition of boundaries where none existed, and the magicking away of productive musical relationships that had existed between forms. As trends in communication, cultural consumption, migration and education coalesced into what, by the end of the century, was thought of as 'globalisation', classifications seemed all the more moribund to many.

The old hierarchies were durable, but efforts to grapple with these musical and social complexities eventually came to the fore. The story of music studies in the twentieth century mirrors that of many other disciplines. In broad terms, musicology began the century subscribing to an idealist and positivist ideology anchored in transcendent *texts*. This disciplinary ideology gave way over the course of the twentieth century, at least in some respects, to a stylistic and methodological pluralism attuned to music's social and cultural *contexts*.

This movement was engineered from both in- and outside traditional music studies. The insiders were those scholars linked to what became known as the 'new musicology', which emerged in the mid-1980s. These writers responded to what Robert Fink (1998: 137–8) called a 'general disciplinary crisis' over the authority and legitimacy of art music and its study both by expanding the methodologies and conceptual approaches used to tackle canonical works, and, perhaps to a lesser extent, by expanding the range of music considered suitable for such study (see Kerman 1985; Kramer 1990; McClary 1991; Rosen 2000). The outsiders were ethnomusicologists and, later, popular music scholars. They questioned traditional musicology's legitimacy by seeking the wholesale expansion of academic study to include both non-Western and popular musics, and by invoking anthropological and sociological methodologies of the kind that allowed the address of music's social meanings.

Yet while inroads were made, efforts to explore new methodologies and repertories continued to be hampered by traditional musicology's positivistic and ethnocentric values and vocabularies (see Middleton 1990; Frith 1996; Tomlinson 2003; Walser 2003; Nettl 2005). For much of the later twentieth century, both ethnomusicology and popular music studies remained under the influence of traditional musicology, just as traditional musicology itself struggled to get free of its own inheritance.

The persistence of these traditional views can be seen in a range of music histories written in the latter decades of the twentieth century. Despite their nominal promise to cover 'twentieth-century music' or 'modern music', they in fact focus almost exclusively on art music. They also focus primarily on the works 'themselves', which are invariably treated as stable entities embodied in written scores largely free of social and cultural context (e.g., Morgan 1991; Schwartz and Godfrey 1993; Whittall 1999; Salzman 2001/

1967; Griffiths 2011). Even Richard Taruskin's monumental six-volume *Oxford History of Western Music*, published across several years in the 2010s, which attempts to move beyond the works-and-composers model of most music histories, includes only a single chapter on popular music. While some attempts at writing social and postmodern music histories have been made – Herbert (2003) and Clarke (2007) provide neat overviews of these attempts – the dominant mode of music history writing remained text-centred and generically exclusive into the twenty-first century.

Many writings did attest to musicology's efforts towards diversification at or following the century's close (Bergeron and Bohlman 1996; Fink 1998; Born and Hesmondhalgh 2000; Shepherd 2003; Clarke and Cook 2004; Clarke 2007; Cook 2008; Born 2010). These books and articles variously historicised musicology's prejudices of repertoire, style and methodology as historically determined and culturally anchored constructions. In addition, various extra-academic or para-academic publications also reflected these shifts. 'Polygeneric' anthologies such as *Audio Culture* (Cox and Warner 2006), *Sound Unbound* (Miller 2008) and the *Arcana* series (2000–12) treated various contemporary music genres in broadly equal terms, although, mashing genres together, they did not attempt to develop a critical account of the ways in which styles interrelated and overlapped.

So, at the time of writing, a growing recognition exists within the music academy that old disciplinary canons and methodologies need to be reinvented for a new era in which the presumed cultural authority and distinctiveness of different repertories has collapsed. Many music departments have attempted to remodel ageing curricula in order to reflect better both this and the increasingly diverse backgrounds and listening habits of their students and professors. Certainly, inequalities of prestige and representation still riddle university music courses, and, indeed, faculties. Nevertheless, in the twenty-first century it is possible not only to study popular music to the highest academic levels at a range of institutions across Europe and America but also to study popular and non-Western musics within general music degrees of an otherwise traditional nature.

How to Use This Book

Our fundamental position is that twentieth-century music is best studied not as a number of parallel or hierarchical traditions but as a proliferation of intersecting practices and problems – the latter technical, cultural and historical. It is by thinking about music in this way that the full significance of styles and acts – their specificities, their commonalities – can most fully be understood and enjoyed.

We hope readers will emerge with a strong sense of chronology, in terms of both twentieth-century history and twentieth-century music. But the book also sets that music amid the more fluid critical discourses that surround it. This period saw the massive expansion of professional music criticism and academic study, and many practitioners were also active writers, analysts and polemicists; these proliferating, competing interpretations of musical activity and worth meant that no form's cultural stature remained stable for long. The interweaving of critical position-taking with practice, and the understanding of both in flux, is one of this text's central aims.

The scope of repertoire covered is governed by the same basic principles. The book addresses what have been considered central works and practices – Stravinsky's *The Rite of Spring*, the Beatles' recording methods – but it also devotes much time and attention to material which, while more marginal to the canons of art music, popular music or jazz, nevertheless offer musically rich and intellectually ripe opportunities for thematic exploration. And while our focus is on musics in 'the West' – an old, meaningful but admittedly problematic category – practices from around the world, and particularly global popular musics, are also addressed.

Certainly, the book's attempt to evolve rather than revolutionise the stuff of musical history, along with its Anglophone, European–North American perspective, marks it out as the product of a particular institutional and cultural environment. But we believe its method allows us to circumvent at least some of the problems attending many canonic constructions, not the least of which has been the systematic exclusion of musicians and thinkers who were women and/or people of colour. It also allows us to avoid the construction of yet another authorised collection of Greats, one perhaps more inclusive, yet similarly bounded; instead, we aim to show numerous local understandings of musical repertoire and value in dialogical but ultimately removed relationships.

The book is divided into four broadly defined parts: (I) Histories, (II) Techniques and Technology, (III) Mediation and (IV) Identities. We aim to offer a new range of perspectives on musics that have too often been presented as having one kind of value – formal interest in the case of art music, sociological import in the case of the popular. Our four sections, then, aim to show: (1) how twentieth-century music can be heard in relation to historical and social change; (2) how, and with what developing resources, musicians constructed that music; (3) how music was fostered, disseminated and valued by commercial agents and governmental organisations; and (4) how music played host to changing notions of the private and public self.

Each of these sections is divided into four chapters. Rather than a particular musical style or moment, the chapters focus on topics important across the twentieth century's genres and decades. In the name of coherence and the appreciation of historical change, each of these topics is framed chronologically. But, forming a series of sixteen juxtapositions rather than a single thread through the century, the chapters are designed to present music history as strata overlaid, or as threads twisted, rather than as a sequence of slices. At many points in the text, we touch on a topic briefly, but, using the ➔ symbol, point to a chapter in which it is dealt with at greater length. Suggested listening is indicated at bullet points. We use English-language titles of works, except where the non-English original title is standard; we use the British rhythmic terms *semiquaver, quaver, crotchet, minim, breve* and *bar* (equivalents to the US terms *sixteenth note, eighth note, quarter note, half note, whole note* and *measure*).

We have chosen chapter topics which, apart from their central importance, maximise cross-cutting between art music, popular music and jazz traditions. Certain chapters, such as Chapter 9, 'Recording and Production', or Chapter 13, 'Gender and Sexuality', suggest themselves easily in these terms. Others, such as Chapter 7, 'Harmony', Chapter 5, 'Work and Notation' or Chapter 15, 'Audiences, Class and Consumption', are more usually studied in terms of either popular or Western art music, but for that reason are often more productive when applied to unexpected musics in unexpected ways.

However, our chapter topics echo shifts far more dramatic than any within music studies. Where our discipline has tarried with concerns around cultural authority, relation, and value, it has been because – in an unstable and often troubled era – such anxieties have occupied the thoughts and actions of many people in general. In line with much musicological work since the 1980s, this book argues that any attempt at musical history must consider the social, cultural, political, economic and technological landscapes from which that music emerged; for that reason, it will be useful to end this introduction by way of a schematic survey of those landscapes as seen from the West, and the ways they changed between 1900 and 2000.

An Outline of the Western Twentieth Century

There are several historical trajectories that we might highlight in sketching the Western twentieth century. These include:

- the changing shape and importance of the nation state, and the challenges posed to sovereignty and nationalist identity by a developing globalisation;
- the changing ways in which class was understood and organised, and related transformations in modes of employment, manufacture and consumption;
- movements aimed at securing equal rights for women, as well as those ethnic groups, religions, and sexualities that had been marginalised or oppressed;
- the widespread withdrawal – but in some important instances, the renewal – of faith from daily life.

In this section we provide a summary of these themes, along with some examples of their musical repercussions.

The State

Nationalist movements, often inspired by the writings of Johann Gottfried Herder (1744–1803), had spread across Europe in the late nineteenth century, and, peaking in the early twentieth, they played a major part in the outbreak of World War I (1914–18). Nationalist sentiment was audible in music across the continent during these decades. But the particular significance of national identity and self-construction in twentieth-century Europe – music's role in which pales alongside the first war's death toll of some 40 million – can be illustrated in a comparison of maps from shortly before and shortly after the conflict (Figure 0.1). Whereas most of the continent had previously been dominated by a small number of nations and regional empires, after the war's final peace treaties were signed Europe resembled a patchwork of small nations. Most of these now strongly asserted their own national languages and cultures.

Yet the end of World War I did not mark the resolution of internationalist tensions within Europe. The 1920s and 1930s saw the transformation of patriotic sentiment into the politics of fascism and National Socialism in Spain, Italy and Germany in particular. Nationalist ideologies – upheld by governments which pressed composers and folk musics from each territory into patriotic and propagandistic service – were not limited to fascist countries: France, Britain, the Netherlands and several other nations maintained empires that stretched across the globe, and the maintenance of these territories depended on continually propagated ideas of the 'mother' countries' racial and cultural superiority. But it was fascist

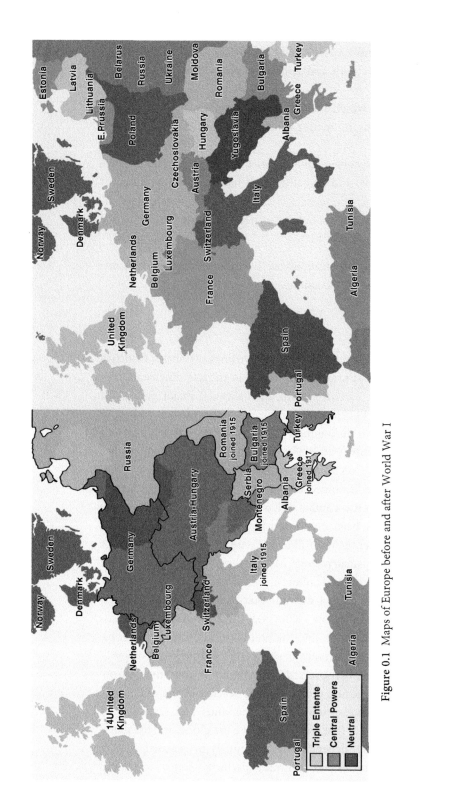

Figure 0.1 Maps of Europe before and after World War I

expansionism that would be the principal cause of World War II (1939–45), contested between alliances headed by Germany on the one side, and Great Britain, the United States and finally the Soviet Union on the other. The war is commonly estimated to have resulted in the deaths of over 60 million people.

If World War I had been fought as a clash of competing national ideologies, then World War II ended as a general defeat for local nationalism. Europe was now divided into liberal economies (such as the United Kingdom, France and West Germany) and those 'Eastern bloc' communist states indirectly ruled by the Soviet Union (such as Czechoslovakia, Romania and East Germany); international alliances were now formed on ideological grounds, and the standoff between the United States-aligned West and the Soviet East, soon known as the Cold War, would last until the Soviet Union's collapse in 1989–91, and arguably beyond. Many of the treaties drawn up and bodies established in World War II's aftermath emphasised international cooperation and co-dependence, and while they aimed to forestall some of the internal conflicts that had led to the world wars, they sometimes tended to bolster the larger East–West divide. These agreements and organisations included:

- The Charter of the United Nations, the founding document of the UN signed by fifty countries in June 1945. The organisation was dedicated to international security, law, dispute resolution, and social and economic cooperation;
- The United Nations Monetary and Financial Conference, held at Bretton Woods, New Hampshire in July 1944, and attended by delegates from the forty-four Allied nations of World War II. Among the agreements signed at the conference were the General Agreement on Trade and Tariffs (GATT; superseded in 1995 by the World Trade Organization, WTO), and documents that led to the establishment of the International Bank for Reconstruction and Development (IBRD, part of the World Bank) and the International Monetary Fund (IMF), organisations that collectively administered what became known as the Bretton Woods system of international monetary regulation;
- The European Coal and Steel Community (ECSC), formed in 1951 between Belgium, France, Italy, Luxembourg, the Netherlands and West Germany. The body aimed to unite national coal and steel resources and so to make future European wars materially impossible. In 1957 the ECSC became part of the European Economic Community, which in turn became the modern European Union, a supranational political and economic group comprising most of the continent's countries;

- The North Atlantic Treaty Organization (NATO), formed in 1949 between eleven western European countries and the United States, and based on an agreement of military cooperation and mutual defence. The organisation's communist counterpart was that formed under the 1955 Warsaw Pact, which comprised seven Eastern bloc countries and the Soviet Union.

The structures that the liberal democracies of the West established postwar were augmented by a different kind of diplomacy, through which the cultural forms of the West – but principally the now-dominant United States – were shown to the world as an enticement towards liberal values, and away from communism. This was 'soft power' (or, to its detractors, 'cultural imperialism'). Hollywood films, globally distributed and promoted, advertised Western freedoms and consumerist lifestyles (Ross 1995).

The expense and attrition of war left the old colonial powers of Europe unable and increasingly unwilling to hold on to their many territories across the world. By the mid-1960s, those powers had withdrawn from almost all the countries in Africa, Asia, Oceania and South America that had been claimed during the eighteenth and nineteenth centuries. Among the main acts of this postwar decolonisation, which had long-lasting effects on the political and economic stability of their respective regions, we might include:

- Vietnam's declaration of independence from France in 1945 (the succession, fought but finally recognised by France in 1954, was the main contributory factor to the 'American' Vietnam War of the 1960s and 1970s);
- the withdrawal of Britain from India in 1946;
- the 1948 creation of Israel, following the British withdrawal from Palestine a year earlier;
- the conclusion of Indonesia's four-year war of independence from the Netherlands in 1949; and
- Algerian independence from France in 1962, following an eight-year war.

Anti-colonial sentiment and celebrations of independence can be heard in the Irish rebel songs or Vietnamese *cai luong* musical theatre of the early twentieth century, or, in the 1950s, 1960s and 1970s, in musics like Trinidadian calypso, Jamaican reggae, and Nigerian jùjú and highlife. The role that music has played in the forging of postcolonial commerce and cultural identities has subsequently been one of the major topics of ethnomusicology.

Advances in transport and communications technology, and the further development of national interdependence through trade and aid, contributed to what became known as globalisation: the process by which cultures, peoples and products from around the world were brought into some kind of contact, whether actual or virtual. Such had begun with the ancient 'Silk Road' trade routes between China, India and Europe, and had grown throughout the modern (and colonial) era (Rosenberg 2012). By the end of the century globalisation was widely understood not just as a macroeconomic phenomenon but as one of the most important forces in everyday life, a single-word explanation for the hugely varied provenance of Westerners' food, clothing and entertainment. As such it had become the subject of widespread political anxiety, critics arguing that it led to a homogenisation of culture, to the overbearing influence of corporations and to the exploitation of the people and resources of the world's poorer countries by those in its wealthiest (see Giddens 1990; Harman 1996; Stiglitz 2002). Indeed, the relationship between corporate power and the labour force forms another central theme of the Western century.

Class, Employment and Consumption

The Industrial Revolution of the eighteenth and nineteenth centuries had drawn great numbers of workers into the cities and factories of the West, and this concentration led both to extreme hardship – living and working conditions were uniformly miserable – and newly sharpened ideas around class and class relations. Karl Marx and Friedrich Engels (Marx and Engels 1848; 1867–94) had drawn intellectual attention to the deprivations of capitalism and the European working classes' plight – not to mention what they believed to be that people's revolutionary destiny – and, in the late nineteenth century, new trade unions had won unprecedented rights for workers. The early decades of the twentieth century were characterised in the United States and Europe by the entrenchment of standardised, assembly-line mass production. After Henry T. Ford's hugely successful mobilisation of the practice in automobile manufacture, the method and its principles became known as Fordism; this became the industrial norm, with low-cost goods being produced cheaply and in huge volumes by a largely unskilled workforce, the latter still involved in struggles to establish and assert labour rights and protection. Similar assembly-line methods were employed in communist countries and, increasingly, in the global south.

Mass production helped swell industrial wealth and accelerate techno-logical development of all kinds; it accelerated urbanisation across the world, often forcing improvements in pay and public health, with popula-tions booming as a result. Amid all this developed a range of new mass cultural art forms, from cinema to radio to the popular music of Tin Pan Alley and Broadway. Mass culture paralleled the mass production of Fordism in its use of new technologies and industrial production (see Adorno 1991a/1938; 1991b; Benjamin 1999/1936), while also speaking directly to the modern working and middle classes by representing and reflecting life in the new urban centres.

These tendencies found further expression in the 1960s, which saw the explosion of popular music in something like its modern industrial form. The performance of popular music itself also offered one of the compara-tively few opportunities for young people from working-class backgrounds to escape the still-constricting social structures of the late twentieth century.

Social Democracy, Neoliberalism and Globalisation

The social democratic movement began in the second half of the nineteenth century, at the same time as – and as an alternative to – Marx and Engels's communism. Drawing influence from the philosopher and political activist Ferdinand Lassalle and the British Fabian Society, social democracy advo-cated a socialism acquired through gradual parliamentary reform rather than revolutionary force. Revolutions leading to communist rule in Russia (1917) and later in China (1949) were salutary to governments struggling to contain working-class dissent in their own countries. By adopting social democratic principles – with an emphasis on mixed economies, in which private enter-prise would exist alongside the governmental regulation and provision of public utilities and services – governments in the USA, Scandinavia, Western Europe and elsewhere sought to promote social reform and the democratic representation of all social classes while managing capitalist speculation. The years following World War II saw the widening of social democratic efforts across the world, exemplified by the widespread development of social security, and by the establishment of a National Health Service in Britain (1948), or by the introduction of Medicaid and Medicare in the USA (1965 and 1966) (Judt 2005: 360–86). Musical organisations and institutions also benefitted from state subsidisation, especially in Europe (➔ Chapter 11, 'States and Markets'; Chapter 14, 'Race and Ethnicity'). To begin with, funding was generally devoted to the production of 'high' art music, but after the 1960s many governments began also to allocate money to jazz and popular music (Rigby 1991; Street 2011: 28–40).

Social democratic and egalitarian politics were consistently, and often successfully, challenged in the last decades of the century. Many of these challenges have been identified with the school of thought and policy known as neoliberalism. Neoliberal principles and practices emphasised the deregulation of markets and the privatisation of industry and public services in deference to finance capitalism (Hayek 1948; Harvey 2007). Union power was undermined, and union membership was often actively discouraged by employers. Heavy industry and production were increasingly 'outsourced' from the West to poor countries in which labour was cheap and legally unprotected – neoliberal economics and trends in globalisation are densely intertwined – and financial service industries were established, partially in place of Western manufacturing. By the end of the century the neoliberal model of market fundamentalism, institutionally supported by organisations like the IMF and World Bank, had been adopted and normalised as the bedrock of economic policy by governments across the world. On the logic that market forces worked as the ultimate arbiter of value, classical, popular and folk musicians in many parts of the world faced declining governmental funding of their forms; the gradual withdrawal of funding for music teaching, and social welfare and housing, also affected those learning and working in music. Various protest and resistance movements sprang up in response to the social inequality and concentration of wealth that this politics produced, but neoliberal precepts were dominant by 2000.

Identity Politics

These were not the only grounds on which battles between the powerful and the disempowered were fought. Some of the century's greatest losses were incurred by minority ethnic groups faced with governmental oppression and murder; during World War II the Nazi Holocaust cost well over 6 million Jews, Roma and other minorities their lives.

But some of the greatest gains were made in rights for women. The campaign for women's equal rights, symbolised first by the right to vote or 'suffrage', began in the late nineteenth century. In Great Britain – where equal rights campaigners, like Emmeline Pankhurst and the composer Ethel Smyth, were known as 'suffragettes' – women won the right to vote in 1918 (although not on equal age terms until ten years later). The same right was added to the US Constitution in 1920. Social and labour rights began to be extended to women through the 1920s. Feminism's so-called 'second wave', sometimes also called the women's liberation movement, began in the 1960s. With fundamental issues of suffrage and property rights in many instances greatly improved, second-wave feminists turned their attention to a much broader spectrum of concerns, including employment rights, reproductive rights (in which the arrival of the contraceptive pill in 1961 played a part) and sexist sociocultural conventions (➔Chapter 13, 'Gender and Sexuality'). As it became intellectualised in the 1970s, feminism became factionalised. The 1980s were characterised by argument and fragmentation. The 'third-wave' feminism that emerged subsequently drew on cultural theory to formulate a more pluralistic perspective that could accommodate women of diverse backgrounds. Further issues now under discussion – in all areas of discourse, music included – were rape (Dworkin 1987), domestic violence (Ylló and Bograd 1988), race (Hill Collins 1990), body image (Orbach 1978–82) and pornography (Dworkin 1981).

Movements for civil rights were seen across the West – and especially in European imperial territories – during the first half of the twentieth century. In the USA, the African American movement for reform reached a peak between the mid-1950s and the late 1960s. Using tactics of civil disobedience and non-violent protest, numerous organisations and leaders – most famously Dr Martin Luther King – campaigned for the end of racial segregation and legalised inequality. Among the movement's great achievements were the Civil Rights Act of 1964, which outlawed most forms of racial segregation across the United States, and the Voting Rights Act of the following year, which extended voting rights to all US citizens, regardless of race. In music this civil rights movement helped shape the themes and reception of contemporary Black musics, from gospel to Motown to free jazz (Ward 1998; Kernodle 2008) (➔Chapter 14, 'Race and Ethnicity').

Rights for lesbian, gay, bisexual and transgender people had also been an issue since the late nineteenth century, with the trials and imprisonment of Oscar Wilde in 1895 perhaps the greatest cause célèbre. Localised advances were made in the first half of the century: homosexuality was decriminalised in Russia after the 1917 Revolution, and in Poland in 1918 (Poland's public homosexuals included the composer Karol Szymanowski). Lesbian and gay periodicals were published, and in Germany an Institute for Sexology was established in 1919, offering sex counselling, transgender operations and research into sexuality. However, the ascent of far-right politics in the 1920s and 1930s set many of these advances back. In fascist

Italy homosexuals were labelled degenerate; in Nazi Germany, between 5,000 and 15,000 were sent to concentration camps.

The postwar years saw a shift in popular attitudes to sex. This was partly enabled and partly symbolised by the work of social scientists such as Alfred Kinsey (1948 and 1953) and William Masters and Virginia Johnson (1966) in the United States, and by philosophers and writers such as Jean-Paul Sartre (1969/1943), Georges Bataille (1986/1957) and Michel Foucault (1978) in Europe, all of whom gave legitimacy to sex as an object for serious investigation and analysis. This development was also aided by the popular music, literature and cinema of the period, which placed a new emphasis on a modern, supposedly liberated sexuality. The social activism of the 1960s gave the fight for the right towards sexual self-determination a new urgency, yet advances were slow to materialise; homosexuality had been decriminalised across most of Western Europe by the 1980s, but it remained illegal in Russia, China, parts of Australia, Ireland and much of the United States until the 1990s or even later. In the second decade of the twenty-first century, homosexuality was still illegal in most of Africa and the Middle East, and rights for same-sex marriage and adoption were not accorded in many countries around the world.

Faith

The century saw a general and gradual decline in religious practice, particularly across Western Europe. This decline had begun long before the twentieth century began, but it was accelerated by many of the forces described above.

However, in many countries and regions – the United States, the Middle East, much of Africa – religious observance remained relatively stable throughout the century, and even increased. The late twentieth century saw questions of faith restored to national and international politics. The Iranian Revolution of 1979 saw the overthrow of the constitutional democracy of the Pahlavi regime and its replacement with an Islamic Republic led by the Grand Ayatollah Khomeini. Meanwhile, the 'culture wars' of the 1980s and 1990s in the United States replaced ideological struggles based on religious, class or ethnic identity with a discourse ostensibly focused on 'values', and issues such as abortion and civil liberties; in practice, however, the culture wars were primarily defined by the opposition of a largely faith-based conservative movement to a secular liberal one. The continued importance in the later decades of the twentieth century of notions of faith, particularly in its role as a carrier of wider cultural identities, was most tragically demonstrated on September 11, 2001.

This outline of a social history partially conceals innumerable 'other' histories; it is perfectly possible to narrate the twentieth century through something as concrete as the period's technological developments, or through something as nebulous as the changes seen in emotional etiquette. Indeed, those kinds of phenomena and many others will make appearances in the present 'other' history of the twentieth century – which is, of course, musical.

PART I

Histories

1 | Place and Space, Local and Global

It is usual for books like this to begin with the momentous changes in art music composition that took place around 1900. That is logical enough. But rather than dwelling on isolated moments, each of our chapters examines a topic as it developed over the course of many decades – and when the twentieth century is seen as a whole, it is clear that what best defines that period is not any single artistic approach but the huge developments in technology, travel and trade that, over the course of 100 years, effectively 'shrank' the planet. Most people in 1900 would live and die where they were born, and the music they made and listened to was often reflective of their immediate cultural surroundings. Certainly, some music cultures already had an international dimension: German, French, Italian and Russian art music was heard across the West and was beginning to take root in Asia (→Chapter 15, 'Audiences, Class and Consumption'). But, by 2000, a hugely expanded version of that internationalism was the norm. Most people in the industrialised West – who, by that time, had commonly travelled and lived far away from their first home – could claim extensive and intimate knowledge, both first-hand and media-borne, of a huge array of musical styles that circulated around the world.

What was at stake in all this change was more than just expanding access to, and participation in, music that had once been local but was now becoming global. As people's experience of the world became broader, so ideas of 'authenticity' – and the ways music could belong to a place or cultural group – became more keenly contested. As growing industrialisation and media dissemination took styles across the world, so local music traditions could seem to be at risk of being subsumed by a blandly international product. And as large population groups were forced into or embraced global dispersion – the Jewish diaspora that fled the nineteenth-century pogroms and twentieth-century Nazism, the Afro-Caribbean diaspora that circulated Black music styles around 'new' and 'old' worlds – understandings of a people's history and identity were rendered complex and multiple.

23

In music as in many other areas of Western life, then, the experience of local *place* was now supplemented by an understanding of the ways that people, culture and goods moved around global *space*. This chapter begins by looking at how musicologists and other scholars defined and developed theories that would enable analysis of these changes. That thinking is then brought to bear on a narrative that explores music making as it occurred across the most important types of place and space: city and country, nation and world. We will see how, with the industrialisation that began in earnest in the 1900s, people moved from the country to newly vast cities, with new music styles and industries springing up in their wake. We will then explore the growing phenomenon of globalisation and the ways that, especially in the century's second half, many musics transcended their point of origin to become international and intercultural endeavours. Central throughout will be the tension between the idea of location and what was a growing experience of *dis*location. That was a major source of anxiety in twentieth-century life; it was a central figure in twentieth-century music.

The Musicology of 'Place' and 'Space'

Music has long been identified with 'place': the place of its creation, the places it depicts. In the art of the nineteenth century, there were few more important settings than the pastoral, with its enchanted woods and soaring mountains. Both real and imaginary versions of these places were endlessly represented in works of all kinds, and always in service of an idea. That idea could be Romantic, in which case the focus was nature's sublime majesty, its mystery, its harshness. Or it could be nationalist, portraying instead the unique characteristics of a particular region, and the always indomitable spirit of its folk.

- Frederick Delius (1862–1934), *Brigg Fair: An English Rhapsody* (1907)
- Jean Sibelius (1865–1957), *Tapiola* (1926)
- Elizabeth Maconchy (1907–94), *The Land* (1929)

As we will see in this chapter, those places and ideas continued to be important. But musicologists like Daniel Grimley (2011) have developed critical approaches that explore the politics underpinning such musical representations of place. As Grimley writes, those projections – idealised depictions of country life, lyrical invocations of hill ranges – concealed real relationships of political and economic power. The bourgeois composer who looked out across the land and saw it as the wellspring of, say, timeless English folk identity, saw something different to the agricultural worker whose relationship with that place was manual, hard and hostile (Grimley 2011: 394–5). Similarly, in a highly influential study, the geographer Edward Relph (2008/1976: 61–2) writes that thinking about place means thinking about the variety of relationships, or kinds of access, that people have to that location. But that does not necessarily mean just distinguishing between people who have first-hand experience of a place and those that do not. The twentieth century was one in which mass media played an increasing role in our understanding of the world, and the ways that places became shaped and known by their representation and consumption in the media – including in music – would complicate that notion of insiders and outsiders.

The sounds and images of places and their musics, circulating on record, film and writing in ever-greater quantity through the century, nevertheless made much use of old ideas – and myths – of authenticity and exceptionalism. These followed the thinking of the German philosopher Johann Gottfried Herder. Writing in the 1760s and 1770s, Herder posited the highly influential notion of 'folk genius': a collaborative, cumulative sedimentation of cultural practices and expressive forms, unique to (and representative of) a singular place and people. This understanding of culture was central to attempts in the latter half of the nineteenth-century to document and safeguard folklore – not least folk music – as developing industrial economies took more and more people from their rural home communities and threw them together in cities; it was a conception of the relationship between place, people and music that remained central in the twentieth century.

This can be seen in early histories of North American blues and country musics. In Paul Oliver's *Blues Fell This Morning* (1960) and Bill C. Malone's *Country Music, USA* (1968), the emergence of those forms is explained by the separation – both cultural and spatial – of the social groups held responsible for each form (enslaved African Americans and sharecroppers on the one hand, white agricultural workers on the other):

[The blues] has evolved from the peculiar dilemma of a particular group, isolated by skin pigmentation or that of its ancestors, which was required to conform to a society and yet refused its full integration within it. This enforced partial isolation produced, in spite of black desires to be accepted on wholly equal terms within the social pattern of American life, a certain cultural separation which bore fruit in, amongst other things, the blues. (Oliver 1960: 4)

The socially ingrown South, from the tidewater of Virginia to the pine barrens of East Texas, produced a population that, in its commitment to and preservation of traditional cultural values, should be considered as a distinct family unit. The music of these people, lying outside the mainstream of American cultural development, provided the origin and nucleus of what we now call country music. (Malone 1968: 5)

These are progressive readings in so far as they recognise, and celebrate, the particularities of different groups and their music. Still, they seem suspiciously neat, not to say conservative: in clinging to old, pseudo-anthropological ideas around race and culture, these narratives enforce a kind of segregation of their own. If Oliver's and Malone's stories are accurate, and cultural and spatial separation accounted for the development of both blues and country, why did those musical forms share so many performance techniques (like falsetto and yodel) and song materials (the I-IV-V harmony)?

- Jimmie Rodgers (1897–1933), 'Blue Yodel No. 1 (T for Texas)' (Victor, 1927)
- Robert Johnson (1911–38), 'Ramblin' on my Mind' (Vocalion, 1936)

Discussing this problem, Peter Manuel (2008) argues that attempts to fix the social 'origins' of a musical style have come to seem misplaced: what is needed is to see society not as a fixed 'thing' but as a 'process', in which forms of social contact and dialogue are always changing.

It is not wrong, then, to claim that place 'makes' music. But it might be more apt to see music as one of the crucial agents that makes *sense* of a place: the relationship is symbiotic, the one impossible to disentangle from the other. The ethnomusicologist Martin Stokes writes that, in this way, music 'evokes and organises collective memories and present experiences of place with an intensity, power and simplicity unmatched by any other social activity'. In this view, a particular form of music making does not just characterise a particular place; it is also a means to transform that place (Stokes 1994: 3–4; see also Leyshon et al. 1998). We will see this in our case study of New Orleans, below (Case Study 1.1).

However, the way things 'really are' is subject to remaking in the image of what people want things to be; once a 'story' about the link between music and place has circulated enough, and once it has enough believers, it acquires a kind of truth. Marybeth Hamilton (2007) and Karl Hagstrom Miller (2010) have written revisionist histories of blues and country that show this remaking at work, with the shared musical practices in country and blues music being segregated by record labels and early historians into distinct 'white' and 'Black' approaches. As Stokes argues, musics and musicians can have their complexities smoothed over as they are made to stand for a place, or a people, as they wish to be seen, especially in an international context (1994: 13–14). Edward Relph argues that a sense of place continued to be vital to humans in the late twentieth century, and that is borne out by many popular discourses around music at that time, in which musicians, audiences, commentators and music businesses can be seen taking pains to construct and represent place as the birth site of inherently local expressive forms. There are few better examples of this than in 1990s hip-hop, central to which were evocations and representations of life in the 'hood, that streetscape in which rappers – at first in the USA, then worldwide – based their claims to experience and authenticity (Forman 2002; Quinn 2005). Even in less fraught contexts, such as the Liverpool rock scene studied by Sara Cohen, such links between place and sound underpin much creative work and listener interpretation (Cohen 1991, 1994).

There are, then, tensions in defining the relationship of music and place: tensions between local particularity and more widely shared generalities; tensions between socio-musical complexity, and the reductive fictions that narrate this music as the indubitable product of that place. As scholars addressing the idea have shown, the challenge for a musicology of place is not to simply buy into local myths or to reject them but to observe and understand these complexities in all their workings.

The concept of 'space' is in some ways more abstract than that of place. Prosaically, spaces can be particular sites with defined boundaries and relatively fixed codes of operation, for instance a stage or a dance hall. But some spaces are broader, imagined spheres of activity, such as 'the classical music world'. A space might be delimited by walls, and it might not. What really defines a space is not so much the material boundaries as the social, practical or cultural affinities constructed within that space, and the type of focal activity they serve – in our case, the experience of music.

The idea of musical space became an important one at the very end of the century. At that time, writers on Western music began more frequently to import from ethnomusicology – and, moreover, from sociology, anthropology and contemporary philosophy – an attention to the ways that social practice, social situation, identity and thought came into being in specific contexts (Berish 2009). Examples came from scholars like Guthrie P. Ramsey (2004: 131–62), who described music in African American homes in the middle-century; Sarah Thornton (1996: 26–86), who wrote about the UK's dance-music club scene of the 1990s; and Wendy Fonarow (2006: 79–121), who investigated British indie rock cultures of around the same time. These works sought to chart not just the social and practical roles played by participants within those musical spaces but often the hierarchies established between them: musical spaces were charged not just with sound but with differing kinds of power and responsibility. In some twentieth-century music cultures, for example, it was the audience's responsibility to listen silently, while in others, they were expected to interact with performers directly and audibly.

Indeed, attempts to transform both social and musical practices often began with a reorganisation of the space in which music was experienced.

Like other pieces of the 1960s and 1970s inspired by a utopian socialist politics, Cornelius Cardew's composition *The Great Learning* (1969–70) puts the performers among the audience, with music makers and listeners mobile in a space full of musicians who come together and move apart from moment to moment. The goal was to overcome the separation between an orchestra and audience, and what musicians like Cardew saw as the alienated relationship between music's workers (musicians) and its passive consumers (the public). The critic Richard Dyer (2002/1979) saw a similar kind of transformation in the gay disco scene of the late 1970s. For Dyer, the rock concert represented a traditional, and indeed reactionary, kind of masculinity: male performers thrust hips and guitars around the stage while an admiring audience looked on. But the 1970s disco lacked that performance focal point. There, the centre of activity was the dance floor and the erotic interactions that dancers constructed among themselves; the music, formed of endless mixes and repetitive grooves rather than climactic and showy instrumentalism, reinforced an idea of whole-body, communal erotic flow. For a gay community still very much marginalised in the 1970s, this social reorganisation – articulated through music – was hugely meaningful.

Those more abstract, imagined kinds of music spaces will be explored in the case studies that follow. Clearly, notions like 'the classical music world', or indeed 'the West', are 'spaces' only in a metaphorical sense. But the spatial metaphor has proven useful and enduring precisely because it groups together what would otherwise be disparate, disconnected people and phenomena; it allows us to think about the ways that sounds, ideas, people and money circulate and interact in that space, in service of something like a common project. That model, as we have already begun to see, was important in a century so defined by flows of people, culture and commerce. There is one final advantage to note here. Conceptions of place tend to produce relationships based on 'central' and 'marginal' status. For example, much of the nationalist music produced in Eastern Europe, Britain and the USA in the late nineteenth and early twentieth centuries, which made use of local folk-music styles, was created in defiance of the dominant Austro-German school (and often, of the Austro-Hungarian Empire's political power); it was often a gesture of self-determination, launched from the margins and aimed at the centre (Chapter 16, ➔ 'Centres and Peripheries'). The same could be observed in later jazz, rock, reggae and hip-hop – musics widely understood to be strongly linked in their early 'authentic' forms to particular places. But a differently conceived spatial metaphor – one in which a musical space is formed of multiple, networked centres of activity – allows us to think beyond simple centre–margin oppositions. Later, we will see this model at work in studies of Afro-diasporic and global rock musics. First, we will consider some places that would prove central to twentieth-century music.

City and Country

The changes that modernity wrought affected everyone in the West, but new arrangements and technologies for working, travelling and living were concentrated in the cities. They came to stand for industry, activity, noise, energy, encounter and change – and for new kinds of drudgery, violence and alienation.

Many cities of the world had seen their limits and populations expand steadily over hundreds of years. But the Industrial Revolution of the eighteenth and nineteenth centuries – which, beginning in Europe and the USA, transformed small-scale artisanal production processes and cottage industries through the introduction of powerful, automated technology – brought many people from the countryside into new urban factories. Cities often exploded in size. By one count, London's population grew from 1,335,000 to 6,480,000 between 1825 and 1900; in the same period Paris' population grew from 855,000 to 3,330,000, and New York City's from 170,000 to 4,242,000 (Sutcliffe 1984: 7).

The extraordinary new density and noise of modern city life made Western cities a favourite theme for writers, politicians, campaigners and artists (see Benjamin 1999/1939; Thompson 2002). Their work can be seen as posing two big questions, whether directly or indirectly. The first asked how people, brought together in such diversity and quantity as had never been experienced, might live together in some kind of harmony; the second asked how industrialisation would affect, and perhaps deform, cultural expression.

In Western art music, images of the urban, the mechanical and the teeming began to blot the musical landscape. In New York City, Charles Ives (1874–1954) was an archetypal modern professional, working by day in Manhattan as the director of an insurance firm, but in his spare time he wrote the music which has since seen him acknowledged as one of the earliest North American composers to comprehensively break away from European models. Ives' piece *Central Park in the Dark* (1906) and the third part of his Orchestral Set No. 2, 'From Hanover Square North' (composed *c.*1915), are often cited as early portrayals of American city life; in both, songs heard, sung and played in public waft over orchestral spaces already occupied by tonally ambiguous and conflictual lines. The orderliness of material and key and the decorum of the fully integrated musical work as it had long been understood are supplanted by a kind of collage, in which elements bump into each other, coexisting rather than obviously co-operating.

• Charles Ives, *Central Park in the Dark* (1906)

Meanwhile, the lyrics of the British music hall, the blues and the Broadway musical alike described, attacked and celebrated metropolitan life and social mores; it is not surprising that these forms and others, despite their geographical and cultural differences, were packed with people articulating new city-life concerns, given that the trends they addressed – arrival from the country, landlords, big-city flash and, as in Figure 1.1, urban sprawl and overcrowding – were being experienced all over the global north.

Figure 1.1 Sheet music copy of 'If It Wasn't for the 'Ouses In Between', as sung by British music hall star Gus Elen (1862–1940)

- Gus Elen (1862–1940), 'If It Wasn't for the 'Ouses In Between' (The Gramophone Co., 1899)
- Bessie Smith (1894–1937), 'Chicago Bound Blues' (Columbia, 1923)
- Cole Porter (1891–1964), 'I Happen to Like New York' (from *The New Yorkers*, 1930)

Case Study 1.1: New Orleans and the Birth of Jazz

Few places were as important to the development of twentieth-century music as New Orleans. As we will see shortly, the city has commonly been thought of as the birthplace of jazz. But its Black churches gave rise to gospel, and stars like Mahalia Jackson; its idiosyncratic colonial and cultural history was made apparent by leading Cajun and zydeco musicians Amédé Ardoin and Clifton Chenier. Through the 1950s and 1960s, important rhythm and blues and soul artists like Professor Longhair, Fats Domino, the Meters and Irma Thomas emerged. In the 1980s, the Marsalis family would play a central role in the resurgence of jazz; and in the 1990s, a local rap scene, with entrepreneur-rapper Master P at its head, would become globally prominent. The richness of this local musical heritage has been internationally acknowledged since the 1930s (Panassié 1936/1934).

   Yet that international status was a cause as much as an effect of this musical vitality. Like any large city, New Orleans concentrated musical talent. But the music developed there very often reflected the city's particular location, and its global cultural and economic networks. The port – founded by the French in 1718, and from 1722 the capital of what was then the French colony of Louisiana – is situated just above the Mississippi delta and the Gulf of Mexico, across which lies central America and the Caribbean. Waterways and shipping routes thus link the city to states in the far north of the USA as much as to Cuba or Trinidad. This coveted trading position saw the city subject to competing colonial interests through the eighteenth century, and New Orleans was under Spanish rule for forty years before the Louisiana Purchase of 1803 made it American. This complex colonial history was reflected in the population's make-up. Creoles, those of mixed French or Spanish background, were joined by Creoles of Color: under French rule, European colonisers and the region's Black and native American residents were not discouraged from intermarrying, and the resultant offspring were legally recognised as *gens de couleur libres*. The *libre* or 'free' nomenclature distinguished this community of colour from enslaved Black Louisianans, very much unfree before 1865, the subject of oppressive sharecropping thereafter and present in large numbers in New Orleans. Indeed, the city's Congo Square, where religious rituals brought from Africa were free to be ministered by leaders both male and female to the accompaniment of drums and dance (Cavin 1975), has often been regarded as the symbolic epicentre of Black music in the USA.

Case Study 1.1: (cont.)

Many Germans, Italians and Filipinos would also arrive during the nineteenth century, and these groups' intermingling meant that the city's ethnic and cultural variety was highly unusual. Social hierarchies and freedoms were partly organised according to nuanced perceptions of class position rather than just skin colour – this in a country in which full liberty was generally accorded only to whites – and musicians of different backgrounds often interacted on those terms (Hersch 2007). For example, an Italian opera company was present from 1837, and its conductor, Luigi Gabici, also worked as a teacher, including for many Creoles of Color; the latter group was identified as an artisan class, not dissimilar from that formed by many newer European immigrants, and this shared class identity was understood to trump any ethnic difference. As Bruce Boyd Raeburn (2009) notes, this model – in which a classically trained European teacher, often Italian, instructed Creole or (more rarely) Black musicians – became a fixture of New Orleans musical life. Different communities also met on somewhat less salubrious ground in Storyville, the centre of legalised prostitution until 1917. That district was home at the turn of the century to characters like Antonia Gonzales, the self-proclaimed 'cornet playing madam' who operated a string of brothels which employed innumerable jazz pioneers, including the pianist-composer Jelly Roll Morton (1890–1941) (Tucker 2004: 22). The streets were themselves filled by sound, and what was a remarkably vibrant culture of public music making. Marching bands, whether Black, Creole or white, processed out of churches, through the streets, into funeral grounds, playing their own repertoires of military, light classical, popular and – in the case of the Black bands – blues music.

- Baby Dodds (1898–1959), 'Shimmy Beat and Press Roll Demonstration' (from *Talking and Drum Solos*, Folkways, 1951)
- Jelly Roll Morton's Red Hot Peppers, 'Black Bottom Stomp' (Victor, 1926)
- Eureka Brass Band, 'Just a Closer Walk with Thee' (from *New Orleans Funeral and Parade*, American Music, 1951)

Yet, as the ring shouts of Congo Square suggest, the city's spaces had often both defined and contained distinct racial identities. This was compounded after 1890, with the introduction of new laws around racial segregation. In 1892, the shoemaker Homer Plessy deliberately violated these laws by demanding to sit in a 'white' train carriage rather than one reserved for citizens of colour. There are few better illustrations of the way that race and racial oppression have always been spatially as well as legally organised; the case led to the 1896 *Plessy*

Case Study 1.1: (cont.)

v. *Ferguson* Supreme Court ruling, which reinforced an illusory doctrine of 'separate but equal' status for whites and Americans of colour and legally enshrined segregation for nearly fifty years.

This legal ruling brutally reinforced the pre-existing grudges, prejudices and hostilities that existed between ethnic groups. But music could sometimes cross boundaries, both literal and metaphorical, that were otherwise rigorously observed. Louis Armstrong, who gained much youthful experience marching with the Tuxedo Brass Band, later recalled how dangerous it could be for Blacks, whites and Creoles of Color to enter each other's neighbourhoods, and that it was only when he gained high musical status in the parades that he could visit any part of New Orleans 'without being bothered' (Brothers 2006: 18).

The *Plessy* v. *Ferguson* ruling began to dissolve the many fine distinctions New Orleanians had made around race and class, and the city's social and cultural life began to be reorganised according to a stark Black/white binary (Hersch 2007: 100–1). These social changes would be central to the development of jazz.

To begin with, Creoles of Color were now obliged to accept the same benighted and disenfranchised legal status that Black Americans had been enduring, even though the Creoles often felt less kinship with them than with the European American cultures with which they had previously identified (Brothers 2006: 23). Further, the new governmental efforts of the 1890s to enforce oppression of people of colour in general also led many Black agricultural workers to flee the violence and vulnerability of the country for a life in New Orleans; as Sherrie Tucker observes, at the moment that jazz began to develop into a distinct form, the city was becoming 'blacker' in every way.

As several jazz historians have argued (Hersch 2007; Shipton 2008), it was not accidental that jazz took its now-recognisable form just as Creoles began to find themselves on the receiving end of legal white supremacy, and Black Americans gathered in ever-greater numbers; the enforced meeting of these two hitherto culturally distinct groups meant musicians with very different approaches to repertoires and performance technique began to share the same stages. Or, more importantly, the same band uniforms, as in Figure 1.2. As Shipton writes, the music of Creole bands such as the Excelsior, and of virtuosi like the cornetist Manuel Perez, had been characterised by sleek, classical-style instrumental techniques developed through rigorous, conservatoire-style teaching (Shipton 2008; see also Brothers 2006: 125). However, 'Uptown', Black bands, and heroes like the legendary (and unrecorded) cornetist Buddy Bolden (1877–1931), worked with equally rigorous blues inflection, elaboration and an early kind of swing. With the new laws in place, these bands – and the places they played – became integrated, and so did their musical approaches (Hersch 2007: 109, 159).

Case Study 1.1: (cont.)

Figure 1.2 Superior Orchestra, New Orleans, between 1908 and 1913. Standing, from left: Buddy Johnson, Bunk Johnson, 'Big Eye' Louis Nelson, Billy Marrero. Seated, from left: Walter Brundy, Peter Bocage, Richard Payne. Photograph courtesy of The William Russell Jazz Collection at The Historic New Orleans Collection, acquisition made possible by the Clarisse Claiborne Grima Fund

It might seem rather too convenient to 'explain' jazz in this way – take Black American blues and expression, add European-derived harmony and instrumentalism, and *voilà*. Indeed, New Orleans' rich cultural mix has long caused both locals and observers to characterise the city's culture as a gumbo, as the quintessential melting pot of American ideal. Yet the historians cited here have been keener to think of the city's culture not as a certain mix but as an ever-changing process. This means imagining the birth of jazz not as the result of a recipe but as a momentary collision of cultural, legal and personal interests in action, in a particular place and time, these subsequently set fast by recording and historical myth-making.

Still, even at the end of the century, George Lipsitz could write that:

New Orleans remains a place of unexpected spaces. Members of social clubs dance in the streets on the way home from funerals. Tribes of Mardi Gras Indians parade through neighborhoods on Mardi Gras Day and St. Joseph's Day, stopping for ceremonies at seemingly ordinary intersections that they treat as sacred sites. (Lipsitz 2011: 274–5)

Case Study 1.1: (cont.)

A place can mean different things to insiders and outsiders, its lived experience radically different from any romantic tale or history-book gloss. Yet New Orleans came to occupy a profoundly meaningful place in the imagination of numberless musicians and listeners across the world. Lipsitz describes how Rampart Street, Congo Square and other important musical sites were disfigured and destroyed by 'urban renewal' projects in the 1960s – even as the city became a place of pilgrimage for jazz-fan-tourists from around the world, seeking, as Richard Ekins (2013) describes, the authentic voice of New Orleans jazz *in situ* at performance spaces like Preservation Hall. The birthplace of jazz is, in popular memory, fixed like a photo; the reality of the place is always in flux.

... City and Country, Continued

Musical enterprise had long been concentrated in the West's urban centres, and the art's educational, professional, and commercial structures had flourished most fully in places like Paris, London and Vienna. Derek B. Scott (2008) has shown how in the latter half of the nineteenth century those cities, joined now by New York, hosted the development of new kinds of music industry based around new kinds of musical production and performance presentation, new technologies of dissemination, and new forms of consumerism and leisure spending. The nascent industries of that era would, in the twentieth century, grow to a value and cultural domin-ance that was hitherto unknown. One particular place came to stand for that business in general. As Keir Keightley recounts:

One day around the turn of the twentieth century, Monroe H. Rosenfeld, an established songwriter and sometime journalist, was visiting West 28th Street [in New York City] as part of his research for a profile of the many music publishers located there. While interviewing the successful publisher and songwriter Harry von Tilzer, Rosenfeld noted the noise of the innumerable pianos used to compose and demonstrate songs, and likened them to clashing tin pans, exclaiming: 'This sounds like a Tin Pan Alley!' (Keightley 2013: 729)

- Collins and Harlan, 'Alexander's Ragtime Band' (comp. Irving Berlin, Victor, 1911)

'Tin Pan Alley' (➔Chapter 10, 'Copyright and the Music Industry') became shorthand not just for new music business centres like West 28th St. in

New York, or Denmark St. in London, but of a whole genre of music: popular songs, sold at first in sheet music form, thought of as cheap and transient, and for some representing the commercial debasement that characterised modern city life. Yet there was always an international aspect to this business, not least because it was one in large part constructed by recent Jewish immigrants from Russia and the Middle East (Zuckerman et al. 2011). That was common across the growing entertainment industries; we shall see later in this chapter how such businesses would soon develop a truly global reach.

Histories of urban music making show how urban networks – throwing together new combinations of cultural groups, audiences, and business interests – continued to develop and to play their part in the creation and diffusion of new musical styles. In the 1920s, Chicago became a key centre of jazz innovation – in part owing to the work afforded there to musicians, like Louis Armstrong, who were decamping from New Orleans in search of higher-profile work. In his 1993 study of Chicago jazz, William Howland Kenney argues that, while jazz histories often describe 'a musical art form evolving in its own isolated world of instrumental masters, chord progressions, and orchestral formations and disintegrations', it is more apt to see that creativity and innovation as part of 'a fabric of economic and political activities designed to improve the standard of living and political power of the black community' (Kenney 1993: 171, 4). The influx of Black migrants from the South (both musicians and audience members), the establishment of new entertainment businesses, the creative attempts on the part of musicians to develop innovative acts and to get ahead in the music business: all these factors played a part, and in Kenney's account, the development of a musical style is shown to be a product not just of creative decision-making but specifically urban social dynamics. Other classic studies of musical cities – such as Suzanne E. Smith's 1999 study of Detroit and Motown, or Ruth Finnegan's 1989 (2013/1989) work on amateur music making in the postwar British 'new town' of Milton Keynes – differ greatly in their detail, while sharing Kenney's methodological starting point.

Urbanisation, of course, was far from universally welcomed. Whatever new cultural riches the cities produced, there were widespread anxieties over what was being lost. Attempts to gather, preserve and revive folk music – conducted in Britain by figures like Cecil Sharp (1859–1924), in the USA by the father-and-son team of John and Alan Lomax (1867–1948, 1915–2002) and by Béla Bartók (1881–1945) across Europe (→Chapter 14, 'Race and Ethnicity') – were, in large part, spurred by the realisation that when rural populations vanished, so would their music traditions.

Many others, including Charles Ives – who was informed by American transcendentalism as cultivated by Emerson and Thoreau – worried about the alienating tendencies of the city and modernity's cost to spiritual life (Botstein 1996). As Paul Allen Anderson notes in his study of music in the Harlem Renaissance, African American writers like Zora Neale Hurston and Jean Toomer saw the flight of southern Black workers to the industrial cities of the north – this the 'Great Migration' that spanned the century's first half – as disrupting a vital Black cultural tradition that flowed from the fields of the former slave states. Anderson discusses Toomer's worry over the 'silencing of "back-country Negroes" and their evangelical "shouting" songs by their assimilationist superiors with "Victrolas and player-pianos"': for Toomer as for many others, vital folk traditions were being replaced by bloodless urban commerce and entertainments (Anderson 2001: 74).

Still, there was no getting away from modernity. For those musicians and commentators shaped by modernist ideals, twentieth-century music that aimed to represent the pastoral seemed hopelessly nostalgic. In Britain during the 1910s and 1920s, many composers – Frederick Delius, Arnold Bax, Arthur Bliss and Ralph Vaughan Williams chief among them – worked in the pastoral idiom, which came almost to dominate British art music of the period. Later, the (younger) composer Elisabeth Lutyens would make a withering public rejection of this style, dubbing it 'cowpat music'; her dismissal was celebrated because it so accurately pricked the bubble of premodern make-believe in which much of that music was held.

- George Butterworth (1885–1916), *The Banks of Green Willow* (1913)

Yet even the pastoral mode could be made to say something profound about twentieth-century experience. Although their music could often be taken as little more than a lyrical evocation and celebration of the English countryside, both Bliss and Vaughan Williams sometimes had something else in mind: the fields of France where they had both seen action during World War I. Bliss wrote:

I found in France, as so many others did, that the appreciation of a moment's beauty had been greatly intensified by the sordid contrast around ... a butterfly alighting on a trench parapet, a thrush's songs at 'stand to', a sudden rainbow, became infinitely precious phenomena, and indeed the sheer joy of being alive was the more relished for there being the continual possibility of sudden death. (cited in Saylor 2008: 40)

The lone trumpet that calls out over a quiet landscape of low strings in the second movement of Vaughan Williams' 'Pastoral Symphony' (1922) was, to the composer's mind, an image of the bugles that sounded over fields of the dead. He wrote in a private letter that the piece was 'really wartime music … it's not lambkins frisking at all as most people take for granted' (Saylor 2008: 48). Despite the apparent conservatism of musical language, the *Pastoral Symphony* is a meditation on the modern; if it sounds an imagined arcadia, it is one pitched in the middle of the greatest horror that had until then been seen.

- Ralph Vaughan Williams (1872–1958), Symphony No. 3, *A Pastoral Symphony* (1922), II. Lento moderato

Nation and World

If nationality is a 'condition', writes Richard Taruskin (2001) in a useful survey of the topic, then nationalism is the 'attitude' that seeks to promote that nationality, to bang the drum for a nation's identity, history and heritage, to campaign for its due recognition. As Carl Dahlhaus has argued, the belief that a citizen's loyalties were primarily owed to their nation rather than to 'a creed, a dynasty, or a class' became the 'governing idea' of the nineteenth and early twentieth centuries (Dahlhaus 1980: 81).

The word's meaning shifted according to social and political currents; before the European revolutions of 1848, nationalism was often staged as a force for inclusive liberal reform, whereas afterwards it increasingly took on an ethnically exclusive, chauvinistic function. But always central was the conflation of the nation, as place, people and heritage, with the nation *state*, that is, a government that would administer that nation (Grimley 2006: 12). The alignment of place and political autonomy was necessary at a time when a number of modern nation states were struggling to establish and maintain a unified form. It was the grandeur of those struggles that made nationalism the pre-eminent organising cultural principle of the age.

Aside from politics proper, nationalist ideas were articulated across cultural forms. Art music composition was one of the most important. Here, nations were musically constructed by the constant, repetitious association of the place with certain musical objects: particular intervals, rhythms, melodic shapes or narrative subject matter. A region's folk music and folk myths were usually key, even if the 'folk' sounds invoked were often heavily generalised. These associations were made and remade across musical repertoires and written discourses on music, in local music pedagogy, in patronage and programming, until they became the 'true' sign of a nation's musical identity, and a sounding symbol of its identity in general. In reality those signs were usually widely shared: as Dahlhaus writes (1980: 95), through these processes of association-building, the sharp fourth came to signify Norway for Grieg, and Poland for Chopin.

Musical nationalism of this sort lingered into the twentieth century, taking on new dimensions as new states emerged from the collapsing European empires, and appeared in jazz and popular music as well as art music. Some of the ways that nationalism helped construct a sense of ethnic identity will be explored in →Chapter 14, 'Race and Ethnicity'. Yet this was primarily a nineteenth-century idea, and one widely, if briefly, believed discredited after competing nationalist claims had led to the carnage of two world wars. After World War II, new internationalist imperatives sought ways forward, both in politics (the United Nations was formed in 1945) and in creative work. The serialists of the 1940s and 1950s (→ Chapter 2, 'Modernism') – and in visual art of the same moment, the abstract expressionists – would purposefully frame their newly developed artistic 'languages' as following universal rather than national principles.

But these were largely elective affinities. The greatest challenge to the nationalist idea that a citizen must be loyal to their nation before 'a creed, a dynasty, or a class' came from a reordering of place and space that no one could escape, and which became known in the late twentieth century as 'globalisation'.

That term described a moment in what had been a centuries-long process, through which developing technologies of travel and communication had, with increasing rapidity, 'shrunk' the distance between far-flung places, compressing them in time and space (Harvey 1989). But it was not just that aeroplanes and television had forged closer connections between places and people. 'Globalisation' also described new kinds of political-economic thinking – on the part of government, business and consumers alike – through which goods or services produced in one place might routinely be consumed in another, far distant location, or in which large groups of people would move across the world in search of work. Those goods included music, and those people included musicians.

As the bonds between nation states and domestic production and consumption began to loosen, (multinational) corporate wealth and power was seen to increase. Businesses selling their products in rich Northern hemisphere markets might manufacture only in countries in which labour was cheap and regulation lax, and where the potential for political influence was much larger; their multinational status might mean they were less accountable to a single government or tax regime. The power of nation states, logically and conversely, was seen to wane. Globalisation in the mid- and late twentieth century radically reordered the world, as people, products and power found themselves thrown from place to place in ways previously unimagined.

To be sure, this complex process brought about many benefits, as people all over the world began to be brought into close contact with cultures and experiences vastly removed from their own. Yet the costs to the cultural and economic fabric of local and national communities – and, given the enormously increased amounts of travel and distribution of goods, to the environment – were also great. Even before the term 'globalisation' was in use, critics were denouncing the apparent sameness that mass-mediated ways of living seemed to be fostering. The folklorist Alan Lomax worried that the spread of recorded music across the world, and its assimilation by local musicians, would lead not to a cultural blackout but a 'grey-out' in which local particularities were smoothed over in favour of a bland, homo-geneous mush (Lomax 1972). This was the sounding equivalent of what Relph, observing the strip developments and shopping malls of the late twentieth century, bemoaned as a growing sense of 'placelessness' (2008/1976: 97).

Whether or not one agreed with their judgements – which arguably clung to old ideas of authenticity – many of these critics' fears would be borne out by the end of the century. In a 1999 study, Keith Negus described the music industry category of 'international repertoire', which had devel-oped alongside the globalised popular music business in the 1980s and 1990s (Negus 1999: 152–72). This was music – commonly ballad-based and sung in American-accented English – that was designed to appeal across international markets, as opposed to 'regional' or 'domestic repertoire', which was at once more focused and stylistically varied. Negus showed how domestic artists thought ripe for international success were 'deterritoria-lized' by their labels – their image and musical style changed, their lyrics, if the artist was from outside the Anglosphere, now written in an inter-national English – and how successful this strategy had been, with inter-national repertoire accounting for some 40 per cent of recorded music sales outside the USA. It is significant that 75 per cent of the sales included in that figure was USA-produced, since the cultural, economic and political power of North American business was by now unrivalled; not for nothing were these processes of cultural homogenisation often referred to as 'Coca-Colonisation' or 'McDonaldisation'.

But that international repertoire was successful because it was meaning-ful to large audiences. There were many writers on culture who were therefore less pessimistic, and who celebrated new forms of creativity rather than decrying that so-called cultural imperialism. Some commentators began to use the term 'glocalisation' to describe what they saw as local adaptations of global practices, as in Tony Mitchell's discussion of the 'glocal' hip-hop cultures he observed outside the USA (Mitchell 2001: 32).

However, for some writers, the simple opposition of 'global' and 'local' could not describe the full complexity of lived experience in the globalised age. For example, even if jazz musicians in Scandinavia or rappers in Europe had repurposed music identified as American to their own ends, it was the American exports that remained all-powerful in terms of artistic influence, music-industrial clout and, often, perceived cultural authenticity. But by the same token, while acts like Marseille's Iam, or London's Roots Manuva might have seemed to trade in American musical forms, their work was profoundly concerned with reimagining life through the lens of postcolonial European, rather than American, experience. The hybrid term 'glocal', then, could seem to represent a smoothing-out of what were complex processes of cultural articulation and contestation (Connell and Gibson 2003: 17).

- Jan Garbarek (b. 1947), 'Reflections' (from *Places*, ECM, 1977)
- Sidsel Endresen (b. 1952), 'Stages I, II, III' (from *Exile*, ECM 1994)
- IAM, 'Tam-Tam de l'Afrique' (from … *de la planète Mars*, Hostile France, 1991)
- Roots Manuva (b. 1972), 'Motion 5000' (from *Brand New Second Hand*, Big Dada, 1999)

If the 'homogenising' model was often perceived as one-dimensional, then, the idea of the 'glocal' was criticised as too binary to deal with the multidirectional cultural flows that were so prevalent by the century's end. Perceiving this, scholars began to look for conceptualisations of global experience that could emphasise this fluidity.

Case Study 1.2: Global Musical Spaces

Motti Regev's 2013 study of what he calls 'pop-rock music' provides a developed theory of globalised music practice. Regev contrasts an account of Swedish youths encountering the Beatles in the early-1960s – and the shock and thrill of what they experienced as something entirely outside their prior experience – and what he saw at the very start of the twenty-first century in Beijing: there, 'Western'-style pop-rock, the distinct

Case Study 1.2: (cont.)

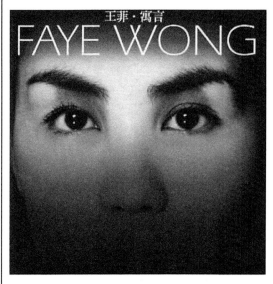

Figure 1.3 Faye Wong, *Fable* (EMI, 2000)

Cantopop of Hong Kong (Figure 1.3), and pop forms from China and Taiwan, mingled without remark with local music and incorporating hip-hop, folk and so on (Regev 2013: 158–61).

- Faye Wong (b. 1969), 'New Tenant' (from *Fable*, EMI, 2000)

For Regev, these two moments demonstrate how the long processes of globalisation – beginning with stark cultural encounters that are then processed, resisted, negotiated, reassessed and so on – had led to pop-rock cultures around the world that, while absolutely of their own place and time, nevertheless participated in a global system of pop-rock. In Regev's view, this musical culture had become a space of 'aesthetic cosmopolitanism', one in which participants from around the world entered so as to seek a kind of musical citizenship and to participate in dialogue across neighbouring and overlapping cultural spaces.

[T]he traditional and modernist perception of world culture as composed of distinct, separate cultural units – be they national, ethnic, local or indigenous – has been replaced by a perception of world culture as one entity composed of numerous sub-units that interact ... The sense of cultural uniqueness shared by any given social entity on earth can no longer stand in real or perceived isolation from that of other entities. Complex forms of connectivity, relations to power, and currents of influence render all frames of cultural uniqueness as sub-units in a single world cultural web. (Regev 2013: 7)

Case Study 1.2: (cont.)

Taking aim at old models of domination and simple hybridity, Regev seeks to foreground the meaningfulness, value and sheer proliferation of contributions to this space, wherever they may have emanated.

Nevertheless, the 'cosmopolitanism' that Regev hails is trickier than it may seem. In a critical discussion of that concept, Martin Stokes cites the anthropologist Anna Tsing: '(p)oor migrants need to fit into the worlds of others; cosmopolitans want more of the world to be theirs' (Stokes 2007: 10). And one need not be a migrant to be on the receiving end of cosmopolitan condescension. Paul Simon positioned his 1986 album *Graceland*, which was recorded in South Africa with local musicians, as an act of musical cosmopolitanism and intercultural dialogue. Yet the politics of social and creative inequality, cultural appropriation and intellectual property were plain throughout the record's production and reception (Meintjes 1990). Musical cosmopolitanism can be a powerful way of engaging with the world, but it can also mask, and even strengthen, inequalities of power and agency.

• Paul Simon (b. 1941), 'Under African Skies' (from *Graceland*, Warner Bros., 1986)

One of the trends that characterised twentieth-century globalisation was mass migration, whether compelled (as in the case of Jews fleeing persecution and murder at the hands of the Nazis before and during World War II) or voluntary (like the many Britons who emigrated to Australia mid-century seeking space and sun). The large-scale dispersal of peoples of shared origin across the world increasingly led theorists of culture to focus on the concept that described that phenomenon: diaspora. Here, in the networks that linked but also marked the distance between members of a scattered cultural group, was a new kind of 'space', one that was apt to be filled with shared cultural expression of all kinds – not least music.

A number of studies have examined the ways that members of the Jewish diaspora, centuries in the making, have maintained and constructed forms of Jewish identity at once stable and evolving: traditional (and often liturgical) musical practices emanating from the Middle East have been safeguarded, even as they have been blended with art, folk and popular forms that migrants have encountered in their new European and American homes (Gottlieb 2004; Bohlman 2008; Botstein 2011). But perhaps the single most influential study of such diasporic cultural dynamics has been Paul Gilroy's 1993 *The Black Atlantic*. Gilroy's book was, in part, a response to the 'Afrocentric' thought that had risen to popularity in African American communities after the 1960s. This work had sought to oppose oppressive, 'Eurocentric' forms of thinking and social

Case Study 1.2: (cont.)

organisation and insisted that an innate 'Africanness' be embraced by Black Americans in their daily life and cultural production. Afrocentrism was developed in Black Studies university programmes and among grass-roots political groups, but at the time of Gilroy's writing, its appeals were most visibly articulated in hip-hop by groups like X-Clan.

In *The Black Atlantic*, Gilroy argued that the 'authentic', 'African' cultural practices that Afrocentrists demanded form the basis of Black American life were reductive, fictional, and 'essentialist' (➔Chapter 14, 'Race and Ethnicity'). But he also saw an alternative 'localism' – in which Black cultures in the West were imagined as discrete, national entities like African American, Anglophone Caribbean, Black British and so on – as equally simplistic (Gilroy 1993: 31–3). Gilroy sought to counter this binarism by describing the dynamics of a Western Black culture that he saw as 'lodged between the local and the global': his 'Black Atlantic' was thus a cultural space around which thought, expression and people circulated, ever open to change – ever resistant to reductive originalism – but ever mindful of what united them (Gilroy 1993: 15).

And that, in the final analysis, was the historical fact of slavery, the transatlantic trade that had first taken Black people westwards. Gilroy argued that, while Black Atlantic culture and identity was endlessly innovative and syncretic, it also kept alive the memory of slavery and the terror of oppression in 'ritualised, social forms', with music – the circulation and recirculation of shared motifs in sound, performance and dance – foremost among them (Gilroy 1993: 73). So, beginning in earnest in the 1950s, American jazz was remade by West Indian and African musicians, many of whom had spent periods living in Europe and the USA, including the Nigerian bandleader Ambrose Campbell, Jamaican saxophonist Joe Harriott, and South African singer and composer (Sathima) Bea Benjamin; in the following decade, soul music was tweaked into ska and reggae by Jamaicans who themselves then moved to the UK, that country becoming a major centre of reggae production with its own local reggae forms, developed by first-generation Black Britons. Meanwhile, African musicians and audiences, most obviously the Nigerian saxophonist and bandleader Fela Kuti, were taking James Brown's American example (➔Chapter 6, 'Rhythm and Time') of funk-based cultural leadership and Black self-determination and adapting it to their own postcolonial situation.

- Joe Harriott Quintet, 'Calypso Sketches' (from *Free Form*, Jazzland, 1961)
- Ambrose Campbell (1919–2006), 'Yolanda' (from *High Life Today*, Columbia, 1966)
- Bea Benjamin (1936–2013), 'Africa' (from *African Songbird*, The Sun, 1976)
- Toots and the Maytals, 'Pressure Drop' (from *Funky Kingston*, Dragon, 1973)

Case Study 1.2: (cont.)

- Janet Kay (b. 1958), 'Silly Games' (Arawak, 1979)
- James Brown (1933–2006), 'Super Bad, Pts. 1 and 2' (King, 1970)
- Fela Kuti (1938–97), 'Zombie' (from *Zombie*, Coconut, 1977)

This led to Gilroy's influential insight that modern identities and cultures might be thought of not in terms of rootedness, but as processes of movement and change: as he put it, not 'roots', but 'routes' (Gilroy 1993: 19).

Conclusion

At the end of the century, discourses around place and space, and all the ideas contained therein – notions of authenticity, identity, centres and margins, belonging and appropriation – were about to be transformed by the massive global uptake of Internet technology. Both 'situation' and 'dislocation' would come to be experienced differently in the thoroughly networked, always-on mediascape that digital culture would engender.

But this was an intensification of trends already long visible; indeed, the term 'mediascape' had been coined by the anthropologist Arjun Appadurai at the turn of the 1990s, as part of what became a celebrated – because apposite – analysis of globalised experience. Appadurai suggested that it was no longer useful to imagine the planet as composed of discrete sets of supposedly 'authentic' places, peoples and practices. The new globalised world, he wrote, could be seen as comprising instead a series of 'scapes': those mediascapes, comprised of images and sounds that circulated the world over, were joined by ethnoscapes (groups of people, often transient), technoscapes and finanscapes (multinational companies and their financial arrangements) and ideoscapes (ideas, like 'democracy', leading different lives in different places). At the start of this chapter, we saw how Romantic landscapes had come to be critiqued as representations that made a place stand for a particular, fixed idea. In contrast, Appadurai argued, the global 'scapes' that characterised the world at the century's end were spaces that were 'fluid' and 'irregular' in size and shape, their identity and meaning constantly changing (Appadurai 1990: 6–7). Appadurai's terms well describe the spaces that twentieth-century music and its makers crossed and recrossed, with ever-increasing speed and reach.

2 | Modernism

From the latter 1700s, new methods of industrial production, concentrated in the cities, had transformed the ways people lived and worked. In the nineteenth century, new modes of travel and communication had reshaped the ways many people experienced space and time. By 1900, developing forms of representative government and administration were giving the citizens of many countries increasing access to power and formal education, and, in the first half of the twentieth century, war and revolution tore through societies across the world. Meanwhile, modern scientific and humanistic study was rewriting what was known about nature, civilisation and the psyche. Across this period, and largely as a result of these events, former mainstays of society and tradition – the church, the monarchies, rigid class systems, patriarchy – were seeing their power challenged and diminished.

These changes characterised what scholars have dubbed modernity. 'Modernism', then, is a term applied to the mass of cultural activity – music, art, literature, design, architecture – which, from around 1890 to 1960, purposefully sought to create new art forms that could articulate the thrill, and bewilderment, of such rapid social change. For Peter Gay (2007), modernist art was that which trashed familiar forms of beauty and expression to pit itself against hypocritical bourgeois conventions and morality. That meant developing new creative techniques and forms, with works that were often fragmentary, sense-disrupting; in music, modernism's first casualty was a traditional notion of tonal harmony, with melody soon following. Central for the modernists was not just what an artwork 'said', but how it would be made. As Mark Fisher (2012a) observes, experimental modernist works were significant not just in and of themselves, but also for the range of further possibilities they conjured: if the rules of harmony could be disregarded, then why not do the same for form, rhythm, instrumentation? That exploration of technique, and the proliferation of creative motives, meant that modernist art was anything but stylistically uniform. This was less a 'movement' than a moment. Nevertheless, modernist art was characterised by its impatient and often radical rejection of norms both social and artistic.

Yet that radicalism, often emphasised in earlier music histories, obscures the extent to which important modernist musicians emerged from, and conducted their entire careers within, an educational and professional establishment that accommodated their revolutions with minimal difficulty. The later reception of modernism has accordingly been shaded with doubt and revisionism. For most twentieth-century commentators and scholars, modernism proper was to be found in the 'high' arts alone: James Joyce's novels, Picasso's painting and sculpture, Le Corbusier's buildings and Schoenberg's atonal musical composition. But towards the end of the century, and with modernism's golden age definitively over, scholars began to reassess the classifications and claims that had long enclosed this exclusive historical terrain. Surely, some argued, modernism had shaped a range of musical approaches beyond Schoenberg's own; strange, others noted, that almost every artist previously deemed to have formulated an important response to the modern experience was highly educated, white and male. In the twenty-first century, scholars have often been eager to bring into the fold people and ideas that had formerly been systematically excluded – women, artists of colour, traditionally minded composition and popular forms – and, while admiring the energy and vision of those modernists who turned musical tradition on its head, to ask questions of the masculine rhetoric or the dubious imaginings of race that, as we will see, were rarely far from the surface.

Still, the debates and manifestos that first articulated modernism's central concerns were initiated in the art music world, so it is there that this chapter begins, exploring the ways that early-century artists tried to rethink relationships between music, society and the self. Because that narrative has been such a central component of twentieth-century music history, the chapter sticks closer to standard histories than does the rest of the book. However, this overview also follows recent scholarship in opening out to include figures who, though significant, were long left out of studies of modernist music; in its second half, the chapter engages with what has increasingly been thought of as 'popular modernism' and musical radicalism that occurred outside the art music sphere. The chapter ends at mid-century, where the next, on postmodernism (➜Chapter 3, 'Postmodernism'), picks up. There, and indeed throughout the book, we will see how early-century modernist attitudes and methods would be echoed by musicians of all stripes for decades to come. But it is important that the differences between musical figures and forms are not dissolved into a happy synthesis: any initial account of modernism which smoothed away all the period's antagonisms – between supporters of high and low forms, between supposed right and wrong ways of sounding the present in music – would miss the point. Not just inclusion, then, but also tension, must be vital in giving a full account of the life, and perhaps death, of the modernist ideal.

Tradition, Progress and the Avant-Gardes

All modernist artists were concerned above all with 'the new'. As we shall see, for many, that meant making music that departed from tradition in order to speak of life *today*. Yet for others, it extended to a belief that the best cultural work not only invalidated the approaches it superseded but also edged humanity towards the fulfilment of its destiny. This thinking was shaped by what has often been termed the 'cult of progress', and assumptions that underpinned latter nineteenth-century discourses of all kinds; in the works of figures as different as the German philosopher G. W. F. Hegel, the philosopher-economist Karl Marx and the historian Auguste Comte, each successive historical stage, it was suggested, had in some way improved upon the last. Following the widespread acceptance and popularisation of Charles Darwin's work on evolution, this thesis came to seem like an observable truth.

This 'teleological' thinking can be seen all over writing about music in that period: debates on the nature of what was called *Zukunftsmusik* – the 'music of the future' – swarmed around the work of self-conscious musical innovators like Liszt and Wagner, those determined to forge the musical tools that would build culture's next stage. In keeping with the progressive doctrine, and the demands for full emotional and spiritual investment also central to art in this Romantic period, the innovating efforts of those composers were seized upon and intensified by their successors. It might seem a rather neat way of seeing music history, but nevertheless there is no little truth in the much-repeated claim that, through the nineteenth century, composers of the Austro-German tradition sought to express an ever-greater degree of emotion by making ever-greater use of chromaticism; unpredictable, surging harmonic movement, and eternally sighing melodic shapes, were used to signify the kinds of fullness of feeling that, for Wagner – and then late Romantic composers like Richard Strauss

(1864–1949) and Gustav Mahler (1860–1911), working at the very limits of traditional tonality by the end of the 1910s – was so important (Taruskin 2010a: 1–20).

Wagner's example was vital to modern art musicians everywhere. Later, we will turn to his Austro-German inheritors, led by Arnold Schoenberg (1871–1951) and congregating principally in Vienna. But the musicians living in what was then *the* artistic capital of the Western world, Paris, reached for a different response. That was no surprise, given that France and the German state of Prussia had frequently been in conflict; most recently in 1870, when a resounding Prussian victory ended with swathes of France confiscated and Paris under occupation. As Richard Taruskin notes, in the war's aftermath, French critics and artistic institutions called for the construction of an 'ars gallica', a specifically French art, amid which the nation's fragile image of its history and future could be rebuilt. Even those given to regarding such official programmes with suspicion were enveloped by the effort to find a way out of a Romantic tradition that was defined by those Germanic avatars; as a result, it has ever since been common for music histories to begin by situating Paris and Vienna as the twin poles of modernist activity (e.g., Salzman 2001/1967).

There were few better exemplars of this attempt than the French composer and pianist Erik Satie (1866–1925). When Satie went to his nightly work as an accompanist at the Parisian cabaret Le Chat Noir in the late 1890s, he walked past a sign that echoed a famous demand of the symbolist poet Rimbaud: 'be modern!', it demanded of the club's patrons. Satie was a member of various sects, orders and brotherhoods, groups of (male) bohemians united by their interest in this or that artistic cause and their waspish, semi-serious intent; 'the best cabaret humour', writes Stephen Whiting in his study of the composer's demi-monde (1999: 416), 'addressed itself to a small circle of insiders or *cognoscenti*, while it sought to mystify outsiders'. Satie's attitude could not have been more distant from Wagnerian high seriousness. But the humour and irony of Satie's music often had serious conceptual impulses and outcomes. His piece *Vexations* (*c*.1893), thought to have been inspired by the austere poetic technique forged by Charles Cros in opposition to the Romantic verbosity of the day, is formed of a dusky line heard alternately alone and harmonised in two ways. But a note on the score directs the whole be repeated 840 times, and whether this ephemeral and long-unpublished work was entirely serious or not, a truly 'modernist' question is posed: what is a musical piece, or a musical performance? What *could* those things be?

Figure 2.1 Erik Satie, *Harmonies*, I (*c*.1893)

A number of composers had begun to work with harmonic vocabularies that did not observe the long-established rules of harmonic movement and resolution, either short or long term. Dating from around the same time as *Vexations*, Satie's page-long sketch *Harmonies* – the first of its three sections is shown in Figure 2.1 in its entirety – embodies this new attention to harmonic colour over procedure.

Satie was a miniaturist, a conceptualist and a provocateur. But his friend Claude Debussy (1862–1918), who enjoyed a highly successful musical education, was given to extending these experiments on a much grander scale. Debussy's approach to harmony – and the structuring of phrase and form to which it gave rise – was not only dramatically unusual for its time, but also remained tremendously influential into the twenty-first century. We will explore this in more detail in a later chapter's case study (➜Chapter 7, 'Harmony'). Here, though, we will note the technical and aesthetic tenets that set Debussy's music at the start of musical modernism proper.

Following Satie, Debussy had begun to take what, in the normal scheme of tonal harmony, would be 'dissonant' harmonies demanding resolution, and to treat them as detachable objects with their own tonal autonomy. No longer, for example, was a dominant seventh chord merely a passing aggregation of voices, laden with tension, that were compelled to resolve to chord I; now, such a chord could be sounded, allowed to linger – allowed to be savoured – and then replaced with one of many others, rather than necessarily giving way to the expected tonic (this can be heard in the example below, *Nuages*). Indeed, traditional leading-note resolution, and the sense of harmonic propulsion that effected – a kind of propulsion which was taken to extremes in the music of Wagner, Strauss and Mahler – was conspicuous by its rarity in Debussy's mature work; his signature use of the semitone-less whole-tone scale – a device that would be so widely adopted as to become one of the clichés of early modernism – represented a further departure from functional harmony's chromatic design, and, moreover, the goal-direction which was of a piece with that wider ideology of progress discussed earlier. Still, a sense of tonal centre was retained. Taruskin's detailed analysis of 'Nuages', from the set *Nocturnes* (completed 1899), shows Debussy employing fragments of tonal, modal and whole-tone grammar in service of the piece's mood (Taruskin 2010a: 79–83).

- Claude Debussy, '1. Nuages', *Nocturnes* (completed 1899)

Debussy's response to Wagnerian, high-intensity chromatic surging was thus cool detachment, and an interest in sonority, sensuality, the surface of sound. His music did not rush to its climax but was content to sit still and shimmer. In its ephemerality and elusiveness, the style recalled the 'Impressionist' painting then regarded as the *dernier cri* of Parisian modernity, and the term – variously embraced and rejected by Debussy and others – was soon applied to music (Albright 2015).

While Debussy's music departed from 'German' norms, his approach owed much to an interest in Russian music, especially the harmonic colour and daring of Rimsky-Korsakov, and the self-designed forms and self-standing textures of Mussorgsky. Debussy was also strongly informed by Javanese gamelan (Fauser 2005). But aspects of his aesthetic were directly owed to the symbolism of modern French poets. Lydia Goehr (2001) provides a reading of Debussy's opera *Pelléas et Mélisande* (completed 1898, first performed 1902) that shows how indirectness was not just a tonal, but also a philosophical outcome. Goehr argues that, while a Wagner work like *Tristan and Isolde* (first performed 1865) had striven and been heralded for its magnificent unity – not just its compositional integrity, but also the synthesis of music, character and drama – *Pelléas* was truly modernist in its questioning of such coherence. As we will see shortly, one of the central modernist preoccupations was with the limits of expressibility of the subjective interior. The opera employs many mysterious, mythical symbols – water, the forest, noon and midnight – which render the action 'unrealistic', resisting simple narrative explanation and instead left hanging as pure idea or mood. Debussy later developed this technique through writing pieces that often had simple but suggestive titles alluding to the pastoral and the natural world (Abbate 1998).

- 'La Cathédrale engloutie', *Préludes*, Book 1 (1909–10)

If early French modernists were apt to see themselves as unpicking the fabric of Austro-German musical tradition, then the German speakers themselves tended to see their work as taking up the thread their elders had left off. The figures who, along with Debussy, are most frequently situated at the beginning of musical modernism – Arnold Schoenberg and his pupils Alban Berg (1885–1935) and Anton Webern (1883–1945), together forming the core of what is known as the Second Viennese School – were typical in this respect, if no other.

Schoenberg has long occupied a central role in histories of twentieth-century music, since it was he who did most to clarify – through both composition and theoretical writing – what music could sound like and how it could work once the rules of tonality were discarded once and for all. We will see in →Chapter 7, 'Harmony' how Schoenberg's works gradually loosened and then broke nearly all bonds with the tonal practice of the day through what he later called (1984/1941) 'the emancipation of the dissonance'. What is important to understand here, however, is that Schoenberg, according to the positivist thinking of his time, saw this not as a rejection of musical history – as was charged by the many listeners and musicians who objected vociferously to his work – but as an inevitable next step in its development, just like those taken by Wagner, Mahler and Debussy in the years preceding. This positioning was not unjustified, and it fairly served an early atonal style that often made use of traditional formal models and gestural shapes – the following example, 'Sehr Langsam', is in simple ABA[1] form – while functioning in a previously unheard world of tonal movement and harmonic colour. We will return to Schoenberg's music, and later developments in atonal composition, below.

- Arnold Schoenberg, 'Sehr Langsam', from *Six Little Piano Pieces* (1911)

Still, the presence of these bonds to tonal tradition did not mean that the new music was supposed to pander to its contemporary audiences. Indeed, music too 'pleasing', too readily comprehended, would likely have rendered the authenticity of the innovation suspect. By definition, the music of the future was not supposed to sit easily in the present, and this was one reason that many members of both early and later modernist schools made much of their disdain for the idea of a popular reception – not least because their music was often subject to critical censure and even ridicule. As Schoenberg put it, with a high-handedness that was entirely unexceptional for its time: 'if it is art it is not for everybody; if it is for everybody it is not art' (cited in Taruskin 2010a: 353).

A somewhat different attitude was articulated by the radical modernist factions known as the 'avant-gardes'. The term avant-garde, 'advance guard', had and would retain military and political connotations; the early socialist theorist Henri de Saint-Simon was the first to apply the term to art and to the idea that new forms were generally created by a few, brave innovators who acted as pathfinders for the many who followed (Scott 2008: 216). Yet, unlike those modernists who tried to position their work as a logical extension of past practice, these groups also showed far less fealty to the grand tradition of bourgeois art and to the institutions that supported them. What became known as the modernist avant-garde was a collection of small groups of self-conscious rebels whose mission was to explode extant artistic practice and aesthetics – often, to make 'anti-art' – and to wrench creative work out of the chilly atmosphere of the museum and concert hall. That did not mean making art that appealed instead to extant popular taste; far from it. Rather, the avant-gardes aimed to situate their experiments in the thick of everyday life, turning the world into the stuff of creative work, transforming both in the process.

Music and sound featured in the activities of a number of the avant-garde groups. The Italian Futurists announced their appearance with the publication Filippo Tommaso Marinetti's 1909 'Futurist Manifesto' in a French newspaper; manifesto-writing was a key element of much avant-garde activity, and this one demanded an art that would celebrate the new machines, speed and the violence of war. We will see in →Chapter 8, 'Instruments' how the Futurists introduced an enduring interest in machine 'noise' to twentieth-century music. But if the Futurists emerged from the political right – as their lust for war, and dalliances with early fascism and anti-feminism suggest – then the members of the Dada group, identified with their early bases in Zurich, Berlin and Paris and emerging during World War I, were their counterparts on the left.

Dada's rejection of bourgeois manners and aesthetics, capitalist society and war, gave rise to a great number of initiatives across art forms and continents: visual art, performance, photography, film and sound poetry all figured in the attempts by artists like Man Ray, Hannah Höch and Marcel Duchamp to subvert the senses and indeed sense itself, to disorient, mock and remake a world brought low by unthinking belief in reason and progress – neither of which were much on display in the slaughter then taking place. The German visual artist and poet Kurt Schwitters was especially interested in music, and his sound poetry makes use of musical approaches and, in the case of *Ursonate*, fully-fledged sonata form.

- Kurt Schwitters, *Ursonate* (1922 onwards)

Before Stalin's policy of socialist realism began to be enforced in the 1930s, Soviet Russia, too, was the site of much avant-garde activity, from the films of Dziga Vertov (1896–1954) to the music of Alexander Mosolov (1900–73), whose early music includes settings of newspaper small ads and the stunning portrayal of a factory in action, *Iron Foundry* (1927). Socialist, anarchist and rightist avant-gardists alike were thus committed to an artistic transformation of daily life, a concern quite distinct from those of the 'concert-hall' modernists; what all these approaches shared was the pre-rogative to give contemporary experience its contemporary creative forms.

Subjectivity

Still, we have already started to see that it would be a mistake to equate modernism with a simple fixation upon the new, even if that is the meaning that most strongly resonates in the twenty-first century. Aside from its continuities with recent artistic, philosophical and scientific tradition, much modernist art also manifested a fascination with something far older: the fundamentals of the human condition. This exploration took several forms.

At the turn of the century, the European colonial powers were at their zenith. As European scholars and functionaries travelled the colonies of Africa, Asia and the Americas – recording what they found and sending back goods, knowledge and even people for display at home – so in the West a modern discourse of 'primitivism' began to emerge (Clifford 1988). Distant non-European cultures, it was thought, represented humanity at an earlier stage of its development than could now be found in the West, and so the study of 'exotic' cultures could give a glimpse of humanity at a time long gone. Theories and histories of music were very much a part of what was a form of white supremacy, and a number of treatises from the late-nineteenth to early-twentieth centuries dealt with African and Asian music – and its supposed foil, 'advanced' European composition – to this effect (Cross 2007).

Yet as we have seen, the modernists were concerned, almost above all, with breaking through what they saw as the now-atrophied structures of art music composition. One way to achieve this was to engage with different musical cultures. As mentioned, Debussy's encounter with a Javanese gamelan group at the 1889 Exposition universelle in Paris helped him clarify his ideas about sound and non-functional harmony (Fauser 2005), and, in the first decades of the twentieth century, folk cultures in general were being mined for ways to help disrupt or invigorate that harmonic and structural system.

There is no better example of that trend – and there are few pieces more central to the twentieth-century canon – than the 1913 ballet *The Rite of Spring*, by the Russian composer Igor Stravinsky (1882–1971). *The Rite* portrays an imagined pagan ritual and makes use of melodies and rhythmic materials affecting a relationship with (and, indeed, directly drawn from) the Russian

Subjectivity   55

folk tradition. In its throwing together of the supposedly old and the inarguably new – Stravinsky's rhythmic, formal and orchestration techniques were astonishing to contemporary audiences, and for many they remain so – the *Rite* was a remarkable fulfilment of the ambitions seen across so much of the contemporary musical world of the century's first decades. Stravinsky's modernist rhythmic innovations, and other modernist mobilisations of 'folk'-derived rhythms, are explored later (➜ Chapter 6, 'Rhythm and Time').

- Igor Stravinsky, *The Rite of Spring* (1913)

More widespread inspiration was found in ragtime and jazz, which began to transform popular music and dance cultures from around 1900, at first in America and then in Europe. This music's rhythmic impulse and play were utterly foreign to Western art music and commercial popular song, and the Black American musicians identified with it were, inevitably, identified with a wider, and as Petrine Archer-Straw's important 2000 study shows, fundamentally racist 'African' primitivism. Yet, owing to its novelty and vitality, jazz was also seen to embody an utterly contemporary spirit. It was natural, then, for a composer like Darius Milhaud to use early jazz rhythms in his music for the ballet *La Création du monde*: the contemporary Blackness it depicted was imagined as tallying with the prehistorical scene in which the piece was set.

- Darius Milhaud, *La Création du monde* (1923)

Clearly, whatever the brilliance of the music made, there was much to regret. Musicians working in the bourgeois art music tradition picked at the styles of 'Other' musical cultures in the search for new musical material that would encapsulate the spirit of the time. Shortly, we will see how some of those supposed Others formulated their own vision of musical modernity. There was, however, a second strand to this modernist exploration of the supposedly primal aspects of human experience; this dwelt on psychology, and the workings of the subconscious.

A large number of modernist artists in all fields were influenced by the (then scandalous) texts that Sigmund Freud had been publishing as he developed his psychoanalytical practice at the end of the nineteenth century; an interest in the subconscious informed modernist music (Carpenter 2010) just as it would Salvador Dalí's surrealist painting, the stream-of-consciousness narratives of James Joyce and Virginia Woolf or Gertrude Stein's 'automatic writing', in which the author attempted merely to transcribe what the subconscious said.

This technique, in which given structures of form and thought were disregarded, was in some ways paralleled in the free atonality being explored by Schoenberg in the first decade of the century. And, though he had likely not read Freud's writing, psychological themes – and the extended meditation on ideas of subjective interiority – became central to his music (Watkins 2008). In his monodrama *Erwartung* (1909, first performed 1924), Schoenberg managed an unprecedented half-hour of music in which there is no thematic repetition, and, the text aside, no conventional formal or tonal framework to follow – just an unbroken compositional stream of consciousness that shadows the singer's character, a woman who wanders, bewildered and alone, in a forest, before finding the body of her lover; it seems, or perhaps she imagines, that she has herself murdered him.

This layering of the imagined, the buried, the desired – and a surface emotion familiar from 'Expressionist' drama and painting of the time – was shared by Alban Berg's opera, *Wozzeck* (1914–22, first performed 1925). The subject matter was also similar: Berg's was the story of a soldier who, in the grip of insanity, kills his lover, Marie. In contrast to Schoenberg's free composition, however, Berg's piece drew upon a gamut of historical compositional devices and forms. Each of its fifteen scenes makes use of a new one, whether passacaglia, rondo or invention on a theme, to realise a piece which is in some ways the summation of the Wagnerian project of through-composed music drama. Berg describes the central character's descent into what Joseph Kerman, in his landmark 1956 study *Opera as Drama*, calls 'psychosis' through material, mood and technique: as Kerman writes, it is not just the 'fantastically chromatic and disjunct lines' demanded of the singers, but also the many uses of ostinato that musically actualise Wozzeck's murderous obsession (Kerman 2005/1956: 182–3). Brass and woodwind choirs burble under the voices summoning a turbulent but unidentified mental disquiet; musical motifs endlessly swim around this musical subconscious in one form or another; material heard in obscure form at the start of the piece is blazingly exposed in Wozzeck's death scene, compositional technique helping to well up Wozzeck's unmanageable, fatal impulses.

- Arnold Schoenberg, *Erwartung* (1909)
- Alban Berg, *Wozzeck*, Act 3, Scene iv (1922)

Modernism and Gender

It is notable that the position of imagined female subjects in the compositions described above is fraught: in a number of modernist dramatic works – *Pelléas et Mélisande*, *The Rite of Spring*, Berg's incomplete *Lulu* (1929–35), Bartòk's *Bluebeard's Castle* (1911–17, first performed 1918), and others – a key element of modernist 'critique' or shock effect is a female lead character's murder, downfall or psycho-trauma. As we described in the →Introduction, one of the fundamental insights of the so-called 'new music-ology' of the late twentieth century was that music, like all cultural forms, was not a neutral observer but a participant in the formation of categories like gender and race; these works, and many like them, constructed and reinforced an imagining of women as somehow 'Other', whether psycho-logically, emotionally or socially. Beyond such representations, feminist scholars also began to scrutinise common modernist claims around innov-ation and the creative destruction of common musical practices. These prerogatives, it was argued, often protected and advanced particularly mas-culine kinds of power. Catherine Parsons Smith (1994) shows how many modernist composers and critics, on both sides of the Atlantic, described and evaluated modern music according to notions of virility, and a particularly thrusting, presumably male kind of energy; drawing on literary theory, Parsons Smith argues that modernists' self-consciously advanced musical languages and techniques sought to mystify musical production and experience, ideally removing them from a public realm to a private circle of initiates, not coincidentally excluding women. Andreas Huyssen (1986: 44–62) has shown how cultural discourses in Europe at this time gendered mass culture, and the masses themselves, as feminine. Both Parsons Smith and Huyssen argue that this 'gendered' specialisation – which we will hear more of later – could be at least partly explained as an anxious male response to the contemporary women's movement, and to a concurrent rise of women in the artistic professions.

After all, the disciplining of women – especially those who had attempted to take some kind of socially unaccepted liberty, like living independently or acting upon desire – was not limited to the narratives of music-drama. It is useful to consider here the example of Germaine Tailleferre (1892–1983). Tailleferre was one of the young French composers, initially brought together by Satie, who would come to be known at the end of the 1910s as Les Six. Milhaud and Francis Poulenc (1899–1963) would come to be the best known of the group, while Tailleferre's music and presence would largely recede from view before World War II. As a young woman, Tailleferre had already taken a tremendously bold step just in studying music, her father having vociferously opposed it. As a wife, she was subject to a near-fatal bout of domestic violence, and marriages that, as was so often the case for women artists, significantly disrupted her career. And as a member of Les Six, her music and talent were subject to strongly gendered criticism. Kiri Heel (2011: 19) notes that one of the ways that Tailleferre negotiated this was to surround herself with a coterie of women patrons, collaborators, performers, supporters and friends. Notable was the ballet Tailleferre created with the artist and writer Hélène Perdriat, *Le Marchand d'oiseaux* (1923), apparently the first to be produced by a team of women. Tailleferre's music for the ballet collaged numerous styles from the baroque onwards, but, Heel writes, '[i]n revisiting previous composers and styles, Tailleferre often modernizes their particular textures and melodic character-istics with dissonant harmonies' (168). This approach was central to her style, as can be heard in *Image*, a piece for octet, with its layers of lyrical melody and counterpoint, each observing its own tonality (or rather modality).

- Germaine Tailleferre, *Image* (1918)

As Jane Fulcher (2005: 193–5) has written, Tailleferre had to plot a careful course through her composition in order to be accepted at all: anything overly adventurous, satirical or obscure was likely to be poorly received, even though these were qualities often celebrated in modernist men. But for Fulcher, Tailleferre demonstrated her 'modernism' just by claiming her place on the modern music scene. After 1918, there was much discussion in France of the 'new woman', and the members of a generation who, following the slaughter of so many men in World War I, were leading independent and public lives in a manner hitherto uncommon for middle-class women. Embodying this figure and yet subject to many gendered constraints, Tailleferre was thus caught between shifting notions of possibil-ity for women, which were key parts of the new, modern European society.

However, the composer who has received the most thoroughgoing re-evaluation since the late twentieth century, Ruth Crawford (1901–53, Figure 2.2), did not emerge from one of that continent's artistic capitals. During the 1920s and 1930s, New York City would be home to a cluster of composers' collectives that provided support and promotion for musicians developing new compositional approaches. The Pan-American Association of Composers was co-founded by the French expat Edgard Varèse (1883–1965) and American original Henry Cowell (1897–1965). Meanwhile, the Composers' Collective was founded by theorist and com-poser Charles Seeger (1886–1979). Cowell and Seeger produced many compelling compositions of their own, but it was in the work of Crawford – who was associated with both groups to varying degrees

Figure 2.2 Ruth Crawford in the 1920s. Reproduced by kind permission of the family of Ruth Crawford Seeger

(Tick 2007) – that American modernist imperatives received some of their most imaginative musical responses.

Crawford's music tended towards a focused austerity, and this, Joseph N. Straus argues (1995: 216–19), represented a fulfilment of Cowell's dictum that American 'ultramodern' music should pull away from the models found in Europe. That often meant focusing less on harmony and more on texture and heterophony, or the play of individual voices. Crawford also explored techniques that systematised control of other musical parameters, like rhythm articulation and that would not be widely taken up by other composers until the 1940s (219).

Such heterophony, and formal heterogeneity, is evinced in Crawford's most celebrated work, the String Quartet of 1931. Ellie Hisama's detailed analysis of the piece's third movement (2006: 12–34) shows two forms of development at work in this extremely unusual, close-textured music. On the one hand, there is a musical narrative that moves towards a rather 'old-fashioned' climax, seemingly some years out of place with its ultramodern musical fabric, which seems more concerned with close-up examination of gestural detail than such bold, Romantic rhetoric. Yet on the other hand, there is a counter-narrative, one which unfolds according to its own rules, excluded from and perhaps subverting the more obvious 'climax' argument. This narrative has each of the quartet's voices constantly ebbing, flowing or in Hisama's term 'twisting', as they tangle, cross and re-cross each other in ways that neither aid the move towards climax, nor reflect the standard registral organisation of the cello, viola and two violins.

- Ruth Crawford, String Quartet (1931)

This conjunction of techniques – which, as we will see shortly, foreshadows the compositional 'processes' of later serial composers – gives the music its teeming unfamiliarity; to Hisama, following the kind of musicological interpretation pioneered by Susan McClary (→Chapter 13, 'Gender and Sexuality') it also articulates something of Crawford's own position in being, by dint of her gender, excluded from full membership of the modernist tide in which she swam. These ideas have been developed by later scholars seeking to locate other female participants in the modernist moment: these are USA-based composers like Johanna Beyer (1888–1944) (Hisama 2006; Allen and Hisama 2007; De Graaf 2008), and the British Elizabeth Maconchy (1907–94), Grace Williams (1906–77) and Elisabeth Lutyens (1906–83) (Halstead 1997; Mathias 2012; Forkert 2017; Brüstle and Sofer 2018).

Case Study 2.1: Twelve-Tone and Serial Techniques

Composers working with atonal materials faced great formal challenges: deprived of the kinds of long-range organisational schemes that tonal harmony had provided, it was overwhelmingly difficult to construct coherent, large-scale pieces.

After several years during which he did not complete any compositional work, in the early 1920s Schoenberg developed a technique to overcome this problem. An Austrian theorist and sometime composer, Josef Matthias Hauser, was independently arriving at a similar system, but it was Schoenberg's formulation and application of what became known as 'twelve-tone' or 'dodecaphonic' composition that would fundamentally reshape modernist music (Schoenberg 1984/1941). Here, the twelve pitches of the chromatic scale were organised into 'rows': an original sequence, arranged to provide whatever thematic and harmonic possibilities the composer wanted, together with that row in its inverted, retrograde and transposed forms. These rows – all forty-eight possible permutations, which could be calculated and set out on a 'magic square' from which the composer could work – were introduced, combined and manipulated in a kind of analogy to chordal derivation and tonal modulation. Yet the feeling of tonal centre was denied by the fact that no pitch in an individual series could be repeated

Case Study 2.1: (cont.)

before the row's remaining pitches had sounded, and composers working with these methods as far as possible avoided intervals and chords too redolent of tonal practice, such as perfect fourths, fifths and octaves – although some analysts have argued that tonal residues, notably the importance of the leading-note/tonic semitone, can be seen in post-tonal music (Milstein 1992).

In this music, composerly invention lies in the initial ordering of the pitch material, which can be designed in order to heighten particular kinds of pitch relationship and their characteristics; it comes from the kaleidoscopic combination and manipulation of row forms that characterise the technique's sophisticated employment. Figure 2.3 shows the scheme, as set out by Robert Morgan, of the Piano Suite's 'Gigue'. The initial or 'prime' row is joined by its retrograde (R), transposed (by six semitones), inverted (I) and retrograde inverted (RI) forms, and those forms' various permutations; these rows' appearance in the realised music is shown on the score extract.

- Arnold Schoenberg. 'Gigue', Piano Suite (1921–3)

Figure 2.3 Tone rows and first two bars of 'Gigue' by Arnold Schoenberg, Piano Suite, Op. 25 (1921–3), as analysed by Robert Morgan (1991: 189–92)

Case Study 2.1: (cont.)

Schoenberg was said to have told a friend sometime around 1921–2 that he had 'discovered something which will assure the supremacy of German music for the next hundred years' (cited in Taruskin 2010a: 704). The twelve-tone system, in his thinking, was the foundation of what the music of the future would be, and later, important pedagogues like the Paris-based René Leibowitz would instil younger composers with a sense of the approach's primacy.

In contrast to the personalised technical endeavours seen earlier, twelve-tone technique was eminently teachable and reproducible, and the systematisation of modern composition helped build an international community of musicians who could feel that they were at work on the same project. As a woman, and as a modernist in a conservative musical culture, the British composer Elisabeth Lutyens (1906–83) felt doubly excluded from musical life in her home country. In 1946, though, she would visit France. 'Among the young composers in Paris', she would write, '12-tone music was, by then, completely accepted so that I lost the sense of utter isolation I had felt in musical England' (Forkert 2017: 281). But Lutyens also saw that codification could bring 'academicism' to a language still in development, a 'grammar', where what was needed was magic. As Annika Forkert argues, Lutyens' cantata from the same year, *Ô Saisons, Ô Châteaux!*, shows that what the composer sought from the apparently ultra-rational twelve-tone technique were expressive means that chimed with her longstanding interests in the esoteric and enchanted. Forkert's analysis suggests how the Rimbaud poem upon which Lutyens' piece was based – at once experimental in structure and drunk with symbolism – could tally with twelve-tone technique's 'obsession with the possibilities of series of numbers and their transpositions, inversions, and retrograde inversions'. For Lutyens, Forkert writes, the technique 'could as well be interpreted as a re-enchantment of music, the return to its alchemy – that is, to Pythagorean experiments with numbers and notes' (Forkert 2017: 285).

- Elisabeth Lutyens, Cantata, *Ô Saisons, ô châteaux!* (1946)

Studies like Björn Heile's mapping of twelve-tone technique's spread across the world – an example of digital musicology that tracks uptake of the method from 1920s Austria to 1970s China – or Stephen Peles' detailed discussion of twelve-tone music's reception and assimilation in the USA, show how far Schoenberg's project spread (Heile, n.d.; Peles 1998). But similarly innovative compositional projects were under way across the global north, and some of these aimed to organise and co-ordinate other musical parameters aside from pitch. In the USA, Henry Cowell began to experiment with the systematising of relationships between a piece's pitches and rhythms as early as 1915, and Ruth Crawford would explore similar ideas in the 1930s (Rehding 2014: 87–8; Straus 1995: 219). In the 1940s, the American composer Milton Babbitt

Case Study 2.1: (cont.)

(1916–2011) worked towards an even more fully integrated approach to the organisation of musical materials (Mead 2011).

However, in the story that has long been told – and told because it was at this moment that these disparate attempts found a concerted and collaborative focus – the next important refinement of twelve-tone technique arrived in 1950s Europe. It was not just World War I that created a disdain for the old-fashioned and outmoded. For many artists, particularly those in central Europe who had come of age during World War II, the violence and destruction of that moment fostered an even more urgent need for renewal and reinvention. As Paul Griffiths has written, 'the ending of the war was an incentive to breathe again, and then to change the world' (Griffiths 2011: 3).

In the minds of many young musicians, this music of the future was to be built upon the achievements of the Second Viennese School – and if that harking back to the recent past seems an odd way to construct a glittering future music, it is vital to remember that modernist art had been denounced and banned by the Nazi regime and its fascist satellites. A new generation, then, saw itself as picking up an unrealised modernist project. The young French Leibowitz student and composer Pierre Boulez (1925–2016) was foremost among those who would herald this moment through composition and writing. Boulez was an extraordinarily gifted musician, but he was also an intellectual and a firebrand. So it was that he wrote in a 1952 tirade that soon became famous: 'any musician who has not experienced – I do not say understood, but truly experienced – the necessity of dodecaphonic language is USELESS. For his entire work brings him up short of the needs of his time' (Boulez 1991a/1952: 113). Yet Boulez and others had come to object to the way that Schoenberg, in the name of musical tradition and continuity, had subjected his 'revolutionary' dodecaphonic language to the constraints of tonal architecture, technique and gesture; however 'necessary' Boulez thought the twelve-tone language, his essay, published not long after the elder composer's passing, was nevertheless titled 'Schoenberg Is Dead'.

By that time, the security of new, more viable models had already been found. An important source of inspiration was found in a piece – in fact, little more than a compositional étude – written by the French composer and teacher, Olivier Messiaen (1908–92). In 1949, Messiaen was teaching at the Ferienkurse für Internationale Neue Musik, or summer school for international new music, in Darmstadt, Germany. There, he demonstrated his piece *Mode de valeurs et d'intensités*, a work that broke new ground by systematically organising not just the order of appearance for each pitch, as in Schoenberg's twelve-tone system, but also duration, attack/articulation and dynamic. As Messiaen explained in the preface to the score, reproduced in Figure 2.4: 'the piece uses a mode of pitches (36 sounds), rhythmic values (24 durations), attacks (12 types) and intensities (7 nuances). It is written entirely in this mode'.

Case Study 2.1: (cont.)

Ce morceau utilise un mode de hauteurs (**36** sons), de valeurs (**24** durées), d'attaques (**12** atta-ques), et d'intensités (**7** nuances). Il est entièrement écrit dans le mode.

Attaques:

(avec l'attaque normale, sans signe, cela fait **12**.)

Intensités: *ppp* *pp* *p* *mf* *f* *ff* *fff*
1   2   3   4   5   6   7

Sons: Le mode se partage en **3** Divisions ou ensembles mélodiques de **12** sons, s'étendant cha-cun sur plusieurs octaves, et croisés entre eux. Tous les sons de même nom sont différents comme hauteur, comme valeur, et comme intensité.

Valeurs:

Division I: durées chromatiques de **1** à **12**

Division II: durées chromatiques de **1** à **12**

Division III: durées chromatiques de **1** à **12**

Au total 24 durées:

Voici le mode:

(la Division I est utilisée dans la portée supérieure du Piano)

(la Division II est utilisée dans la portée médiane du Piano)

(la Division III est utilisée dans la portée inférieure du Piano)

Figure 2.4 Explanatory note to the score of Olivier Messiaen's *Mode de valeurs et d'intensités* (1950). Copyright © 1950 by Editions Durand. All Rights Reserved. International Copyright Secured. Reproduced by kind permission of Hal Leonard Europe on behalf of Editions Durand

- Olivier Messiaen, *Mode de valeurs et d'intensités* (1949)

Case Study 2.1: (cont.)

Messiaen's experimental method necessarily produced a gestural vocabulary and phraseology in no way reminiscent of the Romantic nineteenth century. Similarly suggestive – and, after years of comparative obscurity, suddenly popular among modernist musicians – was the music of Schoenberg's pupil Anton Webern, whose 'pointillism' (and rather ascetic rigour) seemed to offer a cure for Schoenberg's Romantic hangover.

- Anton Webern, Symphony, Op. 21 (1928)

These models were developed, over several years, in what was the annual hothouse of the Darmstadt summer course. In insider commentary from the 1950s on, and in many academic surveys of composed music written later (e.g., Griffiths 2011), Darmstadt – its composers, its aesthetic imperatives – came to be presented as *the* key point of orientation for postwar composition in the West. The course took place in a German city in the midst of postwar reconstruction, and it embodied thoroughly internationalist aims, since the young musicians who gathered there came from many countries (Figure 2.5); Boulez apart, leading figures – a category still off-limits to women,

Figure 2.5 A conversation at the 1962 Darmstadt summer school. (L-R) Margarete Blaar, Mary Bauermeister, Karlheinz Stockhausen, Luis de Pablo (obscured), Pierre Boulez, Aldo Clementi, two unidentified participants. Photograph: Pit Ludwig. Copyright © Internationales Musikinstitut Darmstadt (IMD) and Pit Ludwig

Case Study 2.1: (cont.)

however mixed the company and cosmopolitan the mood – included the German Karlheinz Stockhausen (1928–2007), the Belgian Karel Goeyvaerts (1923–93), and the Italians Bruno Maderna (1920–73) and Luigi Nono (1924–90). Darmstadt remained an important site for the study and performance of what became known as 'new music' into the twenty-first century.

The 'pre-compositional' design of a piece now took on a new importance. With even more organisational rigour than the interwar figures discussed earlier, the Darmstadt composers, and Babbitt in the USA, began work by separating and systematising the basic values, or 'parameters', with which they would work – with pitch, duration and dynamics the most important, but with timbre, register or spatial location also available for similar treatment. Each parameter was given its own row, also now referred to as a 'series', and approached as a plane of material to be manipulated in its own right. This method became known as 'total' or 'integral serialism', and its proponents, 'serialists' (for an overview of this movement, see Whittall 2008).

- Pierre Boulez, *Structures*, premier livre, chapitre 1a (1951–2)

  A good example of the ways that early serialists approached the interaction of these serialised parameters is in the first movement of Stockhausen's *Kreuzspiel* (1951). A series of 12 rhythmic cells is articulated in the tumbas – the cells group 2, 8, 7, 4, 11, 1, 12, 3, 9, 6, 5 and 10 semiquavers – and, reaching its end, this series cycles. Against this, a pitch series does the same. But pitch and rhythm interact not as unified parts of a statement, but like molecules in space, or parts of a system with their own behaviours. Stockhausen described the process in play: 'Each time notes and [percussion] noises occur at the same point of time – which happens fairly frequently – the note in some way or another drops out of the series, alters its intensity, transposes into the wrong register or takes a different duration from the one preordained' (Stockhausen cited in Maconie 1976: 23).

- Karlheinz Stockhausen, *Kreuzspiel*, first movement (1951)

  Not least owing to the energy and determination of figures like Boulez and their administrator-supporters, the postwar modernist music that grew out of Darmstadt serialism came to enjoy a significant institutional presence across the second half of the century. But, just like earlier atonal music, it also met with critical and popular incomprehension and resistance. Negative responses were owed in no small part to the uncompromising rhetoric of its figureheads, and in reaction to what was often portrayed as a strictly policed compositional orthodoxy under construction – even if the musicians concerned were soon occupied by a wide variety of different creative approaches (Heile 2004).

Case Study 2.1: (cont.)

The implications of this institutionalisation will be explored at the end of this chapter. But if their focus on developing new creative techniques was what made them modernists, then it was the extent to which this goal was realised that, in the eyes of more conventionally oriented audiences and musicians, made them scientists and academics rather than artists in the accepted sense. Since one of serialism's early goals was to finally wrench art music out of its Romantic phase, and to discard dead nineteenth-century ideas of inspiration and self-expression, that was not necessarily a problem. The creative approach described above by Stockhausen, in which each parameter would be manipulated and interrelated according to rules native only to the composition, would remain a hallmark of serial and post-serial composition through the century: as M. J. Grant has shown, the serialists' design of such rules and experiments reflected an interest in scientific systems that was prominent in modernist music circles in the 1950s (Grant 2001). The postwar composers' desire to innovate was in keeping with the structural innovations of Wagner and Debussy at the century's beginning. But war had acted as a cure for the investment in myth, the heroic self and the supernatural that earlier innovators had indulged. Now, in music as in many other creative forms, 'modernism' was to assume a new identity, in which – whatever the continuing diversity of its participants' music (Fox 2007; Iddon 2011) – rationalised organisation would be widely perceived as primary.

Popular Modernism

We have seen that 'classic' definitions and accounts have privileged art that often shunned the popular – in our case, music that attempted to outline new emotional and technical parameters, seeking no public acclaim, pitting itself against the commercial musical world. For modernist critics writing in the 1930s, chief among them the German Theodor Adorno (1991a/1938) and the American Clement Greenberg (1989), commercial music – the waltzes of Johann Strauss, the jazz of Paul Whiteman, anything designed for popular consumption – represented a capitalist debasement of music as a spiritual, philosophical and historical power. There had never been a time in which art music was more distant from popular taste than the modernist moment (that was its point); there was no question that commercial 'kitsch' could produce anything with the potential to rethink and remake both self and world, as modernist art should (➜Chapter 15, 'Audiences, Class and Consumption').

But a number of commentators have in the twenty-first century sought to open up a new way of defining and exploring modernism through, rather than against, the 'popular'. In these accounts, earlier avant-garde notions around the artistic transformation of everyday life are transposed out of now-venerable contexts like Futurism, and into a realm of commercial music making previously thought out of bounds for those working in, and thinking about, radical, transformative, critical music making – none of which terms were generally thought applicable to popular music until the late twentieth century.

In this view, any history of modernism that focuses exclusively on the story just told – and which imagines art and the commercial as binary opposites – is myopic. Modernism, it is argued, cannot be fully understood as an idea or as a moment if considered solely through this largely European lens. Indeed, while European artistic preoccupations set the modernist tone from 1900 on – and with that tone, narratives around art music's general direction of travel – the twentieth century was soon to become the 'American' century, the artistic centres of Paris, Berlin and Vienna in some ways superseded by New York and Los Angeles. Scholars such as Ulf Lindberg (2003) and Ronald Schleifer (2011) have contended that it was the USA that played host to many of the most important artistic, technological and ideological innovations of that century, and that all of these things can be seen in American mass culture; (American) popular music, therefore, should be considered a primary site for the study of a different kind of modernism.

This is not just a retrospective, musicological project: modernism was a subject of interest to a great many early-century popular musicians at the time. The musicologist Guthrie Ramsey has developed the term 'Afro-Modernism' as a way of more fully reading into the modernist moment the creative works of African Americans which, so immensely present to global cultural scenes from the 1910s onwards, nevertheless suffered from the banishment from modernism proper that Schleifer describes. For Ramsey (2004), 'modernism' was what resulted when people tried to get a purchase of some kind on the upheavals through which they were living, and amid the turmoil of mass urban migration and racial oppression that characterised the African American early century, this meant that Afro-Modernism was 'the quest for liberation, freedom, and literacy as well as the seeking of upward mobility and enlarged possibilities within the American capitalist system' (Ramsey 2004: 106). Axiomatic of this is the 1940s development of a new jazz style, bebop – 'modern jazz' – which is explored in a case study below (Case Study 2.2).

For some, however, the attempt to find modernism in new spheres of musical activity risks diluting what have long been thought of as that movement's animating impulses: namely, its criticality – those hard-bitten attitudes of rejection, confrontation, challenge to social and aesthetic norms – and its (related) prioritising of disunity, fragmentation, difficulty, estrangement, the creative thorn in the side (Heile 2009). The polished and packaged whole that is a 1930s Cole Porter Broadway musical might be 'modern' in its presentation of twentieth-century city life and gender and sexual mores, but it is hardly 'modernist' in the critical terms just described (Graham 2019).

That does not mean that the idea of a 'popular modernism' should be rejected. Nor does it mean that we should accept the old idea that commercial musics are inherently inauthentic tokens of consumerist conformity, which therefore brook no such critical creative attitude. Following Mark Fisher (2014) and the radical music critic Ben Watson, Stephen Graham (2018: 245–7) argues that all musics must be understood as both implicated in 'official' or commercial cultures – supported by the state and high-art institutions, or else by the market – and yet potentially able to articulate a modernist challenge to such social and aesthetic bonds. In this view, modernism does not sound a certain way: it acts in one. The challenge in identifying a popular modernism worthy of the name is, then, to hear music for its criticality and distancing from accepted norms.

Case Study 2.2: Bebop

By the 1930s, American jazz's principal format was the big band, and its principal function was still to cater for dancers. But, in the following decade, the economic shock of world war reduced touring opportunities for what were expensive ensembles to run. The culture of social dancing would decline further in the 1950s with the advent of television, and, at the same time, new popular music forms (R & B, rock and roll), would render the big band sound even more passé. But if jazz as a mainstream dance music was in decline, then in the same period – and across the world – it was finding a new identity as a popular art form, one in which important intellectual and aesthetic innovations were seen to be made. This was in no small part owed to the musicians who, in the 1940s, had developed a new style known as bebop. The onomatopoeic term 'bebop' was a later, marketable coining. 'We called ourselves modern', remembered drummer Kenny Clarke (1914–85) of the young jazz experimenters (Stewart 2011: 334).

Case Study 2.2: (cont.)

Those players – chief among them the alto saxophonist Charlie Parker (1920–55), trumpeter Dizzy Gillespie (1917–93) and pianist Thelonious Monk (1917–82) – had all cut their teeth in the touring big bands, waiting patiently for their occasional, short solos. But, as they always had been, the most dedicated soloists were keen to develop the possibilities of jazz improvisation beyond those boundaries. The decline of the big band business led to a growth in small-group jazz, where arrangements were necessarily less elaborate and space for soloists much more plentiful.

And this solo space was filled with new musical approaches. Numerous myths surround the invention of bebop's striking technical resources. Charlie Parker recounted how, practising in the kitchen of a restaurant where he had a gig – off-duty Black musicians were often confined to such service areas in the era of segregation – he had realised how to piece together lines that emphasised bold chord extensions (discussed later in this section). Many writers and musicians later described how regular jam sessions at the Harlem club Minton's, where Thelonious Monk was house pianist, acted as a hothouse for collaborative experiment.

These kinds of narratives have come in for some revision (Kelley 2009: 70). But they were important in the ways that they aligned this popular, African American form with tropes familiar from the Euro-American modernist moment: the towering genius' sudden insight into a radical new technique, the band-of-brothers avant-garde meeting almost in secret to plot a musical revolution. When, in 1945, the first bona fide bebop recordings were released, those outside that selective circle were shocked and outraged by a music whose melodic, harmonic and rhythmic codes seemed to have come from the future.

- Dizzy Gillespie and His All Stars, 'Hot House' (Savoy, 1945)

In truth, bebop musicians were contributors to a broad culture of exploratory, innovative approaches to jazz theory and practice, a young generation that learned from and helped enrich the resources of the older. As Scott DeVeaux (1999) argues, leading players of the 1930s, notably the tenor saxophonist Coleman Hawkins (1904–69) – whose recordings like 'Body and Soul' (1939) were influential, and who employed numerous young bebop players – were central to the cultivation of a new approach which aimed, especially, to increase the harmonic density of the jazz canvas. Certainly, European modernism was a reference point for bebop musicians: many spent time with the music of Stravinsky, and bebop's outré sartorial conventions, epitomised by Dizzy Gillespie's beret and professorial glasses, signified an imagined allegiance to a distant intellectual culture rather than local showbiz. Yet, as with European

Case Study 2.2: (cont.)

modernism, what seemed like radical innovations were direct responses to an immediate history of Afro-Modernism in jazz.

The bebop musicians' technical innovations focused on three areas: harmony, velocity and disjunction. We will look at these in turn.

Bebop harmony, like the melodic lines derived from it, was greatly increased in density and dissonance to that found in contemporary popular music. Certainly, in comparison to then-contemporary twelve-tone and serial approaches, bebop's own emancipation of the dissonance was unremarkable, relying as it did on late Romantic and impressionist devices. But context was all. So, beboppers continued to play the blues and popular songs, but with the original melodies removed; in ways previously unseen in that repertoire, jazz musicians now superimposed upon these forms not only their own melodies, but also torrents of passing chords. Meanwhile, improvisers made much use of chromatic neighbouring tones, 'enclosing' chord tones amid a thicket of dissonance. Finally, jazz's harmonic and melodic vocabulary was enriched by way of increased use of chord and scale types found in Western art music as tonality broke down: notably, major and minor seventh chords that were extended upwards to include the ninth, eleventh and thirteenth; dominant-seventh chords that would include a much higher level of dissonance by way of sharpening or flattening one or more of those higher extensions; and augmented chords and the related whole-tone scale. It was often the tritone – the sharp eleventh, or as it was often then called, the flat fifth – that was melodically and harmonically foregrounded, a symbolic dissonance that announced its desire to tear through the fabric of popular song convention with every appearance (see Owens 1995, 28–45; DeVeaux 1999, passim).

The tritone eventually became a bebop cliché to be avoided. But a song by the pianist, composer and arranger Mary Lou Williams (1910–81), 'In the Land of Oo-Bla-Dee', recorded by Dizzy Gillespie's short-lived big band in 1949, shows that device and many others in the thick of popular modernist invention. The flat fifth characterises the melody in its conspicuous presence at the end of each phrase, and this is reinforced by its prominence in the brass-and-sax chords that punctuate each one. The tonal world this constant repetition produces is, to use a word favoured by beboppers, weird. Meanwhile, the lyric acts as a kind of guide, or narrative analogue, of such musical weirdness: it tells us – not without a dash of sexism – that we are in a fantastical country, where jazz scat singing stands in for spoken language and the locals are treacherous aliens. Certainly, the depths of the human condition are not plumbed in the Second Viennese style, and the performance's focal point is not expressionist anguish, but Gillespie's high-stakes trumpet solo. Yet that is exactly why it is a two-and-a-half-minute,

Case Study 2.2: (cont.)

popular modernist equivalent of *Erwartung* or *Wozzeck*: the piece is perverse, technically experimental, a thrilled demonstration of its own potential, but one not afraid to admit that its disorientation works hand in hand with a desire to entertain.

- Dizzy Gillespie and His Orchestra, 'In the Land of Oo-Bla-Dee' (RCA Victor, 1949)

That trumpet solo also serves as a brief introduction to bebop's culture of velocity. This was a performance practice in which improvised lines were much longer, much faster and occupied the extremes of the instrumental range (the presence of vocalists, talents like Sarah Vaughan apart, was unusual, and the increased instrumentalism of the music was another sign of bebop's drift away from the popular). The lodestar of this approach was Charlie Parker (Figure 2.6): 'He used multitudes of notes but never a superfluous one', the jazz critic Whitney Balliett (1976) wrote of the saxophonist. 'His runs exploded like light spilling out an opened door'. Parker's recording 'Ko-Ko' – featuring drummer Max Roach's (1924–2007) amped-up attack and unpredictably placed accents – was an early, and highly influential, announcement of this new method.

- Charlie Parker's Reboppers, 'Ko-Ko' (1945)

What might not be apparent is how any of this was 'critical' of then-current social conventions in the ways that, as we have seen, traditional theorisations of modernism demand. Beboppers were neither accustomed nor, given the precarity of their status as working Black musicians in a racially oppressive society, fully able to make overt 'political' statements. Yet the critique of American segregation and racism was implicit, and immediately recognised as such. As Eric Lott (1988) writes, this often took the form of a 'politics of style' (on show in Figure 2.5): a musical attitude that asserted an artistic autonomy and intellectualism then unexpected of 'mere' entertainers, not least those who were Black; and subcultural codes of dress, speech and behaviour – including heroin use, which would end many bebop lives – that signalled an irrevocable difference and outsiderdom. As LeRoi Jones (later, Amiri Baraka) wrote in his landmark history of African American music, *Blues People* (Baraka 1999/1963: 181–2), bebop was a 'wilfully harsh, *anti-assimilationist*' music that restored to jazz 'its original separateness'. Yet a great many bebop recordings also took more direct forms of political action. By overlaying the chord progressions of Broadway standards with their own melody lines, bebop musicians were able to claim composer copyright while inhabiting an older, shared musical repertoire (Stewart 2011: 339). Social and legal norms that had systematically worked against African Americans were, in largely symbolic but thoroughly modernist ways, continually disturbed.

Case Study 2.2: (cont.)

Figure 2.6 Charlie Parker (alto saxophone), Tommy Potter (double bass), Miles Davis (trumpet) and Max Roach (drums), Three Deuces Club, New York, NY, *c.* August 1947. Photograph by William P. Gottlieb, Library of Congress

Some of this was conveyed in bebop's new techniques of musical disjunction. Phil Ford (2013: 134–5) provides a detailed analysis of Parker's famous solo in his 'Ornithology' (1946) that focuses on these strategies – and on the techniques of improvisational development that balanced them out. Such disjunction worked on two levels. To begin with, the players announced their music's distance from the song material they performed: first through material recomposition of the kind we have discussed, and second through the improvisational exploration of harmonic and melodic possibilities not fully envisaged by the song's original composers. In Ford's example, Parker superimposes his virtuosic solo on his piece 'Ornithology', which itself is superimposed on the chord progression of the 1940 Broadway song, 'How High the Moon'.

The second level of disjunction was closer to the ground: bebop soloists might begin or end phrases in ways that cut against the basic song form, strike single notes or insert uneasy silences at unpredictable moments. These techniques became the hallmark of the pianist Thelonious Monk, in his composition, accompaniment and solo improvisation.

Case Study 2.2: (cont.)

• Thelonious Monk Quintet, 'Evidence' (Blue Note, 1948)

Multiple layers of association and disassociation, virtuosity and innovation, possibility and irony, the whole subjected to fusillades of notes or else oblique undercutting: bebop was true popular modernism. In an important 1959 study of the pianist, the noted French jazz composer and commentator André Hodeir argued that Monk's extreme use of discontinuity meant that the pianist was 'to be hailed as the first jazzman who has had a feeling for specifically modern aesthetic values' (2001/1959: 125). Hodeir had studied in Messiaen's class alongside Boulez, and his critical writing often showed how, despite their very different origins and informing traditions, Afro-Modernist bebop and Euromodernist composition could be seen as part of the same, radical musical project. Indeed, from the 1950s, and at first in Europe especially, modern jazz began to be staged at, taught in and funded by 'official' cultural institutions formerly devoted to art music alone (Lopes 2002; Perchard 2015a).

Institutionalisation

Modernist art was understood to be devoted to the destruction of convention and seen to thumb its nose at the bourgeoisie and popular taste alike. As we have seen, that notion was at best compromised. But in the decades following World War II, modernist precepts and practitioners often found a comfortable home in the institutions that were quite evidently bastions of officialised power and status. Across Europe and North America, former agitators found themselves working with top-flight orchestras and state broadcasters, in universities and research institutions. In part this was because, as already discussed, many modernist composers were products of quite traditional educational institutions – and those institutions were strong proponents of the progress prerogative that had explained the path of Western art music to date and which modernists employed to their own ends.

There was, then, an easy fit between the orientation of those institutions and the many serialist musicians who were minded to cultivate for art music a 'research' methodology, with composition positioned not just as a creative activity but also one which would explore the workings of music and sound in a systematic manner. In seeking such support, composers were able to access the resources, moral support and income needed for the continuation of the serial project: many musicians were keen to engage with cutting-edge technologies of synthesis and magnetic tape recording – with all the potential for editing and manipulation it afforded – and, as noted earlier, with the new mathematics of information theory (Griffiths 2011: 41–2; →Chapter 8, 'Instruments').

Stockhausen was particularly attracted to such possibilities, his interest piqued by his studies with the acoustician and phoneticist Werner Meyer-Eppler. The early tape piece *Gesang der Jünglinge* (1955–6), created at the studios of the German radio station Westdeutscher Rundfunk in Cologne, combines synthetic electronic sounds with a boy treble's recorded vocals, the latter distorted and arranged serially according to seven divisions between comprehensible speech and incomprehensible noise. This was music totally unlike any heard before; Stockhausen's piece and many other contemporary institution-based projects are described in detail by Holmes (2020).

- Karlheinz Stockhausen, *Gesang der Jünglinge* (1955–6).

If music was to become a branch of scientific research, the notion of an audience was nowhere to be seen. In the USA, Milton Babbitt argued that it was only proper for modernist composers to find a home away from the public gaze. In 1958 he published an infamous article outlining his position called 'Who Cares If You Listen?' (the title was the magazine editor's, Babbitt's preferred option being the rather less provocative 'The Composer as Specialist'). In this article – which is often taken as the key document in explaining the mid-twentieth-century split between modernist composers and a wider concert-going public – Babbitt argued that the composers and performers of this hyper-advanced music should not try to appeal to that 'traditional' music audience and marketplace, and should ensconce themselves instead in the university (Babbitt 1998/1958).

By the 1970s, this institutionalisation, and the modernists' establishment power more generally, was increasingly under attack, seen either as a betrayal of the modernist aim to transform society (Bürger 1984/1974: 57–8), or as an affront to the wider audience for whom much of the modernist experiment described in this chapter had continued to prove unpalatable. The observation Andreas Huyssen (1986: 186) made of modern architecture thus seemed to stand for music too: what had begun as an ideology of new beginnings and new techniques had increasingly come to represent power delivered from above. In 1989, the musicologist Susan McClary launched a bitter attack on those university-bound modernist composers that Babbitt had heralded in 'Who Cares If You Listen?', asking them: 'who cares if you compose?' (McClary 1989: 63). The stage was set for the 'postmodern' reaction that will be explored in the next chapter (→Chapter 3, 'Postmodernism').

Conclusion

Regardless of those criticisms of the projects of previous decades, the aspirations, aesthetics and techniques of modernism had been so powerful – and remained so fecund – that the moment has remained the key point of orientation for all studies of twentieth-century music and art in the West. What has changed over time, of course, are the interpretations. J. P. E. Harper-Scott (2012) argues that histories of musical modernism have cohered around three approaches: an older 'positive view', first articulated by Adorno but remaining the guiding principle of twentieth-century histories up to and including works like Griffiths (2011), in which modernist methods were seen as the central aesthetic response to the twentieth-century world; a later 'democratic view', seen fleetingly in McClary's above-cited critique, in which modernism represents the moment at which Western art music and its audiences, actual and potential, parted ways, with art music replaced by other forms; and the 'expansionist view', increasingly prominent and represented by the scholarship on popular modernism explored earlier – and by work on more traditional art music, like Christopher Chowrimootoo's 2018 study of Benjamin Britten and what the musicologist calls 'middlebrow modernism' – which seeks to recover but rethink the celebration of modernist intent, radically expanding its definitions and canons.

It is that expanded view that is taken over the course of this book's following chapters. Musical scholarship in the early twenty-first century has been concerned with identifying and emphasising this huge variety, because in truth, there was no single modernism; rather a number of modernisms, each responding both to local musical traditions and sociocultural conditions. Contrary to earlier accounts, modernism did not claim its great charge and meaning because it represented a club to which only composers of the right kind could belong. Instead, it was an aesthetic imperative – *make it new* – that energised the work of musicians across the board.

3 | Postmodernism

The prerogatives of the new, of progress and the future, had been more important than ever in the wake of World War II. But, by the 1970s, the grand schemes that had characterised Western modernity and modernism seemed all to be failing. This was true on the broadest scale: while Nazi genocide was in the past, the Soviet experiment that had given much early modernist art its force – and postwar Western social democratic reforms their urgency – was now crumbling in totalitarian misery. It was true of people's lived experience: rather than ushering in a life in the sky, new high-rise housing had further ripped at an already tattered social fabric. And it was true of the arts: as much as unveiling a new lingua franca for an international modern music, serial composition had seemed to renounce its own audience, and listeners now turned to popular musics even for the experiment and challenge that art music had once vaunted. Here was the crisis: a loss of intellectual and spiritual confidence in the West's ability – taken as read since the Enlightenment – to envisage and work towards a better future by way of rational means (Berman 1982).

This crisis took place at a moment of global transformation. As we have seen (→Chapter 1, 'Place and Space, Local and Global'), the latter decades of the century were characterised by a new mediatisation and globalisation of commerce and culture, and the information-saturated, consumerist society that resulted would bear little resemblance to the disconnected world that existed in 1900 when the modernist credo emerged (Harvey 1989; Jameson 1991). So, it was not surprising that modernism's claims to power were coming to seem not only hollow, but old hat – aloof and monomaniacal in a world increasingly characterised by communication and multiplicity. As the political geographer David Harvey noted, by the 1980s it was clear that Western culture and society were undergoing 'a profound shift in the "structure of feeling"' (Harvey 1989: 9). They were becoming, to use a term by then in common parlance, 'postmodern'.

One of the primary areas in which this shift was articulated was creative work. The intensification of a mediatised, globalised flow of culture meant that artists and genres from all over the world circulated widely, their music heard in traditional and hybrid forms; what was now celebrated was not the singular modernist project but teeming postmodern variety. Progressivist ideals – which, by the 1960s, had been translated from art music into the popular modernisms of jazz and then rock – were mocked in later decades by musicians' widespread reuse of old styles and techniques. And despite the many anxieties that attended the demise of modernist triumphalism, all this seemed to come as a relief: modernism's high seriousness was now often undercut by a new sense of playful juxtaposition, irony, fun.

Nevertheless, as cultural historians like Andreas Huyssen (1986: 183) pointed out, the very term 'postmodernism' signalled that a relationship endured between the two moments. In music, as we will see, modernist techniques of fragmentation, and the desire to challenge and change, still loomed large. The cultural theorist Linda Hutcheon (1988: 3; 60) argued that postmodernism did not so much overthrow modernist ideals and techniques as inhabit them, destabilising them from inside; the claims of old modernism were treated with what was often called 'radical scepticism', satirised, reshuffled, but rarely supplanted with a programme of postmodernism's own. That would have seemed like the modernist grandstanding that was no longer possible.

Indeed, an overriding interest in critique left postmodern thought and culture open to the charge that it was nihilistic, and had resigned any positive vision of the future (Eagleton 1996). But it also meant that postmodern discourse was marked by an unusually involved relationship between creative work and its interpretive response, not least in the form of the 'new musicology' (see McClary 1991; Kramer 1995; Lochhead and Auner 2002; also Gloag 2012). This chapter reflects that mix and explores episodes in late-century music and its reception by surveying topics central to the postmodern theoretical outlook. These focus in more detail on what we have already identified as the major characteristics of the postmodern moment: the unpicking of grand, future-oriented projects, and the intensification of globalised media and consumption. But, taken together, they also begin to articulate a set of questions that only became more urgent in the twenty-first century, by which time postmodernism itself was regarded as a thing of the past: not just what is happening, but how can we know; not just why is it happening, but who gets to say.

Changing the (Meta-)Narrative

We saw in the last chapter how the 'cult of progress' shaped modernist attitudes towards artistic innovation. But progress was just one of the concepts which would be called into question during the postmodern moment. Tenets such as the primacy of Western scientific rationality and political power, or, more fundamentally, the belief that human society was perfectible, had looked hollow since those things had been pressed into the service of world war, holocaust and nuclear destruction. A number of theorists, then, identified a growing suspicion of 'meta-narratives', that is, 'large-scale theoretical interpretations purportedly of universal application' (Harvey 1989: 9). In place of such grand schemes was a new investment in what postmodernists would come to call 'difference' – between peoples, cultures, beliefs, truth claims, practices – and an aversion to the old hierarchies that existed between them.

This new approach to truth and knowledge was most famously articulated by the French philosopher Jean-François Lyotard, in his book *The Postmodern Condition* (1984/1979). In a postmodern world, Lyotard wrote, a multitude of potentially valid narrative systems – for example, radically different forms of history-telling – could be seen to coexist, sometimes in dialogue, yet not necessarily in agreement: '[c]onsensus', Lyotard argued, 'has become an outmoded and suspect value' (Lyotard 1984/1979: 66). In this section we will look at two musical meta-narratives that were early casualties of the postmodern attitude: the superiority of 'high' culture and the importance of modernist innovation. In both cases, we will see singular narratives around cultural value being supplanted by a new attention to variety and difference.

Early-century conservatives and modernists had been united on at least one point: popular culture was commercial trash, inferior in every way to serious art (Levine 1988). But World War II brought about a decisive reordering of Western society, and if 'high art' started to look like a relic of an old, divided world, then so too were new, creative energies increasingly being expressed in popular idioms. Studies by Andreas Huyssen (1986), Linda Hutcheon (1988) and Phil Ford (2013) show how an emergent postmodern approach took popular culture as the central site for serious investigation of cultural and creative change. In British and American pop art, Andy Warhol, Richard Hamilton and Pauline Boty used commercial products and image-making techniques. The American composer Terry Riley conducted early minimalist experiments using fragments of jazz and Motown recordings; musicians in rock and jazz like the Beatles in the UK, Miles Davis in the USA and Caetano Veloso and Gilberto Gil in Brazil developed entirely new musical forms in the context of commercial record production. At first, pop-cultural works were taken seriously insofar as they could be seen as behaving like high art (Mann 1963). Later, as we will see, postmodern attention fell on forms that did not fulfil that role – but which were taken as signifying something important about the world, nonetheless.

- Terry Riley (b. 1935), 'Bird of Paradise, Part 1' (from *Music for The Gift*, 1963)
- The Beatles, 'Tomorrow Never Knows' (from *Revolver*, Parlophone 1966)
- Miles Davis (1926–91), 'Shhh/Peaceful' (from *In a Silent Way*, Columbia 1969)
- Gilberto Gil (b. 1942), 'Objeto Semi-Identificado' (from *Gilberto Gil*, Philips 1969)
- Caetano Veloso (b. 1942), 'Sugar Cane Fields Forever' (from *Araçá Azul*, PolyGram 1972)

Influential latter-century intellectual work turned to this weakened 'high' culture, and began to chip away at its claims to uniqueness. This work often came from sociologists. Janet Wolff (1981) argued that ideas of 'autonomous' art acted to obscure the murky commercial mediations that made even high culture subject to its paymasters; Pierre Bourdieu (1984/ 1979) showed how aesthetic taste was often employed as a marker of social class and distinction, rather than as a disinterested response to some artistic stimulus; John Shepherd (1991) suggested that understandings of music not as a series of reified works, but as a 'social practice', meant that it was popular rather than art music that should be understood as the century's most significant form, and that it, rather than art music, should be the subject of a transformed musicology. Meanwhile, musicologists like Charles Hamm (1995) were also showing how the social and ideological positions allotted to classical and popular music had been invented only recently, and, indeed, how they were mutually dependent: for classical music to represent the timeless and the civilised to the satisfaction of the nineteenth-century bourgeoisie, 'Other' musics ('tribal', popular) were made to serve as uncivilised or transient foils. We will see more examples of the muddling of 'high' and 'low' styles throughout this chapter, and some of these trends are also discussed further in →Chapter 15, 'Audiences, Class and Consumption'. For now, though, we will note that in both creative and critical realms, and among both musicians and their audiences, the old hierarchies of cultural value were being resolutely flattened.

Naturally, what was identified as a new spirit of 'relativism' was keenly contested by conservatives of various stripes. Allan Bloom's 1987 book, *The Closing of the American Mind*, was a much-cited polemic for the 'point of view' – that is, an anti-relativist sorting of the culturally valuable from the worthless. In Bloom's argument, the massive ubiquity of shallow, hyper-sexualised popular music showed how mass culture impoverished public discourse. And, while high–low hierarchies continued to crumble – arts institutions and universities increasingly concerned themselves with popular musics in the 1980s and 1990s – defences of that distinction continued to be made, as in Julian Johnson's book *Who Needs Classical Music* (2002).

But old meta-narratives were being torn up even within the field of art music. Many musicians and musicologists were questioning the classical canon that had long been taken as an unproblematic description of Western musical and cultural history (→Chapter 4, 'Canons'). And, as we saw at the end of the last chapter, modernist imperatives – chiefly around the historical necessity of serial methods, and the refusal to compromise in the name of a wider audience – were increasingly rejected by those who saw such values as belonging to another time and place. As the minimalist composer Steve Reich (→Chapter 6, 'Rhythm and Time') remarked, 'for composers today to re-create the angst of [Schoenberg's] *Pierrot Lunaire* in Ohio, or in the back of a Burger King, is simply a joke' (Page 1986).

So much was recognised even by those working within the modernist tradition: composers like Helmut Lachenmann, Wolfgang Rihm and Brian Ferneyhough employed post-serial methods, but, in contrast to the sleek rationality of the Darmstadt moment, these techniques were now fractured, effaced, full of echoes of the past. And to be sure, the end of modernism as be-all and end-all also gave comfort to those who had never signed up to the modernist programme of challenge and innovation. The art critic Hal Foster (1983: xi–xii) identified 'a postmodernism of resistance and a postmodernism of reaction', and both tendencies can be seen playing out in musics which, especially from the 1970s on, attempted to recover tonality from the depths of history. Some of this music was radical ('resistant') in its staging of a tonality that was freighted with the memory of a time now inaccessible. Some of it was conservative ('reactionary') in that it imagined a musical world in which atonality and serialism had never happened. Yet all of it was postmodern in that, whether explicitly or implicitly, it responded to modernism as a historical moment, now passed.

- Helmut Lachenmann (b. 1935), String Quartet No. 1, 'Gran Torso' (1972)
- Sofia Gubaidulina (b. 1931), *Offertorium* (1980, rev. 1982, 1986)
- Lorenzo Ferrero (b. 1951), *Canzoni d'amore* (1985)

It is true, though, that many of the meta-narratives that postmodernism most urgently critiqued – and which, of course, were most keenly defended in response – had never been fully believed by those excluded in the first place. The African American literary critic Cornel West (1993/1989) argued that, even after a decade of high-profile discussion, postmodernism remained a 'narrowly Eurocentric' project in which 'First World' culture had belatedly begun to question its own spurious claims to singularity, and with which African Americans could therefore not fully identify. The African American feminist Audre Lorde (1984) demanded that feminist thought escape exclusionary academic contexts – in which 'difference' was often a topic of theoretical discussion, but, she said, rarely a characteristic of that discussion's participants – and be made in newly cooperative ways, since 'the master's tools will never dismantle the master's house'. While such arguments chimed with the observations of Lyotard above, these were more radical rejections of the Western meta-narrative than many post-modern intellectuals and artists who had emerged from within Euro-American culture were willing to make.

Perhaps the artistic tendency dubbed Afrofuturism exemplified what Lorde was demanding: an organic, collaborative and radical revisioning of modern history made very much from outside 'the master's house'. First framed by critic Mark Dery (1994), Afrofuturism was invoked to describe the ways that African American and broader Afro-diasporic creative prac-tices dismantled and rewired those narratives of modernity that often omitted or belittled the experiences of Black people. Dery, and subsequent writers on Afrofuturism like Alondra Nelson (2000), Kodwo Eshun (1998, 2003) and Erik Steinskog (2018), described the ways in which Black music, literature and visual art made use of cosmic and science-fiction tropes – abduction by aliens, life on strange planets, the development of new technologies by turns liberating and oppressing – to retell and redirect the story of transatlantic slavery and its heritage, and to position that experience as modernity's foundational fact. Innovative uses of technology in Black music often complicated ideas of what it meant to be human, or to authentically belong, since slavery had done the same for Black people in the West (➔Chapter 14, 'Race and Ethnicity'); the Afrofuturist imagin-ation, given its fullest early expression in the work of Sun Ra (Figure 3.1),

Figure 3.1 Sun Ra in *Space Is the Place*, directed by Jim Newman (1974)

thus re-visioned a factual historical narrative by way of images from cartoons and film, upsetting Western meta-narratives in which the future, technology and rationality were often positioned as properties of 'white' Western culture.

- Sun Ra (1914–93) and His Solar-Myth Arkestra, *The Solar-Myth Approach* (BYG, 1971)
- Alice Coltrane (1937–2007), *Universal Consciousness* (Impulse! 1971)
- Warp 9, 'Light Years Away' (Prism, 1983)
- Goldie (b. 1965), *Timeless* (FFRR, 1995)
- Dr Octagon (Kool Keith, b. 1963), *Dr. Octagonecologyst* (Bulk, 1996)
- Missy Elliot (b. 1971), 'She's a B**ch' [video] (1999)

Semiotics and Deconstruction

As we will continue to see, postmodern intellectual culture united a wide range of intellectual tools, these drawn from fields as various as sociology and psychoanalysis. But there was one long line of enquiry that under-pinned many of the rest – 'semiotics', the study of signs – and it is vital to grasp its basics in order to understand the moment as a whole.

This work developed out of the insights of a Swiss linguist, Ferdinand de Saussure (1857–1913). For Saussure, language was only functional at all insofar as it pointed to a storehouse of cultural codes and understandings. A word ('violin') was in itself an arbitrary collection of sounds or pen strokes. But it was a sounding and visual 'signifier', by which was 'signified' a concept, that is, a historically and culturally encoded understanding, widely and immediately shared by a language and culture's participants. To those people, the word 'violin' summons an image of what a violin looks like, is used for, sounds like and, crucially, stands for (Romantic expression, high-culture cachet and so on). Additionally, Saussure argued that linguistic signifiers work in contradistinction to what they are not – that violin is emphatically *not* an electric guitar, nor the things the guitar represents.

Later developments of these principles, notably the school of linguistic and anthropological 'structuralism' (Lévi-Strauss 1974/1958; Sturrock 2003), sought to understand all human social and cultural structures as revolving around signs and contradistinctions of one kind or another. A range of semiotic approaches to music analysis would also later develop, often focusing on how particular melodic shapes (like the 'sighing' semitone fall in baroque music) or tonalities (like the 'heroic' key of E♭ major) came to signify particular kinds of movement or mood (Tagg 1982; Nattiez 1990/1987; Agawu 1991). We will return to structuralism in our first case study, and semiotics in our second.

However, in the 1960s a critique of this approach emerged – inevitably, it was dubbed 'post-structuralism' – and this would prove central to the development of postmodern perspectives on the world. The leading figure of this movement, and in some ways the postmodernist par excellence, was the French–Algerian philosopher Jacques Derrida (1930–2004); his philosophical work was forbiddingly complex, but his methods were soon taken up across the humanities, including music studies. In its most basic form, the post-structural observation was that, while semiotics and structuralism had taken signs to work as a system of oppositions or mutual exclusions, it was better to see opposing signs as dependent upon each other for their meaning. Supposedly stable and separate concepts were shown to be meaningful only insofar as they were permeable: 'life' could not be meaningful without understanding that it is framed by, and infused by knowledge of, its opposite, 'death'. Endless similar relationships – between writing and speech, body and mind, violins and guitars – could be imagined.

This meant that texts that were notionally focused on one topic – and for postmodernists, almost any kind of object or activity became a 'text' to be 'read' – could be seen to be infused with worry about another (such as those hymns to the transcendental value of classical music that betray worry over base, but enjoyable, popular music). Derrida called the highlighting and unpicking of such relationships 'deconstruction' (Wolfreys 1998), and, in academic contexts, that term came to describe any kind of work that 'interrogated' culturally accepted conceptual identities and oppositions and aimed to upend the categorical stability, meaning and power hierarchy implicit within them. Deconstruction also became a buzzword in popular culture, where it suggested the critical questioning of a previously accepted norm, or, in creative contexts, the destabilising of a genre or model: a composer might deconstruct the concerto form, or a chef a classic dish.

If the idea of deconstruction caught the popular mood, it was because this line of thinking was contributing to powerful critiques of what had been even the most strictly policed social and cultural categories. This was particularly true of identity (→Part IV, Identities). Judith Butler (1988; 1990) contended that a body does not simply have a gender, but becomes gendered through the performance of a repertoire of behaviours that signify maleness, femaleness and so on. Work by theorists like Stuart Hall (1997) advanced similar arguments around race. Many scholars thus came to see 'race', 'gender' and 'sexuality' as 'floating signifiers' – that is, categories not fixed or meaningful in themselves but socially and historically contingent, made to mean different things in different times and places. Such categories ('man', 'Black', 'gay') were socially produced, and comprehensible only in relation to their supposed opposites ('woman', 'white', 'straight'). This mode of analysis would prove both influential and durable.

Lawrence Kramer's 1996 article on the uses of Black American styles in early twentieth-century concert music is a good example of the deconstructive attitude at work in musicology. While earlier musicologists had approached similar topics by thinking about, for example, how Milhaud or Stravinsky had come into contact with jazz, Kramer instead 'reads' the mobilisation of 'Black' materials for the politics in play, and the ways that a dialectical relationship – between white and Black identities and (supposed) ways of being – was made in music. Kramer argues that in Charles Ives' First Piano Sonata (1902–9), a vision of happy-go-lucky Blackness (this was a popular racist stereotype of the time) is summoned by way of passages that employ ragtime material. These are both marked by their 'raucousness' and quarantined from the contrastingly serious – and putatively 'white' – sections of modernist composition. For Kramer, the piece thus betrays a white desire for Black 'pleasure-as-excess', while ensuring such pleasure is 'safely curbed in the very act of being invoked' (Kramer 1996: 65); the 'white' material gains its identity and meaning by advertising, anxiously, how far it is 'not Black'. Music, then, is shown both to participate in and to police the construction of racial identities – and, however rigorous the compositional attempt to segregate them, these identities are shown to derive their meaning precisely from their interdependence.

Representation

Kramer's article is axiomatic of the postmodern critical attitude: what might, for most people, have previously seemed like innocent sights or sounds were now scoured for the ideologies and power plays that they seemed to support. The scepticism and deconstruction we encountered above were important instruments in this operation. But they were reliant on another central postmodern concept – 'representation', or the ways the people, ideas, values and so on were described and symbolised in texts, music, images or any other form.

There were two insights in play. The first was old: before reaching us through these forms, reality – the 'world out there' – was always mediated, and that act of mediation could not help but divert and reshape the real in such a way as followed the mediator's own methods and values. The second was newer: such representations were not just reports on reality but, since they shaped people's understanding of the world, they also helped construct realities in their turn, as we saw in Kramer's work on Ives (see Hutcheon 1988: 149). The last decades of the twentieth century saw a huge growth in studies and analytical vocabularies around the representation of identities and ideologies in visual culture (Mulvey 1975), anthropology (Clifford and Marcus 1986), media and cultural politics (Hall et al. 2003), music (Born and Hesmondhalgh 2000) and many other fields.

To see how critiques of representation tended to proceed, we will focus on one of the most important studies of this type: *Orientalism*, a 1978 book by the Palestinian–American literary scholar, Edward Said (1935–2003). In illustrating how the 'Orient' was represented in fiction, reportage and history during the age of European colonialism, Said showed how a limited number of picaresque 'tropes' – recurring images and ideas – were used to construct an imagined Far East for European readers. Large and diverse Asian and North African cultures were represented as monolithic, static, at once cruelly hierarchical and tantalisingly eroticised. For Said (1978: 5–6), this 'Orient' did not really exist, except as a discursive creation in the West (1978: 5–6). But while Orientalism was built from mythical written, painted and musical representations, it was not a flimsy thing: the discourse of Orientalism informed, justified and sustained a practice of colonial domination, providing 'teachable wisdom' on the East for those working in the governmental and military institutions involved in that region's imperial domination (Said 1978: 246). Representation begat reality.

Said's book has been controversial on grounds of both evidence and method (Porter 1994). Yet his thesis, and his term, have been enormously influential, and can be seen running through many subsequent musicological treatments of representation and difference (McClary 1992; Born and Hesmondhalgh 2000; Taylor 2007; Locke 2009). An example of how Said's critique was transposed into new contexts is Richard Middleton's commentary on Gershwin's opera, *Porgy and Bess* (1935), in which – whatever the work's humanity – a non-Black composer represents Black life through the employment and framing of a certain number of potentially suspect tropes.

[F]or all the musical eclecticism of *Porgy and Bess* and the tensions that result, one feels that the authorial Gershwin is always pulling at the strings. The characters are allowed a range of idioms, which, in the context of the overall stylistic location of the work, are not difficult to interpret; they range from Sportin' Life's slithery sensual chromatics to Porgy's folky-cum-heroic lyricism, from the 'ecstasy' of the religious pieces to the neoprimitive abandon of the picnic scene. Yet in the end this differentiation of the other is circumscribed by the framework of the genre: the black idioms are encased, put in their place, by the style, orchestration, and structural conventions of late-romantic opera. By choosing to write in this genre, Gershwin is unavoidably constrained by received power-relationships between high and low ... the authentic is *presented* to us; we see through Gershwin's eyes. Thus the honeyman's haunting pentatonic cry is surrounded by a harmonic 'haze' created by drones and ostinatos, which has the effect of magically placing the scene in a distant landscape within the composer's mind – a place of trance and lost innocence. (Middleton 2000b: 67–8)

- George Gershwin (libretto, DuBose Heyward, lyrics, Ira Gershwin): 'Here Come de Honeyman', from *Porgy and Bess* (1935)

As we will see in our second case study, forms of Orientalist representation would long endure. Nevertheless, by the end of the century, an enriched understanding of the workings of representational acts – arrived at in part through works like Said's – was apparent in many different academic and media discourses (see Fürsich and Avant-Miller 2012). A new, albeit imperfect, sensitivity towards the politics of representation might be regarded as one of the most important effects of postmodern thought.

Authorship

By the end of the 1960s, several strains of post-structuralist thought were cohering around one idea: that the individual subject could never be fully considered the author of his or her own thoughts and words. We have seen how Derrida argued that the intended meanings of any writer's text were subject to slippage and self-sabotage. The historian Michel Foucault (2000/ 1969; →Chapter 10, 'Copyright and the Music Industry') contended that what mattered in history was less who said (or did) what, but how those statements and acts formed a 'discourse' that described what was thinkable, sayable and doable in any one place and time. The psychoanalyst Jacques Lacan (1998/1973) suggested that, since we only think, experience and communicate in ways given to us by a language we are born into rather than originate, we do not speak a language: it speaks us.

Naturally, objections were forthcoming. The African American feminist writer bell hooks (1990), for instance, expressed suspicion that notions of subjecthood were being 'decentred' so soon after people of colour in the West had gained the legal and cultural power to voice their own.

Nevertheless, a new emphasis on 'discourses' (the conversation) rather than 'subjects' (the speakers themselves) caught the mood in many creative and critical fields. These ideas' most-cited expression came in the literary theorist Roland Barthes' 1967 essay, 'The Death of the Author'. There, Barthes argued that authors of all kinds trade in phrases, metaphors and images that, whatever the marginal novelty of their combination, have been employed by multitudes of others before; any text is merely a 'space in which a variety of writings, none of them original, blend and clash' (Barthes 1977/1967: 146). Another Paris-based literary theorist, Julia Kristeva (1980/1966), coined the term 'intertextuality' to capture a similar idea. This was a major critical downgrading of the heroic, original, creative subject so idealised in Romantic and modernist culture: authors were now to be understood, first and foremost, as readers like the rest of us, reshuffling what they had found in the past into something approximating their own work.

Critical interventions like these helped clarify, and perhaps intensify, what was already in motion in creative fields. From the 1960s, visual artists, architects, writers and musicians across the West were making increasing use of 'found' materials; by the 1980s, 'postmodern art' was widely identified as that in which quotation, allusion and pastiche of pre-existing styles played a central role (Connor 1997). Frequently introduced into these discussions was the American saxophonist and composer, John Zorn. In Susan McClary's celebrated description, Zorn's collage-like music was a 'revelling in the rubble' of Western culture past and present (McClary 2000: 139).

- John Zorn (b. 1953), *Cat o' Nine Tails* (1988)

Certainly, musicians had incorporated pre-existing materials and styles into their work for centuries. But postmodern quotation practices represented a much more purposeful exploration of music's 'signifying' potential; musical fragments were now widely understood semiotically, as meaning-making signs to be employed in an expression of, or argument about, the contemporary cultural situation. In his study of musical quotation in the twentieth century, David Metzer writes:

It is the ways in which quotation handles the 'what' and the 'how' that make it such an effective cultural agent. The gesture latches on to a specific work, often a familiar one, and places that work squarely in front of us. The borrowed material is tightly gripped and prominently featured rather than being merely alluded to or buried in the background. This directness calls attention to the cultural associations of the original, for the more discernible and intact the borrowing, the more apparent those associations. (Metzer 2003: 6)

Metzer says quotation demands that the listener ask themselves: what is that fragment of music doing *here*?

Case Study 3.1: Polystylism, Quotation and Collage in Post-serial Composition

The Russian-born composer Alfred Schnittke (1934–98) was an important figure in the development of techniques of musical reference. In a 1971 article, Schnittke identified and distinguished between collage, in which snippets of earlier musics were quoted in juxtaposition (as in Stockhausen's national-anthem mashup, *Hymnen*) and polystylism, in which contrasting stylistic languages were inhabited and often interwoven (as in the music of Stravinsky, Henri Pousseur's opera *Votre Faust* or the work of Schnittke himself).

- Henri Pousseur (1929–2009), *Jeu de miroirs de Votre Faust* (1964–5)
- Karlheinz Stockhausen, *Hymnen* (1966–7, rev. 1969)
- Alfred Schnittke, Symphony No. 1, II. Allegretto (1969–74)

Polystylism, Schnittke wrote, was at the turn of the 1970s being newly exploited in reaction to the supposedly monostylistic dogma of 1950s serialism. But Schnittke also anticipated later theoretical descriptions of the postmodern experience: collage and

Case Study 3.1: (cont.)

polystylism, he suggested, reflected the vastly increased rate of cultural contact, changed perceptions of time and space and mass of information and media that had 'polyphonized' late twentieth-century experience (Schnittke 2002/1971: 89).

Schnittke's analysis had much force. But it is worth going beyond general explanations to look in more detail at the ways that quotation and polystylism were employed in different contexts. Doing so will complicate the story somewhat: as we will see – and as already suggested in this chapter's introduction – these putatively postmodern techniques did not so much represent a simple rejection of modernism as a critical dialogue with it.

To begin with, let us look at a single (and singular) compositional practice. The German Bernd Alois Zimmermann (1918–70) was ten years older than most of the postwar musicians identified with serialism; although he turned to serial methods in the 1950s, he was removed in temperament and motive from the modernist projects emerging from Darmstadt. By the end of that decade, Zimmermann had arrived at a very personal intellectual, spiritual and musical orientation, one which synthesised his profound Catholic beliefs with his interests in the early-century philosophies of Husserl and Bergson – these often concerned with the subjective experience of time – and the world-reordering modernism of writers like James Joyce. At root, Zimmermann was concerned with expressing in musical experience what he called 'the unity of present, past, and future that Saint Augustine identified in the essence of the human soul, which in a moment of intellectual expansion reaches past the fleeting instant and brings the past and future into a perpetual present' (Zimmermann 2014/1960: 136).

Clearly, in privileging the spiritual over the hyperrational, and ideas of pastness as much as future-oriented research, Zimmermann was swimming against the modernist tide. Still, serial technique afforded a thoroughgoing pre-planning of the compositional process, and by using that technique to create pieces such as *Tratto* (1965–7), in which material simultaneously unfolds from beginning to end and vice versa, Zimmermann was able to articulate his spiritual and philosophical ideas at a formal level (Dahlhaus 1978: 633). But it was the composer's techniques of collage, which aimed to create a different kind of temporal unity, that brought Zimmermann notoriety. By layering quotations from very different moments in music history – plainchant, classical-Romantic repertoire, jazz – Zimmermann offered what Carl Dahlhaus (1978: 635) called 'a spatial metaphor for the aesthetic-metaphysical experience of an inner simultaneity beyond succession, or the concept of before and after'; he also explicitly challenged modernist claims around the historical necessity, even supremacy, of particular musical techniques.

On occasion, such techniques were employed to critical and even darkly comic ends, as in *Musique pour les soupers du Roi Ubu* (1962–6), where Berlioz, Wagner and

Case Study 3.1: (cont.)

Stockhausen appear in crazed, war-like convergence. But these methods' fullest and most ambitious realisation was in Zimmermann's masterpiece, the opera *Die Soldaten* (1958–65), based on a 1776 play by Jakob Lenz that was also a distant source for Berg's *Wozzeck* (→Chapter 2, 'Modernism'). Here, the plot's chronology is sometimes collapsed, with multiple scenes running simultaneously, an action and its consequences playing out at the same time; likewise, layers of musical quotation offer comment on the drama, as when the soldier protagonist's betrayal of his sweetheart, played out in high-serial style, is underpinned by 'Ich bin's, ich sollte büßen', the chorale that Bach places in his St. Matthew Passion at the moment of Christ's betrayal.

- Zimmermann, *Musique pour les soupers du Roi Ubu*. 'VII. Marche du décervellage' (1962–6)
- Zimmermann, *Die Soldaten*, Act II, Scene ii (1958–65)

We will now turn from Zimmermann to look in more depth at the ways in which quotation practices can function in a single piece.

Luciano Berio's orchestral work *Sinfonia* (1968) contains perhaps the most celebrated use of quotation in twentieth-century music. Berio bases the piece's third movement on the Scherzo of Mahler's Symphony No. 2 ('Resurrection', 1895). The Mahler runs throughout, but it is a palimpsest, often momentarily erased or obscured by quotations from the Western canon as it was then understood: Bach, Beethoven, Berlioz, Richard Strauss, Debussy, Schoenberg, Berg, Stravinsky, Ravel, Boulez and Stockhausen are among those who make appearances. Also present are eight amplified vocalists, who sing and speak fragments of various texts, chief among them Samuel Beckett's novel *The Unnameable* (1952).

- Luciano Berio (1925–2003): *Sinfonia*, III. 'In ruhig fließender Bewegung' (1968)

The smashing together of so much music history is simultaneously awesome, absurd, comic and tragic; in the context of the piece as a whole, and indeed of the modernist tradition to that point, it was a statement of shocking power. What it was all supposed to mean was another question. David Metzer argues that this piling up of music history's rubble critiques the 'avant-garde arrogance' of the serialists (Metzer 2003: 137), and pronounces the death of their future-oriented meta-narrative. But modernist forms of authorship are clearly in play, too. Berio's selection and placement of quotations is anything but haphazard, instead articulating post-serial technique and thought. C. Catherine Losada (2009) has shown how quoted material is incorporated into a post-tonal scheme of chromatic saturation, whereby gamuts of chromatic space are gradually 'gap-filled' by the introduction of new materials, whether Berio's own or

Case Study 3.1: (cont.)

that of his quoted forebears. The singers' texts, too, are often made to comment on structural procedures in play: Beckett's words 'where now?', 'when now' and 'keep going' mark sectional divisions, and announce the reappearance of Mahler's material (Losada 2009: 65). This attention to technical procedure – much in evidence in the *Sinfonia*'s other movements, and across Berio's *oeuvre* as a whole – would seem to suggest the coexistence of what we might think of as 'modernist' and 'postmodernist' creative methods.

Equally suggestive of such continuity is what David Osmond-Smith, in a noted study from 1985, calls the 'semantic' aspect of *Sinfonia*'s materials. Osmond-Smith was writing before theories of the postmodern definitively swept Western intellectual culture, and so he was apt to see the work in the context of the postwar modernist circle from which Berio had emerged. This was not fanciful, as the piece's opening movement sets texts from the French anthropologist Claude Lévi-Strauss' book *The Raw and the Cooked*, a classic work of structuralist anthropology then famous for its analyses of myths, most notably those of the indigenous peoples of South America. It is fragments of text on myths concerning water that Berio sets here, and Osmond-Smith (1985: 40–69) shows how the quotation-laden third movement interacts with this material. Osmond-Smith notes that Mahler's scherzo – in the score marked 'In ruhig fließender Bewegung', with quietly flowing movement – was derived from a song that the composer was simultaneously writing, this setting a text on the biblical story of Saint Anthony's preaching to the fishes. Many other of the movement's prominent quotations relate visions of water, too. Debussy's *La Mer*, 'Farben' from Schoenberg's *Five Pieces for Orchestra* (which the composer described as a study of colours on a lake in the early morning), the drowning scene from Berg's *Wozzeck*, the 'Scene by the Brook' that forms the second movement of Beethoven's Symphony No. 6 ('Pastoral'): these are Western 'myths' of water to compliment those of the indigenous Americans, and Berio's use of them seems to resonate with the modernist universalism that Lévi-Strauss' structuralist anthropology espoused.

So, despite the piece's extensive quotation of existent materials – and despite its lack of obvious 'message' – Berio was clearly meditating upon an authorial idea of his own. But the 'birth of the reader' that, as we have seen, Roland Barthes suggested would follow the death of the author, is delivered by the undecidable richness of Berio's work, and what Osmond-Smith called the challenge of 'learning to be receptive to the peculiarly vivid aesthetic impact of the half-understood'. The posing of that original question – what is this music doing there? – gives us, in Osmond-Smith's estimation, 'a survival kit against the facile nihilism that so easily informs attempts to analyse a disjointed, relativistic environment' (Osmond-Smith 1985: 91). This apparently postmodern work, then, stands somewhat against many of the cultural trends that were taken as characterising that moment.

... **Authorship, Continued**

Those working in popular music were also now forcing together fragments and pastiches of historical styles to make innovative work. Within the space of three songs on the second side of his album *Aladdin Sane* (1973), David Bowie became a cabaret performer evoking the louche, seen-it-all spirit of 1920s Berlin, a mid-Atlantic scenester offering a veiled tribute to French playwright Jean Genet over 1950s-style Chicago blues, and an otherworldly commentator backed by virtuosic piano gestures out of the Romantic nineteenth century. Likewise the work of Patti Smith, who was, in the early 1970s, making her name in the bohemian corner of downtown New York City where contemporary art and garage rock met. The centre-piece of her influential debut album, *Horses* (1975), collages teen Americana, Rimbaudian symbolist poetry – an enduring interest of Smith's – garage-band jamming and Wilson Pickett's 1966 soul hit, 'Land of a Thousand Dances'. In her memoir of the moment, *Just Kids* (2010), Smith recalls fashioning her image by collaging symbols from high and low cultures as they spoke to her – a hat that resembled the poet Mayakovsky's, a sweater like the one Audrey Hepburn wore in the 1957 film, *Funny Face* – and much music from this period reads similarly.

- David Bowie (1947–2016), 'Time', 'The Jean Genie', 'Lady Grinning Soul' (from *Aladdin Sane*, RCA, 1973)
- Patti Smith (b. 1946), 'Land' (from *Horses*, Arista, 1975)
- Steely Dan, *Pretzel Logic* (ABC, 1974)
- Joni Mitchell (b. 1943), 'The Jungle Line', 'Harry's House/Centerpiece' (from *The Hissing of Summer Lawns*, Asylum, 1975)

Dai Griffiths (2007) provides a detailed study of the ways that, in Europe at the end of the 1970s, Elvis Costello was constructing a songwriting technique in which allusion, reference and juxtaposed sources were key methods; Griffiths' article, which provides an excellent introduction to the concept of intertextuality in general, shows how Costello's songwriting worked as a kind of critical as well as creative act, sizing up a source and then saying something about it in an 'original' song. Musicians working in rock music forms were now routinely showing a degree of historical con-sciousness that had largely been absent from mainstream popular music. But rather than entertaining conservative notions of continuity and tradition, this reflection on the past foregrounded a play of creative juxtaposition and, sometimes, irony, that typified the emerging postmodern mood.

Similar innovations were emerging at the same time in early hip-hop culture. In mid-1970s New York City, party DJs like Kool Herc and Grandmaster Flash were developing techniques that involved looping the 'break' of a funk or soul record – a few bars of a particularly danceable hook, often just percussion – by alternating two copies of the same record on two turntables (Toop 1984b: 67). Over this patchwork of recorded rhythm, MCs, masters of ceremony, would lead call-and-response routines and, as the form developed, full verses of rapped lyrics. DJs' use of found materials was eclectic. But following the introduction of Ensoniq and Akai S series digital samplers in the mid-1980s (➔Chapter 8, 'Instruments'), hip-hop producers were able to develop increasingly complex techniques for layering samples. This was, in some ways, a brief flourishing: as we will see later (➔Chapter 10, 'Copyright and the Music Industry'), sampling practices like these were soon subject to legal challenge.

- The Real Roxanne (b. 1967), 'Bang Zoom (Let's Go-Go)' (produced by Howie Tee, Select, 1986)
- Public Enemy, 'Night of the Living Bassheads' (produced by Bomb Squad, Def Jam, 1988)
- Boogie Down Productions, 'My Philosophy' (produced by KRS-One, Jive, 1988)
- De La Soul, *3 Feet High and Rising* (produced by Prince Paul, Tommy Boy, 1989)

It was easier to find a context for hip-hop's intense referentiality than it was for rock. The use of found materials had many precedents in Afro-diasporic creative tradition, whether in the work of visual artists like Romare Bearden, writers like Ishmael Reed, bebop musicians (➔Chapter 2, 'Modernism') or dub producers (➔Chapter 9, 'Recording and Production'). This borrowing tradition was at that moment being theorised by the literary scholar Henry Louis Gates, who showed how reference, collage and irony – those supposedly postmodern discoveries – had long been important in African American creative work, folklore and everyday language use. Gates' 1988 book, *The Signifying Monkey*, was influential in the development of music studies that sought to reframe postmodern intertextuality, especially as found in jazz (Monson 1994) and hip-hop (Potter 1995), through an African American perspective.

But hip-hop's early scholars also understood it as a form that, in tune with other postmodern forms, made use of the past in a newly self-conscious way: one in which recorded history was cut up and reassembled in a creative, even radical, act of meaning-making. In *Black Noise*, a key early text, Tricia Rose called sampling 'a means of archival research, a process of musical and cultural archaeology' (Rose 1994: 79). As much was suggested by the hip-hop cult of 'crate-digging', where producers would scour record shops for long-forgotten but potentially useful sample sources, and by the ways in which some rappers discussed the cultural significance of their sample choices (Perchard 2011). Still, popular music practices were not as routinely defined by a critical-intellectual project as art music, and theorists like Joseph Schloss (2004) disputed this interpretation of sampling. Schloss cites producer Prince Paul's response to a critical interpretation of his work with De La Soul as an exercise in postmodern irony: 'Wow. That's pretty deep', Prince Paul reflected. 'But I think the bottom line is just: [we sampled] a good song! . . . We didn't consciously think . . . you know, "Postmodern". We was just like, "Wow. Remember that song? That's hot!"' (Schloss 2004: 148).

By the final years of the century, referentiality and stylistic eclecticism were so ubiquitous as to be almost unremarkable. These remained productive creative methods, though, and figures as different as György Ligeti, John Adams, Kaija Saariaho and Tan Dun – respectively born in Hungary, the USA, Finland and China, but making their living in countries across the world – brought into contact de- and re-contextualised elements of classical and vernacular languages from many cultures. For younger musicians, including those who identified strongly with a modernist art music tradition, boundaries between musical styles and worlds were now traversed with barely a second thought. In *The Long Rain* (2000), Michael Kreihsl's film of a Ray Bradbury sci-fi story with music by Olga Neuwirth, four astronauts pick their way through the thick vegetation of a hostile planet, increasingly desperate as they are drenched by unending rain, caught up by the tendrils of Neuwirth's post-serial language – until they arrive at a shelter to find a vinyl record playing a smeared, woozy version of a song made famous by Frank Sinatra, 'Here's That Rainy Day', the standard incorporated into the ensemble.

- György Ligeti (1923–2006), Trio for Violin, Horn and Piano (Hommage à Brahms). IV. Lamento Adagio (1982)
- John Adams (b. 1947), *Harmonielehrer* (1985)
- Tan Dun (b. 1957), *Orchestral Theater II: Re* (1992)
- Kaija Saariaho (b. 1952), *Six Japanese Gardens* (1993)
- Nitin Sawhney (b. 1964), *Beyond Skin* (Outcaste, 1999)
- Mr Bungle, *California* (Warner Bros., 1999)
- Olga Neuwirth (b. 1968), *The Long Rain* (2000)

Image and Consumption

The mid-century saw the growth of a new area of intellectual enquiry: media theory. The increasing prevalence of mass-media technologies, not least television – which, like audio equipment, was in the majority of homes in the USA and much of Europe by the 1960s – demanded a new analysis of the relationship between cultural production and its consumption. What kinds of messages did the mass media produce, how was such information understood by audiences and how was this dynamic shaping politics and society? As we will see in our second case study, new thinking about media had a profound impact on the ways that late twentieth-century music and its commercial products were understood by audiences and scholars alike.

A central figure in this project was the Canadian philosopher, Marshall McLuhan (1911–80). One simple but acute observation – 'the medium is the message' – propelled McLuhan to pop-culture fame; for him, what was significant about a medium was not so much the content that it conveyed as 'the change of scale or pace or pattern that it introduces into human affairs' (McLuhan 2001/1964: 8). Meanwhile, in France, the philosopher and film-maker Guy Debord (1931–94) was developing a political critique of the deluge of TV and film images, recorded music and radio and newspapers and magazines that he called the 'spectacle'. In his tract, *The Society of the Spectacle* (1994/1967), Debord aimed to describe the ways that capitalist production and power relations were being restructured. Where nineteenth-century capitalists had controlled industrial production, and thereby the masses who toiled in their factories, twentieth-century capitalists exerted new forms of control through the production of commoditised media images, which were then consumed by the masses. The spectacle was to be thought of not as the images themselves but as the terrain upon which that power relationship was played out, as 'a social relation between people that is mediated by images'. The spectacle was not a 'supplement' to or 'decoration' of the real world. Instead, it made visible capitalist reality, and the 'commodity dominating all living experience' (Debord 1994/1967: paragraphs 4, 6, 37). These analyses from the 1960s would retain much of their edge even in the age of the Internet and social media, fifty years later.

The insight that people's lived realities were increasingly being constructed through their consumption of media images also underpinned the work of another French philosopher, Jean Baudrillard (1929–2007). In his 1960s work, Baudrillard addressed the new consumer society of the postwar period, and the ways in which consumption practices worked as the purchase of selfhood – a purchase that was never completed, a desire never sated – and as the communication of that self to others. But Baudrillard became known as a key contributor to postmodern thought through his work on the concept of the 'simulacrum', which he developed in the 1970s and 1980s. That word had traditionally denoted a simulation of some kind: crocodile tears, feigned illness. However, Baudrillard saw that in the postmodern society – saturated as it was with media in which distant, recorded events were experienced as live, and in which news and feature-film images increasingly resembled each other – the distinction between 'reality' and its 'simulation' was breaking down. Postmodern 'reality' was experienced having passed through a set of photo filters, made 'more real than the real' (Baudrillard 1994/1981: 81). Baudrillard famously dubbed this the 'hyperreal': a situation in which it was no longer possible to distinguish between 'real' objects, events or experiences and their simulation or representation.

Case Study 3.2: Image, Consumption and the Hyperreal in Postmodern Pop

Many of the things that postmodernism was claimed to be are apparent in the video for Madonna's 'Material Girl' (1984). Here, Madonna (b. Madonna Ciccone, 1958), near the beginning of her career and yet already a global superstar, plays a global superstar. Rather than delivering the song to us, the spectators, in a realist manner, we see her filming a grand set-piece performance of it – and one that precisely mimics the set-piece performance of the song 'Diamonds Are a Girl's Best Friend' given by an earlier global superstar, Marilyn Monroe, in the 1953 film *Gentlemen Prefer Blondes* (Figure 3.2). The ironic self-reflection on stardom, the intertextuality and the presentation not just of the image of the star but also of that image's media production: these added levels of knowingness were important elements in the postmodern experience.

Along with Michael Jackson, Madonna was one of the leading, and most complex, icons in 1980s popular culture. She inhabited different personae from one release to the next, swapping from sassy clubland face to Mediterranean peasant, from would-be gay icon to Kabbalist, and this endless play with identity and difference made her the subject of much debate (O'Brien 2007). That was not entirely novel. But one of the chief traits of this postmodern period was the readiness of cultural commentators and academics to apply sophisticated theoretical writing to 'low' popular culture, and discussion of Madonna soon extended into scholarly literature (Street 1993; Vernallis 1998).

Some writers, like the musicologist Susan McClary (1991; →Chapter 13, 'Gender and Sexuality'), argued that, in all the talk about Madonna the icon, her music was being neglected. For most observers, however, the music was not really where the interest lay: Madonna was a 'metatextual' star, and neither her work nor her significance was contained in her songs alone. In this view, Madonna's art form was media celebrity itself, the entire ensemble of images that she took on and cast aside so rapidly:

Case Study 3.2: (cont.)

Figure 3.2 Madonna performs in the video for her single 'Material Girl' (Sire/Warner Brothers, 1984);
Marilyn Monroe performs 'Diamonds Are a Girl's Best Friend' in the 1953 film *Gentlemen Prefer Blondes*

Case Study 3.2: (cont.)

her public persona and life narrative; her films, videos, albums and tours; the very fact of her fixture in public consciousness and debate.

Examples of this metatextual perspective can be found in pieces by David Tetzlaff and Cathy Schwichtenberg (both 1993). For Madonna, Tetzlaff argued, there seemed to be no controlling or 'real' authorial self. Instead, she was 'offering our received images of women back to the media culture that spawned them but decontextualized and piled on top of one another in a way that reveals their contractedness, that subverts their hold on us' (Tetzlaff 1993: 256). Madonna's work could be read as critique, and even, potentially, as emancipatory: Schwichtenberg argued that Madonna's 'shifting persona' and play of visual codes collapsed stifling social categories and hierarchies – female/male, straight/gay and so on – thus signalling a newly fluid approach to gender and sexuality (Schwichtenberg 1993: 130). As Tetzlaff observed (1993: 242–3), Madonna inspired her young fans to think of new ways of being. 'Fictional' representations of identity preceded their real-world employment.

However, any redefinition of roles took place within the framework of consumerism – where the first thing consumed was Madonna's products or personas – and so Madonna's output acted as 'a reinvigoration of the commodity cycle' before even beginning to inspire any social change (Tetzlaff 1993: 256). As we have seen, postmodern trends in creative work were often met in celebratory fashion, and that was a point of contention for those who lamented what they saw as the acceptance of an increasingly inescapable culture of consumption. Tetzlaff's comments, however, suggest that some critics were interested in identifying the ways that postmodern creative approaches made visible their own socio-economic circumstances.

An extended example of this approach can be found in Olivia Bloechl's 2005 study of Madonna's global-pop-star contemporary, Sting (Gordon Sumner, b. 1951), and his hit, 'Desert Rose' (1999). Again, Bloechl does not focus on the song alone. Nor does she even consider that the primary object; instead, she writes about a plurality of '"Desert Rose" texts', treating the song, its video and a tie-in luxury car commercial as equally important parts of an intertextual whole, each part constructed in a different medium, each serving particular creative and commercial aims.

'Desert Rose' begins with some classic Orientalism. Making a guest appearance, the Algerian raï singer, Cheb Mami (b. 1966), decorates the introduction with vocal inflections that, overlaying chattering hand-drums and sweeping strings, conjure the Middle East and North Africa region. These signifiers pile up as the song progresses. For Bloechl, Mami serves as an uncomplicated sign of 'authentic' and 'exotic' Arabness, and throughout the song – and moreover, the video – Mami will function as a 'pure' Other by way of which Sting's identity will be measured and, perhaps, fulfilled; the character that Sting portrays in the video is curiously empty to begin with, and the narrative will track his progression, via encounters of various kinds, towards some new completeness.

Case Study 3.2: (cont.)

Figure 3.3 Sting, opening scenes of the video for 'Desert Rose' (A&M, 2000)

It is a journey, literally. At the video's start, Sting, all but alone in the middle of a desert, climbs into a luxury car, and is taken by his female driver – large sunglasses hiding her face like a veil – down a lonely motorway, across a glittering cityscape and finally to a nightclub (Figure 3.3). Bloechl notes that none of these are identifiable or particular spaces. They are instead tokens of their type – hyperreal – and likewise the lyrics construct an imagined, Oriental space full of imaged Oriental people: 'I dream of gardens in the desert sand'; 'This desert rose/Each of her veils, a secret promise'.

Sting travels in his luxury car through the desert, peering through the window and recording his surroundings through a newly released JVC digital video camera. It transpires that the car is a Jaguar S-Type; the video features a number of shots

Case Study 3.2: (cont.)

of the kind that featured heavily in automobile advertising at the time, and a commercial for the S-Type, aired while the song was on release, features numerous extracts from Sting's video. It had been common to smuggle paid-for product placements into cultural works for many decades. But here, the relationship between the creative text and its supposedly auxiliary commercial purposes is celebrated rather than obscured.

Watching and travelling, Sting is an observer cocooned in luxury, turning from the scene only to close his eyes and, as the lyrics report, to dream of the exotic. His opening vocal is a largely unadorned melodic line rooted in standard Western diatonic-modal practice, but it also incorporates a melodic fillip that is figured as 'Arab'. For Bloechl, this is the start of the white, male, Western subject's fantasising of himself as Other. Arriving at the club, Sting finds Cheb Mami as well as a drummer, a violinist, singers and an audience engaged in 'authentically' social music making. The Others are complete in their exoticism, but also their vibrant conviviality, a contrast indeed to Sting's own incomplete and solitary self. Sting climbs the stage, eyes still closed, still dreaming, but now his hips sway in a manner he seems to imagine as Arab (Figure 3.4).

This compact of creative, commercial and ideological motives was typical of the late twentieth-century culture industries. But Bloechl argues that Desert Rose's many 'texts' make it a particularly telling example. In the Jaguar commercial, intertitles flash up a statement and question: 'Everyone dreams of becoming a rock star. What then do rock stars dream of?' The commercial then cuts to shots taken from the end of the music video, with Sting on stage, eyes closed in a becoming-Arab reverie. We see him participate in the communal music making, Cheb Mami by his side, and we hear Mami's vocal 'arabesques', swirling modal strings and Sting's own voice, double-tracked. What rock stars dream of, Bloechl writes (2005: 151), is a self that is many times multiplied (and, of course, an S-Type). Bloechl recalls Baudrillard's framing of consumption as a method through which people form their subjective identities by purchasing signifiers of Otherness. The ownership of the Jaguar is a banal example of that. But here, the signifiers are also sonic – by taking on musical signifiers of the Orient, Sting is (temporarily) transformed – and they are experiential: by dipping into an Arab cultural social space, Sting borrows an experience of Other life in order to enrich his own.

Bloechl's study provides a rich reading of a particular postmodern situation, but much the same could be said of Madonna's output. Here, systems of representation, consumption, cultural appropriation and identity-making are set to work in what is a fundamentally hyperreal space. Although the accumulation of sounds, objects, identities and cultural practices would seem to create a weight of meaning, those

Case Study 3.2: (cont.)

Figure 3.4 Sting, later scenes in the video for 'Desert Rose' (A&M, 2000)

things are only present as two-dimensional signs, themselves already reproductions. This kind of postmodern experience is shown to be curiously weightless.

Conclusion

For critics both on the left and right, that weightlessness was the problem. For them, 'postmodernism' meant the resignation of seriousness and ambition, the indulgence of vapidity and consumption. Even in the twenty-first century, the term is still invoked by politicians and commentators as they lament the West as it supposedly was: a place of security and order, where 'truth' and 'reality' were not things to be deconstructed but faced and grasped. For that reason, observers who stood with a finger in the wind ready to announce the moment's passing often seized on the terror attacks of September 11, 2001 as the moment that the 'real' – and a clash of competing ideologies that were truly, viscerally, violently believed – wiped the ironic smile off postmodernist faces.

Yet postmodernism was not really the making of 'postmodernists' – that is, the critics, thinkers and artists who identified and articulated the mood of a postwar West which, forlorn of its world-making hopes, had supposedly given up and gone shopping. What those people did achieve was to make it widely understood that narratives, knowledge and truth were not timeless things, but arguments and observations, produced by certain people and certain institutions towards certain ends. Contra postmodernism's critics, this was not a call for a new 'post-truth' era. In many ways, it was a demand for more truth, for the unmasking of hidden and even unthinking forms of power that pressed 'truth' into their own service. Postmodernist thought and creativity emphasised that, for better or worse, the categories we live by – not just notions of truth, but also identity, history – are categories that we *construct*, day after day. And categories we construct are categories we can change.

4 | Canons

As diverse as they may seem, the works of Schoenberg, Ella Fitzgerald, Ligeti, the Sex Pistols and Patti Smith all have something in common. From innovative, extended form to progressive and authentic performance style, the work of these diverse musicians has transcended changing tastes and styles to become firmly rooted in our musical culture. When the music of an artist continues to be played long after their death, or long after the music was released, and has exerted significant influence over subsequent musical practice, it can become part of a musical canon. A canon is a group of works considered by certain social and cultural groups to be the most significant and influential of a time period, style or genre. The consideration of a piece of music as an autonomous and bounded 'work' is a relatively new concept (→Chapter 5, 'Work and Notation'). In music, the Western art-music canon was the first to develop, but during the twentieth century, canons of punk, jazz, rock and pop formed as their commercial and critical apparatus developed.

Here, we explore the ways that musicians, scholars, journalists, record companies, music fans, academics and the media have populated the canons of twentieth-century music. As the century progressed, social and cultural change, together with the emerging post-structuralist, post-colonialist, feminist and Afrocentric critical frameworks that we saw developing in →Chapter 3, 'Postmodernism', encouraged scholars to revisit and repopulate earlier art-music canons. We see how these voices worked with and against each other to interpret and order the century's new music not only into dominant narratives, but also into numerous small and outsider canons. Our case studies will address two of the biggest issues in the study of canons. First, who is responsible for constructing canons, and who are the gatekeepers that determine our ongoing access to music? Second, where are all the women and what does their absence from the dominant music narratives tell us about the processes of value construction and authorship?

The Art-Music Canon

For centuries, the ideology of high art put Bach, Mozart and Beethoven on a pedestal at the heart of the Western art-music canon, and as the twentieth century unfolded, this was reflected in the way music was played, funded and taught. Motti Regev describes the work that populates a canon as representing the 'peaks of the aesthetic power of the art form in question, as ultimate manifestations of aesthetic perfection, complexity of form and depth of expression . . . The works and the authors that comprise the canon are supposedly the undisputed "masterpieces" and "geniuses" of the art form' (2006: 1). But what is important and why? What is worth remembering, repeating and studying? And who decides these things? Many scholars have tackled these questions by investigating the processes used to form canons as well as the music that populates them (Bohlman 1993: 201; Shreffler 2013). Canon formation is a process of writing history that determines what was and remains important and places ideas and works within a narrative according to certain criteria. Once selected, works are ordered into particular groups that enable us to navigate through past music practices and their common values and experiences (Shreffler 2013). Karol Berger sums up this position particularly well:

> *The canon makes it possible to write a narrative history of the tradition of art music.* If a practice left nothing but an unsorted archive of instances behind, it would be possible to write its chronicle but not its narrative history. A chronicle . . . orders the relevant events in a chronological order, one thing after another; a narrative history shows how these events are related, one thing because of another. An archive can be the subject matter of a chronicle; a canon makes possible the writing of a narrative history. (2014: 189, italics his)

For us, this is a very familiar way of thinking about music history. But the idea of a music canon – particular pieces of music that continue to be played across decades and centuries – is relatively recent. Before this, the cult of the new dominated. Despite Bach's (1685–1750) notoriety as an organist and composer of works for the Tomaskirche, for instance, his works were rarely performed after the event for which they were written. However, by 1800, a new sensibility began to emerge that recognised the historical and cultural existence beyond a work's first performance. The performance history of Bach's St. Matthew Passion (1727) illustrates this change well. Although occasionally performed during Bach's life, the work quickly fell out of the repertory and was all but forgotten until Mendelssohn revived it in 1829. Mendelssohn's performance was so

successful that it encouraged a renewed interest in earlier musics in
Germany and the work subsequently re-entered the performance repertoire (Applegate 2005). By the time that Beethoven (1770–1827) was
writing his late symphonies, his work was already beginning to enter the
emerging canon; it has enjoyed constant performance ever since. This
dawn of an historical awareness – not only of music from the past, but
also the place of contemporary music within this trajectory – could also be
found in England (Weber 1994) and France around the same time. It is this
idea of an afterlife for a musical work that gave rise to the possibility of
a canon.

In part, this change in behaviour was enabled by the rise of the bourgeoise in the late eighteenth century, which saw the establishment of the
public concert, as distinct from the performance of court and religious
music. Where before patrons determined what was written and for which
occasion (i.e., when it would be performed), the public concert saw a shift
in power to the general public – and the middle class in particular – and
their tastes and values. Emerging distinctions between high and low art saw
the elevation of certain works and styles above those of others, and concert-
going took the form of a social ritual where audience members could
demonstrate their education, taste, status and opinion to their peers.
Related to this were the new economic possibilities of printed sheet
music. Lydia Goehr describes these changing sensibilities in terms of
intent, arguing that before 1800 composition was a craft; after, it was
a fine art (Goehr 1992). This is an important distinction, as it gave rise to
the modern concept that the value of music is not necessarily rooted in
a particular moment but can transcend time and place.

We will come back to the thorny issue of value later, but for now it is
important to note that the art-music canon is populated by large-scale
works that demonstrate formal and technical complexity. These works are
original and progressive; they offer a form of historical transcendence and
greatness (Bourdieu 1984) that ensures the music continues to be regularly
played, recorded and analysed; and they have been influential for subsequent composers. We can say that these works demonstrate considerable
significance both in their immediate contexts and for subsequent musicians. Most often, these are works of absolute music by a relatively small
pool of male composers: Bach's keyboard works, Mozart's string quartets,
Beethoven's and Schubert's symphonies, Chopin's and Liszt's piano work,
and the concertos of Rachmaninoff, Schumann and Tchaikovsky. Come
the twentieth century and the gender and race of composers showed very
little sign of diversifying, with the music of Debussy, Stravinsky, Bartók,

Shostakovich, Ligeti, Reich, Ives and Vaughan Williams rapidly augmenting, and self-consciously referring to, the historical canon.

What did diversify, though, was the art canon itself, which split into two contrasting strains (Kerman 1983; Kramer 1994): a performing canon centred around late-eighteenth-to-nineteenth-century and tonal twentieth-century music that is enjoyable to perform and listen to; and an avant-garde (or scholarly) one made up of complex and intellectually challenging music like that of the Second Viennese School. Although progressive, works in this canon do not always find easy performance opportunities or large audiences although, as this book attests, they continue to attract significant scholarly attention. Christopher Chowrimootoo (2016) explores this distinction in his work on Benjamin Britten, whose more accessible sound worlds have seen him reside on the edges of the 'scholarly' canon, yet have also afforded him mainstream appeal as part of the repertory (→Chapter 7, 'Harmony').

- Britten, 'Requiem Aeternam', from *War Requiem* (Op. 66, 1962)

The century also saw the development of ancillary canons with a focus on musical type (early repertoires, concertos, opera and so on), instruments (piano, violin, etc.) and people who have traditionally been excluded from the mainstream narratives (women and ethnic minorities), as we shall see in Case Study 4.2.

Popular Music Canons

By the century's third decade, the idea of the canon was so strong that as soon as people started taking popular music seriously (first with jazz in the 1930s, then rock in the 1950s), canonising was a reflex way of organising knowledge about those forms. But whereas the historical art-music canon was formed posthumously (Bach and Mozart found themselves in a canon designed by others after they had died, for instance), popular music in the twentieth century could enter its respective canon almost as soon as it was released. This was partly because canon formation was common practice by the time many popular music genres had developed in the twentieth century, and partly because of the new ways in which people engaged with music through the century's new media forms – recordings, radio, print and online journalism – and the diversifying possibilities of fan participation, whereby underground and alternative histories could be collectively written through fanzines, which were particularly important to the history

Figure 4.1 A selection of punk fanzines from the 1970s. Photograph by J. K. Miloszewski

of punk (Figure 4.1). But it was also due to the unique nature of popular musics. The art-music canon is formed from written texts: notated music that requires interpretation and performance for its realisation. The texts of the popular music canons, on the other hand, are (usually) recordings which have particular performances embedded in them. Referring to this change, Alan Moore refers to the popular music canon as 'a construction made on the act of listening' (2002: 210).

Nevertheless, the main popular music canon resembles the art music one in terms of its focus on narrative, ability to highlight and perpetuate the values of different communities, influence and longevity. Like the art-music canon, it has been populated by large-scale works – here the album – that demonstrate considerable *significance* through authentic style, progressive songwriting, internal coherence and innovative production design. The Beatles' album *Revolver* (1966) is an album that fulfils all these requirements for canonisation: it had immediate impact, presented progressive songwriting and studio techniques and was original yet coherent in style. *Revolver* later influenced the ways that subsequent albums were imagined, created and produced to become an artwork 'without which the history of rock would be very different' (Wyn Jones 2008: 53). It is not surprising, then, that *Revolver* tops a meta-list of albums that Ralf von Appen and André Doehring produced after comparison of 38 '100 greatest albums of all times' lists drawn between 1985–89 and 2000–2004 (2006). They note that the Beatles album was consistently on or near the top of most of the lists analysed and can therefore be considered a pivotal part of the mainstream popular music canon.

Appen and Doehring's analysis throws up several other useful observations. Rock music from the 1960s and 1970s dominates the mainstream popular music canon – also high on their list are albums by the Beach Boys, Pink Floyd, the Rolling Stones, U2, The Clash, Bob Dylan and the Jimi Hendrix Experience – perhaps because this was the time when the idea that popular music was a legitimate scholarly art form worthy of canonisation really gathered pace. It can also be attributable to the value judgements used to assess popular music, but we will come back to this later. Other scholars have noted the canon's narrow focus. Andy Bennett refers to Cleveland Ohio's Rock and Roll Hall of Fame to show how 'many of those artists ... rose to prominence during the 1960s' (2015: 22), while others note the dominance of 'the Beatles, "punk" and Bob Dylan' (Moore 2001: 7) and 'Jimi Hendrix, The Rolling Stones, Stevie Wonder' (Regev 2006: 1). In her book on the rock canon, Carys Wyn Jones (2008) analyses ten albums that she considers to represent the heart of the pop canon, of which only one was produced after 1977: Bob Dylan's *Highway 61 Revisited* (1965), the Beach Boys' *Pet Sounds* (1966), the Beatles' *Revolver* (1966), the Velvet Underground's *The Velvet Underground & Nico* (1967), Van Morrison's *Astral Weeks* (1968), Marvin Gaye's *What's Going On* (1971), the Rolling Stones' *Exile on Main St.* (1972), Patti Smith's *Horses* (1974), Sex Pistols' *Never Mind the Bollocks: Here's the Sex Pistols* (1977) and Nirvana's *Nevermind* (1991).

- The Velvet Underground, 'Venus in Furs' (from *The Velvet Underground & Nico*, Verve, 1967)
- Sex Pistols, 'Pretty Vacant', *Never Mind the Bollocks, Here's the Sex Pistols* (Virgin Records / Warner Bros, 1977)
- Nirvana, 'Smells Like Teen Spirit' (from *Nevermind*, DGC, 1991)

The dominance of rock music and its aesthetics over that of mainstream popular culture saw the omission of numerous other genres from the dominant narrative. Although some lists are more diverse, including artists like

ABBA, Led Zeppelin, Michael Jackson and others, whether or not they have been attributed lasting value by scholars (Frith 1996), exclusions include indie guitar rock (Bannister 2006a, 2006b), disco and club cultures (Thornton 1990), country, hard rock, hip-hop, R & B, blues, soul, metal and pop. During the century, these different genres developed their own, parallel canons that can seem to resist many of the mainstream narrative patterns while at the same time repeating the classic canon parameters. Indie rock, for instance, arises from local scenes, is less dependent on commercial pressures and appears to be 'free of high culture elitism' (Bannister 2006a: 77). However, Matthew Bannister shows how its apparent self-promoted freedoms were actually as hierarchical, and media dependent, as those of many other genres (2006; Hesmondhalgh 1999: 46–7). The same issues have surrounded jazz. As scholars like Krin Gabbard (1995) and Sherrie Tucker (2002) have argued, by the mid-twentieth century a jazz canon had developed according to similar criteria – and with just as many resultant blind spots – as the art-music canon. 'Canonic jazz' was driven by the desire to innovate, not by commercial gain; it was made by great men, and not women; it featured a limited number of 'approved' ensemble formats; and it was made by African Americans to the general exclusion of other people. But the latter factor meant that, in the last decades of the century, musicians led by the trumpeter and educator Wynton Marsalis would purposefully frame the jazz canon as a storehouse of Black American creativity that had usually been maligned by cultural gatekeepers. Again, the canon was shown to be both reactionary and empowering.

Criteria for Entry

How can we say a piece of music has universal value? What exactly is it that determines whether a piece will be studied and played across decades and even centuries? Value is an extremely tricky thing to identify and understand, not least because something that is meaningful to one group of people at a certain time may not remain so for other cultures or eras. In his work on folk canons, for instance, Philip Bohlman shows how 'Different communities shape and express ... canons in various ways' (1998: 106). And yet, in the West, the value judgements underpinning both the classical and popular canons have remained remarkably consistent.

Innovation, complexity, coherence, expression, influence and longevity: these aesthetic criteria can be gathered together to demonstrate a work's significance. Most music in the mainstream canons evidences these characteristics and allows us to construct clear and linear narratives. But above all, a composer is most likely to enter the canon through successful formal innovation. Anne Shreffler, speaking of the twentieth-century Western art-music canon, describes it 'as a series of technical and formal accomplishments, starting with atonality and ranging from the twelve-tone technique to serialism to indeterminacy, polystylism, New Complexity, and beyond' (Shreffler 2013: 11). As we have seen (→Chapter 2, 'Modernism'), the twelve-tone technique of Schoenberg pushes previous expansions of tonality explored by Strauss and others to its extreme. Although complex, his atonal music achieves a great coherence and expressive power even across large structures. Its influence was immediate and far-reaching and can be traced through the music of Berg and Webern to Berio, Messiaen, Arvo Pärt, Ruth Crawford (Seeger) and even the jazz compositions of Bill Evans and others. In terms of longevity, Schoenberg's music continues to be played, studied and recorded and remains an integral part of many university music syllabuses.

Similar criteria determine the main popular music canon. Although many have questioned this borrowed framework, which has generated 'critique and resentment' among some popular music scholars (Regev 2006: 1), it has been very influential. Wyn Jones (2008), for instance, uses concept albums to demonstrate how 'the canonical criteria of originality, complexity and truth . . . associated with an autonomous artist/genius' can emerge through connected songs. To enter the canon, an album must show that it encourages 'repeated listening and can sustain multiple interpretations, has withstood the test of time and influenced subsequent albums, but it is also complete in itself, forming an object of endless study and value' (42). She uses Marvin Gaye's (1939–1984) *What's Going On?* (1971) to show how the combination of innovative song structures, when collected into a coherent suite of shared themes and styles, produces a 'completeness and self-sufficiency' (42) akin to the classical song cycle (43). In this way, *What's Going On?* deviated from previous Motown records, which tended to be collections of singles with fillers added to bring them to album length. Together with the expressivity of Gaye's voice, this coherence became extremely influential for artists working across a range of genres.

- Marvin Gaye, 'What's Going On' (from *What's Going On*, Motown, 1971)

While we can locate similar criteria at play in art and pop music canons, though, there is a fundamental difference. Because popular music is most often sold as recordings – or aural artefacts – rather than written texts, it requires an additional type of assessment that looks not only at compositional process but also at how the music is recorded and performed, often by the songwriter herself. But performance can be harder to evaluate objectively. Many critics have used the concept of authenticity to think about how well a song's message is conveyed to an audience (Appen and Doehring 2006: 31). For Allan Moore (2002), authenticity is generated in two ways: 'first person authenticity' that 'arises when an originator (composer, performer) succeeds in conveying the impression that his/her utterance is one of integrity, that it represents an attempt to communicate in an unmediated form with the audience' (214); and a 'second person authenticity' that persuades the listener that their experiences are valid (220). Nirvana's *Nevermind* (1991), which sits at number 3 on Appen and Doehring's meta-list, shows just how powerful the authentic gesture can be. While the band's music does not offer particularly innovative or complex structures, the raw expressivity of the band's delivery and the recording's lo-fi production provided an authenticity that had an immediate and lasting impact on a whole generation of artists.

Recording technology also provided new ways of assessing influence and longevity. Before it was developed, reviews of live performances and music analysis could help us to understand how dominant a piece of music had been. In the twentieth century, the recording industry, music charts, ticket and record sales, merchandise, magazine and fanzine coverage, fan activities and radio play enabled a more comprehensive analysis of music's commercial success and market value (Desler 2013: 388). However, although using radio play to assess the continuing relevance of music can be useful, it could be argued that such data disadvantage types of music that are unsuitable for prime-time broadcast. The transgressive messages and language of speed, death and black metal, for instance, have kept them out of many radio playlists, which might help explain why these genres remain peripheral to the mainstream canon, despite their virtuosity, complexity, authenticity and embrace of intricate large-scale forms (Kärjä 2006: 14; Walker 1992).

Commercial statistics also sit awkwardly against the criteria used to determine aesthetic value. We noted that, during the century, art music was divided into a scholarly and a performance canon, with the former emphasising 'formal and technical accomplishments', and the latter more popular textures. Appen and Doehring have found a similar divide in the mainstream popular music canon. Their analysis leads them to construct two lists: one created through the traditional forms of value construction outlined above, and the other based on record sales (or popularity; 2006: 23, 25). While some artists – notably the Beatles and Pink Floyd – appear high on both lists, others see a fundamental shift in position. Michael Jackson's *Thriller* (1982) only sits at number 40 in the aesthetically judged meta-list, for instance, yet is the second bestselling album (according to the US sales position and estimated worldwide figures; 25). It is notable that many artists at the top of the bestseller list, including the Eagles, who sit at number 1, do not feature at all in the meta-list: Elton John, Billy Joel, AC/DC, Shania Twain and Garth Brooks are some other notable names here. This is also true of the art-music canon: Schoenberg's atonal *Variations for Orchestra* (1926–8) sits at the heart of the scholarly canon but has not always found regular performance opportunities. This discrepancy between music in the canon and bestselling, or most-performed work suggests that popularity and sales figures are not the main staple of canon construction. In fact, Appen and Doehring point out that chart success and artistic authenticity can have a limited relationship (33).

Although much of the criteria used in canon creation is quite clear, then, there are many aspects that are open to interpretation, and these interpretations can change from one decade to another. Karol Berger (2014) argues that personal taste has a lot to do with how the narratives of canons develop. He points out that if someone considers the most significant composer at the end of the century to be Helmut Lachenmann, they will view the century's main achievements as running from Schoenberg, Webern and Stockhausen through to Nono: 'But if you think that the composer who really mattered late in the century was György Ligeti, your story will make much more room for Debussy, early Stravinsky, and Bartók' (188–9). Different people, working to different criteria, will construct a narrative that privileges the traditionalism of the neo-classicists; the innovation of the modernists and the avant-garde; the experimentation of the postmodernists and polystylists; or the interdisciplinarity of the spectralists and multimedia artists.

Gilbert B. Rodman demonstrates a similar changeability in rock music by outlining at least three 'strikingly different' ways to tell its story, particularly when performance and recording become part of the assessment: emphasising the 'creative, artistic endeavour' perpetuates the story of the 'Great Artists', while focus on the 'shrewd entrepreneurs and media empires' of the recording industry gives another story entirely. And if we assess music's 'powerful social, cultural, and political' influence, the narrative changes again (Rodman 1999: 42).

Who Constructs a Canon?

Value in music, then, can be assessed through aesthetic criteria (by critics, reviewers, academics and fans) but also through material production (sales of tapes, vinyl, CDs and sheet music) and its distribution (airplay, concert programming, tours and so on). Thinking about the criteria used for canon construction can reveal what has been valued and extolled in music and why. And comparing performing/bestselling and scholarly canons can show how those values may not always translate into positive listening experiences or popularity. But once we acknowledge the possible variations in the narrative – as Berger and Rodman do – we need to ask another question: *who* decides these things? Who asserts and legitimises what and how we should evaluate an artwork's value, originality and universality? Or as Joseph Kerman puts it: '*How* are canons determined, *why* and on *what* authority?' (1983: 124, italics his).

Sometimes, musicians themselves play an active role in canon formation. This is particularly true of what Bohlman, in his work on folk music, calls 'small group' canons (1998: 111). Small group canons are constructed by members of a community who know each other and pass down their music, which is often associated with social or ritual activities, through oral traditions. Here, the collection of music emphasises belonging and identity significant to traditional communities. This type of canon can also be found in urban environments, where small groups articulate 'more intimate cultural expression' (111–12). Antti-Ville Kärjä has mapped this process onto popular music beyond the mainstream (2006). It is only when the group gets bigger that more abstract sorting and interpreting comes into play to generate what Bohlman calls a mediated and an imagined canon (1998: 111).

Most often, though, canons are constructed by other people, or what we can call the 'gatekeepers' of music. The gatekeepers in the arts are those responsible for opening or closing the gates between those who create cultural artefacts and those who engage with them: between what gets promoted, and thus heard, and what does not (Bourdieu 1984/1979; Maguire and Matthews 2010). Susanne Janssen and Marc Verboord explain that

The term 'gatekeeping' has been applied when the focus is on judgments whether to admit persons or works into a cultural field; it has to do with accepting or rejecting works or their creators and the consequences of these choices for subsequent works and creators. Driving forces behind gatekeepers' decisions range from political and moral concerns, commercial interests, to 'purely' aesthetic motives. In most cases, they consist of a mixture of these. (2015: 442)

Because value judgements can be subjective, as we have seen, gatekeepers assume an authority over the shape, legitimisation and promotion of aesthetic values and tastes, and thus acquire a degree of cultural capital (Skinner 2006: 58–9). French sociologist Pierre Bourdieu has suggested that, through this process of evaluation, cultural intermediaries actually become significant in the 'production of the value of the work or, what amounts to the same thing, of the belief in the value of the work' (1996: 229). More recently, thinking has focused on the ways in which those in gatekeeping positions have been instrumental in the formation and transformation of genre classifications and canon formation (Matthews and Maguire 2010).

Early canon formation was determined by an elite few – like concert organisers and patrons – who held the cultural and financial power to decide which music would be preserved and repeated. Before the twentieth century, the gatekeepers of musical culture were bourgeois patrons, concert organisers, reviewers, salon owners and music publishers, who decided which sheet music – and thus repertoire – would enter the public domain. But historic gatekeepers were also music scholars responsible for writing the earliest music history books, and Lydia Goehr has called for attention to be refocused from the criteria applied 'to the nationalist anxieties and aspirations that motivate the process of canonizing in the first place . . . the specific process of canonizing works is inextricably tied to how writing and making histories shape the political identity, confidence, and authority of particular groups' (2002: 314). Because a lot of the earliest engagement with music history happened in Germany and Austria, some scholars (Gerhard 2000; Gossett 1992) have argued that the Germanic lineage that underpins the historic art-music canon – running from Bach, Mozart, Beethoven, Brahms and Schumann through to Mahler and Strauss – was put into place by those wishing to promote their own musical heritage. Historians of French, Italian and Russian music have since encouraged us to look to other countries and lineages to form a more well-rounded and representative story. This demonstrates how significant the positioning of those responsible for canon construction is: if the gatekeeper's point of view were different, the narrative might alter; a Finnish historian might privilege Sibelius, a Hungarian Bartók, a Norwegian Grieg. Similarly, behind the 'greatest albums' lists used by Appen and Doehring to explore popular music canons, for instance, we find 'predominantly white males from the Western hemisphere, aged between twenty and forty, having a higher educational level' who 'regard themselves as "experts"' (2006: 34). As the new century dawned and the music industry rose as a significant cultural force, the gatekeeping role expanded to include record companies, radio stations, music magazines, fans, collectors and media personalities. We could argue that canon formation in the twentieth century represented a more democratised process than the elite authority of previous centuries, but as we see in Case Study 4.2, this was not always the case.

Case Study 4.1: Gatekeepers and Mediators of Twentieth-Century Canons

In the main chapter, we have explored the role of gatekeepers in constructing and preserving various music canons. But exactly who are these gatekeepers of the twentieth-century music canons who have in some way shaped access to music through the century?

The Recording Industry

As the century unfolded, different units of power came into being at various points. The rise of the recording industry had one of the greatest impacts on the promotion and preservation of music, and record labels have perpetuated or antagonised existing canons by keeping composers and performers in the popular consciousness (Skinner 2006). Box sets, rereleases and compilations all ensure ongoing coverage and visibility in shops, adverts and print media reviews. Labels also wield power over the canonisation of new musicians. A & R personnel represent the first step in deciding who gets signed, before labels provide the financial backing and artistic guidance and agents ensure adequate exposure and promotion. They also determine which composers have their music recorded and made available for public consumption, which can determine subsequent commissions and help ensure influence and longevity.

The recording industry's National Academy for the Recording Arts and Sciences also exerts significant power over the promotion of both established and emerging artists. Its annual Grammy Awards ceremony performs a sort of canonisation in progress by providing exposure and prestige for innovative popular musicians. In their survey of the Awards, Mary R. Watson and N. Anand (2006) show how the panel of judges are afforded the power to decide how value in popular music is understood and perpetuated and how winners usually enjoy a subsequent surge in sales, making them more likely to achieve the longevity required for canonisation (Negus 2002).

Print Media

Like the recording industry, the twentieth-century print media influenced the construction of canons in a variety of interrelated ways. The publication of notated music was vital if a composer was to have their music played in professional and amateur events, and publishing houses used the criteria of canon formation to decide which artists to support (and which were the most financially viable).

The music press has also performed an influential gatekeeping role. Simon Frith shows how music magazines are created for, and in turn perpetuate and even form, distinct musical communities (1996: 84), while Andy Bennett argues that magazines like *Rolling Stone* and *Mojo* perform a critical role in canon construction by assembling 'a canon of rock artists deemed worthy of retrospective cultural consecration' (2015:

Case Study 4.1: (cont.)

21). We can find similar processes at play in the classical music press (Dowd 2011). As we have seen in the main chapter, best-of lists (Appen and Doehring 2006; Wyn Jones 2008) make visible the value judgements that determine and pin down canon formation (Shuker 2010), while coverage of anniversaries – for example, twenty years since Elvis died – ensure posthumous engagement.

Critical attention is vital. Ratings and reviews of new or reissued work are instrumental in ongoing canonisation, and critics are extremely influential gatekeepers who make use of a range of criteria to lead public opinion, cultivate taste and ultimately determine record sales and a continuing presence.

Educators

While the recording and print industries determined who and what was preserved and heard, music educators assumed the power of shaping the century's musical narratives. Teachers and pedagogical institutions held great authority over how and why music history was portrayed in a certain way, and university courses remain deeply significant to the construction and perpetuation of music canons. The music included in music syllabuses demonstrates what remains significant to scholarship and can determine what students are exposed to. While many university courses expanded through the twentieth century to include jazz, ethnomusicology, popular music and folk (Hill 2009), teaching of the historical Western art-music canon remained remarkably consistent. And yet academics have also been instrumental in dismantling or rethinking traditional canons through new critical methodologies. Speaking of education systems, Philip Bohlman writes that 'some measure of power accrues both to those who advocate central canons and to those who effectively seek to undermine the same canons' (1992: 200).

Museums and galleries are also powerful gatekeepers of musical knowledge. Their permanent collections and exhibition programming both reflect musical popularity and perpetuate popular stories. In her work on pop music museology, Marion Leonard (2007a; and with Rob Knifton 2015) has shown how public institutions are able to reinforce existing canons through shows on major artists while also renegotiating traditional narratives by promoting local ones that activate personal and biographical memory.

Distributors and Institutions

While educators mediated the scholarly curriculum, orchestras, opera houses, venues and music festivals quickly became significant gatekeepers of our live music options. As commercial ventures, their programming and booking lists reveal much about contemporary value judgements. The gatekeeping function of the media operates in similar ways. Radio presenters, for instance, exert control over taste and value by

Case Study 4.1: (cont.)

curating playlists that determine exposure to certain musics (John Peel's promotion of the Undertones' 1978 hit 'Teenage Kicks', which launched their career, is a good example), while college radio has played an important role in supporting alternative musical cultures – particularly indie rock (Bannister 2006a: 78). While radio pro-grammes can perpetuate canons, they can also destabilise them. BBC Radio 3's *Late Junction*, first broadcast in 1999, provided a multicultural mix of music that catered for a rise in a new cultural omnivorism (DiMaggio 1991) and roamed far beyond the boundaries of discrete traditional canons.

Screen media has also played a powerful gatekeeping role. Andy Bennett (2015: 22; 2010) uses the BBC *Classic Albums* TV series (which began in 1997) to show how the narrow focus of the mainstream popular music canon has been reinforced on the small screen. Most of the albums featured are classic rock and were made between 1967 and 1975: The Jimi Hendrix Experience's *Are you Experienced?* (1967), Cream's *Disraeli Gears* (1967) and Pink Floyd's *Dark Side of the Moon* (1973) are three examples. Moreover, of the forty-five episodes, only four feature non-white artists, all but Bob Marley's *Catch a Fire* (1973) are by Anglo-American musicians and only one album features a woman artist.

Fans, Collectors and Retailers

But radio listeners and TV audiences are not simply consumers. In fact, music fans played significant roles in selecting, collecting and sorting the century's music (Shuker 2010). In Chapter 9 (→ 'Recording and Production') we will see how early folklorists were responsible for seeking out, and recording, music from the Mississippi Delta region. John Dougan finds blues record collectors to be just as important in preserving and ordering the tradition, referring to them as 'musical archaeologists, culture brokers, creators, keepers, and through their entrepreneurial efforts . . . disseminators of a blues canon' (2006: 42). These were people collecting hard-to-find artefacts and turning them into history.

Matthew Bannister considers indie rock in a similar way, writing that its evolution 'could be rewritten as a history of record collectors' (2006a: 81). For him, second-hand record shops, particularly in the 1980s when music was not so readily available, were important sites where fans could perform a type of archival musicology by sorting through forgotten or rare recordings and sorting them into collections, thus providing an essential gatekeeping function to a genre (81–2). Significantly, several important record labels, including Flying Nun and Rough Trade (Figure 4.2), were started by record-shop workers (Bannister 2006a: 82; Kruse 2003: 51–5).

Case Study 4.1: (cont.)

Figure 4.2 The Rough Trade record shop opened at 130 Talbot Road, London, in 1976. In 1978 Rough Trade launched its own record label, which became highly influential in post-punk and indie circles

Rethinking the Past: De-canonisation in the Twentieth Century

One way to assess the role played by gatekeepers in canon formation is to explore how historical narratives have been challenged in the twentieth century. As we have seen, canons have many uses: they help to sort and order music history into manageable collections and can both mirror and extend music's social and cultural role and establish strong musical communities. They help to orient the listener and ease the processes of distribution and marketing. In fact, the mainstream musical canons have become so embedded in our culture that they have begun to influence practice. Richard Taruskin, writing about the implications of this influence, has suggested that twentieth-century composers were so aware of the canon and its promotion of artists to greatness that they consciously incorporated many of the main criteria for canonisation into their practice in order to ensure their own heritage, writing not for the repertoire but for the canon (2005: 665–6). In his work on popular music canons, Motti Regev makes a similar point: 'Once established, canons exert cultural power by influencing memory and heritage and by radiating out on the work of musicians. That is, canons influence the narration of the past, and they inspire the radius of creativity for the future' (2006: 2). This is perhaps one of the reasons that canons have continued to flourish, although for Andy Bennett, this can lead to an uncritical reproduction of the dominant narratives (2015: 20).

We will come back to how contemporary composers worked within and against historical narratives later, but for now it is important to note that the European Western art-music canons – both scholarly and perform-ance – remained popular and relatively intact throughout the century as a legitimate form of authority in the classification of musical works, despite evolving aesthetics and tastes. Carl Dahlhaus (1977) went so far as to argue that changing values are subjective and should not interfere with the larger historical forces at play in the elevation of composers like Bach, Beethoven, Mozart, Haydn, Berlioz, Wagner, Tchaikovsky, Chopin, Verdi and others to the greats of music history. While its values remained intact, though, the historical canon was augmented to encompass new works that fulfilled the traditional criteria outlined above, such as the eighteenth-century operas of Handel and others. An increase in scholarly engagement with early music during the century (→Chapter 8, 'Instruments') also saw the canon extend backwards to incorporate the work of Hildegard von Bingen (1098–1179), Gregorian chant and so on.

On the one hand, then, the relative constancy of the canon suggests a lasting ideology able to span centuries. But on the other, its perpetuation of negative attitudes to class, gender and race soon became out of step with twentieth-century values and began to draw criticism. Canons can allow groups to self-identify and share ideologies, but they also exclude artists and styles, as Appen and Doehring write: 'Any kind of canonisation inevitably entails exclusions that can be traced back to the social disposi-tions of the participants. Accordingly, any canon should be examined and critically questioned as it implies latent claims to power' (2006: 34). The risk, in other words, is that gatekeepers exclude people unlike them.

As the twentieth century got underway, scholars began to question these omissions, with some suggesting that the ideologies of the historical

Western art-music canon were devised by white men to preserve and perpetuate certain social hierarchies (Kerman 1983). In response came calls to re-gender and decolonise the musical canons in order to include the work of ethnic minorities, women and working-class communities, as we shall see below. Challenges were launched by post-structuralist, feminist, post-colonialist, Afrocentric and queer-theory scholars, fans, modern gatekeepers and the musicians themselves.

In the later decades of the century, early canon formation was viewed as the work of elite gatekeepers who tended to be white, male and European and perpetuated values associated with complexity and that were intended predominantly for the musically educated (Hallberg 1984; Citron 2007; Whiteley 2000). We can see the change in perception as part of the postmodern critique of knowledge and power outlined in →Chapter 3, 'Postmodernism'. With the money and power to curate concerts and charge for entry, these gatekeepers could also determine who had access to the music (Bourdieu 1984; DiMaggio 1991). But it is not just about accessibility. As we shall see in our second case study, women composers are notable by their absence, with popular and prolific composers like Emilie Mayer (1812–83), Clara Schumann (1819–96), Alice Mary Smith (1839–84), Augusta Holmès (1847–1903), Morfydd Llwym Owen (1891–1918) and Lili Boulanger (1893–1918) usually left out of the canon.

- Morfydd Llwym Owen, 'Gweddi y Pechadur' (1913)
- Lili Boulanger, Psalm 129 (1916)

Black voices are also absent from the main narrative. Joseph Boulogne, Chevalier de Saint-Georges (1745–99), born to a plantation owner and a female slave, was a virtuosic violinist and prolific composer of operas, symphonies, concerto and chamber music, for instance. He famously caught the attention of Mozart, who was apparently so jealous of his success that he folded him into the villainous character of Monostasos in *The Magic Flute* (1791). With a string of violin concertos and string trios dedicated to him and a selection of high-profile conducting positions, Boulogne was clearly an influential eighteenth-century figure (Banat 2006). And yet he appears in few history books and until recently his music was rarely performed. The same fate was afforded English composer Samuel Coleridge-Taylor (1875–1912) (Green 2016/2011).

Postmodernism's critique of grand – or meta – narratives (→Chapter 3, 'Postmodernism') encouraged the destabilisation of single authoritarian viewpoints and leading postmodernist thinker

Jean-François Lyotard questioned the legitimation of canons entirely, calling instead for 'les petites histoires' and local narratives (1984/ 1979: xxiv). To a certain extent, we can see this happening with the addition of new canons – early music, women composers and so on – around the traditional historical one. Arguing along similar lines, Anne Shreffler suggests that it is now harder than ever to squeeze musical diversity into a single grand narrative. She points to postmodernism's critique of universal value, the destabilisation of the intellectual elite, electronic media's ability to instantly broadcast sounds and opinion, gender equality, the cultural and intellectual significance of popular musics and access to world music and global-isation as posing significant opposition to linear histories (Shreffler 2013: 2).

But rather than fragment existing canons entirely, others have argued that a more contextual approach to history can reveal new stories not so dependent on the traditional elitist idea that value is intrinsic to a musical work. If value and significance can be found in the contexts and circumstances of a work's creation, then different groups of composers may come to the fore. Marcia J. Citron (2007), for instance, suggests that the focus on notated works privileges the single author, which in the historical canon, is often male; she calls instead for a range of extramusical factors to be included in our construction of significance that will champion the work of female composers. Philip Tagg finds a similar issue with the popular music canon. For him, the issue lies in the very nature of a canon as a chronology of great works positioned as sublime and transcendent objects, which opposes the culturally and socially embedded nature of popular music (Tagg 2000: 165). Gary Tomlinson calls for a similar contextualisation in his work on jazz and African American traditions, writing that 'Placing the music first will always distance it from the complex and largely extramusical negotiations that made it and that sustain it. It will always privilege European bourgeois myths of aes-thetic transcendency, artistic purity untouched by function and con-text, and the elite status of artistic expression' (1992: 78). This decentring also has ramifications for folk music, and Bohlman (1998) points out that the historical canon's focus on the musical text and notation has excluded a large and diverse body of works transmitted through oral and improvised traditions, performances and recordings.

Case Study 4.2: Women Artists and De-canonisation

History, so goes the cliché, is written by (and largely about) the victors. There is truth in most clichés and that is the case here; music histories have long been dominated by familiar figures and repertoires: Bach, Beethoven, Brahms; symphonies, operas and art songs (Swafford 1992 is a recent example in the genre). More-or-less traditional music histories led by male figures and their masterpieces were being written right up to the end of the century (Whittall 1999). Such an approach contributed to the institutional and cultural production in conventional social terms of both music history itself – that is, the lived experience of musicians and audiences – and music histories written in response. Given the different cultural roots and make-up of each tradition, this problem inevitably impacted classical more than it did popular, jazz and folk music. But it shaped the history and histories of all musics nonetheless.

In her work on art history, Griselda Pollock writes that the canon 'is formed retrospectively by what artists themselves select as their legitimating or enabling predecessors. If, however, artists – because they are women or non-European – are both left out of the records and ignored as part of the cultural heritage, the canon becomes an increasingly impoverished and impoverishing filter for the totality of cultural possibilities generation after generation': to address this, she calls for a 'differencing' of the canon (1999: 4).

It is not hard to see why this is necessary. In their meta-list, Ralf von Appen and André Doehring find that the top 30 albums include no women artists (2006: 23). In fact, the top 100 only throws up 5 albums by female artists, with Patti Smith's *Horses* (1975) the only one to appear in the top 50 (25). A similar picture is painted after a flick through the 1988 version of the *Norton Anthology of Western Music* and Leon Plantinga's *Romantic Music* (1984), which include almost no references to women musicians at all. Twentieth-century anthologies rarely fare better, with only limited reference to musicians like Lili Boulanger (1893–1918), Thea Musgrave (1928–), Ethel Smyth (1858–1944), Tania Léon (1943–), Florence Price (1887–1953), Ruth Crawford (Seeger) (1901–53), Daphne Oram (1925–2003), Meredith Monk (1942–), Judith Weir (1956–), Sally Beamish (1956–), Laurie Anderson (1947–), Eleanor Alberga (1949–), Pamela Z (1956–) and Rachel Portman (1960–), and a whole host of other women composers who made significant and lasting contributions to harmony and form, style and instrumentation.

- Ethel Smyth, 'The March of the Women' (1910)
- Judith Weir, String Quartet, movement 2 (1990)
- Pamela Z, *Bone Music* (1992)

Why? There are two main reasons: the struggle for female artists to find exposure; and the social and gendered positioning of the gatekeepers to music histories. As we will see

Case Study 4.2: (cont.)

in Chapter 13 (➜ 'Gender and Sexuality'), women composers are notably absent from the historical canon for many reasons, including a lack of access to education and social restraints that prevented anything more than an amateur engagement with music composition and performance (Halstead 1997: 101). The innovations of Fanny Mendelssohn's 460 compositions are thought to have preceded her brother's Felix's later development of the piano tone poem, for instance. And yet her work, initially published under her brother's name, has until recently been little discussed, while Felix holds a significant canonical position. It was not that women were not composing, but rather that their work rarely received exposure, and thus not the recognition, required to form part of the historical canon. Yet the social and cultural revolutions of the twentieth century did not immediately lead to more diversity in the contemporary music canons, and until recently female composers remained on the edge of the art-music scene.

  In the main chapter, we looked at several moves towards de-canonisation – or re-canonisation – in the twentieth century. An important move came from feminist scholars, for whom the continued focus, in both the concert and the scholarly canons, on white male composers served to reinforce the cultural hegemony and exclusivity that had kept women from composing in previous centuries. In literature, this resulted in what Lillian Robinson called a 'counter-canon' that included only woman writers (1983), an idea also amply present in the music press in the form of best-of lists: greatest women composers of the twentieth century; twenty significant albums by women artists and so on. But while the formation of a separate canon can highlight women's work in a positive way, it can also be problematic. In her seminal book *Women and the Musical Canon* (1993), Marcia J. Citron warns against simply 'adding-and-stirring' women's names into the extant narrative (43): without challenging the parameters and paradigms of entrenched methods of canon formation, she argues, women's achievements will remain peripheral to the dominant stories of music.

  While some continue to advocate for a canon based on individuals (Berger 2014), others have argued for an approach that decentres attention from the traditional idea of the 'genius' creator, which for many centuries was gendered male (Hallberg 1984). Shelia Whiteley (2000), for instance, argues that the dominance of male artists in the mainstream popular music canon is not just down to the male-centred nature of Anglo-American pop-rock; it is also due to the focus on authorship, which tends to lean towards male performers and masculine genres. For Citron, the idea of a history based on the author and an associated written text 'de-emphasizes process, collaboration, community, the private, and oral transmission, which all played a key role in the lives of historical musical women' (2007: 211). Instead, she advocates for

Case Study 4.2: (cont.)

a sociological-cultural approach able to open up new ways of assessing the contributions that female composers have made to music history.

Inherent in this call for a more contextual reading of music history is an interrogation of the gatekeepers responsible for canon formation. We have seen in the main chapter that the early music canons were compiled by men who held enough cultural, social and financial power to be able to commission, promote and arrange performances of what they considered to be great work (Kerman 1983; Shreffler 2013). But it could be argued that a similarly reductive voice has determined the popular music canon, as Appen and Doehring's lists demonstrate. Andy Bennett has voiced a similar concern over 'the hegemonic grip of white, Anglo-American, middle class values when it comes to defining notions of heritage in this particular sphere of contemporary cultural life' (2015: 23). One way to redress the balance and 'difference' the canon during the century has been to place more women in gatekeeping roles, including women journalists in the early feminist music press (Harris 2014), female artists who set up their own record labels – Ani DiFranco's Righteous Babe Records is a powerful example – and female radio DJs, concert promoters and music critics.

Conclusion

The changes in cultural politics outlined above suggest that canons were becoming more inclusive in the late twentieth century. But the aesthetic values of the historical art-music canon, which threaten to omit entire swathes of society, have proved surprisingly resilient. Despite maintaining a strong and continuing focus on historical music (Kerman 1983), the art-music canons gathered new works as the century progressed. The scholarly canon continued to be populated by music which, as Shreffler pointed out, demonstrates particular 'technical and formal accomplishments' that speak to the criteria of significance. This is particularly apparent in the complex work of composers working in the modernist tradition. The performance canon – or repertoire – comprising the French work of Debussy and Ravel, the neo-classical technique of Stravinsky and Bartók, the minimalism of Reich and Glass, Górecki and Pärt, the Americana of Ives and Copland and the sweeping English tonalism of Elgar and Vaughan Williams also promoted innovation and coherence, although significance was produced through less radical forms of experimentation. While stylistic and technical aspects have remained important, other indicators that a composition has entered the canon include its regularity of performance programming, new recordings, radio play and continuing scholarly and journalistic engagement. Stravinsky's *The Rite of Spring* (1913) is a good example: innovative in texture and theme, and scandalous in its time, the work has since received continual performance opportunities and remains a prominent part of school and university syllabuses.

However, similar issues persist. Do values remain consistent? We can see a shift of tastes, with some composers popular at the beginning of the century – French composer Paul Dukas (1865–1935) and English Frederick Delius (1862–1934), for instance – falling out of the favour as the decades passed (Shreffler 2013: 6). And what about the perpetuation of elitist values? One criticism of twentieth-century canons is that there has been an unbalanced focus on the second Viennese School (Chowrimootoo 2016; McClary 1989), and some (Born and Hesmondhalgh 2000) have argued that modernist music's lack of reference to other cultures and musics has served to perpetuate the elitist 'self-enclosure' (16) and linear narrative of the art-music canon. And diversity? This certainly remains an issue. Twentieth-century art-music canons are still dominated by white men, despite the musical and cultural achievements of composers like William Grant Still (1895–1978), the first African American to have an opera staged by a major company and a symphony programmed by a national orchestra, and Florence Price (1887–1953), whose 1933 premiere of her first symphony by the Chicago Symphony marked the first major orchestral performance of a work by an African American woman. The work of these composers has since fallen out of the repertoire.

- William Grant Still, Symphony No. 1 ('Afro-American': 1930)
- Florence Price, Symphony No. 1 (1932)

Like the art-music canon, the popular music one has also struggled with diversity. The significant dearth of Black musicians in the lists Appen and Doehring analyse (2006: 24) is striking: 'Only sixteen out of the first one hundred artists are persons of colour, and only two of them to be found among the top thirty, although musicians like Michael Jackson or Whitney Houston are commercially successful. African American music styles like soul, blues or hip hop hardly appear in the canon.' Our second case study sees a similarly bleak gender representation in the canon, with only 5 women artists making it into the top-100 best albums meta-list.

In response, scholars have called for alternatives that range from the 'expansionism' of the canon beyond the traits of modernism in the art-music canon (Harper-Scott 2012: xiii) to the development of multiple 'canons' better able to encompass diversity (Citron 2007: 41). Rather than do away with canons entirely, another possibility is for more democratised and conscious ways of regulating canons by treating them as interdisciplinary sites of convergence for issues such as race, masculinity and instrument development (Waksman 2010: 69) or by loosening the hold of the gate-keepers. Anahid Kassabian suggests that we take back power from the universalising values handed down from history and diversify input by producing 'a Wiki where everyone can add and discuss things', thus promoting little-known works and embracing multiple perspectives (2010: 78).

The process of canonisation, then, can tell us how music is mediated and transmitted; it can give us insight into the nature and construction of value as well as the impact of the recording industry on the dissemination and globalisation of musical practice in the twentieth century.

PART II

Techniques and Technologies

5 | Work and Notation

The concept of the work of art is – at least in the West – 'the fundamental category of aesthetics' (Dahlhaus 1987: 210; see also Dahlhaus 1982, 1989 and 1990). Yet although we often talk about musical 'works', it is hard to say what one actually is. In the visual arts, it is easier: the work is generally an object – a painting or a sculpture, perhaps an installation. In literature, it is usually a book. These are things at which we can point: they have definite borders and are fixed in space and/or time. Works are also thought to contain within them all that is necessary for their appreciation, a fact that situates them in a particular functional relationship between the artist, the audience and (in the case of music) the performer. The work, therefore, not only serves as art's central object of contemplation and creation but also determines the social, functional and economic hierarchy between who creates it, who realises it and who appreciates it.

The date at which the musical work-concept emerged is contested, but it is widely agreed that long before the end of the nineteenth century it became situated in the work's written form, as musical notation, with a single author, the composer. The importance of the work-concept is related to our previous chapter (→Chapter 4, 'Canons'). The notion of the canon as the storehouse of high culture was dependent on a conception of musical works as timeless and autonomous: 'things', as it were, that could be set into relatively fixed, objective relations with one another. If works are not stable, or not easily defined or discriminated from one another, the idea of a canon becomes impossible to sustain. This was to a great extent a Romantic invention and was supported by historiographic practices that, since the time of Beethoven, have portrayed the composer, often in heroic terms, as the sole arbiter of 'truth' in their work. Stemming from this emerged, in the nineteenth century, the idea of *Werktreue*, or work-faithfulness, interpreted as faithfulness to the intentions of the composer as captured by the score. This was an ideology that regarded the musical work as fixed by its omniscient composer (rather like a painting or a novel), to be realised more or less perfectly by a passive performer. Finally, as we will see in a future chapter (→Chapter 10, 'Copyright and the Music Industry'), the economy of publishing and copyright was designed to privilege composers: in a time before recording, the written score was the work's only enduring form and therefore the only one to which lasting economic value in terms of royalties (as well as less tangible values such as prestige) could be attached; it made sense, therefore, to define the work as residing in the score.

Yet as we have already seen in →Chapter 2, 'Modernism' and even more so in →Chapter 3, 'Postmodernism', many twentieth-century trends and practices exploded this Romantic notion of authorship and of the singular, autonomous text. In line with these trends, and alongside wider aesthetic debates across the arts that took place throughout the century, philosophers and theorists also engaged with the question of what the musical work was, and what its meaning was. These debates challenged not only the borders of the musical work but also its relationship to its composer, performer and listener.

This chapter will look at some of the ways in which the musical work-concept evolved in response to those debates, and how the respective roles of composer, performer and listener as co-creators of the work were at various points redefined. Although jazz, serialism and recording were already challenging the work-concept in the first half of the century, many of these destabilisations would be most pronounced in its second half, particularly under the banner of postmodernism. This chapter begins in the 1950s, therefore, at the mid-century pivot when the Romantic, score-based notion of the work encountered the nascent postmodernism of the New York experimental school.

Dissolving the Work: Cage, Feldman and Cardew

In a small concert hall overlooking the Catskills mountains, the pianist David Tudor (1926–96) walks on stage and sits at the piano. He positions his music and his stool, glances at a stopwatch and then, carefully and deliberately, closes the lid of the piano. After a minute and a half, he opens the lid and closes it again. Rain begins to fall; the audience starts to become restless. Again he opens and closes the lid. Finally, after just over four and half minutes have elapsed, he opens the lid once more and stands to take his bow. The rain has stopped but sounds from the forest outside can still be heard. The applause begins.

Like the first performance of Stravinsky's *Rite of Spring* in Paris in 1913, the premiere of *4'33"* (1952) by John Cage (1912–92) on 29 August 1952 at the Maverick Concert Hall in Woodstock, New York is a storied moment in twentieth-century music history (for a book-length study, see Gann 2010). Cage's piece – four minutes and thirty-three seconds in which no music is played – is emblematic of the style and aesthetic of the remainder of his career: the quintessential 'silent piece', analogous to (and directly inspired by) the white canvases painted by Cage's friend Robert Rauschenberg (1925–2008). More than any other composition of the twentieth century it poses a direct challenge to what we understand by music, and the musical work. (More than almost any other, it is also widely referenced, satirised and frequently misunderstood, in popular and scholarly discourse.) As the American composer and critic Kyle Gann puts it:

How are we supposed to understand it? In what sense is it a composition? Is it a hoax? A joke? A bit of Dada? A piece of theater? A thought experiment? A kind of apotheosis of twentieth-century music? An example of Zen practice? An attempt to change basic human behavior? (2010: 11)

The challenge posed by *4'33"* is a fundamental one, however. By almost entirely removing himself as a composer of the work (limiting himself to the framing of a section of time in which the work is to take place, a frame which is left to the performer to articulate, as in Tudor's raising and closing of the piano lid), Cage radically subverts the Romantic notion of the work-concept. Instead of the composer acting as the work's single author, it is the listener – and their audition of the unpredictable, unplanned sounds of the surrounding environment – who brings into being the work that is *4'33"* (Figure 5.1).

At around the same time as Cage was devising *4'33"*, on another floor of the Manhattan apartment building in which he lived the composer Morton Feldman (1926–87) was writing works that would challenge in an entirely different way the status of the musical work. Where Cage had shifted the responsibility for completing the work to the listener, Feldman was shifting it to the performer. In several groups of works composed in the early 1950s, Feldman substituted the precise specifications of the five-line musical staff for 'staves' of evenly spaced squares. Each square represented a unit of time (usually a second) in which something would happen: in his first pieces, the five *Projections* (1950–1), this was a single note; in later works he added

I

TACET

II

TACET

III

TACET

Figure 5.1 John Cage: *4'33"* (1952). Edition Peters No. 6777 ('Second Tacet Edition'). © 1960 by Henmar Press Inc., New York. Reproduced by permission of Peters Edition Limited, London

numbers to indicate how many notes each square should contain. Within each instrument's staff the vertical position of the square indicated register – high, medium or low. Despite the radical appearance of Feldman's scores, much remains of conventional notation, including the axial layout of time against pitch, the division of time into regular pulses, and the separation and coordination of instrumental parts. Feldman's innovation is his non-specification of pitch, beyond these vaguely defined registers. The first system of Projection 1 is shown in Figure 5.2.

• Morton Feldman, *Projection 1* (1950)

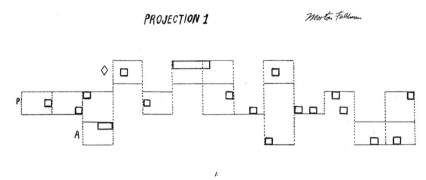

Figure 5.2 Morton Feldman: *Projection 1* (1950). Edition Peters No. 6945. © 1961 by C. F. Peters Corporation, New York. Reproduced by permission of Peters Edition Limited, London

Feldman's 'graphic' approach (he wrote his scores on graph paper, like accountancy charts or an esoteric game) was radical because it gave the performer a degree of autonomy and creative responsibility not seen since the days of baroque-era figured bass. What is more, and unlike the semi-improvisatory practices of the seventeenth century, Feldman was asking his performers to make decisions outside the framework of an established performance practice. Feldman's performer was faced with a large number of creative decisions of their own. Should 'high, middle, low' be interpreted as three consistent pitches (as some performers have done)? Or should the performer strive for the greatest pitch differentiation possible? Should pitches be decided upon in the moment, or might they be planned in advance? (This latter approach was in fact taken by several of Feldman's early interpreters, such as the cellist Charlotte Moorman; see Dohoney 2016.) To what extent were Feldman's scores in fact an invitation – to the performer, to invent – or a prescription, to reproduce?

Although Feldman soon abandoned his box method, the practice of graphic notation – as all notations that exceeded or rejected the practices of five-line staff notation came to be known – diversified and spread rapidly throughout the 1950s and into the 1960s. Inspired by Cage's advocacy of a musical 'indeterminacy' (Cage 1961), and given permission by the recent acceptance of jazz as a serious art form thanks to the work of bebop musicians like Charlie Parker (→Chapter 2, 'Modernism'), composers of both the European and North American avant-gardes began to devise more and more ways to incorporate and regulate freer or more imprecise elements within their music. The results varied from borderline cases, such as Krzysztof Penderecki's *Threnody, to the Victims of Hiroshima* (1960) and

Witold Lutosławski's *Jeux Vénitiens* (1961), which incorporated graphic elements within a framework that was otherwise conventional and to a large extent determined by the composer, to those in which the outcome (beyond the broadest formal outlines) was almost entirely in the hands of the performer. Within Feldman's circle, the latter included examples by Earle Brown (*December 1952*), Christian Wolff (*For 1, 2, or 3 People*, 1964) and many works by Cage himself (most spectacularly his *Concert for Piano and Orchestra*, 1957–8; see Iddon and Thomas 2020). In Europe, examples included Sylvano Bussotti's *Five Piano Pieces for David Tudor* (1959), Karlheinz Stockhausen's *Zyklus* (1959) and Cathy Berberian's *Stripsody* (1966, Figure 5.3). For many more examples, see Cage and Knowles (1969).

Perhaps the most substantial of all of these was the 193-page *Treatise* (1963–7) by the British composer Cornelius Cardew (1936–81). By reason of its sheer size, *Treatise* remains the foremost work of graphic notation and is a classic of its era. Apart from two (blank) five-line staves running along the bottom, each page is different and features symbols and designs that are more or less related to conventional notation. These range from staves of different sizes that seem to fold into and around each other to patterns of lines and curves that resemble by turns hieroglyphic scripts, circuit diagrams or the sketches for a sort of art deco car. Cardew's publisher, Peters Edition, pressed him into writing an accompanying handbook (Cardew 2006/1971), but instead of instructions for the score's

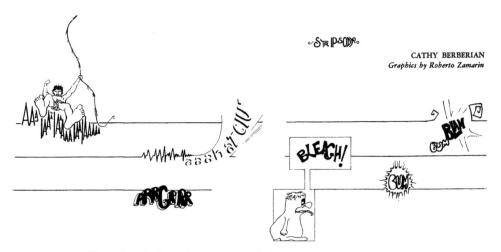

Figure 5.3 Cathy Barberian: *Stripsody* (1966). Edition Peters No. 66164. © 1966 by C.F. Peters Corporation, New York. Reproduced by permission of Peters Edition Limited, London

realisation (which would have brought *Treatise* closer to the Romantic conventions of the work, presumably Peters' goal), this contains various philosophical aims and justifications for the graphic scoring method, combined with diary entries that document Cardew's own attempts to make musical sense out of the piece as he was composing it and further undermine the authoritative voice of the composer. Cardew sometimes makes suggestions for realisation (e.g., matching trills, chords, tremolos, clusters, etc. to shapes that seem close to them), but ultimately leaves the details of its realisation open to his performers.

- QuaX Ensemble, dir. Petr Kotik, *Cornelius Cardew: Treatise* (Mode, 2009, recorded 1967)
- Jim Baker, Carrie Biolo, Guillermo Gregorio, Fed Lonberg-Holm, Jim O'Rourke, Art Lange, *Cornelius Cardew: Treatise* (hat[now]ART, 1999)

Looking back, what is most surprising about the graphic scores of the 1950s and 1960s is not how much they changed the dynamic between composer and performer, but how little. In most cases the composer's intentions remained paramount; the difference was simply that intent was more or less precisely articulated across different musical parameters. (As it always had been, of course: as the composer Christopher Fox succinctly notes: 'Composers make scores and give them names because they want to articulate something unique' (2014: 16).) Stories of Cage's anger at performers who were too free in their interpretations of his music are notorious (see, e.g., Dohoney 2014). Even in *Treatise* – a piece 'whose musical notation was so thoroughly "emancipated" that it was effectively put beyond realisation' (Fox 2014: 11, quoting Stockhausen 1959: 6) – the detail, precision and invention of Cardew's notation encourages at the very least a corresponding degree of respect and imagination from its performers. After the mid-1960s, although some composers went still further in the direction of wholly graphic notation, graphics became a shorthand resource for effects that may have been difficult or inefficient to notate otherwise. In other words, they were used in precisely the same position within the economy of composerly desire and performer convenience as more traditional notational elements had been, from the rubato to the figured bass. The 'highest note possible' notation of Penderecki (1933–2020) is emblematic. As it is used at the start of *Threnody*, the actual pitch produced by each of the fifty-two string instruments is irrelevant to the work's effect; more important is the sense of extremity and collective effort, an expressive effect that would have been lost with a more 'precise', pitch-based notation. So too Feldman's grids: again, pitch precision is not important, but in its place is a consideration of pitch fields and the boundaries between them, as well as a consideration of spontaneity versus consideration and of models of continuity and discontinuity. Such scores still demand interpretive labour in the service of a set of instructions chosen by the composer. The question, as Fox has put it, is the extent to which notations 'constitute the beginning of a creative process or ... an objective to be more or less achieved' (Fox 2014: 9).

- Krzysztof Penderecki, *Threnody, to the Victims of Hiroshima* (1960)

Happenings and Texts: Cage, Fluxus, Oliveros and Stockhausen

As well as determining the relationship between composer and performer, or composer and listener, the score also serves to determine the financial and prestige value of the work. By determining a given, repeatable outcome, the score enables the musical work to become a commodity within a system of exchange. Performances – ephemeral, unrepeatable – are harder to commoditise, however (or at least they were before the advent of performance rights in recordings, →Chapter 10, 'Copyright and the Music Industry'), and for this reason the different types of labour of composer and performer have been valued differently through the century.

Again, Cage offered one possible alternative to this Romantic and early twentieth-century conception. Building upon the Zen-inspired theories of indeterminacy and non-intention that he had been studying and developing for himself (and that lay behind 4′33″ too), in 1952 he co-created an event (*Theater Piece No. 1*) at Black Mountain College with his teaching colleagues Tudor, Rauschenberg and the choreographer Merce Cunningham (1919–2009). The event came to be known as the first 'Happening'. Cunningham and several others danced; Rauschenberg played records by the French chanteuse Edith Piaf (examples of his *White Paintings* hanging overhead); Tudor played piano; Cage gave a lecture and poured coffee to signal the end. Beyond recollections and diary entries, the work was not documented (see, e.g., Larson 2012: 251–5 for descriptions). No score for its recreation exists and no recording was made. It was a collaborative work (created, apparently, within a single day) in which the boundaries between art forms were dissolved and in which performers became creators and creators, performers. A touchstone for almost all of today's multimedia, installation and performance art forms, the Black Mountain College event is remarkable for existing entirely outside the composer-centred framework of the musical work-concept.

Over time, the 'Happening' was refined to the 'event': a single, intentional action from which a large artistic impact could be derived. Event scores were associated in particular with the artistic movement, international but active principally in New York, known as Fluxus. Fluxus was founded by the artist George Maciunas, along with Dick Higgins, Alison Knowles, George Brecht, Jackson Mac Low, Nam June Paik, Ben Patterson and others. Although this group of artists, composers and writers had worked together loosely since the late 1950s, its name was conferred after the 1962 'Festum Fluxorum' festival held in Wiesbaden, Germany, that Maciunas organised to help promote a magazine and publication series that he was calling *Fluxus*. The group's artistic orientation grew out of Marcel Duchamp's Dadaism and Cage's Happenings, and several Fluxus artists ('Fluxartists' in Maciunas' designation) took Cage's composition class at the New School for Social Research in New York. Nevertheless, Higgins (2018) notes that Fluxus itself was distinct from both of these traditions. 'Fluxworks' tended to seek maximal implication from minimal conception or design (indeed, *Composition 1960 #7*, 'To be held for a long time', by La Monte Young (b. 1935), featured frequently in Fluxus concerts, as did his *X for Henry Flynt*, a forearm cluster on the piano repeated x times, at one- to two-second intervals). These were singular events or actions that could be extrapolated outwards by composer, performer or observer. As Higgins observed, there was a sense that 'a Fluxpiece, whether an object or a performance, should be as implicative as possible, that it should imply a maximum of intellectual, sensuous, or emotional content within its minimum of material' (2018: 100).

Not all Fluxpieces were 'musical' in most common understandings of the term (although Higgins has noted that 'musicality', meaning a non-climactic lyricism, is one common criterion; 2018: 98). Many Fluxpieces take the form of poetry, sculpture, theatre or mixed media. Not all employ scores, either. Those that do take a radically direct approach, in which the instructions are often presented as brief aphorisms or injunctions. George Brecht's *Water Yam* (1963) comprises a box filled with notecards, on each of which are printed instructions for a new piece: examples include *Drip Music (Drip Event)* for a source of dripping water and an empty vessel; and *Time-Table Music*, instructions for translating a train timetable into a musical score.

The brevity of many Fluxus scores requires their reader to extrapolate a lot of information for themselves about what might be required for a performance; but they also invite the performer to think about different ways in which the event might be carried out. The greater flexibility and precision of text over traditional or even graphical notation (see Lely and Saunders 2012) allows for other types of dialogue between composer and performer. *Proposition* (1962) by Alison Knowles (b. 1933) simply instructs, 'Make a salad', a direction that not only invites a creative realisation (define a 'salad' . . .) but also radically decentres the work, as Knowles shares the food she has made with her audience, reforming the act of solitary artistic contemplation as an unbounded social occasion. (For another Fluxus-type invitation that brings the audience into the centre of the work's creation, see Case Study 5.1.)

Although not a Fluxus composer, Pauline Oliveros (1932–2016) took up the idea of invitation in her *Sonic Meditations* (1974; see Osborne 2000). Rather than works or scores, she called these 'attentional strategies', that is, aids to the musical practice and aesthetic that she called 'deep listening' (Oliveros 2005). Her text to *One Sound Once*, for example, begins 'First imagine silence'. Oliveros' text pieces do not attempt to express anything as such but invite the reader/listener to find out for themselves what might happen if they pay attention in a particular way; sometimes this means just listening, sometimes it means making sounds as well. The pieces rarely require specialist musical knowledge: they can be read, and performed, by anyone. But to perform them properly requires discipline, attention and concentration.

Oliveros' works intersect with forms of meditative practice. In this regard her pieces may appear close to another set of text pieces written by Karlheinz Stockhausen (1928–2007), *Aus den sieben Tagen* (1968). These fifteen pieces were written in the wake of a personal crisis for Stockhausen – his wife Mary Bauermeister (b. 1934), herself an early Fluxus artist with whom he had two children, had terminated their relationship – and in response to an increasing cultural interest in meditation and spirituality, epitomised by the countercultural 'hippy' movement in the USA (to which Oliveros was also responding). Stockhausen called his pieces 'intuitive music' and regarded them as opportunities for musicians to 'attune' to one another (an idea explored at greater length in another work composed around the same time, *Stimmung*), and to play without the underlying habits and formulae of a received musical language. The fifteen short texts are meditative or koan-like, with instructions such as to 'Play a sound/Play it for so long/until you feel/that you should stop' (*Richtige Dauern*), or 'Play a vibration in the rhythm of the universe' (*Verbindung*). However, as Stockhausen's own words about his work reveal, he found it hard to completely relinquish his own authority over the process:

The music provides spiritual orientation derived from the text . . . Musicians' 'orientation', which I shall also call 'attunement', is not, however, either fortuitous or exclusive (shutting out specific possibilities of musical thinking). It is always focused on a text by me, which invites an absolutely specific response. (Stockhausen 1989: 35–9)

- Karlheinz Stockhausen, *Fais voile vers le soleil,* from *Aus den sieben Tagen* (1968)

The texts of *Aus den sieben Tagen* may leave many gaps to be completed by the players, and indeed involve those players in a process of spiritual transformation, even enlightenment, but the process is nevertheless still controlled, and owned, by the composer. This led to conflict between the composer and his players if they resorted to familiar idioms in their playing (see Maconie 1989: 121–2), and prompted the composer Helmut Lachenmann to describe Stockhausen's role as becoming that of 'a "regulator", perhaps even a manipulator' (Lachenmann and Toop 2004: 46).

Case Study 5.1: Yoko Ono, *Cut Piece*

Although not a formal member of the group, the Japanese American artist Yoko Ono (b. 1933) was associated with Fluxus from around 1960, when (with La Monte Young) she began to host Happenings and events at her Manhattan loft, and in 1961 mounted her first solo exhibition at Maciunas' AG Gallery on Madison Avenue. Ono incidentally became Fluxus' most famous associate when she began an affair with and later married (in 1969) the Beatles' John Lennon (1940–80), an event that subjected her to much racist press attention and for many years damaged her reputation as an artist. More than 150 of her 'event scores' – short text pieces – are collected in *Grapefruit* (1964), a book that is today regarded as one of the founding documents of conceptual art: many of them take the form of (often utopian) instructions for creating (or imagining) works of art. *Cloud Piece* is typical:

Imagine the clouds dripping.
Dig a hole in your garden to
put them in.

Perhaps Ono's most powerful work – and certainly one of her most notorious – is *Cut Piece*, written in 1964. It was performed by Ono five times between 1964 and 1966 (she gave a revised version in 2003) and it has been performed by many others since. The score exists in three different versions, but its 'First version for single performer' may be taken as exemplary. More precise and practical in its directions than many of the *Grapefruit* pieces, it reads:

Performer sits on stage with a pair of scissors in front of him.
It is announced that members of the audience may come on stage – one at a time – to cut a small piece of the performer's clothing to take with them.

Case Study 5.1: (cont.)

Performer remains motionless throughout the piece.
Piece ends at the performer's option. (Quoted in Concannon 2008: 82)

In each of her 1960s performances, Ono would sit on stage, alone and still, wearing one of her finest outfits. As the score instructs, the piece would be over when she chose; Ono often continued until almost all her clothing had been removed. After her initial invitation (sometimes given by a separate announcer), Ono would remain silent and impassive, perhaps only moving to cover her breasts with her arms. The sound content of the work would be in the slicing of the shears, the steps of the audience members as they came onto the stage and occasional giggles and murmurs from the auditorium. The work's form existed in the often-tense interplay of cutting and taking, giving and receiving. Its specific content was not only realised in the minds of its audience (as in Cage's *4'33"*) but visibly and audibly performed by them.

Variously, *Cut Piece* has been read as an originating text of performance art, a feminist manifesto, a violation, a piece of East–West exotica, a titillation and an act of remembrance for the victims of atomic warfare (see, e.g., Bryan-Wilson 2003; Rhee 2005). It is important to note, however, that nearly all these interpretations derive from Ono's own performances – and her own identity as a Japanese American woman. They do not reside in the text itself, which, not least among other things, genders its performer as male. One might argue that the nature of Fluxus-type performance art is to entwine work and artist together; yet other Fluxpieces do not attract such specifically embodied interpretations. It is notable in this context that when Ono performed *Cut Piece* once more, in 2003, the event was described as a 'reenactment' rather than a performance, or even revival, emphasising that the essence of the work resided in Ono's on-stage presence, regardless of the score or its subsequent realisation by artists other than her.

The existence for *Cut Piece* of a score that can be used by others sets it apart from many other examples of performance art. Marina Abramović (b. 1946; →Chapter 8, 'Instruments'), an artist whose work is often compared to Ono's, has noted that by translating performance instructions into scores, as Ono has done, works of performance art might be brought into the marketplace and into 'the academic discourse of history' – that is, the world of critical prestige (Concannon 2008: 92). Even here, then, in the outer regions of the musical work-concept – where the authorial role of the creator is inverted to one who gives, rather than instructs; where it is the audience who create the work, their participation in it their only expectation of reward; and where the identity of the work appears to reside in a single performer and a now-distant sequence of performances – there remains a compulsion to draw the work back in to the commodifying economy of authorship and scores.

Historically Informed Performance

Despite radical reconsiderations such as these, the score-based model of the work has retained a power within Western music that has proved hard to dislodge. At the start of the century, the legendary violinist Joseph Joachim observed in his *Violinschule* (written with Andreas Moser) that 'In order to do justice to the piece which he is about to perform, the player must first acquaint himself with the conditions under which it originated' (quoted in Lawson and Stowell 1999: 1). As scholars extended the Western art-music canon backwards in history as far as the medieval era (➔Chapter 4, 'Canons'), performers of this newly revived repertoire began to use historical data and methods to try to recreate those works so the result was as close as possible to how they would have originally sounded (and, it was assumed, as close as possible to how their composers intended them to sound). In this manner, works that were composed long before the concept of the musical work was established were recast within a Romantic framework that placed the authority of the composer and the score at its head.

Beginning with the work of the French musician and instrument maker Arnold Dolmetsch (1858–1940), the 'early music revival' emerged as a scholarly discipline in the first half of the century through the founding of research institutions such as the Schola Cantorum Basiliensis in Basel, Switzerland (founded 1933) and the Galpin Society in Great Britain (1946), a society dedicated to research into the history and construction of musical instruments, as well as the pioneering work of a number of specialist performers such as the English countertenor Alfred Deller. The 1960s and 1970s saw a large growth in the number of ensembles devoted to the performance of early music, among them the Early Music Consort of London (founded by Christopher Hogwood and David Munrow, UK), Collegium Vocale Gent (Philippe Herreweghe, Belgium) and Musica Antiqua Köln (Reinhard Goebel, Germany). At this time, the goal of the early music revival was 'authenticity'. Using historical documents, advocates sought to perform historical works on instruments similar to those that would have existed at the time the works were composed, often remaking contemporary versions of such instruments (➔Chapter 8, 'Instruments'). They also sought to reconstruct performance techniques and styles such as the realisation of figured bass or ornamentation, tuning (baroque instruments were tuned slightly lower than modern ones), choice of performance space, and even costumes (the exhaustive catalogue of methods for the performance of baroque music found in Donington

1992/1963 is indicative of the degree of historical detail with which performers could engage). Originally works played in this manner dated from the pre-classical era (i.e., music from the medieval period up to the seventeenth century), although the principles were later expanded into performances of music from the eighteenth to nineteenth centuries too.

- Musica Antiqua Köln, *Louis Antoine Dornel: Sonate Pour Trois Dessus*, from *Kammermusik des Franz. Barock auf Original Instrumenten* (aulos, 1975)
- Early Music Consort, *Des Prez: Scaramella va alla guerra*, from *The Art of the Netherlands* (His Master's Voice/Seraphim, 1976)

While the early music revival – later known as historically informed practice or (not without a touch of irony) HIP – emerged from an understandable desire to marry the performance of early music with scholarly discoveries about that music and the context in which it was composed, and while it led to numerous musical revelations and discoveries, in the 1980s Anglo-American scholars began to question the ways in which historical evidence was interpreted. (Fabian 2001 notes that European scholars anticipated some of these arguments by several years.) In particular, Richard Taruskin (1995) and Daniel Leech-Wilkinson (1984) argued that the clean sounds of the early music revival were a reflection of the twentieth-century aesthetics of modernism and contemporary compositional taste, thus disputing the fundamental 'authenticity' that such performers claimed for their work (see also Kenyon 1988). Taruskin, who was once a director of an early music choral group himself, began his critique in response to a lecture given by the conductor Joshua Rifkin (b. 1944) in 1981 (reproduced in Parrott 2000) on the subject of performing Bach's choral music with one voice to a part. (Taruskin's stance was developed over a number of subsequent publications, collected together as *Text and Act* in 1995.) Rifkin's idea was contentious at this time, when Bach's music was typically performed in a Romantic fashion by large choirs and full orchestras. His 1981 recording of Bach's Mass in B Minor with his own Bach Ensemble is his first major realisation of his theory and makes a stark comparison with Herbert von Karajan's recording with the Berlin Philharmonic made a few years earlier.

- Joshua Rifkin, The Bach Ensemble, *Bach: Mass in B minor* (Nonesuch Records, 1981)
- Herbert von Karajan, Berlin Philharmonic and soloists, *Bach: Mass in B minor* (Deutsche Grammophon, 1974)

In his own paper ('On Letting the Music Speak for Itself'), given at the same musicological conference at which Rifkin spoke and reproduced in *Text and Act* (Taruskin 1995: 51–66), Taruskin formulates his critique as follows: 'Like all other modernist philosophies, historical reconstruction views the work of art, including performing art, as an autonomous object, not as a process or activity' (60). His objection, therefore, is that a reconstruction like Rifkin's – whatever its merits – continues to be based on a sanctification of the *text* of the work (its score, and whatever supporting documentation may be brought in to aid its interpretation): a Romantic or modernist invention with 'no demonstrable relevance to the ways people thought about art and performance before the twentieth century'. Historical accuracy, Taruskin says in his introduction to *Text and Act*, is a chimera (9), built on a misguided equivalence between the musical work and its score. His own preference is for a complete overturning of the Romantic, score-based idea of the work and an adoption instead of a view of the work not as a fixed text, but as an open-ended opportunity for conviction, imagination, emotion and delight (71–2).

The Work Beyond the Score

So far, our focus has been on Western art music, but concepts of the work extend also into popular music, even in cases where there is no notation or only a minimal score. Outside art music, it seems at first that it is not hard to find musical forms that exemplify exactly the open-ended, anti-Romantic view of the work-concept that Taruskin espouses. The most notable example is of course jazz, a musical genre with improvisation and spontaneity apparently at its heart. Yet even here, the work is to a large extent defined by historical and cultural ideologies like those expressed in the historically informed performance movement, as well as the economic and legal structures that underpin the music industry itself (→Chapter 10, 'Copyright and the Music Industry'). Jazz improvisations are not created entirely spontaneously but are typically shaped in relation to a song, a set of chords, a melody or just a scale. In order for several players to play together, those frameworks need to be predetermined and agreed upon by the group. Unless the work is to be wholly collaborative (and this does happen, although generally only in some examples of free jazz and free improvisation), this requires someone to assert themselves as 'composer': the one who designs the basic framework.

In many jazz compositions, the framework is borrowed from out-side the group, in the form of a skeleton representation of an existing song (or 'standard'). This skeleton is known as a lead sheet and is as compressed a version as possible of the song: its melody (often a single treble line on a single stave); harmony (often just chord symbols); lyrics; author and copyright information. Note the last of these: the primary function of a lead sheet was and is so that the song can be registered with a copyright institution, and the composer (and lyricist, if applicable) can be remunerated through subsequent per-formance royalties. The implications this has for the division of labour and ownership within the work are clear: whatever creative effort might have been made on the part of the performer in a given performance, it is the composer's labour that is valued most highly. The performers remain subordinate, their solos only realisations of the true 'work', '[n]o matter that chorus after chorus of music has tum-bled from the musician's mind', as the drummer Eddie Prévost has acidly described it (1995: 88). And the impacts go beyond money: in his social history of the drum kit, Matt Brennan (2020) argues that the lower musical status that is commonly given to jazz and rock drum-mers extends from the fact that drumming itself is not based in notation.

Although the lead sheet is the source of prestige and income for the composer (and a source of literacy-legitimacy for everyone but the drummer), it is even less self-sufficient than a full score: at the very least instrumental arrangement, chord voicing, dynamics and phrasing must all be realised by the performer, and all are more or less open to interpretation. One only need compare Coleman Hawkins' 1939 recording of 'Body and Soul' – 'a masterful transformation of this quite ordinary theme' (Prévost 1995: 88) – with the rather more pedestrian version by Paul Whiteman and His Orchestra of nine years earlier to get a sense of the potential flexibility of the 'work'. (For a performance history of this particular standard that critiques Western notions of authority, variation and reproduction of the work, see Bowen 2015.) Although the lead sheet borrows from the com-poser-centred orientation of Western art music, through its scarcity of information it makes clear that an alternative concept of the work is at play: on its own it is not enough for a musically interesting perform-ance. Drawing on jazz's ancestry in oral/aural traditions, folk music, the blues and practices of signifyin' (Gates 1988), the standard is in fact endlessly reworkable, within the loose framework represented by the lead sheet, to an extent that an art-music composition often was not – at least not until the 1950s and 1960s.

- Paul Whiteman and His Orchestra, 'Body and Soul' (Columbia, 1930)
- Coleman Hawkins (1904–69), 'Body and Soul' (Bluebird, 1939)

In fact, within popular music many different alternative landscapes of prestige, remuneration and authorship – and therefore concepts of 'the work' – exist. Several of these appear in other chapters of this book, and include the creative editing, layering and remixing of dub (→Chapter 9, 'Recording', Case Study 9.1) and the highly referential, sample-based language of hip-hop (→Chapter 10, 'Copyright and the Music Industry', Case Study 10.2), both of which reflect a form of creativity in which the original source work – such as a dub riddim – is regarded not as a fixed destination but as a point of departure. Building on the precedent set by the jazz standard, which shifted prestige (if not remuneration) away from the composer to the performer, rock 'n' roll itself grew out of the cover version (→Chapter 10, 'Copyright and the Music Industry', Case Study 10.1), allowing for a form of 'identity in motion' (Griffiths 2002) as songs were reworked by successions of performers of different genders and sexualities, ethnicities, and cultural backgrounds. Finally, from the 1970s onwards, dance musics such as disco, house and techno inaugurated practices of mixing and remixing that reconsidered the work not as a formal unity but as an unstable collection of elements (beats, hooks, vocals etc.) that could be endlessly filtered, reconfigured and supplemented live within a DJ's club set, or in the studio as a new release. Even popular music's most unified work-concept, the album (see Case Study 5.2), could be reimagined in remix form, as in Mad Professor's dub reworking of Massive Attack's *Protection* (1994). Within such practices, the fallacy that Taruskin locates in 'identifying the Romantic work-concept purely and simply with the text' (1995: 12) is neglected in favour of entirely new concepts of work, authorship and authenticity (Middleton 2000a).

- System 7, 'Alpha Wave (Hemi-Sync Mix)', from *Point 3 Water Album* (Butterfly, 1995)
- System 7, 'Alpha Wave (That Sound Mix)' (Butterfly, 1995)
- System 7/Richie Hawtin, 'Alpha Wave (Plastikman Acid House Mix)' (Butterfly, 1995)
- Massive Attack v. Mad Professor, *No Protection* (Wild Bunch, 1995)

Case Study 5.2: The Album

Before the late 1940s, the dominant recording format was the '78', a (usually) 12-inch disc, made of shellac and designed to be played at 78 rpm. Although it was hard-wearing and resistant to warping, shellac was brittle and produced a lot of surface noise. In the 1940s vinyl was investigated as an alternate recording medium. By the end of the decade, two competing formats were officially available: the 33 1/3 rpm 12-inch record, known as the LP (long player), introduced in 1948 by the Columbia Record Company, and the 45 rpm 7-inch record introduced by RCA Victor in 1949. Very quickly, the two media diverged as the preferred formats for different marketing demographics and musical genres: the 45, holding three to four minutes of music per side, became the preferred format for singles sold to the teen market; the LP, holding around twenty minutes of music per side (and costing several times as much to purchase), became the preferred format for 'adult' genres, such as jazz, classical, and easy listening or adult pop artists such as Frank Sinatra (1915–98).

As Keir Keightley has shown in a thorough economic analysis of the early years of the LP format (2004), this difference led the LP (as opposed to the faddish, throwaway single) to become viewed as an object of symbolic capital, 'more and more seen to be related to the book, assembled in libraries, and respected as a repository of cultural tradition' (380). The role of the back catalogue in the economics of the LP – longer-term, steady sales, rather than trend-influenced sharp spikes in attention – helped to establish the LP itself as an important cultural object: a coherent, multifaceted artistic statement that could (in the best case) contribute to a growing canon of recorded music. This approach to the LP is first and most clearly apparent in the jazz recordings of the late 1950s and early 1960s, a time in which the studio album became a medium for unprecedented experimentation with form, style and technique: consider albums such as Miles Davis' *Milestones* (1958) and *Kind of Blue* (1959), the Dave Brubeck Quartet's *Time Out* (1959), John Coltrane's *My Favorite Things* (1961) and Charles Mingus' *The Black Saint and the Sinner Lady* (1963). The same could be said of adult-oriented popular music: consider Sinatra's *Come Fly with Me* (1958), conceived as a musical world tour, from Capri to Hawaii, via New York, Mandalay, Paris and Brazil. As the critic Ian Penman has noted, 'Sinatra was one of the first musicians to see the long-playing album as an opportunity for sustained mood music … a quasi-cinematic reverie for listeners to sink into and dream along with' (Penman 2015).

- Frank Sinatra, 'Moonlight in Vermont', from *Come Fly with Me* (Capitol, 1958)

Case Study 5.2: (cont.)

Within a few years, however, sales of albums of 'teen' music began to overtake those of adult music. At the beginning of the 1960s, the major record labels had shown little interest in rock music; most singles, such as the Beach Boys' first single, *Surfin'* (1961), were released on independent labels. However, in the face of Beatlemania the biggest music companies worked rapidly to capture the new youth market. Capitol signed the Beach Boys in 1962. In the same year, Parlophone (a subsidiary of EMI) signed the Beatles, followed by the Hollies, and Gerry and the Pacemakers. By the mid-1960s, the rock album was established as a coherent artistic statement equal to the jazz or classical album, and one that now led the market in sales.

The money that labels were now investing and earning from such groups meant that bands and producers were able to spend more and more on their music's production. Bands began experimenting with resources and song forms in the studio rather than just recording their live repertoire almost live. They also devoted more album time to original compositions rather than covers. The rapid evolution of the rock album can be traced across the early recordings of many groups, but nowhere more strikingly than over the three albums released by the Beatles between 1964 and 1966. Whereas *Help!* (1965), already the group's fifth studio album, still featured cover versions ('Act Naturally' by country singer Johnny Russell and Voni Morrison, and Larry Williams' rock 'n' roll classic 'Dizzy, Miss Lizzy'), *Rubber Soul* (1965) was comprised entirely of songs devised within EMI's Abbey Road studios by the band's four members and producer George Martin. With *Revolver*, the Beatles were sufficiently confident (and financially supported) to indulge in a new level of experimentation and DIY electronics, in which the studio became an instrument in its own right rather than a more or less passive tool for capturing a performance (→Chapter 9, 'Recording'). 'Tomorrow Never Knows', the album's most adventurous track, featured – as well as the usual guitars, bass, drums and vocals (double-tracked and sent through a revolving Leslie speaker) – piano, organ, tape-loops (Paul McCartney laughing; an orchestral chord; a Mellotron playing 'flute'; a Mellotron playing 'string'; scalar sitar pattern), a sitar, and a tambourine (for a complete analysis, see MacDonald 2008: 184–93).

- The Beatles, 'Tomorrow Never Knows', from *Revolver* (Parlophone 1965)

Shortly after *Revolver*'s release the Beatles gave up on live performance altogether. Not only was the screaming of their fans making it impossible to hear themselves play, but their current music had become too intricate (thanks to their studio experiments) to recreate live (Cunningham 1998: 146). Their fame, and the now-developed mechanisms of music production and dissemination,

Case Study 5.2: (cont.)

meant that they could become a band that only existed in the studio; the Beach Boys' leader Brian Wilson (b. 1942) (if not the rest of his group) made a similar decision, as did the Kinks a little later on.

As the teenagers of the early 1960s grew into young adults, the Beatles and a few groups like them were able to develop their music to keep pace with their audience's changing tastes. Recognising this, major labels began to obtain more 'mature' rock (and folk and soul) acts that appealed to a wider but still youthful market. This often meant moving away from 2.5–3-minute singles to something more expansive. The album – exemplified by *Rubber Soul*, *Revolver* and the Beach Boys' *Pet Sounds* (1966) – thus became conceptualised as a work in itself rather than a collection of singles filled out with quickly run-up tracks. The songs themselves also began to directly thematise the transition from youth to adulthood that their intended listeners were undergoing.

- The Beach Boys, 'Wouldn't It Be Nice', from *Pet Sounds* (Capitol, 1966)

The emergence of the album-as-work created a mythology of the genius singer-songwriter (Lennon and McCartney; Brian Wilson), much like that granted to the classical composer (➔Chapter 10, 'Copyright and the Music Industry'), regardless of the fact that studio albums are inherently collaborative affairs involving technicians, producers, session musicians and more (Wyn Jones 2008). And, as Joshua Friedberg notes, the centrality of the album-as-work to popular music history since the 1960s encouraged a bias towards white male rock musicians who 'mastered' the format before soul and R&B artists like Marvin Gaye, Stevie Wonder and Isaac Hayes did. Friedberg's essay considers one exception to this rule, Aretha Franklin (1942–2018), who he finds 'fits more comfortably in the rock canon than other contemporaries of color, partly because . . . she was a master of the album format' (Friedberg 2018). To Franklin's *I Never Loved a Man the Way I Love You* (1967, ranked no. 1 in *Rolling Stone's* 'Women in Rock: 50 Essential Albums' in 2002) and *Lady Soul* (1968) we might also add more exceptions, among them Laura Nyro's *Eli and the Thirteenth Confession* (1968), Joni Mitchell's *Ladies of the Canyon* (1970), Minnie Riperton's *Come to My Garden* (1970) and Freda Payne's *Contact* (1971).

The mid-1960s development of the album was fuelled by a good-natured rivalry. Brian Wilson, who wrote much of *Pet Sounds* while the rest of the Beach Boys were on tour, was inspired by the artistic cohesion of *Rubber Soul* (Wyn Jones 2008: 56). In turn, McCartney (b. 1942) and Lennon loved the expansiveness of *Pet Sounds*, and in response began to build an album – *Sgt. Pepper's Lonely Hearts Club Band* – around the idea of a show. That concept was abandoned after two songs, as Lennon would have nothing to do with it, but these songs still bookend the record, which hangs together

Case Study 5.2: (cont.)

through shared themes rather than narrative. The recording's half-concept (carried over from the music into the album artwork, which included elaborate costumes for the John, Paul, George and Ringo of Pepper's imaginary band), coupled with a sonic inventiveness that exceeded even that of *Pet Sounds*, helped make it a pivotal moment in the history of the album.

Sgt. Pepper is often credited as the first 'concept album' – a loose term that describes an album whose songs are unified musically or lyrically around a central theme or narrative, and for which the 'concept' itself is key to an appreciation of the whole. Although artists made use of the idea in the 1960s (The Kinks: *The Kinks Are the Village Green Preservation Society*, 1968; the Who: *Tommy*, 1969), in the 1970s the concept album became an important if not essential part of the style known as progressive or prog rock (Borthwick and Moy 2004: 68). Albums by Yes (*Close to the Edge*, 1972), Genesis (*The Lamb Lies Down on Broadway*, 1974) and Pink Floyd (*Wish You Were Here*, 1975) are good examples. Borthwick and Moy (62) write that prog came to be 'an album-based form that valued experimentation and creative integrity over commercial acclaim', yet it also relied upon music industry commercial and economic enablers: double and triple LPs, with complex musical arrangements, layers of studio effects and live shows to match, required large amounts of cash investment. The fact that many prog albums were huge commercial successes certainly helped: at 45 million copies and counting, Pink Floyd's *Dark Side of the Moon* (1973) is one of the best-selling albums of all time.

- Pink Floyd, 'Shine on You Crazy Diamond, Parts 1–5', from *Wish You Were Here* (Harvest, 1975)

The concept album was not limited to prog rock, though; Travis D. Stimeling (2011) has written of three examples from the early 1970s by country musician Willie Nelson. The love of costumes, stage production, elaborate backstory and album artwork introduced by *Sgt. Pepper* and continued in prog can be found in other genres as well, not least the superhero-inspired funk universe of George Clinton's (b. 1941) various Parliament and Funkadelic groups (Figure 5.4), and the Afrofuturism of jazz keyboardist and alleged interplanetary visitor Sun Ra (1914–93), in both cases serving as a means to frame alternative, non-European musical histories (→Chapter 3, 'Postmodernism').

- Parliament, 'Dr Funkenstein', from *The Clones of Dr Funkenstein* (Casablanca, 1976)
- Sun Ra, 'Rocket Number 9', from *Interstellar Low Ways* (El Saturn Records, 1966)

Case Study 5.2: (cont.)

Figure 5.4 Parliament, *The Clones of Dr Funkenstein* (Casablanca, 1976)

The legacy of Clinton in particular can be seen and heard in rap's enduring love of costume and role play, from Grandmaster Flash and the Furious Five to Kendrick Lamar. Indeed, the concept album is an enduring form in rap, perhaps more than in any other genre: a list of significant examples from the end of the twentieth century would range from Lauryn Hill's autobiographical *The Miseducation of Lauryn Hill* (1998) to the dystopian rap opera *Deltron 3030* (2000) by Del tha Funky Homosapien, Dan the Automator and Kid Koala. Although the advent of downloads, MP3s and streaming threatened to fragment the long-form, track-by-track listening experience that characterises the album (a prospect that met resistance from many musicians who placed great value in that aspect of their art), at the turn of the century it remained popular music's most distinguished form.

Conclusion

Earlier in this chapter we noted how the emergence of the multi-authored, multimedia Happening – beginning with the Black Mountain College event of 1952 – contributed to the dissolution of the 'work' within Western art music as a unified category centred upon the figure of the singular composer; by extension, *Theater Piece No. 1* marked an early moment in music's postmodern suspicion of the author and textual autonomy (→Chapter 3, 'Postmodernism'). Yet it is a curiosity of history that at much the same time, popular music was moving in the opposite direction, reifying the album – another multimedia, multi-authored production – as a Romantic-style work-concept of its own, central to the creation of new structures of value and authorial genius (and which we have seen described in →Chapter 4, 'Canons'). The Romantic notion of the work may have faced many challenges in the twentieth century, yet it proved resilient, in large part thanks to the (European, male) economy of prestige and authority on which it was based, and which is described further in other chapters in this book (as well as →Chapter 4, 'Canons', see also →Chapter 10, 'Copyright and the Music Industry' and →Chapter 13, 'Gender and Sexuality'). Bolstered by inherited tradition, ideologies of genius and the complicity of the music industry, the Romantic work-concept retained a hold on the musical imagination – even as some pop practices were overturning the fixed form of the musical work. The rise in the second half of the century of forms such as the album demonstrated well past the century's end, therefore, the enduring value of Dahlhaus' 'fundamental category'.

6 | Rhythm and Time

In the twentieth century as in our own time, 'rhythm' meant different things in different contexts. Popularly, it often suggested a type of beat or musical feel, usually something lively or active. To music specialists, it could also refer to any one of the aspects of the relationship between sound and time: attack, metre or phrase structure (or 'period'). As the century progressed, and the new discipline of ethnomusicology began to suggest to a dominant caste of Westerners ways of understanding local music cultures as local participants did, it became apparent that many peoples had other ways of perceiving and describing what those Westerners described as rhythm (Agawu 1995). In what follows, we will address changing 'cultural' and musicological understandings of rhythm across the century. Yet our attention will often be on the ways that musicians developed rhythmic approaches to particular aesthetic and technical ends; in these discussions we will follow the definition of Anne Danielsen (2010a: 4) and take rhythm to refer to 'an interaction between non-sounding reference structures', such as metre, 'and sounding rhythmic events', such as an attack or beat.

This chapter focuses on two broad themes in the twentieth-century history of rhythm. The first, representing perhaps the most widespread and transformative of all musical developments during that time, concerns the global and cross-cultural dissemination and elaboration of rhythmic practices associated with the African diaspora. A great many approaches to rhythmic conception and performance were taken from Africa to the Americas during the dreadful 400-year epoch of transatlantic slavery that ended in the late nineteenth century. In the twentieth, those practices were carried back across the world through mass media and mass migration, and became profoundly influential in the development of popular and art-music forms on every continent.

The second theme – and one that can be seen in light of the first – concerns the ways in which those working in Western art music used rhythm to ask questions about the articulation and experience of the flow of time. To begin with, this entailed the disruption of regularised metre and pulse, which was a defining trend in early-century art music. It subsequently meant disassociating the notion of 'rhythm' from what had been common-sense ideas of bodily movement (like the 1, 2, 3, 4 of a walking bass line) and gesture (for instance the speech-like rhythm of a melodic line). Instead, in many strands of mid- and late-century compositional practice, 'rhythm' would be framed simply as the marking of specific, abstract points on the canvas of time and space, and a tool with which to construct technical and formal processes. But that did not mean art-music composers simply lost interest in the subjective experience of rhythm: as we will see, the exploration of rhythmic perception was a key feature of new art-music approaches emerging from the 1960s.

We begin by exploring developments in modernist composition early in the century. We then turn to the global uptake of Afrodiasporic rhythmic practices, especially jazz swing and Latin American forms. Investigations into the musical structuring of time and perception are discussed in the context of post-World war II serialist and minimalist composition practices. Finally, we examine the concept of groove, and changes in popular music rhythm practices in the latter half of the twentieth century – including their sudden transformation through new technologies like the drum machine and sequencer.

Modernist Rhythm

As discussed in ➔ Chapter 2, 'Modernism', histories of musical modernism have often described the 'movement' as unfolding across a series of very different, yet interlinked, cultural centres. So while modernist composition emanating from different parts of Eastern Europe, Western Europe and the United States during the early decades of the century showed a variety of rhythmic experiment, there were commonalities in play.

Most important among these was the revolt against what had long been an unassailable regime of metrical discipline. In the so-called 'common practice' period up to and including the late nineteenth century, melodic phrases were usually organised across a regular succession of identical metrical units (like bars of 4/4 time). These units were themselves very often organised into larger, but still regular periods (like groups of 2, 4, 8, or 16). Now, though, the phrase was to be 'set free', released from the bonds of both bar and period. Composers would explore new ways of rhythmically and metrically articulating their material, with metre often becoming subservient to the musical idea, not its organising structure. This new approach would be variously inspired by the vitality and complexities of the folk music practices that had been brought back into art music's orbit during the nationalist moment of the late nineteenth century and by the modernist imperatives of fragmentation, discontent and technical innovation (➔Chapter 14, 'Race and Ethnicity'; Chapter 2, 'Modernism').

There was no more important single figure in this initiative than Igor Stravinsky. The rhythmic vocabulary of Stravinsky's early triumph, *The Rite of Spring* (1913), came to be imitated across twentieth-century music of all kinds. *The Rite* sought to imagine a 'primitive' pagan ritual, the brutality of which was in large part expressed through its rhythmic aggression, and the subjection of rhythmic images of Slavic folk dance to modernist technical procedure – most notably, the creative manipulation of 'additive' rhythms, in which short rhythmic units were bolted together to create longer metres and phrases. We will see this technique at work throughout this chapter.

- Igor Stravinsky, 'Augurs of Spring', from *The Rite of Spring* (1913)

Stravinsky's compositional methods here have been examined by a number of musicologists (e.g., Taruskin 1980), but Matthew McDonald (2010) provides a detailed argument that seeks to account for these rhythmic procedures. Among many examples, the analyst shows the celebrated, irregular accent pattern that begins the section 'Augurs of Spring' – 9 quavers, followed by 2, then 6, then 3 and so on – alongside a vertical arrangement of the pitches that make up the ostinato that interrupts that accent pattern. These vertical intervals (a 2nd, 6th, 3rd and so on) closely match the accent pattern; 'at an initial compositional stage', McDonald writes (502), 'Stravinsky may have used a mechanical procedure to derive the accent pattern, in nearly its ultimate form, from an independently generated succession of intervals.' Elsewhere, the irregular accent patterns that characterise the piece are grouped into rapidly shifting metres, such as the adjoining bars of 2/8, 2/16 and 3/16 in the piece's closing section.

The Rite's instantly identifiable rhythmic innovations became musical shorthand for a kind of contemporary brutality, and echoes of its rhythmic language can be heard in concert music (George Antheil's *Ballet mécanique*, 1925), music for stage and screen (Leonard Bernstein's *West Side Story*, 1957) and countless concert music pastiches.

This work – together with the music of composers such as the Hungarian Béla Bartók (1881–1945) – clarified for other composers the ways in which folk sources and modern technique might be mutually reconciled. Beginning in 1908 and continuing into the 1930s, Bartók collected a large number of folk songs in central and south-eastern Europe, before synthesising them into his own composition. Central here were additive 3+2 and 2+3 groupings, voiced, for instance, by the viola in the complex of cross-rhythms that opens the final movement of Bartók's String Quartet No. 4 (Figure 6.1, bars 11–15; Leong 2004).

• Béla Bartók, String Quartet No. 4. V. Allegro Molto (1928)

This was an especially attractive proposition to those composers who, modernist by disposition, were nevertheless concerned with representing and addressing wider, popular experience. Stravinsky was also among the first to make compositional allusions to the ragtime and early jazz rhythms that were becoming all the rage, but the American Aaron Copland (1900–90) would also explore the polyrhythms of ragtime and jazz, 'experimenting', as he would write in 1927,

with shifting beats by introducing a variety of highly unorthodox and frequently changing rhythms – 7/8, 5/8, 9/8, 1/8, etc., that made the music polymetric – the use of different time signatures one after the other. The challenge was to do these complex vertical and horizontal experiments and still retain a transparent and lucid texture and a feeling of spontaneity and natural flow. (Copland cited in Kleppinger 2003: 87)

• Aaron Copland, Piano Concerto. II. Molto Moderato (1926)

The unpredictable distribution of rhythmic accents across a metrical ground itself rendered unpredictable threw the experience of rhythm into thrilling turmoil. It was this that so appealed to many composers eager to articulate 'the modern'; Copland's words are axiomatic of the ways that many of them were now dealing with rhythm in their work.

If re-versioned Slavic folk and American jazz rhythms represented the east and west of the modernist reinvention of rhythm, then, in what was still widely imagined as the European centre of art-music composition, different things were afoot. Schoenberg, and many of those atonal composers who followed his example in the first decades of the century, would often cling to late Romantic models of rhythm and phrase. As we will see, following World War II this rhythmic traditionalism would become a point of contention for the next generation of modernist composers. Yet not every echo of art music's historical rhythmic practice could be called conservative: once again, it was Stravinsky who led the way in repurposing

Figure 6.1 Béla Bartók, String Quartet No. 4. V. Allegro Molto (1964), bars 1–15

baroque and early classical figurations and rhythmic drive for use in composition that was otherwise thoroughly modern. This 'neo-classical' style foregrounded a relatively familiar sense of continual pulse and remained popular through the 1920s–1940s because of it.

- Igor Stravinsky: Concerto for Piano and Wind Instruments, 1. Largo-Allegro (1923–4)

The sophisticated workings of harmony and counterpoint in the Western tradition had long been highly codified. But while rhythm had often been left to a composer's intuition, modernist musicians had begun to intellectualise that parameter too – to systematise and formalise its use so as to enlarge the field of compositional and experiential possibilities. As a result, many modernist composers across the world were producing music with entirely new rhythmic profiles. Yet the rhythmic revolution was incomplete, and we will return to this line of development below. And as we saw in → Chapter 2, 'Modernism', the modernist impulse reverberated across culture, and in the 1920s and 1930s the rhythmic profile of Western popular music, too, was undergoing profound transformation on its own terms.

The African-Americanisation of Global Rhythmic Practices

The transatlantic slave trade lasted from around 1500 to 1888, when the practice was finally abolished in its last holdout, Brazil. Africans taken as slaves to the Americas brought with them a wide and diverse range of cultural practices, not least of which was music and dance. A fund of Afrodiasporic approaches underpinned a huge range of musics subsequently developed in the Americas (Floyd, Zeck and Ramsey 2017). Through the twentieth century, many of these forms would spread worldwide. While melodic devices like the blue note and structuring principles like call and response became part of the global lingua franca, it was arguably rhythm that exerted the most influence, in both cultural and technical terms; indeed, it is no exaggeration to say that the twentieth century saw the thoroughgoing African-Americanisation of the world's understanding and experience of rhythm – even in societies, and musical forms, where African Americans themselves barely participated. That musicians and listeners of all races were participating in this cultural change was a phenomenon that, initially at least, was far from universally welcomed (Radano 2000).

During the twentieth century, a number of scholars worked to establish and theorise the links between musical forms of sub-Saharan Africa and those that had subsequently developed in the Americas (Johnson and Miller Chernoff 1991; Kubik 1994). This work identified several rhythmic cells fundamental to both African and African American music practices. Most famous among these is the *clave*, of which there are two types, the *son* and *rumba*. Both types are heard in 3–2 and 2–3 forms – that is, with three attacks in bar 1 and two in bar 2, or else the reverse (Figure 6.2).

Closely related, and almost as common, is the 3+3+2 *tresillo* figure (Figure 6.3; Floyd 1999), which, as we will see, would prove tremendously adaptable.

These and other Afrodiasporic rhythmic devices resonated through to the end of the century. But at its start, they could be found underpinning numerous dances and associated musical forms – rumba, cha-cha-cha, mambo, samba – that were developing in Cuba, Brazil, Puerto Rico and other Caribbean, Central and southern American countries. Circulating regionally and then globally, not least through gramophone recordings and cinematic representations, commercialised forms of these dances and musics had dominated the world's ballrooms by the 1920s. This was a time in which semi-formal social dancing was a central leisure activity; before World War II, then, a great many people across the world were spending their spare time engaged with, and attempting to embody, Latin American rhythms, then often only dimly perceived as somehow African.

What excited so many was these styles' syncopation: the ways that their rhythms cut across the beat and across metre. Indeed, in the first decades of the century, a new and hugely widespread approach to syncopation transformed the rhythmic (and melodic) texture of Western popular music, as is shown in Huron and Ommen's 2006 study of syncopation in American

Figure 6.2 *Son* and *rumba* claves

Figure 6.3 The *tresillo* rhythmic figure

popular music during the period 1890–1939. This work is a good example of 'big-data' computational musicology: the researchers fed recordings of 1,131 songs into software that analysed the sound files for both density and variety of syncopated patterns, finding that in terms of both frequency and complexity, syncopation moved from rarity to commonplace over that period.

Latin American styles were important to this shift – but jazz swing was vital. In its simplest terms, swing meant that, where a crotchet was subdivided into quavers, the first of each was rendered slightly longer than the second, and the second was slightly accented (Butterfield 2011). This gave a feeling of push on the '&' of each beat; equally important was the accent on the bar's offbeats (2 and 4 in a 4/4 bar). At both beat and bar level, then, swing reversed the placement of stress as generally expected in Western musical practices of many kinds, and the upset was compelling.

Within this framework, jazz musicians were developing increasingly complex approaches to syncopation. These rhythmic games of anticipation, repetition and retardation were played across the jazz ensemble, whether in a drum or bass accompaniment, an arranged ensemble passage or a singer or instrumentalist's solo line. Brian Harker (2011) shows one aspect of this development in his study of one of the form's global stars, Louis Armstrong. In his first recordings, in 1923, the young Armstrong – at that point playing cornet – had based his solos on stock figures that included discrete rhythmic units and licks: snatches of cakewalk, ragtime and fanfare, these assembled and juxtaposed in the course of an improvised solo. This was standard early jazz practice. However, by 1926 and the recording of the song 'Big Butter and Egg Man', Armstrong had developed a much more integrated approach to rhythm, whereby ideas introduced during a solo were subject to extended rhythmic variation and development. In Armstrong's solo on the recording of that song (Figure 6.4), the first three notes of Armstrong's paraphrase of the melody (quaver-crotchet-quaver) are reworked in many ways in the first half of the solo in a game of variation of the anacrusis, as Harker describes:

We move from the original (mm. 0, 4) to a modified version in four eight notes (mm. 2, 8) to an expanded version (m. 6), to a contracted version (m. 12), to one splintered into six eighth-note triplets (m. 16). Then, as if to compensate for the digression, Armstrong returns to the original motive, emphatically stating it four times without variation (mm. 20–22). (Harker 2011: 52)

- Louis Armstrong and His Hot Five, 'Big Butter and Egg Man' (Okeh, 1926)

Figure 6.4 Louis Armstrong's solo on 'Big Butter and Egg Man' (Okeh, 1926). Words and Music by Louis Armstrong and Percy Venable. Copyright © 1926 UNIVERSAL MUSIC CORP. All Rights Reserved. Used by Permission. Reproduced by kind permission of Hal Leonard Europe Ltd

The solo contains other games of rhythmic and melodic variation. This extended sleight of hand would become standard jazz practice following Armstrong, as the solo – the extended, improvised variation of material, of which Armstrong was a foundational exponent – succeeded collective improvisation as jazz's basic performance practice.

Armstrong himself described this jazz approach as '"swinging" around, and away from, the regular beat and melody you are used to' (Armstrong 1999/1936: 75). Much later in the century, African American cultural theorists like James A. Snead (1984) and, as we saw in →Chapter 3, 'Postmodernism', Henry Louis Gates (1988), would argue that these kinds of methods, in which repetition and surprising variation acted not just to decorate but to intensify, ironise or otherwise make meaningful an original statement, had long been a central part of Black American cultural meaning-making. But equally important is the relationship between this rhythmic play and dance. As Harker points out, Armstrong's move away from stock figures towards a more fluent rhythmic language coincided with a Chicago residency during which he played onstage nightly alongside virtuosic 'rhythm tap' dance teams. Musician contemporaries later remarked on how Armstrong had developed his playing to mimic each step of the routine, and Harker finds a number of tap-dance-like rhythms in the cornetist's solo (Harker 2011: 60–7).

Dance rhythm was joined in jazz improvisation by an increasing use of speech-like rhythms. Armstrong switched to trumpet, and soon his playing was virtuosic in its mix of the declamatory and the muttered aside: a recording such as 'Tight Like This' (1928), with its quick semiquaver figures that seem to stretch the music's basic triplet-feel swing like elastic, shows how far and how quickly he had developed the techniques of improvised discourse. These approaches were taken up and adapted by jazz musicians across the world; if the British trumpeter and vocalist Nat Gonella was a capable imitator, then Django Reinhardt (1910–53), star guitarist of Quintette du Hot-club de France, would come to be recognised as the most outstanding non-American jazz improviser of the middle century.

- Nat Gonella and His Georgians, 'Tiger Rag' (Odeon, 1935)
- Quintette du Hot-club de France, 'Chicago' (Swing, 1937)

By the 1930s and 1940s, the jazzified popular song – the genre identified as 'swing' – would be the West's dominant commercial form, with the approaches described above being further developed by composers, singers and instrumentalists. Vocalist Billie Holiday (1915–59), for example, would often cast a lyric and its accompanying melodic line this way and that, inflecting it with speech rhythms and surprising accents, often reforming the lyric's meaning as she did so. Huang and Huang (2013: 288) write that Holiday's performance style 'undermines our ability to pinpoint the instant of a word's onset and thereby renders uncertain the precise duration of a note', generally a key aspect of melodic articulation; Holiday's art, they continue 'is one of melodic shape without abrupt boundaries of pitch or rhythm . . . Rather, her lines are supple, continuously sliding trajectories'.

- Duke Ellington, 'It Don't Mean a Thing (If it Ain't Got That Swing)' (Brunswick, 1931)
- Chick Webb and His Orchestra (Ella Fitzgerald, vocal), 'A-Tisket, A-Tasket' (Decca, 1938)
- Billie Holiday, 'All of Me' (Okeh, 1941)

While the rhythm of Western popular music had been effectively 'African-Americanised' by the 1940s, only a few Black musicians reaped the full benefit of this. At a time in which Black artists were only rarely accorded the commercial and cultural standing of their white counterparts, it was generally white musicians – Benny Goodman in the USA, Jack Hylton in Europe – whose bands popularised such music. Major stars like Glenn Miller often traded in highly traditional popular material, updated through the application of a rather gentle swing feel.

- Glenn Miller and His Orchestra, 'Danny Boy' (Bluebird, 1940)

Against this backdrop, the new rhythmic dash of bebop (→Chapter 2, 'Modernism') seemed astonishingly powerful. Later in the 1940s, a number of jazz musicians – bebop leading-light Dizzy Gillespie and Cuban-born mambo bandleader Machito (1909–84) chief among them – would further reaffirm jazz's broader Afrodiasporic rhythmic heritage by pioneering what became known as Latin jazz, putting jazz improvisation techniques in an even-quaver setting.

- Machito and his Orchestra: Tangá, pts. 1 and 2, rec. 1949 (from *Machito Jazz with Flip and Bird*, Mercury, 1952)

As the following case study shows, these new syntheses of Afrodiasporic rhythmic approaches would continue to play a role in the forging of new communities and ways of life, particularly as, in the 1950s, many Puerto Ricans migrated to the United States.

Case Study 6.1: Salsa

What became known as salsa emerged from Cuban popular forms of the 1930s, 1940s and 1950s – especially son. But the music in its modern form was chiefly developed by the newly swelled Puerto Rican community of New York City in the 1960s. New York would remain the spiritual home of salsa, not least because local label Fania was largely responsible for the music's commercial framing, production and dissemination. Yet, in the 1970s, the music would come to represent a powerful, transnational *Latinidad*, Latin-ness; salsa was a form through which Latin Americans in the USA began to assert a newly singular identity, and those in the Caribbean and countries such as Venezuela and Colombia described and experienced new, urban, cosmopolitan ways of life. As Lise Waxer (2002) notes, the intrinsically diasporic nature of the music – where the rhythms that made up the music were understood as being just as migratory as the people who played them – meant that those participating in salsa scenes usually saw themselves as part of a regional, and eventually, global network of culture.

Case Study 6.1: (cont.)

Though the rhythmic vocabulary of salsa was drawn from circum-Caribbean forms like son, guaracha, mambo, cha-cha-cha and bolero, in New York this was married with brassy instrumentation and arrangements that echoed 1940s Latin jazz. In the early 1960s, Eddie Palmieri (b. 1936) incorporated trombones into a traditional *charanga* flute-and-violin ensemble to produce a sound that came to define salsa. This syncretism, as Marisol Berríos-Miranda writes (2002: 25), is in part what ensured that salsa was 'stylistically and sonically distinctive' from those older Caribbean forms.

- Eddie Palmieri and His Conjunto 'La Perfecta', 'Tema La Perfecta' (from self-titled album, Alegre, 1962)
- Celia Cruz and Johnny Pacheco, 'Toro Mata' (from *Celia and Johnny*, Vaya, 1974)
- Larry Harlow and Orquesta Harlow, *La Raza Latina, A Salsa Suite* (Fania, 1976)
- Willie Colón & Rubén Blades, 'Siembra' (from *Siembra*, Fania, 1978)

Equally subject to local adaptation was salsa's lyrical content. As the music travelled to Europe and Asia (Hosokawa 1999), and aimed for mainstream success in the USA, the gritty narratives of working class-life that had characterised the music's earlier subject matter were replaced with less specific, and perhaps more traditional, popular music themes.

Still, in the minds of many musicians and audiences, it was rhythm that remained of primary importance: specifically, the ways in which the rhythmic parts of a salsa performance would lock together. Fundamental to any salsa song's rhythmic patterning was one of the two claves, and here is one of those rhythmic phenomena that musicology has often described in inappropriately 'Eurocentric' terms. In that understanding, the clave can seem like a repetitive, surface rhythmic figure, yet, as perceived in Afrodiasporic theory and practice, it also fulfils some of the functions of metre: that is, it works as a regularising, recursive form upon which a much more complex rhythmic architecture is built. As Simpson-Litke and Stover write in their analytical study of salsa dancing (2019: 78), clave thus 'defines a liminal space that is neither rhythm nor metre, yet interacts essentially with both'. Also central, and playing a related structural role, is the tresillo rhythm. In practice, this means that the clave and tresillo, continuing throughout, articulate the down- and upbeats, as well as co-determining the song's other repeating rhythmic patterns: these are carried by percussion like timbales, bongó, conga and piano, as well as horns, vocals and other instruments, and all lock into the basic grammar dictated by clave and tresillo. So too do they lock in with each other, as Figure 6.5's illustration of a typical salsa passage shows.

Case Study 6.1: (cont.)

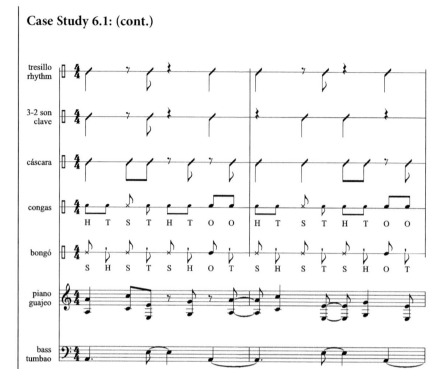

Figure 6.5 A typical salsa passage. The H and T markings in the conga and bongó parts indicate strokes from the 'heel' and 'toe' of the hand, while S indicates a slap and O the drum's open tone. Simpson-Litke and Stover, 'Theorizing Fundamental Music/Dance Interactions in Salsa', *Music Theory Spectrum* 41 (2019): 76. DOI: 10.1093/mts/mty033. Reprinted by permission of Oxford University Press on behalf of Society for Music Theory

Transcriptions like this belie the fact that salsa was, at least originally, arranged and described orally rather than in notated form – and, indeed, that it was the unnotated, minute differences of feel and interpretation that were most valued by musicians and audiences. Berríos-Miranda (2002) describes salsa musicians characterising and evaluating performance styles using terms like *afinque* (locked) or *mantecoso* (buttery). Historically, the *afinque* designation was important: Berríos-Miranda writes that it was this feeling of fixity, in which musicians did not elaborate their part at all, that defined salsa in its early Puerto Rican form, while in Cuba and elsewhere more individual variation was likely to be heard. However unifying salsa rhythm could be, it was also the ground for regional rivalries and self-definition. When, in 1968, the Fania label formed a supergroup, the Fania All-Stars – which became hugely important in the dissemination of the style – salsa purists of the old school criticised what they saw as the individualistic, jazz-like improvisational approaches taken by the New York musicians.

Case Study 6.1: (cont.)

In salsa as in many other forms indebted to Afrodiasporic rhythmic practices, the play of beat, syncopation and accent was articulated almost as often by the music's dancers as by musicians and composers. Simpson-Litke and Stover (2019: 79) describe the poly-rhythmic play cultivated by the skilled salsa dancer, which, the authors suggest, puts 'the ribcage, shoulders, and arms swaying in opposition to the hips, knees, and feet in a complex set of body articulations that characterizes many forms of Latin dance'. The authors cite salsa percussionist Steve Smith's expert observations of some of the highly nuanced ways in which dancers respond to rhythmic invention in music. In the transcription above, there is a strong accent on beat 4, this determined by the *tresillo*, and articulated by bongó, tumba and tumbao. But '[t]he most common variation in the percussion', Smith says,

is to shift the beat 4 accent in the 2 half of clave to the '&' of 4 . . . Consequences of this accent include giving the dancer a syncopated 'bump' directly after their accent on beat 4 of the 2 half, which good dancers often express in a backwards shoulder movement after they plant their foot, as if you gave them a shove in the chest. It also serves to create a suspension that is resolved on beat 4 of the 3 half, making that note an even more solid anchor as it includes a clave note, open tones on both drums and a foot plant from the dancers on the same beat. It's kinda like you pull the rug out from under them on the 2 half and then plant 'em back on track on the 3 half. (Simpson-Litke and Stover 2019: 83)

In salsa as in many other Afrodiasporic forms, expert participants were to be found on the dance floor as well as on stage. The communal nature of dance – and a shared approach to rhythm, in which technical comprehension, imaginative response and collaborative cohesion were all essential – made it a key site in the construction, and celebration, of shared cultural identity.

Mid-Century Compositional Experiments in Rhythm

The rhythmic experiment that characterised early modernist music con-tinued through the mid-century in both Europe and the USA, and while these efforts were largely made in isolation, they converged to a considerable degree.

In the USA, the 1930s saw a flourishing of works for percussion ensem-ble, a genre introduced to Western composition by the French expat Edgard Varèse with his piece *Ionisation* (1929–31). For young composers in North America like Johanna Beyer (several pieces including *Percussion Suite*, 1933), Henry Cowell (*Ostinato Pianissimo*, 1934) and John Cage (three *Construction* pieces, 1939–41), the medium promised results that were not only new, but also far removed from those arrived at by the pitch- and harmony-obsessed European modernists. Cage had taken lessons with Schoenberg, who was by then living in Los Angeles. But the American soon developed a pre-compositional process which was devoted to plotting a piece's durational and proportional characteristics, rather than – as was the norm for those working with twelve-tone technique – its pitch rela- tionships. This gave Cage a set of formal boxes to fill with 'material', an inversion of the Schoenbergian, modernist norm, in which a piece's formal shape only emerged as pitch materials were 'worked out'.

As Paul van Emmerik shows, although Cage sometimes worked with additive rhythms like those we saw earlier in this chapter, his principal structuring method at this time was one of proportion. Cage's 'rhythmic structures' were thus

based on numerical relationships between the durations of sections and of groups of measures of a composition in such a way that the durations of both levels were governed by a single series of proportions . . . [*First Construction (in Metal)*, 1939] consists of sixteen periods of sixteen measures each, which are grouped into five large sections composed of 4, 3, 2, 3 and 4 periods – or 64, 48, 32, 48 and 64 measures – respectively. Similarly, each individual period is subdivided into five groups of 4, 3, 2, 3 and 4 measures respectively. (van Emmerik 2002: 218)

- Cage, First Construction (in Metal) (1939)

In pieces like *A Room* (1943), and up until the time of *String Quartet in Four Parts* (1950), Cage developed this approach to include repetition and cycling structures that would create different, coexisting layers of rhythmic stasis and change (Latartara 2007).

Meanwhile in France, the French composer Olivier Messiaen was devel- oping a technique in which pieces were underpinned by rhythmic pat- terns – these, coincidentally like Cage's in the USA, often cyclical – to which pitch and other parameters were then attached. Messiaen was a keen student of both Indian classical music and Western medieval music, which used similar techniques. Characteristic of the patterns Messiaen con- structed was the use of additive technique, a transformative process con- ceived as a means, in Anthony Pople's words (1994: 36), 'of irregularising regular patterns', and of endlessly varying small component rhythmic cells. In Pople's illustrative example (Figure 6.6), a semiquaver is added to a cell, rendering each impossible to metre in any conventional way. This was one of the elements that gave Messiaen's music its strangely out of kilter, other- worldly air.

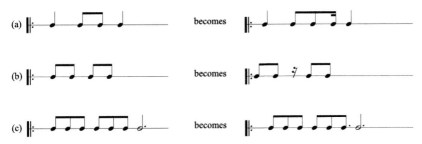

Figure 6.6 Typical additive rhythms used by Messiaen (Pople 1994: 36)

- Olivier Messiaen, *Quatuor pour la fin du temps*. I. 'Liturgie de cristal' (1941)

We saw in →Chapter 2, 'Modernism' how varied and conflicted the modernist 'movement' was, and how, following the cataclysm of World War II, a young generation of art-music composers struggled to construct a new music that would challenge even the achievements of the early-century revolutionaries. For many among the avant-garde of the 1940s and 1950s, early modernist uses of propulsive folk, jazz and 'neo-classical' rhythm now seemed dated. Indeed, repetition of any kind was viewed with suspicion: the Schoenbergian principle of continuously developing variation, even if recast in new theoretical language, generally meant that repetitive statements of blocks of material, whether rhythmic or pitched, were viewed as immature – a crutch for the listener, and an obstacle in the piece's logical unfolding. It was for this reason that the philosopher-critic Theodor Adorno, at first an influential figure for the young serialists, railed against Stravinsky's highly influential, highly repetitive rhythmic language, and it also formed a major part of his arguments against popular music (Adorno 2019/1949; Adorno 1991a/1938; Kronfeld 2019). But Schoenberg also came in for criticism from the postwar generation; leading figures like Pierre Boulez judged the late Romantic vocabulary of rhythm and gesture to which Schoenberg had cleaved, and which was still much used by other twelve-tone composers, to be a throwback that hampered the development of a truly new music (Boulez 1991b).

Serialist composers began to treat rhythm as just another a parameter to be set in processes designed according to the aims of the composition. The strikingly disembodied, studiously non-repetitive rhythmic patterning that resulted helped characterise postwar modernism almost as much as did its pitch aspect. Certainly, more traditionally minded postwar composers, including leading figures like Benjamin Britten and Dimitri Shostakovich, had continued largely to adhere to rhythmic conventions of late Romantic music. And, from the 1960s, a new generation of composers, at first in the USA and then elsewhere, began to reintroduce regular pulse and other forms of rhythmic repetition to composed music. But not because they were returning to tradition: rather, many of these musicians were exploring the radically new compositional processes and aesthetics that later came to be characterised as minimalism.

Case Study 6.2: Minimalism and Repetition

The term 'minimalism' was first used to describe the work of 1960s visual artists in the USA – including Donald Judd, Agnes Martin and Sol LeWitt – which was characterised by a dramatic reduction (and interrogation) of its material (Figure 6.7).

The epithet soon came to be applied to a coterie of young American musicians active in contexts very close to those artists, and with good reason, since their work, too, made do with as little material 'content' as possible (Strickland 1993). Yet several of those central to minimalism's development – Terry Riley (b. 1935), La Monte Young (b. 1935) and Steve Reich (b. 1936) – began in the 1960s to compose with repeated rhythmic patterns that recalled the jazz and R & B they had been drawn to in their earlier life. That basic orientation, which contrasted with that of many of their generation, was central to their embrace of pulse and repetition.

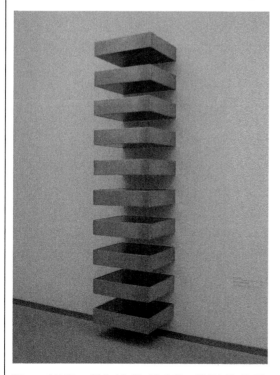

Figure 6.7 Donald Judd, *Untitled (Stack)* (1968–9). Photograph by Oliver Kurmis

Case Study 6.2: (cont.)

For young composers trained in the Western art-music tradition, and thereby steeped in twelve-tone and serial technique, this was a radical step. As noted above, in Romantic-modernist thinking, a piece that repeated itself, or stayed the same, represented a kind of simple-mindedness or regression; *real* music represented becoming and transformation. Minimalist music would come to challenge this thinking and describe a new kind of compositional process and listening experience, one in which small-scale rhythms became synonymous with their larger-scale repetition, and in which repetition gave rise to a different experience of musical duration and time.

An important early method in both Riley and Reich's work was the compositional use of tape, and the recording, editing and layering of 'found' sounds. The most noted example was Reich's piece *It's Gonna Rain* (1965). In New York, Reich recorded an African American street-corner preacher, Brother Walter, in the midst of an emphatic retelling of the story of Noah's Flood. Reich then experimented with edits and loops of Walter's voice, and eventually arrived at what would become his central early compositional technique.

In the process of trying to line up two identical tape loops in some particular relationship, I discovered that the most interesting music of all was made by simply lining the tapes up in unison, and letting them slowly shift out of phase which each other ... Sampling each channel in synchronisation with the voice rhythm will give you 'it's gonna, it's gonna ...' over and over again. Speed up the sampling rate, however, and the result will move from 'it's gonna', inching into the 'r' of 'rain', then into 'ain', 'nnn', and finally back to 'it's gonna'. (Reich cited in Potter 2000: 166, 169)

- Steve Reich, *It's Gonna Rain* (1965)

The startling simplicity and effectiveness of the technique – Reich called it 'phasing' – led the composer to adapt it for instrumental works such as *Piano Phase* (1967). That piece's three sections are each based on a single figure. These phrases are in no way altered or 'developed'; instead, they are gradually realigned. The two pianists begin playing each section's phrase in unison; in transition passages, one player gradually shifts one semiquaver ahead, until the players lock back into tempo. This process repeats until the initial unison is regained.

- Steve Reich, *Piano Phase* (1967)

Reich had hit upon a developmental process that was based on rhythmic material that, despite that development, somehow also stayed the same; unlike other modernist rhythmic designs – especially those of Reich's serialist contemporaries – the simplicity of both material and compositional strategy meant that the nature of the process was to be entirely audible, not hidden in a piece's inner workings. In his important 1968 essay 'Music

Case Study 6.2: (cont.)

As a Gradual Process', Reich described such music as unfolding 'so slowly and gradually that listening to it resembles watching a minute hand on a watch – you can perceive it moving after you stay with it a while' (Reich 2002/1968: 35).

A similarly influential approach was forged by Philip Glass (b. 1937), who in the late 1960s began making use of repeating, moto perpetuo figures that referenced antique Western art-music styles. In *Music in Fifths* (1969), an instrumental line is forever starting, restarting or allowed to spool on, before beginning again. The pulse remains absolutely constant, yet the feeling of the line's syncopated reiteration is of a piece with jazz and rock practices at mid-century – this is perhaps not coincidental to Glass' widespread acceptance and mainstream promotion in the 1970s.

- Philip Glass, *Music in Fifths* (1969)

Glass' early works were based on intuitive, additive rhythmic processes, with simple motivic cells expanding from repetition to repetition. But from *1+1* (1968) onwards, that additive approach was rigorously systematised, with structure now unfolding in a more audible way as a result (Potter 2000: 272ff). Like Messiaen before him, Glass was influenced in this technique by his study of Indian classical music.

Why were the minimalists working in these ways? In a speculative study, Robert Fink (2005a) argues that minimalist music was part of a broader 'cultural practice' emerging in the American mid-century, where new forms of consumption – of mass media with its endless reels of images, of shopping with its endless aisles of soup cans – chimed with a music that had purposeful repetition at its centre.

Yet this work more directly reflected the rise of phenomenological approaches in philosophy and their application to (musical) aesthetics (Langer 1953). An important theoretical articulation of the ideas underpinning early minimalist art of all kinds was Susan Sontag's celebrated essay, 'Against Interpretation' (Sontag 2009/1966). Sontag argued that trying to provide verbally explicable 'meanings' for contemporary art works belied their true purpose, which was to inspire a sensuous encounter with form and material. While Sontag's visual artists asked viewers to look at physical materials in space, musicians were bound to ask their audiences to hear material in time. The slipping synchronisation of phrases in Reich's phasing pieces produced a series of rhythmic-acoustic effects that were particular to the listener's position relative to the sound source, their attentiveness to isolated strands of the process and so on. Patterns thrown up in two different hearings could give the same listener two entirely different acoustic perceptions of the piece, a lack of fixity that Reich welcomed (Reich 2002/1968: 35). Similarly variable experiences were furnished by pieces like Glass' monumental, four-hour *Music in 12 Parts* (1971–4). Minimalist innovations in compositional approaches to rhythm and musical time, then, also heralded a new attitude to musical understanding. In contrast to

Case Study 6.2: (cont.)

an art-music tradition that had long lionised the composer and 'his' vision, minimalist art of all kinds enabled, invited and celebrated its audience's subjective experience (Potter 2000: 15). The minimalist work would be 'achieved' not through its composed, structural coherence, as the Romantic-modernist doxa demanded, but at the moment of its individual, idiosyncratic perception.

The moment did not last. By the mid-1970s, both Reich and Glass were structuring their pieces very differently, and often, rather more traditionally. Yet the use of repetitive figures endured. A piece like Glass' *The Photographer* (1982) still made use of those endlessly repeated moto perpetuo arpeggios and accompaniment figures, its material still extremely limited; now, though, there was much more play in metrical change – and, as was true also of Reich's mature music, more harmonic movement – with figures suddenly pausing or vaulting as they were articulated as syncopations or polyrhythms over the continuous pulse.

- Philip Glass, *The Photographer*, Act III (recorded version, CBS, 1982)

Similar approaches came to characterise the music of very different 'post-minimalist' composers like John Adams, Julius Eastman, Louis Andriessen or Meredith Monk. Monk (b. 1942) incorporated dance and – most importantly – her own voice into her work, as well as an extended repertoire of vocal techniques that drew on a wide variety of approaches. In her 1970s work, Monk would often sing lines comprised of small repetitive rhythmic modules, these often formed of plosive sounds that gave the modules percussive intent. Such lines were often extended or contracted by the addition of syllables, in ways that did not sound like, but nevertheless were not dissimilar from, the additive techniques we have seen at work in both European modernist and American minimalist composition. Added to this were repetitive ostinati, often articulated by an accompanying piano but sometimes by other, overlapping voices, which were as much about attack and propulsion as they were harmony.

- Meredith Monk, 'Tablet' (from *Songs from the Hill/Tablet*, Wergo, 1979)

Minimalist uses of rhythmic repetition were extremely influential both in and outside art music. And the style's early theoretical concerns were shared by – and helped usher in – a wider interest in the phenomenology of musical experience. Music theorists of the late twentieth century would begin to foreground the idea of the listener's subjectivity; understandings of rhythm and other musical events as tied only to specific points in time came to be thought of as reductive, given that listeners know what has come before, are always predicting what comes next and experience a performance cumulatively (Clifton 1983; Kramer 1988; Hasty 1997; London 2004).

Rhythm and Blues, Funk and Rock

Time and again, artists working in African American popular forms, in which rhythmic repetition and cycle were central, developed new approaches to pulse and time that were soon taken up by musicians across the world. Rhythmic innovation and expertise came to form a significant part of African American and Afrodiasporic cultural identity and pride.

We have seen how swing feel came to dominate Western popular music. But the 1960s saw an equivalent shift back from swing to even-quaver feels. As Stewart (2000) describes, shuffle and swung rhythms were still central to the Black popular music newly dubbed rhythm and blues (R & B) in the early 1950s, as a hit like Big Joe Turner's 'Honey Hush' (1953) shows. But by the 1960s, African American musicians and their disciples were tending to straighten out their triplets. This was a gradual shift: so gradual, indeed, that on R & B and rock 'n' roll recordings of that time – Elvis Presley's 'Hound Dog', Little Richard's 'Long Tall Sally' (both 1956) – some band members can be heard playing even, while others play shuffle. On James Brown's 'Think' (1960), the whole band plays a finely calibrated compromise between the two feels.

- James Brown and the Famous Flames, 'Think' (Federal, 1960)

By the mid-1960s, Brown's basic rhythmic approach was even rather than swung. The new attitude soon begat a new genre descriptor: funk. In this style, as Stewart writes, the semiquaver was the basic unit, whether played or implied. And crucially, the first beat of the bar – the 'one' – became the stressed focal point, 'permitting deviations from the accented second and fourth beats (backbeats) and offbeat eighth notes [quavers] found in jazz and R & B shuffles'. This newly liberated, syncopated play filled the last three beats of the 4/4 bar and was found in the bass and other instruments as much as drums.

- Marva Whitney, 'What Do I Have to Do to Prove My Love to You' (King, 1968)

Certainly, new swung rhythms continued to appear, notably the reggae 'one-drop' of the 1960s and 1970s, with its heavy emphasis on beat 3 of the 4/4 bar and, often, an implied 12/8 shuffle underneath.

- Bob Marley and the Wailers, 'Trenchtown Rock' (Tuff Gong, 1971)

Yet 'even' feels and a strong backbeat by now defined a great many popular styles, such as the soul of Motown, or rock. The latter form was identified with white musicians and mass audiences, and was by the second half of the 1960s the defining style of mainstream youth culture. But, as with swing, decades before, rock still evinced its Afrodiasporic rhythmic roots at every turn. Nicole Biamonte (2014) shows how the phrase structuring and syncopation practices in 'classic' rock of the 1960s and 1970s – she analyses songs by the Beatles, Black Sabbath, Kansas – were based on clave and the 3+3+2 *tresillo*, even though those terms were alien to rock terminology. Biamonte's analysis reveals cultural relations, and debts, that had vanished from view. What she calls the 'double tresillo' – in which a phrase is grouped 3+3+3+3+2+2 – can be heard in jazz from the 1930s and in rock from the 1970s and 80s, as in this example:

- AC/DC, 'For Those About to Rock' (from *For Those About to Rock*, Albert, 1981)

Rock developed into a form in which sonic experiment was highly valued (➔Chapter 5, 'Work and Notation'). Leading groups like the Beatles and the Beach Boys had made much use of irregular phrase structures, but in the late 1960s, musicians developed these practices into a self-consciously modernist irregularisation of metre. Biamonte's corpus analysis of Beatles songs shows the band introducing metric shifts and juxtapositions around the experimental high point of *The Beatles* (known as the 'White Album', 1968); the form dubbed 'progressive rock' – represented in the early 1970s by groups like Pink Floyd and Yes, and later to inform the work of bands like Rush and Radiohead in the 1980s and 1990s – made extensive use of odd (5/4, 7/4) and quickly changing metres (Covach 1997).

- The Beatles, 'Martha My Dear' (from *The Beatles*, Parlophone, 1968)
- Yes, 'Close to the Edge' (from *Close to the Edge*, Atlantic, 1972)
- Pink Floyd, 'Money' (from *The Dark Side of the Moon*, Harvest, 1973)
- Radiohead, 'Pyramid Song' (from *Amnesiac*, Parlophone, 2001)

Groove and the Machine

The term 'groove' had been in use among jazz musicians since the first decades of the twentieth century. Through soul and funk – in which groove was often the topic of a song's lyrics, as well as its rhythmic driver – the term was further popularised in the 1960s and 1970s (Danielsen 2006). But defining groove has been as tricky for commentators as the definition of 'swing' had been. Jazz drummer Charli Persip's explanation, made to ethnomusicologist Paul

Berliner (1994: 349), would have rung true for many: 'When you get into that groove, you ride right down with that groove with no strain and no pain – you can't lay back or go forward.' Rhythmic interlocking between musicians, dancers and listeners, a sense not just of urgent forward motion but of solidity and inevitability: that was 'groove'. When that interlocking failed, when the motion seemed sloppy or sluggish, the groove was not happening.

However, a number of scholars studying rhythm in Afrodiasporic dance forms have suggested that groove is, in fact, not reliant on the total co-ordination (or 'entrainment') of, say, drums, bass, horns and feet. Instead, what the ethnomusicologist Charles Keil (Keil and Feld 1994) called 'participatory discrepancy' – that is, the micro-rhythmic rub between the anticipated pulse and its articulation, the slight but vital feeling of 'laying back', or 'playing on top' of the beat – this is what, for Keil and others, made jazz, soul, funk and other kinds of Afrodiasporic music groove.

These precepts were called into question from the 1970s by the increasingly widespread adoption of new rhythm technologies, principally the drum machine and sequencer. Here, there were not necessarily any 'people' to co-ordinate, and those machines knew little nuance – they did not play in front of or behind the beat but snapped it out in regulated (or 'quantised') perpetuity. In the early 1980s, these machines became central to the sound and development of genres like electro, synth pop, house and techno, the latter building on 1970s disco's 'four-on-the-floor' kick-drum demarcation of the 4/4 bar (➔Chapter 8, 'Instruments').

- Donna Summer, 'Bad Girls' (from *Bad Girls*, Casablanca, 1979)
- Cybotron, 'Clear' (Fantasy, 1983)
- Depeche Mode, 'Everything Counts' (from *Construction Time Again*, Mute, 1983)
- Rhythim Is Rhythim, 'Nude Photo' (Transmat, 1987)

Audiences and dancers knew – and later, the musicologist Mark Butler (2006: 76–116) would show – how electronic dance music producers were layering rhythmic patterns in ways that played with the expectations of what was almost always 4/4 metre. But many commentators railed against what they saw as music's dehumanising. The rock critic Ian MacDonald (2003) bemoaned the 'radical absence of innerness in modern dance music' owed to the drum machine and sequencer, suggesting that this was music by robots, for robots. Yet it was their very distance from analogue instruments and human performance – their novel, futuristic sound – that made them apt for experimental adoption by popular musicians. In hip-hop from the late 1980s to early 1990s, stark, high-impact drum machine kick and snare sounds – which leant their name to the form's onomatopoeic 'boom-bap' sound – were often paired with flowing, sampled drum fills and loops from older Afrodiasporic styles.

- MC Lyte, 'MC Lyte Likes Swinging' (from *Lyte as a Rock*, First Priority, 1988)
- Pete Rock and C. L. Smooth, 'They Reminisce over You (T. R. O. Y.)' (from *Mecca and the Soul Brother*, Elektra, 1992)

To the end of the century and beyond, musicians exploited the characteristics of the technology to take rhythm in directions that spoke of a new relationship between human touch and machinic ability. By the late 1990s, musicians who had grown up in the 1980s with newly technologised rhythm – but who themselves played traditional rhythm instruments – were developing styles that imitated and reframed the sound of the drum machine. Many such examples can be heard in D'Angelo's album *Voodoo* (2000). D'Angelo (b. 1974) directed drummer and producer Questlove to play the drums in an imitation, 'non-quantized' style (King 2013), and this 'crooked' approach gave rise to a rhythmic lope that would become much used across R & B and hip-hop in the first years of the twenty-first century.

- D'Angelo, 'Left and Right' (from *Voodoo*, Virgin, 2000)

Anne Danielsen (2010b) has used spectrograms like the one shown in Figure 6.8 to analyse recordings so as to get a precise view of these phenomena. In her analysis of 'Left and Right', Danielsen remarks on the comparatively large discrepancies between the point at which bass drum and rhythm guitar articulate the pulse; while notionally occurring at the same point in the bar, in fact a significant amount of time, shown by the highlighted area below, elapses between drum and guitar attacks. Danielsen writes that this asynchronisation will often sound incongruous at first, but will then seem to fade as the listener becomes accustomed to a much wider 'beat shape' – in other words, as the listener enters into the specific groove the music offers.

Conclusion

In a 1998 lecture, 'Rap, Minimalism and Structures of Time in Late Twentieth-Century Culture', musicologist Susan McClary pondered the prevalence of pulse and cyclic repetition in music of very different kinds at the century's end. Yet she was wary of ascribing some single motive to the use of repetition in styles as different as rap and minimalist composition. McClary argued that, rather than the product of a single cultural

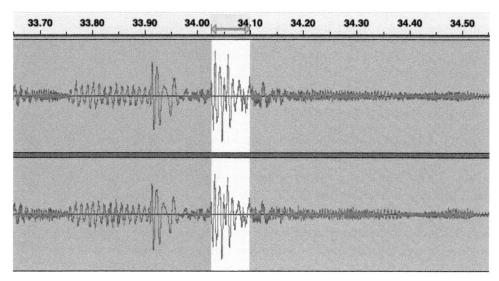

Figure 6.8 Spectrogram representation of D'Angelo's 'Left and Right' (2000)

phenomenon, the widespread presence of rhythmic repetition was the result of a complex intertwining of music traditions that we have seen spreading across the world: Afrodiasporic and Indian classical music techniques, the modernist recuperation of folk music drive and the conceptual approaches taken by minimalist composers (McClary 2004).

But if the phenomena observed by McClary seemed central to the world's musics at late century, perhaps it was because they always had been: only during art music's modernist moment had rhythmic rupture, disjunction and discontinuity become a subject of interest. Asking why these repetitious uses of rhythm were suddenly everywhere might betray the fact that that Western canon, and its particular stylistic concerns, had – temporarily, and to certain people – come to overshadow a much broader, global music history of continual pulse and propulsion. Yet McClary was surely right to say that this shared rhythmic concern was now of a fundamentally different order. If widely dispersed cultures had long built their musics on repetition and the cyclical, then the twentieth century – with its recordings and radio, its transcontinental journeys and intercultural borrowings – brought all those practices into closer and more productive contact than ever before.

7 | Harmony

Harmony is a very large area of musical debate and practice. As with our previous chapter on 'Rhythm and Time' (→Chapter 6), we must begin with a brief definition. In popular usage, the word 'harmony' often refers to something pleasurable, calming and consonant: think of 'sweet harmony' or 'peace and harmony'; things are also good when they are 'harmonious'. In this chapter, however, 'harmony' will be used in a more pragmatic way to refer to the sound of two or more pitches sounding together to create intervals and chords, and the various practices developed by musicians to organise those chords, not only in isolation from one another but also in larger networks to create harmonic languages and musical structures. Nevertheless, those popular idioms reveal something of harmony's potential to invoke ideological, social and even political systems of value, and it is these that will be the subject of this chapter.

These are big issues, but how they play out can be illustrated through a small example. For this, we turn to a form of African American amateur music-making that emerged around the 1890s in Florida and across the American South and that had at the heart of its sound a single chord: the major triad with an added minor seventh (Figure 7.1). This was barbershop music, so named for the informal spaces, such as barbershops, out of which it emerged. In Western art music this chord is known as a dominant seventh and has a very particular function in creating tension that needs to be resolved by a move to the tonic (as, for example, at a perfect cadence). As Frédéric Döhl (2014) argues, however, in its guise as the so-called barbershop chord, the chord was used within African American vocal and instrumental groups for its specific sound qualities, and not for any functional role. The practice of adding non-functional sevenths like this was known as 'cracking up a chord', the basic idea being 'to improvise, linger on, and bask in the immediate warmth of hair-raisingly unusual close-harmony chords' (Abbott 1992: 290). As Döhl shows, such chords

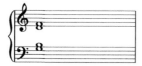

Figure 7.1 A typical 'barbershop' chord

could be heard in all forms of American music in the early twentieth century, both popular and classical, low and high, and African American and white: around 1900, 'the rise of the "barber shop chord" as a harmonic style and its name as a musical term took place on every level as an all-American musical phenomenon' (2014: 131).

Much later, the harmonic style characterised by the barbershop chord was absorbed into the genre of vocal music known as barbershop singing, an invented genre, codified in the 1940s through a culture of highly regulated singing competitions and dominated by white performers (often male, but not exclusively so). Here, the chord is ubiquitous (it is also known as the 'meat 'n' taters' chord) and serves as a defining characteristic of the genre: barbershop arrangers are even said to assert that songs should contain approximately 35 to 60 per cent dominant-seventh chords in order to sound authentic (Averill 1999: 44), and much of the artistry of barbershop singing lies in tuning these chords precisely. Indeed, barbershop quartets gain their particular timbre (and, according to their practitioners, a quasi-spiritual power) from singing in just intonation rather than equal temperament (the artificial division of the octave into twelve equal parts established in European art music in the eighteenth century): this is another example of the importance of harmony to the genre's identity and sense of value.

• The Mills Brothers, 'Sweet Adeline' (Decca, 1939)

Within this small example, then, we can see how harmony can play a role in determining musical, social and even ideological values (Averill 1999; Garnett 1999). Adding the seventh to a chord without sufficient preparation went against the principles of Western art music, where it would have been regarded as a dissonance; but in the barbershop context it becomes a focus of aesthetic pleasure and a means of distinguishing the genre and its values. This definitional function of harmony can be seen not only in the institutionally conservative world of barbershop singing but across many musical genres, including (especially, even) Western art music, jazz and rock. Inspired by African American barbershop musicians, this chapter follows a process of 'cracking up' the Western-art-music-dominated practices and assumptions around harmony that existed at the start of the century, along three lines: the expansion of harmonic resources that took place through the twentieth century, the effect this had on new kinds of musical form and genre, and the use of consonance and dissonance as a framework for defining and regulating musical value.

The chapter begins with the specific application and language of harmony known as tonality, or common-practice tonality, that defined Western art music through the eighteenth and nineteenth centuries, and one influential response to it represented by the music of Arnold Schoenberg (1875–1951). Schoenberg's music and theories – which we have already encountered in our chapter on →'Modernism', Chapter 2 – greatly expanded the harmonic resources available to composers in the early years of the twentieth century, but they also raised questions of musical value that were debated throughout that century; the chapter considers next a series of responses and alternatives to this new ideological framework, including the implications for rock and popular music of alternative harmonic structures derived from the blues and other non-Western sources. We conclude with a consideration of the role harmony played in the twentieth century in shaping musicological discourse.

One note before we begin: this chapter cannot offer a comprehensive survey of harmonic practices as they were developed and used throughout the twentieth century, although it does offer brief summaries of some key examples. These are covered in more detail in other texts. For art music, writings on (and often by) individual composers are the best place to seek more specific information. Similar attention has also been given to the harmonic practices of some jazz musicians; see, for example, Martin (2012–13) and Waters (2016). More general surveys, for both classical and popular music, also exist; among the most useful of these are Russell (1953); Strunk (1988); Björnberg (1989/1984); Moore (1992); de Clercq and Temperley (2011); and Wörner, Schneider and Rupprecht (2012, 2017).

Art Music's Break from Tonality

Schoenberg was not the first art-music composer to cut ties with common-practice tonality. By the end of the nineteenth century, progressive composers – among them Richard Wagner (1813–83) and Franz Liszt (1811–86) – were using all twelve notes of the chromatic scale in elaborations so rich that the hierarchy of interval relations that underpins common-practice tonality was almost completely obscured. Wagner's opera *Tristan und Isolde* (1857–9), with the famous 'Tristan chord' of its prelude, stretched the inherent tensions of the tonal system to unprecedented limits (those tensions are reflected in the sheer number of attempts that have been made to analytically define this chord's tonal function, a summary of which can be found in Nattiez 1990/1987: 216–29), while occasional pieces like Liszt's *Bagatelle sans tonalité* (1885) hinted at the possibility of music detached entirely from a tonal centre. By the start of the twentieth century Claude Debussy and Charles Ives (1874–1954), whom we will discuss further shortly, as well as Alexander Scriabin (1872–1915), were all writing works that had dispensed with tonality almost entirely.

Yet it was Schoenberg who took the most decisive (and, as we will see, self-conscious) steps towards formulating an alternative practice that could be generally applied. Schoenberg's early works, notably the mammoth cantata *Gurre-Lieder* (1900–10), are – like several works by Liszt or Wagner – in a late Romantic harmonic style rooted in tonal practice, albeit elaborately ornamented. With *Das Buch der hängenden Gärten* (1908–9), however, a song cycle on poems by Stefan George, Schoenberg completed his first work entirely without a central tonality. Schoenberg's preferred term for his new approach was 'pantonality', that is, music that was not in any one key but in all of them at once. Nevertheless, it would become more commonly known (with disparaging implications) as atonality, or (acknowledging its non-systematic basis) free atonality. The debate over terminology already hints at the ideological undercurrents at work: pantonality stresses an elaboration and extension of existing practice and tradition; atonality suggests a complete rejection of the past and an undesirable radicalism.

As he moved further away from tonality, Schoenberg was presented with two challenges. The first was to find an alternative way to coherently structure large-scale forms. One advantage of common-practice tonality is that it establishes a 'home' key – the tonic – as well as a hierarchy of degrees of distance from it that can be used to create structures that move away from, and then back towards the tonic. Before Schoenberg, this network of connections was what underpinned the forms of Western art music, from the counterpoint of Bach to the sonatas and symphonies of Mozart and Beethoven and the operas of Wagner. In the absence of this tonal hierarchy, many of Schoenberg's earliest atonal works – the *5 Pieces for Orchestra* (1909), *6 Little Piano Pieces* (1911) – are very short, or they rely on a text to provide formal coherence, as in the monodrama *Erwartung*

(1909). The fact that music for stage or screen can draw coherence from its dramatic context helps explain why a musical, for example, may be stylistically more diverse than any symphony: examples such as *West Side Story* (1957, music by Leonard Bernstein), *Fiddler on the Roof* (1964, music by Jerry Bock), *Into the Woods* (1986, music by Stephen Sondheim) or *Starlight Express* (1984, music by Andrew Lloyd Webber) move fluidly between pop, jazz, dance and classical idioms of different eras and origins. Indeed, as Scott McMillin suggests in his pioneering study *The Musical as Drama* (2006), the ability of characters to break into spontaneous song without the need for those songs' integration into a larger Wagnerian (i.e., harmonic) plan is one of the characteristic features of the musical. The power of story to give form to music also partly explains why dissonant harmonic languages have received much wider acceptance in film than in concert music. Influenced by the mid-century modernism of Stravinsky and Bartók, the scores written by Bernard Herrmann (1911–75) for Alfred Hitchcock's films (notably *Vertigo* (1958) and *Psycho* (1960)) are exemplary, as is the use by Stanley Kubrick (1928–99) of even later concert music by Krzysztof Penderecki and György Ligeti in his films *2001: A Space Odyssey* (1968), *The Shining* (1980) and *Eyes Wide Shut* (1999).

The limitations on formal coherence that atonality presented to purely instrumental music are what led Schoenberg in the 1920s to develop the 'twelve-tone method' of composition that we encountered in our chapter on →'Modernism' (Chapter 2). Having devised his new method, Schoenberg's second challenge was to legitimise the radicalism of his approach in the face of public incomprehension and rejection. As one of the century's first and most prolific composer-theorists (among those who followed were Messiaen (1944 and 1949–92), Harry Partch (1979), Stockhausen (1963–2017) and James Tenney (1964)), Schoenberg used his writings as a way to provide historical context and justification for innovations that struggled to command widespread audience acceptance. His *Theory of Harmony* (*Harmonielehre*, 1983/1911) remains an important textbook, although it does not yet deal extensively with post-tonal harmony, and three more books were published posthumously: *Structural Functions of Harmony* (1954), *Preliminary Exercises in Counterpoint* (1963) and *Fundamentals of Musical Composition* (1967). Most forceful of all is the retrospective essay 'Composition with Twelve Tones' (1984/ 1941), in which he argues for the 'necessity' of his method of twelve-tone (or serial) composition from the basis of harmony, and the musical equivalence of dissonances and consonances, leading to his famous and loaded description of 'the emancipation of the dissonance'. Through texts such as these; the music of his students, particularly Alban Berg (1885–1935) and Anton von Webern (1883–1945); the support of some of the century's most important critics, including Theodor Adorno (1903–69; see 2007/1947) and Carl Dahlhaus (1987); and his music itself, Schoenberg is remembered as one of the greatest influences on post-tonal harmonic practice.

As we have already seen, Schoenberg sought to emphasise the continuity of his own practice with that of the nineteenth century rather than its modernistic rupture. As he left tonality behind, he considered it nonsensical to think of 'consonance' and 'dissonance' as opposing forces, the latter a mere decoration of the former. Atonality, and later serialism, was thus the logical continuation of a process that had begun in the late nineteenth century:

> The ear had gradually become acquainted with a great number of dissonances, and so had lost the fear of their 'sense-interrupting' effect. One no longer expected preparations for Wagner's dissonances or resolutions of Strauss's discords; one was not disturbed by Debussy's non-functional harmonies, or by the harsh counterpoint of later composers ... The term *emancipation of the dissonance* refers to its comprehensibility, which is considered equivalent to the consonance's comprehensibility. A style based on this premise treats dissonances like consonances and renounces a tonal centre. (Schoenberg 1984/1941: 216–17)

Yet in practice Schoenberg unlocked a series of oppositions that mark out the territory on which many of the aesthetic battles of the twentieth century would be fought, and that align with many of the recurring themes of this book: complexity vs. simplicity, high art vs. low pop, European vs. non-European, revolution vs. reaction and legacy vs. ephemerality. From a harmonic viewpoint, all of these oppositions – despite Schoenberg's 'emancipation' – might be aligned with the enduring harmonic opposition of dissonance and consonance. We will return to this opposition throughout this chapter as a way of interpreting a range of musical aesthetics and ideologies.

Case Study 7.1: Harmony after Debussy

As they were for Schoenberg, twentieth-century debates about the relative progressiveness or radicalism of a musician's work were frequently framed around the relative complexity of their harmonic language. The more chromatic that harmony – the further it departed from the consonant intervals of the major or minor third – the more advanced it was considered to be. Yet dissonance was not the only way in which

Case Study 7.1: (cont.)

twentieth-century modernity could be expressed. Counterexamples are rife within popular music, from the rhythm-and-blues riffs of Bo Diddley (1928–2008) to the stabbing keyboard loops of Detroit techno pioneer Frankie Knuckles (1955–2014). Within art music, a prominent alternative is offered by Claude Debussy (1862–1918).

Although Debussy has been acclaimed as one of the most important composers of the turn of the century (➔Chapter 2, 'Modernism') he was only moderately successful in his lifetime. Despite winning the Prix de Rome in 1884, widespread recognition came only eight years later, with his anti-Wagnerian opera *Pelléas et Mélisande*; this was followed by years of personal scandal and then a final decade grappling with ill health, the breakdown of his second marriage and the onset of World War I. As Matthew Brown argues, although Debussy's career was distinguished, 'his legacy must also be judged in terms of his impact on other composers' (2012: 2) – an impact that extends surprisingly broadly, as Brown shows, up to the present day.

That impact (which is also explored in Johnson 2020) can be keenly felt in his approach to harmony and form. As we have already outlined, Debussy's approach may be summarised as an 'impressionistic' interest in surfaces and sensuality, and a separation of tonality's vocabulary (its chords) from its grammar (its deployment of those chords within a hierarchically organised system). This surface 'prettiness' was the source of many early critiques of Debussy's music: upon hearing *Pelléas* in 1907, no less a figure than Richard Strauss (1864–1949) remarked 'There's nothing in it. No music. It has nothing consecutive. No musical phrases. No development . . . There's not enough music in this work. Delicate harmonies, excellent orchestral effects, in very good taste. But it amounts to nothing, nothing at all' (quoted in Holloway 1979: 55). These same factors were at the heart of Adorno's criticism (2007/1947; see also Johnson 2020) that Debussy's musical language was unable to express the fragmentation of modernity.

Yet while Adorno's preferred branch of twentieth-century music to a great extent moved past harmony into serialism, Debussy represents the beginning of another strand of harmony-based modernism, one that resists the opposition of tonal/atonal. Only after World War II, when the composer and conductor Pierre Boulez (1926–2016) brought together the influences of Debussy and the arch-serialist Webern, as he did in a lecture given at Darmstadt in 1955, could the implications of the older French composer's work for musical form begin to be fully appreciated and the legacy of his harmonic practice start to emerge.

Julian Johnson (2020) argues for an alternative (or supplementary) history of art music in the twentieth century that begins with Debussy. This would be a non-Schoenbergian (and non-Adornian) lineage in which the organisation of sound –

Case Study 7.1: (cont.)

rather than pitch – is paramount: 'The history of music "after Debussy" is thus one in which composers increasingly foreground the concrete particularity of sound' (13). That history would run from 'the primacy of sound in *musique concrète* and electronic music to the centrality of the body in the work of Helmut Lachenmann or Mauricio Kagel, from the imitation of natural processes in the music of Iannis Xenakis to the exploration of the borders of silence in the work of Morton Feldman and Giacinto Scelsi' (11).

- Pierre Schaeffer (1910–95), *Etude aux chemins de fer* (1948)
- Iannis Xenakis (1922–2001), *Herma* (1961)
- Giacinto Scelsi (1905–88), *Xnoybis* (1965)
- Helmut Lachenmann (b. 1935), *Pression* (1969–70)

Johnson's list focuses on art music – and to it might be added Debussy's impressionistic colleague Maurice Ravel (1875–1937) and the spectral analysis of timbre as a source of compositional material in the music of Gérard Grisey (1946–98) and Tristan Murail (b. 1947) – but examples of Debussy's influence can be found elsewhere. Among the most important of these is a strand of jazz impressionism that began with the work of artists such as Bix Beiderbecke (1903–31) and Duke Ellington (1899–1974). The titles of Beiderbecke's piano songs 'Candlelights', 'Flashes' and 'In a Mist' already nod towards Debussy's own piano music, an allusion strengthened by their use of parallel chords and repeated gestures that seem to float free of any tonal organisation. Ellington was introduced to Debussy's music by the African American composer and arranger Will Vodery (1885–1951), best known for his work on Jerome Kern and Oscar Hammerstein's *Show Boat* (1927). On Vodery's recommendation, Ellington conducted the William McGuire Broadway musical *Show Girl* (1929), for which Vodery had provided orchestrations of George Gershwin's music. It was through this experience that Ellington came to know the orchestrational and harmonic techniques of Debussy and Ravel, which Vodery was greatly influenced by. That influence may be heard on the slower, more atmospheric style and airy textures of Ellington's recordings of the early 1930s, most notably his own composition 'Mood Indigo'. Meanwhile, the stride pianist James P. Johnson (1894–1955) would in 1929 record his piece 'You've Got to Be Modernistic', a piece in which the whole-tone and parallel harmony so beloved of Debussy and his French colleagues was subjected to massive rhythmic disruption, as it is in the 1933 recording made by Fletcher Henderson (1897–1952) of Coleman Hawkins' piece 'Queer Notions'. Highlighted in these pieces, and their titles, was an eager fascination with the new – represented here by Debussian harmonies – and with the convention-breaking use of techniques radically unfamiliar to the form.

Case Study 7.1: (cont.)

- Bix Beiderbecke, 'Candlelights' (1930)
- Duke Ellington, 'Mood Indigo' (1930)
- James P. Johnson, 'You've Got to be Modernistic' (Brunswick, 1929)
- Fletcher Henderson Orchestra, 'Queer Notions' (Vocalion, 1933)

Partly due to Ellington's own significance as a composer, orchestrator and performer, Debussy's influence on jazz continued through to the end of the century. As Brown notes, musicians from Chick Corea (1941–2021) to Branford Marsalis (b. 1960) have cited that influence, or recorded versions of Debussy's music (Brown 2012: 3–4). What is clear is that, contrary to Schoenberg's view, embracing consonance has proved no barrier to either historic legacy or high-art legitimacy, and atonality is not a prerequisite of modernity. Furthermore, there is no clear relationship between these and a dichotomy of European and non-European musics: musicians in both traditions have explored related ideas and influenced each other across that putative divide.

Lingering Tonalities

Despite Schoenberg's efforts – and despite the symbolic value often given to atonality and serialism in histories of the twentieth century – in the event it was only the 'common practice', rather than the 'tonality' of common-practice tonality that composers abandoned. The formal coherence (as well as the sonic familiarity) offered by tonality proved hard to replace, and many composers throughout the century found ways instead to extend or elaborate it without deserting its underlying principles. Reactionary or nostalgic post- (or anti-) modernism may account for tonality's continuing presence in the work of composers such as David Del Tredici (b. 1937) or Ellen Taaffe Zwilich (b. 1939) (although for discussion of tonality's reappearance in some more radical art-music contexts, see Mosch 2017). The cultural store of musical affects built up through the nineteenth-century symphonic and operatic traditions also account for its presence in scores written for film, TV and musical theatre, which often rely on an emotional synchronicity between dramatic action and musical score. In his scores for leading Hollywood films (among them *Jaws* (1975), *E. T.* (1982), *Schindler's List* (1993) and the *Star Wars* franchise (1977–2019), the composer John Williams (b. 1932) draws heavily on the music of Dvořák, Tchaikovsky and other nineteenth-century symphonists (as well as

Wagnerian leitmotivic technique; →Chapter 12, 'Music and the Moving Image'). As the popular success of composers like John Adams (b. 1947) and Philip Glass (b. 1937) further indicates, by the end of the century the modernist narrative of the exhaustion of tonality was itself becoming overtaken by a new delight in consonance and euphony, examples of which might have been heard at almost any point in the century.

- John Adams, *Grand Pianola Music* (1981)

Nevertheless, many adaptations of tonality still took place within the same framework of oppositions as underpinned the modernist project – or they were interpreted in that way by scholars and critics. Philip Rupprecht gets to the heart of the matter with his identification of a style he calls 'triadic modernism' in the early music of Benjamin Britten (1913–76), one of the most prominent tonal composers of the mid-century (Rupprecht 2012). However, Rupprecht's term points to a critical anxiety around triadic and consonant harmony, such as Britten employs in mature works such as the *War Requiem* (1962) or his first opera, *Peter Grimes* (1945), as indications of a conservative or reactionary aesthetic – an anxiety that continued to accompany reactions to the music of Glass or Adams much later in the century. Rupprecht's analysis does not deny the essentially non-dissonant nature of Britten's music but emphasises by way of compensation the complexity of its harmonic relations and its legacy and influence at the start of the twenty-first century:

While for many writers in the Twenties and Thirties, the survival of a living tonal tradition seemed a distinctly open question in the face of the revolution of atonality, the landscape several decades later appears very different. ... Britten's shifting attitude to triadic consonance in the Thirties and beyond can shape our own evolving historical view of tonality as an expressive resource, the center of an old and a new art. (243)

In seeking a defence against those who would characterise Britten's music as reactionary, Rupprecht highlights the enduring logic of modernism and its dualistic framework of value.

Debussy's fellow countryman Olivier Messiaen (1908–92; see also →Chapter 6, 'Rhythm and Time') also retained elements of triadic and consonant harmony within his work, while also inventing a completely original harmonic practice. From a harmonic point of view, the most important element of his music is the self-invented system of 'modes of limited transposition': a set of seven scales made up of repeated units of tones and semitones. Because of their internal repetitions, these modes (unlike the conventional major or minor scales) can only be transposed a few times before they duplicate themselves. They give Messiaen's music a distinct harmonic character while avoiding the extremes of expressionistic free atonality or over-regulated serialism. They also create a harmonic language that can be overtly appealing without depending on the goal-directed structures of common practice tonality: diatonic chords remain part of Messiaen's harmonic vocabulary, but they are removed from their conventional tonal context (see Neidhöfer 2005 for an analytic approach to this matter) and are treated equally to chords of much more dissonant character (as in Figure 7.2). Often indulgently sensual, and full of non-European influences, Messiaen's harmonic language is far removed from Schoenberg's self-conscious dissonances. Yet the theoretical basis he contrives for it (asserted in his 1944 treatise *Technique de mon langage*

Figure 7.2 Olivier Messiaen, 'Prière du Christ montant vers son Père', from *L'Ascension* for orchestra (1932–3), bars 1–3. Copyright © 1932 Editions Musicales Alphonse Leduc All Rights Reserved. International Copyright Secured. Reproduced by kind permission of Hal Leonard Europe Ltd.

musicale) has ensured its assessment in terms of revolution, legacy and complexity, in spite of its frequent consonance; as with Britten, musicologists (see, e.g., Bernard 1986; Neidhöfer 2005) – this time with the collusion of the composer himself – have sought to expand the definition of modernity in order to legitimise the consonant or tonal aspects of their subject's practice.

- Olivier Messiaen, 'Prière du Christ montant vers son Père', from *L'Ascension* for orchestra (1932–3)

Outside Europe, the American Charles Ives (1874–1954) pursued a still different course. As a young composer, he experimented thoroughly with forms of polytonality (the simultaneous use of more than one key), but always in search of new forms of unity and consonance, rather than opposition and dissonance. Ives' music is dense with quotation, allusion and paraphrase (described exhaustively in Burkholder 1995), but he also employed systematic methods such as inversion and augmentation as well as structural models such as wedges and palindromes (Lambert 1997). In these respects his methods were similar to the atonal and serial practices of Schoenberg, Berg and Webern. At times Ives even pre-empted developments in Europe. *The Unanswered Question* of 1906, characterised by Leonard Bernstein as a portrayal of post-tonal uncertainty, was written two years before *Das Buch der hängenden Gärten* and has some claim to be the first atonal composition. Yet like Messiaen's, Ives' music does not easily fit the Schoenbergian view of musical evolution through the emancipation of dissonance. In fact, he rejected the necessity of the tonal/atonal dualism: 'Why tonality as such should be thrown out for good, I can't see', he wrote. 'Why it should be always present, I can't see. It depends, it seems to me . . . on what one is trying to do, and on the state of mind, the time of day or other accidents of life' (quoted in Lambert 1996: 106). As Magee notes (2008: 103), Ives' experiments in collage and polytonality – formal principles remote from Schoenberg's late Romantic origins – were 'a crucial part of questioning and circumventing the European tradition'.

- Charles Ives, *The Unanswered Question* (1906)

Alternative Practices

Let us return to the first of Schoenberg's two challenges: how to create musical structure without the network of harmonic relationships provided by tonality. Without tonality as a support, composers after Schoenberg pursued a variety of different ways in which to establish musical unity and coherence. Serialism, as we have seen, was one approach, with its own radical implications for musical form. Others included forms of symmetry, such as those mentioned in the music of Messiaen but also present in the minor-third-based 'axis system' that Bartók used to create a form of functional harmony based upon the modality of south-eastern European folk music (described in Lendvai 1979), or the symmetrical twelve-tone harmonies of Witold Lutosławski (see Bodman Rae 1994). More radical examples include drones, as heard in some minimal music, for example, or alternative tuning systems, such as the just intonation systems used by Harry Partch (1901–74) and Ben Johnston (1926–2019) (see, e.g., Partch 1979; Johnston 2006). These examples lie far enough outside the tonally derived consonant/dissonant framework that they can be considered in entirely new terms. Johnston developed a practice based on the harmonic series, rather than equal temperament, using simple frequency ratios between pitches. Partch went further, however, using an application of the harmonic series to divide the octave into forty-three pitches, a move that required him to design and build entirely original instruments (some with Johnston's assistance) that could navigate this unique harmonic terrain.

- Ben Johnston, String Quartet no. 4 'Amazing Grace' (1973)
- Harry Partch, 'Exordium: The Beginning of a Web', from *Delusion of the Fury* (1964–6)

All these approaches might be seen as ways to replace the principle of the tonic chord with alternative forms of 'home' that can serve as points of departure and arrival, or mark degrees of continuity and difference. 'Home' tones or chords are present in much jazz and rock, even that which departs a long way from its generic norms, as in the drones that underlie John Coltrane's music of the early 1960s, for example, or the tonal recapitulation, reminiscent of classical sonata form, of Queen's 'Bohemian Rhapsody' (see Brown 2012). In jazz, the head motive often provides the pretext for a return to the home key. In rock it might be the riff. Both are sufficiently strongly identified to allow for elaborate harmonic and melodic departures that radically extend the underlying form without losing a sense of 'home'.

An important source here is the blues. As it is for Western art music, harmony is central to defining the blues as a musical aesthetic and genre. As well as the so-called blues scale, which tweaks the equally tempered scale with partially flattened 'blue notes' on its third, fifth and seventh degrees, fundamental to blues music is its twelve-bar harmonic progression. Yet although this can be described in terms recognisable to Western art music (as the chord sequence I–I–I–I–IV–IV–I–I–V–IV–I–I, one chord to a bar, where I is the tonic, IV the subdominant and V the dominant), it is distinct on at least three points. The first is its stasis: the drone-like emphasis on the tonic (making up eight of the twelve bars) is highly unusual; common-practice tonality tends to emphasis faster harmonic rhythms, and goal-directed harmonic patterns of tension and release. The second is its circularity: the twelve-bar blues is designed to be played as a loop, repeating for each chorus. Although harmonic loops of this kind are present in Western art music, they are rare in the common-practice era, fading out of use between the chaconne and passacaglia of the seventeenth and early eighteenth centuries and the minimalism of the late twentieth. The third point is perhaps the most telling. This is the emphasis on the subdominant (IV) as the second most important chord after the tonic: art-music tonality is based on the tonic–dominant (I–V) relationship, not the tonic–subdominant (I–IV). The harmonic language of the blues – its hierarchy of relationships between chords – is, therefore, fundamentally different from that of Western art music, no matter what else it may have in common.

As de Clercq and Temperley have shown in a corpus analysis of rock harmony from the 1950s to 1990s, it is the harmonic language of the blues, and in particular the tonic–subdominant relationship, that defines the language of rock music. (Just as harmonic practice in Western art music is closely related to instrument design, one reason for the emphasis on fourth-based harmonic relationships in the blues and later rock may be the fact that they are more idiomatic to the fourth-based tuning of the electric guitar; see Koozin 2011.) The role of modality and the de-emphasis of tonic–dominant relationships are also highlighted in an important early study by Alf Björnberg (1989/1984). Writing in the mid-1980s, Björnberg observes that rock harmony was frequently viewed by musicological theory (dominated as it was by the ideology of common-practice tonality) as of little significance, and that when it was discussed it was described as 'downright deficient, or more or less explicitly judged according to the standards of traditional functional harmony' (n. 1). This particular criticism is less relevant today, and harmony has become a focal point of musicological attention for rock music (just as it is for art music and jazz); yet the originality of Björnberg's study highlights the way in which rock tonality is considered differently from classical or functional tonality.

In place of functional tonality, Björnberg uses the term 'aeolian harmony' to describe a form of modal harmonic practice based on triads formed not from the major or minor scale (as in functional tonality), but from the aeolian mode: that is, chords i, ♭ iii, iv, v, ♭ VI, and ♭ VII. This system is tonal in the sense of being rooted on a tonic chord, but it lacks several defining features of common-practice tonality, notably the dominant-major chord essential to perfect cadences (V–I/i), and likewise the highly directional semitonal leading note–tonic melodic step that this contains. Instead, it relies predominantly on minor chords, with the semitone steps of the major scale replaced by whole tones that have a weaker need for stepwise resolution.

Björnberg's aeolian harmony covers a large amount of rock music from the 1960s and 1970s (examples from the 1980s, 1990s and more recently may also be found). The specifics of aeolian harmony are less significant than the conclusion that Björnberg draws, however. This is that the shift away from tonic–dominant relationships in rock, as outlined in his study and more comprehensively catalogued by de Clercq and Temperley twenty-five years later, encouraged chord progressions that were more static and more 'tension-less' (1989/1984: 4). This in turn enabled an explosion of the conventional song form within rock (and later pop and electronic music) as traditional tonal relationships and tensions no longer needed to be maintained. We can hear these relationships already being stretched in the Beatles' 'Ticket to Ride' (1964), in which the extended A-major tonic chord of the introduction and verse is briefly interrupted by a ii–V imperfect cadence into the chorus and then a V–I perfect cadence back to the opening riff. Yet by removing the inherent tensions of functional harmony altogether (often replacing them with pedals or drones, like those hinted at in 'Ticket to Ride', or looping patterns of three or four chords), musicians were able to focus on other musical parameters, such as rhythm or texture, as means to create structural patterns of tension and release.

- Martha Reeves and the Vandellas, 'Dancing in the Street' (Gordy, 1964)
- Rolling Stones, 'Sympathy for the Devil', from *Beggar's Banquet* (Decca, 1965)
- Led Zeppelin, 'Whole Lotta Love', from *Led Zeppelin II* (Atlantic, 1969)

By the end of the 1970s, the complete dissolution of song form that such static, tension-less, looping harmonies had created allowed for much more extended structures, no longer based on the verse–chorus alternations and tonic–dominant changes of conventional song form (although, as Everett

2004 argues, there was still a place for functional harmony in rock too). Such forms may be heard across a range of popular music genres, from disco to funk to the so-called Krautrock or kosmische music of German groups like Neu! and Kraftwerk. Within these static harmonic fields, other forms of variation were possible, often straying far from the song's establishing riff and extending across long periods without risking any loss of formal coherence.

- Neu! 'Für Immer', from *Neu! 2* (Grönland, 1973)
- Donna Summer (1948–2012), 'I Feel Love' (Patrick Cowley Mega Mix) (Casablanca, 1982)
- Sonic Youth, 'Total Trash, from *Daydream Nation* (Enigma/Blast First, 1988)

In the place of traditional song structures, alternative ways of creating musical anticipation and change emerged. Among these is what Mark Spicer (2004) has called 'accumulative form', in which harmonic stasis combines with the controlled addition and subtraction of individual parts enabled by multitrack recording to draw the listener into the unfolding musical process. Although it is possible, as Spicer argues, to create moments of musical culmination when the various layers of a groove all come together, more often accumulative forms provide a series of points of interest by permutating the various layers that are available. Spicer's references come from rock music from the 1970s to 2000s, but the technique was especially characteristic of garage, house and techno music from the 1980s onwards. Using multitrack sequencers, DJs and producers composed music in series of stratified layers that could be juxtaposed in a potentially endless and always varied range of combinations – as well as overlaid with parts from other records, the basis of the seamless DJ mix that emerged in the New York dance clubs of the 1980s.

- Jesse Saunders (b. 1962), 'On & On' (Jes Say, 1983)
- Manuel Göttsching (b. 1952), *E2–E4* (In Team, 1984)
- Orbital, 'Lush 3-1', 'Lush 3-2' and 'Impact (The Earth Is Burning)', from *Orbital 2* (Internal, 1993)

Around the same time as the rise of disco, kosmische and house, the dissolution of harmonic tension that accompanied the turn away from functional tonality was also encouraging the exploration of static and elongated forms within art music. Many works by Morton Feldman (1926–87) of the late 1970s and 1980s are very long (several last more than an hour; String Quartet No. 2 (1983) can last up to six hours without pause), a feat made possible in large part by their non-hierarchical language of attractive harmonic fields and delicate instrumental gestures which can simply be extended or juxtaposed without the need for long-term harmonic planning. Feldman's late works contain a lot that sounds like repetition, but are carefully written so as not to be strictly repetitive (*Crippled Symmetry*, the title of his 1983 trio for flute, percussion and piano, is indicative of his compositional aesthetic at this time). As a consequence, his music retains an air of erudition (partly due also to the high degree of precision and concentration required to perform such regulated non-repetition) that maintains its high-art status. However, it was the minimalist composers of a younger generation, such as Philip Glass (b. 1937), Steve Reich (b. 1936) and La Monte Young (b. 1935) (→Chapter 6, 'Rhythm and Time'), who were able to merge the post-tonal harmonic stasis and experimental aesthetics that Feldman was exploring with the riff-like repetitions and tension-less, immersive sounds of popular and non-Western musics. These were composers who had grown up in the 1950s and 1960s listening to jazz, R & B and rock (in Young's case, offering a direct influence too, through his association with the Velvet Underground's John Cale), as well as music from India, South East Asia and West Africa, thanks to the emergence of ethnographic recordings during this time. Few musical styles better demonstrate how the move towards non-functional, modal harmony – and away from functional or common-practice tonality and atonal dissonance – offered a way to break down the ideological separation of art and popular musics, a fact supported by the wide influence minimalist composers have subsequently had on popular music.

Case Study 7.2: Destiny's Child and *Fin-de-Siècle* Tonality

Rock modality emerged as an alternative to what until then had been a hegemonic norm of functional tonality. Yet as that modality itself became a norm it is not surprising to find examples of functional (or functional-like) tonality emerging in response. One such example was the brief trend in the music of female R & B artists in the 1990s such as TLC, Destiny's Child, Pink and Britney Spears for highly functional chord patterns and voice-leading borrowed directly from common-practice tonality. As with barbershop's 'cracking' of harmony through the addition of dominant-seventh chords a century before, the sounds of common-practice tonality were here repurposed or even signified upon by Black musicians or those influenced by Black music. This time, the language of tonality was used as a symbol of prestige and distinction to serve an image of empowered femininity.

Case Study 7.2: (cont.)

Pop has always co-opted sound worlds in its shaping and chasing of new trends. By the end of the century – thanks in part to sampling and in part to an increasing need to make products that grabbed listeners' attention within a crowded soundscape – it had become especially adept at such borrowings. Among the most notable examples was the emergence of South Asian bhangra tropes in the mid-1990s. Spears again offers an example ('Toxic'); see also Missy Elliott's 'Get Ur Freak On', as well as the popular success achieved by actual South Asian artists such as Punjabi MC. The late-1990s use of common-practice tonality may be heard as another example of this phenomenon, and its borrowed status is only reinforced by a baroque-like sound world of (synthesised) harpsichord and string arpeggios.

These elements are particularly clear in 'Bills, Bills, Bills' (1999) by Destiny's Child, an American girl group comprising Beyoncé Knowles, Kelly Rowland and Michelle Williams. The group's fourth single, and their first US no. 1, it was taken from their second album *The Writing's on the Wall*. Notably, the song was co-written by husband-and-wife team Kevin 'She'kspere' Briggs and Kandi Burruss, among whose other credits are P!nk's 'There You Go' and TLC's 'No Scrubs'. All three songs were released between February and July 1999, beginning with 'No Scrubs' – the biggest hit of the three. All three share a musical language of baroque-like string timbres, arpeggiated chords, jittery R & B rhythms and lyrics of female empowerment and self-determination.

- TLC, 'No Scrubs' (LaFace, 1999)
- Pink (b. 1979), 'There You Go' (LaFace, 1999)
- Destiny's Child, 'Bills, Bills, Bills' (Columbia, 1999)

'Bills, Bills, Bills' is about financial independence (a theme to which Destiny's Child would return with their even bigger hit, 'Independent Woman', a year later). Fed up with her partner using her car and phone but not paying his way, the song's protagonist decides she has had enough and must leave him. This miniature story is played out in the song's harmony. The verses, in which the details of the situation are set out, are based around simple perfect cadence formulations. These are already notable because of their use of a major V–i cadence – common enough (textbook, even) within common-practice tonality but, as we have seen, rare in popular music. Emphasis of this leading note and its semitonal movement up to the tonic within the cadence aurally signifies 'classical' music more than 'pop' (or, European more than African American).

This impression is elaborated in the chorus. Over a chromatically descending bass, the harmony outlines a chain of imperfect cadences, each using a pivot note to move by a minor third: B minor–F ♯; A–E; G ... As the lyrics enumerate the protagonist's

Case Study 7.2: (cont.)

financial grievances (car, phone, etc.) the chain could continue indefinitely (. . . –D; F–
C; and so on). However, as the bass reaches the dominant, F ♯, we are abruptly brought
to a halt – the only moment in the song when the chord progression (G–F ♯) does not
follow common practice – and a sudden realisation: 'You and me are through'. With
another perfect cadence, F ♯–B minor, we are back to the verse's tonally rooted self-
assertions.

Chromatic descents like that in the chorus of 'Bills, Bills, Bills' are common
throughout the history of rock: two famous examples are Led Zeppelin's 'Stairway to
Heaven' and the Beatles' 'Michelle', both of which feature a progression sometimes
known as the 'minor drop'. However, the harmonisation of 'Bills, Bills, Bills' (shown in
Figure 7.3) owes more to baroque and classical practice, rooted in keyboard-based
tonality rather than fretboard modality. Indeed, a chromatic bassline that descends
a fourth from tonic to dominant such as this is known as a 'Lamento' bass and was
common in seventeenth- and eighteenth-century music (see, e.g., Caplin 2014).
Perhaps the most famous example is 'Dido's Lament' from Purcell's *Dido and
Aeneas*; the particular harmonisation of 'Bills, Bills, Bills' bears a closer resemblance
to that used by, for example, Vivaldi in his motet *O qui coeli terraque serenitas*,
although its use of movement across a minor third also incorporates post-baroque
harmonic practice such as found in Beethoven or Schubert – and indeed in later
adaptations, such as Led Zeppelin's 'Stairway to Heaven' (1972).

• Led Zeppelin, 'Stairway to Heaven' (Atlantic, 1972)

In any case, the immediate aural impression is of a distinctive sound that is
markedly removed from the norms of modally inflected rock and pop. Yet while
Briggs and Burruss' use of such motifs is no doubt partly commercially motivated –
'Bills, Bills, Bills' and 'There You Go' surely wished to build on the success of 'No
Scrubs' – it is not a meaningless appropriation made only for the sake of marketplace
distinction. The use of the lament motif deliberately draws upon musical affects
developed in the Western European classical tradition, resituated as a complaint
about financial exploitation and cathartic independence: harmonic practice used as
a way to reimagine Enlightenment-era values of stateliness, grace and autonomy
through a late twentieth-century feminist prism.

Figure 7.3 Harmonic reduction of chorus to Destiny's Child, 'Bills, Bills, Bills' (1999)

Harmony and Musicology

The example of 'Bills, Bills, Bills' highlights harmony's continuing potency as a carrier of musical affect in terms that can be analytically described and categorised. This power partly explains why harmony has been fundamental not only to the making of music in the twentieth century but also its study in musical analysis and musicology.

Harmony's role in shaping the discourse of twentieth-century music history is closely bound to the emergence of analytical musicology and its attendant skill sets, and with the significance of the notated score as the 'legitimate' form of musical documentation (➔Chapter 5, 'Work and Notation'). Pitch is the parameter that can be most completely represented in conventional musical notation (enharmonicity and microtonality notwithstanding). Timbre is almost impossible to notate with precision; dynamic is relative and highly subjective; and even rhythm is context-dependent – consider swing in jazz or rubato in Chopin. Pitch is also, at least within the context of equal temperament, the musical parameter most easily described in terms of discrete numerical values and therefore most susceptible to analysis: Allen Forte's (1926–2014) pitch-class set theory, a method of analysing atonal music via the use of numbers to represent pitch classes and relationships between them, is the paradigmatic example (Forte 1973). For these reasons, many of the most influential methods of musical analysis that developed in the twentieth century focused on harmony; consequently, a large amount of the musicological discourse based upon these analyses also concentrated on harmony as the most important musical parameter.

One of the most influential analytical methods developed in the twentieth century is that of the Austrian music theorist Heinrich Schenker (1868–1935). Schenkerian analysis is a method of reducing musical works to a limited number of underlying structural models, on the basis of common-practice principles of harmony and counterpoint. Although Schenker's method has been adapted by other theorists to a wide variety of contexts, it works best for compositions of the Austro-German classical school, from Bach to Brahms. This is not a coincidence: Schenker's goals were tied to early twentieth-century German nationalism, and his method is a self-fulfilling demonstration of the 'genius' of the Austro-German classical school. As Philip A. Ewell (2020) has explained, the intertwining of nationalism and racism with the theorisation of common-practice tonality that takes place within Schenker's theory (a link explicitly acknowledged by

Schenker himself) has become deeply embedded within twentieth- and twenty-first-century music theory itself; the robust reception Ewell's article received serves, if nothing else, to indicate how thoroughly absorbed those connections are.

Harmony – particularly the forms of goal-directed functional harmony that are characteristic of Western art music – is an arbiter of value in the work of another influential theorist writing a few decades later than Schenker, the American Leonard B. Meyer (1918–2007). Writing in the late 1950s, Meyer applied the then-new discoveries of information theory to the analysis of music, arguing for the importance of 'the arousal and subsequent inhibition' (1967: 5) of expectations as 'the psycho-stylistic conditions which give rise to musical meaning'. Pitch relationships, in Meyer's analysis, are where such expectations may be established; the relative probability of any given pitch appearing next (and the satisfaction or deferral of that expectation) is what creates meaning; meaning is, therefore, established by the surrounding harmonic context. The more richly these meanings are created and conveyed, Meyer argues (i.e., the more successfully expectations are created and deferred; or, in information theory terms, the greater the degree of redundancy within the message), the greater the work of music. That is to say, musical greatness is to be understood as a function of harmony; and non-harmonic music cannot be 'great'.

Harmony's extended legacy of analysis and its centrality to the identity of Western art music also made it a frequent site for new musicological critique towards the end of the century. The readings of sexual violence and sexual pleasure in the music of Beethoven, Madonna and Janika Vandervelde made by the musicologist Susan McClary (b. 1946) are grounded in harmonic analysis. Indeed, the title of the book in which those essays are collected, *Feminine Endings*, derives from what was a long-accepted categorisation of cadences into strong and masculine, and weak and feminine (→Chapter 13, 'Gender and Sexuality'). McClary's analyses originate in her observations that music theorists have gendered features of common-practice tonality for centuries: she notes a mid-eighteenth-century description of major and minor triads as, respectively, 'complete' and 'male', and 'not as complete . . . but also lovely and pleasant to hear' and 'female' (1991: 11), and a similar designation made more than a century-and-a-half later in Schoenberg's *Theory of Harmony* that 'The dualism presented by major and minor has the power of a symbol suggesting high forms of order: it reminds us of male and female and delimits the spheres of expression according to attraction and repulsion . . . The will of nature is supposedly fulfilled in them'

(Schoenberg 1983/1911: 96; quoted in ibid.). McClary and others have also examined historical descriptions of Schubert's chromatic, third-led harmonies (against the dominant-tonic patterns of Beethoven) as attempts to regulate alternative masculinities and sexualities in post-Enlightenment Europe (McClary 2006; see also Kramer 1998, esp. ch. 4, and Clark 2011: 56–145; for related arguments in a different context, see Fred E. Maus on the Pet Shop Boys, 2001; also →Chapter 13, 'Gender and Sexuality'). And, as we have already seen (→Chapter 2, 'Modernism'), Catherine Parsons Smith has demonstrated how new modes of musical discourse requiring insider knowledge – such as the treatises on harmonic practice that were invariably written by men – developed in resistance to the emergence of feminism after World War I. Serialism, writes Parsons Smith, 'with its claims to have superseded romantic concepts of melody and harmony' (and their feminising influence), is an obvious example of such a discourse (1994).

The emphasis on harmony within the study of Western art music has led to it being given greater weight in studies of other musical practices too. Laurent Cugny's *Analyser le jazz* (2009), for example, devotes three chapters to harmony and only one each to 'rhythm' and 'form, sound, melody'. And when Forte turned his attention away from atonal art music to American popular ballads he began with a chapter on harmonic practice, which itself outlines the role of harmony in defining the style and genre under discussion: 'When we experience, as listeners or performers, the elegant popular ballads of the Golden Era we may be aware of a special sonic aura that emanates from the individual harmonies and their combinations' (Forte 1995: 6). Whether or not they study popular music, most music theorists, Robert Fink has suggested, 'tend to argue that it is the presence of coherent melodic and harmonic progressions that determines whether a musical work can organize experiential complexes of sound into the orderly, syntactic progressions of "linear musical time"' (2011: 182).

Conclusion

In his article 'Goal-Directed Soul? Analyzing Rhythmic Teleology in African American Popular Music', Fink outlines forcefully why a focus on harmony as music's principal structuring feature is problematic. Referring back to Meyer's information-theory-based teleological arguments (and, implicitly behind them, the analyses of Schenker), Fink argues for alternative theories of goal-direction that would allow similar notions of greatness and goal-direction to be applied to music that is rhythmically rather than harmonically determined. 'Meyer hypothesizes that information theory can distinguish between "sophisticated art music" and more "primitive" forms of musical expression [Fink notes that Meyer is probably referring here to rock 'n' roll], since the primitive rejects the complex patterns of tendency inhibition, favouring "immediate gratification" of his impulses' (Fink 2011:188). Because 'groove-based music' – Fink's term – is supposedly unable to create patterns of tension and release (an assertion that relies upon the racialised opposition of European music as harmonic, sophisticated and intellectual, and African music as rhythmic, spontaneous and bodily), it is accorded lesser value in this framework, he argues. 'Secondary parameters like beat and groove are of course highly variable in this music, but these variations have not been conceptualized by most hermeneutics as having goal-directed syntax, which is a structuring potential usually reserved, even within popular-music scholarship, for pitch relationships' (183). Fink's own analyses of late 1960s soul and Motown, which combine close musical readings with a detailed social history, show the untenability of this position. And they restate once more the potency of harmony as a carrier of ideology that was its story throughout the twentieth century.

8 | Instruments

'I happen to think that computers are the most important thing to happen to musicians since the invention of cat-gut which was a long time ago' (Moog, in Williamson 1990). Electronic music pioneer Robert Moog's (1934–2005) words point to the two main stories of instrument development in the twentieth century. One was concerned with newness and saw traditional instruments undergo transformation through extended performance techniques, electrification and amplification and the creation of brand-new devices. Equally radical, the other was concerned with the past. Focusing on preservation, it saw renewed interest in ancient and early instrument restoration (and a return to cat-gut strings), performance practice and musicological research. While it is tempting to establish a stark binary between these two stories, in many cases we will find that a rich dialogue flowed between them.

This dual nod to the past and the future characterised many art forms in the twentieth century, as artists, writers and musicians began to grapple with their place in history amid the rapidly changing cultures of contemporary life. We touched on the Italian Futurists in →Chapter 2, 'Modernism', and their work is also important here. In his 1913 manifesto, 'The Art of Noises', leading Futurist Luigi Russolo (1885–1947) bemoaned the symphony orchestra as a 'hospital for anaemic sounds' (1913: 6) and encouraged musicians to respond to the tempo and noise of the new industrial world through refreshed sonic textures. Three years later, Edgard Varèse (1883–1965) voiced a similar sentiment: 'We have a great need for new instruments . . . I refuse to submit to sounds that have already been heard' (Varèse, in Patteson 2016: 1). For these very different musicians, existing instruments could only create outdated music. In order to produce newer, weirder, louder and more complex sounds, instruments needed to be extended, reappropriated or invented from scratch. Fast forward through the century and we find John Lee Hooker heightening the blues with his amplified guitar, Pauline Oliveros using tape as a compositional tool,

Daphne Oram pioneering electronic music, Kraftwerk using the synthesiser to change the sound of pop and Pharoah Sanders using extended techniques to move free jazz into new sound worlds. Some of these transformations required new performance gestures, while others got rid of the need for human engagement altogether.

These rapid innovations were part of the large cultural, social and political shifts that vibrated through the century and have required refreshed forms of musicological engagement. Contextual studies of the guitar (Waksman 1999b), the piano (Rowland and Cross 1988) and the vocoder (Tompkins 2010), for instance, have decentralised the study of sound-making. Rather than treating instruments as fixed, physical objects, these authors explore how the objects and their sounds produce meaning in a variety of cross-cultural settings. Kevin Dawe articulates this methodological change particularly well in his promotion of a 'guitarscape', a way of viewing the instrument as 'a large-scale musical-cultural-social occurrence' (2010: 41). This repositioning was later developed by Matt Brennan, who asserts that '[t]he drum kit in all its forms (acoustic, electronic, physical, virtual, and symbolic) participates in the drumscape': '[f]raming musical worlds from the perspective of an instrument (as opposed to an artist, genre, or scene) encourages us to think across traditional musical boundaries' (2020: 317). This chapter takes us through the main innovations in instrument design and use during the century and considers how these newly emerging instrument-scapes have helped to destabilise ideas about class, race and gender.

Looking Back: The Early Music Revival

Let us begin with the engagement with existing instruments and their histories that blossomed as the century unfolded. The development of modern musicology saw a reinvestment in organology – the study and classification of musical devices and their cultures – and several major studies in categorisation appeared, including the Hornbostel–Sachs system (1914), *The Grove Dictionary of Musical Instruments* (1984) and Bart Hopkins' *Experimental Musical Instruments* magazine (1985–99). While the first two documented well-established instruments, the work of Hopkins charted more experimental musicians and instrument builders, such as American outsiders Harry Partch (1901–74) and Moondog (1916–99), who created homemade instruments (Figure 8.1) able to extend tonalities and tuning systems based on unequal interval scales in just intonation and microtonality

Figure 8.1 Harry Partch's Boo 1 (1955–6), a marimba made from bamboo, oak and gum plywood and played with felted mallets. The instrument uses Partch's system of just intonation. Photograph by HorsePunchKid

(Rasch 2013). This renewed scholarly interest in instrument design and manufacture extended into performance practice and in the century's first decades, several groups of musicians embarked on painstaking historical research to recreate early instruments and forgotten playing techniques. Through the historically informed performance movement (→Chapter 5, 'Work and Notation'), neglected instruments such as harpsichords, forte-pianos, viols and recorders were reintroduced. One side effect of this was contemporary composers' renewed interest in such instruments: see, for example, Iannis Xenakis' or György Ligeti's works for harpsichord, or Mauricio Kagel's *Music for Renaissance Instruments*, 1965–6.

- Harry Partch, *Delusion of the Fury* (1966)

This early music revival developed alongside the Arts and Crafts movement and shared its promotion of simple manual workmanship over the methods of mass production that characterised many aspects of post-Industrial Revolution life. The instrument maker Arnold Dolmetsch (1858–1940), who was born in France but spent most of his life in England, pioneered a research-practice approach from his workshop in Haslemere, Surrey. There, he reconstructed and built harpsichords, clavichords, viols, lutes and recorders (Figure 8.2) and used historical treatises

Figure 8.2 Arnold Dolmetsch performing with his family, 1928

on performance practice to provide guidance on 'authentic' performance styles in his pioneering book (1915).

Although for some scholars the engagement with (an imagined) past practice resulted in 'the atmosphere of a modern museum' (Scruton 1999: 448), historical performance practice flourished, becoming a significant part of twentieth-century music culture, with ensembles, such as David Munrow's Early Music Consort, Christopher Hogwood's Academy of Ancient Music and John Eliot Gardiner's Orchestre Révolutionnaire et Romantique, performing scholarly versions of early music on original (or recreated) instruments, often without vibrato or excessive Romantic sensibility. As we have seen, however, the claims to authenticity were fraught, and the historically informed performance movement may appear to have been as much about innovation as it was preservation.

Looking Forward: The Twentieth-Century Soundscape

For other twentieth-century musicians, innovation was more explicitly valued. While Schoenberg and Debussy were rejuvenating composition through atonality, timbre and structure, more experimental artists felt that musical progress had gone as far as it could with existing instrument capabilities. In 1907, for instance, Italian writer and composer Ferruccio Busoni (1866–1924) lamented that 'It may be that all the possibilities of traditional instruments have not yet been exploited. But we are certainly well along the way of the path toward exhaustion' and called for 'a new, virginal beginning' (Busoni 1907: 42). Below, we will encounter many new beginnings, but one of the most radical came early in the century. As we have seen in several other chapters, the first decades were marked by rapid modernisation, technological change and the speed, sounds and smells of modern industrialisation: as soundscape artist R. Murray Schafer (1933–) famously remarked, 'modern man is beginning to inhabit a world with an acoustic environment radically different from any he has hitherto known' (1977: 2–3). Russolo and Varèse, mentioned above, considered the sounds of existing instruments to be too far removed from this new 'acoustic environment' to produce music meaningful to a twentieth-century society. For them, the modern ear, attuned to an urban soundscape, required refreshed musical timbres. Russolo's modernist-driven manifesto is one of the earliest promotions of non-traditional instruments. Penned in response to the *Manifesto dei musicisti futuristi* (1909) by founder of the Futurist movement Filippo Marinetti, which called for the art world to start afresh and for galleries and concert halls to be abandoned, the manifesto fed into Russolo's experimentation with a group of homemade-sounding devices – his *intonarumori* (Figure 8.3) – that sought to break from 'the limited circle of pure sounds' in order to conquer the 'infinite variety of "noise-sounds"' (Russolo 1967/1913: 1298). The twenty-seven *intonarumori*, referred to by names such as howler, gurgler, roarer and buzzer, were sounding boxes with acoustic horns on the front, a crank on the back and a noise machine inside and were used for several of Russolo's compositions, including *Risveglio di una città* (*Awakening of a City*).

- Luigi Russolo, *Risveglio di una città* (*c*.1913–14)

The Instruments of Everyday Life

While Russolo's *intonarumori* produced new sounds sympathetic to urbanised soundscapes, another way to respond to the contemporary environment was through the musical appropriation of sounding objects from everyday life. The use of non-musical artefacts as creative material also reverberates through the century's visual art practice. The ready-

Figure 8.3 Luigi Russolo's *intonarumori*, 1913

mades of Dada artist Marcel Duchamp (1887–1968) are a good example. Duchamp famously recontexualised a urinal by putting it into an art gallery (*Fountain*, 1917) to demonstrate that anything could be art if we choose to see it that way. Later, pop artist Andy Warhol (1928–87) performed similar gestures when he put piles of soap boxes and soup cans into gallery spaces. Like these visual artists, musicians made use of non-musical objects in numerous, aesthetically divergent ways. Some used existing artefacts specific to the century to punctuate familiar musical textures: American composer George Antheil (1900–59) accompanied pianos, tam-tams and xylophones with sirens, electric bells, airplane propellers and player pianos in *Ballet Mécanique* (1923–4), for instance, while Varèse included sirens in his percussion ensemble for *Ionisation* (1931). Others were less specific in the choice of object. German composer Karlheinz Stockhausen (1928–2007) asked the two percussionists of *Mikrophonie 1* (1964) to create 'squeaking', 'scratching', 'whistling' and 'clanging' sounds by hitting a tam-tam with various household 'implements' (1974, his term; Maraš 2017: 52) and recorded them with a microphone.

- George Antheil, *Ballet Mécanique* (1923–4)
- Edgard Varèse, *Ionisation* (1931)

Despite incorporating new sounding objects into musical practice, though, these examples remain rooted in the Western tradition of notated music. A different strand of experimentation engendered radical new relationships between composers, performers and audiences. John Cage's

(1912–92) quest to expand musical material through non-traditional instruments is particularly important here: 'I never stopped touching things, making them sound and resound, to discover what sounds they could produce. Wherever I went, I always listened to objects' (Cage 1981: 73). Feeding into his reconceptualisation of music as the 'Organisation of Sound' (1961/1937: 3), Cage's interest in non-musical objects, radios and sensors decentred music practice by highlighting the context of performance, a realignment articulated most famously in *4'33"* (1952), a piece in two movements that asked the performer to simply sit in front of their instrument without playing for the exact time stated in the work's title. *4'33"* is often mistakenly thought of as a piece of silence. In fact, it is not about silence at all, but rather encourages audience members to consider any sound heard during the time frame to be musical material. Like Duchamp's urinal, Cage's piece asks us to rethink what music is and who holds the authorial control. Because the composer gives us no sound, creative control is repositioned onto the audience: any sound they make becomes part of the piece. As a result, *4'33"* can be fundamentally different in each performance, depending on the audience members.

We can think of this promotion of non-musical objects as a step towards destabilising the high–low divide and the boundaries between the arts and everyday life: some have gone so far as to consider Cage 'the first postmodernist' (Gloag 2012: 43; Williams 2002), while for other critics, the fusion more readily demonstrates an intensification of hyper-modernist tendencies (Bernstein 2002).

The refreshed view of instruments had a direct impact on how performers and audiences behaved, as we saw in the discussion of happenings and events in →Chapter 5, 'Work and Notation'. La Monte Young's (1935–) Fluxus event, *Poem for Chairs, Tables and Benches Etc. (or Other Sound Sources)* (1960), for instance, demands no particular musical skill to perform as it simply requires participants to push furniture around the recital space. Other performances required direct involvement from audience members, which not only destabilised centuries of performance rituals (Small 1998), but also opened the space to a variety of political ramifications (Rogers 2013). Serbian performance artist and film-maker Marina Abramović's (1946–) *Rhythm 0* (1974) constructs a tense and gendered form of expression, for example. An endurance piece of body art lasting six hours, *Rhythm 0* invites attendees to choose from an array of objects laid out on a table, and to use them on the artist in any way. Positioning herself in both a passive and objectified role, Abramović allowed her identity to be constructed through the actions of others by providing the audience with objects that could give her pain or pleasure and giving them a space in which, removed from normal consequences, they could push the boundaries of acceptable behaviour.

All the examples above are driven by different aesthetics, of course, but connecting them is the desire to deconstruct traditional ideas of what constitutes an instrument and, by extension, the way in which performers and audiences could engage with sound.

Case Study 8.1: The Piano

In the nineteenth century, the piano represented a powerful middle-class ideology based on etiquette, education, social standing, wealth and taste. In particular, the parlour instrument, prohibitively expensive to all but the gentry and the aristocracy, became a popular female pastime, and was used to indicate a very particular, often gendered, social standing (Leppert 1988). As the twentieth century unfolded, the piano retained its position at the heart of art-music practice, driving the music of Debussy, Schoenberg, Messiaen, Bartók and others. Like several other instruments, it was used in various ways to press into modernist agendas. The player piano, or pianola, which became fully automated in 1904, for instance, was employed by composers like Conlon Nancarrow (1912–97) to achieve speed and complexity beyond the capabilities of a human performer. Firmly rooted in the industrial age, the instrument fulfilled the modernistic and avant-garde desire for technology, innovation and precision.

- Nancarrow, *Study for Player Piano #21 (Canon X)* (1961)

At the same time, however, the piano's past associations began to be troubled, and for other many composers the bourgeoise history and elite commodification of the instrument, with its virtuosic concerto displays, was something to be reclaimed and reimagined. Scholars like Trevor Pinch, working within the field of science and technology studies, have argued that culture, society and politics influence technological development and scientific research; these developments then feed back into culture and society (Pinch and Oudshoorn 2005) and this reciprocal flow of influence can be seen throughout the twentieth century. In 1968, for instance, musician and video artist Nam June Paik (1932–2006) declared that 'the piano is taboo, it must be destroyed'. One way in which Paik performed this rejection of the instrument's cultural heritage was through physical destruction in a piece of interactive installation art called *Klavier Intégral* (1963, Figure 8.4). The four pianos in this work each required different responses from visitors. For one, visitors were asked to walk on the keys to defamiliarise normal bodily interaction; another was silenced by a wooden panel across the strings. The other two were covered to the point of destruction by various household objects: a doll's

Case Study 8.1: (cont.)

Figure 8.4 Nam June Paik, *Klavier Intégral*, 1958–63. Photograph © mumok - Museum moderner Kunst Stiftung Ludwig Wien, Former Hahn Collection, Cologne. Courtesy of the Nam June Paik Estate

head, wires, photographs, a padlock, parts of a record player. This work destabilised the accumulated symbolisms of the nineteenth century in a literal and forceful way.

Other composers worked in more subtle ways. Appearing in compositional practice from the mid-century, the use of toy pianos highlighted and questioned many of the facets of the instrument's legacy, with pieces like John Cage's *Suite for Toy Piano* (1948) lampooning the social privilege that a concert grand, a symbol of high art, had come to represent. This happened in two ways: first by drawing attention to its social position, second by deconstructing it. This double unravelling also drove more conceptual events. La Monte Young, in his theatrical *Piano Piece for David Tudor #1* (1960), for instance, instructs the performer to 'Bring a bale of hay and a bucket of water onto the stage for the piano to eat and drink. The performer may then feed the piano or leave it to eat by itself. If the former, the piece is over after the piano has been

Case Study 8.1: (cont.)

fed. If the latter, it is over after the piano eats or decides not to' (quoted in Nyman 1999/
1974: 84).

One persistent way to refresh the piano's social and cultural position was through the
disruption of its expected sounds and the bodily gestures usually required to sound it.
Although others had manipulated pianos before, it was John Cage who began to enlarge
the sonic potential of the instrument in 1938, intervening in its history with a variety of
objects and unusual sounds. His prepared pianos lie somewhere between a tuned and
a percussion instrument, with the keys producing rattles, bangs, overtones or harmonics
once screws, bolts, string, weather stripping, bamboo strips and/or coins are placed
within its casing. A key at the start of each of his scores indicates where and how each
object should be located and, once set up, the performer simply follows standard
notation to perform the piece. The level of detail given on how to prepare a piano varies
between composers. George Crumb, for instance, provides meticulous notes on the
inside-the-piano techniques for *Makrokosmos* (Volume 1, 1972).

Andrea Neumann's (1968–) work destabilises the social and cultural values of the
instrument not only through modification but also through a fusion of acoustic and
amplified possibilities. Neumann spent the last decades of the twentieth century
preparing the piano into a hybrid form – what she calls her 'inside piano' – that is
both acoustic resonator and synthetic, electronic instrument that requires expanded
techniques. Part of Berlin's 'echtzeitmusik' scene, which fused noise, composed
sound, electronica and sound art, Neumann used electric guitar magnetic pickups
to amplify the sounds of her modified piano through a mixing board.

The prepared piano has also been a powerful tool for the diffusion of genre boundaries.
The sound worlds produced were not confined to experimental art practice but can also be
found across styles, from John Cale's use of paper clips in the piano for the Velvet
Underground's 'All Tomorrow's Parties' (1967), the gyroscope that spins on the instru-
ment's soundboard in the Grateful Dead's *Anthem of the Sun* album (1968) and Brian
Eno's prepared sounds, which drive 'Little Fishes' (1975), all the way through to Aphex
Twin's prepared-piano track 'Ruglen Holon' (2001), which sits on the temporal threshold
of our study.

- John Cage, *Sonatas and Interludes* (1946–8)
- The Velvet Underground, 'All Tomorrow's Parties' (from *The Velvet Underground
  & Nico, Verve*, 1967)
- The Grateful Dead, 'That's It for the Other One (Part IV)' (from *Anthem of the Sun*,
  Warner Bros.-Seven Arts, 1968)

In its natural state, the piano deconstructed many of the nineteenth century's race and
class symbolisms by becoming a key player in popular music, from the ragtime of African
American Scott Joplin, which influenced the Harlem stride-piano style of early jazz artists

Case Study 8.1: (cont.)

Fats Waller and James P. Johnson, through to the more avant-garde free style of Thelonious Monk and Cecil Taylor (Givan 2009), to its position at the heart of rock 'n' roll in the songs of Little Richard and Jerry Lee Lewis. Later in the century, subversions of the 'feminine' bourgeois pianist stereotype can be seen in Elton John's and Liberace's flamboyant performance styles and Tori Amos' outspoken feminist songs. The piano's many transformations – from the Fender Rhodes, Clavinet and Wurlitzer, through to the synthesiser – also located the keyboard at the heart of 1980s electropop, with artists and bands like Gary Numan, the Human League and Soft Cell using it to drive their sounds.

- Scott Joplin, *The Entertainer* (1902)
- Little Richard, 'Tutti Frutti' (Speciality Records, 1955)
- Tori Amos, 'Silent All These Years' (from *Little Earthquakes*, Atlantic, 1992)

To return to Nam June Paik, then, the piano did not need to be destroyed to find a new voice. Used in different contexts, manipulated with non-musical objects, amplified, mechanised and processed through digital media, the instrument became an integral and radical part in the many histories of twentieth century music. Following Kevin Dawe's notion of a 'guitarscape' and Matt Brennan's exploration of a 'drumscape', both mentioned at the start of this chapter, it is possible to identify a powerful pianoscape that threads through issues of class, gender and race during the twentieth century.

Technology, Recording and Sampling

So far, we have focused on acoustic non-musical instruments, yet arguably, real-world sounds entered music practice most significantly with the arrival of electronic instruments of reproduction. As the century progressed, technology not only reconfigured the ways in which instruments were designed and used but also gave rise to new performance and compositional techniques. This confluence has caught the attention of many scholars. For instance, Richard Middleton observes that '[t]echnology and music technique, content and meaning generally develop together, dialectically' (1990: 90), while Keith Negus asserts that '[t]echnology has never been passive, neutral or natural. Music has for centuries been created through the interaction between "art" and technology' (1992: 31). Jason Toynbee has opened out the implications of this interaction even further, arguing that '[t]echnology and the social and cultural are always imbricated. . . . technologies take off because they are congruent with an emerging aesthetic among musicians: they must literally be imagined into existence' (2000: 99).

If we follow the story of non-musical objects and sounds sideways, into the commercial availability of magnetic tape recorders in the 1940s and 1950s, Toynbee's idea of congruence becomes clear. Composers were quick to embrace tape's creative possibilities, with Cage referring to it as the first real 'twentieth-century means for making music' (1966: 6). From the beginnings of tape culture in the 1940s – signalled by Egyptian Halim El-Dabh's 1944 recording of a public exorcism which became known as *The Expression of Zaar*, and Pierre Schaeffer's 1948 piece of *musique concrète*, *Étude aux chemins de fer*, created entirely from the sound of trains – to the sound art of Pauline Oliveros and Morton Subotnick and foundation of the San Francisco Tape Music Center in 1962, magnetic tape allowed composers to distance non-musical sounds from their sources, and to cut and splice previously recorded music into new sonic collages. This initiated new and complex levels of auditory attention (Hegarty 2007) that required that 'conventional listening habits imparted by education first be unlearned' (Schaeffer 2017/1966). Unlike Russolo above, who created noises evocative of contemporary sonic life, the early tape music movement sought what Schaeffer referred to as reduced listening (1966/2017), whereby audiences were encouraged to abstract the sounds from all possible sources and to experience them as independent sonic objects with their own aesthetic integrity, although more recent scholars have questioned the possibility of this dislocation (Kane 2014: 9).

- Halim El-Dabh, *The Expression of Zaar* (1944)
- Pierre Schaeffer, *Étude aux chemins de fer* (1948)
- Pauline Oliveros, *Time Perspectives* (1959)

While those working in the middle of the century used tape to transform everyday sounds into absolute music, the use of sampling equipment that propelled several different areas of 1970s and 1980s music culture emerged not from the remediation of real-world sounds but from recorded music. The year 1979 is pivotal here, as it saw the birth of first commercially available electronic sampler, known as the Fairlight CMI (Computer Musical Instrument, Figure 8.5). Designed by Australians Peter Vogel and Kim Ryrie, the instrument could sample a second of sound, which the user could then play back at different pitches. Artists were enticed by the instrument's reproductive qualities, as we can hear on Peter Gabriel's eponymous 1980 album, which includes the sampled sounds of glass bottles smashing and bricks breaking. Kate Bush made significant use of the Fairlight CMI for several of her albums, including *The Dreaming* (1982) and *Hounds of Love* (1985). 'Running Up That Hill (A Deal with God)' from

Figure 8.5 Fairlight CMI

the latter album makes heavy use of the Fairlight's CELLO2 sample, which you can hear throughout the song.

- Kate Bush, 'Running Up That Hill (A Deal with God)' (from *Hounds of Love*, EMI, 1985)

Despite a hefty price tag of $25,000, the series two, which boasted a larger capability, helped some of the century's most prominent sounds, including hip-hop, Detroit techno and house, although musicians working in these genres rarely used the series two itself, relying instead on material resampled using the cheap Akai and Ensoniq samplers. Nevertheless, it can be argued that these genres developed in direct response to the new instrument and it is important to note that electronic media called for a renegotiated relationship not only between instrument and performer but also between art and commercial venture. Paul Théberge views the development of digital synthesisers, samplers and other components of the emerging home studio as a game-changing moment in the history of instruments and their relationships with musicians, arguing that a different form of consumer practice arose that placed unprecedented emphasis on instrument manufacturers: in fact, for him, instrument design and production became 'a driving force with which musicians must contend' (Théberge 1997: 4).

If we return to Toynbee's theory that technology 'congruent with an emerging aesthetic among musicians' was most likely to influence musical culture, we can suggest that the sampler's success came from the potential it held for those already engaged with turntabling, mixing, rap and MCing. The musicological perspectives that have formed around hip-hop have alighted on this tension between past music and contemporary technology. As we saw in →Chapter 3, 'Postmodernism', sampling instruments were used by hip-hop artists as an articulation of political critique and cultural lineage, allowing artists to link back to earlier African American pop music traditions and jazz, but also to the 'multimedia borrowings' from 1970s blaxploitation film soundtracks (Demers 2003: 42) and Black womanhood and representation (Pough 2004).

One of the most famous Fairlight samples was named 'ORCH5'. An easily recognisable orchestra stab taken from Stravinsky's *The Firebird* (1910), and available in the Fairlight's catalogue of preset samples, ORCH5 can be used to trace the instrument's broad influence during the 1980s: it sounds throughout Kate Bush's 1982 album *The Dreaming* (1982) and punctuates songs as diverse as Bronx DJ Afrika Bambaataa's 1982 hit 'Planet Rock', Duran Duran's 'A View to A Kill' (1985) and Miles Davis's 'Tutu' (1986). Robert Fink has focused on the ways in which the ORCH5 sample became 'thoroughly naturalised in hip hop' (Fink 2005b: 353), enabling the 'classical ghost' of Stravinsky, a symbol for the death of European art music, to become trapped in the 'hip hop machine' (340).

- Afrika Bambaataa, 'Planet Rock' (Tommy Boy Records, 1982)
- Duran Duran, 'A View to A Kill' (EMI, 1985)

The availability of cheaper digital samplers like the Akai S-series (1984), the MPC60 (1988) and the Ensoniq Mirage (1985), together with the rise to prominence of drum machines like the Linn LM-1 (1980) and Oberheim DMX (1981), which used sampled kit sounds as well as those created from circuits, pushed the earlier avant-garde ideas of remediated sound and collage into mainstream contexts. The MPC60 sampler, for instance, was used by DJ Shadow (1972–) for *Endtroducing* (1996), an album created almost entirely from sampled vinyl records. A serious issue for remixed work based on musical samples, however, is copyright infringement (Negus 1999: 95; Schumacher 1995; →Chapter 10, 'Copyright and the Music Industry'). Real-world sounds can be the safer bet, and at the end of the century we find a re-emergence of *concrète* soundscapes and non-musical instruments, with Fourtet's *Dialogue* album (1999), Matthew Herbert's *Bodily Functions* (2001) and Matmos' *A Chance to Cut is a Chance to Cure* (2001) using analogue and digital technologies to form sustained works from non-musical samples.

- DJ Shadow, 'Best Foot Forward' (from *Endroducing*, Mo' Wax, 1996)

Despite contrasting aesthetics, then, the remediating drive behind analogue tape machines and digital samplers threads through *musique concrète*, sound art, pop, hip-hop, techno and electronica. The reuse and sampling of musical material was discussed in →Chapter 3, 'Postmodernism', and a basic postmodern atmosphere was in operation during the evolution of the synthesiser. But a related and more contemporary way of reading these reused sounds is through the idea of 'hauntology'. Although the idea was developed by Simon Reynolds and Mark Fisher for twenty-first-century British electronica and hip-hop, we can see these earlier artists delighting in the retromania of collocating 'delectable morsels of decaying culture-matter' (Reynolds 2006: 273). We could even argue that such reappropriation falls into Fisher's description of hauntology as a 'confrontation with a cultural impasse: the failure of the future' (2012c: 16). Here, then, we see how new instruments enabled a complicated interplay between the past and the future, reuse and innovation, old sounds and new.

Electronic Music

For other artists, however, it was all eyes to the future, and early electronic instruments like the ondes martenot (favoured by Varèse, Messiaen and Radiohead) and Daphne Oram's Oramics machine gave rise to completely new sounds.

- Messiaen, *Turangalîla-Symphonie* (1946–8)
- Daphne Oram, *Four Aspects* (1960)
- Radiohead, 'How to Disappear Completely' (from *Kid A*, Parlophone, 2000)

We saw in →Chapter 2, 'Modernism' that postwar modernist musicians were quick to seek out the resources of new state-run broadcasting services. Especially important to this part of our story is the rise of the electronic music studio (EMS) during the 1950s, particularly that of the Westdeutscher Rundfunk in Cologne (WDR, West German Radio). The WDR was a radio studio able to issue emergency broadcasts in the event of nuclear attack. In the meantime, it became a hub for mid-century experimentation with electronic instruments; it was here that Stockhausen worked with sine-wave generators, and Gottfried Michael Koenig and Mauricio Kagel appropriated the radio station's electronic apparatus, including oscillators, filters and, as we shall see in our second case study, the vocoder. Unlike Schaeffer's electro-acoustic work with tape, composers at the WDR created music that was entirely electronic. Despite the newness of these sounds, however, as in so many other instrument stories of the twentieth century, the avant-garde creativity emerging from the radio station troubled the boundary between past and future. Jennifer Iversen suggests that the electronic work created in the WDR 'was emblematic of a Janus-faced Cold War attitude toward technologies', as the gadgets reappropriated as musical instruments harboured 'memories of wartime trauma' while at the same time promising 'optimistic visions of a timbral utopia, animated by ever-new sonic innovations' (Iversen: 2, 3).

- Karlheinz Stockhausen, *Studie 1* (1953)
- Gottfried Michael Koenig, *Klangfiguren II* (1955–6)

Sounds created through purely electronic means could be disquieting, and the century is awash with anecdotes about audiences walking out of concerts equipped with technology but lacking discernible human presence. Yet Simon Emmerson sees electronic technology as a 'third party' that can operate as 'partner, mediator, or intruder', while for Théberge, digital instruments become a 'hybrid', existing somewhere between the production of music and its reproduction (1997: 2–3). In many new instruments, this hybridity is clearly apparent. The Theremin, for instance, is a responsive and interactive instrument that establishes an electromagnetic field between two antennae, which emits a sound when an electrical conductor interferes with the signal; when hands and bodies are used to create this interference, the instrument becomes an organic extension of the body. Léon Theremin (1896–1993), the Russian physicist who first developed the instrument around 1928, was adamant that these bodily interventions prevented 'automatic technology and soullessness' (Glinsky 2000: 68), as became clear in its use by musicians as diverse as Percy Grainger, film composer Bernard Herrmann, the Beach Boys, Jimmy Page and the Pixies.

- Bernard Herrmann, *The Day the Earth Stood Still* (20th Century Fox, 1951)
- Pixies, 'Velouria', *Bossanova* (4AD / Elektra, 1990)

Among the most influential electronic instruments we find the synthesiser – an electronic instrument able to imitate other instruments or generate new sounds. Erupting onto the popular music scene in 1962 with Joe Meek's electronic studio effects for the Tornados' 'Telstar', early analogue synths quickly crept into the electroacoustic sounds of Pierre Henry and the minimalist textures of Philip Glass. Moog's early modular synthesiser with a keyboard user interface in the mid-1960s appeared on 'Daily Nightly' by the Monkees (1967) and the Doors' *Strange Days* (1967), before the development of the Musical Instrument Digital Interface (MIDI) meant that synths could be synchronised with other electronic devices. The availability of a simplified mini-Moog in 1970 heightened its popularity, and it became the driving force for Kraftwerk's *Autobahn* album (1974) and the bassline for Michael Jackson's 'Thriller' (1982). Although the polyphonic capabilities of the Yamaha GX-1 in 1973 was a significant development, it was the arrival of digital models by Korg, Roland and Casio and of Yamaha's DX7 from the end of the 1970s that kickstarted a real music revolution.

- The Tornados, 'Telstar' (from *The Original Telstar: The Sounds of the Tornadoes*, Decca, 1962)
- Michael Jackson, 'Thriller', *Thriller* (Epic, 1982)

The new compositional and performance possibilities enabled and afforded by these new instruments changed the face of the popular music landscape, driving 1960s pop, the 1970s synth sounds of Jean-Michel Jarre and Vangelis, the emergence of 1980s new wave and the electropop of Gary Numan and David Bowie. One of the most significant instrument-dependent genres arose during the mid-1980s thanks to the electronic bass synthesiser-sequencer the Roland TB-303 (Figure 8.6), a synth that helped to move electronic music into mainstream culture. Although not successful at producing bass guitar effects, the synth projected a chirping sound that became a fundamental component of 1980s acid house, Detroit techno, Chicago house and ensuing subgenres like drum and bass, ambient and dark wave. The TR-808 (1980), on the other hand, became one of the most important drum machines ever made (see →Chapter 6, 'Rhythm and Time'), with its bass-drum, clap and cowbell sounds pervading most areas of popular music, driving the sound worlds of Run-DMC and Beastie Boys and featuring prominently on 1980s hits from Marvin Gaye's 'Sexual Healing' (1982) and Talking Heads' 'Psycho Killer' (1977) to Whitney Houston's 'I Wanna Dance with Somebody (Who Loves Me)' (1987).

Acoustic Extensions and Amplification

Not all instrument innovations arose from new forms of technology, of course. In fact, some of the most avant-garde extensions of sonic possibility came from traditional instruments played with radically transformed

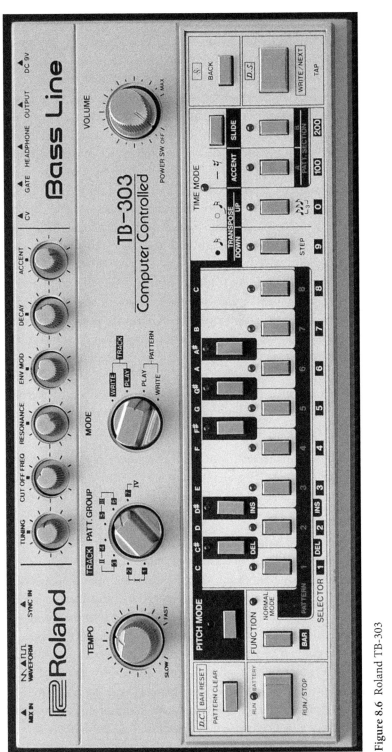

Figure 8.6 Roland TB-303

technique, as Théberge writes: 'the manner in which you play an instrument can transform both the instrument itself and the nature of the musical sounds produced' (1997: 166). We find extended techniques dominating the free improvisations of avant-garde jazz in the 1960s, with John Coltrane and Ornette Coleman overblowing and manipulating the saxophone to create unfamiliar sounds and tonalities, while experimental composers explored and manipulated unused areas of traditional instruments: in *Pression* (1969), for instance, German composer Helmut Lachenmann (1935–) asks the cellist to bow behind the bridge, hit the instrument's body and tap and rub the soundboard. Extended vocal techniques were often a vehicle for politically charged messages and diasporic links to other cultures (Maultsby 2005). American pioneer Meredith Monk (1942–), who we encountered in →Chapter 6, 'Rhythm and Time', combines wordless and acrobatic chants, cries, whispers and folk-derived ululations over modal drones to highlight her strong feminist agendas, while the more operatic growling, screaming, hissing and panting of Greek American Diamanda Galás (1955–), who has collaborated with Xenakis as well as members of Led Zeppelin and Erasure, took influence from Eastern folk traditions, blues and gospel to produce a form of sonic activism, particularly against the AIDS crisis during the 1980s. In some of her work, she uses up to thirteen languages to form what Freya Jarman calls 'glossolalic speech', a type of enunciation that rejects masculine 'rational(ist)' and 'semiotically structured language', in a radically feminist move (Jarman 2011: 145).

- John Coltrane, 'Pursuance' (from *A Love Supreme*, Impulse!, 1965)
- Helmut Lachenmann, *Pression* (1969)
- Diamanda Galás, 'There Are No More Tickets to the Funeral (Were You A Witness)' (from *Plague Mass*, Elektra, 1991)

Although extended techniques were often a hallmark of avant-garde practice, they made their way into mainstream culture during the 1980s, with the development of human beatboxing, which emulated the sounds of early drum machines and the quickly shifting rhythms of the DJ's turntable. Beatboxing's almost immediate move into popular culture can be seen in Michael Winslow's performance as 'the man of 10,000 sounds' in the *Police Academy* films.

Despite the cultural and aesthetic diversity of these examples, it is clear to see that the radical reconfiguration of acoustic instruments through physical gesture became a prominent creative force across genres and styles. Amplification took the development of traditional instruments and performance practice in another direction. Andrew Ford writes that '[t]he most important instrument in pop music is the microphone . . . What the microphone made possible in pop music was a complete range of vocal manners, from the most hectoring to the most intimate' (Ford 2014). From whispering and physical proximity (Young 2019), through the emergence of the crooning style of singing (Frith 1986) to the evolution of hip-hop collaborations (Katz 2012: 70), the microphone opened up new possibilities for vocal technique and its position within musical textures.

Similarly, the electrification of the guitar had a profound influence on twentieth-century music culture. Richard Middleton charts the rise of guitar amplification, from practical necessity (in order to allow the guitar to be heard within the loud textures of big bands) to gestural experimentation, writing that electrification 'facilitated an expansion of certain traditional guitar solo techniques (fast runs, inflection and glissando, vibrato), while demanding certain new playing techniques in the process, which then resulted in new effects (sustained tone). Exploitation of possibilities for tonal modulation led to demands for extra technology in this area (wah-wah, fuzz, and so on)' (1990: 90).

The electric guitar was truly boundary-crossing. It was used by minimalist composers like Steve Reich and Rhys Chatham, in the avant-garde compositions of Glen Branca, combined with traditional acoustic ensembles in the work of Gavin Bryars and made into soundtables for the free improvisations of guitarist Keith Rowe. However, its cultural importance really lies in its position as a key player in the rise and diversification of popular music. As part of the leading formation of drums, bass, guitar and voice line-up that came to dominate popular music in the second half of the century, the electric guitar drove the chugging rhythm sections of rock 'n' roll, the distorted howls of psychedelia, the irreverence of punk and thrash metal and the melodic lines of indie rock.

- Steve Reich, *Electric Counterpoint* (*Steve Reich: Works 1965–1995*, Nonesuch Records, 1997)

The electric guitar was immortalised by Leo Fender, who set up his Californian business in 1946, producing the Telecaster in 1950, the Precision Bass a year later – the instrument Paul Simonon smashes to smithereens on the cover of the Clash's *London Calling* (1979) – and the Stratocaster in 1954. With the help of Fender and other innovative designs from Rickenbacker and Gibson, the electric guitar's rise to prominence was rapid, yet its success was reliant on another electric device. Although various models of amplifier were available before 1965, it was then that Pete Townshend (1945–), guitarist of the Who, struggling to compete with the volume of Keith Moon's drums with his 50-watt amp, visited Jim

Marshall's shop and requested a new sonic 'weapon' (Townshend, quoted in Motter and Schu 2015). The result was the development of the 100-watt valve amplifier, a 4 x 12" speaker cabinet powered by the Marshall Super Lead Model 1959 head, which became known as the iconic Marshall Stack, a staple of the rock gig ever since (the late Lemmy Kilmister of Motörhead famously used two customised Marshall stacks named Murder One and Murder Two). The combination of electrified guitar and new modes of amplification paved the way for new approaches to sound manipulation, and artists such as Jeff Beck (1944–) seized the opportunity to play with distortion and manipulated the unavoidable side effect of high volumes into nuanced forms of expression.

Not surprisingly, there have been several major studies of the instrument, including Dawe's study of guitarscapes mentioned at the start of this chapter, and the work of Steve Waksman who, in his seminal book on the electric guitar, suggests that '[t]he issue is not whether the instrument created volume, distortion and other new sonic effects, but whether the creation of these effects, the noise of the electric guitar, marked a reorganization of musical practice or a reconceptualization of social and political differences' (1999b: 12). While some sought to tame the instrument (Chet Atkins and Les Paul), others (like Jimmy Page) embraced its potential for anarchy, a capacity for disruption immortalised by the images of Pete Townshend smashing his guitars and Jimi Hendrix burning his. This upheaval has often been read in masculine terms, with the instrument morphing into a 'technophallus' (Waksman 2003: 257) that rapidly became central to the 'thrusting, grinding . . . phallo-centric' nature of rock (Dyer 2002: 155).

The interventions of the sonic 'weapon', however, were not always welcome, and the integration of electric instruments into traditions with well-established acoustic histories were often problematic. Bob Dylan's (1941–) infamous performance at the Newport Folk Festival in 1965, where his use of an electric guitar undermined the authentic, grass-roots aesthetics of folk ideology and saw him booed offstage, is the most famous example of this. In other circumstances, the electric guitar's potential to undo ideology was more complex. Jimi Hendrix's (1942–70) intervention into the predominantly white 1960s counterculture of Woodstock (1969) exemplifies the multilayered symbolism the electric guitar could embody. His rendition of the 'Star-Spangled Banner' (Figure 8.7), the USA's national anthem, was unique to the instrument, embodying many of the expansions identified by Middleton above. Using extreme distortion, Hendrix punctuates the

Figure 8.7 Jimi Hendrix performing 'The Star-Spangled Banner' at Woodstock, 9 September 1969

familiar melody with the screaming wails of warfare to comment on America's involvement with the Vietnam War. Reactions were contrasting. For some, the interjected mimicry of bombs falling suggested the call-and-response traditions of African callers, a technique that also infuses early blues music (Floyd 1995: 201–3), but for others, his choice of rock music undermined and betrayed a Black aesthetic (Waksman 1999b).

- Jimi Hendrix, 'Purple Haze', from *Are You Experienced?* (Track, 1967)

Case Study 8.2: The Vocoder

The history of the vocoder offers a glimpse into the interconnections between the creative arts and science. Its increasing popularity as a musical tool in the avant-garde and in popular culture as the century progressed transgressed many deeply entrenched high–low boundaries and gave rise to refreshed forms of expression around race, gender and sexuality.

In 1928, Bell Labs began work on the vocoder (the voice-coder), a speech-synthesis device for military communication, patented by Homer Dudley in 1939. At first, the technology was used to secure sensitive communication by transforming a voice into

Case Study 8.2: (cont.)

ten channels of random noise, each with a separate frequency. At the other end, the receiver used another vocoder that played the same noise which, when synced with the original transmission, could synthesise and decode the information, returning the frequencies to their initial state. The message was then presented in what the instrument's phonetic engineers described as a 'spectral description' of speech (Tompkins 2010: 4). While the process was simple, without the key to the transposed frequencies, the message was virtually undecipherable. During World War II it became a significant weapon, used by Churchill and Truman to encode correspondence regarding major events such as D-Day.

The vocoder's early appropriation by musicians began in electronic music studios, like the WDR, Cologne. Werner Meyer-Eppler (1913–60), one of the WDR's founders, is particularly important to the story of the vocoder. Applying his background in physics and acoustics to experimental phonetics, Meyer-Eppler explored the creative possibilities of vocal transformation, producing a book in 1949 that focused on the boundaries between electronic music and synthesised speech (Grant 2001). This work on phonetics fed into the vocoder experimentation of the studio's musicians, who explored the instrument's potential for radical fusion – of human with machine, of organic with inorganic and of the real and the mediated (a phenomenon discussed further in →Chapter 14, 'Race and Ethnicity'). Although speech synthesis was significant to much of the WDR avant-garde, the vocoder itself was incorporated into the work of Mauricio Kagel (in *Sur Scène*, 1959/1960, created with equipment from the Siemens Studio for Electronic Music, Munich) and Karlheinz Stockhausen (in his opera *Freitag aus Licht*, 1996). In her work on the Cold War avant-garde, Jennifer Iversen notes that neither composer was aware of the vocoder's military implications or telecommunication history but that they were intrigued by its possibility for 'body-machine interchangeability' (Iversen 2019: 188) and capacity for sonic Otherness, created either through rupture and transformation, or synthesis and transgression.

- Mauricio Kagel, *Sur Scène* (1959/1960)

It was not long before the possibilities afforded by this 'interchangeability' of the subjective and the mechanical drew the attention of musicians working to very different aesthetics. Innovations were rapid. In 1968 Robert Moog created one of the earliest musical vocoders while electronic pioneer Bruce Haack created the 'Farad', a prototype he used on his *The Electric Lucifer* album (1970). 1970 also saw Wendy Carlos' (1939–) vocoder prototype transfigure the vocal textures of Beethoven's Symphony No. 9 into the dystopian anthem for *A Clockwork Orange* (Stanley Kubrick, 1971). By the late 1970s, the appearance of early analogue renditions with

Case Study 8.2: (cont.)

chorus and string effects was producing a surge of exploration in popular culture, and the Korg polyphonic VC-10 (1978) was quickly appropriated by Kraftwerk, Rick Wakeman, Pink Floyd and later Goldfrapp, while the Roland VP-330 (1979) can be heard in the work of Tangerine Dream, Air and Royksopp as well as Vangelis' futuristic *Blade Runner* score (1982). While most examples of vocoder use can be found in isolated songs, like Phil Collins' 'In the Air Tonight' (1981), for others, like Mike Oldfield, Herbie Hancock and Daft Punk, it became a recurring feature.

- Wendy Carlos, 'March from A Clockwork Orange (Ninth Symphony, Fourth Movement, Abridged)' (from *A Clockwork Orange*, Columbia Records, 1972)
- Laurie Anderson, 'O Superman', *Big Science* (Warner Bros., 1982)

In disturbing the voice, the vocoder disguises and mediates presence. While many – like Wendy Carlos and Vangelis above – have used its robotic sounds to suggest a futuristic aesthetic, the rupture of bodily utterance from transformed voice has enabled dominant ideologies around race, gender and camp to be troubled. Dave Tompkins, for instance, notes that for 1980s electro hip-hop artists, the removal of voice from body was emancipatory: 'the black voice removed from itself, dispossessed by Reaganomics, recession and urban renewal' could escape the weight of its cultural oppression (2010: 22). For others, the instrument's potential for transformation could renegotiate gender representation. In Laurie Anderson's (1947–) 1981 hit, 'O Superman', for instance, layers of the singer's voice are fed through a Roland VP-330. Susan McClary points to the multiplicity of this mediation: 'the closer we get to the source, the more distant becomes the imagined ideal of unmediated presence and authenticity. Anderson deliberately plays with those anxieties provoked when a voice is not securely grounded in a particular body. She insists on and problematizes her mediation' (1991: 137). While promotion of the vocoder's destabilising capacity can symbolise the dehumanising and 'alienating' (137) potential of media, McClary reads Anderson's estrangement of voice from body as an empowering gesture able to critique the cultural objectification of the woman's body by affording her voice a creative and authorial agency and her presence 'multiple identities' (141).

This multiplicity is also explored by Kay Dickinson (2001), who finds similar modes of gender construction in Cher's (1946–) 1998 hit 'Believe'. Dickinson mistakenly attributes the diffusion of Cher's voice to the vocoder, when in fact its transformation was due to Autotune, a technology introduced in 1997 to help performers correctly pitch their voices in live settings, yet quickly adapted to creative rather than corrective means. Nevertheless, the similar aesthetic of vocal processing muddles 'what is natural, what is the original and what the surface'. This confusion troubles 'staid notions of reality, the body, femininity and female capability' (345) and gives rise to a camp aesthetic. If we return to the early understanding of coded speech synthesis as

Case Study 8.2: (cont.)

producing a 'spectral description' of the original utterance, we can begin to understand the significance of the vocoder to contemporary forms of representation. With its routes in military communication, it is a quintessential twentieth-century instrument able to both humanise technology and de-familiarise traditional musical timbres. Where once it was used to conceal a message, its use in popular music embraces rupture and transformation as positive ways to rethink significant ideological positions.

Conclusion

The stories of instruments in the twentieth century, then, are complex. On the one hand, the sonic possibilities of existing instruments were expanded through performer behaviour (extended technique) and technical intervention (amplification). On the other, brand-new instruments were created that either emulated contemporary soundscapes (*intonarumori*), remediated old music (the sampler) or formed brand-new timbres (the Theremin and synthesiser). Many of these histories contend with the fragile borders between the old and the new, particularly in the use of innovative technologies to remediate pre-existing sounds and music. In light of these complexities, creative forms of musicology have emerged that deal with instruments not as isolated objects but as a framework for cultural activities in which social and political meaning can be reshaped or constructed anew. In our case studies, we focused on two instruments, one with a long- and well-established history, the other brand new. The entrenched gender and class associations of the piano were destabilised by twentieth-century performance practice, while the vocoder and its ability to displace cultural identity prompted audiences to think differently about musical material and the politics of performance.

PART III

Mediation

9 | Recording and Production

'The first thing about recording' ambient music composer Brian Eno has written, 'is that it makes repeatable what was otherwise transient and ephemeral' (Eno 2004: 127). Some of the biggest changes to musical culture in the twentieth century were the result of newly emerging recording technologies. As Brian Eno (1948–) suggests, sounds that once had to be performed live could now be captured, packaged, collected and distributed in ways unimaginable in the previous century. This affected both the creation and consumption of music. When used as an instrument to manipulate or make music – a process known as 'phonography' (Eisenberg 1987) – the tools for sound reproduction generated textures and structures difficult to replicate in live performance. In fact, audio engineering technologies saw the advent of reverb, echo, overdubbing, splicing and digital processing, techniques essential to genres as diverse as *musique concrète*, acousmatic sound art, dub, electronica, hip-hop and turntablism. Not only did these technologies give rise to new types of musician, from the studio engineer and producer to the DJ, they also encouraged collaborative ways of working rarely seen before.

The new technologies also had a profound impact on the ways in which music was created and consumed. Local oral cultures, significant performances and innovative styles could easily reach global audiences, enabling influence to move rapidly through musical communities, while the ability to reproduce sounds at the flick of a switch generated new ways of listening. For the first time, music lovers could enjoy private listening in their own homes on the radio and via home audio technology, or, as the century progressed, on the go via mobile media like transistor radios, Walkmans and MP3 players; on the other hand, communal forms of listening became commonplace, as music was piped into a variety of public spaces and experienced in the background of everyday activities. Sound recording technology also enabled changes in creative practice so radical that scholars like Eric Clarke have argued that 'it is recording that changed music so profoundly in the twentieth century, rather than the changes in "musical language"' (Clarke 2007: 48).

Building on Mark Katz's (2010) identification of seven ways that sound recording technologies have transformed musical practice – tangibility, portability, (in)visibility, repeatability, temporality, receptivity, manipulability – this chapter traces the celebrations of recording across the century. But it also outlines the considerable anxieties that the new technology caused for musicians and listeners alike, particularly in the century's early decades. For our case studies, we first focus on how early dub artists used the recording studio as an instrument in 1970s Jamaica, before exploring the different ways of listening that recorded music generated across the century.

Technology through the Century

Although technological progression was rapid, it is useful to identify four broad periods of profound change. The first begins in 1877 with Thomas Edison's phonograph (Figure 9.1), closely followed by Emil Berliner's gramophone in 1887, two inventions that enabled sound to be captured and reproduced for the first time. By the dawn of the new century, wax records could preserve and disseminate sonic material, and early recordings of Italian tenor Enrico Caruso and the Original Dixieland Jazz Band (1917) provide a fascinating glimpse into the century's early musical culture, tastes and aesthetics.

- Enrico Caruso singing Verdi's 'Questa o guella' from *Rigoletto* (1832): recorded in 1904 in Room 826, Carnegie Hall (Victor)

With the advent of radio in the 1920s, with its associated electrical microphones, the early period of acoustic reproducibility gave way to the electrical era. In the hands of HMV and Bell Telephone Laboratories, radio technology was used to extend the frequency range of recordable material to acquire a greater sound fidelity. The new microphones also enabled a spatial fidelity by capturing the sonic ambiance of performance space to give a greater sense of aural realism (Doyle 2004: 33) on the one hand, while also encouraging 'softer and more intimate' (Dibben 2016: 319) vocal styles through close miking. This technique, particularly apparent in the recordings of Bing Crosby and other crooners of the time (Doyle 2004), increased

Figure 9.1 Thomas Edison showcases the second version of his phonograph, 1878. Photograph by Levin Corbin Handy

the proximity between singer and audience and had a lasting impact on future songwriting and performance practice. As we shall see below, the mediation enabled by the microphone affected both pop and art musics.

• Bing Crosby, 'White Christmas' (Decca, 1942)

Although these early years saw the advent of audio engineers, who specialised in studio equipment, at this stage the role most often involved faithfully capturing what was in front of the microphone, as the editor of *High Fidelity* magazine wrote in 1951: a record should 'recreate as perfectly as possible, for the individual listener in his home, the *illusion* of the live performance' (Fowler 1951: 8). The idea of an 'individual' listener engaging with music at 'home' marks an extremely significant moment in our story. Short-playing shellac phonograph records (or 78s) and their eventual replacement by the long-playing vinyl disc (LPs), were tangible, portable and repeatable (to use three of Katz's points), making music readily available for domestic consumption. In the previous century, unless you played an instrument yourself, engaging with music was usually a communal activity, undertaken in a public space. Recorded music took music into the home, where people could listen on their own as and when they liked. Although we will learn more about this in our second case study, it is important to note here that as music performance became tied to physical objects, it became a commodity (Adorno 1941: 17–48) and the music industry as we now know it began to emerge. By the years following World War II, the industry was in full force, as Albin Zak III writes: 'Columbia Records alone reported a sales increase of 850 per cent from 1945 to 1946, and all the other large companies registered profit increases of at least 100 per cent in the same year' (2012: 43). By the end of the 1940s, the vinyl 45 rpm single (also known as the 7") and increasing radio play were revolutionising the production and sale of popular music yet again (Peterson 1990). These developments in the US music industry would soon be mirrored in other countries across the world.

By now, the third period of technological change was in full swing. The 1950s saw record companies moving away from direct-to-disc recording in favour of magnetic tape, which had undergone significant development in Germany during the war. Not only did the format offer an enhanced sound quality, it also enabled audio information to be manipulated and edited after capture. As we have seen, it became one of the first technologies to be treated creatively by mid-century composers like Pierre Schaeffer, Pauline Oliveros, Daphne Oram and Pierre Henry (→Chapter 8, 'Instruments'). By 1955, one of the most significant developments in the history of recording occurred. Multitrack tape recording, pioneered by Les Paul (1915–2009) among others, allowed users to mix, splice, sample, reverse and drop in sounds rather than simply capture live performance, a process that marked the transition of recording from a process of preservation to an art form (Eisenberg 1987). Whereas before, records were usually cut live following intense rehearsal, now different takes could be combined, multiple parts added and sounds fundamentally altered in post-production. Virgil Moorefield, in his aptly named book, *The Producer as Composer* (2015), charts this process, describing the changing soundscape as a move from the 'illusion of reality' to the 'reality of illusion' (109). British producer and audio engineer Joe Meek (1929–67), for instance, was a pioneer of composite recording and kickstarted techniques that were later to become normal studio practice, like close miking and the compression of an audio signal to reduce loud sounds and amplify quiet ones into the mid-range.

The century's fourth period of recording began in the 1970s, with the development of digital sound encoding, pioneered by Sony, and signalled by the first all-digitally recorded album to be released by a major label; Ry Cooder's 1979 *Bop Till You Drop* (Warner Bros.). In 1982, ABBA's *The Visitors* became the first all-digital pop record to appear on compact disc (CD). By the 1990s, digital audio had replaced analogue technology in most major studios. Digital Audio Workstations (DAWs) and software such as Pro Tools could record, edit and produce audio files from a single work-station – the computer – giving engineers and producers precise control over a sound's treatment and placement. Because digital capture enabled a larger dynamic range without degradation of signal quality no matter how many tracks were added, the new workstations could accommodate unlimited overdubs, which could be easily moved around and edited.

One of the most controversial studio interventions of the digital age came with the pitch-correcting technology Auto-Tune, which launched in 1997 as a hardware and a DAW plug-in. Although the manipulation of a voice to evoke particular connotations in listeners – what Serge Lacasse calls 'vocal staging' (2001: 56) – can be found throughout recording history, Auto-Tune enabled engineers to re-pitch off-key notes and smooth out the tiny fluctuations natural to the singing voice, a practice that has since been embraced by many performers. Auto-Tune has also attracted many detractors, however, who complain that the retuned voices sound inauthentic and de-humanised. Although for many the idea of recording and technology remained a source of anxiety, as we shall discuss below, others turned these negative attributes into positive creative material by setting Auto-Tune to its highest level and embraced the resultant 'unset-tlingly robotic tone' (Milner 2009: 232: →Chapter 8, 'Instruments'). By the beginning of the twenty-first century, pitch-altering software had become so prevalent that Simon Reynolds called it both '[e]poch-defining' and 'epoch-defacing': 'Few innovations in sound-production have been simul-taneously so reviled and so revolutionary' (2018).

The last decades of the century also saw an important shift in audio dissemination. As the 1980s unfolded, the medium of tape augmented the possibilities for engagement. Where the LP enabled home listening, the compact cassette and portable tape recorders (like the Walkman, released in 1979) gave rise to the beginnings of mobile media and a diversification of listening practices. The next shift came in 1988, when CD sales began to overtake vinyl. Able to produce the entire sound spectrum without distor-tion, CDs offered an enlarged storage capacity and, read by a laser beam rather than a record stylus, did not degrade when played. However, by the

1990s, their dominance over the market was being challenged by digital audio storage like WAV and MP3, which reduced file sizes through digital signal compression to allow large amounts of virtual data to be easily stored and transported. By the end of the century, Apple's iTunes and the iPod (both 2001) had signalled the beginning of a new era of sound reproducibility.

Echo, Reverb and the Virtual Spaces of Rock 'n' Roll

The increasingly specialised nature of the studio gave rise to new types of musicians who were highly skilled in certain technologies. The audio engineer, for instance, provided the technical skill necessary to capture and manipulate sounds in a certain way, and there sprung up several significant collaborations, including Leanne Ungar, who engineered records for Leonard Cohen, and Susan Rogers, who worked with Prince on his *Purple Rain* album (1984). The music producer, on the other hand, would usually assume overarching control over all aspects of the recording session, and could be involved with writing and arranging the material as well as managing the actual recording sessions. Forging unique sonic aesthetics, producers like Quincy Jones, Nile Rodgers, John Culshaw, Rick Rubin, T Bone Burnett, Denis Bovell, Daniel Lanois and others (whom we will meet later in this chapter), became as renowned as the artists they recorded. The examples below show how a producer can create an artist's unique sound.

- Michael Jackson, 'Bad' (from *Bad*, produced by Quincy Jones, Epic, 1987)
- Emmylou Harris (with Daniel Lanois), 'Goodbye' (from *Wrecking Ball*, Elektra, 1995: song written by Steve Earle)

While these roles became increasingly distinct as the century wore on, the formative years saw a more unified approach to recording, with many early studio owners like founder of Sun Records Sam Phillips, who produced work for Elvis, Roy Orbison, Johnny Cash and Howlin' Wolf, taking on multiple roles not only to maintain their independence but also to keep costs down (Williams 2006; Bell 2008). This is particularly apparent for Cordell Jackson (1923–2004) who, in 1956, became one of the first women producers when she sidestepped the male-dominated environment of Sun Records to engineer and arrange rock 'n' roll albums in her home studio for her self-founded Memphis label, Moon Records (Currans-Sheehan 2009).

It was during these years that some of the most notable developments in studio technique began to coalesce into a style that was to have a lasting effect on popular culture. Several musicologists (Lacasse 2001; Dibben 2003; Doyle 2004) have identified a history of real and imagined sonic ambiance that exists around the edges of recorded music, with Nicola Dibben suggesting that '[t]he history of recording contains within it a chronicle of virtual space' (2003: 319). Early on, virtual space was most often signalled by the (often artificial) addition of echo – 'the presence of one or more slightly delayed repetitions of a discrete source sound' – and reverb – a 'reverberant-sounding continuation of the source sound as though the sound has been recorded in a highly resonant acoustic space' (Doyle 2004: 32).

In his work on the recording strategies of early popular music production, Peter Doyle (2004) argues that room ambiance and reverberation entered practice during the 1920s, when electric sound recording gained greater fidelity, noting that more room tone was used for orchestral recordings than popular songs, while dance music had little or no reverb. By the 1940s, Bill Putman, working with tape, became an early pioneer of the techniques, producing the first hit song to add artificial reverb, the Harmonicats' instrumental hit 'Peg O' My Heart' (1947). Four years later and Les Paul introduced the mainstream audience to tape echo, close miking and multitracked voices in his number 1 hit, 'How High the Moon' (with Mary Ford, 1951).

- Les Paul and Mary Ford, 'How High the Moon' (Capitol Records, 1951)

But it was with the advent of rock 'n' roll in the latter half of the 1950s that echo and reverb were pushed to the front of recordings at the hands of Leonard Chess at Chess Records, as well as Sam Phillips at Sun Records, who pioneered his own unique technique known as slapback echo delay. Most often, echo was added from the control room rather than the studio, so the musicians were unaware of the manipulation as they performed (Guralnick 1994: 237). Doyle (2004) refers to the result as '"pictorial" spatialising – reverb and echo effects deployed in combination with certain lyrics to render aural vistas' (32) and uses Elvis' (1935–77) 'Heartbreak Hotel' (1956), recorded with Chet Atkins in Nashville's RCA studio, as a clear example of such a construction. The sonic ambiance was taken from the studio's hallway and fed into the studio, allowing the performers to play into and respond to the reverb as the song developed. This ensured that the effect integrated into the song and made aesthetic sense: 'the reverb is more or less "authorised" by the references in the lyrics to the baroque, horror film-like hotel located in the noirish "Lonely St"' (45).

- Elvis, 'Heartbreak Hotel' (RCA Victor, 1956)

The Music Producer as Creator

When the input of a producer became such that new sounds and textures were formed, their role transformed from what Adam Bell describes as 'a recording *facilitator* to a recording *creator*' (Bell 2008: 33). At this point, Michael Chanan explains, 'the essential activity of the musician, the performance of music, becomes more and more fragmented' (Chanan 1995: 144). This creative involvement could be structural: in the 1930s and 1940s, for instance, American producer Teo Macero developed a cut-and-paste tape editing method of production that he later used to manipulate the sounds of Miles Davis' (1926–91) *Bitches Brew* (1970), famously using nineteen edits and loops during the post-production of the first track, 'Pharaoh's Dance' (Tingen 2001).

- Miles Davis, 'Pharaoh's Dance' (from *Bitches Brew*, Columbia Records, 1970)

But it could also be ambient: Paul Théberge argues that stereo sound complicated authorship as 'the overall musical texture was increasingly given to the sound engineer and producer' (Théberge 1997: 216). Sometimes, the sonic stamp of a producer could be such that entirely new genres were generated. Jamaican Sonia Pottinger (1931–2010), who produced albums for Culture, Toots & the Maytals and the Ethiopians among others, was instrumental in forming the reggae sound for the 1960s and 1970s, for instance, while Silvia Robinson (1935–2011), founder of hip-hop label Sugar Hill Records in Harlem, produced the Sugarhill Gang's 'Rapper's Delight' (1979), widely regarded as the first rap track to reach a wide audience.

It was American producer Phil Spector (1939–2021), however, who became known as pop's 'first "auteur"' (Bannister 2006b: 36). His 'wall of sound' aesthetic, which drove tracks like the Crystals' 'Da Doo Ron Ron' (1963, co-written by Spector) and the Ronettes' 'Be My Baby' (1963), was created by using Ampex three-track recorders (Figure 9.2, shown here with a later digital addition) to build a wash of instruments doubling and tripling parts to create an unprecedented depth of texture and sound. Capturing backing tracks live in a single take, Spector would then place the lead vocal on the second track, before filling out the third to form reverberant echo chambers unlike anything heard before. His unique sound and deep involvement in most areas of the recording process led to a diffusion of authorship and initiated what Chanan describes as 'power struggles for aesthetic control of the finished product' (1995: 144–5).

Figure 9.2 The Ampex three-track tape recorder. Photograph by Cliff

- The Crystals, 'Da Doo Ron Ron' (produced by Phil Spector, Philles Records, 1963)

But the distribution of authorship did not have to result in a power struggle: it could also generate productive collaborations. The work that resulted in the long partnership between the Beatles and their producer George Martin (1926–2016), was highly creative, for example (Williams 2006: 297–8; Zagorski-Thomas 2014) and Olivier Julien (2008: 162) notes a 'gradual integration of arranging and recording into one and the same process' from 1963 to *Sgt. Pepper's Lonely Hearts Club Band* (1967). While *Sgt. Pepper* was hailed a great success, some reviewers critiqued the 'special effects', which they saw as 'dazzling but ultimately fraudulent' (reprinted in Skinner Sawyers 2006: 99). Others questioned whether the complicated textures could be performed live (Moorefield 2005: 55). The integration of arranging and recording is also apparent in the 1967 single 'Strawberry Fields Forever', whose innovative techniques, like reverse-recorded instruments and tape loops, took fifty-five hours of studio time to perfect (2005: 194). However, the song marks an important moment in the shared creative process between musicians and producer. Martin and sound engineer Geoff Emerick decided to splice the song together from two separate takes. Because both had been played at slightly different tempos, when placed together, they created a small shift in the pitch: 'Although the splice is nearly undetectable', writes Katz, 'the slightly altered speed of Lennon's voice helps give the song it's dreamlike quality' (2010: 47). Martin used a similar technique on *Sgt. Pepper* to juxtapose two very different fragments – one by Lennon, the other McCartney – to produce 'A Day in the Life'. This intervention was so significant that album reviewer John Gabree was compelled to ask 'whether we are to credit the group, the producer or the engineer ... Shouldn't we laud Martin instead of the quartet?' (speaking in 1991; quoted in Kimsey 2008: 125).

• The Beatles, 'Strawberry Fields Forever' (Parlophone, 1967)

In other cases, the notion of authorship did not arise. The recording process for the Beach Boys' *Pet Sounds* (1966), one of the century's first concept albums (Lambert 2008), is a key example here. While his band-mates were on tour, Brian Wilson wrote, arranged, recorded and produced most of the album. After extensive rehearsals with carefully chosen musicians, Wilson shunned Capitol Studios in order to make use of the different equipment and strengths of a variety of recording spaces (Granata 2017: ch. 5). When the other members of the band returned from their tour, he taught them their parts individually before overdubbing their vocals, making extensive use of multitracking to layer the different components, a process that afforded him ultimate control over the final mix. For more on the rock album, see →Chapter 5, 'Work and Notation'.

Case Study 9.1: Lee 'Scratch' Perry and the Emergence of Dub Music

In the main chapter, we have seen how recording technology profoundly impacted twentieth-century musical culture. Here we focus on dub, a genre characterised by heavy bass and rhythm that developed in the 1970s studios of Jamaica and flourished at the hands of producers and studio engineers like King Tubby (1941–89) and Lee 'Scratch' Perry (1936–2021). The music emerged as a positive space away from the postcolonialism, economic depression and political instability that was shaking Jamaica at the time, as Michael Veal (2007) explains: 'Infused with Rastafari-influenced themes of African repatriation and Old Testament allusion, dub provided a collective imaginative escape, an optimistic teleology for the displaced victims of the African diaspora' (80–1). This positive space was crafted by dub artists who worked the studio to forge distinctive new sonic and cultural aesthetics that became a fundamental motivator of punk, trip-hop, jungle, drum and bass, ragga and electronica.

Case Study 9.1: (cont.)

Dub is hard to define. Although primarily a studio practice, it originated as part of Jamaica's live sound-system culture. Some (Barrow and Dalton 1997: 199) have broken the emergence of dub into three phases beginning with 'instrumentals' of existing reggae songs, and the more creative intervention known as 'versions', which were produced for local sound-systems deejays to 'toast' over (a particular style of rap). Versions were cut on 'dub plates', acetate discs that could be made cheaply, but degraded swiftly. In the small Jamaican market, studios were able to generate income through multiple customised versions for different sound systems to use.

Dub music emerged from these early live-music practices. The verb 'to dub' evolved in the industry to refer to the process of making a double of a recording. In music, the term also involves copying, but refers more positively to the creative remixing and layering of pre-existent tracks to produce characteristic echo- and reverb-heavy rhythm sections (the 'riddim'). Original vocals are often removed or edited into ethereal snippets, keyboard and guitar tracks are temporarily omitted to give a greater sense of space, and samples – from other songs, TV, the natural world – are mixed into the riddim or combined with new vocal lines. The genre emerged around 1972 when engineer King Tubby, having found success with his Kingston sound system, got hold of a dub cutting machine, a two-track tape recorder and a four-track mixing desk (Partridge 2007: 316) and began to overdub and mix music brought to him by other producers. Christopher Partridge (2007) explains that 'The renewing and reinventing was not simply musicological, but it was also technological, in that the very equipment used to produce the music was itself often a modification, a version of an original piece of equipment' (316). Having worked as an electrical engineer, Tubby, for instance, made his own echo delay unit 'by passing a loop of tape over the heads of an old two-track machine' (Barrow 1994). In 1973, Tubby worked on *Blackboard Jungle Dub* with Lee 'Scratch' Perry and the Upsetters, a record many consider to be the first fully dub album (although this is debated; see Katz 2000: 173).

- The Upsetters, 'Rubba, Rubba Words' (from *Blackboard Jungle Dub*, Clocktower Records, 1973)

Perry (Figure 9.3) quickly became one of the genre's pioneers, collaborating with Bob Marley and the Wailers, the Congos, the Beastie Boys, Mad Professor and the Clash, whose punk anthem 'Complete Control' (1977) marked an important merging of aesthetics, cultures and radical political views. Having worked in other studios as a vocalist, songwriter, producer and engineer, Perry had wide-ranging skills that enabled him to set up his own studio in his garden, the Black Ark (1973–83), named after the Ark of the Covenant, with its house band – the Upsetters. Although Perry's equipment was good quality, it was not cutting edge. While European and US studios

Case Study 9.1: (cont.)

Figure 9.3 Lee 'Scratch' Perry in his Black Ark studio

were working with sixteen or twenty-four tracks, many Jamaican studios were still working with eight. Perry supported his Echoplex delay unit, Roland space echo and phaser unit with a four-track Soundcraft board and a TEAC 3340 recorder (Partridge 2007: 326; Bradley 2001: 325; Katz 2000: 180).

- The Congos, 'Solid Foundation' (from *The Heart of the Congos*, Black Art, 1977)
- The Clash, 'Complete Control' (from *The Clash*, CBS, 1977)

Perry turned the potential restrictions of his equipment into innovative techniques, and Steve Barrow and Peter Dalton explain that 'the Black Ark sound exemplified the Jamaican approach of making maximum demands of minimal resources' (1997: 183). Limited to four tracks, Perry had to bounce material to make room for more layers, resulting in a reduced sound quality that quickly became a unique part of his disorientating aesthetic – or as David Toop puts it, 'supernatural soundworlds' (1995: 114) – characterised by a density of distorted echoes, reverb and jump-cuts: 'the sound that I get out of the Black Ark studio, I don't really get it out of no other studio. It was like a space craft. You could hear space in the tracks' (Perry quoted in Toop 1995 114). Space resonates through tracks like 'Rubba, Rubba Words', from *Blackboard Jungle Dub*: 2:40 minutes in, and an abrupt yet playful oscillation between raucous ensemble and quiet bass solo draws attention to Perry's studio techniques. But it is also more than this. Veal (2007) notes that 'dub's deconstruction of traditional song structures evokes a sense of discontinuity and ominous indeterminacy and reflects the psychic spatial and temporal discombobulations of ganja, the Rastafari's sacramental herb' (2007: 80–1).

Case Study 9.1: (cont.)

Spatial and temporal discombobulation can also arise from Perry's use of real-world sounds. In 'Kojak', from his *Revolution Dub* album (1975), for instance, snippets from radio and British comedy and samples from Bunny Clarke's 'Move Out of My Way' (1973) are scattered over a pre-existent track propelled by an early drum machine. Here, echo, repetition and the remediation of existing sounds conjure up the aesthetics of alienation, recollection and dislocated time that fuel the 'collective imaginative escape' mentioned above.

- Lee Scratch Perry, 'Kojak' (from *Revolution Dub*, Cactus, 1975)

Here, then, we have an example of a genre born in the recording studio and driven by producers who far exceed our traditional understanding of the role. In fact, for many, a more creative designation has been preferred. Veal (2007), for instance, refers to the dub mixer as a '"soundscape" composer concerned with regulating the musical parameters of (electronically manipulated) texture and soundscape as much as the traditional parameters of melody, rhythm, and harmony' (18), while Jeff Stratton refers to King Tubby as a 'postproduction composer' (2005). It is clear to see from this brief introduction that dub is a genre sculpted by technology (Bradley 2001). For early producers like Perry, the studio was an instrument that could generate new material from old.

Liveness, Authenticity and the Ideal Performance

By now it should be clear that the twentieth-century recording studio was not simply a place to capture and transmit sounds but also a site to create and manipulate them (Bell 2008: 37). While the producers above used technology creatively to craft new and imaginative sound worlds, others, including those working in the art-music sphere, explored its potential for generating perfect renditions of particular pieces. Composers who perform have often recorded and rerecorded their own works to demonstrate 'the right way' to play a certain piece, for instance. In one example, Stravinsky made a point of recording his changing interpretations of his own works (see Chanan 1995: 122–4). Evan Eisenberg (1987: 113) says that some composers – he names Stravinsky, Schoenberg and others – have used recording to reinforce the idea of the 'Masterpiece'. But the lure of a reconstructed, 'perfect' rendition was also appealing to producers and performers. Walter Legge, arguably the first art-music producer to assemble pieces from multiple (sometimes microscopic) takes to produce a performance that would be impossible live, explained: 'I decided that recording must be a collaboration between artists and what are now called "producers". I wanted better results than are normally possible in public performance' (Legge cited in Eisenberg 1987: 96). For Canadian pianist Glenn Gould (1932–82), one of the earliest musicians to embrace recording technology, the promise of 'a more cogent experience than is now possible' (Gould 1966, quoted in Andersson and Andersson 2006: 97) led him to retire from public performance in 1964 to concentrate entirely on studio work. For him, the opportunity to cut and splice takes in order to cut mistakes, accidents and inelegant passages threatened the very future of live concerts. Instead, music could be constructed and manipulated over time, using takes from different sessions, locations, equipment and engineers, enabling the performer to 'assume something of an editorial role. Inevitably . . . the functions of the performer and of the tape editor begin to overlap' (Gould 1966, quoted in Cox and Warner 2004: 118). Writing of his recording (Columbia Records, 1964) of Bach's Fugue No. 20 in A Minor from Book 1 of *The Well-Tempered Clavier* (BWV 865, 1722), Gould explains that although takes 6 and 8 appeared at first satisfactory, the privilege of subsequent and repeated listening revealed 'monotonous' defects (118) that prompted him to create 'one performance to consist alternately of takes 6 and 8' (118). This opportunity for combination, he argued, enabled musicians to 'transcend the limitations that performance imposes upon the imagination' (118).

- Bach, Fugue No. 20 in A Minor from Book 1 of *The Well-Tempered Clavier* (BWV 865, 1722) recorded by Glenn Gould (Columbia Records, 1964)

Ideal performances represent a technological intervention into the precarities of live performance. But this was not always desired, and other artists sought to maintain – or give the illusion of – the spontaneity of a live setting. For some, this involved extreme measures: John Cage (1912–92), who famously hated records and claimed he did not own any, sought to actively incorporate recording materials – digital tape, microphone, speakers, record players – into live performance to keep music live and relevant. In fact, David Grubbs begins his book, *Records Ruin the Landscape* (2014), with a general observation that:

Most genres in experimental and avant-garde music in the 1960s were ill suited to be represented in the form of a recording. These various activities – including indeterminate music, long-duration minimalism, text scores, happenings, live electronic music, free jazz, and free improvisation – were not only predicated on being experienced in live performance, but they can also be said to have actively undermined the form of the sound recording. (2014: 1)

For Grubbs, such music was intended to be different in every performance, so to pin it down to a single ideal iteration made little sense.

This question was also pertinent for other types of music. To capture the 'authenticity' of liveness, for instance, became particularly important for many recording folk musicians. Bob Dylan (1941–), for instance, is often seen as a primarily performing artist who is wary of the studio: there are many anecdotes about his reluctance to spend time laying down tracks, and many of his recordings give the appearance that they were captured live (which is not to say that multiple takes and versions were not worked through beforehand: for more on the intellectual and obsessive study of Dylan, known as Dylanology, see Weberman 1969). Building on the myth of spontaneity, Paul Williams (1990, 1992, 2004) has suggested that the artist's apparently dismissive position on his recorded material, together with his proclivity for radically rearranging songs in live settings, destabil-ises the idea that his studio recordings represent his definitive voice. The cult of the specific performance that developed around Dylan pervades his reviews, which regularly describe live renditions of songs (even in their mediated, recorded form) as more instinctive and expressive than the recorded versions. This view positions Dylan's recorded material as work-ing drafts to be later developed in a live setting (Negus 2010: 213–14).

The impression of a raw, live performance is also important to other genres and requires skilful production knowhow to reduce the studio's mediating presence. A good example of this can be found in Steve Albini's production work for Nirvana's *In Utero* (1993). The album is described by drummer Dave Grohl as sounding

like a band in a room but there's some sort of sonic element to it that nobody else could get ... I remember when we were making *In Utero*, one of the things Steve [Albini] talked about was trying to record or mix or equalise a band in a way that seemed natural without the vocals seeming disconnected from the music, like, I think what he tried to do was present the song to the listener in a way that sounded entirely real ... I swear we would do one take and he would hit stop and say 'what's next?' (Boilen and Hilton 2013)

• Nirvana, 'Heart-Shaped Box' (from *In Utero*, DGC, 1993)

Of course, such appearance of liveness in fact involves extremely careful technological skill. Sound planes, spatialisation and stereo, compression and equalisation, amplification and proximity have produced artificial forms of crystal sonic clarity – or hyperreality – that have become naturalised (Zagorski-Thomas 2014; Théberge 2004). For Roquer González (2018: 17), 'the truth is that technology has substantially conditioned our perception of sound reality: we have been seduced to participate in an audio virtual reality experience that we now accept as natural'. Drawing our attention to Dylan's thirty-four studio albums, for instance, Keith Negus finds significant 'audible evidence' (2010: 214) of a producer's input. For him, studio rearrangements and Dylan's songwriting process demonstrate a 'phonographic imagination' that has been shaped by listening to recorded music and the development of a clear studio aesthetic.

For some musicians and scholars, the normalisation of a perceived and idealised performance has changed our expectations of music in concert. Recorded music, in other words, has influenced our musical ears, as Mark Katz writes: 'When the phonograph was invented, the goal for any recording was to simulate a live performance, to approach reality as closely as possible. Over the decades, expectations have changed. For many – perhaps most – listeners, music is now primarily a technologically mediated experience. Concerts must therefore live up to recordings' (2010: 26). Katz uses music historian Joseph Horowitz's description of the Chicago Symphony's '"machine-like" and "precision-tooled"' live performance of Brahms' Symphony No. 1 (Op. 68, 1876) as an example of a concert rendition that sounded as though the orchestra had been '"fed through the giant speakers". In other words, "they sounded like a phonograph record"' (Katz 2010: 267).

The Studio as an Instrument: Deskilling versus Enabling

The reception of recorded music was not without its anxieties. Throughout the century there was concern that with ample access to reproduced sounds, people may be less compelled to learn instruments or specific skills. This worry was voiced early on by one of the very earliest stars of the phonograph, the marching band composer J. P. Sousa (1854–1932), who speculated that the availability of recorded music would lead to what we now call 'deskilling' – the progressive loss of musical skill among the population as a whole, as people could rely on recorded sounds rather than learning to make them themselves (Eisenberg 1987: 148). The worry was that this would result in a reduction of communal music making.

We could argue, however, that in fact, the opposite has happened: technology has enabled new types of musician, from the producer and audio engineer to the studio-based performer. Offering room to experiment, the studio has also drawn the attention of composers, from those working in the electronic music studios to those sound-tracking films (→Chapter 8, 'Instruments'; →Chapter 12, 'Music and the Moving Image'). Like performers, composers have used studio technology to fundamentally change compositional methods. Speaking of his creative process, Brian Eno, who cannot read or write music, refers to

in-studio composition, where you no longer come to the studio with a conception of the finished piece. Instead you come with actually rather a bare skeleton of the piece, or perhaps with nothing at all … Once you become familiar with studio facilities … you can begin to compose in relation to those facilities … In a compositional sense this takes the making of music away from any traditional way that composers worked. (2004/1979: 129)

- Brian Eno, *Ambient 1: Music for Airports* (Polydor, 1978).

Recording technology may have led to fewer people taking up acoustic instruments, then, but it also gave access to techniques of music making which do not require traditional performance or instrumental skills. It is not that producers and engineers lack musical skills; it is that they have developed newer kinds of creative ability. Aden Evens, for instance, says that music that arises through digital processes replaces the physical and acoustic gestures of fretting, bowing, picking and hitting with the technological gestures of cutting, pasting, dubbing and duplicating, so it is not a matter of what instrument someone plays but rather what part of the production process they enable (Evens 2005: 124–5: 90).

We have noted above that the recording studio saw the advent of new and specialised roles in the process of music recording and production. And yet, as the tools for digital music reproduction became more affordable, the merging of roles became increasingly common. It was not long after major recording studios turned to DAWs in the late 1980s that home studios became readily available, giving rise to the bedroom producer, an artist who can work alone with low-cost technology. Folktronica artist Fourtet, whose first two albums (*Dialogue*, 1999; *Pause*, 2001) span the turn of the new century, for instance, produced his work using just a DAT recorder, a Creative Labs Soundblaster Live soundcard on his Windows PC and a hi-fi.

During the century, the technological process and the equipment for reproduction have been foregrounded as intensively creative forces in and of themselves. Turntablism is an excellent example of this. As we saw in →Chapter 3, 'Postmodernism', early hip-hop DJs isolated and manipulated pre-existent beats and samples in live, sometimes competitive ('battle') settings. Although by the 1980s the turntablist was being displaced by the rapping MC and digital sampling equipment, later artists Kid Koala, DJ Shadow and DJ Spooky moved into more experimental areas, while DJ networks like San Francisco's Sister SF helped to promote and support female DJs in this male-dominated arena.

Where Are All the Women?

During this brief foray through the history of music producing, you will have noticed that the role has been dominated by men. In fact, writing in the 1970s, Simon Frith and Angela McRobbie (1990) noted how the whole music industry, including 'popular musicians, writers, creators, technicians, engineers and producers' was 'male run' (373–4). And yet the under-representation of women in studio roles has been particularly enduring for several reasons. First, and particularly in the early years, women were largely excluded from studio spaces, as Paula Wolfe explains: 'Historically, music production knowledge and skill have been accessed and developed in the professional recording studio, a site gendered as a male space of creativity', not only because of the enduring association of technology with male-dominated expertise but also because of the producer's strong association 'with notions of power and control' (Wolfe 2012). In fact, in 1959, Decca Records told electronic music pioneer Delia Derbyshire, who later assumed a revolutionary role at the Radiophonic workshop alongside Daphne Oram and became a founding member of White Noise, that 'they didn't employ women in the recording studio' (Derbyshire quoted in Niebur 2010: 98).

- White Noise, 'Here Come the Fleas' (from *An Electric Storm*, Island Records, 1968)

Second, the hostility of mainstream studios and its impact on the gendered perceptions of recording creativity have had a lasting and negative effect on women assuming audio production or engineering roles (Théberge 1997: 451). Several musicologists (Whiteley 2000; Leonard 2007b) have identified how far-reaching the gendering of music production and its technologies has been, noting how media outlets and even journalism have tended to perpetuate these 'patriarchal assumptions' (Mayhew 2004: 232) in their language. To help counter this, the more recent feminist discourse of Tara

Rodgers, developed in her *Pink Noise* project, introduced an alternative and more organic female (rather than 'feminine') language around music technology and sound (re)production (2010: 26).

But this does not mean that women did not produce music during the twentieth century: rather, that their work has not always been recognised. Above, we have acknowledged the pivotal work of Cordell Jackson, Sonia Pottinger and Silvia Robinson, but there were also others. Ethel Gabriel, for instance, became the first female producer to work for a major label (RCA Victor from the late 1950s to 1984). Not only did she oversee significant developments in early stereo sound in her production work with Elvis, Henry Mancini, Perry Como and on two Grammy-nominated albums (1967 and 1969), but she also pioneered computer restoration techniques (for Caruso's early recordings). Kate Bush has produced all her work since *The Dreaming* (1982), while Sylvia Massy produced Tool's extremely successful *Undertow* album in 1993. Although not always highly visible, then, there has been an important female presence in the history of music production, so it is astonishing to note that during the century, not a single (non-classical) Grammy was awarded to a woman producer, despite nominations including Janet Jackson (1990), Sheryl Crow (1998) and Lauryn Hill (1999). Notably, these nominations are for women who produce their own music, which suggests that power conflicts and studio accessibility prevented women from successfully infiltrating studio practice even as the century closed.

Collectors and Curators of Sounds and Cultures

If we now turn our attention to recorded music as a product, to be sold, bought, collected and distributed, we can see that audio technology has played an important part in the shaping of musical tastes and the configuration of canons during the century. Speaking about the arrival of records, Evan Eisenberg notes that 'Music is now fully a commodity, exchangeable for the universal commodity, money' (1987: 20). Music's emerging double role as a live and recorded medium at the start of the century connected it to the art-versus-commerce debate that was already underway in the other arts (➔Chapter 10, 'Copyright and the Music Industry'). In the 1940s, Adorno became one of the most vocal opponents of the commodification of music, targeting the collector whom he regarded as one who amasses music's *objects* without real concern for its *content*: the point for these music collectors is the collecting, not the music. When the music object is part of a 'lifestyle' rather than a specifically musical interest, music, he argues, can be said to have been commoditised (1941; we will explore this more in Case Study 9.2, 'Listening to Recorded Music').

Yet for others, recorded material played a positive role in the preservation of musical events and cultures. Dying or changing traditions could be sonically preserved, ensuring access to lost or changing practice. The recordings made of Alessandro Moreschi (1858–1922), the last castrati, in 1902 and 1904 give us a glimpse into a world that no longer exists, for instance, while ethnomusicologist Gilbert Rouget's 1946 recordings (released in 1948 by Pathé and La Boîte á Musique) of Pygmy culture in Gabon and Middle Congo, open doors to remote locations and cultures. Oral traditions – like Irish traditional music – can be frozen in time (Eisenberg 1987: 102) to capture part of an ongoing process, and the behaviour of audiences (did they participate, listen attentively, go about their business?) can provide vital historical clues about the tastes and behaviours of earlier concert practice. Also embedded in recorded music is significant detail about gesture and nuance that can reveal essential information about the techniques, rhythms or performance styles that were important to particular groups of musicians and their audiences. Lillian McMurray's (1949–98) label Trumpet Records (1951–5), for instance, produced early recordings of Mississippi Delta musicians such as Elmore James, whose raw, vivid and unique style is extremely difficult to convey in words.

The dissemination of these frozen archival moments quickly assumed significant pedagogical importance. Although access to all kinds of music is commonplace for us today, at the start of the twentieth century the opportunity to easily experience new and diverse sounds was revolutionary. In 1919, for instance, an article in *Musician* stated that recorded music could provide music teachers with 'a world-laboratory and Musical History Museum at small cost, no matter how remote . . . from the acknowledged centres of music' (quoted in Katz 2010: 69). Recorded music also opened new avenues of influence among musicians, who used records to expand their practice by emulating and responding to a great range of performers. A good example of this is the way that many jazz musicians in 1950s Philadelphia learned to play, as saxophonist Sam Reed (1935–) explains:

Well, we would listen to whatever the guys would play on the records at that time, everybody had a record machine, and whenever anything new came out we had it. Everybody was basically listening to what the other person was doing . . . and trying to imitate whatever they did, in sound or in structure, and then work it out to see exactly what he was doing. (Reed quoted in Perchard 2006: 28).

While Reed treats recorded sounds as part of a learning process, they could also initiate a revival of interest in forgotten styles. Harry Smith's (1923–91) compilation of blues, jazz, folk and gospel 78s recorded between 1927 and 1932 in his six-album *Anthology of American Folk Music* (1952), for instance, has been credited with initiating the subsequent American folk music revival. For the first time, collectors and curators could shape and disseminate aural historiographies and cultural narratives, choosing what to save and what to leave out (see →Chapter 4, 'Canons' for more on this process). At times, the perspective of the collector drew criticism. In her work on the early blues folklorists, for example, historian Marybeth Hamilton (2007) argues that what has become known as the Delta blues is a mythology created by the 'Blues Mafia' that included Alan Lomax, who recorded Lead Belly in the Southern penitentiaries, sociologist Howard Odum who used a cylinder phonograph to capture simple, repetitive folk tunes and Oxford- and Columbia-educated Dorothy Scarborough (Figure 9.4), who journeyed for four years from 1921 to collect Black folk songs. For Hamilton, these educated, white, middle-class folk scholars and collectors were instrumental in crafting stories of Black, poor musicians that ultimately determined what

Figure 9.4 Dorothy Scarborough, 1918

we have come to understand about artists like Robert Johnson, Muddy
Waters, Howlin' Wolf and others. And yet, these folklorists, she points
out, 'were born in the era of segregation' and 'made racial assumptions
that were hackneyed, condescending and often offensive' (2009: 18).

Case Study 9.2: Listening to Recorded Music

Recorded music allows us to re-listen. Where previously music was experienced as
a live, often social activity, audio technology enabled new forms of private and
communal engagement that altered 'the site, situation and practice of consuming
music' (Clarke 2007: 48). Although the personalised listening experience was not
new to the century – think of Wagner's speculation (1870) that Beethoven's deafness
attuned his inner ear to a more profound realm, or the transformation of rowdy opera
audiences into the attentive, emotionally involved ones of the nineteenth century who
often listened with eyes shut (Johnson 1995), for instance – the increasing affordability
of domestic listening devices in the 1950s allowed engagement with music to now
become a solitary activity.

The changes to listening practice that recorded music afforded were not universally
embraced. Leading the early negative response was Theodor Adorno (2002/1934), who
argued that phonograph music represented 'nothing more than ... acoustic photographs', which turned embodied events into a 'two-dimensional model of a reality that
can be multiplied without limit, displaced both spatially and temporally, and traded on
the open market' (278). For him, the poor sound quality and restricted dynamic range
of early recordings prevented full engagement with the music and failed to provide the
same aesthetic sophistication as a live concert. This, he argued, resulted in a distracted
attention that prevented listeners from forming critical and informed judgements.
Even worse, such distracted attention could lead to a regression in the quality of
listening that took place in the concert halls. Although coming from a completely
different position, John Cage also reviled the embalming and stultifying nature of
recorded material, arguing that captured music lost its fleeting, immediate, spontaneous life; moreover, repeated listening to such music reduced it to a museological
artefact (Grubbs 2014).

While Cage's position remained consistent, Adorno's did not, and he later suggested
that the repeatability of long-playing records (LPs) in fact gave rise to a more
musicological and studied form of listening: the ability to re-listen to certain passages
'foster[ed] a familiarity which is hardly afforded by the ritual of performance' (Adorno
2002/1969: 285). As time passed, and the quality of recorded material improved,
engaging attentively with recorded music became increasingly complex. Listeners

Case Study 9.2: (cont.)

not only had to grapple with musical material, but also with the subtleties of recording itself, as Axel Volmar (2019) argues: spatiality, definition and studio practice formed 'new ideals of listening emerged that shaped the ways listeners engaged with reproduced music' (297).

These new ideals of listening produced different forms of engagement that Keir Keightley (1996) has described in terms of location within the sound: 'Initially omnidirectional microphones gave a faithful point of audition that sounded like being seated at a concert; stereo sound gave a hyperrealism, immersion' that allowed the listener to be 'transported (mentally) elsewhere' (169). This enabled 'a virtual escape from domestic space' (150). For Volmar (2019), such sonic escapism was particularly significant during the Cold War, when recordings 'nurtured the evolution of affective, subjective listening practices' (405).

Initially, immersion and subjective listening practice was restricted to the home by the cumbersome equipment. With the advent of mobile media later in the century, all this changed. Earphones augmented the intensity of the interior experience yet again, enabling sound to seemingly emanate from 'inside the head of the listener' (Toop 2011: 44), and 'transform[ing] what it means to "hear" in the world' (Bull 2014: 105). With the release of the Sony Walkman in 1979, this profound sonic experience could be taken out of the home for the first time. By the time of the arrival of the iPod at the century's end (2001), mobile media allowed users to individually soundtrack their environment. Michael Bull (2014) explains this in terms of a new introversion: 'users often report being in dream reveries while on the move, turned inward, away from the historical contingency of the world, into the certainty of their own past, real or imagined, enclosed safely within their own auditory soundscape', and this 'realigns the relationship between public and private space' (109).

While home stereos and mobile media could provoke intensely personalised experiences, recorded music could also do the opposite. In a speech given in 1964, Benjamin Britten (1913–76) lamented that:

Bach wrote his *St Matthew Passion* for performance on one day of the year only – the day which in the Christian church was the culmination of the year, to which the year's worship was leading. It is one of the unhappiest results of the march of science and commerce that this unique work, at the turn of a switch, is at the mercy of any loud roomful of cocktail drinkers – to be listen to or switched off at will, without ceremony or occasion. (Britten 1978/1964: 119)

For Britten, music like the Passion was written for a particular occasion and suffers when removed from that ritual. At the heart of his criticism is the notion of attention. If private listening could induce profound and attentive listening, then music that

Case Study 9.2: (cont.)

jostles with other activities and sounds runs the risk of being ignored. This does not necessary mean that the music is not being heard, however, nor that it is unable to affect those within earshot. Anahid Kassabian has described the 'ubiquitous listening' of contemporary life (2013b) as a catalyst for new modes of auditory engagement, for instance. Muzak – a brand name for background music production, but also now used as a generic term – has been used throughout the century to encourage certain forms of communal behaviour. Piped into shops and lifts, background music remains unobtrusive yet works on the subconscious of those in earshot to encourage them to behave in a certain way; either for marketing purposes, by encouraging shoppers to linger and buy more, or as a mood modulator to keep people calm in stressful situations.

Of course, we must be mindful that not everyone hears music in the same way (Drever 2019). As the final decade of the century gave rise to new audio formats, such as the MP3 (→Chapter 10, 'Copyright and the Music Industry'), the complicated concept of an 'ideal' listener was taken seriously by production companies. Jonathan Sterne (2012: 149), for instance, identifies a 'composite listening subject written into the MP3'. The format's development, by the International Organization for Standardization (ISO) and International Electrotechnical Commission (IEC), involved a series of listening tests conducted in 1990–1 that sought to shape a sound acceptable to people in a variety of listening situations: 'MP3s may confront an almost infinite and unmeasurable multiplicity of listeners, but they do so within a surprisingly limited set of contexts and aesthetics of "good sound"' (Sterne 2012: 182–3).

Recorded music, then, created an anxiety among musicians and listeners due to its reductive aspects. But it has also encouraged us to listen differently, to engage with more sonic elements and to shift between levels of attention as we pass through our everyday lives.

Conclusion

Audio recording has had a profound impact on the ways in which music has been created, performed and 'consumed' in the twentieth century. New technologies have refreshed creativity, given rise to different types of musicians and opened the doors to original sounds and effects. Recording technology has enabled music to be disseminated and curated in ways that have brought together communities and forged exciting ways to learn about and respond to existing practice. It has also been used as a musicological tool for creating canons and collecting histories.

10 | Copyright and the Music Industry

Is music property? If so, can it be owned? And by whom? Can it be stolen? Who gets to make money from it – and who risks being exploited? Answers to these questions all hinge on the issue of copyright: the legal instrument that defines the owner of a musical work and gives them exclusive rights to make copies of it. Copyright may seem like a marginal, even bureaucratic subject for a music textbook. Yet it is central to the history of music in the twentieth century. Without copyright, music publishing – and therefore a music industry – is almost unimaginable (Frith and Marshall 2004: 1). And copyright is the framework through which music in the twentieth century was understood legally and economically – and, consequently, morally.

The principles of copyright in music date back to the early eighteenth century and they have changed surprisingly little since. Although they were originally established to control the copying of books and were built upon basic (and legally definable) conceptions of the artistic work and of its authorship and ownership, they were later applied more or less without change to the copyright of music. This is obviously problematic, as the identity of a musical work is not always clear, and it is sometimes even harder to determine who its author is (and who, therefore, has claims upon its copyright), whether performer or composer (→Chapter 5, 'Work and Notation'). Fixing these definitions in law has implications for how we value different kinds of musical labour. And as this chapter will show, because these definitions originate in white European, post-Enlightenment thought, they also have implications for how different kinds of musical creativity are recognised, and regarding who is rewarded and who is exploited.

Through the twentieth century, as different kinds of musical creativity came into play under the same legal regime, at a time in which those concepts of authorship and the bounded, singular work were called into question (➔Chapter 3, 'Postmodernism'; ➔Chapter 9, 'Recording and Production'), these fundamental principles faced a series of challenges. This chapter will review several of these, as well as some of the impacts – both positive and negative – that they had on musical creativity, focusing in its case studies on two particular moments: the birth of rock 'n' roll in the mid-1950s and the 'golden age' of hip-hop in the late 1980s. But first, it begins with a summary of the history of copyright in music, followed by some examples of how the legal and economic principles of the 'culture industry' intersect with several strands in twentieth-century aesthetic theory. This historical overview is necessarily brief and focuses on musical copyright in the United Kingdom and USA. For more detailed histories, see, among others, Demers (2006), Frith and Marshall (2004) and Vaidhyanathan (2001).

The Music Industry 1: Publishing

Put simply, copyright is a legal concept that gives the author of an original creative work certain rights as to how that work may be used. Although international standards exist (first and most importantly through the Berne Convention of 1886), the specifics of copyright law itself differ from country to country. In general, however, the law confers upon copyright holders a set of exclusive rights to adapt, perform, distribute and make copies of an original creative work. By applying a fee to those who wish to access or make use of their work (selling a physical copy, uploading to a commercial streaming service, broadcasting on the radio, licensing for an advert soundtrack, etc.), copyright holders are thus able to earn money. Note that a copyright holder is not always the work's original author: copyright may be assigned to a larger third party, such as a publisher or record label. Indeed, this is often the case, and such transfers of ownership – and accumulations of what we might call creative capital – form the economic basis of the cultural industries (for more on the economics and politics of copyright and the music industry, see Laing 2004 and Greenfield and Osborn 2004).

At the heart of most copyright regimes is an essential dichotomy: between an *idea*, and its *expression*. An idea in itself is not copyrightable, but its expression is. The idea of a novel tracing a day in the life of a middle-class lady in 1920s London is not protected by copyright, but Virginia Woolf's *Mrs Dalloway* (1925) is. In the case of literature or art, this dichotomy is relatively clear: the idea of the work (what it is 'about', let's say) is generally fairly easy to separate from its realisation or expression. Within music this divide is harder to determine: what is the *idea* of Mozart's 'Jupiter' Symphony or Stockhausen's *Klavierstück IX*, as distinct from the *expression* of that idea?

One famous example will illustrate the problem. When Igor Stravinsky was planning to take up US citizenship in 1945, his three best-known ballets (*Firebird* (1910), *Petrushka* (1911) and *The Rite of Spring* (1913)) were not in copyright in that country: they were owned by the Russian house Editions Russe. Since Russia was not a signatory to the Berne Convention, these works were effectively in the public domain outside that country. In order for Stravinsky to bring his works under the control of a US publisher (who could pay him royalties on international performances), a few light revisions were deemed sufficient to create a new expression, and thus versions of those works that could be separately copyrighted. Compare, for example, the two versions of the *Firebird* suite from 1919 to 1945 – the latter is a hurried rewrite, extended only with some additional pantomimes orchestrated from the original ballet (see Walsh 2006: 173–5).

- Igor Stravinsky, *Firebird Suite* (1919)
- Igor Stravinsky, *Firebird Suite* (1945)

The course of copyright legislation has been closely tied (although often slow to respond) to the development of new creative technologies. A pattern has been repeated through history from the printing press to the Internet: a new technology emerges; this leads to an explosion in creativity, often including entirely new artistic forms; there is some sort of crisis as these forms conflict with an established legal order; and new laws are written that bring the technology within the legal framework. This last step brings together the conflicting interests of an artistic avant-garde and the self-protective state or industry; it is therefore usually the point of most controversy. Legislation was challenged through the twentieth century, however, by alternative models of authorship, ownership and the work that originated outside the post-Enlightenment, European framework.

A full history of copyright is complex and falls outside the remit of this chapter; nevertheless, a brief outline will be useful. Copyright's origins lie in the invention, in the mid-fifteenth century, of the printing press: in the face of a proliferation of pirated copying through unregulated presses, states gave selected printers (in exchange for a fee) monopoly rights to print. Since the state granted these privileges, however, they also became a means for controlling the dissemination of new ideas. Beginning with the

Statute of Anne (1710) in the UK, and later the US Constitution (1776), legal principles began to be developed that shifted the function of copyright law away from censorship and idea management and towards the creation of ideas and artworks as a public good. Authors were encouraged by legal provisions that gave them a copyright monopoly for a limited period (initially fourteen years), during which time it would be expected that they would recoup whatever investment of time and energy had been required to create the work, after which the work would enter the public domain for anyone to copy, adapt and distribute.

As already mentioned, early forms of copyright law were drawn up only with literary works in mind. This served music in its form as sheet music – which for legal purposes was identical to a written text – but not as live performance. Over time, beginning with the US Dramatic Compositions Copyright Act of 1856, copyright provisions around music were extended to include performances and, as the technology emerged, broadcasts and recordings. The turn of the century saw rapid progress in the codification of national and international copyright standards for music. The ontological complexity of music that is reflected in three separate sets of rights (what *is* music? a score? a performance? a recording?) interacted with the history of music through the twentieth century. Table 10.1 summarises some of the key acts of legislation.

Table 10.1 Important acts of US, UK and international copyright legislation

Date	Name	Country	Key points
1710	Statute of Anne	UK	
1776	US Constitution	USA	
1856, amended 1897	Dramatic Compositions Copyright Act	USA	Extended composers' rights to performances of their music
1886	Berne Convention	International: currently 176 signatories (excl. USA)	Attempt to coordinate copyright legislation and enforcement globally
1909	Copyright Act	USA	Creation of compulsory mechanical licence
1971	Sound Recording Act	USA	Copyright extended to recordings themselves
1976	Copyright Act	USA	
1998	Digital Millennium Copyright Act	USA	

The creation of rights for music's composers and performers is all very well. In practice, however, few musicians have the time or skills necessary to negotiate licences, collect royalties, pursue infringements and so on. For this reason, the creation of the modern copyright system in the late nineteenth and early twentieth centuries also saw the creation of collecting societies: institutions with whom artists could register to protect their copyright interests. The first of these, the Société des auteurs, compositeurs et éditeurs de musique (SACEM) was founded in France in 1851. As control of copyright across different media became an increasingly pressing issue, other societies followed in the early years of the twentieth century, many of them, like SACEM, founded by composers themselves. Among them are Germany's Anstalt für musikalische Aufführungsrechte (AFMA, 1903), the precursor to the Gesellschaft für musikalische Aufführungs- und mechanische Vervielfältigungsrechte (GEMA, 1933); the American Society of Composers, Authors, and Publishers (ASCAP, 1914); and the UK's Performing Rights Society (PRS, 1914), founded by a group of music publishers. Acting as middlemen between an artist (or rights holder) and their fee-paying public, collecting societies are an important element of the musical culture industry, offering essential administrative and legal support to artists, and economies of scale to rights users such as broadcasters, music venues and so on. (For more detailed histories of individual societies and some of the challenges they have faced, see, e.g., Ehrlich 1989 and Ryan 1985; for a picture of the music economy before such societies, see Scherer 2004.)

Philosophical Objections

The centrality of copyright to the development of music and art in the twentieth century may be inferred from its shadowy presence in seminal essays by three of the century's most important cultural critics, Walter Benjamin, Theodor Adorno and Michel Foucault.

In his essay 'The Work of Art in the Age of Mechanical Reproduction', written in 1935 (and also discussed in →Chapter 15, 'Audiences, Class and Consumption'), Benjamin argues that photography, film and sound recording have removed the 'aura' that gave unique works of art their cultural and commercial value. Although Benjamin does not make the connection, the legal scholar Thomas Schumacher notes that 'aura' is deeply connected to copyright: 'the structures of intellectual property rights are founded on notions of the work of art that has its aura intact.

Statute and common law definitions of originality and authenticity still presume that the aura of the author remains intact after the processes of technological mediation' (2004: 448). Without that aura, what exactly is it that copyright is protecting? Benjamin is not especially concerned, however, with the collapse of systems of authorship and property, or the ethics of reproduction. Instead, he finds a political good in the loss of aura. The reproducibility of works of art, he argues, is emancipatory: works may leave the private sphere and enter that of the (mass) public (218), a consequence that Benjamin concludes will serve in the fight against fascism that was becoming increasingly urgent as he was writing.

Benjamin's view was taken up polemically by his friend and colleague Adorno, in his wide-ranging essay 'On the Fetish Character in Music and the Regression of Listening' (1938, also discussed in →Chapter 15, 'Audiences, Class and Consumption'). In this text Adorno decries the 'standardization' of commercial music ('the street ballad, the catchy tune and all the swarming forms of the banal', p. 34) and outlines his fear of what that standardisation may be doing to our ability to listen critically and fully to complete works. In essence, his argument is that the culture industry's need for commodifiable products (i.e., hummable tunes) breaks up our ability to grasp formal complexity and the true uniqueness ('greatness') of large-scale classical works. Such tunes are almost generic; authorship (and therefore, by implication, copyright) should reside in their large-scale formal manifestation as a particular symphony, sonata or string quartet.

Both Benjamin and Adorno were concerned with the status of the artistic work. But in his 1969 essay 'What Is an Author?', the French philosopher Michel Foucault challenges instead the concept of authorship. (Foucault's title plays on Barthes' 'Death of the Author' (see →Chapter 3, 'Postmodernism'), and his essay extends some of its ideas.) Foucault builds his argument from the notion of 'discourse', developed in texts such as *The Archaeology of Knowledge* (1997/1969) and *Discipline and Punish* (1991/1975). For Foucault a 'discourse' is a body of statements, behaviours and practices that are organised according to relationships of power. Examples from his own studies include medicine and sexuality: in each case, Foucault demonstrates how the definitions that lie at the heart of how we understand such contexts are determined by discursive statements, interpreted across a framework of power and authority (What is health? What is sexually normative? And who gets to decide?).

In 'What Is an Author', Foucault identifies the concept of the 'author' itself as a topic that binds together notions of identity and status, authenticity and property (2000/1969: 211). The discourse of authorship – in which copyright plays a crucial role – polices how we determine authorship.

Apparatuses of scholarship and publishing determine, for example, what is and what is not part of the written output of a given author. Those apparatuses depend themselves on structures of power, finance, prestige, authority and value (Is a scholarly edition of Nietzsche's journals worth publishing? What about his laundry lists?). Ultimately, Foucault argues, it is the author's name that defines these boundaries: 'The author's name manifests the appearance of a certain discursive set and indicates the status of this discourse within a society and a culture' (2000/1969: 211); furthermore, the meaning and value we ascribe to a literary text today depend on how we answer the question of authorship.

Who we decide is an 'author' is related to our own relationship with the text, and how we understand it within a larger cultural framework; it is a matter of choice (Schumacher 2004: 450). Consider, for example, the many different constructions of authorship – individual and collective – we apply to a performance of Mahler's Fifth Symphony (1901–2) by Simon Rattle and the London Symphony Orchestra, versus 'Love Child' (1968) by Diana Ross (b. 1944) and the Supremes. Authorship resides not only in the particulars of the musical work or act (the originality of a melody, the tone of the voice, the repertory of solo licks) but in how structures of publishing and reception – legally codified as 'copyright' and named by Adorno as 'the culture industry' – define authorship. Thus the Funk Brothers, who played on most Motown recordings between 1959 and 1972, including 'Love Child', and were as responsible as anyone for the creation of an entire musical genre, can be relegated from the legal status of 'author' and denied the prestige and remuneration that goes along with that. The discourse here is reflected in the structures of power at Motown Records: the tightly controlled corporate structure determined by founder and owner Berry Gordy (b. 1929); the marketing power of the star performers (differentiated, at Gordy's insistence, between the Supremes and Ross herself); the publishing rights of the songwriters R. Dean Taylor, Frank Wilson, Pam Sawyer and Deke Richards; and the function of the Funk Brothers (in fact a flexible pool of session musicians) as hired artisan-labourers within Gordy's production-line method. Through the discourse of authorship, copyright can become a framework that not only remunerates musicians but also exploits them (see Ryan 2012: ch. 20).

The Music Industry 2: Recording

As we have already discussed, the copyright regimes of the late nineteenth and early twentieth centuries were designed around the Western art-music tradition and the concept of the musical work as a written artefact (score) with a single author (the composer). However, the increasing importance of musical recordings during the twentieth century – and the multiple forms of authorship just described – necessitated new legal definitions of the musical work and new rights of ownership.

The invention of musical recordings meant that music no longer existed exclusively – at least in copyright terms – as a notated score. Recordings could be also conceived as copyrightable objects. One of the first legal responses to this new scenario was the 1909 US Copyright Act. Among other things this created what is known as a 'compulsory mechanical licence'. This was a legal mechanism that made it possible for anyone to make a mechanical reproduction (i.e., recording) of a musical work without the consent of the original copyright owner, upon payment of a small licensing fee. The licence was originally intended to protect the then-thriving piano roll industry, but by the mid-century had been adapted to the recording and distribution of cover versions: beyond the fee, the only requirement for the licence was that the song being covered had already been released to the public as a recording. In this way, a cover had the legal status of an *imitation* of the recording (a collection of non-copyrightable sounds), and not a *realisation* from its printed sheet music (a copyrightable arrangement of notes and lyrics).

The compulsory mechanical licence made it possible for emerging recording artists to develop and assert their own performance style without the trouble and expense of hiring songwriters. There were other benefits too. Performers of a cover were also able to depend upon a certain amount of familiarity of the original song among their target audience; they could be confident that a given song had been successfully 'road-tested' by another artist; and the existing performances provided a useful template against which they could distinguish themselves. As Case Study 10.1 shows, this copyright framework – which favoured sonic and stylistic innovation over original songwriting – was one element crucial to the development of rock 'n' roll. The challenge to the law of trying to define recordings artists' rights as opposed to composers' rights lies in the different statuses of recordings and compositions as works. A composition, by definition, is written down – and therefore qualifiable in legal terms. Put simply, if one notation resembles another above a certain threshold (measured by similarity of melodies, rhythms, harmonies), then a claim for copyright infringement may be successfully pursued. This is relatively easily done on paper, comparing one score to another. Where the resemblance is purely timbral – a sampled drum or vocal sound, for instance – it is very much harder to prove infringement. That *might* be a sample of James Brown's characteristic grunt you are hearing (in which case, there is a copyright issue to resolve); or it could be a very good impersonation of it (in which case, there is not). The difference between recording rights and composer rights therefore reflects conceptions of the musical work developed around Western art music (and the discourse of the author to which Foucault draws attention), but which are profoundly challenged in philosophical and practical terms when confronted by models of authorship and creativity from outside that tradition. As Schumacher observes in relation to rap music in particular, sampling

forces us to reconceptualize these bases of copyright doctrine for both technological and cultural reasons – the former because digital reproduction accentuates existing understandings of 'copying' and poses its own challenge to the ways in which we have to think about the process of production, the latter because rap highlights how different cultural forms and traditions are founded on different understandings of creativity and originality. (2004: 443)

Case Study 10.1: The Origins of Rock 'n' Roll

The complete story of rock 'n' roll's origins is contested, but broadly speaking it grew out of an amalgam of different styles of American popular music, including rhythm and blues, gospel and country. Essential to the creations of the environment of fusion, crossover and evolution that eventually coalesced in the mid-1950s into what we recognise as the rock 'n' roll style was the cover and the copyright framework that followed the 1909 US Copyright Act (but see Peterson 1990 for a thorough analysis of all the contributing social, technological and economic factors).

That crossover spirit is personified in rock 'n' roll's greatest star, Elvis Presley (1935–77). Born and brought up in the segregated South, Presley listened extensively to country, blues and gospel musicians as a young man, both live and on record. Significant influences on his musical style included the gospel singers Jake Hess and Sister Rosetta Tharpe, the blues musicians Arthur Crudup and Rufus Thomas, and the country singers Jimmie Rodgers, Ernest Tubb and Bob Wills. A rendition by Presley of Crudup's 'That's All Right' (1946) late into an otherwise fruitless early recording session at Sun Studios, Memphis, proved the catalyst for unlocking Presley's unique crossover talent (Guralnick 1994: 94–7): when it was first played on the radio, many listeners assumed Presley was Black. As if to affirm the two sides of Presley's art, the song's release in 1954 as a single was backed by a bluegrass number, a cover of Bill Monroe's 'Blue Moon of Kentucky'.

Case Study 10.1: (cont.)

While Elvis understood the essence of African American styles such as gospel and rhythm and blues (and was careful to credit the Black artists whose music he was borrowing or adapting), others were less respectful. Most notorious was Pat Boone (b. 1934), a singer whose fame in the late 1950s was exceeded only by that of Presley himself. Boone made his name with covers of rhythm-and-blues songs tempered for a white market: famous is his cover of Little Richard's 'Tutti Frutti' (one of rock 'n' roll's founding documents), which substitutes Richard's anarchic howl and hyper-active piano work for clean vocals and a crisp arrangement. Accusations that Boone was 'whitening up' African American music (and hence denuding it of its energy and soul) have also been levelled against Elvis: a telling comparison might be made between his 1956 recording of 'Hound Dog' and that made four years earlier by the rhythm-and-blues singer Willa Mae ('Big Mama') Thornton (1926–84). (This is a simplification; the much more complex network of interracial influences, grievances and crossovers that runs through the history of rock 'n' roll and rhythm and blues is explored in detail in Ward 1998.)

Most notably – and controversially – white artists were able to put their own spin on blues and rhythm-and-blues recordings by Black artists, often to much greater commercial success than the original performers (a dynamic that Steve Chapple and Reebee Garofalo describe as 'black roots, white fruits'; Chapple and Garofalo 1997: ch. 7; see also Garofalo 2002). The 1950s were still a period of segregation, and the American music industry had a history of exploiting and unfairly remunerating Black songwriters and performers. The aesthetic of the blues itself did not help either. As shown in ➔Chapter 5, 'Work and Notation', definitions of authorship within blues culture are very different from the European model. Little value is placed on the written musical work; originality comes from performance, and from signifyin' on models that are in general circulation (see Ferris 1970). The music's essence lay in its *expression* – the particular spin a performer gave to a song – rather than its *idea*, or how it might appear on the written page. The 1909 Copyright Act required that compositions be fixed (on paper) before their expressions (as recordings or performances) could be protected. This left musicians from an oral culture like the blues particularly exposed to exploitation.

The abuses of copyright and financial remuneration that lie behind a lot of early rock 'n' roll parallel the issues of cultural appropriation and exploitation while at the same time putting a specific price on them. And yet, rock 'n' roll was one of the most vibrant, most important popular art forms of the twentieth century. Sixty years later its cultural power and presence remain irresistible, not least because of its power to cross boundaries at a time of segregation and exclusion. In a less permissive copyright

Case Study 10.1: (cont.)

regime, such as that which existed after the Copyright Act of 1976, it might not have happened at all. Some Black musicians were, no doubt, exploited for their work – particularly under today's copyright framework – but others, among them Muddy Waters, Bo Diddley and Robert Johnson, achieved great secondary acclaim after their work was referenced by those white musicians (such as Elvis; and later the likes of Eric Clapton and the Rolling Stones) who credited their inspiration. Copyright scholar Siva Vaidhyanathan has even argued that a 'loose and balanced' copyright system, such as existed in the USA between 1909 and 1976, 'can amplify the positive elements of the West African aesthetic tradition. In principle, copyright law does not prevent artists from taking from the "commons". It supports the idea that new artists build upon the work of others' (Vaidhyanathan 2001: 125). It was a copyright regime that encouraged the sort of stylistic cross-fertilisation and creation of recording personalities that made rock 'n' roll possible. But it was also one that, by affording greatest protection to the written work and not the performance or recording, invited the exploitation of Black artists, particularly within the wider context of political segregation, even as many rock 'n' roll musicians fought against it – Elvis and his Sun Records producer Sam Phillips among them. In 1976, a new Copyright Act offered greater protection for recorded works. However, as Case Study 10.2 will show, the consequences of this were also unpredictable.

Folk and Popular Practices

Schumacher highlights an even greater difficulty for a music industry whose basis lies in the principles of Western art music. Although recording presented a significant challenge to the accepted framework of musical copyright, in the end the law's response was simply to supplement that framework rather than to alter its fundamental principles. A musical work could still be identified as a unique, commodifiable entity in law – a recording no less than a score – and its author could be named as a single entity, whether as an individual or a collective, such as a band. With these extensions, the definitions of 'author', 'work' and 'ownership' remained much the same as before. What Schumacher highlights, in the context of rap, is that outside the European/Western art-music tradition such concepts are fundamentally different.

   Although the principle of copyright is based on the literate tradition of Western art music, within many folk and popular traditions very little is written down. Music is passed between musicians orally – through listening, imitating, teaching and adapting. An Irish *sean nós* singer may lay claim to his interpretation of a particular song (and there will be much about that song, in particular its words, that is 'fixed'), but no one person is identified as the song's original composer. Usually, this is not a problem – most musical cultures around the world have flourished without the framework of a Western-style music industry. The advent of recording in the twentieth century brought traditional musics into the commercial sphere, however, and these differences in systems of authorship and ownership came into conflict: who should be credited (or paid) for a song that has been transmitted orally through generations of singers?

A widely studied example is the blues, which in the early twentieth century transitioned from a folk music of the American South to a commercial success and then to the bedrock of rock 'n' roll itself: 'Within the [folk-blues] tradition ownership of a song might be claimed by demonstrating a singular *approach* to, or treatment of, otherwise floating verses and phrases. This offered no practical application for commercial composers: "approach" was not a copyrightable commodity' (Abbott and Seroff 1996: 412). Similarly, in Jamaica, a fusion of oral and recorded traditions emerged in the 1970s out of reggae. With a low priority given to copyright laws in Jamaica (which were in any case outdated), reggae producers worked in an economy in which authorship was unclear and little valued, and artists worked not for royalties but for the sales of short-run recordings and the prestige of having their music played by the big sound systems. As described by Wayne Marshall and Peter Manuel (2006), this fostered an environment in which 'riddims' (the instrumental tracks that are the building blocks of reggae and dub) could circulate freely and be endlessly remixed and re-versioned, creating an aesthetic logic that outlasted the eventual arrival of copyright norms (→Chapter 10, 'Recording and Production', Case Study 10.1).

Practices of versioning, sampling and remixing (→Chapter 5, 'Work and Notation') – all manifestations of the African American practice of signifyin' that lies behind such open-ended models of authorship – destabilise the author function of Western art music. Copyright, as Porcello notes, is 'based on assumptions that one can clearly separate producers from consumers and texts from their readings'. As these distinctions fade, as in the creative 'reading' that is encapsulated in reggae versioning, the fundamental model of copyright becomes 'frustrated' (1991: 77, quoted in Schumacher 2004: 451).

Schur notes the particular challenges that hip-hop aesthetics present to 'the romantic conception of genius that underlies intellectual property law'

(2009: 64–5) and, indeed, Foucault's author function. Sampling, he suggests, is akin to finding a productive use for a hitherto useless element or turning wasteland into something economically useful. Drawing on John Locke, the seventeenth-century English philosopher who first developed a labour theory of property, Schur argues that a recorded break only becomes a commodity – something worthy of ownership and subjection to property law – once someone has laboured over it and marked it as their own. In this case, that labour is undertaken by the hip-hop artist in the form of discovery and refinement; in the law's eyes, the labour was undertaken by the original recording artists. Something similar might also be said about the way in which the reggae producer or the DJ makes use of riddims or pre-existing recordings within their own works. Musical authorship on these terms rests upon a model of creative (rather than re-creative) genius.

The distinction rests upon where one situates the 'expression' component of a sample, riddim or track. As a solo or fill on the underlying beat of a song, the four-bar break of the Winstons' 'Amen, Brother' is an expression, and therefore subject to copyright. After circulating on a number of hip-hop records in the 1980s, this particular break was used explosively by hundreds of producers in the 1990s as the fundamental DNA of the new genres of hardcore, jungle and drum 'n' bass; see Harrison (2004).

- The Winstons, 'Amen, Brother' (Metromedia Records, 1969)
- Salt 'n' Pepa, 'I Desire', from *Hot, Cool & Vicious* (Next Plateau Records, 1986)
- Carl Cox (b. 1962), 'Let the Bass Kick' (white label, 1991)
- Peshay (b. 1970), 'Piano Tune' (Good Looking Records, 1994)

Only when it was extracted from that context by a digital sampler, however, did the 'Amen' break begin to take on the status of an 'idea' within the cultural commons (analogous, perhaps, to a perfect cadence, or a samba rhythm)? Could, in fact, a single musical artefact like the 'Amen' break speak to more than one 'idea', and appear in more than one 'expression'? What about a much larger, more complex musical component, like a riddim? To what extent was Winston Riley's 'Stalag riddim' (originally the basis of Ansel Collins' 'Stalag 17') a musical idea and not an expression? And within the enormous network of versions made upon this legendary riddim (the online riddim database Riddim-ID lists more than 300), where did the idea reside? Finally, what about the reuse of an entire track within the stream of a DJ's set? While individual musicians may be paid for the use of their recordings, all the prestige – and much of the remuneration – accrues to the superstar DJ. As Case Study 10.2 suggests, these are questions that copyright law has struggled to resolve: 'The idea/expression dichotomy breaks down when applied to hip hop producers because their verbatim copying frequently shows how multiple ideas exist within a single expression' (Schur 2009: 66). Yet, as Marshall and Manuel note in their study of Jamaican dancehall, alternative metrics of value, ownership and recognition are possible and, indeed, musically productive (Marshall and Manuel 2006). In Foucauldian terms, 'not every discourse stands equal before the law' (Schumacher 2004: 451).

- Ansel Collins, 'Stalag 17' (Techniques, 1973)
- Dillinger, 'Melting Pot' (Techniques, 1975)
- Sister Nancy, 'Bam' (Techniques, 1982)

Case Study 10.2: Hip-hop from the Golden Age to G-funk and Beyond

In the 1980s, hip-hop was defined by its use of the newly invented technology of digital sampling (➔Chapter 8, 'Instruments') to create beats and instrumentals from short edits and cuts (samples) from recordings by other artists. At this time, most sampling – although it infringed copyright – took place beyond the attention of the law. Hip-hop had not yet reached the mainstream, and copyright holders at the major record labels either were not aware of what was going on or did not consider it financially significant enough to make it worth pursuing legal claims. Artists such as Eric B and Rakim, Public Enemy, the Beastie Boys and Queen Latifah were able to sample freely and prolifically, creating their music from dense collages of samples (see also ➔Chapter 3, 'Postmodernism'). Many of the records made at this time – an era from the mid-1980s to the early 1990s often referred to as the 'golden age' of hip-hop – are venerated by fans, musicians and scholars. Yet the laissez-faire environment that had made them possible came to an abrupt halt in the early 1990s with a series of high-profile copyright lawsuits (McLeod and DiCola 2011). Isolated suits were brought in the 1980s, notably Jimmy Castor's suing in 1986 of the Beastie Boys and Def Jam Recordings for sampling his break and vocal ('Yo, Leroy!') on the Beasties' 'Hold It Now, Hit It'; and the Turtles' 1989 case against De La Soul for the rap trio's sample of their 1968 single 'You Showed Me', used on De La Soul's 'Transmitting Live from Mars'. Yet these cases were settled, albeit expensively, out of court. In 1991, sampling came to the courts for the first time when Grand Upright Records sued Warner Bros. Records for an unlicensed sample of Gilbert O'Sullivan's 'Alone Again (Naturally)' on a track by the rapper Biz Markie, also titled 'Alone Again'. Warner Bros. lost the case, and Markie's album was recalled and banned from sale, effectively ending his career

Case Study 10.2: (cont.)

(for more details on all these cases and their outcomes, see McLeod and DiCola 2001: 132–47; Vaidhyanathan 2001: 132–48).

- Jimmy Castor, 'The Return of Leroy, Pts 1 & 2' (Suss'd Records, 1977)
- The Beastie Boys, 'Hold It Now, Hit It', from *Licensed to Ill* (Def Jam, 1986)
- The Turtles, 'You Showed Me' (White Whale, 1986)
- De La Soul, 'Transmitting Live from Mars', from *3 Feet High and Rising* (Tommy Boy, 1989)

Vaidhyanathan (2001: 140–5) notes that the chilling effect of cases such as these (that is, the suppression of sampling practices through the threat of legal sanction) turned several previously sample-heavy artists towards live instruments. Other artists changed their production approach to focus on fewer samples, in turn inaugurating new styles of hip-hop – such as gangsta rap and g-funk – whose beats were more streamlined, more linear and less collage-like. In time, as samples became lucrative commodities in their own right, some artists came to 'wear' those samples they had been able to pay clearance for as badges of wealth and status (Marshall 2006: 2); one of the most notorious examples was Puff Daddy's (Sean Combs; b. 1969) seventeen-second loop of an iconic riff by the Police (as well as a reworking of the original song's melody and lyric) as the basis of his 'I'll Be Missing You' (1997).

- Beastie Boys, 'Sabotage', from *Ill Communication* (Capitol, 1994)
- Warren G and Nate Dogg, 'Regulate', from *Regulate ... G Funk Era* (Violator Records, 1994)
- Puff Daddy and Faith Evans, featuring 112, 'I'll Be Missing You' (Arista/BMG, 1997)

Although the practices of quotation, versioning and signifyin' are fundamental to hip-hop practice, sampling itself is not, in fact. Many pre-golden-age records were made using live musicians – on their 1988 album *In Full Gear*, Stetsasonic brag about being 'like a hip hop band, so to say': 'We have a human percussionist, that's the human mix machine Wise, and DBC on the keys, and the drum machines live themselves, and we have two turntables with the devastating Prince Paul.' Even hip-hop's foundational document, 'Rapper's Delight' by the Sugarhill Gang (1979), relies not on recorded samples of disco and funk riffs, but on session musicians paid to reproduce those sounds within the studio. Nevertheless, sampling's association with the so-called golden age has reinforced the idea that sampling, and its particular sonic qualities, is authentic to 'classical' hip-hop practice.

Yet authenticity within hip-hop is not always what it may seem. Wayne Marshall (2006) notes the way in which another group, the Roots, use studio techniques to give live instruments an 'authentic' sound. Dr Dre's *The Chronic* (1992), one of the most

Case Study 10.2: (cont.)

acclaimed post-golden-age albums, is a masterful example of layers of signification. 'Let Me Ride' builds up layers of reference through its explicit reworking of Parliament's 'Mothership Connection', which draws heavily on the spiritual 'Swing Down, Sweet Chariot', itself a humorous reworking of the more well-known 'Swing Low, Sweet Chariot'; the song's video turns these references to chariots away from the spiritual to the material, and a celebration of California's lowrider car culture. (NB: Warren G's 'Regulate', mentioned above, itself signifies upon 'Let Me Ride', adding another, subsequent, layer.) Yet Dre used live musicians to replicate the recorded source material: the record's sonic authenticity was created in post-production by the addition samples of vinyl pops and scratches (Demers 2006: 82–4).

- Parliament, 'Mothership Connection (Star Child)', from *Mothership Connection* (Casablanca, 1975)
- Dr Dre (b. 1965), 'Let Me Ride', from *The Chronic* (Interscope Records, 1992)

Schloss (2004: 63–78) summarises many of the debates around authenticity and what he calls 'aesthetic purism' in hip-hop. Copyright restrictions did play a role in changing the direction of hip-hop around the turn of the 1990s. But this effect can be overstated, perhaps because it serves a narrative of hip-hop's noble resistance to white commodification. By the end of the century sampling was ubiquitous, not only within hip-hop but across the spectrum of popular music. In large part, hip-hop's rise between the late 1980s and mid-1990s from local underground phenomenon to global music was responsible for this. The tighter copyright regime that emerged in the early 1990s did not halt that rise, although some adherents to the 'golden age' narrative might dispute this.

- The Roots, 'Proceed', from *Do You Want More?!!!?!* (Geffen Records, 1994)

Sampling offered a convenient way to quickly access and play with signifying practices across the corpus of African American popular culture. It carried certain sonic signifiers, especially as it had been used in the 1980s, and these – thanks to the golden age narrative – set the terms of a certain sonic authenticity. But this authenticity, as the different approaches of Dr Dre and the Roots show, could be recreated by different paths. What remained consistent was hip-hop's attachment to an idea of culture as circulatory, comprised of repetitions, quotations, versions and a cultural commons. Hip-hop's eventual ubiquity as the most globalised of all musical genres helped it to change copyright practice as much as it was changed by it, forcing industry and the law to find ways to make sampling – and, more broadly, non-Western models of authorship and intellectual property – acceptable to all sides.

The Birth of the Internet

Just as the twentieth century was bookended at its start by the creation of international copyright standards, and the formation of the 'culture industry', so it ended with the greatest challenge yet to that industry: the Internet and file-sharing. Once again, music was the setting for this particular cultural battle.

The initiating step was another technological one: the invention of the MP3 audio codec in 1995. A way of making sound files smaller without a significant loss in quality (→Chapter 9, 'Recording and Production'), the MP3 made digital audio files easier to store, an issue in the 1990s when hard-drive space was still expensive. However, it also made them easier to transfer over the World Wide Web. With a 28.8-k dial-up modem, of the sort available when the MP3 codec was released, a one-minute MP3, coded at the standard bit rate of 128 kbps, would take just over four minutes to download. Although still slow, compared to the fifty minutes that would be required for the same download at CD quality it was easily fast enough to be practical. Internet users began sharing music files with each other, and by the end of the 1990s faster modems and dedicated file-sharing (peer-to-peer, or P2P) sites had made it trivially easy for users to share entire MP3 collections.

The most popular P2P network for sharing music was Napster, launched in June 1999 (Figure 10.1). With tens of millions of registered users at its peak, Napster began attracting the attention of artists, notably the heavy metal band Metallica, who in March 2000 filed the first copyright suit against a P2P company. Metallica were followed by Dr Dre (who shared Metallica's lawyers) and then a number of labels themselves. In July 2001, Napster was forced to close by the US Ninth Circuit Court and eventually agreed to pay copyright owners $36 million to settle past infringements and as an advance against future royalties.

However, this court victory for the recording industry did not erase the fact that the Internet, MP3s and file-sharing had transformed consumers' relationship with music. The Napster generation – predominantly teenagers, who are naturally one of the music industry's largest sources of income – had become used to listening to music on demand, at their computers, and at minimal (ideally zero) financial outlay. This was a model that conflicted profoundly with the industry's preference for selling physical artefacts (CDs and records) in physical stores, exploiting values such as scarcity, objecthood and fetish character. Although record labels and copyright holders initially fought this change hard in the early twenty-first century, with the launch of Apple's iTunes Store in April 2003 the argument in favour of online distribution – and the need

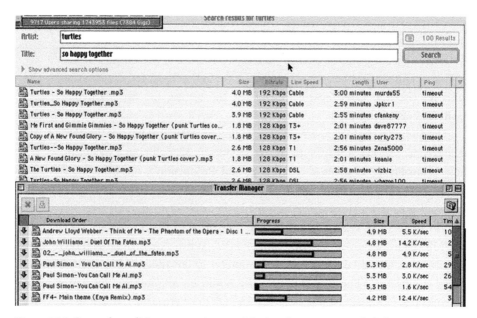

Figure 10.1 Screenshot of Napster running on a Macintosh computer with dial-up connection, 2001. Image by Njahnke

for new commercial models that could counter the threats of piracy and file-sharing – was effectively conceded. In turn, downloading was itself over-taken by streaming (Napster itself re-emerged as a legitimate music-streaming service.)

Conclusion

Streaming represents an endpoint (so far?) in a century-long shift from musical objects to musical services, and from artists to corporations: the major players in the music industry in the early twenty-first century were no longer even record companies but online distribution services: Apple, Amazon and Spotify. The music industry has so far struggled to re-organise around this new landscape, and artists (who are reported to receive minute payments from streams of their music) are finding it harder to be properly paid for their work. It remains to be seen whether these conditions will precipitate further changes to copyright law comparable to those seen a century earlier, or what musical outcomes may emerge.

11 | States and Markets

States and state-like supranational bodies have always sought to control music's creation and dissemination. As early as the fourth century BC, Plato made explicit (in *The Republic*) the laws that a state should enact in response to the social benefits and threats posed by different musical scales. Twelve centuries later the Council of Trent considered the role of music among its many reforms to the Catholic Church, recommending intelligibility of text, avoidance of secular expression and 'only the divine phrases of hymnody' be used in its music, such that 'the hearts of listeners should be ravished by longing for heavenly harmony and by contemplation of the joys of the blessed'. Later still, in nineteenth-century Vienna, Franz Schubert laboured under a censorial regime promoted by Emperor Franz I and his anti-liberal foreign minister Prince Clemens von Metternich. In each of these examples, the battle can be seen as one between conservatism and modernity. The intervention of the state (or the church, as it may be), is almost always an attempt to regain control of meaning in the face of change. As the sociologist Howard S. Becker summarises, 'the state and its agents act in pursuit of their own interests, which may or may not coincide with those of the artists making the works' (2008/1982: 165).

In the twentieth century, the apparent ability of national, international and supranational bodies to exert such control (whether effectively or not) increased with the invention of broadcasting and the development of the publishing and recording industries (although see also Jacques Attali's arguments in *Noise: The Political Economy of Music* (1985) about recordings' ability to neuter the social and political power of music). The legal frameworks that were created around these (➔Chapter 10, 'Copyright and the Music Industry') brought a large proportion of the activities involved in the creation, dissemination and reception of music under the auspices of bodies that were, ultimately, answerable to the state and to government policy.

Across the century, these tools were used by political regimes both authoritarian and benign in ways that determined music's dissemination (what music might be available to audiences); its reception (how it might be accessed or packaged); and, in certain extreme cases, its composition (what form that music took). Furthermore, as the century progressed, those frameworks began to operate at a supranational level. This realm is sometimes known as the 'free market' but, as we shall see, the marketplace has acted in a similar fashion to the state in its attempts to control the dissemination, reception and composition of music. Whether in the form of states (see Case Study 11.1) or markets, industry regulations or national broadcasters (see Case Study 11.2), economic and political institutions continue to invest in the creation and understanding of music; throughout the century, musicians, hoping to have their work heard and appreciated within these frameworks, have had to consider that work in relation to such forces.

The Authoritarian State

Some of the century's most heavy-handed actions to censor or shape music took place in the authoritarian regimes of Nazi Germany and the Soviet Union. In both instances, music (and the other arts) was seen to pose a threat to the unitary power and ideology of the regime, which sought ways to control their form and dissemination. Although there were important differences between the ideologies of each regime – and therefore their reasons for seeking control of music – there were also striking parallels in how this control was enacted, which reveal that in practice the targets and means of repression were to a great extent shared.

The censorship and repression of music in the Soviet Union is perhaps the better known of the two examples (one reason for this being the Cold War-inspired impetus to study and expose the shortcomings of communism in order to shore up support for liberal capitalism). In the years immediately after the 1917 Revolution, avant-garde and modernist art and music flourished in Russia: artists such as Kasimir Malevich and Vladimir Tatlin pioneered forms of abstract and symbolist painting; composers like Alexander Mossolov (1900–73; →Chapter 2, 'Modernism') experimented with forms of noise, dissonance and mechanical repetition. However, under Joseph Stalin (1878–1953), who in 1924 became leader of what had become the Soviet Union in 1922, these experimental outlooks were soon suppressed by a class-based political ideology that gave priority instead to accessibility, to realism and to usefulness. Where possible, the arts were to uphold the heroism of the Soviet worker and the narrative of the communist revolution. Music that could be performed and enjoyed by the masses was preferred; music that was complex, abstract or ambiguous in meaning (however defined) was denounced as bourgeois. Broadcasters and publishers were state-controlled, and from 1932 composers had to submit their work for approval by the Union of Soviet Composers. Works that did not pass ideological muster were not approved for performance; in the worst cases, musicians could find their lives threatened by the state. One impact of this policy is described further in Case Study 11.1.

As Case Study 11.1 also shows, the interpretation of these diktats was frequently unclear. The Third Reich's relationship to music was even more complicated. Nazism's basis was in distinctions of nation and race, rather than class. The high position of music within Germany's cultural heritage – exemplified in the music of Bach, Beethoven and Brahms – made it a particularly potent carrier of nationalist and racialist discourse. Hitler himself acknowledged this in his description of Wagner as his only prede-cessor. To oversee its cultural policy, Germany could enlist internationally recognised composers and conductors: the first president and vice-president of the Reichsmusikkammer (RKM; Reich Chamber of Music) in 1933 were Richard Strauss (1864–1949) and the conductor Wilhelm Furtwängler (1886–1954). Strauss proclaimed the founding of the RKM 'an important step in the direction of the reconstruction of our total German musical life'. The Nazi ideology of 'cleansing' could be applied to both race and musical style: part of the RKM's attraction for musical conservatives like Strauss and Furtwängler was no doubt the priority given to supporting German (i.e., non-Jewish) musicians, and to reconstructing a Romanticised musical culture after the modernistic experiments of the 1920s (although both soon left their posts when the true aims of the RKM became apparent). As Erik Levi notes in one of the first and most substantial studies of music within the Third Reich, 'It is possible to divide the main tenets of Nazi cultural policy into two halves: one concerned with the preservation of German racial purity, the other with the upholding of reactionary attitudes against "modernism" in the arts' (1994: 82). Within the logic of cleansing, the tonal triad was claimed as 'the purest expression of the German essence' (Dümling 2002: 50), and even Wagner (1813–83) was not immune: by emphasising harmonically simpler works like *Parsifal* and *Die Meistersinger* (as opposed to *Tristan und Isolde* and *Die Walküre*), German musicologists were able to paint him not as 'a pioneer of the avant-garde . . . but rather as a sustainer of archaic simplicity' (ibid.).

The range of music that could fall foul of these criteria was large: as Dümling notes, on the basis of race alone, composers of light opera such as Léon Jessels and twelve-tone composers such as Arnold Schoenberg were equally at risk (2002: 60), in spite of the latter's claim a few years earlier to have secured 'the supremacy of German music for the next 100 years' with his twelve-note system (Levi 1994: 103; see also →Chapter 7, 'Harmony'). In 1934 a proposed performance of the opera *Mathis der Maler* by Paul Hindemith (1895–1963), one of Germany's leading composers and seemingly a natural successor to the contrapuntal tradition represented by Bach, was prohibited by Hermann Göring, leading to Furtwängler's resignation from the RMK. Hindemith left his post at the Berlin Academy and in 1936 was forced to sign an oath of loyalty to Hitler in order to continue working in Germany. In 1938, concerned for his safety, he left Germany and eventually emigrated to the United States.

In the same year, Hindemith's music was included in an exhibition devoted to works of 'degenerate music'. On opening the exhibition (which followed a notorious one the previous year devoted to 'degenerate art'), its curator Hans Severus Ziegler (author in 1930 of the essay 'Against Negro Culture, For the German Heritage') described its contents as 'what was and is diseased, unhealthy, and highly dangerous in our music and that for this reason must be eliminated' (quoted in McKee n.d.). Other composers in the exhibition included Alban Berg, Kurt Weill, Ernst Krenek and Igor Stravinsky. The cover of the exhibition's catalogue featured a grotesquely racist caricature of a Black saxophonist.

Yet it is indicative of the Third Reich's confused policy on music that both Stravinsky and jazz maintained ambivalent relationships to the regime. As Joan Evans (2003) notes, Stravinsky's music was hugely popular in Germany, even at the time of the 'degenerate music' exhibition. Jazz, meanwhile, although distasteful to the regime on racial grounds (it was viewed as both Black and Jewish in origin) and for its Americanism, eventually won tacit support because of its sheer popularity: it was reasoned that if German radio stations stopped broadcasting jazz, listeners would simply retune to British or American stations instead, where they would also encounter anti-German propaganda (Kater 1989).

State crackdowns on forms of musical expression such as those found in Germany and the USSR were not limited to outwardly authoritarian regimes. In liberal democracies such as the US and UK, threats were often perceived to come from young, working-class and/or non-white cultures (→Chapter 15, 'Audiences, Class and Consumption'). In the United States, the Parents Music Resource Center (PMRC) was founded in the 1980s by a group of prominent women (all were married to political figures in Washington, DC) with the aim of educating and informing parents about pop music lyrics that were violent or sexually explicit, or that glorified the use of drugs, alcohol or the occult. Although an independent body, the PMRC wielded enough influence to instigate a series of Senate Committee hearings into its cause (Deflem 2020: 7). The hearing proposed no legislation, but it did draw a response from the Recording Industry Association of America (RIAA), which volunteered to place 'Parental Advisory' stickers on all records deemed to contain explicit material (Figure 11.1). The PMRC's early targets were rock and pop (an early list of fifteen target songs included tracks by Prince, Madonna, Cyndi Lauper and AC/DC), but by the 1990s the Parental Advisory stickers were more frequently found on rap records. Although the PMRC's initial aim

Figure 11.1 Cover of Eminem, *The Slim Shady LP* (Interscope, 1999), showing PMRC 'parental advisory' stickers

was to provide information to parents, it has been argued that the consequences of its actions (which continue today in the labelling of music as explicit, and the parallel release of 'clean' versions of tracks, with explicit content removed or masked) amounted to a form of censorship in that many records were pulled from sale (Chastagner 1999).

In the UK, public anxiety at the end of the century centred on dance music, particularly the unlicensed electronic music festivals known as raves that were held in the early 1990s in outdoor locations such as quarries, disused airfields and racetracks. (For an enthusiastic and rich study of rave culture, see Reynolds 1998.) In 1994, this prompted a legal response from the Conservative government in the form of the Criminal Justice and Public Order Act (CJA). Raves, it was felt, disturbed the peace of rural life; the music was loud, electronic and made for taking ecstasy and dancing through the night; land, property and livelihoods were deemed to be under threat. The collision of middle-class anxieties with a culture fuelled by technology, drugs and folk mysticism (and a heavy dash of peasant revolt inspired by historical rebels like the seventeenth-century Levellers) proved a potent site of ideological conflict that was notably different from the concerns of the PMRC with sex, violence and the occult, although drug use was a fear in both cases. The final straw was the Castlemorton Common Festival of 1992, a week-long free festival held in the Malvern Hills (an area of countryside associated musically with Edward Elgar) that was attended by an estimated 20–40,000 people, many of them travellers, which was the 'high-water mark and absolute climax' of the rave era (Reynolds 1998: 137).

The wide-ranging CJA, introduced in the wake of Castlemorton, included restrictions on the right to free assembly and protest as well as the right to silence. It also included a prohibition on outdoor events playing 'sounds wholly or predominantly characterised by the emission of a succession of repetitive beats'. The law's definition of rave music was derided for its bureaucratic language (in 1994 the electronica duo Autechre released a track, 'Flutter', with no rhythmic repetitions, but sardonically advised that DJs have 'a lawyer and a musicologist present at all times . . . in the event of police harassment'), but it also highlighted the cultural divide at the heart of the controversy: an open-air orchestral concert featuring Holst's *Planets* (1914–16) or Ravel's *Bolero* (1928) would fall foul of the same description, yet such events were implicitly held to be exempt. Like the PMRC – and indeed, on a more extreme level, the policies of the USSR and Third Reich – the CJA was an attempt by the dominant classes to curb and control cultural expressions that they found threatening (Rietveld 1998: 60).

Case Study 11.1: Shostakovich, His Fifth Symphony and the State

Even more than his German contemporary Hindemith, the Russian composer Dmitri Shostakovich (1906–75) had an uneasy relationship with his home country's political regime. His prodigious First Symphony (1924–5), premiered when he was nineteen, saw him hailed as 'first composer of the Revolution'. Yet his second and third symphonies, much more experimental in nature, were not public successes, despite their pro-Soviet programmes (the second, 1927, subtitled 'To October' featured a choral finale in praise of Lenin and the October Revolution; the third, 1929, 'First of May', celebrated the triumph of the workers' revolution). His surrealistic first opera, *The Nose* (1928), begun while he was writing the Second Symphony and seemingly even more aligned with the modernist tastes of post-Revolutionary Russia, won the disapproval of the conservative Russian Association of Proletarian Musicians and soon disappeared from the stage.

- Dmitri Shostakovich, *The Nose*, Act I: Interlude (1928)

Shostakovich's second opera, *Lady Macbeth of the Mtsensk District* (1933), fared better. Based on a story by the novelist and playwright Nikolai Leskov – of an unhappily married woman who commits a series of murders after falling in love with another man – it was widely acclaimed after its first performances in Moscow and Leningrad in January 1934. In the next two years it received more than two hundred performances in Russia alone. Yet this reception changed dramatically in January 1936 when Stalin himself attended a performance at the Bolshoi Theatre in Moscow. Stalin's party – who had alternately mocked and winced at the production – left before the end. Shostakovich saw all of this and was filled with dread. Two days later, his fears were realised by the publication in the newspaper *Pravda* of an unsigned tirade against his opera, titled 'Muddle Instead of Music'. Like Hans Gerigk's condemnation of Carl Orff's *Carmina Burana* (1935–6) a year later, the review's objections were aesthetic, moral and political. Shostakovich's music was decried as 'deliberately dissonant', 'a confused stream of sound', and 'chaotic'; its story was 'vulgar'; its spirit was 'bourgeois' and 'wrong-headed'. All three charges together resulted in a complete condemnation, chillingly captured in one notorious line: 'The power of good music to infect the masses has been sacrificed to a petty-bourgeois, "formalist" attempt to create originality through cheap clowning. It is a game of clever ingenuity that may end very badly.' (For a detailed retelling of this story, see Wilson 2006: ch. 3; for a critical analysis, see Taruskin 1997: 511–44.)

- Dmitri Shostakovich, *Lady Macbeth of the Mtsensk District*, Act IV: 'Vstaváy! Po mestám! Zivo!' (1933)

Case Study 11.1: (cont.)

Shostakovich did not fail to notice the threat. For several years already, the Soviet regime had been censuring artists who did not meet its demands of class-appropriate work. Yet 1936 had marked the beginning of an escalation in attacks on those seen as enemies of the revolutionary project: the Great Purge of 1936–8 saw the mass removal of political figures, as well as genocidal acts against kulaks and ethnic minorities. Artists were not immune, and hundreds were executed or exiled; many more were forced into effective silence.

The impact of the *Pravda* editorial was swift. Soviet critics who had hailed *Lady Macbeth* quickly revised their views to condemnation. Shostakovich prepared himself for the worst. He kept a suitcase packed in case of his arrest and began sleeping in his clothes. His Fourth Symphony, begun in September 1935 and completed in May 1936, was withdrawn from its first performance. Whether the composer did this willingly or whether he was forced is a matter of conjecture (the work was finally premiered in 1961 by the Moscow Philharmonic), but the cancellation notice disingenuously states that the work 'in no way corresponds to his creative convictions and represents for him a long-outdated creative phase' (quoted in Fay 2000: 95). Shostakovich himself may have been dissatisfied with the work, which, despite many inventive passages, exhausts itself long before its end.

The real artistic breakthrough was achieved with the Fifth Symphony. Shostakovich's strongest and most coherent artistic statement up to that point, it is also one of his most conservative, avoiding the experimentalism of the early symphonies, the surrealism of *The Nose* or the lurid expressionism of *Lady Macbeth*. Instead, across its conventional four-movement structure, it draws on the nineteenth-century symphonic tradition from Beethoven to Mahler. It was a huge success. At its first performance, in Leningrad on 21 November 1937, listeners wept openly during the stark, funereal third movement, and were lifted out of their seats by the resounding finale. Shostakovich was presumably greatly relieved by the work's acceptance by public and Party (he would soon be showered with official prizes).

- Dmitri Shostakovich, Symphony no. 5, III, Largo (1937)

Shortly before the symphony's first performance in Moscow a few months later, a newspaper article appeared under his name with the title 'My Creative Response'. In it, Shostakovich, or whoever was writing on his behalf, acknowledges the *Pravda* criticisms and the need to 'turn toward greater clarity and simplicity' in his music (quoted in Taruskin 1997: 523). The article's subtitle, 'A Soviet artist's creative response to justified criticism' – whether written by Shostakovich or not – became emblematic of this apparent restructuring of his career towards the demands of the

Case Study 11.1: (cont.)

state. (For the wider effects of the *Pravda* article on music in the Soviet Union, see Mikkonen 2010.)

The story of the Fifth Symphony, already freighted with a dense biographical narrative, was made even more complex in 1979 with the publication of *Testimony* by the Russian journalist Solomon Volkov. Volkov claimed that *Testimony* was a memoir of Shostakovich, conveyed to him in conversations with the composer conducted between 1971 and 1974. In it, Shostakovich describes much of his music as veiled or coded criticism of the Soviet regime, serving a construction of himself as a subversive dissident, always working against the regime even when he appeared to be acceding to its demands. Yet doubts have been raised about the veracity of *Testimony*, most notably by the American musicologist Laurel E. Fay (1980, 2005), who notes – among other discrepancies – that several passages of *Testimony*, supposedly written from face-to-face conversations with Shostakovich, are copied almost verbatim from articles published by the composer thirty or more years earlier (for the opposite view, see Ho and Feofanov 1998). *Testimony* reshaped the international image of Shostakovich nevertheless. Works like the Fifth Symphony, which appeared to have effected an uneasy compromise with the requirements of the Soviet system ('justified criticism'), now seemed full of codes against that system, the work of an avowed and heroic dissident: the militaristic march of the first movement a satire of Soviet pomp; the triumphant ending a hollow smile through gritted teeth.

In the years since the symphony's first performance, responses to it have changed dramatically according to the context of its reception. In the Soviet Union in 1937 it was heard autobiographically within the context of Shostakovich's denunciation of the previous year, his own words of submission and his restoration to Party favour. In 1961 (five years after the USSR's new leader Nikita Khrushchev had denounced the repression and violence of the Stalinist regime), Shostakovich's message was regarded as more universal than specific (see Taruskin 1997: 525). In the USA, meanwhile, the autobiographical aspect was revived for inverted political ends: Shostakovich was not in fact a servant of the USSR but a dissident hero and a symbol of the West's moral rectitude in the Cold War; Leonard Bernstein (1918–90) and the New York Philharmonic performed the symphony in Moscow in 1959 as part of a concert tour of the Soviet Union, and later produced a famous recording for Columbia Records. Bernstein's account – controversial, but apparently approved by the composer – took the work's finale at double the marked tempo, emphasising its heroic aspects.

- Leonard Bernstein, New York Philharmonic, Shostakovich: Symphony no. 5, IV, Allegro non troppo (Columbia, 1959)

Case Study 11.1: (cont.)

The publication of *Testimony* supported this view: here, apparently in his own words, was Shostakovich at the end of his life confirming that he had been playing a joke on the regime all along; that the Fifth Symphony was a work of subversion, full of coded satire and bitter irony ('the secret diary of a nation'; Taruskin 1997: 475). However unlikely it was that this was actually true (ibid.: 535–41), the symphony became an icon of Soviet dissidence in the West. Recordings, like that of 1995 by Shostakovich's friend and compatriot Mstislav Rostropovich (1927–2007) with the National Symphony Orchestra, began to take a much more subdued approach to the finale than Bernstein's example. *Testimony* itself became a matter of bitter musicological dispute (see Brown 2005), and with so much at stake – particularly with the Soviet Union's invasion of Afghanistan the year after its publication – it was inevitable that debates over musical interpretation would become heated. As Fay noted in a return to the controversy two decades later, Shostakovich 'was much too good and much too important a composer for the West ever to digest easily that he was a true believer in communism and the Soviet system' (2005: 55).

- Mstislav Rostropovich, National Symphony Orchestra, Shostakovich: Symphony no. 5, IV, Allegro non troppo (Teldec, 1995)

The example of the Fifth Symphony demonstrates how the lives of the state and of the artist can become intertwined. Whichever way one turns, it seems impossible to avoid the influence of the state – whether the USSR or USA – on our understanding of Shostakovich's music both during his life and after his death in 1975. Perhaps one way forward is that suggested by the American musicologist Richard Taruskin. Writing in the 1990s, after the end of the Cold War and the ideological defeat of the Soviet Union, Taruskin suggests that attempts to establish whether or not Shostakovich intended this or that response to his music are 'naïve, unanswerable, and irrelevant' (Taruskin 1997: 472). 'Sometimes the composer's intention is manifestly irrelevant to the meaning of his work, and to insist on limiting meaning to original intention can only, and obviously, impoverish it' (ibid.: 473).

The Democratic State

States have not only sought to censor, suppress or control musical expression. In the aftermath of World War II, institutions such as the UK Arts Council (founded 1946; see Sinclair 1995), the French Ministry of Culture (1959; see Loosely 1995) and the National Endowment for the Arts (1965,

USA; see Binkiewicz 2004; Uy 2020; for a detailed analysis of the relationship of the NEA to contemporary music, see Robin 2021: ch. 4) were
founded by governments as a response to the sort of authoritarianism
described in the previous section, and to provide artists with financial
and other forms of support. The argument ran, in the words of the historian Tony Judt, that 'only the state had the resources to service the cultural
needs of its citizens ... It was the responsibility of a well-run public
authority to deliver cultural nourishment no less than food, lodging, and
employment' (Judt 2005: 377; for a detailed introduction to state funding in
the UK and North America, see also Upchurch 2016). Nevertheless, such
bodies still sought to promote social or national agendas, albeit ones that
we might consider relatively benign in comparison to the authoritarian
regimes of the 1930s.

Nowhere was this change in cultural policy more pronounced than in
West Germany. Following the catastrophe of World War II, here the
reconstruction of a German artistic culture served the urgent task of re-
educating and reorientating citizens away from Nazism and towards democracy. High art (including classical music) was enlisted in this endeavour.
In the years immediately after the war, as Germany was divided into four
zones of occupation (by France, the UK, the USA and the USSR), the US
Military Government was especially keen to help fund the country's 'cultural
re-education'. Under instructions from Washington, the United States
Office of Military Government in Germany (OMGUS) supported, guided
and gave approval to cultural activities in Germany from concerts to radio to
publishing. Leading musical figures like Bernstein were sent as cultural
ambassadors, the German radio network was re-established and concerts
and music festivals were supported. American OMGUS cultural officers
such as John Evarts and Everett Helm wrote articles and reviews, brokered
contacts and procured musical scores. Most famous among the events that
OMGUS assisted was the Internationale Ferienkurse für Neue Musik (INM),
or Darmstadt Summer School, founded in 1946 by the music critic
Wolfgang Steinecke. As described in →Chapter 2, 'Modernism', the INM
grew in the 1950s to become one of the most important meeting places for
the European and North American avant-garde, and a symbol of postwar
high modernism in music. Although it was not an OMGUS initiative, it was
frequently supported by it, with the Military Government providing money,
performance spaces, bedding and food; on one occasion, a Steinway grand
piano was donated by American soldiers and transported on the back of an
army jeep (Beal 2006: 38). In this, as in many other instances, many of them

detailed by Amy Beal (ibid.), OMGUS allowed German musical activities to follow their own path.

Once denazification and the reconstruction of German culture stopped being a priority in the 1950s, the American government began to regard the arts – and particularly the contemporary arts – as a propaganda tool against the repressive regimes of the communist world. In the face of the conservatism and conformity of socialist realism promoted in the Soviet Union (see Case Study 11.1), American arts, from abstract expressionism to Hollywood, could be cast as symbols of freedom, democracy and Western values: as demonstrated by the historian Frances Stonor Saunders in her seminal work on the period, *Who Paid the Piper?*, it was felt to be particularly important to draw the attention of the European intelligentsia away from Marxism and towards 'the American way' (Saunders 1999: 1; for studies of music, both classical and jazz, as a weapon in the USA's Cold War, see Carroll 2003; Davenport 2009; Fosler-Lussier 2007; Von Eschen 2004). One tool in this operation was the Congress for Cultural Freedom (CCF; 1950–67). Covertly funded by the CIA until this fact was scandalously revealed by the press in 1966, the Congress published numerous cultural journals around the world; sponsored exhibitions, conferences and prizes; and supported artists and musicians. Its reach was extensive: as Saunders notes, few European artists, scientists or writers – whether they knew it or not – 'were not in some way linked to this covert enterprise' (1999: 2).

Yet in terms of music, the preferences of the CCF were somewhat conservative, at least at first. Its secretary general was a former composer, Nicolas Nabokov (1903–78). Cousin of the author Vladimir Nabokov, Nicolas had had one of his own works – the ballet-oratorio *Ode* (1928) – presented by Diaghilev in Paris. He emigrated from Russia in 1933 and became a US citizen in 1939. In 1945 he was appointed a cultural adviser for OMGUS in Berlin. His experience, as well as his understanding of Russian culture, made him an ideal candidate for leadership of the CCF, which he held from 1951 until its dissolution. His own tastes were not for the avant-garde, however. No admirer of serialism, his musical hero was the neo-classical Stravinsky (whom he knew personally), and these tastes are reflected in the programming of one of the CCF's first major activities, the festival L'Oeuvre du Xxe siècle held in 1952 in Paris. As Mark Carroll (2003) observes, many of the musical pieces programmed at this international art festival could equally have been written in the USSR, and did not necessarily promote the CCF's ideological goals – in spite of Nabokov's typically swaggering assertion that 'Practically all the works [to be] performed belong to the category branded as "formalist, decadent and corrupt" by the Stalinists and the Soviet aestheticians' (quoted in Saunders 1999: 116). Nevertheless, the same programme that was dominated by works by Stravinsky and Ravel also featured the unexpected premiere of Pierre Boulez's (1925–2016) *Structures, Book 1* (1951–2) for two pianos, played by the composer and his teacher, Olivier Messiaen. Carroll describes the challenge this pioneering work of the postwar avant-garde presented to Nabokov's aesthetic (ibid.; see also Wellens 2002). Yet two years later, at the CCF's next musical event, La Musica del XX secolo in Rome, works by composers of the twelve-tone avant-garde – including Nono, Dallapiccola, Carter and Varèse – made up around half of the programme (Carroll 2003: 170). The transition between the two events marked 'the Congress's shift from a policy which in essence held that to attack socialist realism was the last form of defence to one that attempted to present the organisation as a patron of the latest trends in Western music' (ibid.: 168).

While culture affairs in Germany after the war were largely determined by its occupying powers, in 1958 France became the first country to establish its own ministry for the arts. The aims of its first minister, the novelist and art theorist André Malraux (1901–76), were to preserve French cultural heritage and to improve the cultural education of the masses. To this end, Malraux diverted state funding away from the elite Parisian institutions (the Opéra, the Comédie Française, the major museums) and towards regional venues and festivals. Yet although this move sought to democratise access to culture, in practice French regional institutions continued to stage only elite works; there was not yet an expansion of repertoire or outreach.

Two decades after L'Oeuvre du Xxe siècle, the French government began making plans for the creation of the Institut de Recherche et de Coordination Acoustique/Musique, otherwise known as IRCAM (Figure 11.2). Opened in 1977, alongside (and beneath) the Centre Pompidou, with which it is associated, IRCAM is one of the world's largest computer music research facilities. It was conceived by President George Pompidou (1911–74) to aid in the reconstruction of French artistic life after the protests and political upheavals of 1968, and in 1970 Pompidou invited the composer and conductor (and France's leading musical modernist) Pierre Boulez to direct its planning, in conjunction with the French Ministry of Culture. Boulez remained IRCAM's director until 1992. As the musicologist Georgina Born notes in her groundbreaking anthropological study of IRCAM in the early 1980s, IRCAM is 'a uniquely authoritative and

Figure 11.2 IRCAM building on the Place Georges Pompidou, Paris. Photograph by
Fred Romero

well-funded' contemporary music institution, one that represents 'an
extreme of legitimacy and subsidy in the contemporary music world'
(Born 1995: 4).

Yet its success, at least in its early years with which Born is most
concerned, may be questioned. Despite millions of francs of state support,
in its first decade or so IRCAM produced only a small number of important
musical works (Boulez himself produced only one major work involving
computer technology, *Répons*, 1984). Its research into acoustics and music
and computing remained closely guarded and often self-justificatory. Its
impact on commercial music and software was minimal. Works were
composed to showcase new technologies, which were themselves created
by technicians to meet the bespoke wishes of individual composers. This
began to change in the 1990s as Boulez retired as director and was replaced
by another composer, Laurent Bayle. IRCAM improved its public access
with an extensive multimedia library and authoritative online resources.
Education and marketing departments were created. The former offers
opportunities ranging from children's workshops and software training
up to graduate courses that are an essential part of the education of many

young composers. The latter department has thoroughly embedded IRCAM and its work in global commercial, industrial and academic networks, placing the institution 'at the center of societal and economic concerns combining culture and information technologies'.[1] Among its most widely adopted products in the twenty-first century are the programming languages Max and OpenMusic, which are commonly used by both art and popular musicians. Initially designed purely for the advancement of French musical culture – albeit an extremely expensive example of its type – IRCAM has become, and arguably found a more effective purpose in becoming, a pillar of France's national culture industry.

• Boulez, *Répons* (1984)

Similarly to France, in the UK the arts came to be seen as 'important for their contribution to national prestige, and for their role in "civilizing" the [working-class] population' (Gray 2000: 37). This aim is reflected in a number of large-scale initiatives undertaken by British authorities in the postwar years, including the National Theatre (proposed in 1946 and founded in 1962), the Royal Shakespeare Company (established 1961), the Royal Festival Hall (built for the 1951 Festival of Britain) and, not least, the founding of the Arts Council itself. The Arts Council's origins date back to the war and the establishment in 1940 of a Council for the Encouragement of Music and the Arts (CEMA). Initially funded by a private charity, CEMA intended 'to defend British culture and the arts against the threat of fascism' (ibid.: 39). Sensing potential benefits to national morale as well as a propaganda opportunity, the UK government took over CEMA's funding by 1941, in which year the economist (and adviser to the treasury) John Maynard Keynes (1883–1946) was appointed chair. What CEMA demonstrated was the benefits that could come from the state funding the arts at arm's length, without having to be involved in artistic decision-making (as in the Soviet Union, for example). These organisations in turn led to the founding of the Arts Council after the end of the war, with Keynes at its head.

In the two decades after the war, the Arts Council carefully separated high art (painting, theatre, classical music, ballet and opera) from craft or entertainment. In a hangover from nineteenth-century concepts of genius (→Chapter 10, 'Copyright and the Music Industry'), true artistic talent was deemed to be such a rare phenomenon that only a few examples could be supported. The result was an exclusive focus on large professional

---

[1] https://www.ircam.fr/innovations, accessed 9 April 2020.

institutions (most of them in London) and a neglect of amateur or local organisations, as well as of 'low' arts such as film, photography, children's theatre, literature, and jazz and popular music. (This was also the case in other countries; for an analysis of the situation in France, for example, see Rigby 1991.) The role of the UK Arts Council, as it saw itself, was to preserve artistic excellence, not broaden access.

This view was challenged by the MP Jennie Lee (1904–88), who in 1964 became the UK's first Minister for the Arts (a post she held until 1970). In 1965 she wrote the UK's first (and until 2016, only) policy document on the arts. Titled 'A Policy for the Arts: The First Steps', it argued that the arts should play a central role in everyday British life and set out the case for expanding the Arts Council's work, particularly outside of London. Unlike Keynes' Arts Council, Lee did not regard excellence and access as antithetical. It was not the job of the state to decide where excellence lay, she argued, only to provide the circumstances in which it could emerge (for more on Lee, see Hollis 1998).

In both France and the UK, commercial mass culture, such as popular music, which had emerged in the postwar years was regarded for many years as a threat to state power and cohesion, threatening values of prestige, civilisation and class hierarchy. Yet as colonial empires were dismantled in the postwar years, particularly by countries such as France, Spain and the UK, and waves of migration into those countries took place – to France from North Africa and Vietnam; to Spain from Central and South America; and to the UK from the Caribbean, the Indian subcontinent and West Africa – state cohesion faced a different challenge, and art policy in the 1970s and 1980s was forced to respond. Under the banner of what was now known as multiculturalism (a political principle that recognised the particular needs of different cultural groups and sought to ensure equality of opportunity between them), state-funded bodies such as the UK Arts Council or French Ministry of Culture now had a responsibility to support the arts beyond the forms of white European high culture.

This case was made particularly clearly in France under François Mitterand's socialist government of the 1980s. Jack Lang (b. 1939), Minister for Culture from 1981 to 1986 and from 1988 to 1993, proved particularly ready to give cultural legitimacy (i.e., state support) to mass cultural forms such as comics, cartoons and popular music. His signature initiative was the founding, in 1982 (with the Ministry's Director of Music and Dance, Maurice Fleuret), of the *Fête de la musique*, an annual celebration on 21 June of free and public music making that now takes place worldwide. By being 'willing to accept the validity of what every group had to offer', Lang was refusing to use 'hierarchical, traditional, conformist norms of culture as a way of excluding what had previously been perceived as inferior, but which, it was now recognised, had been excluded simply because it was different'. Lang's objective, then, was 'less a case of providing access to high culture', in the mode of postwar cultural policy, 'than of supporting a whole diverse range of cultural practices' (Rigby 1991: 182; see also Loosely 1995).

In the UK, although there was no arts minister with quite the same vision or ambition as Lang (and no socialist government, either), numerous grass-roots organisations benefitted throughout the 1970s and 1980s either directly or indirectly from Arts Council funding, or from association with other regional funding bodies. Social democratic welfare policies, established in the postwar years, also played an invisible role in supporting artistic activity, allowing musicians and artists the time to experiment and rehearse, free from the pressures of having to work to pay the bills: as the late cultural critic Mark Fisher notes, 'Most of the innovations in British popular music which happened between the 60s and the 90s would have been unthinkable without the indirect funding provided by social housing, unemployment benefit and student grants' (2012b). Beneficiaries of such largesse range from the London Musicians' Collective (1975–), a charity devoted to contemporary, experimental and improvised music partly supported by the Arts Council, to internationally acclaimed rock groups like the Smiths and the Stone Roses, whose members relied on unemployment benefit in their groups' early days. Nevertheless, there are some caveats to this: opera and classical music remain by far the largest beneficiaries of funds, and, as some critics of multiculturalism have argued, liberalised funding policies were not always successful in helping minority communities (see, e.g., Phillips 2003: 158–9).

Case Study 11.2: Paternalism at the BBC

As radio broadcasting grew in the years immediately following World War I, countries began to issue national licences to broadcasters in order to control and apportion the available frequency spectrum. Among the most significant of these was that of the British government to the British Broadcasting Company (as it was then known) in October 1922, granting the exclusive right to broadcast across the UK. The BBC began broadcasting on 14 November and, after growing rapidly in its first few years, in 1927 it was established as an independent, public body, the British Broadcasting Corporation.

As its sole broadcaster, the BBC assumed responsibility for shaping the nation's cultural tastes. In an article written in 1924, John Reith (1889–1971), the BBC's

Case Study 11.2: (cont.)

managing director (later its first Director General), described this succinctly as a desire 'to entertain, to interest, to enlighten'; later this would become an ambition 'to give the public what we think they need, and not what they want' (see Doctor 1999: 25–38). As a transmitter of cultural values, the BBC saw itself in an educational role, disseminating art and ideas to a population that had previously had little access to them. In seeking to create a national culture, however, the choices of both what was 'culture' and what was of 'national' interest quickly became points of contention.

Music was central to the BBC's output from the beginning. In 1929 around two thirds of the total hours broadcast were given over to music. Almost one third of that was given to live classical music, another 40 per cent to light music and the remainder was divided between recordings and dance music (Doctor 1999: 40). From 1927, the BBC took over responsibility for Henry Wood's Promenade Concerts, and this annual summer festival of (mostly) classical music remained a prominent feature of the corporation's live musical output into the twenty-first century. In 1930 the BBC Symphony Orchestra was founded, with the ambition of providing not only the broadcaster, but the whole UK, with its first world-class ensemble.

Classical music was clearly used to serve the Reithian goals of enlightening the British public and of fostering a national culture. There were, however, different schools of thought as to how this goal might be realised. The BBC's first director of music, Percy Pitt (1869–1932), was director of the British National Opera Company. He had been educated in France and Germany, but his tastes for European modernism were not shared by the BBC's board of advisers, drawn from elite British establishments such as the Royal Academy of Music and the Royal Military School of Music.

In 1930, however, they found a more cooperative partner in Pitt's successor Adrian Boult (1889–1983), who also become the first conductor of the BBC SO. Under Boult, the BBC's music programming became distinctly more parochial, and this pattern continued under his immediate successors, among them the composer Arthur Bliss (1942–4) and the tenor Steuart Wilson (1948–50). British composers were championed, and in a manner that was not only non-European, but also anti-European. In the 1940s, this anti-European (and especially anti-German) sentiment grew, not only at the BBC but across the country. An internal BBC document from 1942 states that 'The BBC regards it as a matter of first importance to develop a strong sense of national pride in British music' (quoted in Edmunds 2006: 239). The source of that pride was to be music that in some way reflected 'British', rather than 'European' qualities. Music that was inspired by British folk or historical traditions was especially valued. Not only was this music programmatically tied to British (in fact, more often English) musical traditions and (idealised) landscapes (→Chapter 1, 'Place and Space, Local and Global') but it was remote from European modernist trends such as

Case Study 11.2: (cont.)

serialism and atonality. The BBC's twenty-four-part series *Contemporary British Composers*, broadcast from July 1947, serves as a statement of values. Of the twenty-four composers profiled, only two – Elisabeth Lutyens (1906–83) and Humphrey Searle (1915–82) – were serialists. In 1972 Lutyens reflected on the Boult era, and its paradoxical confluence of nationality with aesthetic:

> Apparently it is not un-English to study Palestrina and Bach at every musical institution; to be influenced by Brahms, Hindemith or Bartók; but to adopt a technique, like the twelve-tone associated with a German, Schoenberg . . . was '*mittel*-European'; un-English and iconoclastic. (Quoted in ibid.: 240)

Lutyens and her modernist colleagues, among them the young members of 'the Manchester school', Harrison Birtwistle (b. 1934), Peter Maxwell Davies (1934–2016) and Alexander Goehr (b. 1932), had better luck with William Glock (1908–2000), the BBC's Controller of Music from 1959 to 1972 (and Controller of the Proms, 1960–73). Glock came to the BBC as a critic and administrator rather than a composer or performer. His particular interests were in contemporary and early music, evidenced by the programmes of the Bryanston (later Dartington) Summer School of Music that he established in 1948, where courses might be given alongside one another in plainchant, contemporary opera, madrigals and Bartók. Glock carried these interests into his programming at the Proms and the BBC, bringing music by Stockhausen, Elliott Carter, John Cage and others from the European and American avant-gardes to the UK for the first time. Boulez was particularly favoured, and Glock did much to further the French composer's reputation in Great Britain, including appointing him chief conductor of the BBC Symphony Orchestra in 1969 – a symbolic inversion of the Boult years. His decisions were controversial, however. Tonal composers previously championed by the BBC found themselves out of favour; some even spoke of a 'lost generation'.

- Elisabeth Lutyens, *Quincunx* (1960)
- Peter Maxwell Davies, *Worldes Blis* (1966–9)

Yet Glock and his predecessors were, in fact, all responding to the BBC's paternalistic instinct. Boult and the directors of the 1940s and 1950s were responding to a sense of national inferiority (especially with regard to Germany) and therefore sought to bolster the nation's cultural output and identity. Glock was responding, as he would see it, to the 'enlightenment' part of the equation, by introducing British audiences to the most advanced music being written around the world: his stated ambition was to offer listeners 'What they will like tomorrow'. The Thursday Invitation Concerts series he developed provided, he said, the 'clearest image' of the BBC's ethos, 'based on illuminating contrasts and depending on a repertory of twentieth-century music that will . . . compare proudly with the many masterpieces of the past' (Glock 1991/1963,

Case Study 11.2: (cont.)

quoted in Edmunds 2006: 241). The logic of sandwiching unfamiliar or difficult contemporary works between more familiar pieces extended into Glock's Proms programming – a practice that recalls the BBC's policy of using lighter music as a hook to attract listeners to higher cultural fare that we have seen elsewhere in this chapter. (One of Glock's most innovative Proms programmes introduced progressive rockers Soft Machine to the Albert Hall in 1970.) Although Glock left the BBC in 1972, this combinatory approach perhaps reached its apogee with the premiere of Birtwistle's loudly frenetic *Panic* for saxophone, drums and wind band at the 1995 Last Night of the Proms. This high-profile premiere by Britain's leading composer, broadcast to a global television and radio audience of many millions, attracted an unprecedented number of complaints to the BBC. For all the Last Night's atmosphere of flag-waving national celebration, the division between national identity and aesthetic appeared still strong.

- Harrison Birtwistle, *Panic* (1995)

Instrumentalisation

Multiculturalism may have helped redistribute at least some state support beyond the large, elite institutions, yet it raised an uncomfortable question: if the arts were to be funded for reasons other than the preservation of high culture and the 'civilisation' of the population, what should the state expect in return for its investment? Or, in other words, what were the arts for?

The answer lay in instrumentalisation, or the view of the arts as having a useful, or instrumental, function within society. The idea may be traced back to the arguments Plato makes in *The Republic* for certain forms of poetry and music being beneficial (or detrimental) to the state. In the 1990s, the idea re-emerged as a way to argue for the public funding of culture in the wake of the postmodern dismantling of ideals of high culture, and the civilising power of art per se. (Instrumentalisation has also been used to argue for the funding of arts education in schools and universities, against more obviously 'useful' subjects such as science and technology.) Ways in which music might be instrumentalised include highlighting its economic benefits or its contribution towards community cohesion. In its transformation in the 1990s from a secretive academic institution to a creator of industrial goods (notably the music software OpenMusic and the visual programming language Max/MSP (developed in partnership with the company Cycling '74)), IRCAM has been something of a model of the process of instrumentalisation.

There were already hints of instrumentalisation in Jennie Lee's reform of the Arts Council, but the evolution of public funding in the 1980s and 1990s in the UK and Europe saw it increasingly emphasised. In the UK this view was cemented by the Arts Council's publication in 1993 of *A Creative Future: The Way Forward for the Arts, Crafts and Media in England*. This lengthy policy document makes clear a case for 'Why [it should] be the business of government to pay for the arts' (p. 8): that there are collective benefits to society as a whole; that the absence of the arts is damaging to society; and that as well as economic benefits, the arts support emotional and spiritual health and the identities of individuals and groups. (Similar goals of community cohesion within a multicultural context might also be found in Lang's Fête de la musique in France.) The distance established by this document from the 'high arts' role of the postwar Arts Council is graphically told in the document's title: arts, crafts and media are addressed on an equivalent basis.

The recommendations of *A Creative Future* were taken on by Tony Blair's New Labour government from 1997, by which stage, the instrumentalising process may be said to have turned full circle. Keen to attract younger voters, and to distance itself from the ageing, fusty image of John Major's Conservatives, the Blair government recruited rock artists such as Blur and Oasis to bolster its Cool Britannia brand (see Harris 2003). Blur, and in particular their lead singer Damon Albarn, were courted by New Labour ahead of Blair's 1997 election victory for support and cultural legitimacy; Oasis, infamously, were invited to a reception at 10 Downing Street in July that year to provide some of the 'simple currency of celebrity' (ibid., 343, Figure 11.3). Although more benignly enacted than in the Soviet Union, here was music once more enlisted in the service of the state. Yet now the desire was for mass appeal and brand identity rather than social improvement, and popular music was felt to be a more potent tool than classical. Between the USSR of the 1930s and the UK of the 1990s the political uses of music had changed; as a consequence, so too did the type of music that was used.

The Marketplace

Nazi Germany and Soviet Russia were command economies, in which the state could set the rules for what music could and could not be freely produced and sold: most communist countries of the second half of the century, for example, operated state-run publishing houses and recording

Figure 11.3 Noel Gallagher of Oasis meets UK Prime Minister Tony Blair at a reception held at No. 10 Downing Street in July 1997. Photograph Rebecca Naden/PA

companies, which held a monopoly on officially approved releases. This is not to say that there were no substantial black markets in unofficial music making, of course; however, such activities came with serious penalties.

The tension between state media and the free market was, however, not limited to authoritarian regimes. In the UK in the 1960s, the BBC held the monopoly on radio broadcasting. Following its stated goals of educating the masses and improving popular tastes (see Case Study 11.2), the BBC regarded commercial pop with disdain, and played very little of it on radio or TV. What popular music was broadcast was confined to the 'Light Programme' and comprised less serious forms of classical music by composers such as Eric Coates, Ernest Tomlinson and Ronald Binge. The idea – possibly fanciful – was that it would act as a gateway for listeners to explore the more serious and avant-garde music available on the BBC's Third Programme (Simonelli 2007: 97). Although there was a huge demand for broadcasts of pop and rock 'n' roll, this was not something the BBC could countenance, as it would remove airtime from forms of music it deemed more worthwhile.

With such a large gap in the market, other actors could not help but fill it. On 29 March 1964 the pirate radio station Radio Caroline began broadcasting across the UK from a ship anchored in international waters in the North Sea and beyond the reach of British law. Within two years, pirate radio was listened to by more than a third of the British population and was generating advertising revenue in excess of £2 million. In order to stifle this illegal activity, Parliament passed in 1967 the Marine Offences Act, which made it an offence for British businesses to advertise on pirate radio, thus cutting off its income. The justification given was that pirate broadcasts interfere with radio stations already operating on internationally agreed wavelengths (such as the BBC) and, more tendentiously, that 'They may also jam ship's radio and interfere with distress signals, shipping forecasts, gale warnings and other essential messages.' Yet even Parliament could not ignore the vast demand for popular music radio, and in order to regain control of the market the Marine Offences Act was preceded by the decision to create a new BBC radio station devoted entirely to pop and rock: Radio 1, with the Light Programme renamed as Radio 2. David Simonelli notes that, 'The creation of two radio stations that broadcast popular music with no overt attempt to educate the public's taste appeared to be a major reversal of everything the BBC had stood for through-out its existence' (2007: 95). And yet the pattern would be repeated more than once in the BBC's history: the creation of the digital channel Radio 1Xtra in 2002 was intended to draw a young, mostly Black audience away from the pirate radio stations broadcasting genres such as drum 'n' bass and UK garage that had proliferated in the 1990s. Some former pirate DJs were even recruited into Radio 1Xtra's early roster of presenters.

By the end of the century, not even contemporary art music was untouched by the marketplace. The unexpected popular success in the early 1990s of recordings of music by Henryk Górecki (1933–2010), Arvo Pärt (b. 1935) and John Tavener (1944–2013) – a recording of Symphony no. 3 by the first of these reached number 6 on the *popular* album charts – led to a fashion for 'spiritual' or 'holy' minimalism that shaped record companies' marketing strategies and the characterisation (often retroactively applied) of numerous composers and their music (see Rutherford-Johnson 2017: 24–38).

- Henryk Górecki, Symphony no. 3 'Symphony of Sorrowful Songs' (Nonesuch, 1976)
- Arvo Pärt, *Tabula rasa* (ECM, 1977)
- John Tavener, *The Protecting Veil* (Virgin Classics, 1988)

In the wake of widespread cuts to state funding in the 1990s (partly a result of the end of the Cold War and the requirements of soft power; partly thanks to a worldwide turn towards neoliberal policies that favoured market-led dynamics over state intervention; and, in the USA, partly a result of a 'culture war' against the liberal arts led by Republican politicians), and encouraged by the popularity of recordings like Górecki's, performers and composers began to develop entrepreneurial skills, identifying or creating market niches for their music and developing their own audiences. Two American groups proved especially adept at this: the trio of composers Michael Gordon, David Lang and Julia Wolfe, who founded the Bang on a Can (BOAC) music festival as well as numerous associated ventures; and the Kronos String Quartet, one of the first classical ensembles to capitalise upon the possibilities of a youthful, MTV-influenced brand image (casual clothes, lighting, pop informality) in their concerts. BOAC benefitted from the popularity of minimalism and a public appetite for classical/rock crossovers. Alongside smart branding, Kronos benefitted from a confluence of world music and spiritual minimalism (they several times recorded works by Pärt and commissioned three quartets from Górecki) that tapped into the hip, touristic countercultural vibe of the 1990s.

- Kronos Quartet 'Purple Haze', from *Kronos Quartet* (Nonesuch, 1986)
- Bang on a Can All-Stars, '1/1', from *Brian Eno: Music for Airports* (Point Music, 1998)

Conclusion

Both the Kronos Quartet and BOAC evince an ideological desire born of late twentieth-century-free-marketplace thinking: that contemporary art music (i.e., high culture) can no longer depend upon the support of the state – and, indeed, should no longer expect it – for its future success. Instead, like popular cultural forms, it must survive according to its acceptance within the marketplace, among a broad, non-specialist audience. This ideological position is the focus of William Robin's study of BOAC (2021), which notes that groups like BOAC were in the late twentieth century adapting to a widespread shift away from state patronage and a centralised bureaucracy to a more ad hoc, patchwork system of support – 'the default mode of American arts funding in the twenty-first century'. 'At the close of the [twentieth] century', he writes, 'the marketplace was no longer a rhetorical position – an ethos that could be embraced or defied – and no longer a choice. It was an imperative, and its "magic" … could no longer be resisted' (137). Of course, as other examples throughout this book show, both popular and art music continued to resist the 'magic' of the market – or at least engage with it in more complex ways. Nevertheless, at the end of a century of state interventions, music in many forms had reached an uneasy peace with those national and supranational powers that had sought to control it.

12 | Music and the Moving Image

The first public screening of projected moving images by the Lumière Brothers in Paris in 1895 marked the beginning of an artistic revolution. Almost immediately, music became an integral part of the film industry, first being performed live to silent film screenings before becoming fully integrated into the cinematic apparatus on the advent of sound film. While the placement of music against the moving image for commercial film built on centuries of dramatic practice, it also developed forms of audiovisual communication unique to the twentieth century. In fact, we can say that moving-image art is a form exclusive to modern life. As the decades passed, many of the audiovisual conventions established in early film practice began to be appropriated by other moving-image genres, from television (1950s) and music video (1980s) to the interactive forms of video art (1960s), gaming (1970s) and online culture (1990s). These new audiovisual textures were also used by composers and artists to refresh the processes of music composition, while screen media quickly became an integral part of live music performance, from opera to stadium rock.

Like many other musics of the twentieth century, the sonic component of audiovisual culture reached far into other disciplines and creative practices. In this chapter, we will explore how the century's musicians sought and developed collaboration with the visual and moving-image arts to either radically extend creative practice or develop new art forms altogether. Convergence – the fusion of two or more media forms – is the key theme of this chapter: of the aural and visual arts, film and music industries, live and recorded music, film, music video and live performance, high and low cultures, art music and pop, and music and sound. The notion of convergence also dominates the diverse body of theoretical work that grew around these new multimedia forms. Case studies, taken from two prominent areas of audiovisual practice – music video and contemporary opera – illustrate how twentieth-century musical form and aesthetics have been challenged and extended through combination with the moving image.

Music, Film and Immersion

We will start by looking at the twentieth century's largest screen media industry: film. Music has accompanied the filmed image from its earliest days. Before the technology to produce sound and image at the same time emerged in the late 1920s, silent films would usually be supported by live music. Claudia Gorbman, one of the first to treat film music in a theoretically engaged way (1987, chs. 2 and 3), suggested several practical reasons for this: during the nineteenth century, music was a common component of dramatic productions, from opera to music theatre and vaudeville, so early film audiences would have been accustomed to experiencing sound with visual narratives; music could help to cover the distracting noise of primitive film projectors; conversely, sitting in silence can be uncomfortable, so music was used to help an audience relax and become more thoroughly immersed in the film's world; and, along similar lines, seeing images without accompanying sounds can appear ghostly, so music, even if not closely synchronised with an image, could help to embody and substantiate what was on screen.

Most significantly, however, Gorbman drew attention to narrative coherence. In silent film, where information was provided only through physical gesture and the odd intertitle card, a story could be difficult to follow. Music could help to provide the image with emotion, nuance and purpose. When synchronised music, sound and speech – which enabled dialogue and sound effects to link with on-screen events – hit cinemas with the 1927 film *The Jazz Singer* (Alan Crossland), it seemed at first as though soundtrack music was no longer needed. After all, most aural information could now be delivered through the spoken word, while sound effects made two-dimensional images appear fully embodied and more realistic. And yet, it would not be long before film companies, directors and audiences realised the extraordinary power the placement of newly composed or pre-existent music against a filmed image could exert over our emotional responses; by the mid-1930s, the sweeping orchestral scores of Max Steiner and Erich Wolfgang Korngold were driving Hollywood's biggest blockbusters with styles and techniques that continue to influence film-music composers today.

- Erich Wolfgang Korngold, 'Main Title', *The Sea Hawk* (Michael Curtiz 1940)

These scores are intriguing. The music does not appear to come from the film's world; at least, the characters do not appear to hear or respond to it. So what, or who, is it for? Traditionally, film-makers have used music to give a sense of realism by placing it within the film (this being referred to as 'source music') and have helped to support the narrative by providing music that accompanies, or drives the image (this referred to as 'dramatic music'). Film theorists have been fascinated by these two types of musical placement, and have used different words to describe each state: diegetic or source music, which comes from a locatable place in the film's world – a radio playing, someone singing and so on; and non-diegetic, or dramatic, music, which appears to have no discernible on-screen source. While diegetic music sets a scene and can provide key plot information, non-diegetic music can focus our attention on specific characters, events or feelings, draw out significant narrative moments, form subtle connections between scenes and encourage us to respond to events in very specific ways. And yet, in order to do so, it occupies a paradoxical space within a film's world. Mel Brooks' 1974 comedy *Blazing Saddles* plays on the strange presence of non-diegetic music in a clever way. Accompanied by big-band music, Sheriff Bart (Cleavon Little) rides his horse through the desert. Focussed on the image, we are at first only vaguely aware of the upbeat big-band music that accompanies his journey, which assures us that the Sheriff is doing well; he is joyful and energised. Then, the roaming camera picks up the edge of something. Panning back, it reveals American bandleader Count Basie conducting his orchestra, seated on chairs in the sand (Figure 12.1). This is not non-diegetic music, but diegetic – on-screen – sound! While this is an arresting comedic moment, a more subtle blurring of non-diegetic and diegetic music is not uncommon, and film history throws up many examples of intricate narrative levels. When Audrey Hepburn sings Henry Mancini's (1924–94) 'Moon River' on her balcony in *Breakfast at Tiffany's* (Blake Edwards 1961), for instance, she is at first accompanied diegetically by her guitar (Figure 12.2). But as the song develops, a full orchestral underscore joins in. We can assume that there is not an orchestra hiding on the street, and yet diegetic and non-diegetic merge into one unified track. When Hepburn stops singing, the orchestra continues, moving back into the underscore and our conscious attention moves to the ensuing dialogue. With examples like this aplenty, some film-music scholars have rethought the terms non-diegetic and diegetic (Stilwell 2007), called for a greater variety of terms to describe the different types of overlap (Winters 2010) and suggested getting rid of them altogether (Kassabian 2013a).

Figure 12.1 Sheriff Bart comes across Count Basie conducting his orchestra in the middle of the desert: *Blazing Saddles* (Mel Brooks, 1974)

The unexpected visual revelation in *Blazing Saddles* is funny because it highlights the strangeness of a cinematic convention in which visual narratives are awash with sounds that have no clear place in the world depicted. While these non-diegetic sounds are not always immediately noticeable as our attention is so focussed on the moving images (scholars like Caryl Flinn (1992) have gone so far as to suggest that we do not process such music at a conscious level, but rather at a powerful subconscious one), their place within the on-screen world is ambiguous. After all, mainstream narrative film is constructed to resemble a plausible and realistic world: edits are seamless, film equipment is never in shot and point of view is consistent. So why threaten this with disembodied music?

While some scholars understand non-diegetic music to be an external narrator situated between the spaces of the film and the real world (Levinson 1996), others suggest that the characters may be aware of it because films do not emulate our world but rather form a brand-new type of cinematic reality (Winters 2010). Whatever the reason, all understandings rely on the music being tightly stitched into the image, rhythmically or aesthetically. This can happen in several ways. A score is said to be Mickey-Mousing when the music closely mimics every visual action, for

Figure 12.2 Holly Golightly sings 'Moon River' on the balcony in *Breakfast at Tiffany's* (Blake Edwards, 1961)

instance. As the name suggests, this is something common to cartoons: think of Tom and Jerry's famous chase scenes, where the music is co-ordinated with the characters' footsteps and physical gestures to such an extent that it almost functions like sound effects. A stinger – a musical stab found in horror films that coincides with an unexpected or sudden visual occurrence – operates in a similar way. But audiovisual synchronicity can also be more subtle. Leitmotivic composition, developed in the previous century by Berlioz and Wagner, involves the transformation of small musical cells over the course of an opera – or in this case a film – to help tell a story. In opera, a semantic connection is made when a character sings about a particular person, emotion or action. The melody heard when the words are uttered takes on that meaning. When the melody recurs again, that meaning is evoked, even if it is no longer part of the lyrics. The melody can then transform through mode, rhythm, speed, instrumentation or other musical development to shape the meaning or give nuance to current events. In this way, music can take on and transform specific meaning. In film, leitmotivs work in a similar way, although strong semantic associations can also be formed through the placement of melody against image.

Once connected with a character or an emotion – love, jealousy, fear, bravery – the music can be used to direct our attention to specific readings of the image. In this sense, music can gather meaning throughout the film, ultimately acquiring the power to undermine or contradict what we see.

Although the transformation of leitmotivs in film is different from its operatic forebear for various reasons – there is often less overall music as film soundtracks do not flow continuously, dialogue is spoken, not sung, and close-ups enable conjunctions to be made visually, not just through text – many film composers generate coherent narratives from this technique. In Rachel Portman's Oscar-winning score for *Emma* (Douglas McGrath 1996), the opening titles become a leitmotiv for love that spans the whole film. John Williams' (1932–) work on all nine of George Lucas' *Star Wars* films (1977–2019) demonstrates how complex musical meanings can develop, with over fifty transforming themes driving character development and plot lines (Paulin 2000).

For studios and composers working with early sound film, the technique was extremely useful. European émigrés such as Austrians Steiner and Korngold brought to Hollywood a rigorous schooling in tonal, nineteenth-century orchestral textures, which not only proved a perfect match to the sumptuous tales of Hollywood's Golden Age, but also allowed composers to write quickly, offering a cost-effective way of producing a lot of music in a short space of time. Time was of the essence. Composers were often brought in at the last minute and given an edited print of the film and just several weeks to compose the entire score, with very limited collaborative opportunity with a director. Exceptions to this working practice could result in some powerful sonic moments, and strong director collaborations – many resulting in a leitmotivic score – spanned the twentieth century: John Williams and Steven Spielberg, Bernard Herrmann and Alfred Hitchcock, Michael Nyman and Peter Greenaway, and Tim Burton and Danny Elfman. In these instances, composers were often brought into the process early on and could help to structure and pace a visual narrative.

- Bernard Herrmann, 'Prelude', *Psycho* (Alfred Hitchcock 1960)
- John Williams, 'The Imperial March', *Star Wars: The Empire Strikes Back* (Steven Spielberg 1980)
- Danny Elfman, 'Introduction – Titles', *Edward Scissorhands* (Tim Burton 1990)
- Michael Nyman, 'Prospero's Magic', *Prospero's Books* (Peter Greenaway 1991)
- Rachel Portman, 'Main Title', *Emma* (Douglas McGrath 1996)

Dissonant Film Scores and Experimental Music

Despite the potential power of leitmotivic scores, they drew many detractors, including Theodor Adorno (2007/1947), who argued that the tonal sound worlds were not only out of date but also did little more than reiterate information available in the images. Contemporary critics pitted 'serious' composers against the 'Hollywood brand of composer' – musicians who were 'excellent' but made 'no pretence at artistic creation' (David Ewan): Hollywood's music was 'almost composing but not quite' (Irwin Bazelon) (both quoted in Flinn 1992: 39). Despite this, concert-hall composers like Shostakovich and Prokofiev made strong contributions to the world of film scoring, while Bernstein's score for *On the Waterfront* (Elia Kazan, 1954) has become a soundtrack classic. Other examples include Benjamin Britten (1913–76), who was commissioned to soundtrack rousing British documentaries for the General Post Office Film Unit, including *Coal Face* (Alberto Cavalcanti 1935) and *Night Mail* (Basil Wright / Harry Watt 1936); John Cage (1912–92), who scored a piece by artist Marcel Duchamp for Hans Richter's surreal classic 1947 film, *Dreams That Money Can Buy*; and, later in the century, Philip Glass (1937–), who appropriated his minimalist style to propel scores for experimental films like *Koyaanisqatsi* (Godfrey Reggio 1983) and mainstream blockbusters like *Candyman* (Bernard Rose 1992) and *The Truman Show* (Peter Weir 1998). Many composers working almost exclusively for film have also pushed into more dissonant textures, from Leonard Rosenman's serialist score for psychological drama *The Cobweb* (Vincente Minnelli 1955) to Bernard Herrmann's modernist work for Alfred Hitchcock, including the leitmotivic score for *Psycho* (1960). In other cases, more experimental sounds have been appropriated for a cinematic context: in 1968, for instance, Stanley Kubrick famously placed György Ligeti's *Lux Aeterna* (1966) in his *2001: A Space Odyssey* (1968). It is notable from this list that those making the transition from concert hall to the film studio tended to be white male composers (see → Chapter 13, 'Gender and Sexuality' and Chapter 4, 'Canons'). This was not only due to the difficulties women composers faced during the century in general, but also the difficulties they encountered when attempting to enter the film industry: it is notable that only four women were nominated for an Oscar in the Best Original Score categories during the century, and only two won (Rachel Portman for *Emma*, 1996, and Anne Dudley for *The Full Monty*, 1997).

- Benjamin Britten, 'This Is the Night Mail Crossing the Border', *Night Mail* (Basil Wright/ Henry Watt 1936)

- John Cage, 'Discs', *Dreams That Money Can Buy* (Hans Richter 1947)
- Leonard Rosenman, 'Main Title', *The Cobweb* (Vincete Minnelli 1955)
- György Ligeti, *Lux Aeterna* (1966)
- Philip Glass, 'Vessels', *Koyaanisqatsi* (Godfrey Reggio 1983)

Beyond Hollywood and mainstream film practice, examples of experimental music are plentiful. One of the most radical film sound techniques came early in the century, when film-makers began to explore the direct translation of image into music through a method known as hand-drawn, or synthetic, sound. Unlike the examples above, where collaboration between a director and a musician produced a visual and an aural track that were stitched together during post-production, synthetic sound produced sound and image together and was often the work of a single practitioner, such as avant-garde Russian composer Arseny Avraamov, German animator Rudolf Pfenninger and Scottish Canadian film-maker Norman McLaren (Rogers 2014b). Music was created when the artist or musician drew, photographed or etched shapes onto the optical soundtrack strip of film stock. When run through a film projector, image translated *directly* into sound, without any interpretation to form visual music. In 1932, German American animator Oscar Fischinger suggested that his experiments with what he called Sounding Ornaments produced 'drawn music … when run through a projector, these graphic sounds broadcast tones of a hitherto unheard-of purity, and thus, quite obviously, fantastic possibilities open up for the composition of music in the future' (1932). English electronic music pioneer Daphne Oram (1925–2003) (who we met in ➔ Chapter 8, 'Instruments') developed the technique further, using her Oramics machine (which she developed throughout the 1960s) to draw shapes onto 35-mm film stock and translate them directly into sounds by running the stock through a scanner (Niebur 2010). Because these drawn sounds were created artificially without any external sources or instruments, they can be considered a precursor to electronic music, and we will see below how technological developments later in the century led to such fluency that visual music could arise in live music settings.

Soundscapes: The Relation between Sound and Music

There are many ways that the sound of twentieth-century film fed into contemporary music practice. While visual music had links with later forms of electronic music, the creative use of film sound – rather than music – also forged significant connections with the *musique concrète* of Pierre Schaeffer and the sound-art practices of the mid-century. As we saw in →Chapter 8, 'Instruments', the creative uses of real-world sounds gave rise to new forms of deep listening (Oliveros), engagement with everyday sonic environments (Russolo) and the expansion of musical material (Cage). The history of film sound treads similar ground in two ways. First, by using real-world sound creatively, a practice we can trace right back to the beginnings of sound film; and second, and more recently, by combining it with traditional instruments. Sometimes these two forms of convergence can occur simultaneously. Alan Splet's soundtrack for David Lynch's *Eraserhead* (1976) is created entirely from *musique concrète*, yet is so musical it was subsequently released as a soundtrack album (1982), for instance, while Björk's music for Lars Von Trier's *Dancer in the Dark* (2000) arises from diegetic sounds that gather into musical rhythms (Rogers 2020).

- David Lynch and Alan Splet, 'Side A', *Eraserhead* (David Lynch 1977)
- Björk, 'Cvalda', *Dancer in the Dark* (Lars von Trier 2000)

For big-budget films, sound is a complicated business. Foley artists produce sound effects in a studio, using various objects to mimic or create the sound of something happening on-screen. Sound designer Ben Burtt's famous lightsabre sound from *Star Wars* (George Lucas 1977), for instance, was created from a microphone feeding back from a tube TV; to create the T-Rex's roar in Steven Spielberg's *Jurassic Park* (1993), sound designer Gary Rydstrom combined the slowed-down noises of howls of a baby elephant with the sounds made by a Jack Russell, an alligator and a tiger. Like music, these sounds can be heightened or focussed to draw attention to certain events or emotion (Chion 1994; Wierzbicki 2016). ADR (automated dialogue replacement), where actors overdub their voices for clarity, is synched separately. These are extremely important steps, as they ensure that what we see and what we hear match closely enough that the moving image appears realistic and fully dimensional (Chion 1999: 125), even if this embodiment is entirely illusory. The synchronisation of sound and image is the job of the Sound Effects Designer. Scholar William Whittington explains that 'sound is often one of the most highly constructed aspects of cinema ... it is understood that sound design does not simply capture reality, but rather constructs an entirely new "cinematic reality"' (Whittington 2014: 64). To make an audience believe what they hear, audiovisual synchronisation must be perfect. In fact, sound designer Walter Murch (1943–), who worked with Francis Ford Coppola on *The Godfather* (1972) and *Apocalypse Now* (1979), argued that the re-association of image and sound during post-production is the 'fundamental pillar upon which the creative use of sound rests, and without which it would collapse' (Murch 2000). In the meantime, a composer works on the score in relative isolation, while a music supervisor compiles any required pre-existent material. Finally, a sound editor or designer prepares all dialogue, background sounds, sound effects and music for the final mix.

In →Chapter 8, 'Instruments', we saw how the development of the sampler and the synthesiser enabled early experimental work by Pierre Schaeffer, John Cage and others with non-musical objects and sounds to eventually enter mainstream music practice through hip-hop and other sampling-heavy musics. A similar movement happened in cinema. The arrival of the digital audio workstation (DAW) in the early 1990s saw the three elements of a film's soundscape combine in new ways, as Kevin Donnelly explains: digital audio software allowed

sound designers and editors to manipulate sound effects in precisely the same way musicians do when they compose music. Indeed, sound designers use 'musical software' and digital products designed primarily for the production of music (such as ProTools) for processing both dialogue and sound effects. (Donnelly 2013: 365)

The result is a more integrated aural track, where sound effects can be used musically, dialogue can be treated rhythmically and music can draw every-thing together. Although many films at the end of the century demonstrate this sonic integration, examples like *Chocolat* (Lasse Hallström 2000) and *Amélie* (Jean-Pierre Jeunet 2001) demonstrate particularly stylised, hyper-real soundtracks (Smith 2013: 338) that operate very differently from the 'inaudible' scores of the Golden Age. In response to these changes in process, there has been a theoretical turn towards a more integrated study of film soundscape (Greene and Kulezic-Wilson 2016), where all aural elements are analysed as a united sonic track, rather than divided into diegetic sound, ambient sound and non-diegetic music.

Case Study 12.1: Opera and the Moving Image

Some of the century's most notable operas, like Puccini's *Tosca* (1900), developed the grand dramatic gestures and familiar tonal arcs of large-scale nineteenth-century practice. But at the same time, different forms of staged work developed that demonstrated a radical undoing of traditional opera form. Linear and coherent narratives were compli-cated by multiple events that unfolded at the same time (Luigi Nono's *Intolleranza 1960*, 1961), were rejected entirely for static tableau (Philip Glass' *Einstein on the Beach*, 1976) or offered plots delivered from different viewpoints (Harrison Birtwistle's *The Mask of Orpheus*, 1986). Many of these new works made use of shorter forms, expanded tonality

Case Study 12.1: (cont.)

and unusual ensembles that included non-musical instruments and extended techniques. They could also include the screened image, either as an element of the staging, or as an integral part of the plot with a pivotal, structural role.

Before the TV screen first entered the musical stage in the 1960s, moving images were already intervening in opera performance and dissemination in several ways. From cinema's earliest years, film was used to retell, refresh and augment familiar opera narratives in silent films, from Cecil DeMille's trailblazing *Carmen* (1915), with a score based on the music from Bizet's opera (1875) of the same name, to new and highly cinematic adaptations such as Robert Townsend's African American *Carmen: A Hip Hopera* (2001), featuring Beyoncé (Figure 12.3). Although replacing the spontaneity and energy of a live performance with prerecorded footage, opera films such as these opened the doors for exciting new interpretations. Scenes could be set outside; cars, trains and planes could be depicted; actors had a greater freedom of movement, and traditional tales could easily be transported into a setting – and a format – familiar and accessible to contemporary audiences (Joe and Theresa 2002; Citron 2010; Citron 2013). Some scholars have argued for a reciprocal flow of influence between screen media and staged opera (Ward-Griffin 2018). Influenced by the intimate gestures of film and television and the success of opera on the small screen, many directors took their live opera performances to smaller venues unencumbered by the high-art, bourgeoise connotations of traditional opera houses, opting for contemporary settings and smaller, less flamboyant gestures from their singers.

Figure 12.3 Beyoncé starring in *Carmen: A Hip-Hopera* (Robert Townsend, 2001)

Case Study 12.1: (cont.)

- Beyoncé and Mekhi Phifer, 'The Last Great Seduction', *Carmen: A Hip Hopera* (Robert Townsend).

But it was not long before moving-image technology itself moved into live settings, and by the century's end, most major opera houses were making creative use of screened media to give the proscenium stage space an illusion of greater depth. When set around the stage, TV screens and projected images could depict urban and rural backdrops and enlarge an opera's cast with filmed crowds and choruses, while close-ups of singers via live-circuit feeds could help to direct an audience's gaze to particular narrative events or emotions.

Although screened images could reinvigorate the scenography of pre-existent operas, in new works they could assume an integral narrative role if incorporated during the composition stage. The earliest examples of audiovisual amalgamations are found in New Music Theatre, an avant-garde operatic form that developed between 1955 and 1975. Distinctive for postwar experimentation in musical language and dramatic tradition, these works were distinctive for their political content and multi-media performance styles that included dance, mime and various forms of current media. In fact, so eclectic were these works that Robert Adlington has argued that they are more like an 'anti-genre . . . characterised by a refusal to conform to traditional or pre-existing genres and categories, rather than by any other consistent traits. Music theatre tends to illuminate the awkward interstices between art forms, the gaps between categories' (Adlington 2005: 230).

Within these gaps, the moving image became a powerful tool. Early examples of filmed elements on stage include Manzoni's *Atomtod* (1965), Bernd Alois Zimmermann's *Die Soldaten* (1965) and Carl Orff's *Prometheus* (1970). Luigi Nono's *Intolleranza 1960*, which weaves a hard-hitting tale of immigration and political upheaval, was the first work of New Music Theatre to integrate screened images with staged action. Nono worked closely with Czech stage director Alfréd Radok and set designer and scenographer Josef Svoboda, who had collaboratively pioneered a type of multimedia theatre known as Magika Laterna (Burian 1970). These magic lantern shows used a combination of live and prerecorded moving images to augment and complicate the traditional space of theatre to such an extent that it became a dramatic component of the action. One of the most famous examples of this activation can be seen in the second performance of *Intolleranza*, held in Boston on 21 February 1965 with set design by Svoboda. Spread across screens of different sizes were scenes of violent demonstrations juxtaposed with natural landscapes,

Case Study 12.1: (cont.)

prerecorded footage of the onstage actors and inflammatory text slogans. A live feed – controlled by an off-site television studio – projected close-ups, unusual angles and, radically, images of the audience themselves. This mixture of prerecorded images, contemporary news footage and a live feed of the whole auditorium folded audience members into historical and current events for an immersive and powerful call to arms (Příhodová 2011; Rogers 2019).

- Luigi Nono, Act 1: Scene 3, *Intolleranza 1960* (1960)

As the capabilities of moving-image technology expanded through the century, film, video and live opera could be used in more complex ways. Steve Reich's (1936–) multimedia theatre project with video-artist wife Beryl Korot *The Cave* (1993), for instance, relies on an intricate interplay between a live vocal-instrumental ensemble and a bank of screens projecting both text and talking heads (Figure 12.4). Although only working with a single screen, Philip Glass' *La Belle et la Bête* (1994) requires a mathematical synchronisation between the images of Jean Cocteau's 1946 film and the new opera, which replaced the original dialogue and soundtrack.

Figure 12.4 Steve Reich and Beryl Korot, *The Cave* (1993). Image from Beryl Korot's video of a performance by Ensemble Modern and Synergy Vocal at the Palais de la Musique et des Congrès, Strasbourg, 2011

Case Study 12.1: (cont.)

Moving-image technology, then, was used by directors and composers in numerous ways throughout the century. It allowed traditional opera scenography to be refreshed and contemporised, it opened up alternative channels of dissemination from domestic TV to cinemas and new performance spaces, it provided composers with an additional narrative voice and it allowed new forms of audience immersion and engagement.

Pop Scores and Pre-existent Music

Film's ability to blur the boundaries between high and low art made it a great force for the dissemination and interpretation of music during the century. Popular music has been routinely used in mainstream film since the 1950s, when major film production house Universal Pictures was taken over by Decca Records (in 1952). By 1958 there had been a significant reshuffle in film and music industries, with several major companies making film and representing musicians (Smith 1998). The result was a cross-fertilisation of influence and a diversification of risk. In 1960, *Billboard* magazine stated that: 'The record and motion picture industries are working in closer and more effective harmony today than they have since the golden days of movie musicals' (quoted in Smith 2003: 71). The appearance of prominent musicians, like Elvis Presley, in big-budget films could maximise both film and records sales, as well as providing a third outlet: the soundtrack album. But film musicals could also make big stars, who could break from the screen to become touring artists in their own right, a process particularly common for Bollywood stars.

Early on, there were several ways in which popular music could integrate into a film's texture. *The Graduate* (Mike Nichols 1967) soundtrack, for instance, is a compilation of Simon and Garfunkel's work from previous albums, with the addition of one newly worked-up track, 'Mrs Robinson' (released later in 1968). The film was woven around this familiar, pre-existent music, initiating a reversal of the scoring practices outlined above. Mancini's newly composed score for *Breakfast at Tiffany's*, on the other hand, worked the other way around. Integrating traditional orchestral textures with a new song, 'Moon River', the music is essential to the narrative, appearing both non-diegetically and diegetically, as we have seen. The song and score both became subsequent hits, and earned Mancini Best Original Song and Best Score at the 1961 Academy Awards.

The Beatles used the promotional cross-fertilisation between music and cinema particularly well and were involved in five full-length films. Mockumentary *A Hard Day's Night* (Richard Lester 1964) saw the four musicians deal with Beatlemania, with the music forming Side One of their third studio album of the same name (1964), while the soundtrack to *The Beatles: Yellow Submarine* (George Dunning 1968) formed the basis of their tenth album (1969). Subsequent examples of an established artist both acting in and creating the soundtrack for a commercial film include Prince (*Purple Rain*, Prince / Albert Magnoli 1984; Number 1 for 24 weeks; 13 million record sales) and Whitney Houston (*The Bodyguard*, Mick Jackson 1992: Number 1 for 20 weeks; 17 million sales). Even when a musician did not appear in the film, the exposure given to the music could be significant. The soundtrack for *Saturday Night Fever* (John Badham 1977), for instance, which included five original songs by the Bee Gees, topped the Billboard album charts for 24 weeks, since selling over 54 million copies.

Pop songs can signify in many ways in a film. When pre-existent music is used, images can be edited to fit to the musical structure; they can also pick up on the social and cultural connotations acquired in the music's previous life (Kassabian 2001). This is also true for art music: long sections of Luchino Visconti's *Death in Venice* (1971) are cut to excerpts from Gustav Mahler's third (1866) and fifth (1901-2) symphonies, for instance. Because they are often relatively short, popular songs can work differently from art music, punctuating events in an audible way and introducing lyrics as another level of commentary. Spike Lee's use of contemporary hip-hop in *Do the Right Thing* (1989), a film about a race war in Brooklyn, demonstrates many of these possibilities. Public Enemy's 'Fight the Power' (1989), written for the film, appears as a leitmotiv in both the non-diegetic score and the on-screen protest speech of protagonist Radio Raheem (Gibson 2017; Millea 2019). With samples taken from various aspects of African American culture, including the voices of civil rights activists, the song not only adds a nuanced commentary on filmic events but also stitches the film into the current social and political climate that it was commenting on.

Case Study 12.2: Music Video

In the second half of the twentieth century, moving-image technology enabled new ways of visualising music. As we have seen in several other chapters, the development of speakers and the emergence of the recording industry dislocated

Case Study 12.2: (cont.)

music from the physical gestures required to make it. Screen media could offer musicians the opportunity to re-embody their sounds in interesting ways. A live performance could be captured, new aesthetic interpretations generated, an artist's image tightly controlled and the commercial reach of the music greatly augmented. Almost immediately, television, a common addition to homes after World War II, offered a powerful alternative to radio for mass dissemination. Live and prerecorded performances could be broadcast into the heart of domestic life, giving musicians and record companies immediate access to the general public. Artists were not always in control of how they appeared, however: Elvis' hips were censored on his third appearance on *The Ed Sullivan Show* (1957), for instance, with the camera only shooting him from the waist up. They were not even in control of how they sounded: Nirvana, in retaliation for being asked to sing to a backing track of 'Smells Like Teen Spirit' on *Top of the Pops* in 1991, deliberately sabotaged the performance by theatrically miming on their instruments and offering a radically reconfigured vocal part.

By contrast, music video offered artists more control not only of their image and performance, but also over a song's interpretation. Although short promotional films for songs have enjoyed a long history – early defining moments include Bob Dylan's 'Subterranean Homesick Blues' (1967), the Beatles' 'Strawberry Fields Forever' (1967) and Queen's 'Bohemian Rhapsody' (1975) – the 1981 launch of MTV, followed quickly by the Music Video Charts and MTV's Video Music Awards (first held in 1984), gave the form a powerful new platform. Comprehensive airplay and a well-received video could significantly boost a record's popularity. A good example of this is Michael Jackson's 'Thriller' (1982; music video 1983, Figure 12.5). After the release of his 14-minute long-play video with its parody-driven 1950s B-Movie introduction featuring spoken dialogue and its infamous zombie dance, sales of the track doubled.

Although certain music genres have developed consistent visual styles – Carol Vernallis (2004) notes how alternative bands often prefer large, fanciful and barren locations while rap artists favour street locations and documentary-like handheld camera work, for instance – music videos come in so many shapes and sizes that it is difficult to talk about them in a coherent way. There are some useful generalisations that we can make, however. Although often emulating the cinematography of mainstream film, music videos are most often confined to the temporal limits of a 2–3-minute song. With scant opportunity to develop intricate narratives or well-rounded characters (although many try, as we shall see), the focus lies on capturing the music's essence through gesture, colour, texture, props, imagery, close-ups and audiovisual rhythm, with visual leitmotivs reinforcing the song's structure and scenes of singing and playing promoting the artist.

Case Study 12.2: (cont.)

Figure 12.5 Michael Jackson, 'Thriller' (John Landis 1983)

In the main body of this chapter, we have seen how a film composer traditionally works to a roughly edited visual structure. Music video operates the other way around: the director must work to a pre-existent sonic structure. As a result, images can be closely synchronised with musical beats, leading to a rhythmic, fast-paced editing style that jumps between scenes, locations and styles with great rapidity. Staged band performances that drive videos like Nirvana's 'Smells Like Teen Spirit' (1991) can mediate the energy and chaos of live music, while highly aestheticised videos like Prince's 'Raspberry Beret' (1985) fuse performance with saturated cinematic gestures. On the other hand, carefully crafted videos like A-ha's 'Take On Me' (1985) and the Fugees' cover of a Roberta Flack song, 'Killing Me Softly With His Song' (1996) weave fanciful narratives from small kernels of lyric information to generate what Mathias Korsgaard (2017) calls a 'polyphony' of voices. Other videos, like Guns N' Roses' 'November Rain' (1991) intersplice elements of both, offering scenes of performance within the staged narrative: in this video, the narrative cuts to a long scene of Slash performing a guitar solo in the desert. But there are exceptions. The sustained close-up

Case Study 12.2: (cont.)

Figure 12.6 Sinéad O'Connor, 'Nothing Compares 2 U' (John Maybury 1990)

of Sinéad O'Connor in her video for 'Nothing Compares 2 U' (1990, Figure 12.6) and Thom Yorke in Radiohead's 'No Surprises' (1997, music video 1998) forgo visual interpretation for a stillness that focuses attention on the lyrics.

Music videos can help an artist make a great impact. Madonna's videos, for instance, have consistently generated publicity through controversial topics and iconic styling. Most provocative was her 'Like a Prayer' (1989) video, which was condemned by the Vatican as anti-religious for its images of the singer dancing in front of burning crosses, seducing a Black saint and revealing her stigmata. The video was linked to a commercial as part of her $5 million endorsement with Pepsi, which led to a mass boycott of their products and eventually saw the commercial pulled.

As we have seen in the main chapter, commercial moving-image media usually requires collaboration. Music video is no exception, and the format has attracted well-known film-makers, like Tim Burton and Martin Scorsese, and artists, like Andy Warhol and Damien Hirst, whose infamous Britpop video for Blur's 'Country House' (1995) powerfully captured the contemporary cultural aesthetic. However, music video's unique creative and commercial demands also saw the emergence of specialist directors such as Floria Sigismondi, Michel Gondry, Spike Jonze and David Fincher, whose work with Björk, Fatboy Slim, Kylie Minogue, David Bowie, the Chemical Brothers and others encouraged the development of techniques, technologies and aesthetics unique to the visual music form.

As with many twentieth-century art forms, it was not long before these unique aesthetics began to transfer to other disciplines. Most notable has been their influence on (or back into) feature-film production and style (Korsgaard 2013; Vernallis 2013). In part, this was due to Gondry, Fincher, Jonze and others trying their hands at film directing. Taking with them a nuanced understanding of music, as well as great skill in specific audiovisual

Case Study 12.2: (cont.)

technologies not common to mainstream film-making, these directors produced surreal, quirkily edited narratives very different to traditional film form. But it was also due to the rise of the genre that would become known as hyperreal postclassical cinema. Exemplified by films like *Run Lola Run* (Tom Tykwer 1998), *Fight Club* (David Fincher 1999) and *Moulin Rouge!* (Baz Luhrmann 2001), this cinematic style is characterised by rapid editing, erratic camera movements and multiple storylines that resemble the fragmented narratives of music video and the multi-window nature of what was then a new online culture (Bordwell 2002; Smith 2013).

Interactive Media: Video Games, Video Art and Live Music Performance

So far, we have looked at the use of music within recorded audiovisual media. But in other cases, relationships between music and the moving image can be forged in real time. This can happen in several ways, ranging from allowing audience members to choose how music and image progresses to the live manipulation of music and/or image in a performance setting by an artist or musician. To explore this, we will take three contrasting examples of interactive audiovisual media: video games, video art and the VJ (or video jockey). The gaming industry emerged during the 1970s with coin-operated arcade games like *Pong* (1972) and *Space Invaders* (1978), which were placed in large public spaces. As the 1980s got underway, the development of consoles that could be linked up to domestic television sets, like the Atari Video Computer System (1982) and the Nintendo Entertainment System (1983), and of handheld devices like the Game Boy (1989), provided portable and affordable opportunities for home gaming. These consoles quickly became one of the most commercially successful audiovisual ventures of the century. Consoles gave players varying levels of choice over the actions of on-screen avatars, from simple yes–no options to the complex and immersive strategy-based decisions seen in games like the fantasy-driven *Legend of Zelda* (1986). Like film, music quickly became an integral part of the gaming industry, with users suggesting that moving images without sound and music felt not only less fully dimensional but also less immersive.

The element of choice, however, posed significant challenges for composers. As we have seen, when writing for film composers often worked to edited structures, even when they were involved in the process from early on. The interactive nature of gaming meant that every user option had two or more possible outcomes: so, in theory, the texture, style, mood, instrumentation, speed and/or motives of the music must also be able to move in several different directions. As games became more sophisticated and user choice augmented, however, the financial ramifications of numerous musical pathways demanded a different solution. Early on, the lack of computing power, together with the technical limitations for both visual and aural tracks, meant that narratives were simple and options limited, so continuous music that did not respond to small changes in the game play could be used. In *Space Invaders* (1978), for instance, the soundscape is consistent, punctuated only by sound effects, while *Super Mario Bros* (1985) made use of different samples – or patches – that kicked in during platform changes. But by the end of the century, the improvements in the memory and processing power of console hardware that had taken place over the decades (an evolution often referred to as the 'bit wars') had increased opportunities for game play, graphics and audio design (Harris 2014). Particularly significant for audiovisual textures were developments that occurred during the third – or '8-bit' – generation (1983–2003) of game design. While sound in first- (1972–80) and second-generation (1976–92) consoles was limited by processing power, subsequent processor developments enabled more audio channels, as well as advanced graphics, enhanced colour and the capacity for complex levels of game play. The fourth (1987–2004), fifth (1993–2005) and sixth (1998–2013) generations – like Sony's PlayStation 2 (2000) – saw a rapid increase in capability, resulting in an increasingly cinematic feel to big-budget games. This was particularly apparent in games that were released as part of film franchises like *Star Wars*. In such examples, sweeping orchestral scores quickly became commonplace. While main motives were used in filmic ways – at the start of the play and to represent certain characters and so on – two main dynamic scoring practices developed to allow for the element of choice. Horizontal sequencing involves sometimes drastic changes in motive, texture or mode as a player moves between locations or challenges, while vertical rescoring sees patches added to create textural changes according to a player's actions (McAlpine, Bett and Scanlan 2009; Collins 2008a). The first is preset and helps to set a general scene. As a result, it can be musically quite complex. The second, on the other hand, is highly responsive to gameplay but must remain in a single key, or stick to a short, simple modulation. When a player makes a decision, a new patch is initiated that adds to the music's texture, instrumentation and/or rhythm to reflect the altered mood. The more sophisticated the game, the more likely the music is to use a variety of techniques. While the early *Star Wars* games appropriated the original film music of John Williams, other composers developed working techniques specific to game culture. The composer for the first nine games (1987–2000) of the *Final Fantasy* franchise, Japanese Nobuo Uematsu (1959–), for instance, developed a game-specific leitmotivic score that was so popular it was released as a soundtrack album that appeared in the classical music charts, enjoyed concert tours and has been arranged for several other instruments.

Game culture, then, developed ways in which music could respond when a user participated in the narrative. But while this enables an interactive relationship between game and user, in most cases this is in fact limited, as all possibilities have been preprogrammed and composed. Our other two examples manipulate audiovisual relationships more spontaneously. Video art is an audiovisual practice that developed in the mid-1960s when video technology first became commercially available. It took two decades to be fully established as an art form accepted by galleries and museums, but since the mid-1980s it has occupied a significant position in the art world. This is significant for two reasons: first, moving-image media has been treated with suspicion by art institutions as its connection with film culture suggests to many a mass-media, commercial venture, so this inclusion represented a more open approach to contemporary art; and second, the aural side of much video work – which ranged from composed and improvised music to the sounds of the performance environment – problematised the traditional notion that art was a silent genre. The second point is important to our story of twentieth-century music because it marks the moment that compositional practice and music performance crossed over into the art world to produce a new interdisciplinary form, encouraging the development of not only refreshed forms of artistic expression but also new audiences for contemporary music. Unlike film technology, which took a great deal of time to process, video enabled sound and image to be recorded and projected at the same time. It was also more user-friendly and less cumbersome than the tools needed for film-making, and this allowed composers to work with the moving image with little or no training. Earlier in this chapter, we encountered the visual music of Fischinger and others, who worked laboriously with film stock to produce sounds from visual material. Video enabled a more impulsive form of visual music. Icelandic classical violinist Steina Vasulka (1940–) was one of the first to explore video's possibilities in the work *Violin Power* (1970–8). For this piece, Vasulka modified her violin so that different notes or bowing patterns interfered with an electronic signal hooked up to a closed-circuit projection focussed on her performance. As she played, her own videoed image was warped and manipulated by the sound in real time.

Works incorporating video link to other compositional experiments in many ways, including the inclusion of audience members, which we have seen in several other chapters and in the work of John Cage in particular. Korean musician Nam June Paik (1932–2006) was particularly good at this; in a 1969 collaboration with cellist Charlotte Moorman he made an instrument out of three TV screens, strung like a cello. On the screens was prerecorded footage but also images of the audience that could be warped when the instrument was played. The audience could then participate in the work, determining if and when their images became part of the piece. Holly Rogers has argued that, like Like other Fluxus events and expanded performance situations of the century, *TV Cello* dissolved not only the boundaries that separate composer from performer but also those separating artwork and performers from audience (Rogers 2013).

While video art straddled the music and art worlds, our third example used the moving image to revolutionise live music performance. Because the filmed image required extensive post-production before it could be shown, early examples of live audiovisuality tended to combine pre-existent visual material with live performance. The multimedia events of the Exploding Plastic Inevitable in New York (1966–7), for instance, saw the Velvet Underground perform alongside Andy Warhol's pre-filmed images of the regulars from his Factory. In order to give the images a more spontaneous feel, the regulars also appeared live, bathed in psychedelic light shows and improvising and dancing with their own filmed images (Joseph 2002).

As technology developed to include video and digital media, it became possible for screened images to be more reactive. Live feeds enabled onstage gestures to be relayed directly onto the big screen to give a clear view of the performance, while multiscreens could weave complicated readings of the music. An early example of audiovisual extravagance is U2's 1992–3 Zoo TV Tour (Figure 12.7), which made use of a massive bank of different-sized screens operated by 12 directors from a $3.5 million media control and a roaming crew of 19, to deliver a mix of prerecorded footage, live and manipulated shots of the stage and audience, scrolling text that acted as media headlines and glimpses of the current Sarajevo war delivered via satellite link (Phelan 1993). Created to form a counterpoint to the music, the wall of screens not only evoked the media saturation of a channel-surfing

Figure 12.7 U2, Zoo TV: Live from Sydney, 27 November 1993 at Australia's Sydney Football Stadium. Photograph by David Mallet

generation but also drew attention to the desensitisation to events caused by continual news coverage.

The closest relationships between music and image – and the most closely related to the early visual music – developed as part of the 1970s New York club scene. Like a DJ, a VJ mixes, loops and manipulates samples from pre-existent media, or creates newly generated images, to move in close rhythmic and aesthetic synchronisation with live music. Like our other examples, the possibilities open to the VJ were technology dependent. In the 1970s, bands like Cabaret Voltaire and Throbbing Gristle relied on lo-fi video to visualise their performances, before early analogue video processors such as the Sandin Image Processor and the Rutt-Etra and Paik synthesisers enabled more fluid forms of audiovisuality. The Fairlight Computer Video Instrument in the 1980s could manipulate videoed images through digital effects, and by the 1990s, Max/MSP and Macromedia Director had enabled more sophisticated audiovisual manipulation. Berlin's 1990s techno club scene, for instance, saw visual collective Pfadfinderei (Pathfinders) build apps that helped them to play their laptops like pianos to form intermedial (between-media) textures. Although striving for an audiovisuality as closely intertwined as Fischinger's 'visual jazz', however, Pfadfinderei's work was ephemeral: 'It's there for a night and then it vanishes again' (Völker quoted in Melfi 2018).

Conclusion

Screen media, then, feeds into many of the investigations in this book. During the century, it initiated new art forms and instruments, gave composers and artists new ways to collaborate and paved the way for creative uses of technology. The convergence of music and the moving image influenced the music industry and gave a long-established genre a new lease of life.

PART IV

Identities

13 | Gender and Sexuality

The twentieth century saw a huge shift in social attitudes towards gender and sexuality. The story of this shift can be told through a series of major landmarks – the suffragettes and universal suffrage, the postwar sexual revolution, Stonewall and gay liberation, second- and third-wave feminism – though social change was always both compromised and fitful, unevenly distributed and caught up in political compromise. Music both reflected and reinforced this complex pattern of social change. It served throughout the century as a powerful 'technology of the self' (Foucault 1988; DeNora 2000), allowing individuals to express personal and collective identities through music making or listening. These identities very often pivoted around gender and sexuality, such that musicians and audiences engaged with music that expressed their gendered and sexual identities and experiences. This took very different forms depending on the time, place and musical tradition in play; now out in the open and bold, now heavily coded or repressed. We will see this as we move through the chapter, which takes a broadly chronological look at intersections of music with gender and sexuality in the twentieth century. Along the way, its first case study pauses the chronological narrative to examine gender and sexual symbolism in sound, while its second takes an extended look at gender and sexuality in (particularly late-century) classical music.

We should note here that we use 'men' and 'women' and 'heterosexual' and 'homosexual', since these were the preferred terms for much of the period we are writing about. However, it is important to emphasise that the debates we examine would lay the groundwork for twenty-first-century discourses that did not see gender and sexuality (and, indeed, sex, which is the implicit synonym of gender here) as being confined to such monolithic and reductive categories.

Early-Century Musical Constructions of Gender and Sexuality

The first few decades of the twentieth century were filled with struggles over how modern society would be organised. Battle lines in this culture war were drawn particularly around questions of gender and sexual roles and identities. Early twentieth-century movements such as the suffragettes fought successfully on behalf of women for improved access to education and the workforce, the right to vote and equal status under the law, while figures such as the 'New Woman', as embodied in characters like Nora from Ibsen's *A Doll's House*, acted as important cultural symbols of emerging tensions and fault lines. Pockets of relative sexual freedom could be found in the period too, particularly in Berlin, Zurich, Amsterdam, New York and other cities in the Roaring Twenties, where an underground blossoming of then-unconventional sexuality could be seen. On the other hand, forces ranged in opposition to all this claimed powerful victories both large and small, from the Nazi repression of non-traditional sexuality to the late-1940s re-establishment of the Victorian housewife following the great shakeup of the social order that had taken place during World War II. Music embodied these tensions between social progress and restoration in various ways.

Music-hall (or similar) stages across the UK, mainland Europe and the USA around the turn of the century provide a fascinating early example in the realm of music of the way that norms of gender and sexuality could be played with or, on the other hand, anxiously obeyed. Music hall at this time featured both progressive and conservative elements, often cheek by jowl with each other. Genres such as popular song and comedy, ballet and vaudeville, for example, all routinely included sexually suggestive poses, subversive themes and empowering narratives, these elements regularly rubbing up against more conservative imagery and/or expectations. With reference to the relatively lewd costumes and poses of female music-hall performers in the UK at this time, for example, Patricia O'Hara makes the point that although

the music hall was widely regarded by respectable Victorian society as a disreputable and tawdry place, and the women who performed there were often held as morally suspect and socially 'low' ... in their different ways, the New Woman's direct and deliberate demands for a wider sphere of action for women and the music hall girl's appearance in the footlights' flare unsettled conservative and traditional minded Victorians. (1997: 142–3)

Sarah Gutsche-Miller echoes this in writing about Parisian music halls in the same period, arguing that 'music-hall ballets mirrored both the broadening of gender norms and the societal fears which accompanied these changing social mores; they helped reinforce shifting perceptions of women while simultaneously undermining them' (2017: 187). In these examples, sexually suggestive imagery and risqué performance served to create opportunities for women to participate in an expansion of social attitudes while also contributing to their hardening, such challenges to Victorian ideology often getting caught in the cross hairs of bourgeois respectability politics.

In a different cultural context and with different cultural pressures in play, early female blues and jazz singers explored musical themes that spoke to their own experiences of what we would now call 'intersectional' gendered, sexual and indeed racial and class subjugation. In examining blues music as a repository of collective feelings tied to both emancipation and ongoing discrimination, Angela Davis argues in this spirit that female blues singers expressed a particularly potent form of double consciousness where racial, class and gender repression was both embodied and challenged (1998). Davis points out that the music of artists such as Gertrude 'Ma' Rainey (1886–1939), Billie Holiday (1915–59) and Bessie Smith (1894–1937) 'addressed urgent social issues and helped to shape collective modes of black consciousness'. This 'mode of black consciousness', however, was not the expected 'strong consciousness of race against a backdrop of prevailing patriarchal constructions of gender' (1998: xiv), such as had been suggested to Davis through biographies. Instead, these singers managed to stage 'seemingly antagonistic relationships as noncontradictory oppositions', which for Davis in turn suggests a kind of 'historical feminist consciousness' (xv). This feminist consciousness can be seen, argues Davis, in the way that both Rainey's and Smith's versions of 'Oh Papa Blues' (called 'Oh Daddy Blues' by Smith) express subservience to male desire but also, in the words and in what we might hear as the yearning frustration (Rainey) or building regret (Smith) of the performances, embody both resistance to that male desire *and* autonomous female desire of their own.

- Bessie Smith, 'Oh Daddy Blues' (Columbia, 1923)
- Ma Rainey, 'Oh Papa Blues' (Paramount, 1927)

Davis underlines the way in which this working out of such conflicting forces through musical performance speaks powerfully to the interweaving of gender, class and race in the experiences of both female artists such as Smith and Rainey and the working-class audiences that bought their recordings in such large numbers across the 1920s and 1930s:

The more I listened to their recorded performances, the more I realised that their music could serve as a rich terrain for examining a historical feminist consciousness that reflected the lives of working-class black communities. That their aesthetic representations of the politics of gender and sexuality are informed by and interwoven with their representations of race and class makes their work all the more provocative. (1998: xv)

Billie Holiday's account of her experiences touring with Count Basie's and Artie Shaw's bands in 1937 and 1938, respectively, provides vivid proof, if any were needed, of the way in which these different forms of subjugation were indeed wrapped up in the everyday experiences of female artists and audiences in this period.

Getting a night's sleep was a continual drag too . . . I had to double up with another vocalist. I don't think she liked Negroes much, and especially not me. She didn't want to sleep in the same room with me. She only did because she had to. Artie had asked me to help her to phrase her lyrics; this made her jealous . . . There were some places where the management wouldn't let me appear, and I'd have to sit in the bus while she did numbers that were arranged for me. She was always happy when she could sing and I couldn't. I'll never forget the night we were booked at this fancy boys' school in New England. She was real happy because she was sure I was going to have to sit in the bus all night again because I was too black and sexy for those young boys. But when the time came to open, the head man of the school came out and explained that it wasn't me, they just didn't want any female singers at all. So the two of us had to sit in the bus together all night and listen to the band playing our songs. (2018: 67)

In both music hall and the blues, then, we find women working within powerful social constraints but pushing back against those constraints in different ways. The nature and impact of these constraints varied according to the example: clearly, Holiday and other Black blues and jazz singers invariably had to contend with racial discrimination on top of the gender- and potentially class-based limitations visited on those music-hall performers who were, or passed as, white. And yet, such pushing back can be seen across all these different contexts.

Other music traditions in the early-twentieth-century period were visited by different kinds of discrimination. Classical music at this time was largely dominated by white, often privileged people. And yet, there again we find structural discrimination against women and girls reaching right back from this period into earlier centuries. Such discrimination took the form of gendered divisions of labour, restrictions of opportunities and other socially accepted forms of inequality. Jill Halstead writes on this topic that

Female music tuition up until the later decades of [the twentieth] century consisted primarily of learning to sing or play a keyboard instrument, lute, violin or guitar. Any instrument that demanded an unusual posture, energetic movement or distortion of the face was discouraged as 'unladylike'. The study of musical instruments was thought to suit women both intellectually and socially. To play a musical instrument was considered an employment of the hands rather than of the intellect ... Learning to play an instrument had the added advantage of being home based; lessons and practice rarely required the woman to leave her home. Performances on her instrument were mainly for domestic enjoyment, access being controlled by her husband. This perpetuated the view of women as amateur (private or domestic) rather than professional (public) musicians. (1997: 101)

Marcia Citron, similarly, writes that women were largely excluded from the study of counterpoint until the end of the nineteenth century and from score reading until on into the twentieth (1993: 59). Citron also points out that women were generally denied the kind of familial support and early tuition routinely offered to sons, while accomplished female composers were correspondingly obliged to all but give up their musical activities and aspirations after marriage (60–2). Letters from the early 1920s between Ruth Crawford (later Seeger; 1901–53) and her mother, Clara, embody many of these expectations and attitudes. In 1922, after Ruth had travelled to Chicago to study piano, Clara Crawford praised the pianist Augusta Cottlow as 'the beautiful finished American lady artist', and suggested that 'I would be proud to have you like her'. Clara indeed wanted her daughter to become 'a real lady musician, with nice manners and poise and self-confidence and pretty clothes' (cited in Tick 1997: 24). Meanwhile, in a letter from 1921 that criticised Ruth's eager study of musical composition and harmony, Clara suggested that 'You will be judged when you come home by what you can show *when you play*, and not by what you know of the science of music composition' (ibid.: 31). Halstead, on this point, shows both that some early-century female composers' careers were socially limited but also, conversely, how some others' successes often relied on the absence of such limitations. Halstead mentions the English composer Elizabeth Maconchy (1907–94) as an example in this latter regard. Maconchy was encouraged by her family to study music from an early age and to a high level, eventually being sent to the Royal College of Music in London. Maconchy also had a supportive husband who encouraged her musical activities and acted as the main breadwinner throughout their fifty-four years of marriage. Maconchy, finally, did not have children until the then relatively advanced ages of thirty-two and forty-one, by which time she had already established herself as a composer (Tick 1997: 76–7). Without this family support and indeed privilege (Maconchy was from an upper-middle-class background), it is difficult to imagine Maconchy achieving the level of success she did.

Gender and sexual constraints impacted classical music in this period in many different ways, of course. Corissa Gould has written about the way in which early-twentieth-century figures such as Edward Elgar struggled with 'pressure to conform to the prevalent codes of manliness in order to gain social and professional acceptance' (2009: 161). As Gould notes, 'the establishment of music as an academic profession made composition as a career thus distinct from the amateur and domestic aspects of music associated with women' (171). As such, and as we have seen in the example of Ruth Crawford and others, musical composition gained masculine associations. This masculine image was reinforced by the macho imagery and language associated with movements such as modernism, where figures such as Schoenberg were hailed as conquering heroes struggling out on the modernist frontier (see Smith 1998 for context on these links between modernism and masculinity). And yet, with composers such as Elgar being engaged in creative pursuits often characterised both by lofty sentiment and, perhaps more importantly, economic insecurity, many male composers were only able to construct partial and fragile masculine self-images. Indeed, Elgar would remain essentially and often precariously self-employed for much of his life. Even if creativity was conceived very much in masculine terms for much of the nineteenth and early-twentieth centuries (Taylor-Jay 2009: 183–4), then, such composerly masculinity could not help in many cases but be configured in what we might now call 'beta' terms.

Social Norms and Music in the Twentieth Century

The social traditions and norms we have just discussed drove far-reaching male domination of music across Western society throughout the twentieth century. Musics such as the blues, jazz, music hall, classical music and many other forms struggled within, and in many ways were defined by, gendered structural impediments around childbirth and educational opportunity (as well as, of course, by deep-rooted systems of racism and class exclusion). Susan McClary has even gone as far as to suggest in this vein that 'although there are some notable exceptions, women have traditionally been barred from participating in Western music' (1991: 15). Until the later twentieth century women were indeed systematically excluded from the kind of nurture, training and professional opportunities that would allow them to become independent, successful musicians. As a result, women in music had to struggle against social forces that restricted their ability to work independently and create with impunity, even as local exceptions such as Crawford, Maconchy, Rainey, Smith and Holiday either benefitted from personal circumstances that allowed them to sidestep structural constraints or pushed against those constraints in creative ways. Such pushing against constraints would become commonplace later in the century (as we will see after the next case study, once we return to our chronological story), as all sorts of artists played with or embodied unconventional sexual or gender identities in their music and public lives.

The social norms we have been discussing relied on a complex process of what is sometimes called 'sedimentation' for their authority (D'Silva and St. Clair 2008), whereby everything from established patterns of familial support to cultural gender roles and other habitual social traditions help establish such gender and sexual conventions. Sara Cohen's study of the Liverpool indie rock scene of the 1980s and 1990s illustrates very clearly how music has been actively 'sedimented' with social values in this way. Cohen shows how the scene is actively 'produced' as male through a web of interlocking habits, from the self-reproducing dominance of white males (whether as audience members, musicians or business owners), through entrenched gendered divisions of labour in the city, to the subtle but politically powerful sensuous experience of the scene as one in which certain kinds of sounds, movements and energies are normalised (1997). Such social dynamics are shared with many other music genres, from the international heavy metal scene, to Western classical music, to noise (Walser 1993; Gould 2009; Novak 2013). Musics like these are not 'naturally' 'male' or 'female', or 'straight', or 'white', but are actively produced as such. This has had significant impacts on people's lives, such that, for example, key decisions around choice of livelihood were (and continue to be) affected. But such production or sedimentation often had impacts that were less decisive and that were musically reinforced or reshaped in ways that were less obvious. A good example of this more understated musical expression of gender and sexual ideologies is in the area of musical sound.

Case Study 13.1: Gender, Sexuality and Musical Sound

The association of musical sound with gender and sexuality is a many-layered and complex process. A common way for the two to be brought together is in the cultural framing of particular genres within particular gender or sexual identities. Such framing can be found in a general sense throughout the century. We saw this earlier with the idea of 'masculine' classical composition, and just now with the example of Cohen and Liverpool indie rock. The latter, in fact, is just one applied instance of perhaps the most famous example of gendered musics; the gendered opposition of rock and pop music. Simon Frith and Angela McRobbie's 1978 essay, 'Rock and Sexuality' (1990), identifies a version of this opposition *within* rock music, where the more aggressively masculine 'cock rock' contrasts with the more feminised, softer 'teenybop' (this opposition eliding gender and sexuality). The explicit discussion of music being gendered and sexualised, though found throughout the century, became more pervasive from the 1960s on, first with the explosion of popular-music journalism and then again with the advent of so-called 'new musicology' in the 1980s and 1990s, a scholarly approach in which a concern with social concepts such as gender and sexuality was to the fore. All of the subsequent examples in this case study are therefore drawn broadly from these two areas.

Echoing McRobbie and Frith's characterisation of 'cock' rock, Richard Dyer writes that, for him, rock music in the last few decades of the century was 'thrusting, grinding – it [was] not whole body, but phallo-centric'. By contrast, disco was 'an open-ended succession of repetitions . . . it restore[d] eroticism to the whole of the body for both sexes, not just confining it to the penis' (cited in Negus 1996: 128). Similarly, both Robert Fink and Keith Potter have heard echoes of female sexuality in disco and minimalism. Fink compares the cyclical 'recombinant teleology' in Donna Summer's (1948–2012) 'Love to Love You Baby' (from *Love to Love You Baby*, Casablanca, 1975) to similar effects in Steve Reich (b. 1936) pieces such as *Four Organs* (1970) and *Music for Eighteen Musicians* (1976), where intense but temporary moments of climax – Fink mentions the sudden and forceful 'F#' of *Eighteen Musicians*' Section VI – emerge out of the music's wave-like interlocking patterns. These moments act as climactic release amid a more general rolling wave of pleasure. The links between sexuality and 'Love to Love You Baby' are more obvious in one sense; Summer spends much of the track moaning in imitation of sexual ecstasy. But Fink argues that, as with *Eighteen Musicians*, the track also embodies sexuality in its form, with its sparse, periodically climaxing disco-funk groove rolling out a languid, cyclical flow (2005a: 55–60). Though this flow extends through several builds and breakdowns across the track's seventeen minutes, it climaxes around the halfway point, where thickening textures and a sudden shift from the tonic note of C to D (and back again) serve as an arresting pivot point. This C/D oscillation runs throughout the next

Case Study 13.1: (cont.)

passage of music, before the music releases with a return to C and the re-entry of the main vocal hook. The track's prolonged builds, momentary release and final ebbing away therefore mirror *Eighteen Musicians'* 'recombinant', cyclical flow. For Fink, indeed, 'both pieces use the systematic build-up and breakdown of a basic groove to gather musical energy that is released in a single, relatively isolated moment of teleological breakthrough'. In this, both evoke a kind of 'musical erotic' that, in Summer's case at least, is 'as virtuosic, exigent and blunt as any ever committed to record' (2005: 60). Potter, for his part, agrees with Fink but goes further, comparing *Eighteen Musicians'* 'pulsing notes played or sung, for the length of a breath, mainly by voices and clarinets, rising and falling from silence to *forte* and back to silence', to nothing less than the female multiple orgasm (2016).

- Steve Reich, *Music for Eighteen Musicians* (1976; ECM, 1978)
- Donna Summer, 'Love to Love You Baby' (from *Love to Love You Baby*, Casablanca, 1975)

Other, more heavily coded evocations of gender and sexuality have been heard in examples from even later in the century. Fred Maus, for example, addresses what he identifies as 'evasion' and 'ambivalence' in the work of the Pet Shop Boys (2001). For Maus, these double meanings connect the band's music to the gay culture and history with which they would become so strongly identified. Maus illustrates this via the lyrics of the Pet Shop Boys' 1993 track 'To Speak Is a Sin' (from *Very*, Parlophone). This song 'can be heard as a sad song about an evening in a pub, but it evokes, quite precisely, experiences of cruising in gay bars (of a rather dated kind): "To speak is a sin/ You look first, then stare/And once in a while/A smile, if you dare"' (2001: 383). Maus goes on to argue that the almost total absence of explicitly or nominally gay subject matter in much of the group's work is part of a more general historical strategy of queer 'deniability'. Maus indeed finds a related 'ambivalence' in the band's song titles; 'You Have a Different Point of View' (from *Very*, Parlophone, 1993); 'Happiness Is an Option' (from *Nightlife*, Parlophone, 1999); 'I Wouldn't Normally Do This Kind of Thing' (from *Very*, Parlophone, 1993). 'This ambivalence about direct expression', Maus suggests, 'these bizarre formulations that embody the desire to express and the desire to withhold, are continuous with the discretion that homophobia enforces' (385).

Moving more directly to musical sound, Maus writes that the group's 'combination of sensuous, opulent sound and evasive or withdrawn expression can itself be heard as a gay-coded configuration, whatever the specific content of the lyrics' (385). Maus contends in this spirit that the Pet Shop Boys' use of ambiguous tonal schemes helps

Case Study 13.1: (cont.)

establish the sense of indirectness and ambivalence described above. For example: '"Dreaming of the Queen" [from *Very*, Parlophone, 1993] opens with a grand-sounding introduction in D ♭ major (0:00–0:10). The verse follows, in B ♭-minor, narrating a dream of a visit to Queen Elizabeth and Princess Diana (0:11–0:52) . . . The chorus (0:53–1:24) is ambiguous between relative major and minor (D ♭ and B ♭). It cadences into the glowing major of the introductory passage (1:25–1:36)'. For Maus, this 'glamorous, glowing music' can be heard 'as an official intervention, as though these textless passages appear in order to silence Tennant's voice: "There are no more lovers left alive, no one has survived"'. Maus concludes that 'this is not only a guarded, indirect song, but also a song about evasive language, about what social norms, personified by the Queen, may discourage you from saying directly' (2001: 388).

It is easy to see here how this succession of gay-associated imagery and icons suggest a so-called 'gay sensibility'. But the question arises of whether the Pet Shop Boys' use of alternating major and minor tonalities arises out of queer ambivalence or simply out of common properties of the tonal system. This question connects us to a common issue with such concrete semiotic interpretations of musical sound (indeed, see Maus' discussion of the supposed intersection of thematic and tonal ambivalence in the band's 'West End Girls' for similar issues: 379–80 and 386). Maus' analysis cannot really prove that musical sound and style in the Pet Shop Boys connote generally queer-anchored ambiguity and in this sense act somehow as carriers of queer identity in themselves. Instead, Maus demonstrates how the music contains suggestive echoes of the clear themes of ambiguity and double meaning in the band's titles and lyrics. Such echoes would most likely have been picked up on by sensitive listeners and, as such, would have carried real emotional weight and are worth attending to in analysis. But they fall short of the clear interpretation Maus imposes on them.

- Pet Shop Boys, 'Dreaming of the Queen' (from *Very*, Parlophone, 1993)
- Pet Shop Boys, 'West End Girls' (from *Please*, Parlophone, 1986)

Equally conditional, and equally symptomatic of what tends to happen when critics attempt to project concrete social meanings onto musical sound, are Susan McClary's gendered readings of Madonna. In this case, the tonic key on the one hand, and more distant key areas on the other, are seen to equate in turn to (masculine) 'self' and (feminine) 'other'. For McClary, Madonna's manipulation of such symbolism creates narratives in which she is able to 'operate within a persistently repressive discourse to create liberatory musical images' (1991: 148–149). The primary example McClary uses to make this point is Madonna's 1986 track 'Live to Tell' (from *True Blue*, Sire Records, 1986), though she also highlights the ambiguous resistance to 'narrative closure' found in 'True Blue' (from *True Blue*, Sire Records, 1986) and 'Like a Prayer' (from *Like a Prayer*,

Case Study 13.1: (cont.)

Sire Records, 1989). McClary argues that, in 'Live to Tell', the central convention of tonal music – the introduction but eventual subduing of secondary key areas – is destabilised, which in turn destabilises expected hierarchies of masculine and feminine. McClary describes the main musical material of 'Live to Tell' to evidence this. On the one hand a dark pedal on D minor alternates with softer, more energetic patterns and verses on or around F major, and on the other the choruses lean towards a warmer F major. She writes that a 'traditional' reading would understand D as fundamental and F major as the 'feminine' region, which – even if it offers the illusion of hope, escape and freedom – 'must be contained and finally purged for the sake of satisfactory closure' (158). But this does not happen. Instead, Madonna retains ambiguity at a couple of key points in the song. For example, on the way out of each chorus Madonna sings a cadential 'D' over a rising B♭-C-D bass progression, in this partly seeming to 'avoid closure' in either F major or D minor. This is redoubled in the 'blurred' D/F oscillations of the coda's fade-out. McClary argues of these moments that 'to settle for an option – either option – is to accept a lie, for it is flexibility in identity rather than unitary definition that permits her to "live to tell"'. This song, for McClary, therefore resists closure 'wherever it lies in wait', and in doing so refuses 'to choose between identity and Other' (160).

- Madonna, 'Live to Tell' (from *True Blue*, Sire Records, 1986)
- Madonna, 'Like a Prayer' (from *Like a Prayer*, Sire Records, 1989)

As with Maus above, we can ask some critical questions in response to this analysis. For example, how much does the identity of the artist herself – her gender, her reputation, her image – shape the interpretation? McClary herself indeed points out that 'male musicians could construct forms along these lines if they wanted to do so' (161). Given the prevalence of these kinds of issues across the two main examples in this case study, we can therefore ask what the true nature of the link between musical sound on the one hand, and gender and sexuality on the other, actually is. Cultural forms such as music, we could argue, have no *essential* social qualities but can nevertheless easily be construed in social terms. Such social readings often prove compelling, chiming with audiences' felt sense of their favourite music as being immersed in the same struggles over identity and belonging as them. According to this line of argument, then, neither *Eighteen Musicians* nor 'Love to Love You Baby' are therefore *essentially* sexual but instead can be said to *evoke* sexual qualities. Similarly, Maus' and McClary's analyses of the Pet Shop Boys and Madonna can be read as suggestive rather than strict accounts of what the music 'means'. For all their fragility as analytical arguments, all these positions can be said to draw productively on a key quality of music, its 'implicitness', which has allowed it to be used to tell personal, socially expressive stories (Koestenbaum 1993: 189–90).

Late-Century Musical Constructions of Gender and Sexuality

As discussed in the previous section, 'Early-Century Constructions of Gender and Sexuality', musicians across the first half of the century both struggled within and pushed beyond social constraints of gender and sexuality. As some of those constraints began to loosen quite dramatically in the wake of the 1960s counterculture, gay liberation and second-wave feminism, musicians of all stripes took the opportunity to explore and even help to forge new cultural norms around sexual and gender identities. The most well-known examples here come from popular music, where mainstream musicians from David Bowie (1947–2016) to Grace Jones (b. 1948), Prince (1958–2016) to Boy George (b. 1961) and k. d. lang (b. 1961) to Annie Lennox (b. 1954) explored what were then highly unconventional modes of gender – and, in Jones' and Prince's cases, racial – presentation.

Jones' androgynous (or what was later called 'genderqueer' and/or 'non-binary') and cyborg-like appearance on the cover of albums such as *Nightclubbing* (Island Records, 1981) and in videos such as 'Living My Life' (Island Records, 1983) struck a stark contrast with most other female singers from the period, where pop, rock and other artists from Chrissie Hynde to the Runaways, Kate Bush to Karen Carpenter, all still presented in broadly traditional feminine terms. For Bennett Brazelton (and many others, at least in spirit), Jones' unique blend of 'robotic, alien, futuristic, diasporic, Afro Caribbean, sexual, queer, black, feminine, masculine, dominating, intimidating, androgynous … coalesce[d] into provocative performances which disturb[ed] dominant modes of being/thinking'. Jones, in this way, decisively subverted and, in Brazelton's language, 'confronted race and gender through the manipulation of blackface, minstrelsy and transmasculine drag' (2020: 54). Meanwhile, Prince played with sexual positioning in various ways. For example, he had a female alter ego in the 1980s called 'Camille', who sang songs such as 'If I Was Your Girlfriend' (1987). An earlier song, 'I Would Die 4 U' (1984), featured the provocative opening lyric, 'I'm not a woman, I'm not a man, I am something that you'll never understand'.

- Grace Jones, 'Living My Life' (Island Records, 1983)
- Prince, 'If I Was Your Girlfriend' (from *Sign 'O' The Times*, Paisley Park, 1987)

Prince also explored unconventional gender presentation on album covers such as *Dirty Mind* (Warner Bros, 1980) and in videos such as

'Kiss' (from *Parade*, Warner Bros, 1986), where he used female-coded make-up, clothing and movement. Prince has therefore been seen as offering a similarly powerful mainstream challenge to traditional social norms compared to that of Jones (Reynolds 2016). Jones' and Prince's challenges were mounted at the level of music, too; Jones' bionic techno-disco and Prince's lissom, louche rock-funk played as much of a role in queering expectations as their visual imagery and verbal cues (Figure 13.1).

Prince's glam-like gender play and Jones' hard-edged Afro-cyborgism served both as revolutionary cultural act and canny commercial strategy: both artists rode gender and sexual notoriety to huge critical and/or commercial success in an era where such ambiguity was catnip to audiences eager for new sexual symbols and myths. This can be seen, indeed, in the prevalence of such popular-music challenges to sexual and gender norms. Beyond especially significant individual cases of this, from Bowie to Lennox, perhaps the most notable further example of this trend can be seen in the late-1970s and 1980s goth subculture, which circled around bands such The Cure, Siouxsie and the Banshees and Bauhaus, and attained a great amount of exposure at least partly as a result of its unorthodox gender and sexual imagery:

In the late 1970s a new incarnation of androgynous masculinity claimed to represent what Wilde called 'the artistic temperament in our inartistic age'. A bricolage of the hyperromantic, gothic youth culture culls from its glam, punk, and new wave subcultural antecedents; from Gothic literary culture; from vampire cults and B-movie camp; from religious iconography; from cyborg and technoculture; from oppositional sexual cultures including queer, fetish, BDSM, drag, and bloodsports; and from a historical canon of the gothic avant-garde ranging from the

Figure 13.1 David Bowie, *The Man Who Sold the World* (Mercury, 1970), Prince, *Dirty Mind* (Warner Bros., 1981), Grace Jones, *Nightclubbing* (Island Records, 1981)

Pre-Raphaelites, Nietzsche, and Lautreamont, to Dali, Sartre, and the Velvet Underground. (Goodlad 2007: 107)

In the spirit of this quote, male goths such as Robert Smith (from The Cure, b. 1959) would habitually deploy 'feminine signs', from long hair to make-up and flowing skirts, to suggest a 'feminized interior: a realm of forbidden depth, antirationality, and sensitivity'. These musicians in this way evoked 'a feeling, crying man: a postmodern evocation of aesthete, dandy and tragedian' (ibid.).

As with Jones and Prince, then, goth musicians called on a host of culturally potent symbols to signal non-traditional sexual and gender imagery to popular audiences. For some members of that audience such signalling must have appeared as an exotic marker of a typically outré, bohemian and even alien artistic identity. But for others, it served as an entry point into an empowering world of imaginative and performative self-liberation. And so, even though it was inevitably the case that the vast majority of popular artists in this period either adhered to traditional identities or dissimulated less traditional ones, as in the case of closeted stars such as George Michael, Freddie Mercury and Michael Stipe, the exploration of unconventional gender and sexual identities by all of these artists would prove particularly significant, presenting new and clearly welcome cultural symbols and standards of representation. These would be taken up and embraced by at least some corners of the twenty-first-century audience, for whom identity politics based on struggles over gender, sexual and racial identities would play an increasingly central role.

Such liberatory gendered and sexual images existed, of course, as part of a tapestry of musical intersections with gender and sexuality in the second half of the century. We just alluded to traditional or closeted identities above, and in the case study below (Case Study 13.2) we explore aspects of classical music's relationship with gender and sexuality in the period. It is also important to acknowledge that, in partial contrast to the outwardly progressive artists just examined, a whole underbelly of more transgressive and in some cases perhaps retrogressive late-century artists explored gender and sexuality through music. Notable here are the various artists that self-consciously tried to embody and therefore explore what they saw as the pathological aspects of maleness and heterosexual male sexuality. Throbbing Gristle, for instance, regularly incorporated themes of pathological masculinity into their music. 'Persuasion', from 1979's *20 Jazz Funk Greats* (Industrial Records), builds a chilling narrative of sexual predation out of a throbbing two-note bass pulse, interpolations of distortion and distressed female voices and the coldly lascivious narration of singer Genesis P-Orridge. 'Hamburger Lady', from 1978's *D. O. A: The Third and Final Report of Throbbing Gristle* (Industrial Records), pairs delayed, deadpan description of a burn victim with whooshing and bleeping noises and static. While the latter track does not necessarily invoke pathological male sexuality in the manner of 'Persuasion', its unnerving musical staging of male-coded clinical, quasi-scientific distance grotesques masculinity in a related fashion all the same. Power electronics act Whitehouse, UK contemporaries of Throbbing Gristle, went farther than perhaps any other twentieth-century musical act into the exploration and, for some, embodying of pathological masculinity. The group's fourth album, *Dedicated to Peter Kurten* (Come Organisation, 1981), an ostensible tribute to the early-century German serial killer, contains a series of upsetting titles, from 'Prosexist' to 'Rapeday', 'Dom' to 'Ripper Territory'. The latter track is typical for the album, with its marrying of sampled speech (in this case, news reports discussing the arraignment of Yorkshire Ripper, Peter Sutcliffe, in court), whirring, sometimes overwhelming feedback and abstracted electronic noise, and fragmented screams and wails. Music and theme blend here to evoke intense and dehumanising abjection.

Somewhat less aesthetically challenging but nevertheless still interested in exploring masculinity as pathology were the Birthday Party and the Bad Seeds, interrelated Australian post-punk and rock groups active in the same era as Throbbing Gristle. Mark Fisher argues that these groups' pathologising of masculinity reached an apex with the 1984 track 'From Her to Eternity', with its idea that 'the desire to possess her is a wound', and its gurning, churning masculine depredation. Fisher points out that both the words and the 'form' of tracks such as this embody pathologised masculine desire. With this music,

Masculinity was no longer some invisible normativity, but came into view as something diseased, grisly. This is crucially not just about (lyrical) content but also form – the lurching funhouse-cum-torture chamber topographies of the music capturing the chaos of a seething reptile brain stewed in hormones and programmed by pornoscopic junk, the whole racket kept from devolving into the totally inchoate by the dumb implacability of drive, impersonated in the Birthday Party and the Bad Seeds by Pew and Adamson's bass. (2009)

- Throbbing Gristle, 'Persuasion' (from *20 Jazz Funk Greats*, Industrial Records, 1979)

- Whitehouse, 'Ripper Territory' (from *Dedicated to Peter Kurten*, Come Organisation, 1981)
- The Birthday Party, 'From Her to Eternity' (from *Her to Eternity*, Mute, 1984)

It is possible to identify the political tactic of 'overidentification' at play in all of these examples, where controversial subjects are taken up and explored from the 'inside' with the intent to expose their contradictions (Graham 2016: 189–201). For some, though, the manner in which these acts engage with such subjects leaves them beyond the political pale. Either way, these artists present another side to the late-century musical engagement with gender and sexuality, paralleling the subversion of norms found in Jones and Prince but pushing through those norms in different directions and with a different energy.

Case Study 13.2: Gender and Sexuality in Western Art Music

Experiments with norms of gender and sexuality were perhaps less obvious in Western art music in this period, though they were far from absent. As in popular music, many well-known classical musicians and composers who were gay or gender-non-conforming, from John Cage to Wendy Carlos, Pierre Boulez to Aaron Copland, Leonard Bernstein to Virgil Thomson, did not necessarily address sexuality or gender explicitly in their music (and indeed in some cases lived closeted for some or all of their lives). Others, like Benjamin Britten (1913–76), incorporated queer themes into their music only in coded or ambiguous fashion. Clifford Hindley compares Britten's operatic treatment of homosexuality to the more open attitude found in Britten's contemporary, Michael Tippett (1905–98):

A close study of Britten's operas suggests that for him homosexuality constituted a problem which was at once difficult to deal with and impossible to avoid. In this the composer differs from many other creative artists who also happened to be attracted to their own sex. A comparison with Michael Tippett, who also has introduced same-sex love into his operas, is natural and revealing. The relationship between Mel and Dov in *The Knot Garden*, for example, and even the fleeting encounter in the same opera between Dov and Faber, are far more explicit than anything in Britten – and far less problematical. The love affair between Mel and Dov may be breaking down – but it is the kind of breakdown which may occur between any couple, irrespective of sexual orientation and irrespective of society at large. There is no sense of special mystery, let alone guilt, around the existence of a gay love affair in itself. The reverse is true in many of Britten's operas. Except for *Death in Venice*, the homosexuality is almost entirely below the surface. (1995: 63)

Case Study 13.2: (cont.)

Though it is possible to read Britten's operas in a variety of ways (a point Hindley acknowledges), many have indeed identified a kind of closeted, subtextual component to Britten's life and work. Most famously, Phillip Brett described the 'open secret' of Britten's sexuality and the anxious encodings of same in *Peter Grimes* in a 1977 article for *The Musical Times* (McClatchie's 1996 article on *Owen Wingrave* offers further context here).

- Benjamin Britten, *Peter Grimes* (1945)
- Michael Tippett, *The Knot Garden* (1970)

And yet, other queer composers and musicians working in the classical tradition in the second half of the century found ways to deal with their sexual or gender identities in much more explicit, often challenging ways. Julius Eastman (1940–90) is a notable figure in this regard. Active as a pianist, performer and composer in the New York downtown scene (→Chapter 16, 'Centres and Peripheries') from the late 1960s to the 1980s, Eastman explicitly engaged themes of race, gender and sexuality both in the titles of his compositions and in his performances. Notable examples of the former include *Five Gay Songs* (1971), *Nigger Faggot* (1978) and *Gay Guerrilla* (1980). Though the improvisatory, chiming, pattern minimalism of such pieces does not necessarily parallel the combative political intent of the titles, some have seen their loose, open structures and mode of organisation as a subversion of typical Western musical strategies; George Lewis, in this respect, uses Houston A. Baker's concept of a 'deformation of mastery' to describe Eastman's music (in Packer and Leach 2015: xi).

- Julius Eastman, *Gay Guerrilla* (1980)

The most infamous example of Eastman in performance is surely the notorious 1975 Buffalo concert by the S. E. M. Ensemble, which featured an Eastman-led performance of 'Solo for Voice No. 8', from John Cage's *Song Books* (1970). The score of 'Solo' asks performers to 'perform a disciplined action, with any interruptions, fulfilling in whole, or in part, an obligation to others', an instruction that can obviously be responded to in any number of ways. Eastman's decision to invite two people – a Black woman named Suzyanna and a white man named Charles – on stage to strip, as Eastman delivered lewd commentary about their physiques, race and so on, before getting into a clinch with the man as he removed the last few items of his clothing, can therefore presumably be considered as valid a performance as any other. And yet, the usually mild-mannered John Cage looked on stonily at the performance before confronting Eastman aggressively afterwards: Cage was apparently disappointed that the deeper, Zen-related intent of his score as a prompt to ego transcendence had been ignored (see

Case Study 13.2: (cont.)

pp. 9–74 in Packer and Leach 2015 for an account of the incident). But it is easy to read a kind of generational conflict of racial and sexual values into the incident, such that the older gay composer was made uncomfortable by Eastman's radical, open relationship to sexual and racial themes and self-presentation.

This radical gender, sexual and indeed racial positioning meant that Eastman stood out in terms of queer visibility in the contemporary classical field. But he was far from alone. As with Tippett above, a range of other composers, from Michael Finnissy to Pauline Oliveros, Sylvano Bussotti to Samuel Barber, lived proudly as queer musicians. Not all of them addressed sexuality explicitly in their music – notable exceptions here include Finnissy (b. 1946), where works such as *Unknown Ground* (1989–90), *Shameful Vice* (1994–5) and *Seventeen Immortal Homosexual Poets* (1997) all include gay themes as central programmatic-musical reference points (Cross and Pace 2001). But the presence of such queer composers was important. Alongside this, the increasing importance and visibility of radical female composers and artists such as Galina Ustvolskaya, Annea Lockwood, Charlotte Moorman, Joan La Barbara and Cathy Berberian, all of whom worked within the social constraints surveyed earlier but equally benefitted from openings up later in the century of gender and sexual norms, was equally key. The presence of such queer and female musicians helped shift the cultural field of classical music to a more inclusive and somewhat more diverse position by the end of the century.

- Michael Finnissy, 'Seventeen Immortal Homosexual Poets' (1997)
- Cathy Berberian, *Stripsody* (1966)
- Annea Lockwood, *A Sound Map of the Hudson River* (1982)

Perhaps the most interesting comparison for Eastman, and a useful final point of discussion for this case study, is Claude Vivier (1948–83). Vivier was a French Canadian near-contemporary of Eastman who suffered a similarly early death; Vivier was stabbed to death in strange circumstances by a male prostitute, having just written the line 'Then he removed a dagger from his jacket and stabbed me through the heart' on a score he was working on. Vivier, like Eastman, spoke openly about his own sexuality. Vivier indeed positioned himself and his music in opposition to what he saw as the masculine Western tradition: 'Male discourse, the way it is presented to us in western civilisation, is a discourse that obliges us to be strong, great, dominating, which obliges music to be goal-oriented, which obliges opera to have conflicts, to put the universal on stage' (cited in Hind 2015). Paul Griffiths echoes this point: 'Vivier thought that music in the Western classical tradition was conditioned by the conventional attributes of maleness: determination, purposefulness,

Case Study 13.2: (cont.)

independence'. According to Vivier, 'gay music would be different. It would hover; it would glisten. It would be the music of angels' (1996: 31).

Though Vivier's music never engaged queer themes in quite so explicit a manner as Eastman's (titles, at least), his shimmering, floating spectral scores nevertheless place precisely the kind of non-goal-orientated aesthetic at their core as described above. The most obvious example of this is perhaps the opera (or, 'opera-death-ritual') *Kopernicus* (1980), which stages a kind of non-narrative rite around the fire god Agni and a set of mythic-historical characters, including Mozart, Lewis Carroll and Merlin. But a piece like *Lonely Child* (1980), for soprano and orchestra, provides an even more vivid illustration. *Lonely Child* uses the Tristain Murail-derived, ring-modulation-like technique of 'combination tones' (or '*les couleurs*', in Vivier's language), where pairs of tones in turn generate sum and difference tones that serve as the basic building blocks of the music (Gilmore 2007: 5). These tones create glistening sound arrays and sonorities that chime, bell-like, with sonic variety. And yet the piece is far from new-age ambience: thwacking drums and gongs and tense, distraught declamation are as much a part of the sound world here as chiming, metallic spectra.

- Claude Vivier, *Kopernicus* (1980)
- Claudie Vivier, *Lonely Child* (1980)

This last point is important, because as much as Vivier and others might have proudly proclaimed a new aesthetics of gay (g)listening in his and others' music, and as much as it is possible to hear new relationships to cultural theme and aesthetic narrative in this work, it is just as easy to detect clear, perhaps even traditional, emotional arcs and musical patterns. As with many other examples discussed in this chapter, then, Vivier's music, though thematically rich and suggestive, cannot ultimately close the unavoidable gap between political ideal and musical idea that we find in all examples of queer or feminist music. Music is always both implicitly rich and explicitly elusive.

Conclusion

Music, as we have seen, was a site of both repression and liberation for female, queer and gender-non-conforming musicians and audiences throughout the twentieth century. Where inherited patterns of social behaviour often held such groups back from the kinds of musical experiences they may have otherwise enjoyed, white men continued to experience levels of access to and control of music that far surpassed that of other groups (even if such control was very unevenly distributed among those white men, of course). And yet broader cultural change over the course of the century, including novel musical performances of gender and sexuality, meant that an increasingly wide range of people accessed and were represented in music as the century wore on. As we will see over the next few chapters, this gradual opening up of the twentieth-century musical field to groups of people previously excluded from it is not only characteristic but also potentially misleading, since both cultural representation and wealth distribution in the music business at the end of the century were still radically uneven.

14 | Race and Ethnicity

This chapter explores twentieth-century music's entanglement in various racial and ethnic (or national) struggles. We start by looking at the concepts of 'essentialism' and 'constructivism', two ideas that shaped how music was talked about and/or experienced in the period. We extend that discussion in turning to ethnicity and nationalism in twentieth-century music. Our first case study examines Béla Bartók's (1881–1945) folk-song collecting through the lens of national and ethnic identity. We then discuss the concept and traditions of Black music in the twentieth century, in turn looking at the post-human in Black and white music in our second case study. The final section draws together previous discussions in looking at end-of-the-century transnational musics as symbols of changing racial, ethnic and national dynamics. We should acknowledge the complexity of 'race' and 'ethnicity' at the outset. Though the shorthand of race as biology (physical characteristics) and ethnicity as culture (customs tied to heritage or nationality) is useful, it masks a more complex reality where race is shaped by cultural experience, and ethnicity can refer to shared physical as much as cultural characteristics. The choice of topics and examples in the chapter draws that complexity out as much as possible.

Essentialism and Constructivism

Essentialism and constructivism are hugely important ideas. They crop up across lots of different intellectual disciplines under one or other guise – chauvinism, conservativism, puritanism on one side; relativism, deconstructionism, post-structuralism on the other. They also, perhaps more crucially (and often implicitly), shape a lot of everyday, ordinary thinking and beliefs. Essentialism is, in simple terms, the idea that people or things have fixed essences; that if you are born (or present as) a woman, for example, you will necessarily have a 'womanly' character or personality.

This conflation is already difficult in this case of gender/sex. It becomes especially so with race and ethnicity; the kind of essentialism that sees, say, Black or Irish or Jewish people as sharing sets of (positive or negative) stereotypical characteristics can obviously lead to racist, chauvinistic world views. Though there is more to the story of essentialism than this, as we will see, it is nevertheless easy to see it as dangerously reductive. In comparison with essentialism, constructivism offers a more flexible account of how things are. It is the view that identities are social constructs; that they change over time and are always in the process of (re)formation. So, your character will be informed but not determined by, for example, your race, ethnicity or nationality.

Essentialism and constructivism have been especially important in the field of music. Different genres of music have often been 'essentialised' in one or other racial or ethnic image such that they start to be seen, for example, as 'Black' or 'white'. But music is not *essentially* Black or white, or indeed Asian, Swiss or any other racial or ethnic category. Instead, it is actively *constructed* as such (→Chapter 13, 'Gender and Sexuality' for a related discussion of the 'production' of music as white and male). Such constructions often make sense, for instance when a musical form largely originates among a specific group of people and speaks to their experiences. But even there the reality is invariably messier than essentialising labels would suggest; such labels always leave things out of the picture. Essentialist thinking can, in this way, some-times lead to negative stereotypes and racist behaviours. However, it is also true that some 'essential' categories can, on the other hand, play a positive, empowering role, for example by giving members of a beleaguered commu-nity a shared sense of cultural history and tradition. The example of 'Black music', considered below in 'Black Music and Essentialism', will allow us to dig deeper into this tension between the reductive but also potentially positive sides of essentialist thinking.

Nationalism (and Ethnicity) in Twentieth-Century Music

Nationalism and ethnicity are based in some of the same tensions between essence and construction that have just been introduced. The process of constructing national musical traditions indeed resembles the process of actively 'constructing' music in a certain racial (or gendered or sexual) image. Music has been 'nationalised' in this sense through its anchoring in different national communities and its association with a set of 'essential' national symbols, stories and sounds. In the latter respect, folk music and folk myths have usually been key, even though the 'folk' sounds invoked were often heavily generalised. These 'essential' materials were routinely combined with modern and/or 'non-folk' musical sounds – usually of an orchestral variety, given how frequently different projects of national identity have traded on the prestige of European classical music – and media messages such that a 'national' musical style was born. In the nineteenth century, musical nationalism of this sort became profoundly useful as cultural propaganda in a Europe where empires and individual nation states were often in conflict. Such conflicts continued into the twentieth century, though they took on new, postcolonial dimensions in the second half of the century. We will look at two brief examples to illustrate these points and to see how arguments in support of musical nationalism have tended to be made.

Daniel Grimley (2001) hears nationalism in Danish composer Carl Nielsen (1865–1931). Citing the importance of flattened sevenths and horn calls – particularly horn-rich fifth sonorities sounding plagal cadences – in Nielsen's music, Grimley reads such features as potential signifiers of national character. And yet, these do not seem to be particularly 'Danish' sounds, given that they occur across a wide variety of musics. Grimley does indeed acknowledge the pervasiveness of horn calls and flattened sevenths in non-Danish Romantic and early-modern music, comparing Nielsen's work in this respect to Schubert and Schumann lieder as well as to Mahler song cycles and symphonies (2001: 129–31). In Nielsen, however, Grimley suggests that there was a kind of condensing or 'elementalisation' (see 128–9) of these core features. This is such that at key moments – for example in the 'proto-minimalism' of the first two movements of his third symphony, 'Sinfonia Espansiva' (1910–11), or at the climax of his song, 'Genrebillede' (1891) – they take on a pastoral, even 'archaic' aspect. (The suggestive term 'archaic' does a lot of work here, as we will discuss in a moment.) Grimley asserts that this elementalisation represented 'the uncovering of a pure musical state that is distinctly Nordic in tone and character' (132).

In a separate piece, Grimley makes a similar argument with respect to Nielsen's piano music. For Grimley, pieces such as *Chaconne* (1916) bore a 'tension between modernist elements and archaic musical material' (2005: 209) – most audible here across Variations 16 and 17 (bb. 130–45), with their chromatic right-hand figures played in baroque style that abruptly switch to 'archaic', simple modal material at bar 146, all of this leading to a typically hazy, 'Arcadian', pastoral coda (218) – that loosely depicted a struggle between Austro-German over-intellectualism and Nordic physical health (216–17).

- Carl Nielsen, 'Sinfonia Espansiva' (1910–11)
- Carl Nielsen, *Chaconne* (1916)

To further his nationalist case, Grimley parallels Nielsen's preoccupation with 'archaic' musical elements with Danish painter Vilhelm Hammershøi's (1864–1916) similar focus on 'bleak open landscapes' (➔Chapter 1, Space and Place, Local and Global) and 'quiet or unpeopled interiors'; his 'tendency towards a geometrical division of space that verges on the minimalist' (2001: 132). Hammershøi's reduction of landscape 'to its barest and most essential elements' (134) is seen to mirror Nielsen's 'elementalisation' of music to some of its own barest ingredients. Similarly, Grimley suggests, Hammershøi's invocations of the 'Golden Age' of Danish Art at the beginning of the nineteenth century parallel Nielsen's use of the horn call as a symbol of Danish musical style. 'Both Hammershøi and Nielsen's work', Grimley finally argues, 'can be seen to enact a process of elementalisation, in which Danish identity is explicitly associated with a state of extreme simplicity and sparseness' (134).

This comparison of (supposedly) nationalist painting with (supposedly) nationalist music is of course intended to strengthen the nationalist interpretation on both sides. But whether the music or the painting are explicitly Danish or not is an open question. It is true that aspects of the Nordic landscape and environment *might* be traced in Hammershøi's paintings and Nielsen's music, thereby lending weight to the nationalist interpretation (though even there the comparison can only be suggestive, since it is extremely hard to depict such things in abstract musical language). But this says little about any broader nationalist character or identity. And in any case, the Nordic environment, already spreading to a territory far beyond just Nielsen's Denmark, is hardly unique. The 'Danish' character of Nielsen's music is therefore far from clearly established by Grimley. Instead, in order to support his case, Grimley has to make a number of mental leaps in constructing arguments by adjective, where terms such as 'archaic' and 'elemental' somehow equate to 'Denmark'. This reminds us that, as Grimley himself acknowledges, 'all "musical nationalisms" are fictitious constructs' (125).

Similar intellectual issues tend to be found across all accounts of supposed musical nationalism. From famous examples such as Taruskin (1997) or Frolova-Walker's (2007) analyses of Russian music to perhaps lesser-known ones such as Harry White's work on Irish music (1998), musical nationalism is always staked on fragile processes of association and extramusical messaging. Music can be made to sound nationalist tones without ever truly 'being' national. White's analysis of Irish cultural history is germane here in how it underlines the multifaceted position music is often made to occupy in relation to various, sometimes competing intra-nationalist discourses. In a twentieth-century Ireland riven by colonial and postcolonial tensions, White argues, music was torn in different directions. On the one hand, the 'corpus of ethnic melody' that was represented by Irish traditional folk music was made to carry an 'irreducibly nationalist aesthetic', expressing above all a 'nationalist feeling, aesthetics and culture' (1998: 6–7). On the other, Irish (and European) art music was compara-tively neglected, its supposed associations with colonial occupiers ensuring it would always be 'mediated through the harsh tonalities of foreign occupation and social dysfunction' (9). Even as composers such as Seán Ó Riada (1931–71) sought to reconcile this tension, as for example in his imaginative integration of traditional airs and marches into a broadly late-Romantic symphonic canvas in the 1959 score for the documentary *Mise Éire*, White argues that the nationalist tension between Irish art and folk music was never truly resolved.

• Seán Ó Riada, *Mise Éire* (1959)

It should also be added here that it is easy to contradict White's sweeping reading of both Irish folk and art music. Folk music clearly served purely musical functions for many listeners, for example, while art music's neglect can just as easily be attributed to the relative poverty and youth of Ireland as a postcolonial state as it can to the music's supposed embodiment of colonial feeling. Both within and without White's account, then, Irish music was caught across different nationalist stalls.

And yet, the point with all these examples of musical nationalism is not so much how tightly the music demonstrated its national identity but rather the emotional battle it was made to wage on behalf of its nation. Nielsen's music in this sense evoked Denmark emotionally without having to achieve ontological 'Danishness', just as Black musical forms have often evoked Black cultural experiences without always 'being' Black. Similar things could be said of Ó Riada, whose *Mise Éire* became an important symbol and sounding of nationalist feeling for many Irish people without ever 'being' Irish. And, it should be underlined, both music and nation benefit from these kinds of associations, each plugging in to the other's powerful appeal to listen-ers and citizens alike.

In discussing musical nationalism, we have focused on classical and folk music. Though musical nationalism was far from absent in twentieth-century popular music, its function was less clearly established. This is partly due to musical nationalism often being a function of, or in service to, official expressions of state identity, something that the established pomp and circumstance of classical music has traditionally been better placed to serve. It is also the case that twentieth-century popular music was, in many ways, culturally monolithic, with the USA and to a lesser extent the UK dominating the global pop industry. Though there were notable local exceptions, for instance the critically respected 'Krautrock' scene of the 1970s or Scandinavian pop of the 1970s–1990s, even these examples operated within an industrial framework that flattened local identity, assimilating everyone to the anglophone majority (the anglicisation of Abba is a case in point). A notable exception to this rule is the example of 1990s Britpop. Comprised of indie, alternative and mainstream rock acts such as Oasis, Suede, Blur and Elastica, Britpop attained huge commercial and critical success in the UK (and elsewhere) at this time. Britpop represented a schism within the US/UK ruling pop alliance, the lesser party yearning for older imperial glories. In this spirit, Britpop groups used symbols such as the Union Jack, most famously on Oasis' Noel Gallagher's guitar, and locally accented geographical and social references, as for example on Blur songs such as 'Parklife' and 'This Is a Low' (both from *Parklife*, Food Records, 1994), to place themselves within a British tradition of popular music that extended back to 1960s acts such as the Kinks.

- Blur, 'Parklife' (from *Parklife*, Food Records, 1994)

Andy Bennett and Jon Stratton examine Britpop through this lens of tradition, seeing the musicians and journalists on the scene as consciously playing with and inserting themselves into a pre-existing set of images, attitudes and myths that had accrued around British history and contemporary life (2010). And yet, as with other traditions and musical nationalisms, Britpop's Britain was largely fictional. It was also, crucially, exclusive. In this case, a confected image of an idyllic 'Albion' ignored 'actual ravages of de-industrialisation and unemployment', while an ethnocentric emphasis on white identity airbrushed other forms of British culture (2). Musical nationalism here served typically contradictory ends, on the one hand bringing people together under an imagined cultural banner, and on the other, excluding others from that banner.

Case Study 14.1: Béla Bartók and Changing Ethnic and National Tides

As we will see again in the case of Black music in the next section, essentialist thinking from earlier in the century often evolved into or existed alongside more flexible and pluralistic frameworks later on. Katie Trumpener's essay, 'Béla Bartók and the Rise of Comparative Ethnomusicology: Nationalism, Race Purity and the Legacy of the Austro-Hungarian Empire' (2000), encapsulates this emblematic twentieth-century move from essentialism to pluralism in one composer's experience as a collector of folk music in the early twentieth century.

Working across modern-day Hungary and Romania amid rising nationalism in the first few decades of the century and in the context of the multinational Austro-Hungarian state, Béla Bartók started out as a committed nationalist eager to promote what he saw as the purity of Hungarian identity: 'I shall have one objective: the good of Hungary and the Hungarian nation' (cited in Trumpener 2000: 407). Bartók saw Hungarian peasant music and the Hungarian language as vital to this project, these acting for him as twin poles of a kind of ancient national patrimony that could serve as 'a site of resistance to the cosmopolitanising force of the Austro-Hungarian Empire' (404). Meanwhile, Bartók's early compositions saw him similarly invested in national patrimony. Bartók's first real critical success, *Kossuth* (1904), celebrated the nationalist leader of Hungary's unsuccessful 1848 uprising against Austria, Lajos Kossuth, in its parodying of the Austrian national anthem and its use of Hungarian march rhythms.

• Béla Bartók, *Kossuth* (1904)

At this time, then, Bartók subscribed to an essential idea of Hungarian identity as being fixed and superior to that of other countries. He railed against what he saw as the cosmopolitanising influence of the Jews and of Austrians in the Dual Monarchy while also criticising Gypsies and other minority groups within Hungary. Bartók saw these groups as rootless, contrasting their culture with the rooted, indigenous musical tradition he saw in the peasant folk music of Hungary (409). For Bartók, Gypsies' use of many different musical styles only saw them 'contaminating' those sources: Gypsies, he thought, could only offer 'a deformed and deforming version of Hungarian folk' (410). In someone like the Hungarian Liszt, by contrast, such assimilation and appropriation of Hungarian peasant music was instead seen as a sort of repurification, a stamping with composerly authority and individuality (411).

However, changing cultural mores and national tides, as well as deepening personal experience as a collector of folk music – indeed, Donna Buchanan tracks the expansiveness and importance of Bartók's activities as an ethnomusicologist working across the whole of the Balkans (2000) – helped to change Bartók's views (Figure 14.1). Notions of an essential, inviolate indigenous Hungarian culture became untenable.

Case Study 14.1: (cont.)

Figure 14.1 Bartók collecting folk music in Zobordarázs (now Dražovce, Slovakia), 1907

Though Bartók continued throughout his life to advance Hungarian nationalism, he would in fact go on to describe the Austro-Hungarian Empire as 'a place of multi-national cooperation' (2000: 416). In addition, Bartók's attitude towards Gypsies shifted quite substantially, with the composer eventually seeing them less as internal enemies and more as victims of social oppression. Bartók would even emphasise the importance of Romanian and Slovakian culture to Hungary; Bartók began collecting Slovak songs in 1906 and Romanian songs in 1908. This latter interest found its way into his own music, too, with pieces such as 'Four Slovak Folksongs' (1917) mixing local dances, drones and work songs. Bartók's 1937 essay 'Folk Song Research and Nationalism' provides further context for this broadening of perspectives. Bartók emphasised in that essay that his extensive collecting experiences showed him that 'the neighbouring nation was also in possession of the treasure which up to that point had been considered as an ancient, original national property' (cited in Trumpener 2000: 418). Bartók, in this spirit, ultimately acknowledged interaction as a key dynamic within all cultural formations: 'people ... come into contact with one another, influence one another – it is these interactions that we, as research workers, must endeavour to unravel with the utmost impartiality' (419).

In an essay published in *Western Music and Its Others* in 2000, Julie Brown echoes many of Trumpener's points about Bartók's dualistic attitude to 'good' Hungarian peasant music on the one hand and 'bad', supposedly rootless Gypsy music on the other. Brown articulates even more strongly the way in which this psychic split shaped Bartók's own compositional voice as well as his publicly stated attitudes. For Bartók,

> **Case Study 14.1: (cont.)**
>
> Brown argues, the construction of a progressive, nationalistic Hungarian compos-
> itional modernism depended upon a kind of purification process in which any residual
> (supposedly) non-Western, anti-modern Gypsy elements would be removed. However,
> as we have seen, Bartók's attitude to Gypsy music shifted towards one of tolerance, in
> which it would now be seen as a valuable stream within the broader 'hybrid' currents of
> Hungarian national patrimony. Brown proposes in this light that the admixture of
> modernist and Gypsy elements in Bartók's 1942 *Concerto for Orchestra* – which can
> be heard in the dissonant 'night' music of the opening and the whole-tone theme of
> the second movement on the one hand, and in the *verbunkos* (a Hungarian dance)
> gestures across the first and third movements and the tumbling folk rhythms of the
> finale on the other – represents a musical reconciliation and even integration of these
> different influences. This musical reconciliation can be seen as a complement to the
> verbal reconciliations expressed by Bartók in such essays as the 1937 one cited above by
> Trumpener.
>
> • Béla Bartók, *Concerto for Orchestra* (1942)
>
>   As all of this demonstrates, Bartók ultimately shifted from a kind of chauvinistic or
> essentialist nationalist position to a more pluralist, even cosmopolitan one. Though
> this newly pluralist position remained, from a modern vantage point at least, notice-
> ably nationalist and even to some degree essentialist in spirit, its more inclusive
> acknowledgement of different traditions within the Hungarian framework marked
> a clear contrast with Bartók's earlier perspective. In this evolution Bartók embodied
> what can be seen as an emblematic twentieth-century shift.

Black Music and Essentialism

'Black music' in the twentieth century reflected similar tensions between
essence and construction as the Bartók example. Black music in that period
indeed very often embodied what on the one hand the postcolonial theorist, Gayatri Spivak, described as 'strategic essentialism' (1990), whereby, in
the words of Paul Gilroy, categories such as 'black music' act as positive
'affirmations' of minority groups' shared experiences (cited in Negus 1996:
106)), and on the other, more contested or complex cultural flows that
transcend essentialist accounts. Music was after all a key, but unavoidably
messy, site of Black memory and identity throughout the century. Social
participation in different musical contexts provided Black audiences with

an opportunity to experience shared cultural memories and modes of expression in a heightened emotional setting. The importance of music to such rituals of Black identity formation was recognised by a whole range of Black writers throughout the century, many of whose accounts, as we will see, take an essentialist position in their close elision of Black music, experience and people. Such essentialism, as we will also see, was often a deliberate attempt to claim the music as an important piece of cultural patrimony for Black communities; a shared heritage where Black-diasporic themes and experiences received unique expression. This is even as that expression was messier and less uniform than such accounts sometimes suggested.

Written in 1903, W. E. B. Du Bois' (1868–1963) *The Souls of Black Folk* provided a powerful testimony to the central place of music in various Black experiences and rituals (as with other cases here, Du Bois speaks primarily to a North American context but refers to broader diasporic circumstances). Du Bois described 'Sorrow Songs' – songs sung and passed down the generations by enslaved African Americans – as 'the articulate message of the slave to the world'. For Du Bois, such songs 'are the music of an unhappy people, of the children of disappointment; they tell of death and suffering and unvoiced longing toward a truer world, of misty wanderings and hidden ways' (2020/1903: 117–18). Du Bois goes so far as to suggest that Black religious music, which he traces back to 'African forests' and thinks of as one of the primary elements of Black religious ritual, stood at that time as the 'one true' expression of the sorrow of the Black experience:

Three things characterized th[e] religion of the slave – the Preacher, the Music, and the Frenzy . . . The Music of Negro religion is that plaintive rhythmic melody, with its touching minor cadences, which, despite caricature and defilement, still remains the most original and beautiful expression of human life and longing yet born on American soil. Sprung from the African forests, where its counterpart can still be heard, it was adapted, changed, and intensified by the tragic soul-life of the slave, until, under the stress of law and whip, it became the one true expression of a people's sorrow, despair, and hope. (2020/1903: 88)

This close elision of Black music and the Black experience can be found in the work of other Black leaders and thinkers in this early part of the century. For example, though Booker T. Washington (1856–1915) and Du Bois would ultimately come to political blows on the matter of Black progress, Washington agreed with Du Bois about the cultural importance of Black music. For Washington, that music served to 'remind the race of the rock whence it was hewn', and 'foster race pride' (cited in Hansell 1978:

17). The poet and intellectual Langston Hughes (1901–67) took a similar position, basing much of his poetry on forms such as the blues and jazz – something that can be seen clearly in the titles, subject matter and language of poems such as 'Jazzonia' (1923) and 'The Weary Blues' (1925) – and seeing those forms as an encapsulation of the Black experience. As Hughes put it in his 1940 autobiography, *The Big Sea*, Black music both shaped the mood and style of his work and could be heard as embodying the 'pulse-beat' of the Black community.

On Seventh Street in 1924 they played the blues, ate watermelon, barbecue, and fish sandwiches, shot pool, told tall tales, looked at the dome of the Capitol and laughed out loud. I listened to their blues: 'Did you ever dream lucky – Wake up cold in hand?' . . . I tried to write poems like the songs they sang on Seventh Street – gay songs, because you had to be gay or die; sad songs, because you couldn't help being sad sometimes. But gay or sad, you kept on living and you kept on going. Their songs – those of Seventh Street – had the pulse-beat of the people who keep on going. (2015/1940: 208–9)

A number of Black scholars and writers of the 1960s and 1970s built on these earlier-century accounts of Black music and culture in constructing a kind of 'long' Black musical tradition that connected disparate examples of African American music and culture within the essentialised framework of a shared Black-diasporic tradition. Eileen Southern's 1971 book *The Music of Black Americans* offered the most thorough account that had yet been published of such a tradition, reaching all the way back to the 1619 arrival of Africans in the English colonies and working its way up through Revolutionary War music, minstrelsy, various folk musics, ragtime, jazz, the blues, concert music and rhythm and blues and rock. Southern's intention was very much, as she put it, 'to record the facts of history' (1971: xvi). As such, she offers no overt argument about what musical or cultural features might unite Black music. Nevertheless, in building such a detailed account of so many disparate but interconnected musical traditions, Southern could not help but offer both implicit and explicit observations about what she saw as the cohesive nature of Black music and culture. For example, early in the book Southern claims that 'Afro-American music is primarily a vocal music' (xvii). Meanwhile, in describing the place of Black musicians within the 'Black' or 'Harlem' Renaissance of the 1920s, Southern emphasises the shared cultural materials, and racially driven concerns, of Black cultural practitioners of the period:

Black musicians participated in the movement by turning to the folk music of the race as a source of materials in composition and performance. To be sure, some black composers had been drawing on such materials for a number of years . . . but now they became more race conscious than ever . . . The composers used poems by black poets in their art songs; they exploited the rhythms of Negro dances and the harmonies and melodies of the blues as well as spirituals, and of the newer music called jazz in their composed concert music. Almost without exception black concert artists began to include on their programs the folk and composed music of Negroes, and some artists staged recitals consisting exclusively of Negro music. (1971: 413)

Moreover, Southern goes on to note other examples of 'race consciousness', including public criticism of discrimination; the sponsoring of recitals of less-well-known Black musicians; and the setting up of scholarship funds for younger Black musicians (1971: 417–18). Both the overarching framework of Southern's book and the connections it drew between different musical traditions point towards an essential vision of Black music as being based in shared diasporic, biographical and cultural reference points.

Famously, and by contrast, Amira Baraka (1934–2014) – then known as LeRoi Jones – offered a clearly defined, and clearly polemical, vision of essentialised Black culture. Baraka argued that African American music was based in both the shared traumas of the Middle Passage and in a broad but interconnected cultural heritage reaching back to African modes of expression (1999/1963). In his 1966 essay, 'The Changing Same (R & B and New Black Music)', Baraka summed this up in the concept of the 'changing same', where 'through many changes', the 'blues impulse . . . remained the exact replication of the Black Man in the West' (1998/1968: 180). Baraka described a sort of hierarchy of Black culture in this essay, where 'weakened' forms such as mainstream or avant-garde jazz were in the process of '[becoming] whiter', their 'middle-class' musicians supposedly finding it easier to 'make believe in America' as a result of their relative privilege and integration into American society (ibid.).

Despite these reservations, however, Baraka nevertheless drew deep lines of ascent from R & B back through the blues, religious music and all the way to African music. This kind of long historical arc mirrors both the Eileen Southern example already covered and those of later writers such as Cheryl Keyes, who traces rap back through street-corner jive, radio disc jockeying, rural storytelling, game songs and the blues to West African griots (2004: x), and Paul Gilroy (1993), whose 'Black Atlantic' concept of a shared Black-diasporic tradition has proved hugely influential (➔Chapter 1, 'Place and Space, Local and Global'). For his part, Baraka's vision of Black music was united in a set of central stylistic and cultural features, from an emphasis on call and response and vocal forms to religious 'spirit worship' (of African and Christian varieties) and ritual. In all this, the music, argued Baraka, 'still [made] reference to a central body of experience'. Baraka ultimately summed up his vision of the cohesive essence of the music: 'Black music is African in origin, and African American in its totality, and its various forms (especially the vocal) show just how the African impulses were redistributed in its expression, and the expression itself became Christianized and post-Christianized' (181–2).

Southern, Baraka, Keyes and Gilroy's constructions of a long Black musical and cultural tradition, building on or echoing earlier figures such as Du Bois, are in some ways 'essentialist' in nature and, as such, incomplete and/or reductive. In some cases, this is deliberate and 'strategic', as with Gilroy, though in others perhaps it is not. Either way, these essentialisms make political and moral sense; writers such as Southern and Baraka were attempting to stage radical acts of recovery in the face of the widespread extermination and suppression of Black culture (see also Floyd, Zeck and Ramsey 2017).

Given the complexity of the intellectual history of the concept of Black music, scholars both Black and white have more recently attempted to nuance how Blackness and Black music are framed. Guthrie Ramsey, for instance, has distinguished between 'blackness as practice' and 'blackness as essence', with the first concept designed as a heuristic to allow writers to think about how Black identity might be heard in music without resorting to essentialising arguments about the racial identity of that music (2007). Others, in a somewhat similar vein, have made use of a kind of 'post-essential' approach that draws together musical 'essences' with more adaptive models of flow and variety, as with the discussions of sampling and hip-hop (→Chapter 3, 'Postmodernism') in Tricia Rose (1994) and Russel A. Potter (1995). However, some white writers have run into problems in attempting to construct such anti-essentialist accounts. For example, Brian Ward (1998) and Ronald Radano (2003) each tried to unsettle typical traps of Black/white essentialism. Though Ward and Radano were clearly well intentioned in attempting to think beyond racial binaries, they were nevertheless criticised by Black scholars Robin D. G. Kelley (2000) and Samuel A. Floyd, Jr (Floyd and Radano 2009), respectively, for imposing a vision of race-criticality that was too distanced from its object (for more on this see Perchard 2015b: 343–4). Black music as both concept and lived experience is still, very understandably, charged with history and feeling.

Case Study 14.2: Post-human (But Not Post-racial) Cyborgs, Robots and Machines

Alexander Wehileye's '"Feenin": Posthuman Voices in Contemporary Black Popular Music' (2002) describes essential continuities across the history of Black popular music but explores ways in which those continuities are rearticulated and fused with post-human concerns in late-century Black electronic music. This fusion mirrors similar thematic concerns and preoccupations across popular and other musics in that period, where acts such as Kraftwerk, Laurie Anderson, Pauline Oliveros and many others grappled with machinic or cyborg themes in their work. This case study explores this post-humanist meeting of late-century music and machine, drawing out the racial dimensions that defined the spirit of many of these meetings.

Post-humanism was a popular theoretical and cultural concern by the 1970s and 1980s. Though it had many well-known applications and aspects, from cyberpunk scenarios exploring powerful artificial intelligence, or AI (e.g., Gibson 1993/1984) to theoretical considerations of the cyborg (as in Donna Haraway's famous 'Cyborg Manifesto', 1987), post-humanism most fundamentally sought to address a universe in which humans no longer occupied the centre of the story. This displacement of the human was often in the face of developments in technology that seemed to threaten humanity (though not always – growing environmental awareness also inspired a new ecological ethics in this period that similarly de-centralised the human; Wolfe 2009). This all generated a great deal of both anxiety and excitement, new (bio-)technological futures in turn inspiring a range of artistic responses. In music, these responses often had a normative racial dimension running through them.

Wehileye, for his part, argues that the vocoderised blending of 'audibly mechanized' and 'more traditionally melismatic and "soulful"' voices in late-century R & B songs such as Zapp and Roger's 'Computer Love' (1985) and 702's 'You Don't Know' (1999) served to challenge normative post-human (and human) whiteness (22).

- Zapp and Roger, 'Computer Love' (from *The New Zapp IV U*, Warner Bros, 1985)
- 702, 'You Don't Know' (from *702*, Motown, 1999)

R & B's intertwining of the human and the machine in this sense 'co-articulate[d] black subjectivity and information technologies' in such a way as to underline Black culture's 'aporetic relationship' with 'the category of the "human"' (21). In other words, the post-humanism of this music exposed the already fragile relationship Black identity had with the category of the human. Wehileye connects this to the dehumanising process of slavery, which, as he later points out, for Black people 'rendered the category of the human suspect' (30): 'Because New World black subjects were denied access to the position of humanity for so long, "humanity" refuses to signify any ontological primacy within Afro-diasporic discourses' (25). Wehileye

Case Study 14.2: (cont.)

argues, in fact, that *all* modern Black musical forms have expressed one or other form of this post-humanism:

Black sacred and later secular music took on two simultaneous functions: proving black peoples' soul and standing in for the soul of all US culture, keeping the racially particular and national universal in constant tension. Thus spirituals ushered in a long history of white appropriations of black music, ranging from the 'slumming' patrons of the Cotton Club, Norman Mailer's 'white negroes', to today's hip hop 'whiggers'. As a result of the dehumanizing forces of slavery, in [Kodwo] Eshun's frame of reference, certain kinds of black popular music stage black subjectivity, bypassing the modality of the human in the process of moving from the subhuman to the posthuman. (28)

On the one hand, then, spirituals and other forms such as soul and the blues were bound up, for Wehileye, in a tension between humanism and dehumanisation. On the other, more recent forms, from Afrofuturist free jazz to Jamaican dub to British jungle music, transcended this tension in articulating a future-facing post-human Black subjectivity. This is at least how Kodwo Eshun – cited above by Wehileye – figured things in *More Brilliant Than the Sun* (Eshun 1998), where he contrasted Black post-humanism with the strong, expressive humanism of forms such as soul and the blues. However, Wehileye's central argument is built on a resolution of this contrast from Eshun. For Wehileye, *all* Black (American) popular music is at its essence post-human, or at least is mounted on a productive dynamic tension between humanism and post-humanism. As Wehileye puts it:

If we consider the history of black American popular music, we can see both forces, the humanist and posthumanist, at work. From nineteenth-century spirituals through the blues, jazz, soul, hip hop, and techno, the human and the posthuman are in constant dynamic tension. It is precisely because slavery rendered the category of the human suspect that the reputedly humanist postslavery black cultural productions cannot and do not attribute the same meaning to humanity as white American discourses. (30)

Speaking more directly to late-century technological experiments in some of these Black forms, Wehileye goes on to underline the vividness and uniqueness of such Black post-human 'coarticulation' of human and machine.

By embracing new technologies such as remixing, scratching, and sampling, black popular music producers and performers persistently emphasize the virtuality of any form of recorded music. Acknowledging the effects of these technologies on these musical practices, black popular musical genres make their own virtuality central to the musical texts. Instead of pulling the strings in the background – that is, being disembodied – these producers, who plug the

Case Study 14.2: (cont.)

performers into the technological apparatus, take front and center stage with the artists. This creates a composite identity, a machine suspended between performer and producer that sounds the smooth flow between humans and machines. (31)

Wehileye's central point – that post-humanism is the central motive force of Black, American popular music, which he hears initially through vocodered R & B music and then extends to other forms – can perhaps be seen not so much as a 'post-essential' but a 're-essential' point, since it identifies a core essence running through all Black popular music. Unlike some other essentialist accounts of Black music, however, Wehileye's orientation is Afrofuturist and aspirational; Black popular music for him does not echo and restate Gilroy's 'pernicious dualism', identifying Black people with the (implied primitive) body and white people with the (implied civilised) mind, but instead looks to the future in interrogating colonial subjugation. Such re-essentialising rings true since it is able to acknowledge (and in this case rearticulate) the clear continuities present across various Black musical traditions while also exploring differences and contrasts within them.

Though operating in a different frame and context to the Black musicians cited above, white female artists such as Pauline Oliveros (1932–2016) and Laurie Anderson (b. 1947) engaged post-human themes and ideas in their music in such ways as to parallel the deconstructive political work of those Black artists with feminist deconstructions of their own. For example, Oliveros theorised her long history of work with technologies such as tape (as in *Time Perspectives*, from 1959) and various forms of live electronics as a kind of 'disembodied', 'transhumanist' practice; 'As I continue to adopt new technologies as tools, I am participating in transhuman activity' (2005). Such transhuman activity moved musical practice beyond gendered codes and limitations, offering a kind of 'empowering shape-shifting' for female artists (Dickinson cited in Auner 2003: 106). Similarly, Laurie Anderson's 'posthuman ventriloquism' in vocoder-rich songs such as 'O Superman' (Warner Bros, 1981) created 'technologised alter-egos' that served as 'emblems of the power of choosing and refashioning identity' (ibid.). So, while the empowering aspects of post-humanist music clearly worked along both racial and gender lines, deconstructing inherited norms and offering Black and/or female musicians the opportunity to explore new forms of identity, it is also the case that the effect of 'post-humanist' music was often very different when it came from more hegemonic, white, male perspectives.

The German electronic music group Kraftwerk offer an important point of comparison here. Kraftwerk's 1974 album, *Autobahn* (Philips), was made almost entirely using Moog, Arp and EMS analogue synthesisers, vocoders and electronic percussion. The group's next four albums expanded the techno-modern horizons of *Autobahn* into

Case Study 14.2: (cont.)

a totalising mission statement. *Radio-Activity* (1975), 1977's *Trans-Europe Express*, 1978's *Man-Machine* and 1981's *Computer World* (all on Kling Klang) saw the group embody and explore a distinctive aesthetics of post-human futurism that both called back to the thwarted modernism of 1920s and 1930s Europe, and forward to the world-to-come of post-human cyborgs enmeshed in digital webs. On songs such as 'Geiger Counter' (from *Radio-Activity*), 'Showroom Dummies' (from *Trans-Europe Express*), 'The Robots' (from *The Man-Machine*) and 'Computer Love' (from *Computer Love*), the sounds, lyrics and even the musicians themselves become *Gesamtkunstwerk* (i.e., 'total art work') projections of a modernity defined by the automatisation of subjectivity and the subjectivation of machines. Actual robots even began to appear in place of the musicians in live shows from the *Computer World* tour onwards. Perhaps reflecting this elegant elision of human and machine, Kraftwerk's music in this period displayed an almost classical poise and balance in form, melody, metre and harmony. Songs such as 'Neon Lights' (1978), from *The Man-Machine*, and 'Trans-Europe Express' (1977), from *Trans-Europe Express*, were in this sense based on simple and repetitive song designs featuring repeated diatonic motifs. But while this music was classically, even machinically balanced, it also featured processed voices singing with a cyborgian glower over then-unusual analogue synthesiser timbres. This intimate and casual juxtaposition of simple musical material with cutting-edge tools and processing methods was typical. While chromaticism and sonic abrasion appeared from time to time in Kraftwerk's music – as for example in the curious rising chromatic scales and the industrial banging of 'Hall of Mirrors' (1977), or the scrunchy and clangy sonic interjections of 'Pocket Calculator' (from *Computer Love*, Kling Klang, 1981) – on the whole its novelty and charge came from the group's engagement with and complex performative and sonic embodiment of technological, post-humanist modernity.

- Kraftwerk, 'Neon Lights' (from *The Man-Machine*, Kling Klang, 1978)
- Kraftwerk, 'Pocket Calculator' (from *Computer Love*, Kling Klang, 1981)

Kraftwerk's post-humanism therefore shared much with that of Black artists such as Zapp and Roger, with both tools and sounds overlapping. And yet, as alluded to above, white, male artists such as Kraftwerk and similar or derivative examples such as Gary Numan inhabited a very different post-human space as compared to Black and/or female musicians. Where those latter musicians could be seen to come at post-humanism from a position already somewhat outside the hegemonic centre, Kraftwerk and Numan were instead operating from that centre. Moreover, where Anderson, Zapp and Roger and the others deliberately conjoined expressive emotion with post-human modes, Kraftwerk often deliberately renounced obvious emotion in

---

Case Study 14.2: (cont.)

favour of a total embrace of the robot. Joseph Auner indeed argued that 'the machine-like or android persona [in these artists' music] became a means for representing dehumanisation, sometimes with ironic or critical intent, sometimes as an affirmative sign of a new hard-edged, emotionless objectivity'. Auner ultimately concluded, in this spirit, that the 'juxtaposition of the human and technological in Kraftwerk and Numan thus does not call into question the essential categories' – as, we could point out, the work of the Black artists did – 'but rather might be seen as a shift in allegiance from one sphere to the other' (2003: 110). White males might therefore be seen to have thrown in their lot with their new technological overlords, while Black and/or female artists like 702 and Laurie Anderson seemed to want to project a more ambiguous, chimeric fusion of human and machine through their music.

New Racial, Ethnic and National Codes in the Globalised Late Twentieth Century

The plural cosmopolitanism at which we saw Bartók eventually arriving grew out of local patterns of porous cultural exchange, which of course themselves grew out of and reflected broader globalising dynamics. These dynamics expanded profoundly over the course of the century. By the century's end, everything from industry to economics, technology to culture had all become global phenomena, information and capital circulating around the world at unprecedented speeds (Giddens and Hutton 2000). Music, of course, played a huge role in all this. Case studies in each of the next two chapters – first on East Asian audiences for classical music and then noise music in Japan – explore this late-century globalised cultural space. This final section thinks in a broad sense about some of the roles that race, ethnicity and nationality took on within globalised musical flows in this period.

Transnational and intra-national musical flows in the last few decades of the century were unevenly distributed. The global proliferation of Western, invariably anglophone culture, for example, was unmatched by any corresponding proliferation of non-Western culture. This is even as various local patterns of exchange complicate this picture, as for example with the popularity of late-century Japanese pop in China and South Korea, and the converse growth of Korean television and pop music across East Asia from the late 1990s on (Eun-Young 2010: 219–20). And yet, even as the late-century global dominance of anglophone culture was undeniable, many postcolonial theorists argued against the traditional image of a culturally imperial, hegemonic monoculture. Such figures instead saw transnational, globalised culture as a battleground of identity and power. Globalised dynamics, according to this argument, would produce a 'creolisation' rather than a homogenisation of global culture (Cohen 2007).

Carl Wilson's 2007 analysis of Céline Dion's (b. 1968) 1996 album, *Let's Talk About Love* (→Chapter 15, 'Audiences, Class and Consumption'), musically illustrates such ideas (2014). Discussing what he sees as Dion's 'pidgin otherness', Wilson makes the point that Dion's personal and musical identity did not fit neatly into traditional North American 'racial and ethnic matrices' (37). In this spirit, Dion's French-language movement between cheap, variety-like so-called *kétaine* songs on the one hand and *chanson* respectability on the other created a sense of 'otherness' that does not quite fit with sanctioned stories of resistance or domination (33–5).

- Céline Dion, 'D'amour et d'amitié' (from *Tellement j'ai d'amour . . .* , Saisons, 1982)
- Céline Dion, 'Ziggy (Un garçon pas comme les autres)' (from *Dion chante Plamondon*, Columbia, 1991)

This bridging of local music traditions, in addition to various public displays of her heritage (including a famous few words of Quebec *joual* slang at the 1997 Grammy Awards), shored up Dion's relatively unique *Québécoise* identity. In another vein, Dion's recording of Spanish versions of songs, theme songs for Japanese shows and songs for internationally distributed films all complemented the localised code-switching of the *katéin/chanson* examples with broader, globally orientated marketing decisions. Such decisions once again ran counter to the simple image of globalised Americanised monoculture, even as Dion songs such as 'My Heart Will Go On' from *Titanic* undoubtedly contributed to anglophone cultural imperialism (released on *Let's Talk About Love*, Columbia, 1997).

The complexity of globalising dynamics led to a variety of musical expressions of unusual, unprecedented racial and ethnic identities to go alongside Dion's 'pidgin otherness'. The Japanese salsa act, Orquestra de la Luz, are a useful case in point here. Formed in the 1980s and most active in the 1990s, the group evinced a lively if deeply and perhaps overly faithful allegiance to Cuban salsa. The pastiche aspect of their work would have been basically unremarkable, however, were it not for their Japanese identity, which infused their music with an aspect of intercultural novelty and even tension. And yet such unusual mixes should perhaps be seen as a natural corollary of globalisation. In discussing the group's typically

Japanese emphasis on tradition and imitation rather than innovation (at least as it's often coded in Western culture), Shuhei Hosokawa indeed argues that Orquestra de la Luz should be seen as a 'vivid demonstration of the intertwined nature of the global and the local' in late twentieth-century culture. Hosokawa, in fact, reads this global/local overlap as a 'key dynamic' in globalised musics (1999: 510).

Loren Kajikawa's analysis of the 1999 single, 'My Name Is' from white American rapper Eminem provides a similarly fascinating example of an artist skilfully negotiating emerging racial and ethnic codes. Eminem did this, argues Kajikawa, through a dual tactic of signalling 'immersion' in Black culture through dextrous rapping and the presence of mentor Dr Dre (a leading figure in 1990s hip-hop), and, conversely, acknowledging but 'inverting' his own whiteness through the inclusion of white pop-cultural reference points in his lyrics and stereotypical white characters in his videos. This dual tactic allowed Eminem to gain both commercial success and critical credibility, something largely unprecedented for a white artist in the history of hip-hop at that time. This success, alongside the broader, global mainstream success of Black hip-hop artists that coincided with this, illustrated what Kajikawa calls 'the dynamic nature of racial categories' (2009: 342), such that a form like hip-hop was now being listened to by huge, mixed audiences and even becoming accessible to a wide variety of racially mixed artists.

- Eminem, 'My Name Is' (from *The Slim Shady LP*, Interscope, 1999)

This dynamic vision of race and ethnicity at the end of the century is supported by Timothy Brown's 2006 article, '"Keeping It Real" in a Different 'Hood: (African-)Americanization and Hip Hop in Germany'. Brown's article uses examples of German and Turkish German hip-hop groups to explore 'the subtleties of the process by which something like hip hop finds a new home in a foreign culture'. Brown shows how the global impact of hip-hop allowed musicians around the world 'to create new identities for themselves out of the raw material of globalized culture' (2006: 138). This employment of hip-hop 'for local effect' (142) could be seen in everything from Advanced Chemistry's rapping in German and their discussion of themes of multiculturalism in songs like 'Fremd in eigenem Land' (Foreign in your own country), to Islamic Force's sampling of the Turkish folk genre *Arabesk* in a number of songs.

- Advanced Chemistry, 'Fremd in eigenem Land' (12', MZEE Records, 1992)
- Islamic Force, 'My Melody'/'Istanbul' (12', First Class Records, 1992)

Conclusion

Timothy Brown ultimately argues that, in using hip-hop both to eke out a place in German society and create new identities for themselves, such artists exploited the 'underdog' ethnicity and spirit of resistance already coded into the music. This is such that the 'structural outsiderism' (2006: 147) some have heard in American hip-hop is recognised by immigrant and working-class communities in other countries and adapted to new ends, turning globalised musical forces to specific local purposes in doing so. Though it needs to be considered against the backdrop of anglophone cultural imperialism, this point echoes across the examples considered in this final section, in which various 'essential' or 'authentic' musical identities and forms were adapted and inflected amid the globalised flows of late twentieth-century culture. What is more, finally, it also echoes the complex local, national and global tussles over identities (musical or otherwise) that we saw across the various musical examples from earlier in the century.

15 | Audiences, Class and Consumption

One of the most significant developments of the cultural twentieth century was the related emergence of 'mass' cultural practices and an urban, diverse, 'mass' audience to go along with them. The industrialising late eighteenth and nineteenth centuries had set the scene, with explosions in wealth, technology and population generating new leisure activities, from pleasure gardens to music halls, galleries to museums, street theatre to vaudeville, all of which were populated by an increasingly mixed crowd (Storch 1982; Cunningham 1980; Oldcorn Reid 1976). Consumption habits were changing, as were audiences. But it was the twentieth-century introduction of mass media and propulsive economic policies such as the New Deal that would most fully realise this drift towards large, mixed audiences and new forms of culture, something that would impact both mass and more specialised culture in profound ways.

This chapter tells the story of these twentieth-century shifts in audience and culture. We start with an overview of Western musical audiences in the first part of the century. We use sociological concepts such as 'subculture' to examine the changing nature of music audiences in the mid-to-late century. Growing out of that, our first case study examines various musical 'taste cultures'. We then consider the impact of various late-century social and political developments on contemporary musical audiences. The chapter closes with its second case study, which looks at the growth of Western classical music in East Asia, an example that brings some of the political complexities underlying earlier discussions to the fore.

Mass Media, Mass Culture: Mass Regression?

Large and mixed nineteenth-century audiences got even larger and even more mixed in the twentieth. Early-century shifts in the means of production towards Fordist assembly-line models of high-volume, low-cost manufacturing drove up discretionary income, further increased leisure time and undergirded the development of sound-recording technology and mass media such as radio and television. As a result, huge national and international audiences were now able to come together around leisure and consumption habits in an entirely new way.

What was it like to be part of and experience this new mass culture? Art from the first half of the century is littered with depictions of busy urban life that capture in images, sounds and words both its excitement and its inherently bewildering, even alienating nature. From the gleaming and noisy art-deco city in Fritz Lang's *Metropolis* (1927), whose scale was conveyed both in Lang's images and in Gottfried Huppertz' grand score, to the bustling Soviet montage of *Man With A Movie Camera* (1929); the urbane city dwellers of Cole Porter and the bustle and clatter of much Golden Age musical theatre to flinty, lurid *Zeitopern* from Kurt Weill and Georges Antheil; the teeming city-theatre of Joyce to the wide-visioned characters of Zora Neale Hurston, modern life was represented as a blur and whizz of machines, movement and metropolitan mass. The experience on the ground was obviously not as uniform as this might suggest; for every louche, suave attendee at the Cotton Club, on Broadway or at a Berlin cabaret you could probably have found any number of less urbane audience members. But this was clearly a time that saw itself at the vanguard of newly massed, modern life.

Historians and cultural critics paint a similarly vivid picture. Richard Hoggart's *The Uses of Literacy* (2009/1957) identifies a turn-of-the-century working-class life in which communal entertainment and leisure activities such as music hall and working-men's clubs glued close-knit but rapidly expanding communities together. Mixed crowds attended such popular and/or middlebrow cultural events as musical theatre, cabaret and operetta, seeing themselves and their lives reflected in modern characters, settings and concerns, as for example in the case of Broadway with the industrial disputes of Marc Blitzstein's *The Cradle Will Rock* (1937), the psychoanalytical themes in Kurt Weill's *Lady in the Dark* (1944) and the metropolitan gamblers and 'sinners' of Frank Loesser's *Guys and Dolls* (1950). Audiences for mass media such as cinema and the radio were likewise mixed in character, often in subtle or perhaps unexpected ways. Isadora Helfgott provides a detailed history of the ways that art foundations and museums in the 1930s and 1940s used mass media such as radio to construct and cultivate racially and often class-mixed audiences for visual art (2015). The Ziegfeld Follies (1907–31), to take a contrasting example, drew on traditions of Parisian music hall and American vaudeville in staging popular musical revues whose audiences were characteristically mixed in gender and class profile (McGee 2008).

Walter Benjamin (1892–1940) famously praised the radical potential of such class-, gender- and even sometimes racially mixed mass audiences. Benjamin's 'The Work of Art in the Age of Mechanical Reproduction' (1999/1936) argued that the assembly-line-anchored mechanical reproduction that was at the heart of mass culture withers both the 'aura' of discrete pieces of premodern art and the social rituals attached to them, such as going to an art gallery or concert hall. Mass culture had the potential, as a result, to 'brush aside a number of outmoded concepts, such as creativity and genius, eternal value and mystery', replacing these with a more democratic model of art and culture. In this vein, Benjamin praised what he saw as active critical-aesthetic encounters in mass culture, which, he argued, could lead to greater political sensitivity and awareness on the part of audiences.

And yet, cultural critics were also quick to highlight what they saw as dilution and degradation in mass culture and mass audiences. Such criticism came from both the left and right of the political spectrum. From the left, figures such as Hoggart pointed to a loss of class cohesion from the 1910s and 1920s on, with newly mixed mass audiences coming to be defined less by distinct class positions and community solidarities and much more by (passive) consumption habits (2009/1957: 310). Lizabeth Cohen provides an account of consumption in Chicago in the 1920s that support's Hoggart's contentions, demonstrating how even contemporary popular commentators saw reduced working hours, increasing discretionary income and an explosion of advertising as leading to a kind of homogenisation of class through shared consumption habits (1989). Theodor Adorno's (1903–69) 1938 'On the Fetish Character of Music and the Regression of Listening' is one of the most notable left-leaning critiques of mass culture (see also Greenberg 1989). Adorno's essay, which was written in response to the Benjamin piece cited above, focused on the impact of music's newly commodified character on the aesthetic perception and taste of audiences (Adorno 1991a/1938). Adorno argued that music in its commodity form became merely another unit of economic value. The social process of buying in this way came to prioritise 'exchange-value' over 'use-value' (1991a/1938: 38–9). Audiences, in this understanding, bought for the sake of buying rather than for the sake of listening: 'the consumer is really worshipping the money he himself has paid' (38). For Adorno, all of this turned modern mass music into a fetish experience

where aesthetic contact was subsumed into a ritualistic exercise of consumer will. This, Adorno argued, led to a 'regression of listening' and,
importantly, a concomitant regression of music, the one being superficial,
deconcentrated and 'pseudo-active' (49–52), the other homogenised and
inauthentic.

These images of regressive listening and a subservience of expression to
economics parallels right-leaning critiques of mass culture from that same
period. Perhaps the most famous examples of such critique, at least in the
anglophone world, are those mounted by F. R. Leavis and his circle from
the 1930s on (alongside related perspectives from the likes of T. S. Eliot, as
in his famous 1919 essay 'Tradition and the Individual Talent'; 2000).
Leavis' critique was mounted on a number of fronts, from teaching to
publishing, but manifesto-like texts such as *Mass Civilisation and Minority
Culture* (1930) are probably the most famous surviving sources. Leavis'
position has often been caricatured as a starkly elitist one. But at its
conservative heart, it wanted to preserve what Leavis saw as important
aspects of national culture and tradition, often setting these against the
encroaching spread of Americanising, modernising forces as embodied by
mass culture, industry and, as the below quotation from *Mass Civilisation*
has it, the 'machine'.

In support of the belief that the modern phase of human history is unprecedented it
is enough to point to the machine. The machine, in the first place, has brought
about change in habit and the circumstances of life at a rate for which we have no
parallel . . . It seems unlikely that the conditions of life can be transformed in this
way without some injury to the standard of living: improvisation can hardly replace
the delicate traditional adjustments, the mature, inherited codes of habit and
valuation, without severe loss . . . It is a breach in continuity that threatens: what
has been inadvertently dropped may be irrevocable or forgotten. (1930: 13–14)

Leavis' position as set out here is typical of both right and left critiques of
mass culture in its despairing attitude towards industrialised modern life.
Indeed, Adorno's condemnation of the way that mass-cultural commodities might be seen as creating passive, docile audiences parallels Leavis'
reproaches of what he saw as the damaging impact of Hollywood film
(1930: 14–15). Both accounts, moreover, anticipate thinking from later in
the century in which, for example, the intense focus on sales figures in
popular music embodies a similar displacement of 'use' by 'exchange' value
(see Greil Marcus on 'Jacksonism', for instance; 1989).

And yet, however powerful these right and left critiques of mass culture
might remain, their pessimism seems to go against the grain of much

everyday experience of music in twentieth-century mass culture. For many audience members, music was rarely just, or indeed ever, simply a means to a ritual economic end. Instead, music listening and music fandom acted as a crucial source of emotional, personal and social support (DeNora 2000). And so, just as Leavis and Adorno's largely pessimistic attitude would be picked up by later thinkers, Walter Benjamin's more varied account of 'active' mass audiences would in this spirit itself be picked up and adapted. Most notable here are the cultural studies set, led by figures such as Stuart Hall, whose descriptions of resistant, politically active popular audiences would prove hugely influential (1980/1973). Perhaps unsurprisingly, in fact, as pop culture moved to the centre of cultural life in the second half of the twentieth century, it would be the more positive, Benjaminian perspective that would come to dominate sociologically orientated studies of musical audiences.

Technologies of the Musical Self: Subcultures

A whole series of youth cultures organised around the conspicuous consumption of popular culture emerged in the booming postwar West. One of the earliest and most important examples of such youth cultures was what would be called the 'subculture': a group of people marked out from a dominant or 'parent' culture through shared tastes and values. Subcultures were first theorised by Chicago School sociologists David Riesman and Howard Becker in the 1950s and 1960s, with a focus on delinquency, crime and socially disadvantaged groups such as recent immigrants and gangs (Gelder 2005: 19). The term was taken up by figures such as Albert K. Cohen and Stuart Hall in the 1970s and 1980s at the Centre for Contemporary Cultural Studies (CCCS) in Birmingham. The CCCS retained the Chicago School's focus on lower/working-class subject groups but dropped the criminological angle in favour of a new attention to mass-mediated cultural consumption.

For CCCS thinkers, 'subculture' had two quite simple ideas at its heart. First, that displaying one's taste in culture through visual, behavioural and performative cues sent messages to other people about the type of person you were or aspired to be (seen as); not least in contrast to other members of your social class such as parents and peers. As a key CCCS text has it, 'through dress, activities, leisure pursuits and lifestyle, [members of a subculture] may project a different cultural response or "solution" to the problems posed for them by their material and social class position and experience' (Clarke et al. 1997/1975: 101). In these 'rituals of resistance', 'subculture' built on Erving Goffman's sociological analysis of self-presentation (1956), and likewise echoed Foucault's 'technologies of the self', wherein individuals effect 'certain operations' on their bodies and behaviour 'so as to transform themselves' (1988). This brings us to the second key idea, which is that subcultures were a way for 'outsiders' in the dominant culture to become resisting 'insiders' in a smaller subculture within it. By making different lifestyle choices to peers or parents and by expressing anti-mainstream values through those choices, the thinking goes, individuals could withdraw their implied 'consent' for cultural hegemony and, through this, become part of a meaningful counter-hegemonic action – *resist* the powers that be.

Key examples of musical subcultures include mods, who evolved from smartly dressed, Europhile modernist jazz fans in the late-1950s and 1960s to Fred-Perry-wearing, scooter-driving, Anglophile Small Faces fans in the later 1960s and beyond; punks, whose anti-establishment and 'DIY' 1970s values inspired decades of imitators and derivations; and later, somewhat more localised examples, from ravers to goths, emos to teenyboppers. Each of these subcultures embodied CCCS-type ideas in different ways. So, writing about punk, Dick Hebdige discusses the safety pins with which punks adorned their bodies and clothes as 'mundane objects which have a double meaning . . . they warn the "straight" world in advance of a sinister presence – the presence of difference' (1979: 3). Hebdige describes this repurposing technique as 'bricolage', a 'cut-and-pasting which re-situates a sign within a different sign system to change its meaning' (104). The late-1970s and early-1980s 2-tone ska revival is a case in point here, with its admixture of Jamaican rude boy and mod visual styles and its musical blend of ska, reggae and punk. To echo Hebdige, we can see the interplay of Black and white style and musical languages in bands like the Specials as both reflecting and redoubling interracial class solidarities, 'resignifying' existing symbols in order to express both local belonging and more general difference.

Though CCCS writers largely focused on subcultures tied to British and American popular culture of the 1960s and 1970s, the concept has had a long and varied shelf life. For instance, sticking with the British popular terrain for a moment, Sarah Thornton developed CCCS ideas of authenticity and cultural capital in her 1996 study of 1980s and 1990s acid house and other dance musics, *Club Cultures*. Thornton focused on what she called 'subcultural capital' in analysing how the 'alternative hierarchies' of subcultures actually worked (104–5). For Thornton, subcultures were based on a kind of 'social logic' in which constantly shifting 'mental maps' relating to standards of dress, dancing, music and other 'prestige symbols' allowed members of the subculture to compete with each other for status and capital (102–3). Others have identified similar subcultural dynamics farther afield. From Klezmer music (Slobin 2002) to extreme metal (Purcell 2003), bhangra (Maira 1999) to contemporary chamber music (Burgess 2004), subcultural tenets have been found in a wide variety of late-century musical audiences.

But despite this evident popularity and usefulness, 'subculture' has also proved conceptually limiting. For starters, it is clearly most at home in the spectacular, stylish arena of popular culture. For the most part, too, CCCS theorists depicted music fandom as the preserve of white, male, working-class youths, when of course the reality was both far more complex and far more fluid than that (Bennett 2006). Angela McRobbie, for one, offered a feminist rereading of subcultural theory that points to gendered social restrictions as having fostered a very public stage for male-identity forma-tion and, in turn, encouraged female fans to explore pleasure and identity in private (2000). Mavis Bayton likewise argued that 'subcultural theorists took for granted young people's ability to choose what to do in their leisure time'. Since female fans' choices in this area were restricted compared to those of their male peers, their relative absence from the public subcultural stage was then only to be expected (2006: 347). A similar critique can and has been made along racial lines, with for example twenty-first-century texts on grime and goth pointing out the racialised norms of the subcultures concept in its classic form (Fatsis 2018; Taylor 2019). Many others, finally, have been sceptical of the supposed 'counter-hegemonic' function of subcultures, see-ing in them and related concepts a merely symbolic resistance (Gitlin 1997). Indeed, subcultures themselves were deeply commodified from the get-go. The outsider aspects of punk and mod, for example, were easily incorporated into high-street and suburban spectacle across the Western world (Liptrot 2014; Lowy 2010). As the decades wore on, the commercial aspect of mod even seemed to supersede any hunger for resistance that might have ener-gised the movement in its early years. Ian Penman sums up mod's typical subcultural trajectory:

Mod became more about buying the right records and wearing the approved uniform, but in the nervy modernist dawn there was a real hunger for films, books … Everything was up for grabs: music and clothes, sex and sexuality; the speech and language of put-down and put-on and pop fandom; transport and travel; nights out and nights in. Everything, in fact, we now take for granted as 'youth culture'. It was a heady time of redefinition; but we also get the first migraine flash of a paradox that would split Mod, and define other subcultures: what began as a principled refusal of the nine-to-five wage-slave grind found its most vivid street-level expression in avid consumerism. (2013)

'Subculture', then, provided a powerful conceptual image of group behaviour, class alliances and social empowerment as organised through the consumption of music in the second half of the twentieth century. But the term's orientation towards popular culture, its users' overestimation of its supposed political dimensions and the reductive images of subcultural audiences meant that it ultimately served as an incomplete description of music audiences in the period.

Other Musical Selves in the Second Half of the Century

Lucy Dearn and Stephanie Pitts contrast the self-identities of music audiences across popular and 'classical' musics. Where the first group have been happy to identify as 'fans' or even consumers, Dearn and Pitts argue, 'audiences for classical music, by contrast, tend to be portrayed – both by themselves and by researchers – as communities' (2017: 3). Dearn and Pitts describe these classical communities as relatively close-knit groups of 'like-minded people' united by class, age, interests and appearance. In this quality of peer alignment and identity reinforcement, and in the close relationship of class and taste running through them, classical music communities across the twentieth and on into the twenty-first century resembled subcultures: both fundamentally served as heavily coded arenas in which narratives of personal identity could be explored and performed.

And yet, some clear differences persisted between late-twentieth-century classical and popular audiences. These differences were most visible in the specific media culture, the particular social etiquette and the typical age and class profile of each group. On the whole, for example, classical audiences later in the twentieth century were smaller and their media more specialised than those for mainstream popular forms. In terms of social etiquette, twentieth-century classical concerts presented (at least superficially) more sedate, behaviourally passive scenes as compared to stereotypically rowdy popular audiences (Pitts 2005). Finally, the general profile of classical audience members as compared to those for popular music, at least before baby boomers aged into maturity later in the century, tended towards older, seemingly wealthy professionals. Prieto-Rodríguez and Fernández-Blanco cite a number of studies that support this point about relatively older and wealthier late-century classical audiences across different territories, from older audiences in Switzerland and Japan to more professionalised ones in the UK (2000: 148–9).

Just as these classical 'communities' expand our frame for understanding late-century music audiences beyond the youth and style-led resistance of subcultures, other sociological terms speak to aspects of audience behaviour not captured by the subcultural model. Attempting to transcend the local boundaries of subculture theory, 'scene' has been used to evoke both a looser and a broader context for music making and listening (e.g., Shank 1994). In contrast to the classic subculture, traditional limitations of social class, cultural capital, physical location and so on did not necessarily apply here. Keith Kahn-Harris' work on extreme metal underlines the flexibility and global perspective of this kind of 'scenic methodology', as contrasted with the 'overdetermining' local attitude of subcultures (2006: 134). 'Neotribe' similarly expands the frame for music fandom in the period. The term rests on Michel Maffesoli's account of a certain tribal 'ambience, a state of mind' (1996: 98), expressed in our case in allegiance to this or that musical artist or genre. These allegiances shifted depending on context; Barry Shields describes neotribal audience identities as dramatic 'postmodern personae' (in Bennett 2006: 108). 'Fan cultures', finally, is a similarly flexible term that embraces different kinds of fan regardless of geographical and/or class location (Hills 2002). What is unique here is the way fan cultures spread across both very commercial and anti-commercial communities or individuals. Unlike the resisting subculturalist, a fan in this respect could express more-or-less consumerist, mainstream allegiances just as much as they could enter into obscure, anti-commercial fan communities (see Hills 2002: 27–45, and in particular 44–5). Terms such as fan culture therefore recognised the wider variety of music audiences in the second half of the century than might be otherwise suggested by useful but limiting terms such as 'subculture'.

Case Study 15.1: Taste Cultures High and Low, Elite and Mass

As we pointed out in the introduction, and as we have just seen in the case of subcultures, one of the cornerstones of audience studies in the twentieth century was an assumed alignment or 'homology' between class identity and cultural taste. As we also suggested, however, this alignment shifted across the century, with audiences becoming increasingly mixed and the social position and meaning of different musical

Case Study 15.1: (cont.)

forms likewise becoming more complex. This case study steps aside from our broadly chronological story of music audiences in the twentieth century to delve into this topic of the evolving nature of twentieth-century audiences and, in particular, their associated taste cultures.

Pierre Bourdieu's (1930–2002) famous study of the sociology of taste in the twentieth century, *Distinction: A Social Critique of the Judgement of Taste* (1979, translated into English in 1984), homes in on the 'homological' twentieth-century relationship between class and taste, where class-based distinctions between elite and mass culture were said to structure much of how audiences related to music. For Bourdieu, taste is closely intertwined with our sense of our identity and social position: 'taste classifies, and it classifies the classifier' (1984/1979: 4). Bourdieu constructs a tripartite hierarchy of taste cultures arising out of this basic theoretical principle that one's education, class and profession all determine one's taste; each of Bourdieu's three categories connote particular class identities and world views and are attached to typical art works or traditions (17).

- Legitimate taste: J. S. Bach's *Well-Tempered Clavier* (1722–42); jazz; Breughel or Goya.
- Middlebrow taste: Gershwin's *Rhapsody in Blue* (1924); Jacques Brel; Renoir.
- Popular taste: Strauss' *Blue Danube* (1866); Petula Clark; *Mona Lisa*.

Each of these three categories, argues Bourdieu, expresses something clear about its member's social position. For example, 'legitimate'-type taste choices were made so as to reinforce a bourgeois self-image. Bourdieu repeatedly argues in this context that music, literature and so on that can be seen as more 'abstract', 'purposeless' and removed from the concerns of everyday life were more often liked by those of middle- and upper-class backgrounds. This is because seeking the 'aesthetically' satisfying rather than the immediately gratifying, as in 'mere' entertainment, was a luxury. The time spent acquiring these aesthetic tastes represented conspicuous consumption – that is, an obvious waste! – of time (1984/1979: 281). Only elites, the thinking goes, had the resources necessary for the cultivation of such expertise. Note that in the examples given above, so-called 'legitimate' taste culture contained the most 'abstract', non-representational cultural works (instrumental baroque and jazz). This kind of music, Bourdieu says, 'is the "pure" art par excellence. It says nothing and has nothing to say' (1984/1979: 19). By contrast, the supposedly lower, vulgar sphere of 'profane' popular culture was based on a 'continuity between art and life', where music or art would be easily digestible even to those with little familiarity with it (32–3). These sharp contrasts between 'pure' and 'profane' culture, and the strong links between artistic

Case Study 15.1: (cont.)

quality and personal character they represent, reinforce Bourdieu's argument that art and cultural consumption fulfil a social function of legitimating social differences (7).

It is easy, by century's end, to identify residues of Bourdieu's elite and mass distinctions, as indeed we saw earlier with Prieto-Rodríguez and Fernández-Blanco (2000). The fact that it was also possible to apply Bourdieusian frameworks within more localised contexts provides further support for his arguments: self-fashioning through music existed in all social settings and ran according to finer and finer Bourdieusian logics of distinction. Carl Wilson's study of Céline Dion's 1997 album *Let's Talk About Love* (Columbia), for example, shows that hierarchical division into 'legitimate' and 'vulgar' wings does not just happen across but also *within* music genres. Here, the supposedly legitimate strains of alternative rock music contrast with the 'vulgar' lilt of, and 'vulgar' listeners to, Dion (2014, and →Chapter 14, 'Race and Ethnicity' for more on Wilson's Dion).

Bourdieu, Wilson and others therefore take a primarily sociological view of taste. For them, a clear homology exists between one's perceived or claimed personal identity and the kind of music one listens to; or at least presents oneself as listening to. This was as true in the early decades of the century as it was in the 1960s and 1970s of Bourdieu or the 1980s and 1990s of Wilson: Adorno treads this ground, for instance, in criticising elite audiences of the 1930s and 1940s for superficially using classical music to convey their supposed cultivation (1991b: 81). And yet, some have nevertheless rejected the sociological model as being overly reductive and deterministic (e.g., the magazine *N+1*, in an editorial in 2013). In this view, Bourdieu ignores the key and unavoidable complexity of aesthetic desire and interests, which are never fully reducible to social function. Music exists within society, the argument goes, but is not simply reducible to that society (Rosen 2012: 210–39, and 217).

Others have sought to adapt the Bourdieusian model in order to describe with more accuracy the increasingly mixed audiences and blurring taste cultures evident later in the century. Peterson and Kern's analysis of the 'shifting ground of status-group politics' in the latter decades of the century, for example, describes an evolution in the exemplary model of elite (or 'highbrow') behaviour from exclusive snob to inclusive postmodern omnivore (1996: 905). The omnivore was characterised by a breadth of knowledge *across* different styles, from commercial to classical, rather than conspicuous consumption within more traditional 'high' art styles. Peterson and Kern argue that the emergence of the omnivore can be linked to a number of historical, social and cultural factors, from an increasing accessibility of elite artistic forms, to growing geographic and class mixtures of people, to the proliferation of culture across mass media:

Case Study 15.1: (cont.)

Rising levels of living, broader education, and presentation of the arts via the media have made elite aesthetic taste more accessible to wider segments of the population, devaluing the arts as markers of exclusion. At the same time, geographic migration and social class mobility have mixed people holding different tastes. And the increasingly ubiquitous mass media have introduced the aesthetic tastes of different segments of the population to each other. Thus the diverse folkways of the rest of the world's population ... are increasingly available for appropriation by elite taste-makers. (1996: 905)

These points resonate with one of Taruskin's observations, that 'maybe it is not such a riddle after all that the traditionally "high" musical genres should have amassed unassailable cultural capital in the [earlier] "gilded" age of intensely concentrated wealth and increasing social stratification' (2007). For both Taruskin and for Peterson and Kern, supposed class mobility and dispersal of wealth led naturally to a democratisation of music such that formerly 'illegitimate' forms ascended to positions of authority. This kind of movement towards pluralism and variety was evident not only in the 'internal' dispersal of cultural authority to different Western musical forms in the second half of the century but also in the expanded frame of culture in that same period; chains of globalised exchange led to the development and exportation of characteristically international forms such as Bollywood, where films like *Sholay* (1975) and *Amar Akbar Anthony* (1977) demonstrated both global and local markers of style across sound, image and story, such that Western film genres and musical styles were given local shape in characteristically heady stylistic blends.

So, taste in one or other specific musical form was no longer necessarily a clear signal of one's social status by the century's end. If, for example, you wanted to appear elite, you might attend the opera on a Wednesday and then a club night featuring some French house music the following Friday. Plugging in to popular culture was no longer a clear indication of illegitimacy. Navigating these complex social waters with any degree of success required dedication and immersion on the part of audiences, whose range of options and roles were now unprecedentedly large.

Globalised Personal Omnivory: Music Audiences at the End of the Twentieth Century

Scholars developed a variety of approaches to characterise the changing social identities of music audiences in the second half of the century, as we have seen. Outside such sociological contexts, we can see a number of interrelated features of music audiences coming to the fore at this time. Most obvious, perhaps, would be the widespread emergence of individualist modes of consumption amid an increasingly globalised spectacle of popular culture, and, as we have just seen, omnivorous, potentially 'post-class' taste preferences (Peterson and Kern 1996). These two interrelated features fed off each other as well as off broader technological, social and political changes. In terms of the latter, the 1979 introduction of the Walkman and subsequent development of other 'mobile' personal listening technologies, such as the Discman and the MP3 player, played a key role. Michael Bull has even suggested that such personal stereos 'revolutionized the everyday experiences of millions of people daily as they move through the city', these stereos' 'individualiz- ing' capacity forming 'a critical tool for users in their management of space and time, in their construction of boundaries around the self and as the site of fantasy and memory' (2000: 2–3).

Personal listening technologies in this sense reflected, and in some senses contributed to, broader cultural shifts towards individualist modes of urban living. Though these were hardly novel in the 1980s and 1990s – Bull himself quotes Georg Simmel's famous declaration in *The Metropolis and Mental Life*, from 1903, that 'the deepest problems of modern life derive from the claim of the individual to preserve the autonomy and individuality of his existence' (2014: 110) – they were lent weight and immediacy by broader political and cultural forces. Chief among these were the emerging post-Fordist, neoliberal 'regimes of accumulation' that were based on the impos- ition of precarious labour and just-in-time, deregulated global circulation of commodities. In this situation, collective working-class institutions such as unions and related phenomena such as public utilities and lifetime employ- ment went into decline in the face of a rush towards individualist market success. Personal identity would be defined within this context through individualist consumer choices and personal affective expression rather than collective social action or solidarity, echoing Hoggart's earlier analysis of mass culture as an agent of class disintegration.

The collective identities that might have been embodied in or repre- sented by subcultures or similar groupings in the immediate postwar period therefore became more and more fragmented in such contexts. In this spirit, Jeffrey Paris and Michael Ault point to social fragmentation and the consequent weakening of subcultures as collective political entities from the 1970s on:

Whereas the 1960s heralded a Cultural Revolution on a global scale, the subcultures that emerged in its wake were forced to carve out individualized, local spaces (for example, Temporary Autonomous Zones or TAZs) in which their signifying practices of resistance would be encouraged and protected. Lines were sharply drawn between and even within competing subcultures, as demanded by survival and influenced by the broader hyper-individualism then rampant in society. (2004: 403)

In the absence of subcultural or other forms of collective social solidarity in the field of music fandom, constructs such as 'world music' were created in order to bind late-century musical audiences together in different consumer 'blocs', where, for example, traditional vocal music from Bulgaria, Bollywood soundtracks, Indonesian Gamelan and ancient court music from Japan would all be turned into so many consumer options. Such constructs were obviously market-led and, as such, necessarily delimited as sociological and/or political characterisations of music audiences. In the case of world music, this limitation is expressed in how the concept, consecrated at a series of 1987 meetings between many of the leading independent record companies selling 'international/roots music', relied on false, neo-colonial images of non-Western musicians as constituting some coherent 'other' category that would be appreciated and consumed in turn by some assumed Western collective subject (see Whitmore 2016 for context). Even though not all share this reading (Anderson 2000), it is clear that for many observers 'world music' rests on dual ahistorical, apolitical images, of Western audiences as relating to non-local musics merely as passive or, worse, paternalistic consumers, and of those non-Western musics as representing a somehow homogenised 'other'.

This configuration of audiences simply as consumers was typical of late-twentieth-century music culture. Indeed, it is at the root of the omnivore concept we have just examined. The omnivore could only have emerged amid the liquid flows of a transnational, transhistorical consumer society in which listeners suddenly had unprecedented access to music of other times and other places. The race to adapt and integrate music from other territories and times into one's consumerist self-concept – and even into different national cultural identities and practices – was on.

Case Study 15.2: East Asian Audiences and Western Classical Music

Western culture had taken deep root across the Far East by the end of the twentieth century. Western fast-food chains and high-street shops, Hollywood cinema and anglophone popular music were all impossible to avoid in Japan, China and Korea by the 1980s, even if these were infused with subtle or not-so-

Case Study 15.2: (cont.)

subtle local inflections. A far-reaching historical process lies behind this global spread of Western culture to East Asia. This is vividly illustrated in the case of classical music's growth in East Asia over the course of the nineteenth and twentieth centuries. Perhaps of most importance in that case were the way that state support and the founding of key institutions such as orchestras and Western-influenced music schools came together to embed the music in Asian society at the most basic level. A good example of this is the 1872 Japanese incorporation of Western classical music into the new national education system. Inspired at least in part by the modernising philosophy of the Meiji Restoration of 1868, as embodied in the slogan 'Japanese spirit, Western technology', this decision saw the formerly isolationist Japan looking to the West for cultural and educational models. Meanwhile, the 1879 founding and then decades-long evolution of what would eventually become known as the Shanghai Symphony Orchestra represents a key example of how Western concert music gradually gained a foothold in Chinese society. In that spirit, the Shanghai orchestra went from being a pick-up band of foreign musicians playing to largely European audiences in 1879 to a mixed line-up of locals and European musicians playing to similarly mixed 1920s audiences, and then ultimately to an orchestra of international standing later in the century. Finally, Naomi Matsumoto's discussion of the Japanese assimilation of Bizet's *Carmen* between 1885 and 1945 provides a fascinating local example of the penetration of Western culture into Asia in this period (2020).

Kayoung Lee's article on the reception of J. S. Bach (and other Western composers) in Korea between 1900 and 1945 is particularly revealing both of the impact of Western music in the Far East in this early-century period and of the mechanisms and values that usually underlay such impact (2013). The Korean promotion and adaptation of composers like Bach indeed can be seen to parallel and even serve as a microcosm of the more general process of Japanese-led modernisation of the country in the first half of the century. The Kanghwa treaty that Korea had signed with Japan in 1876 had been the first step towards such modernisation, opening the country up to Western culture and Western education largely in the form of Christian hymns, churches and missionary schools. By the 1920s, information about and performances of 'old masters' such as Bach had begun to spread in cities such as Seoul. These performances often carried an ideological message, with audiences didactically instructed about the music's apparently improving educational and social qualities. Bach, Beethoven and others were presented and promoted in this way as an embodiment of the very enlightened modernity that the country more generally aspired to (2013: 32–3). Lee uses the writer

Case Study 15.2: (cont.)

Hong Nana Pa as an example of this kind of ideological presentation of Western classical music. Hong's journalism was indeed often openly didactic, seeking to instruct Koreans in how to listen to Western music and, in so doing, to establish a dichotomy between developed, 'modern' Western music on the one hand and static, 'primitive' Korean music on the other.

In 1929, Hong wrote an article that appeared in one of the most important daily newspapers of the time, *The Chosunilbo*. In this article, as in his piece that appeared in the journal, *Sinyösöng* in 1924, Hong focuses on the question of how to listen to Western art music, lamenting the fact that even though concert halls were crowded, audiences were not aware of what they were listening to ... Hong's writings about Western art music were all instructive and didactic in tone. If we read them more closely, however, we see that he had a fairly clear idea of the dichotomy between Western art music on the one hand, and Korean music on the other. In Hong's dichotomy, Western art music was advanced and developed, therefore 'modern', while Korean music was primitive and static, hence, 'non-modern'. (2013: 35)

In many ways, Hong's attitude can be seen as symptomatic of a more general Asian cultural cringe towards the West at that time, where the importance of modernisation along the cultural and social lines set out by the West over the previous few centuries threatened local cultural traditions and identities. Lee gives a number of examples of Korean composers and writers who wrestled with how they could integrate their Eastern heritage into a supposedly enlightened and modern Western culture (2013: 39–41). Western classical music became in this way a lightning rod for a whole range of complex struggles over national identity and positioning. Of course, East Asian audiences were being inculcated into modernity at this time on many fronts. But we can see in this Korean example how musical performance and music journalism were crucial in building ideological consensus around new cultural forms and new ways of life that contrasted sharply with local Asian traditions.

With some notable exceptions, for the most part the kind of spread and embedding of Western classical music that we have just discussed with reference to Korea continued apace throughout East Asia for the rest of the century. The international influence attained later in the century by Japanese and Chinese composers and musicians such as Toru Takemitsu, Toshio Hosokawa, Sarah Chang, Mitsuko Uchida and Tan Dun attests to this. The development of a significant audience for classical music across the region in the same period is another key indicator of the music's penetration. A 1981 survey by NHK (the Japanese Broadcasting Corporation), for example, demonstrated just how rooted classical music was in Japan by that time, with the music's audience share for over-forties comparing favourably with those for forms of Western popular music (Kurabayashi and Ito 1992). On a more exceptional

Case Study 15.2: (cont.)

but perhaps equally telling note, the French pianist Richard Clayderman's first Chinese TV performance in 1987 is said to have been watched by approximately 800 million people (Lebrecht 2017). Indeed, Jindong Cai and Sheila Melvin emphasised in 2004 just how deeply embedded and even pervasive classical music had become in China by the end of the century.

Many of the world's top composers and performers of classical music are Chinese-born and educated. So, too, are many of the rank-and-file orchestra musicians, music school professors, private violin and piano teachers, and students who are classical music's backbone and future. Although it is less remarked upon, even the production of instruments like pianos, violins, and cellos is ever more a Chinese speciality. But China is not just an exporter of classical music, musicians and instruments – it is also a voracious consumer. Classical music has become so deeply embedded in urban China that the performance of a Western opera may draw a bigger audience than that of a Peking opera. (Melvin and Cai 2004: 1)

The popularity and embeddedness of classical music in China and other East Asian countries at the end of the twentieth century could seem like a good news story; young, booming populations taking up the mantle of what might otherwise have been seen as a cultural tradition in decline. But as was explicit in the example of Korea and Bach above, broader political dynamics infuse the deliberate, complex construction of new audiences and cultures of classical music. Mina Yang, for example, sees the spread of classical music to Asia as embodying a number of uncomfortable political dynamics, from an affirmation of Eurocentric imperialism to a playing into Asian 'abjection', to the exploitation of multiculturalism as a marketing tool (2007). On the first count, Yang points out the false universalism that underlies much of the discourse around classical music:

Classical music adherents often characterize the music of Bach and Beethoven as a universal language that transcends historical and geographical boundaries and stands apart from the complex realities of politics. Recent scholarship strongly challenges this assertion, divulging classical music's complicity in nationalist and racialist projects of the last two hundred years, and argues that Western music's 'universal' qualities have been invoked in the past to avow the superiority of European culture. (2007: 2)

Yang expands on this, suggesting that 'Classical music gained a foothold in East Asia because of western imperialism' (2–3). This was such that, as we have partly seen, nation-building projects in Japan, Korea and other countries closely aligned Western technologies, practices, paradigms and culture with modernity writ large. As a result, cultural traditions like that of Western classical music were enthusiastically taken on as gateways to modernity.

Case Study 15.2: (cont.)

East Asia's inculcation in the practices of Western classical music proceeded coincidentally with the project of modern nation building, often framed by Western nationalist ideologies. The states' political and cultural divisions worked, for the most part, in concert. Nationalist policies that equated science and technology, i.e. modernity, with greater economic opportunities and sovereignty promoted the conversion to the 'scientific' rigor of Western music, with its rationalized notation, theory, and industrialized instrumental production. Having assimilated Western associations of classical music with bourgeois ideals of refinement and gentility, the expanding middle classes of the postwar era readily adopted the foreign music as a marker of social distinction. (2007: 3)

Classical music therefore made significant headway in the East Asian twentieth century off the back of complex geopolitical and geocultural dynamics. These dynamics were anchored in centuries of Western imperialism but given new force by the upheavals of the world wars, the breakdown (or, at least, serious transformation) of colonialism and the interlaced but divergent project of Asian modernisation. The latter, in particular, saw countries such as Japan and Korea striving to express sovereignty and expand economic opportunity through their cultural choices. As part of the latter, Western classical music served as a useful tool, delineating each country's membership of an international community of refined, sophisticated, rational, 'modern' nations. That this membership often came at the price of promoting local cultural traditions seems to have been a price worth paying for governments and cultural authorities who were keen to align with the global (consumerist) experience.

Conclusion

The global dissemination of once-local musics, and the growing cultural omnivory that was both cause and effect of that spread, led to many interesting twentieth-century cultural admixtures and adaptations. The popularity of American country music in Northern Ireland, the emergence of various forms of acculturated rap music in countries like Turkey and Morocco, the twentieth-century spread of Western classical music across East Asia: such examples make visible complex webs of transnational cultural dynamics that were increasingly the norm across the century. They also suggest ways in which typical (or, in some cases, stereotypical) earlier-century associations between particular musics and class positions, and between individuals and musical communities, had been transformed. Such associations of audience and music had not been completely left behind by the end of the century. Indeed, as we have seen, many musical audiences remained somewhat homogenous and predictable in character even in this late-century period. And yet, the easy, global circulation and consumption of music that we have been discussing clearly unsettled such associations in many cases making it extremely difficult to track the subtle shifts in musical value and cultural position that ricocheted around the musical world with such pace and energy in the last years of the century.

16 | Centres and Peripheries

The concept of the 'centre and periphery' was a key one in twentieth-century music and culture. It took many forms: 'mainstream and margins' or 'culture and counterculture' oppositions; more personal 'insider and outsider' dynamics; and spatial relationships between centres of cultural power and their peripheries. This chapter examines such centre-and-periphery dynamics from a number of angles, picking up threads of transnationalism, globalisation, mass and minority audiences and different forms of identity from previous chapters as it goes. It starts by tracking countercultures across the century, looking at the 1960s counterculture as a typical example in which competing values eventually become absorbed in the mainstream. The first case study surveys free jazz as a countercultural or marginal practice that either largely resisted or bypassed incorporation into the mainstream. The chapter then pivots to examine the insider and outsider dynamics inherent in noise music, where both aesthetic and social separation from the mainstream is prized as a core value. The second case study, on noise in Japan, extends and develops that discussion, examining the transnational dynamics that underpin even this obscure, marginal musical form. The chapter closes with a discussion of 'downtown' and 'uptown' music as a typical struggle between official and unofficial centres of musical power in the last decades of the century.

Culture/Countercultures across the Century

The twentieth century featured a number of countercultural movements, from the 1960s counterculture and its roots in 1950s Beat, folk and jazz scenes, right back to Dadaist and avant-garde artists active in the first half of the century. All of these movements were based in one way or another on an idea of generational liberation and upheaval. Greil Marcus' 'secret history' of the twentieth century, *Lipstick Traces* (1989), indeed suggests that 'spectral connections' between figures distant in time and place, from

381

Dadaist Walter Mehring and Johnny Rotten to Luis Buñuel and Bob Geldof, arch out the coordinates of a deep-rooted and widespread twentieth-century popular revolt. That revolt was built on 'absolute demands' which, for Marcus, served to 'breach the screen of received cultural assumptions'. These efforts to attack the centre from various different positions contributed, he argues, to a transformation of everyday life and, in turn, society (1989: 2–4). These popular-modernist-like transformations of social reality point to an omnipresent twentieth-century centre–periphery tension between massified, standardised urban life on the one hand and anti-mass-culture revolts on the other.

This tension played out in interesting ways across the century. By the 1950s, for example, those on the political left wing in the USA and across the West saw mass cultural products – pop music, TV, films, comics – as mere commodities that were intended to be consumed quickly and thoughtlessly. The 'trad' jazz movement and the folk revivals of the USA and Europe in the 1950s sat very much on that left wing, and therefore aspired to an 'authenticity' that mainstream mass culture did not seem to possess. In the UK, traditional jazz was often associated with the Campaign for Nuclear Disarmament, and New Orleans-style parade bands often accompanied protests and marches. In the USA, similarly, many folk revivalists were aligned with the Civil Rights Movement of the late 1950s and early 1960s; Joan Baez and Bob Dylan's famous performance at the March on Washington is just the most visible example of this connection between left politics and music.

However, things shifted during the 1960s when, as Phil Ford argues (2013), it became possible to articulate a politics of resistance to the mainstream *through* mass cultural forms. Dynamics of centre and periphery shift here, as mass forms themselves came to occupy a critical, peripheral position in relation to the cultural or political centre (though, of course, it could equally be argued that such mass forms comprised the centre as much as any government or state did). The advent of rock, whose musicians and critics each drew on paradigms of authenticity borrowed from folk music, played a particularly important role here. This was even though, as Keir Keightley writes, rock was a music born in the midst of commercial production and, unlike the intergenerational folk and traditional jazz scenes, was a youth music. 'These differences', Keightley argues,

crucially affected the way rock culture played out its folk-influenced world view, because they allowed rock to emerge in the simultaneous embrace of anti-mass ideology and mass commercial success. Raised on Top 40 and unafraid of popular success for select, authentic rock performers, the newborn rock culture featured a massive youth audience which saw itself, nonetheless, as opposed to the mass mainstream and all that stood for. (Keightley 2001: 122)

Alessandro Bratus' history of the 'underground' music press in the UK from 1966 to 1973 picks up on the conflicted nature of rock as a kind of nucleus of the broader 1960s counterculture, and as a resistant but populist form (2011). The late 1960s, Bratus suggests, saw this 'commercially oriented music [join] with the idea of an experimental and disruptive art, borrowed from contemporary avant-garde trends, in which artistic research was linked to the critique of mass society' (2011: 249). Indeed, alongside an avant-garde culture with which it shared a 'desire to break away from middle-class social conventions and offer a new approach to society as a whole' (228), rock at this time can be seen to have played a key countercultural role in a 'complex network in which art, politics, aesthetics, and ideology joined in the attack against the "system"' (248).

The 1960s counterculture in this sense crested a wave of postwar Western prosperity and related booms in technology, population and culture to effloresce supposedly new modes of living, thinking and creating. These spoke to a generational shift in attitudes to race and sex, recreation and procreation, such that liberation from the established cultural centre was suddenly on the table. Even if such promised liberation was in most cases either crushed or found to be counterfeit – to act as cover for merely redesigned inequalities based in misogyny, racism and class prejudice – the 1960s counterculture has endured as both a symbolic and real moment of cultural change. Richard Taruskin has gone so far as to describe the period as one in which 'sociostylistic categories' were 'blurred' and a 'new approach to society as a whole' was established (Taruskin 2005). The 'watershed years of the 1960s' (McClary 2000: 114), in this respect, can be seen to have generated new musical genres and new social mores that would go on to form the bedrock of Western youth culture for decades to come.

In describing the early years of the Grateful Dead in the San Francisco music scene of the 1960s, Sarah Hill gets at many of the key features of the counterculture (2015; though we should point out that key aspects such as the Civil Rights Movement are not covered at length in her analysis). The Grateful Dead, says Hill, 'grew organically out of the student and dropout populations in the Bay Area' and, 'like other contemporary Bay Area bands in the mid-1960s – Big Brother and the Holding Company, Jefferson Airplane, Country Joe and the Fish – in their formative years did not have a contract with a major record label'. Moreover, the Dead 'lived communally in a house at 710 Ashbury Street, in the Haight district of

San Francisco, and played innumerable free concerts for neighbors and friends' (2015: 3–4). It was, though, to be the group's participation in the infamous 'Acid Tests' of Ken Kesey and the Merry Pranksters, communal psychedelic gatherings based on the large-scale consumption of LSD (immortalised in Tom Wolfe's 1968 book *The Electric Kool-Aid Acid Test*), that exposed them to national and international audiences. It also ultimately both cemented their place at the centre of the counterculture and in turn helped create the wider image of that counterculture as a fundamentally psychedelic, collective and communal movement.

> The Grateful Dead became the de facto house band for the Acid Tests, and from that point onward their philosophy of performance – and their audience's experience of it – was informed by a kind of higher group consciousness … The Dead's live performances were deeply encoded with this psychedelic experience, this forward momentum into the unknown, and the audience's understanding of the musical, visual, and lyrical codes was aided by their own hallucinogenic consumption. (5)

As with all drug trips, however, the peak of the counterculture as a movement that could potentially radically shift established values and priorities while retaining its own radical edge – as approached here with the Grateful Dead's participation in the Acid Tests – was intense but brief. A coalescing of the movement indeed occurred across Europe and the USA with the Summer of Love in 1967 and the student protests and, in the US, the passing of the Fair Housing Act, in 1968. This coalescence or peak extended far beyond popular cultural contexts. Luciano Berio's dense, allusive 1968 composition *Sinfonia*, for example, has been seen as 'carrying the fresh-found voices of its world' (Griffiths 1996: 167). Ben Piekut's history of what he calls the 'mixed avant-garde' in London likewise speaks to the musical variety and freshness of music making in this period. Piekut demonstrates how the London scene played host to interactions and cross-contaminations of artists as diverse as Soft Machine, Spontaneous Music Ensemble, AMM, Sun Ra, Karlheinz Stockhausen and the Beatles (2014).

But these various high-water marks, with their sense that, according to Hunter S. Thompson, an 'inevitable victory over the forces of Old and Evil' beckoned (1998: 68), were not to last. As with many other initially radical cultural movements, the 1960s counterculture could not resist the allure of the economic and cultural centre, which found creative ways to incorporate and, in some ways, neuter the original liberatory political messages of the movement. Indeed, the example of San Francisco provides a useful illustration of this dynamic, with celebration turning sour as the rot of the late 1960s set in. Sarah Hill captures the speed of the San Francisco decline, where commercialism and dilution quickly and inevitably followed hot on the heels of initial waves of publicity and popularity:

By late 1966, the sense of vitality in the San Francisco Bay Area musical scene had already been the subject of exposés in the mainstream press; 'hippies' had entered the public consciousness; tour companies began to haul busloads of frightened out-of-towners through the Haight-Ashbury in search of flower children. In October 1967, the end of the Summer of Love, members of the head community staged a symbolic funeral for the hippie. (2015: 5)

In describing the rich but ultimately conflicted legacy of the underground papers he is writing about, Bratus in fact captures well the similarly rich but conflicted legacy of the 1960s counterculture as a whole, which sought and, in some cases, achieved significant change but yet can easily be placed in a long line of similarly compromised, similarly impure, twentieth-century 'countercultural' movements:

After 1968 had shown the success of youth-oriented expressive forms, their contents were progressively softened as their dissemination and the artistic pretentions that went along with them became generalized ... Paradoxically, and especially where popular music was concerned, the underground papers seem in the end to have been a vehicle for the definitive integration of the counterculture within the system of mainstream cultural production. In fact they came to act as agents in the accreditation of 'rock ideology'. (2011: 248–9)

As the 1960s counterculture was 'integrated' in this fashion, as materialist, Marxist or otherwise radical wings of the movement became neutered, the counterculture increasingly merged into the established cultural centre. Hippy music, fashion and lifestyle choices, as a result, became just one more consumer option within that culture. The liberatory freedom so promoted by the movement was therefore easily turned into an individual, market-based freedom to buy 'ethical' goods, use recreational drugs and have long hair, these countercultural signifiers now shorn of any real political or moral weight. In a similar way, the broader countercultural energies alluded to by Marcus above were likewise easily absorbed into the parade of images in consumer society. This was such that everything from punk to Dada to psychedelia ended up, by the end of the century, incorporated and commodified, another style to be consumed and sold in the global marketplace (Fisher 2009). This is not necessarily a problem in and of itself, though it would certainly be seen as one from the perspective of the original broad aims of the movement. And yet, as we will see in the next section, not all countercultural energy was able to be incorporated and commodified in this fashion.

Case Study 16.1: Free Jazz

In →Chapter 2, 'Modernism', we saw how bebop musicians and their supporters had begun in the 1940s to apply in earnest modernist ideas of technical innovation and progress to jazz. In the late 1950s, this understanding of the music grew to incorporate another modernist shibboleth, that of avant-gardism, and the idea of a music that might grow out of and away from the entertainment industry mainstream.

One of the leading figures of the new jazz avant-garde was the alto saxophonist (and later, trumpeter and violinist) Ornette Coleman (1930–2015). The titles of Coleman's early records show how his music was being positioned for an audience *au fait* with and attracted to the idea of avant-garde visual art and literature: *Tomorrow Is the Question* (Contemporary Records), *The Shape of Jazz to Come* and *Change of the Century* (both Atlantic) were all released in 1959. The 1960 album *Free Jazz* (Atlantic) gave its name to the new jazz style, in which standardised chord changes and regular pulse would often be disregarded. This album cover featured a painting by the abstract expressionist painter Jackson Pollock – by then famous for his 'drip paintings', of which this was one – making the associations with avant-garde visual art clear for potential record buyers (Figure 16.1).

- Ornette Coleman, 'Eventually', from *The Shape of Jazz to Come* (Atlantic, 1959)

Coleman's example helped suggest new directions for musicians like Sonny Rollins, Eric Dolphy and John Coltrane. As we have seen (→'Introduction'; Chapter 8, 'Instruments'), Coltrane in particular had become identified with a jazz attitude that was defined by its relentless search for new modes of expression, be they formal or instrumental; the cascading harmonies of *Giant Steps* (Atlantic, 1960) and the surging modality of *A Love Supreme* (Impulse!, 1965) would eventually be joined by the fully fledged free jazz heard on records like *Ascension* (Impulse!, 1966) and *Interstellar Space* (Impulse!, 1974 [rec. 1967]).

Figure 16.1 Ornette Coleman, *The Shape of Jazz to Come* (Atlantic, 1959), *Tomorrow Is the Question* (Contemporary, 1959), *Free Jazz* (Atlantic, 1960)

Case Study 16.1: (cont.)

- John Coltrane (1926–67), 'Leo' (from *Interstellar Space*, Impulse!, 1974 [rec. 1967])

It's easy to see why this music was framed by the American jazz press and recording industry as avant-garde: since it often did away with conventional tonal centres and treated musical parameters such as ensemble hierarchies or synchronicities with great flexibility, this jazz seemed to re-enact the kind of break that modernist / avant-garde composers had made from the tonal tradition. And just as that music had ignited debates as to the expected nature of the 'new' music's audience – a common-practice tonal tradition had served a popular audience, but any truly new music, it was often claimed, could appeal only to specialist initiates – so the jazz avant-garde emerged as jazz's status as a truly popular music was in the process of waning, and an idea of the music as a bona fide art form was in the ascendant (Lopes 2002).

But other free-jazz musicians and critics brought to their work an explicitly political angle. After all, this was the high point of the great Civil Rights Movement, and for many musicians and commentators, avant-garde jazz's technical developments in some way articulated that turbulent social experience; the notion of a 'free jazz' was especially resonant in a context in which Black people were also seeking full political freedom and autonomy.

In the late 1960s, the Civil Rights Movement – and African American political visibility, power, and action in general – had grown to such a level that the open resentment of white-owned businesses operating in Black communities could now be matched with numbers of organizations that strived to give Black America a greater economic autonomy. In as far as they can be said to have formed a community, African American jazz musicians were similarly economically indebted to the white record labels, promoters, club owners and media which gave an outlet to jazz music. Some jazz musicians began to demand booking agencies, concert venues and media exposure that would gain for them a degree of economic self-sufficiency (Wilmer 1999). In a famous article in *Down Beat* magazine in 1965, the saxophonist Archie Shepp – already a key figure in the free-jazz movement – wrote about what he saw as the position of Black jazz musicians in America, serious artists who were forced to work in nightclubs, which were according to Shepp 'crude stables where black men are run until they bleed, or else are hacked up outright for Lepage's glue' (cited in Perchard 2006: 93).

More polemics were provided by the members of the Black Arts Movement, a loose collective – like many avant-garde groups – of politically engaged African American writers, artists and musicians. One member, Ron Welburn, wrote that Black music was, again using a significant term, the 'vanguard' of 'black feeling', and 'the continuous repository of black consciousness' (Wellburn [*sic*] 1971: 132). Since music was a central 'site' for the definition and redefinition of a wider African American cultural identity, it was to be safeguarded at all costs. 'For the 1970s and beyond', wrote Welburn:

Case Study 16.1: (cont.)

the success of the political, economic and educational thrusts by the black community will depend on both an aesthetic that black artists formulate and the extent to which we are able to control our culture, and specifically our music, from theft and exploitation by aliens. . . . The degree to which we shape our music and *protect* it will dictate the full range and extent of our survival in the United States. (Wellburn [*sic*] 1971: 133)

Part of this protection meant 'sequestering' a Black music that held no similarity to Western art music's values, nor attraction to Western art music's audiences and practitioners. 'We must turn these [Western] values in on themselves', wrote the saxophonist and music theorist James Stewart, so that Black artists 'can not be "successful" in any sense that has meaning in white cultural evaluations' (Stewart 1968: 6). A system of 'Black' artistic values would, in this way, be protected from theft and exploitation by those 'aliens' to whom Black musicians invariably lost out, an embattled new centre working from the periphery 'in' to forge new models of belonging, creating and living.

- Albert Ayler (1936–70), 'Ghosts: First Variation', from *Spiritual Unity* (ESP Disk, 1964)
- Giuseppi Logan (1935–2020), 'Dance of Satan', from *The Giuseppi Logan Quartet* (ESP Disk, 1964)

It is important to note that these were critical positions elaborated by theorists of the music rather than its primary players, who – like Coleman and Coltrane – often spoke in rather different terms. Nevertheless, groups like Chicago's Association for the Advancement of Creative Musicians and New York City's Collective Black Artists (Perchard 2006) were established to clear these kinds of autonomous spaces. And this avant-garde music was often seen as sectioning itself off from a wider, philistine culture; once again the medium, and the technique, was the message, and opposition to one or other perceived centre the engine to drive that message forward.

The avant-garde imperatives of rejection and futurity remained here, but they were reshaped by local, particular race politics: what was rejected was still the widespread and commonplace ('white' participation in 'Black' musical forms), and the future to be embraced was still more authentic (Black music for Black people).

A great many critics attempted to interpret free jazz's importance in terms of a contemporary African American sociocultural situation, often with no little justification (see for instance Baraka 1998/1966). Even so, free jazz never came close to being the 'defining' Black American musical style, and many of its artists failed to find a large Black audience or to generate enough economic or commercial support to remove themselves from an American mainstream. This is, even if they would have wanted to – it is important not simply to conflate the aims of all these musicians with those of some polemical writers. By the early 1970s, in any case, the black avant-garde theorists' hope

Case Study 16.1: (cont.)

that free jazz would suddenly 'take' with a widely (and solely) Black audience had been shown to be wishful thinking. The music would, in this sense, remain something of a peripheral interest.

Indeed, by that time, jazz musicians of all stripes had been facing declining performance and recording opportunities for some years (both in the USA and elsewhere). In response, some began to work with rock and R & B styles, creating a marketable 'jazz fusion' genre. But others, knowingly or not, echoed Milton Babbitt's call for 'serious' music (➔Chapter 2, 'Modernism'): to resituate jazz within a mainstream institutional world and to gain for it some of the security that the Western art music tradition received from government subsidies and educational institutions. This call is ever-present in A. B. Spellman's classic study of the mid-1960s jazz scene, *Four Lives in the Bebop Business*. Spellman continually emphasises the 'cultivated' nature of the music he discusses; he argues that, gradually, '[j]azz's entertainment value has decreased as black artists have conscientiously moved out of the realm of folk art and into the realm of high art' (Spellman 1967: 215). Spellman quotes the saxophonist Jackie McLean's call for the music to receive state patronage because of it:

I think that the United States, to make up for what happened to Charlie Parker, and to make sure that there are no more Charlie Parkers – that is, no more geniuses going to waste like Charlie Parker did, should subsidize jazz. Jazz is the only true art form that this country has come up with, since the US certainly did not produce classical music nor any art form except jazz, and maybe the atomic bomb. This country should make sure that young musicians are paid. (Spellman 1967: 216)

In the 1970s, McLean, and a number of other jazz musicians associated with the free players of the 1960s, had in fact found employment in the university system, there constructing educational courses and controlling programming budgets that allowed their work to continue apart from the strictly commercial music world. These musicians had, albeit precariously, moved from an antagonistic, peripheral position, filled with ambitions of constructing a fresh new autonomous zone for Black musicians and Black audiences, to a position that enabled them to gain entry into mainstream and semi-mainstream cultural institutions. So went free jazz more generally, even if the radical, challenging core of the music meant that it could never be fully incorporated into the musical mainstream in the manner of other forms of 'heritage' jazz.

Music and Noise

Music's sonic and aesthetic parameters expanded radically in the twentieth century, as we saw in ➔Chapter 8, 'Instruments'. In *Noise/Music: A History*,

Paul Hegarty plots a similar historical narrative to the one covered in that chapter, with musicians from John Cage to the Stooges expanding the field of musical sound to incorporate non-traditional sound and noise (2007). But Hegarty eventually focuses on noise music itself, which serves as a kind of logical endpoint of that sonic expansion: 'all previous noise is there' (2007: ix). Noise music was influenced and inspired by a wide range of musics; notably, avant-garde rock and other forms of challenging music from the 1960s, including 'free' music from artists like AMM and Peter Brötzmann (b. 1941), the latter of whose spiky and threshing saxophone (as on 1968's *Machine Gun*, BRÖ) can itself be seen to pivot on the kind of sonic intensity later found in noise. The most direct and important influence on noise, however, was the power electronics and industrial music of the late-1970s and 1980s, from which the noise scene itself later grew. Out of these broad-based musical antecedents, noise music emerged as a stand-alone genre in Japan, the USA and Europe at some point in the late 1980s.

Noise music came out of and relied heavily upon a global nexus of marginal, alternative, independent cultural production. As we will see in more detail in the next section, everything from college radio stations in the USA to global snail-mail networks and the prominent international presence of Western culture would prove crucial in fostering such marginal scenes as noise. Indeed, noise music provides a fascinating example to consider within the broader context of centre and periphery, insider/outsider dynamics. After all, noise was based from the very beginning on a kind of self-conscious antagonism towards conventional music scenes. This is even as it relied on the institutional and cultural undergirding of those scenes' record shops, venues, music technologies (and so on) to survive. This outsider position and attitude – at a remove from but looking towards the centre – was (and indeed still is) absolutely central to the music's appeal. Noise audiences and musicians positioned themselves in this way at the edge of music scenes, their presence in even (most) specialist record shops and venues shadowy and transient at best. The music existed in this sense at the 'edge of circulation', to paraphrase David Novak (2013), leeching off, but happily distant from, established scenes and networks. Similarly, noise music rejected mainstream musical norms. Many key noise artists' embrace of transgressive subject matter, for example – which included everything from autopsy videos to Nazi imagery to overt themes of sexual abuse and perversion Chapter 13, 'Gender and Sexuality' – marked the scene out as taboo-busting and extreme. Musical style itself was likewise a marker of extremity. Noise musicians used static, feedback, distortion and various forms of found and abstracted sound as self-sufficient expressive resources. A prominent 'harsh' noise (one of the main subgenres of noise) album such as Macronympha's *Pittsburgh, Pennsylvania* (Praxis Dr. Bearmann, 1995), for example, consists of forty minutes of chaotic and intense gurgle, bang and rumble, these sounds produced by playing scrap metal with contact mics and processing the results through rudimentary mixers and effects pedals. British artists Smell and Quim, for a contrasting but related example, created dense and unpredictable sound collages that mix together lewd (and funny) sexual imagery, scrappy loops, banal drum patterns, everyday sounds and more into absurdly unwieldy noise performance art.

- Macronympha, *Pittsburgh, Pennsylvania* (Praxis Dr. Bearmann, 1995)
- Smell and Quim, *The English Method* (Stinky Horse Fuck, 1988)

Many other noise acts from this 'classic' 1980s and 1990s period, from Grunt in Finland to Black Leather Jesus in the USA to Monde Bruits in Japan, likewise made music in which recognisable patterns of hook or theme, melody, form and even volume were sidelined. Leading noise artist, Crawl Unit (Joe Colley), describes his own approach to noise at this time (and beyond) as one in which he aimed for a 'sense of instability', where the sound behaves as if it's going to 'eat itself' and the listener feels like the ground is 'crumbling beneath [their] feet' (Colley in Connelly and Mike 2020), a description that can stand in for a lot of noise in the late-century period. Paul Hegarty, for his part, suggests that in its constant undermining of stable gesture, pattern and form, noise music fundamentally asked and asks what he calls the 'question of genre–what does it mean to be categorized, categorizable, definable?' (2007: 133).

Noise music can be seen in all its extremities as a key representative of the gradual, late-century emergence of an international scene of avant-garde, exploratory music and art that was not based in or tied to institutional 'high' art. It was not, in other words, reliant on public subsidy or public infrastructure such as large arts venues and companies, or well-established institutions such as music conservatoires and university music departments and studios. Noise sat and sits alongside related but discrete musics in this emergent international scene, from extreme metal to free improv, experimental techno to fringe composition (Graham 2016). All of these musics were, and continue to be, positioned somewhere outside or between the structuring centres of art and popular musics, inaccessible to mainstream audiences but also antipathetic in one or other respect to established, 'high' cultural institutions. On the one hand, they therefore represented a kind of fluid transcultural network creatively exploiting the force field of resources projected outwards by subsidised and/or popular music, from technologies to funding, listeners to venues. They used these resources to carve out alternative physical and virtual spaces on the peripheries of established traditions. On the other hand, this emergent international scene represented its own kind of 'inside', its own centre of gravity, where uniquely modern patterns of cross- and intercultural exchange generated niche, often marginal centres of musical production and consumption. These peripheral, marginal 'centres' achieved small but self-sufficient identity amid globally flowing mainstream culture.

Case Study 16.2: Japanese Noise Music on the Global Periphery

This kind of marginal or peripheral self-sufficiency characterises the thriving Japanese noise music scene that emerged during the 1980s and 1990s (with important antecedents in the 1970s). This scene, known colloquially by Western audiences as 'Japanoise', built on what was by then a well-established local tradition of Western-influenced experimental, jazz and popular music making. Based on the growing importance and presence of Western culture in Japan in the second half of the century (Chapter 15, 'Audiences, Class and Consumption', such transnationally shaped music making was embodied in Japan in this period in everyone from experimental improv acts such as Group Ongaku to free-jazz musicians like Motoharu Yoshizawa and experimental rockers Les Rallizes Dénudés and Taj Mahal Travellers. The noise scene was no different, with tools, techniques and styles all deriving in whole or part from Western avant-garde and popular forms of music and culture.

Centring initially around Osaka-based musicians, record shops and labels (especially Jojo Hiroshige's Alchemy Records), the Japanese noise scene started getting local and then international recognition via performance-art-influenced, noise or noise-rock Osaka acts in the 1980s such as Hanatarash, Solmania, Masonna, Hijokaidan and Incapacitants. These acts existed alongside contemporary Tokyo groups and artists such as Nord, Ghost and Fushitsusha, among whom a pronounced psychedelic, even Krautrock sound could be detected. This is not even to mention the talismanic Tokyo figure of Merzbow (Masami Akita, b. 1956, with collaborators along the way), whose early style ranged across noise, free jazz and electronics.

In terms of musical style, the Osaka acts were mostly based on a seemingly traditional rock line-up of guitars, drums and vocalists. But such traditional elements were invariably turned to extreme and/or unusual ends. For example, Hijokaidan's 1985 album, *King of Noise* (Alchemy Records), is comprised almost exclusively of detuned, highly distorted and wild guitar playing; agonising, scorching screaming; clattering, unmetered drums; and smeared theremin and analogue-synth sounds. Hanatarash, for their part, overlaid drills, saws and other power tools on to wild guitar and drums, echoing similar tactics in contemporary European and American noise acts such as the

Case Study 16.2: (cont.)

Figure 16.2 Hijokaidan live in 1981

New Blockaders and the Haters. Solmania became known for their use of modified and mangled guitars in the context of churning, clattering harsh noise. Both Hanatarash and Hijokaidan, moreover, turned live shows into confrontational performance art, the former regularly featuring mutilation and venue destruction, and the latter using nudity, urination and defecation as part of their all-out visual and musical live assault.

- Hijokaidan, *King of Noise* (Alchemy Records, 1985)
- Hanatarash, *Take Back Your Penis!!* (Condome Cassex, 1984)
- Solmania, *Vexation* (Fatagaga Tapes, 1985)

   From these confrontational beginnings anchored in punk, free-jazz and performance-art aesthetics, Japanese noise evolved throughout the late 1980s and 1990s into a musically diverse set of practices spread across Osaka, Tokyo, Kyoto and other parts of the country. And yet, this broad Japanese noise scene was united by its particular emphasis on musical and performative extremity and harshness. For Adam Potts, indeed, the scene embodied 'a sonic excess that overflows the form and contours of music ordinarily understood'. 'Japanoise', Potts goes on, in an echo of Hegarty's point above about genre, 'aestheticises excess in such a way that the possibility of it being a type of music is wagered . . . Japanoise wills a world of formlessness and pure chaos, away from the material world of bodies, meaning and formation' (2015: 379–80). Similarly, as Hegarty suggests when attempting

Case Study 16.2: (cont.)

to describe Merzbow's music, 'it is impossible to avoid a vocabulary based on excessiveness, extremity and harshness' (2007: 155).

In addition to extremity and harshness, a very particular approach to sound sources and quality likewise united Japanese noise across the 1980s and 1990s. Japanese noise artists at this time, in partial contrast to the somewhat dirtier American sounds heard in acts such as Macronympha and Black Leather Jesus, indeed tended to base their work in comparatively 'cleaner' sound sources and tools. For instance, both Government Alpha and MSBR, two key Tokyo 'pedal noise' artists from the 1990s, made extensive use of internal system feedback as a sound source, where a closed loop or 'chain' of sound mixer and effects pedals created squealing, trebly system feedback that would then be filtered and otherwise manipulated. Set-ups like this, alongside the modular synths favoured by acts like Merzbow or the more traditional line-ups of groups like Hijokaidan above were perfectly placed to generate sounds of extremity, harshness and sonic dexterity such as came to characterise the scene in this period. We can indeed hear all three qualities running through the chaotic noise beats of Merzbow's run of high-impact 1990s' albums, the wide dynamic and textural range of MSBR's work, the electrical storms found on releases by Masonna and the sustained and burning feedback intensity of a group like C. C. C.

- Merzbow, *Venereology* (Relapse, 1994)
- MSBR, *Ultimate Ambience* (MSBR Records, 1992)
- Masonna, *Spectrum Ripper* (Cold Spring, 1997)
- C. C. C. C., *Love and Noise* (Endorphine Factory, 1996)

Japanese noise gained notoriety, and indeed achieved profound influence on the worldwide noise scene at this time, partially as a result of its particular sonic character. However, its influence also crucially depended on various non-musical factors; most particularly, on the late-century emergence of new mechanisms of transnational exchange such as radio, television, international mail networks and so on. Special-interest record shops, zines and various other marginal media in this way allowed the global periphery of noise to form connections and build networks beyond what would have been feasible only one or two generations previously. Indeed, the very identity and existence of these scenes was in some very real senses made possible by these new global connections. Small noise scenes in places like Japan, Europe and America thus attained a new kind of international visibility through transnational networks of independent distribution. Such networks were born out of both local patterns of taste and activity and broader historical relationships, cultural kinships and material partnerships. For example, the robust economic and cultural associations that had developed by the 1970s between North America and Europe on one side and Japan on

Case Study 16.2: (cont.)

the other meant not only that emerging Japanese noise musicians were heavily and directly influenced by earlier Western styles and artists but also that such Japanese noise music was easily channelled into the fabric of the international scene via American and European independent record stores, radio stations and zines. David Novak expands on this point, showing for example not only how much of an impact Japanese noise music made on the American fringe and alternative scene in the 1980s and 1990s, but also how vital that impact was to the growth of the music back in Japan:

By the early 1990s, recordings by [Japanese noise artists] Hijokaidan, Incapacitants, C. C. C. C., Solmania, Masonna, Monde Bruits, Astro, Aube, Government Alpha, Pain Jerk, K. K. Null, k2, msbr, Geriogerigegege, Violent Onsen Geisha, and Merzbow had swept into North American reception. College radio stations and independent record stores circulated releases from Osaka's Alchemy, Public Bath, Japan Overseas, and New York's Shimmy Disc and Tzadik labels. Underground fanzines like San Francisco–based Mason Jones's Ongaku Otaku informed fans of the archetypal examples of Noise and helped them assemble a rudimentary map of its generic boundaries in Japan. North American tours, especially by Merzbow and Masonna in the mid-1990s, allowed select fans to experience Japanese Noise live and relate legendary stories for those who missed the chance. It was increasingly possible to talk about a 'Japanese Noise scene', and maybe even see some of its representatives in live performance. By the time I really began to tune into what was going on, the layers of feedback from North American reception had already shifted the ground for Japanese musicians. (2013: 11)

The transnational exchanges described by Novak here were crucial in the development of the wider international noise scene. This is evident in the strong presence Japanese noise artists had in the American and European scenes, with leading zines such as the USA-based Bananafish devoting extensive coverage to them; at the same time, various key American and European artists, from the Haters to Smegma, Lasse Marhaug to Speculum Fight, recorded split releases with Japanese artists, toured in Japan or released music by Japanese artists (or did all three). *The Japanese/American Noise Treaty*, an album released on Relapse Records in 1995 that collected together many leading Japanese and American noise artists, is merely the most literal embodiment of a relationship that was pivotal to noise music at this time. Indeed, in a more general respect Novak goes as far as to suggest that 'any story of Noise must account for the transnational circuitry of its subjects ... It was exchanged as an object of transnational musical circulation that touched down in particular places and eventually came to be imagined as a global music scene' (2013: 15 and 5).

What is striking about the example of Japanese noise, and indeed other examples of fringe music on the global periphery, is the way it could exploit those international relationships and channels while staying very much outside centres of culture and

Case Study 16.2: (cont.)

power. As Novak also suggests, on this point, noise was after all ultimately based on the 'dogged pursuit of antisocial, anti-historical, antimusical obscurity' (2013: 15). It was, in this sense, a fringe interest defined by distance from the mainstream in terms of both commercial appeal and musical language. And it very much wanted to remain so. Periphery here, therefore, very much benefitted from centre, using established international networks to form its own international webs of exchange and relationship and in this way to build its own archipelago of marginal centres, while at the same time remaining self-consciously distinct from it.

Downtown and Uptown

'Downtown' describes a kind of non-institutional, collectivist, DIY, stylistically varied approach to culture making, which is often, though not always, based in literal downtown locales physically separated from more official, 'uptown' centres of power. Partly born out of both the 1960s counterculture and the broader twentieth-century popular revolt discussed earlier in this chapter, such an attitude expressed itself in New York across a scene that flowered mostly in the 1960s–1980s, in which low rents and a concentration of young artists inspired a vibrant, cross-media set of cultural practices spreading across small galleries, lofts, bars and clubs (Gann 2006; Masters 2008). In music, this saw the gradual development of experimental, disco and no-wave music scenes in lofts and, later, clubs and venues across the city; notably, lofts such as those of Yoko Ono and La Monte Young, clubs such as The Loft and venues such as The Kitchen and the Mudd Club.

'These downtown sounds', writes Tim Lawrence in addressing the emblematic significance of downtown composer-musician-producer Arthur Russell,

> didn't exist as a series of discrete scenes but instead began to meet and blend until downtown resembled a mashed-up jukebox of illegitimate fusions. Revealing the way downtown New York came to function as a space of explorative flows, Russell's blurry movements between pop, rock, folk, dance, hip hop and orchestral music did indeed resonate more widely still ... his biography could help articulate the contours of a dynamic network: downtown New York during the 1970s and 1980s. (2009: xviii)

Lawrence provides a vivid image here of the kind of peripheral, 'borderline aesthetic' described by Bernard Gendron in *Between Montmarte and the*

Mudd Club. Gendron sees such an aesthetic as a 'symmetrical practice of merger and synthesis', where different downtown musicians, video and fine artists and others worked so comfortably across traditions or centres as to transcend them (2002: 310). In this image, musicians and audiences male and female, Black and white, gay and straight, experimental and popular were thrown together in such a way as to create exciting new genres, relationships and even identities. Gendron mentions the distinctive blend of micro and macro patterns in the downtown guitar music of Glenn Branca (1948–2018) and Rhys Chatham (b. 1952) as an example of such new genres. Branca and Chatham's music was based on a hyper-classical structuration of sound that yet, in its loud and heavy realization, accessed key components of rock, such as a trance-inducing sensation and feel. Branca and Chatham pieces such as the former's *The Ascension* (1980) and the latter's *Drastic Classicism* (1982) presented in this way a kind of 'seamless synthesis of classical and rock', an uncompromising borderline music that even 'erases the borderline' in its organic inhabiting and blending of different traditions (295).

Even if the image of racial and social harmony presented above is evidently an idealistic one – it is notable how white and indeed male the downtown scene was, beyond a few individual exceptions and outside disco's radical commingling of different sexualities and ethnicities – similar musical and cultural blends can be found across the broader downtown scene. Keith Potter, quoting John Rockwell, argues in this spirit that in this

> new version of the 'happy babble of overlapping dialogues – not just cultivated and vernacular, but European and American, white and black, male and female, East Coast and West Coast, Occidental and Oriental' … this 'downtown' community offered much more than radical art practice spiced with the *frisson* easily gained via a few 'vernacular' borrowings. (2000: 18)

Downtown music, in this understanding, came to embody a potent post-modern settlement, where geographical proximity, shared cultural circumstances and blurring cultural boundaries led to unprecedented mixes of people and musics. This was such, according to this line, that the very concept of a stable musical centre with peripheral styles orbiting around it was superseded by a more fluid sense of genre and musical allegiance.

The 'no-wave' wing of the scene provided a particularly interesting example of such cultural blending. For Gendron, no wave's explosion of new-wave pop sensibilities in an avant-garde melange of noisy guitar distortion, thwacking drums and screamed vocals represented a 'true art/pop fusion'. And yet such fusion, such 'aesthetic in-betweenness' (2002: 278), centred on hostile, modernist negation rather than positive conciliation. And it's as much in this dynamic of rejection and self-differentiation as in a notion of happily babbling social equanimity that the truth of downtown culture lay. No wave, for its part, indeed rested on a *double* rejection, first of what Simon Reynolds has called the 'rama-lama riffing or bluesy chords' of Chuck Berry-loving punk (2005: xvii), and second of the cleaner, more commercially orientated sounds of new wave. No wave's characteristic rejection, its 'no', was expressed as much in the confrontational performances of key figures such as Lydia Lunch (b. 1959) as it was in the scraping, sliding dissonances of bands like Lunch's Teenage Jesus and the Jerks. The musical simplicity and accessibility of punk indeed became corrosion in the hands of the no wavers, punk's political burden in this way being expanded from visual imagery and agitprop verbal testimony to the realm of aesthetics too. This point is vividly illustrated by the two main streams of no-wave style: first, the thumping, brutally basic sound of Teenage Jesus songs such as 'The Closet' (from *No New York*, Antilles, 1978) or the noise-chaos of Mars' clattering, clanging 'N. N. End' (1980, later released on *Mars Archive Volume Three: N. N. End*, Negative Glam, 2019), and, second, the gangly, jerky, sharp angles of songs like D. N. A.'s wild 'New Fast' (from *A Taste of DNA*, Rough Trade, 1981) or the Contortion's crunchy, sprung 'Contort Yourself' (from *Buy*, Ariola, 1979). Each of these styles, grimy thump on one hand and springy judder on the other, can be heard as portals into the kind of pulverising, uncompromising popular modernism alluded to by Fisher (2014b; Graham 2019), where, to echo Gendron, unprecedented mixes of avant-garde and pop sensibilities were in evidence.

But for all this talk of overlaps and fusion, notable differences clearly persisted both within the downtown scene and more generally in New York music. Comparing downtown with so-called 'uptown' and 'midtown' music provides a nice illustration of such tensions. Kyle Gann suggests on this note that 'for years, downtown composers ferreted out a middle way; how to make music intelligent without being elitist, fun without being stupid or conventional, and socially relevant but still universal' (2006: 103). By contrast, uptown composers such as Milton Babbitt and Roger Sessions represented 'the musical culture of academia, with its own concerts, stable of expert performers, and well-funded support system' (2006: 3; see also McClary 1989). Between these two, Gann locates 'midtown' composers such as Joan Tower and John Corigliano, whose tuneful, quasi-romantic music came to occupy a stable institutional position, patronised by venues such as the Lincoln Center and backed by establishments such as the Juilliard School.

We can see a complex layering of multiple centres and peripheries in this example. On the one hand, downtown figures like Branca, Chatham, Lunch and Arthur Russell existed outside more stable midtown and uptown institutions such as the Lincoln Center and university departments. On the other hand, such downtown figures stood at something of a distance from the commercial music world around them. Although downtown music in this sense was 'a deliberate rejection of uptown elitism', at the same time it shared some clear parallels with it nonetheless: 'what downtown composers admired in and shared with uptown ones was the felt necessity to flee from mass culture' (Gann 2006: 4). Indeed, even disco and other forms of commercial music that were fomented at least in part on the downtown scene separated themselves as subcultural phenomena from the cultural mores of mainstream, 'straight' society. Looked at every which way, downtown music was engaged in a series of stand-offs and antagonisms both with itself and with external forms of music. Subtle or small differences between practices – differences that actually may not have been all that different when looked at from the outside – provided a degree of self-definition and oppositional energy that could lift up these musicians and musical forms and give them the momentum to keep going.

Conclusion

The complex self-positioning of different musics on the downtown scene injected that scene with great energy, its motley crew of outsiders and experimenters united around a shared purpose of separation from mainstream commercial and cultural centres. That many downtown musicians, from Phillip Glass to John Zorn, would later gain at least a degree of 'official' acceptance simply emphasises the importance of ever-changing centre–periphery dynamics in the development of twentieth-century music scenes and musician. Indeed, such struggles between a marginal, oppositional 'us' and a dominating, all-powerful (or at least all-wrong) 'them' defined much musical activity across the century, where the human compulsion to define oneself against others, to pit one's choices against enemies or foes real or imagined, serious or fun, was as widespread as it was anywhere else.

Bibliography

Abbate, Carolyn. (1998). Debussy's Phantom Sounds. *Cambridge Opera Journal*, 10, no. 1, 67–96.

Abbate, Carolyn. (2004). Music – Drastic or Gnostic? *Critical Enquiry*, 30, no. 4, 505–36.

Abbott, Lynn. (1992). 'Play That Barber Shop Chord': A Case for the African-American Origin of Barbershop Harmony. *American Music*, 10, no. 3, 289–325.

Abbott, Lynn and Doug Seroff. (1996). 'They Cert'ly Sound Good to Me': Sheet Music, Southern Vaudeville, and the Commercial Ascendancy of the Blues. *American Music*, 14, no. 4, 402–54.

Abramović, Marina and Klaus Biesenbach. (2010). *Marina Abramović: The Artist Is Present*. New York: MoMA.

Adlington, Robert. (2005). Music Theatre Since the 1960s. In M. Cooke, ed., *The Cambridge Companion to Twentieth-Century Opera*. Cambridge: Cambridge University Press, 225–43.

Adorno, Theodor W. (1941). On Popular Music. *Studies in Philosophy and Social Science*, 11, no. 1, 17–48.

Adorno, Theodor W. (2002/1934). The Form of the Phonograph Record. In T. Adorno, *Essays on Music: Theodor W. Adorno*, ed. R. Leppert. Berkeley and Los Angeles: University of California Press, 277–82.

Adorno, Theodor W. (2002/1969). Opera and the Long-Playing Record. In T. Adorno, *Essays on Music: Theodor W. Adorno*, ed. R. Leppert. Berkeley and Los Angeles: University of California Press, 283–7.

Adorno, Theodor W. (2019/1949). *Philosophy of New Music*. Minneapolis: University of Minnesota Press.

Adorno, Theodor W. and Eisler, Hanns. (1947). *Composing for the Films*. New York: Oxford University Press.

Adorno, Theodor W. (2019/1949). *Philosophy of New Music*. Ed. and trans. Robert Hullot-Kentor. Minneapolis: University of Minnesota Press.

Adorno, Theodor W. (1938/1991a). On the Fetish Character in Music and the Regression of Listening. In Theodor W. Adorno, *The Culture Industry: Selected Essays on Mass Culture*. London: Routledge, 26–52.

Adorno, Theodor W. (1991b). The Schema of Mass Culture. In Theodor W. Adorno, *The Culture Industry: Selected Essays on Mass Culture*. London: Routledge, 53–84.

Adorno, Theodor W. (2007/1947). *The Philosophy of Modern Music*. New York: Continuum.

Agawu, Kofi. (1991). *Playing with Signs: A Semiotic Interpretation of Classic Music.* Princeton, NJ: Princeton University Press.

Agawu, Kofi. (1995). The Invention of 'African Rhythm'. *Journal of the American Musicological Society*, 48, no. 3, 380–95.

Albright, Daniel. (2015). *Putting Modernism Together: Literature, Music, and Painting 1872–1927.* Baltimore, MD: Johns Hopkins Press.

Allen, Ray and Ellie Hisama. (2007). *Ruth Crawford Seeger's Worlds: Innovation and Tradition in Twentieth-Century American Music.* Rochester, NY: University of Rochester Press.

Anderson, Ian. (2000). World Music History. In *fRoots* 201 (March), https://frootsmag.com/world-music-history, accessed 16 June 2019.

Anderson, Paul Allen. (2001). *Deep River: Music and Memory in Harlem Renaissance Thought.* Durham, NC: Duke University Press.

Anderson, Virginia. (2009). Comfy Cushions and Golden Grandiosi: Instruments of British Experimentalism. *The Galpin Society Journal*, 62, 273–86.

Andersson, Åke E. and David Andersson. (2006). *The Economics of Experiences, the Arts and Entertainment.* Cheltenham: Edward Elgar Publishing.

Ansari, Emily Abrams. (2011). Aaron Copland and the Politics of Cultural Diplomacy. *Journal of the Society for American Music*, 5, no. 3, 335–64.

Antokoletz, Elliott. (1984). *The Music of Béla Bartók: A Study of Tonality and Progression in Twentieth-Century Music.* Berkeley and Los Angeles: University of California Press.

Appadurai, Arjun. (1990). Disjuncture and Difference in the Global Cultural Economy. *Public Culture*, 2, no. 2, 1–24.

Appen, Ralf von and André Doehring. (2006). Nevermind the Beatles, Here's Exile 61 and Nico: 'The Top 100 Records of All Time': A Canon of Pop and Rock Albums from a Sociological and an Aesthetic Perspective. *Popular Music*, 25, no. 1, 21–39.

Applegate, Celia. (2005). Beyond 1829: Musical Culture, National Culture. In Celia Applegate, *Bach in Berlin: Nation and Culture in Mendelssohn's Revival of the 'St. Matthew Passion'.* Ithaca, NY and London: Cornell University Press, 234–64.

Armstrong, Louis. (1999/1936). What Is Swing? In Robert Walser, ed., *Keeping Time: Readings in Jazz History.* New York: Oxford University Press, 73–6.

Attali, Jacques. (1985). *Noise: The Political Economy of Music.* Trans. Brian Massumi. Manchester: Manchester University Press.

Auner, Joseph. (2003). 'Sing It for Me': Posthuman Ventriloquism in Recent Popular Music. *Journal of the Royal Musical Association*, 128, no. 1, 98–122.

Averill, Gage. (1999). Bell Tones and Ringing Chords: Sense and Sensation in Barbershop Harmony. *The World of Music*, 41, no. 1, 37–51.

Babbitt, Milton. (1998/1958). Who Cares If You Listen? In Robert Morgan, ed., *Source Readings in Music History.* New York and London: W. W. Norton & Co., 35–41.

Baily, John. (2009). Music and Censorship in Afghanistan, 1973–2003. In Laudan Nooshin, ed., *Music and the Play of Power: Music, Politics and Ideology in the Middle East, North Africa and Central Asia*. Aldershot: Ashgate, 143–63.

Baily, John. (2015). *War, Exile and the Music of Afghanistan*. Farnham: Ashgate.

Balliett, Whitney. (1976). Bird: The Brilliance of Charlie Parker. *The New Yorker*, 1 March. www.newyorker.com/magazine/1976,03/01/bird-whitney-balliett.

Banat, Gabriel. (2006). *The Chevalier de Saint-Georges: Virtuoso of the Sword and the Bow*. Hillsdale, NY: Pendragon Press.

Bannister, Matthew. (2006a). 'Loaded': Indie Guitar Rock, Canonism, White Masculinities. *Popular Music*, 25, no. 1, 77–95.

Bannister, Matthew. (2006b). *White Boys, White Noise: Masculinities and 1980s Indie Guitar Rock*. Farnham: Ashgate.

Baraka, Amiri [Le Roi Jones]. (1998/1966). The Changing Same (R&B and New Black Music). In Amiri Baraka, *Black Music*. New York: Da Capo Press, 180–211.

Baraka, Amiri [Le Roi Jones]. (1999/1963). *Blues People: Negro Music in White America*. New York: William Morrow.

Barrow, Steve. (1994). Dub Gone Crazy/Liner Notes). *Dub Gone Crazy: The Evolution of Dub at King Tubby's 1975–1979* (Audio recording). Blood and Fire (BAFCD 002).

Barrow, Steve and Peter Dalton. (1997). *Reggae: The Rough Guide*. London: Rough Guides.

Barry, Malcolm. (1989). Ideology and Form: Shostakovich East and West. *Music and the Politics of Culture*, ed. Christopher Norris. London: Lawrence & Wishart, 172–86.

Barthes, Roland. (1977/1967). The Death of the Author. In Roland Barthes, *Image, Music, Text*, ed. and trans. Stephen Heath. London: Fontana Press, 142–8.

Bataille, George. (1986/1957). *Erotism: Death and Sensuality*. Trans. Mary Dalwood. San Francisco: City Lights Publisher.

Baudrillard, Jean. (1994/1981). *Simulacra and Simulation*. Ann Arbor: University of Michigan Press.

Bayton, Mavis. (2006). Women Making Music: Some Material Constraints. In Andy Bennett, Barry Shank and Jason Toynbee, eds., *The Popular Music Studies Reader*. New York: Routledge, 347–54.

Beal, Amy. (2006). *New Music, New Allies: American Experimental Music in West Germany from the Zero Hour to Reunification*. Berkeley and Los Angeles: University of California Press.

Becker, Howard S. (2008/1982). *Art Worlds*. Berkeley and Los Angeles: University of California Press.

Bell, Adam Patrick. (2018). *Dawn of the DAW: The Studio As Musical Instrument*. Oxford: Oxford University Press.

Benjamin, Walter. (1999/1936). The Work of Art in the Age of Mechanical Reproduction. In Walter Benjamin, *Illuminations*. London: Pimlico, 211–44.

Benjamin, Walter. (1999/1939). On Some Motifs in Baudelaire. In Walter Benjamin, *Illuminations*, ed. Harry Zohn. London: Pimlico, 152–96.

Benjamin, Walter and Theodor Adorno. (1999). *The Complete Correspondence 1928–1940.* Trans. Nicholas Walker. Cambridge: Polity Press.

Bennett, Andy. (2006). Introduction to Part Three. In Andy Bennett, Barry Shank and Jason Toynbee, eds., *The Popular Music Studies Reader.* New York: Routledge. 95–7.

Bennett, Andy. (2009). 'Heritage Rock': Rock Music, Representation and Heritage Discourse. *Poetics*, 37, nos. 5–6, 474–89.

Bennett, Andy. (2015). Popular Music and the 'Problem' of Heritage. In S. Cohen, R. Knifton, M. Leonard and L. Roberts, eds., *Sites of Popular Music Heritage: Memories, Histories, Places.* New York: Routledge, 15–27.

Bennett, Andy and Steve Baker. (2010). Classic Albums: The Re-presentation of the Rock Album on British Television. In I. Inglis, ed., *Popular Music on British Television.* Aldershot: Ashgate, 41–54.

Bennett, Andy and Jon Stratton, eds. (2010). *Britpop and the English Music Tradition.* Farnham: Ashgate.

Berger, Karol. (2014). The Ends of Music History, or: The Old Masters in the Supermarket of Cultures. *The Journal of Musicology*, 31, no. 2, 186–98.

Bergeron, Katherine and Philip V. Bohlman, eds. (1996). *Disciplining Music: Musicology and Its Canons.* Chicago: University of Chicago Press.

Berish, Andrew. (2009). Negotiating 'A Blues Riff': Listening for Django Reinhardt's Place in American Jazz. *Jazz Perspectives*, 3, no. 3, 233–64.

Berliner, Paul F. (1994). *Thinking in Jazz: The Infinite Art of Improvisation.* Chicago: University of Chicago Press.

Berman, Marshall. (1982). *All That Is Solid Melts into Air.* London: Verso.

Bernard, Jonathan. (1986). Messiaen's Synaesthesia: The Correspondence between Color and Sound Structure in His Music. *Music Perception* 4, no. 1, 41–68.

Bernstein, David. (2002). Cage and High Modernism. In David Nicholls, ed., *The Cambridge Companion to John Cage.* Cambridge: Cambridge University Press, 186–213.

Bernstein, David. (2008). *The San Francisco Tape Music Center: 1960s Counterculture and the Avant-Garde.* Berkeley and Los Angeles: University of California Press.

Berríos-Miranda, Marisol. (2002). Is Salsa a Musical Genre? In Lise Waxer, ed., *Situating Salsa: Global Markets and Local Meanings in Latin Popular Music.* New York and London: Routledge, 23–50.

Bettig, Ronald V. (1996). *Copyrighting Culture: The Political Economy of Intellectual Property.* Boulder, CO: Westview.

Biamonte, Nicole. (2014). Formal Functions of Metric Dissonance in Rock Music. *Music Theory Online.* 20 no. 2, 1–19.

Bijsterveld, Karin. (2008). *Mechanical Sound: Technology, Culture and Public Problems of Noise in the Twentieth Century.* Cambridge, MA: The MIT Press.

Binkiewicz, Donna M. (2004). *Federalizing the Muse: United States Art Policy and the National Endowment for the Arts 1965–(1980).* Chapel Hill: University of North Carolina Press.

Björnberg, Alf. (2009). Learning to Listen to Perfect Sound: Hi-Fi Culture and Changes in Modes of Listening, 1950–80. In D. Scott, ed., *The Ashgate Research Companion to Popular Musicology*. Farnham: Ashgate Publishing, 105–30.

Björnberg, Alf. (1989/1984). *On Aeolian Harmony in Contemporary Popular Music*. Nordic IASPM Working Paper DK1.

Bloechl, Olivia. (2005). Orientalism and Hyperreality in 'Desert Rose'. *Journal of Popular Music Studies*, 17, no. 2, 133–61.

Bloom, Allan. (1987). *The Closing of the American Mind*. New York: Simon and Schuster.

Bloom, Harold. (1994). *The Western Canon: The Books and School of the Ages*. New York: Harcourt Brace & Company.

Bloom, Harold. (1997). *The Anxiety of Influence: A Theory of Poetry*. 2nd ed. New York: Oxford University Press.

Bodman Rae, Charles. (1994). *The Music of Lutosławski*. London: Faber.

Bohlman, Philip V. (1992a). Epilogue: Musics and Canons. In K. Bergeron and P. Bohlman, eds., *Disciplining Music: Musicology and Its Canons*. Chicago and London: University of Chicago Press, 197–201.

Bohlman, Philip V. (1992b). Ethnomusicology's Challenge to the Canon: the Canon's Challenge to Ethnomusicology. In K. Bergeron, and P. Bohlman, eds., *Disciplining Music: Musicology and Its Canons*. Chicago and London: University of Chicago Press, 116–36.

Bohlman, Philip V. (1998). *The Study of Folk Music in the Modern World*. Bloomington: Indiana University Press.

Bohlman, Philip V. (2002). *World Music: A Very Short Introduction*. Oxford: Oxford University Press.

Bohlman, Philip V. (2004). *The Music of European Nationalism: Cultural Identity and Modern History*. Santa Barbara, CA: ABC-CLIO.

Bohlman, Philip V. (2008). *Jewish Music and Modernity*. New York: Oxford University Press.

Boilen, Bob and Robin Hilton. (2013). Dave Grohl and Krist Novoselic Share Memories, Unreleased Tracks From 'In Utero'/Podcast. *NPR Music*, uploaded 10 September. Available at: www.npr.org/sections/allsongs/2013/09/09/220657501/dave-grohl-and-krist-novoselic-share-memories-unreleased-tracks-from-in-utero?t=1576592285989, accessed 17 December 2019.

Bordwell, David. (2002). Intensified Continuity Visual Style in Contemporary American Film. *Film Quarterly*, 55, no. 3, 16–28.

Born, Georgina. (1995). *Rationalizing Culture: IRCAM, Boulez, and the Institutionalization of the Musical Avant-Garde*. Berkeley and Los Angeles: University of California Press.

Born, Georgina. (2010). For a Relational Musicology: Music and Interdisciplinarity, Beyond the Practice Turn. *Journal of the Royal Musical Association*, 135, no. 2, 205–43.

Born, Georgina and David Hesmondhalgh, eds. (2000). *Western Music and Its Others: Difference, Representation, and Appropriation in Music.* Berkeley and Los Angeles: University of California Press.

Borthwick, Stuart and Ron Moy. (2004). *Popular Music Genres: An Introduction.* Edinburgh: Edinburgh University Press.

Botstein, Leon. (1996). Innovation and Nostalgia: Ives, Mahler, and the Origins of Modernism. In J. Peter Burkholder, ed., *Charles Ives and His World.* Princeton, NJ: Princeton University Press, 35–74.

Botstein, Leon. (2011). The Jewish Question in Music. *The Musical Quarterly,* 94, no. 4, 439–53.

Boulez, Pierre. (1967). Liner notes to *Boulez Conducts Debussy.* CBS LP 32110056.

Boulez, Pierre. (1971). *Boulez on Music Today.* Trans. Susan Bradshaw and Richard Rodney Bennett. London: Faber and Faber.

Boulez, Pierre. (1991a/1952). Possibly . . .. In Pierre Boulez, *Stocktakings from an Apprenticeship.* Trans. Stephen Walsh. Oxford: Clarendon Press, 11–40.

Boulez, Pierre. (1991b). Schoenberg Is Dead. In Pierre Boulez, *Notes on an Apprenticeship.* New York: Alfred A. Knopf, 268–75.

Bourdieu, Pierre. (1996). *The Rules of Art: Genesis and Structure of the Literary Field.* Cambridge: Polity Press.

Bourdieu, Pierre. (1984/1979). *Distinction: A Social Critique of the Judgement of Taste.* Cambridge, MA: Harvard University Press.

Bowen, José Antonio. (2015). Who Plays the Tune in 'Body and Soul'? A Performance History Using Recorded Sources. *Journal of the Society for American Music,* 9, no. 3, 259–92.

Bradley, Lloyd. (2001). Bass Culture. In Lloyd Bradley, *When Reggae Was King.* London and New York: Penguin.

Brantlinger, Patrick. (1983). *Bread and Circuses: Theories of Mass Culture as Social Decay.* New York: Cornell University Press.

Bratus, Alessandro. (2011). Scene through the Press: Rock Music and Underground Papers in London, 1966–73. *Twentieth-Century Music,* 8, no. 2 (September), 227–52.

Brazelton, Bennett. (2020). The Futures of Grace Jones: Queer, Black, Dystopian, Eternal. *Fire!!!,* 5, no. 2, Examining the Humanity of Blackness, 53–82.

Brennan, Matt. (2020). *Kick It: A Provocative Social History of the Drum Kit.* Oxford: Oxford University Press.

Brett, Phillip. (1977). Britten and *Grimes. The Musical Times,* 118, no. 1618, 995–7; 999–1000.

Britten, Benjamin. (1998/1964). On Winning the First Aspen Award. In E. Schwartz, B. Childs and J. Fox, eds., *Contemporary Composers on Contemporary Music,* expanded edition. New York: Da Capo Press, 115–23.

Brothers, Thomas. (2006). *Louis Armstrong's New Orleans.* New York: W. W. Norton.

Brown, Julie. (2000). Bartók, the Gypsies, and Hybridity in Music. In Georgina Born and Philip V. Bohlman, eds., *Western Music and Its Others*. Berkeley and Los Angeles: University of California Press, 119–42.

Brown, Malcolm Harrick, ed. (2005). *A Shostakovich Casebook*. Bloomington: Indiana University Press.

Brown, Matthew. (2012). *Debussy Redux: The Impact of His Music on Popular Culture*. Bloomington: Indiana University Press.

Brown, Timothy. (2006). 'Keeping it Real' in a Different 'Hood: (African)-Americanization and Hip Hop in Germany. In Dipannita Basu and Sidney Lemelle eds., *The Vinyl Ain't Final: Hip Hop and the Globalization of Black Culture*. London: Pluto, 137–50.

Brüstle, Christa and Danielle Sofer, eds. (2018). *Elizabeth Maconchy: Music as an Impassioned Argument*. Vienna: Universal Edition.

Bryan-Wilson, Julia. (2003). Remembering Yoko Ono's *Cut Piece*. *Oxford Art Journal*, 26, no. 1, 99–123.

Buchanan, Donna. (2000). Bartók's Bulgaria: Folk Music Collecting and Balkan Social History. *International Journal of Musicology*, 9, 55–91.

Buckley, David. (2002). *R. E. M. |Fiction: An Alternative Biography*. London: Virgin Books.

Bull, Michael. (2000). *Sounding Out the City: Personal Stereos and the Management of Everyday Life*. Oxford and New York: Berg.

Bull, Michael. (2014). iPod Use, Mediation, and Privatization in the Age of Mechanical Reproduction. In Sumanth Gopinath and Jason Stanyek, eds., *The Oxford Handbook of Mobile Music Studies*. New York: Oxford University Press, 103–17.

Bürger, Peter. (1984/1974). *Theory of the Avant-Garde*. Trans. Michael Shaw. Manchester, UK: Manchester University Press and University of Minnesota Press.

Burgess, Jean E. (2004). High Culture as Subculture: Brisbane's Contemporary Chamber Music Scene. (Masters by Research thesis, the University of Queensland)

Burian, J. M. (1970). Josef Svoboda: Theatre Artist in an Age of Science. *Educational Theatre Journal*, 22, no. 2, 123–45.

Burke, Seán. (2008). *The Death and Return of the Author: Criticism and Subjectivity in Barthes, Foucault and Derrida*. Edinburgh: University of Edinburgh Press.

Burkholder, J. Peter. (1995). *All Made of Tunes: Charles Ives and the Uses of Musical Borrowing*. New Haven, CT: Yale University Press.

Busoni, Ferruccio. (1962). *Three Classics in the Aesthetics of Music*. New York: Dover Publications.

Busoni, Ferruccio. (2012/1907). *Sketch of a New Aesthetic of Music*. Ed. A. Harper and W. Daly, trans. Pamela Johnston. London: Precinct.

Butler, Judith. (1988). Performative Acts and Gender Constitution: An Essay in Phenomenology and Feminist Theory. *Theatre Journal*, 40, no. 4, 519–31.

Butler, Judith. (1990). *Gender Trouble: Feminism and the Subversion of Identity*. New York: Routledge.

Butler, Mark J. (2006). *Unlocking the Groove: Rhythm, Meter, and Musical Design in Electronic Dance Music*. Bloomington: Indiana University Press.

Butterfield, Matthew W. (2011). Why Do Jazz Musicians Swing Their Eighth Notes? *Music Theory Spectrum*, 33, no. 1, 3–26.

Cage, John. (1961). Composition as Process II: Indeterminacy. In John Cage, *Silence*. Hanover, NH: Wesleyan University Press, 35–41.

Cage, John. (1961/1937). The Future of Music Credo. In John Cage, *Silence: Lectures and Writings*. New York: Bloomsbury, 25–8.

Cage, John. (1966). *Silence: Lectures and Writings by John Cage*. Cambridge, MA: The MIT Press.

Cage, John. (1981). *For the Birds: John Cage in Conversation with Daniel Charles, Richard Gardner and Tom Cora*. London: Marion Boyars Publishers.

Cage, John and Alison Knowles. (1969). *Notations*. New York: Something Else Press.

Callinicos, Alex. (1995). *Theories and Narratives: Reflections on the Philosophy of History*. Cambridge: Polity Press.

Caplin, William E. (2014). Topics and Formal Functions: The Case of the Lament. In Danuta Mirka, ed., *Oxford Handbook of Topic Theory*, 415–52. New York: Oxford University Press.

Cardew, Cornelius. (1969). A Scratch Orchestra: Draft Constitution. *The Musical Times*, 110, no. 1516, 619.

Cardew, Cornelius. (2006/1971). Treatise Handbook [extract]. In Cornelius Cardew, *Cornelius Cardew: A Reader*, ed. Edwin Prévost. Matching Tye: Copula, 95–134.

Carpenter, Alexander. (2010). Schoenberg's Vienna, Freud's Vienna: Re-examining the Connections between the Monodrama *Erwartung* and the Early History of Psychoanalysis. *The Musical Quarterly*, 93, no. 1, 144–81.

Carroll, Mark. (2003). *Music and Ideology in Cold War Europe*. Cambridge: Cambridge University Press.

Cavin, Susan. (1975). Missing Women: On the Voodoo Trail to Jazz. *Journal of Jazz*, 3, no. 1, 4–27.

Chanan, Michael. (1995). *Repeated Takes: A Short History of Recording and Its Effects on Music*. London: Verso.

Chapple, Steve and Reebee Garofalo. (1997). *Rock 'n' Roll Is Here to Pay: The History and Politics of the Music Industry*. Chicago: Nelson Hall.

Chastagner, Claude. (1999). The Parents' Music Resource Center: From Information to Censorship. *Popular Music*, 18, no. 2, 179–92.

Cheng, William. (2014). *Sound Play: Video Games and the Musical Imagination*. New York: Oxford University Press.

Chion, Michel. (1994). *Audio-Vision: Sound on Screen*. Trans. Claudia Gorbman. New York: Columbia University Press.

Chion, Michel. (1999). *The Voice in Cinema*. Trans. Claudia Gorbman. New York: Columbia University Press.

Chowrimootoo, Christopher. (2016). 'Britten Minor': Constructing the Modernist Canon. *Twentieth-Century Music*, 13, no. 2, 261–90.

Chowrimootoo, Christopher. (2018). *Middlebrow Modernism: Britten's Operas and the Great Divide*. Berkeley and Los Angeles: University of California Press.

Citron, Marcia. (2010). *When Opera Meets Film*. Cambridge: Cambridge University Press.

Citron, Marcia. (2013). Opera and Film. In D. Neumeyer, ed., *The Oxford Handbook of Film Music Studies*. Oxford: Oxford University Press, 44–71.

Citron, Marcia J. (1993). *Gender and the Musical Canon*. Cambridge: Cambridge University Press.

Citron, Marcia J. (2007). Women and the Western Art Canon: Where Are We Now? *Notes*, 64, no. 2, 209–15.

Clark, Susannah. (2011). *Analyzing Schubert*. Cambridge: Cambridge University Press.

Clarke, David. (2007). Elvis and Darmstadt, or: Twentieth-Century Music and the Politics of Cultural Pluralism. *Twentieth-Century Music*, 4, no. 1, 3–45.

Clarke, Eric. (2007). The Impact of Recording on Listening. *Twentieth-Century Music*, 4, no. 1, 47–70.

Clarke, Eric and Nicholas Cook, eds. (2004). *Empirical Musicology: Aims, Methods, Prospects*. Oxford: Oxford University Press.

Clarke, John, Stuart Hall, Tony Jefferson and Brian Roberts. (1997/1975). Subcultures, Cultures and Class. In Sarah Thornton and Ken Gelder, eds., *The Subcultures Reader*. London: Routledge, 100–3.

Clifford, James. (1988). Histories of the Tribal and the Modern. In James Clifford, *The Predicament of Culture: Twentieth-Century Ethnography, Literature, and Art*. Cambridge, MA: Harvard University Press, 189–214.

Clifford, James and George E. Marcus, eds. (1986). *Writing Culture: The Poetics and Politics of Ethnography*. Berkeley and Los Angeles: University of California Press.

Clifton, Thomas. (1983). *Music as Heard: A Study in Applied Phenomenology*. New Haven, CT: Yale University Press.

Cline, David. (2016). *The Graph Music of Morton Feldman*. Cambridge: Cambridge University Press.

Cohen, Lizabeth. (1989). Encountering Mass Culture at the Grassroots: The Experience of Chicago Workers in the 1920s. *American Quarterly*, 41, no. 1, 6–33.

Cohen, Robin. (2007). Creolization and Cultural Globalization: The Soft Sounds of Fugitive Power. *Globalizations*, 4, no. 3, 369–84.

Cohen, Sara. (1991). *Rock Culture in Liverpool: Popular Music in the Making*. Oxford: Clarendon Press.

Cohen, Sara. (1994). Identity, Place and the 'Liverpool Sound'. In Martin Stokes, ed., *Ethnicity, Identity and Music: The Musical Construction of Place*. Oxford and New York: Berg, 117–34.

Cohen, Sara. (1997). Men Making a Scene. In Sheila Whiteley, ed., *Sexing the Groove: Popular Music and Gender*. London: Routledge, 17–36.

Cohen, Ted. (1993). High and Low Thinking about High and Low Art. *Journal of Aesthetics and Art Criticism*, 51, 151–6.

Collins, Karen. (2008a). *From Pac-Mac to Pop Music: Interactive Audio in Games and New Media*. Aldershot: Ashgate.

Collins, Karen. (2008b). *Game Sound: An Introduction to the History, Theory, and Practice of Video Game Music and Sound Design*. Cambridge, MA: The MIT Press.

Collins, Karen. (2013). Implications of Interactivity: What Does it Mean for Sound to Be 'Interactive'? In C. Gorbman, J. Richardson and C. Vernallis, eds., *The Oxford Handbook of New Audiovisual Aesthetics*. New York: Oxford University Press, 572–84.

Concannon, Kevin. (2008). Yoko Ono's *Cut Piece*: From Text to Performance and Back. *PAJ: A Journal of Performance and Art*, 90, 81–93.

Connell, John and Chris Gibson (2003). *Sound Tracks: Popular Music, Identity and Place*. London and New York: Routledge.

Connelly, Tara and Mike Shiflet. (2020). Noisextra. In Conversation with Joe Colley (Crawl Unit). *Noisextra*, 5 August. www.noisextra.com/2020/08/05/in-conversation-with-joe-colley-crawl-unit/. Accessed 25 September 2020.

Connor, Stephen. (1997). *Postmodernist Culture*. London: Blackwell.

Cook, Nicholas. (1998). *Music: A Very Short Introduction*. Oxford: Oxford University Press.

Cook, Nicholas. (2008). We Are All (Ethno)musicologists Now. In Henry Stobart, ed., *The New (Ethno)musicologies*. Lanham, MD: The Scarecrow Press, 48–70.

Cook, Nicholas. (2013). *Beyond the Score: Music as Performance*. Oxford: Oxford University Press.

Coombe, Rosemary. (1998). *The Cultural Life of Intellectual Properties: Authorship, Appropriation, and the Law*. Durham, NC: Duke University Press.

Covach, John. (1997). Yes, Close to the Edge, and the Boundaries of Rock. In John Covach and Graeme M. Boone, eds., *Understanding Rock*. New York: Oxford University Press, 3–31.

Cox, Christoph and Warner, Daniel, eds. (2004). *Audio Culture*. London: Continuum.

Crawford, John C. and Dorothy L. Crawford. (1993). *Expressionism in Twentieth-Century Music*. Bloomington: University of Indiana Press.

Cronin, Charles. (1998). Concepts of Melodic Similarity in Music-Copyright Infringement Suits in Melodic Similarity: Concepts, Procedures and Applications. *Computing and Musicology*, 11, 187–210.

Cross, Ian. (2007). Music and Cognitive Evolution. In Robin Dunbar and Louise Barrett, eds., *Oxford Handbook of Evolutionary Psychology*. Oxford: Oxford University Press, 649–67.

Cross, Jonathan and Ian Pace. (2001). Finnissy, Michael (Peter). In *Grove Music Online*. Oxford: Oxford University Press.

Cugny, Laurent. (2009). *Analyser le jazz*. Paris: Outre Mesure.

Cunningham, Hugh. (1980). *Leisure in the Industrial Revolution, 1750–1880*. New York: St. Martin's Press.

Cunningham, Mark. (1998). *Good Vibrations: A History of Record Production*. London: Sanctuary Press.

Currans-Sheehan, Rachel Henry. (2009). From Madonna to Lilith and Back Again: Women, Feminists, and Pop Music in the United States. In Lilly J. Goren, *ed.*, *You've Come a Long Way, Baby: Women, Politics, and Popular Culture*. Lexington: University Press of Kentucky, 53–70.

Cutler, Chris. (2004). Plunderphonia. In Christoph Cox and Daniel Warner, eds., *Audio Culture: Readings in Modern Music*. New York: Bloomsbury, 138–56.

Dahlhaus, Carl. (1977). *Foundations of Music History*. Cambridge: Cambridge University Press.

Dahlhaus, Carl. (1978). 'Kugelgestalt der Zeit': Zu Bernd Alois Zimmermanns Musikphilosophie. *Musik und Bildung: Praxis Musikunterricht*, 10, 633–36.

Dahlhaus, Carl. (1980). Nationalism and Music. In Carl Dahlhaus, *Between Romanticism and Modernism: Four Studies in the Music of the Later Nineteenth Century*, trans. Mary Whittall. Berkeley and Los Angeles: University of California Press, 79–101.

Dahlhaus, Carl. (1982). *Esthetics of Music*. Trans. William Austin. Cambridge: Cambridge University Press.

Dahlhaus, Carl. (1987). *Schoenberg and the New Music*. Trans. Derrick Puffett and Alfred Clayton. Cambridge: Cambridge University Press.

Dahlhaus, Carl. (1987/1969). Plea for a Romantic Category: The Concept of the Work of Art in the Newest Music. In Carl Dahlhaus, *Schoenberg and the New Music*, trans. Derrick Puffett and Alfred Clayton. Cambridge: Cambridge University Press, 210–19.

Dahlhaus, Carl. (1988). Progress and the Avant Garde. In Carl Dahlhaus, *Schoenberg and the New Music*. Trans. Derrick Puffett and Alfred Clayton. Cambridge: Cambridge University Press, 14–22.

Dahlhaus, Carl. (1989). *The Idea of Absolute Music*. Trans. Roger Lustig. Chicago: University of Chicago Press.

Dahlhaus, Carl. (1990). *Nineteenth-Century Music*. Trans. J. Bradford Robinson. Berkeley and Los Angeles: University of California Press.

Danielsen, Anne. (2006). *Presence and Pleasure: The Funk Grooves of James Brown and Parliament*. Middleton, CT: Wesleyan University Press.

Danielsen, Anne. (2010a). Introduction: Rhythm in the Age of Digital Reproduction. In Anne Danielsen, ed., *Musical Rhythm in the Age of Digital Reproduction* Aldershot: Ashgate, 1–16.

Danielsen, Anne. (2010b). Here, There and Everywhere: Three Accounts of Pulse in D'Angelo's 'Left and Right'. In Anne Danielsen, ed., *Musical Rhythm in the Age of Digital Reproduction*. Aldershot: Ashgate, 19–36.

Davenport, Lisa E. (2009). *Jazz Diplomacy: Promoting America in the Cold War Era*. Jackson, MI: University Press of Mississippi.

Davis, Angela. (1998). *Blues Legacies and Black Feminism*. New York: Vintage Books.

Davis, Mary E. (1999). Modernity à la Mode: Popular Culture and Avant-Gardism in Erik Satie's *Sports et divertissements*. *The Musical Quarterly*, 83, no. 3, 430–73.

Dawe, K. (2010). *The New Guitarscape in Critical Theory in Critical Theory and Musical Performance*. London: Routledge.

Dearn, Lucy and Stephanie Pitts. (2017). (Un)popular Music and Young Audiences: Exploring the Classical Chamber Music Concert from the Perspective of Young Adult Listeners. *Journal of Popular Music Education*, 1, no. 1, 43–62.

Debord, Guy. (1994/1967). *The Society of the Spectacle*. New York: Zone Books.

de Clerq, Trevor, and David Temperley. (2011). A Corpus Analysis of Rock Harmony. *Popular Music* 30, no. 1, 47–70.

Deflem, Mathieu. (2020). Popular Culture and Social Control: The Moral Panic on Music Labeling. *American Journal of Criminal Justice*, 45, 2–24.

De Graaf, Melissa J. (2008). 'Never Call Us Lady Composers': Gendered Receptions in the New York Composers' Forum, 1935–1940. *American Music*, 26, no. 3, 277–308.

Demers, Joanna. (2003). Sampling the 1970s in Hip-Hop. *Popular Music*, 22, no. 1, 41–56.

Demers, Joanna. (2006). *Steal this Music: How Intellectual Property Law Affects Musical Creativity*. Athens, GA: University of Georgia Press.

DeNora, Tia. (2000). *Music in Everyday Life*. Cambridge: Cambridge University Press.

Dery, Mark. (1994). Black to the Future: Interviews with Samuel R. Delaney, Greg Tate, and Tricia Rose. In Mark Dery, *Flame Wars: The Discourse of Cyberculture*. Durham, NC: Duke University Press, 179–222.

Desler, Anne. (2013). History Without Royalty? Queen and the Strata of the Popular Music Canon. *Popular Music*, 32, no. 3, 385–405.

DeVeaux, Scott. (1999). *The Birth of Bebop: A Social and Musical History*. London: Picador.

Dibben, Nicola. (2016). Vocal Performance and Emotional Authenticity. In D. Scott, ed., *The Ashgate Research Companion to Popular Musicology*. London: Routledge, 317–34.

Dickinson, Kay. (2001). 'Believe'? Vocoders, Digitalised Female Identity and Camp. *Popular Music*, 20, no. 3, 333–47.

DiMaggio, Paul. (1991). Social Structure, Institutions, and Cultural Goods: The Case of the US. In P. Bourdieu and J. Coleman, eds., *Social Theory for a Changing Society*. Boulder: Westview Press, 133–55.

Doctor, Jennifer. (1999). *The BBC and Ultra-Modern Music, 1922–1936: Shaping a Nation's Tastes*. Cambridge: Cambridge University Press.

Döhl, Frédéric. (2014). From Harmonic Style to Genre: The Early History (1890s–1940s) of the Uniquely American Musical Term Barbershop. *American Music* 32, no. 2, 123–71.

Dohoney, Ryan. (2014). John Cage, Julius Eastman, and the Homosexual Ego. In Benjamin Piekut, ed.,*Tomorrow Is the Question: New Directions in Experimental Music Studies*. Ann Arbor: University of Michigan Press, 39–62.

Dohoney, Ryan. (2016). Charlotte Moorman's Experimental Performance Practice. In Corinne Granoff, ed., *Charlotte Moorman and the Avant-Garde*. Evanston, IL: Northwestern University Press.

Dolmetsch, Arnold. (1915). *The Interpretation of the Music of the XVIIth and XVIIIth Centuries*. London: Novello. Available at: https://archive.org/details/cu31924021793314/page/n10, accessed 28 July 2019.

Donington, Robert. (1992/1963). *The Interpretation of Early Music*. Rev. ed. New York: Norton.

Donnelly, Kevin J. (2013). Extending Film Aesthetics: Audio Beyond Visuals. In John Richardson, Claudia Gorbman and Carol Vernallis, eds., *The Oxford Handbook of New Audiovisual Aesthetics*. Oxford: Oxford University Press, 357–71.

Dougan, John. (2006). Objects of Desire: Canon Formation and Blues Record Collecting. *Journal of Popular Music*, 18, no. 1, 40–65.

Dowd, Timothy J. (2011). Production and Producers of Lifestyles: The Fields of Popular and Classical Music in the United States. *Kölner Zeitschrift für Soziologie und Sozialpsychologie*, 63, no. 51, 113–38.

Doyle, Peter. (2004). From 'My Blue Heaven' to 'Race with the Devil': Echo, Reverb and (Dis)ordered Space in Early Popular Music Recording. *Popular Music*, 23, no. 1, 31–49.

Drever, John. (2019). 'Primacy of the Ear' – But Whose Ear? The Case for Auraldiversity in Sonic Arts Practice and Discourse. *Organised Sound*, 24, no. 1, 85–95.

D'Silva, Margaret and Robert St. Clair. (2008). The Sedimentation of Cultural Space. *Intercultural Communication Studies* 17, no. 1, www-s3-live.kent.edu/s3fs-root/3fs-public/file/02-Margaret-DSilva-Robert-StClair.pdf, accessed 19 October 2020.

Du Bois, W. E. B. (2020/1903). *The Souls of Black Folk*. London: Dover Thrift Editions.

Dümling, Albrecht. (2002). The Target of Racial Purity: The 'Degenerate Music' Exhibition in Düsseldorf, 1938. In Richard A. Etlin, ed., *Art, Culture, and Media under the Third Reich*. Chicago: University of Chicago Press, 43–72.

Dunn, David. (2013). *Harry Partch: An Anthology of Critical Perspectives*. New York: Routledge.

Durham, Aisha, Gwendolyn Pough, Rachel Raimist and Elaine Richardson. (2007). *Home Girls Make Some Noise: Hip Hop Feminism Anthology*. Mira Loma, CA: Parker Publishing.

Dworkin, Andrea. (1981). *Pornography: Men Possessing Women*. New York: Perigree.

Dworkin, Andrea. (1987). *Intercourse*. New York: Free Press.

Dyer, Richard. (2002). *The Matter of Images: Essays on Representations*. 2nd ed. London and New York: Routledge.

Dyer, Richard. (2002/1979). In Defence of Disco. In Richard Dyer, *Only Entertainment*. London: Routledge, 151–60.

Eagleton, Terry. (1996). *The Illusions of Postmodernism*. Oxford: Blackwell.

Edmunds, Neil. (2006). William Glock and the British Broadcasting Corporation's Music Policy, 1959–73. *Contemporary British History* 20, no. 2, 233–61.

Ehrlich, Cyril. (1989). *Harmonious Alliance: A History of the Performing Right Society*. Oxford: Oxford University Press.

Eisenberg, Evan. (1987). *The Recording Angel: Music, Records and Culture from Aristotle to Zappa*. New Haven, CT and London: Yale University Press.

Eisenstein, Sergei. (1949/1928). Statement on Sound. In J. Leyda, ed. and trans., *Film Form: Essays in Film Theory*. New York: Harcourt, Brace, and World, 257–60.

Ekins, Richard. (2013). The Social Construction of a Music Mecca: 'Goin' Home. New Orleans and International New Orleans Jazz Revivalism. *Popular Music History*, 8, no. 1, 5–22.

Eliot, T. S. (2000). *The Sacred Wood and Major Early Essays*. New York: Dover.

Emerson, Simon. (2009). Combining the Acoustic and the Digital: Music for Instruments and Computers or Prerecorded Sound. In R. T. Dean, ed., *The Oxford Handbook of Computer Music*. New York: Oxford University Press, 167–90.

Eno, Brian. (2004/1979). The Studio as Compositional Tool. In Christoph Cox and Daniel Warner, eds., *Audio Culture: Readings in Modern Music*. New York: Bloomsbury, 127–30.

Eshun, Kodwo. (1998). *More Brilliant Than the Sun*. London: Quartet Books.

Eshun, Kodwo. (2003). Further Considerations of Afrofuturism. *CR: The New Centennial Review*. 3, no. 2, 287–302.

Eun-Young, Jung. (2010). Playing the Race and Sexuality Cards in the Transnational Pop Game: Korean Music Videos for the US Market. *Journal of Popular Music Studies*, 22, no. 2, 219–36.

Evans, Joan. (2003). Stravinsky's Music in Hitler's Germany. *Journal of the American Musicological Society*, 56, no. 3, 525–94.

Evens, Aden. (2005). *Sound Ideas: Music, Machines, and Experience*. Minneapolis: University of Minnesota Press.

Everett, Walter. (2004). Making Sense of Rock's Tonal Systems. *Music Theory Online*. 10, no. 4, www.mtosmt.org/issues/mto.04.10.4/mto.04.10.4.w_everett.html

Ewell, Philip A. (2020). Music Theory and the White Racial Frame. *Music Theory Online* 26, no. 2, https://mtosmt.org/issues/mto.20.26.2/mto.20.26.2.ewell.html.

Fabian, Dorottya. (2001). The Meaning of Authenticity and the Early Music Movement: A Historical Review. *International Review of the Aesthetics and Sociology of Music*, 32, no. 2, 153–67.

Fatsis, Lambros. (2018). Grime: Criminal Subculture or Public Counterculture? A Critical Investigation into the Criminalization of Black Musical Subcultures in the UK. *Crime, Media, Culture: An International Journal*, 28 June. DOI: doi/ 10.1177/1741659018784111.

Fauser, Annegret. (2005). *Musical Encounters at the 1889 Paris World's Fair*. Woodbridge: Boydell & Brewer.

Fay, Laurel E. (1980). Shostakovich versus Vokov: Whose *Testimony*? *The Russian Review*, 39, no. 4, 484–93.

Fay, Laurel E. (2000). *Shostakovich: A Life*. Oxford: Oxford University Press.

Fay, Laurel E. (2005). Volkov's Testimony Reconsidered. In Malcolm Harrick Brown, ed., *A Shostakovich Casebook*. Bloomington: Indian University Press, 22–66.

Ferris, William. (1970). *Blues from the Delta*. London: Studio Vista.

Fink, Robert. (1998). Elvis Everywhere: Musicology and Popular Music Studies at the Twilight of the Canon. *American Music*, 16, no. 2, 135–79.

Fink, Robert. (2005a). *Repeating Ourselves: American Minimal Music as Cultural Practice*. Berkeley and Los Angeles: University of California Press.

Fink, Robert. (2005b). The Story of ORCH5, or, the Classical Ghost in the Hip-Hop Machine. *Popular Music*, 24, no. 3, 339–56.

Fink, Robert. (2011). Goal-Directed Soul? Analyzing Rhythmic Teleology in African American Popular Music. *Journal of the American Musicological Society*, 64, no. 1, 179–238.

Finnegan, Ruth. (2013/1989). *The Hidden Musicians: Music-Making in an English Town*. Middletown, CT: Wesleyan University Press.

Fischinger, Oskar. (1932). Sounding Ornaments. Available at: www.oskarfischinger .org/Sounding.htm, accessed 20 December 2018.

Fisher, John A. (2005). High Art Versus Low Art. In Berys Nigel Gaut and Dominic Lopes, eds., *The Routledge Companion to Aesthetics*, 2nd ed. London and New York: Routledge, 527–40.

Fisher, Mark. (2005). We Aren't the World. *k-punk*, 26 February. http://k-punk .abstractdynamics.org/archives/005071.html, accessed 15 July 2019.

Fisher, Mark. (2009a). Avant-Conservatism. *k-punk*. http://k-punk.abstractdynamics .org/archives/011115.html, accessed 6 March 2014.

Fisher, Mark. (2009b). *Capitalist Realism*. Winchester: Zero Books.

Fisher, Mark. (2012a). From 1984. *K-Punk*. http://k-punk.abstractdynamics.org/ archives/007364.html, accessed 4 April 2022.

Fisher, Mark. (2012b). Time Wars. *Wired*. 11 August. www.wired.com/2012/08/ time-wars-by-k-punk/, accessed 20 March 2022.

Fisher, Mark. (2012c). What Is Hauntology. *Film Quarterly*, 66, no. 1, 16–24.

Fisher, Mark. (2014a). The Slow Cancellation of the Future. In Mark Fisher, *Ghosts of My Life*. Winchester: Zero Books, 2–29.

Fisher, Mark. (2014b). *Ghosts of My Life*. Winchester: Zero Books.

Fishman, Joseph P. (2018). Music as a Matter of Law. *Harvard Law Review* 131, no.7, 1861–1923.

Flinn, Caryl. (1992). *Strains of Utopia: Gender, Nostalgia and Hollywood Film Music*. Princeton, NJ: Princeton University Press.

Floyd, Samuel A., Jr. (1995). *The Power of Black Music: Interpreting Its History from Africa to the United States*. New York: Oxford University Press.

Floyd, Samuel A., Jr. (1999). Black Music in the Circum-Caribbean. *American Music*. 17, no. 1, 1–38.

Floyd, Samuel A., Jr., and Ronald Radano. (2009). Interpreting the African-American Musical Past: A Dialogue. *Black Music Research Journal*, 29, no. 1, 1–10.

Floyd, Samuel A. Jr., Melanie Zeck and Guthrie Ramsey. (2017). *The Transformation of Black Music: the Rhythms, the Songs, and the Ships of the African Diaspora*. New York: Oxford University Press.

Fonarow, Wendy. (2006). *Empire of Dirt: The Aesthetics and Rituals of British Indie Music*. Middletown, CT: Wesleyan University Press.

Ford, Andrew. (2014). Amzplified Intimacy. *Inside Story*. Available at: http:// insidestory.org.au/amplified-intimacy/, accessed 28 July 2019.

Ford, Phil. (2013). *Dig: Sound & Music in Hip Culture*. New York and Oxford: Oxford University Press.

Forkert, Annika. (2017). Magical Serialism: Modernist Enchantment in Elisabeth Lutyens's *O Saisons, O Châteaux!* *Twentieth-Century Music* 14, no. 2, 271–303.

Forman, Murray. (2002). *The 'Hood Comes First: Race, Space, and Place in Rap and Hip-Hop*. Middletown, CT: Wesleyan University Press.

Forte, Allen. (1973). *The Structure of Atonal Music*. New Haven, CT: Yale University Press.

Forte, Allen. (1995). *The American Popular Ballad of the Golden Era: 1924–1950*. Princeton, NJ: Princeton University Press.

Fosler-Lussier, Danielle. (2007). *Music Divided: Bartók's Legacy in Cold War Culture*. Berkeley and Los Angeles: University of California Press.

Fosler-Lussier, Danielle. (2015). *Music in America's Cold-War Diplomacy*. Berkeley and Los Angeles: University of California Press.

Foster, Hal. (1983). Postmodernism: A Preface. In Hal Foster, *The Anti-Aesthetic: Essays on Postmodern Culture*. Seattle, WA: Bay Press.

Foucault, Michel. (1978). *History of Sexuality: Volume 1*. Trans. Robert Hurley. New York: Pantheon Books.

Foucault, Michel. (1988). Technologies of the Self. In Michel Foucault, *Technologies of the Self*. Amherst: University of Massachusetts Press, 16–49.

Foucault, Michel. (1991/1975). *Discipline and Punish: The Birth of the Prison*. London: Penguin.

Foucault, Michel. (1997/1969). *The Archaeology of Knowledge*. London: Routledge.

Foucault, Michel. (2000/1969). 'What Is an Author?' In Michel Foucault, *Aesthetics: Essential Works of Foucault 1954–1984, vol. 2.*, ed. James D. Faubion. London: Penguin, 205–22.

Fowler, Charles. (1951). As the Editor Sees It. *High Fidelity* (Summer), 8.

Fox, Christopher. (2007). Darmstadt and the Institutionalisation of Modernism. *Contemporary Music Review.* 26, no. 1, 115–23.

Fox, Christopher. (2014). Opening Offer or Contractual Obligation? On the Prescriptive Function of Notation in Music Today. *Tempo*, no. 269, 6–19.

Friedberg, Joshua. (2018). 'Aretha Franklin: Context, Intersectionality, and the Rock Canon'. *Popmatters.* www.popmatters.com/aretha-franklin-music-criticism-2623060199.html, accessed 8 March 2022.

Frith, Simon. (1986). Art vs Technology: The Strange Case of Popular Music. *Media, Culture and Society*, 8, 263–79.

Frith, Simon. (1996). *Performing Rites.* Cambridge, MA: Harvard University Press.

Frith, Simon and Angela McRobbie. (1990). Rock and Sexuality. In Simon Frith and Andrew Goodwin, eds., *On Record: Rock, Pop and the Written Word.* London: Routledge, 271–89.

Frith, Simon, ed. (1988). *Facing the Music.* New York: Pantheon.

Frith, Simon and Lee Marshall, eds. (2004). *Music and Copyright*, 2nd ed. Edinburgh: Edinburgh University Press.

Frolova-Walker, Marina. (1998). 'National in Form: Socialist in Content': Musical Nation-Building in the Soviet Republics. *Journal of the American Musicological Society* 51, no. 2, 331–71.

Frolova-Walker, Marina. (2007). *Russian Music and Nationalism from Glinka to Stalin.* New Haven, CT and London: Yale University Press.

Fulcher, Jane. (2005). *The Composer as Intellectual: Music and Ideology in France 1914–1940.* New York and Oxford: Oxford University Press.

Fürsich, Elfriede and Roberto Avant-Miller. (2012). Popular Journalism and Cultural Change: The Discourse of Globalization in World Music Reviews. *International Journal of Cultural Studies*, 16, no. 2, 101–18.

Gabbard, Krin. (1995). Introduction: The Jazz Canon and its Consequences. In Krin Gabbard, ed., *Jazz Among the Discourses.* Durham, NC: Duke University Press, 1–30.

Gann, Kyle. (2006). *Music Downtown.* Berkeley and Los Angeles: University of California Press.

Gann, Kyle. (2010). *No Such Thing as Silence.* New Haven, CT: Yale University Press.

Garnett, Liz. (1999). Ethics and Aesthetics: The Social Theory of Barbershop Harmony. *Popular Music*, 18, no. 1, 41–61.

Garofalo, Reebee. (2002). Crossing Over: From Black Rhythm & Blues to White Rock 'n' Roll. In N. Kelley, ed., *Rhythm and Business: The Political Economy of Black Music*, New York: Ashakit Books, 112–37.

Gates, Henry Louis, Jr. (1988). *The Signifying Monkey*. Oxford: Oxford University Press.

Gay, Peter. (2007). *Modernism: The Lure of Heresy*. London: William Heinemann.

Gelatt, Roland. (1977). *The Fabulous Phonograph, 1877–(1977)*, 2nd ed. London: Cassell.

Gelder, Ken. (2005). The Field of Subcultural Studies. In Ken Gelder, ed., *The Subcultures Reader*, 2nd ed. New York: Routledge, 1–18.

Gendron, Bernard. (2002). *Between Montmartre and the Mudd Club*. London and Chicago: Chicago University Press.

Gerard, Charley and Marty Sheller (1998). *Salsa! The Rhythm of Latin Music*, 2nd ed. Tempe, AZ: White Cliffs Media Company.

Gerhard, Anselm. (2000). 'Kanon' in der Musikgeschichtsschreibung, Nationalistische Gewohnheiten nach dem Ende der nationalistischen Epoche. *Archiv für Musikwissenschaft*, 57, no. 1, 18–30.

Gibson, Casarae. (2017). 'Fight the Power': Hip Hop and Civil Unrest in Spike Lee's *Do the Right Thing*. *Black Camera*, 8, no. 2, 183–207.

Gibson, William. (1993/1984). *Neuromancer*. London: Harper Collins.

Giddens, Anthony. (1990). *Consequences of Modernity*. Stanford, CA: Stanford University Press.

Giddens, Anthony and Will Hutton, eds. (2000). *Global Capitalism*. New York: The New Press.

Gilbert, Sandra M. and Susan Gubar. (1991). *No Man's Land: The Place of the Woman Writer in the Twentieth Century*. New Haven, CT: Yale University Press.

Gilmore, Bob. (2007). On Claude Vivier's 'Lonely Child'. *Tempo*, 61, no. 239, 2–17.

Gilroy, Paul. (1993). *The Black Atlantic: Modernity and Double Consciousness*. London: Verso.

Gitlin, Todd. (1997). The Anti-political Populism of Cultural Studies. In Marjorie Ferguson and Peter Golding, eds., *Cultural Studies in Question*. London: SAGE, 25–38.

Givan, Benjamin. (2009). Thelonious Monk's Pianism. *The Journal of Musicology*, 26, no. 3, 404–42.

Glinsky, Albert. (2000). *Theremin: Ether Music and Espionage*. Chicago: University of Illinois Press.

Glitsos, Laura. (2018). Vaporwave, or Music Optimised for Abandoned Malls. *Popular Music*, 37, no. 1, 100–18.

Gloag, Kenneth. (2012). *Postmodernism in Music*. Cambridge University Press.

Glock, William. (1991/1963). *BBC's Music Policy*. Reprinted in *Notes in Advance*. Oxford: Oxford University Press.

Goehr, Lydia. (1992). *The Imaginary Museum of Musical Works*. Oxford: Oxford University Press.

Goehr, Lydia. (2001). Radical Modernism and the Failure of Style: Philosophical Reflections on Maeterlinck Debussy's Pelléas et Mélisande. *Representations*, 74, no. 1, 55–82.

Goehr, Lydia. (2002). In the Shadow of the Canon. *The Musical Quarterly*, 86, no. 2, 307–28.

Goffman, Irving. (1956). *Presentation of Self in Everyday Life*. London: Random House.

Goodlad, Lauren. (2007). Looking for Something Forever Gone: Gothic Masculinity, Androgyny, and Ethics at the Turn of the Millennium. *Cultural Critique*, no. 66. 104–26.

Goodwin, Andrew. (1990). Sample and Hold: Pop Music in the Digital Age of Reproduction. In Simon Frith and Andrew Goodwin, eds., *On Record: Rock, Pop, and the Written Word*. New York: Pantheon, 258–73.

Gorbman, Claudia. (1987). *Unheard Melodies: Narrative Film Music*. London, IN: Indiana University Press.

Gossett, Philip. (1992). History and Works That Have No History: Reviving Rossini's Neapolitan Operas. In Katherine Bergeron and Philip V. Bohlman, eds., *Disciplining Music: Musicology and Its Canons*. Chicago and London: University of Chicago Press, 95–115.

Gottlieb, Jack. (2004). *Funny, It Doesn't Sound Jewish: How Yiddish Songs and Synagogue Melodies Influenced American Popular Music*. Albany: State University of New York Press.

Gould, Corissa. (2009). Aspiring to Manliness: Edward Elgar and the Pressures of Hegemonic Masculinity. In Ian Biddle and Kirsten Gibson, eds., *Masculinity and Western Musical Practice*. Farnham: Ashgate, 161–82.

Gould, Glenn. (2004/1966). The Prospects of Recording. In C. Cox and D. Warner, eds., *Audio Culture: Readings in Modern Music*. New York: Bloomsbury, 115–26.

Gracyk, Theodore. (1996). *Rhythm and Noise: An Aesthetics of Rock*. Durham, NC: Duke University Press.

Graham, Stephen. (2016). *Sounds of the Underground*. Ann Arbor: Michigan University Press.

Graham, Stephen. (2019.). Modernism for and of the Masses? On Popular Modernisms. In Bjorn Heile and Charles Wilson, eds., *The Routledge Research Companion to Modernism in Music*. London: Routledge, 239–57.

Granata, Charles. (2017). *Wouldn't It Be Nice: Brian Wilson and the Making of the Beach Boys' Pet Sounds,* revised ed. Chicago: Chicago Review Press.

Grant, Morag Josephine. (2001). *Serial Music, Serial Aesthetics: Compositional Theory in Post-War Europe*. Cambridge: Cambridge University Press.

Gray, Clive. (2000). *The Politics of the Arts in Great Britain*. Basingstoke: Macmillan.

Green, Jeffrey. (2016/2011). *Samuel Coleridge-Taylor: A Musical Life*. Oxford and New York: Routledge.

Greenberg, Clement. (1989). Avant Garde and Kitsch. In Clement Greenberg, *Art and Culture*. London: Beacon Press, 3–21.

Greene, Liz. (2016). From Noise: Blurring the Boundaries of the Soundtrack. In Liz Green and Danijela Kulezic-Wilson, eds., *The Palgrave Handbook of Sound*

Design and Music in Screen Media: Integrated Soundtracks. London: Palgrave Macmillan, 17–32.

Greene, Liz and Danijela Kulezic-Wilson (2016). *The Palgrave Handbook of Sound Design and Music in Screen Media: Integrated Soundtracks*. London: Palgrave Macmillan.

Greenfield, Steve and Guy Osborn (2004). Copyright Law and Power in the Music Industry. In Simon Frith and Lee Marshall, eds. *Music and Copyright*, 2nd ed. Edinburgh: Edinburgh University Press, 89–102.

Greenhill, Larry. (1983). Quad ESL-63 Loudspeaker Larry Greenhill Part 3. *Stereophile* 12, no. 2. Available at: www.stereophile.com/content/quad-esl-63-loudspeaker-larry-greenhill-part-3, accessed 6 November 2019.

Griffiths, Dai. (2002). Cover Versions and the Sound of Identity in Motion. In David Hesmondhalgh and Keith Negus, eds., *Popular Music Studies*. London: Arnold, 51–64.

Griffiths, Dai. (2007). Allusion and Influence in Elvis Costello. *Popular Music History*, 2, no. 2.

Griffiths, Paul. (1996). From the Edge of Experience, a New Sound. *New York Times*, 1 December, Section 2, 31.

Griffiths, Paul. (2011). *Modern Music and After*, 3rd ed. Oxford: Oxford University Press.

Grimley, Daniel. (2001). Horn Calls and Flattened Sevenths: Nielsen and Danish Musical Style. In Harry White and Michael Murphy, eds., *Musical Constructions of Nationalism: Essays on the History and Ideology of European Musical Culture 1800–1945*. Cork: Cork University Press, 123–41.

Grimley, Daniel. (2005). 'Tonality, Clarity, Strength': Gesture, Form, and Nordic Identity in Carl Nielsen's Piano Music. *Music and Letters*, 86, no. 2 (May), 202–33.

Grimley, Daniel. (2006). *Grieg: Music, Landscape and Norwegian Identity*. Woodbridge: The Boydell Press.

Grimley, Daniel. (2011). Music, Landscape, Attunement: Listening to Sibelius's *Tapiola*. *Journal of the American Musicological Society*, 64, no. 2, 394–8.

Grubbs, D. (2014). *Records Ruin the Landscape: John Cage, the Sixties, and Sound Recording*. Durham, NC: Duke University Press.

Grunfeld, Frederic. (1969). *The Art and Times of the Guitar: An Illustrated History of Guitars and Guitarists*. New York: Collier Books.

Guralnick, Peter. (1994). *Last Train to Memphis: The Rise of Elvis Presley*. New York: Little, Brown.

Gutsche-Miller, Sarah. (2017). Parisian Music-Hall Ballet, 1871–1913. *Dance Research*, 35, no. 2, 286–7.

Hagstrom Miller, Karl. (2010). *Segregating Sound: Inventing Folk and Pop Music in the Age of Jim Crow*. Durham, NC: Duke University Press.

Hall, Stuart, Jessica Evans and Sean Nixon. (2003). *Representation*, 2nd ed. Thousand Oaks, CA: SAGE.

Hall, Stuart. (1980/1973). Encoding/Decoding. In Stuart Hall, Dorothy Hobson, Andrew Lowe and Paul Willis, eds., *Culture, Media, Language: Working Papers in Cultural Studies, 1972–79*. London: Hutchinson, 128–38.

Hall, Stuart. (1997). *Race: The Floating Signifier*. Film directed by Sut Jally. Media Education Foundation.

Hallberg, Robert. von. (1984). *Canons*. Chicago and London: University of Chicago Press.

Halstead, Jill. (1997). *The Woman Composer: Creativity and the Gendered Politics of Musical Composition*. Farnham: Ashgate.

Hamilton, Andy. (2007). *Aesthetics and Music*. London: Continuum.

Hamilton, Marybeth. (2007). *In Search of the Blues: Black Voices, White Visions*. London: Jonathan Cape.

Hamm, Charles. (1995). *Putting Popular Music in Its Place*. Cambridge: Cambridge University Press.

Hansell, William H. (1978). Black Music in the Poetry of Langston Hughes: Roots, Race, Release. *Obsidian*, 4, no. 3 (Winter), 16–38.

Haraway, Donna. (1987). A Manifesto for Cyborgs: Science, Technology, and Socialist Feminism in the 1980s. *Australian Feminist Studies*, 2, no. 4, 1–42.

Harker, Brian. (2011). *Louis Armstrong's Hot Five and Hot Seven Recordings*. New York: Oxford University Press.

Harman, Chris. (1996). Globalisation: A Critique of a New Orthodoxy. *International Socialism*, 73, 3–33.

Harper-Scott, J. P. E. (2012). *The Quilting Points of Musical Modernism: Revolution, Reaction, and William Walton*. Cambridge: Cambridge University Press.

Harris, Amanda. (2014). The Spectacle of Woman as Creator: Representation of Women Composers in the French, German and English Feminist Press 1880–1930. *Women's History Review*, 23, no. 1, 18–41.

Harris, Blake J. (2014). *Console Wars: Sega Vs Nintendo and the Battle that Defined a Generation*. New York: It Books.

Harris, John. (2003). *The Last Party*. London: Fourth Estate.

Harrison, Nate. (2004). *Can I Get an Amen?* (Audio installation and video). https://archive.org/details/NateHarrisonCanIGetAnAmen

Harvey, David. (1989). *The Condition of Postmodernity: An Enquiry into the Origins of Cultural Change*. Cambridge: Blackwell.

Harvey, David. (2007). *A Brief History of Neoliberalism*, new ed. Oxford: Oxford University Press.

Hasegawa, Robert. (2009). Gérard Grisey and the 'Nature' of Harmony. *Music Analysis* 28, no. 2–3, 349–71.

Hasty, Christopher F. (1997). *Meter as Rhythm*. New York and Oxford: Oxford University Press.

Hayek, Friedrich. (1948). *Individualism and Economic Order*. Chicago: University of Chicago Press.

Hebdige, Dick. (1979). *Subculture, The Meaning of Style*. London: Routledge.

Hebdige, Dick. (1987). *Cut 'N' Mix: Culture, Identity, and Caribbean Music*. London and New York: Methuen.

Heel, Kiri L. (2011). Germaine Tailleferre Beyond *Les Six*: Gynocentrism and *Le Marchand d'oiseaux* and the *Six Chansons Françaises*. (Unpublished PhD thesis, Stanford University)

Hegarty, Paul. (2007). *Noise Music: A History*. London: Bloomsbury.

Hegarty, Paul. (2017). Grid Intensities: Hearing Structures in Chantal Akerman's Films of the 1970s. In Holly Rogers and Jeremy Barham, eds., *The Music and Sound of Experimental Film*. Oxford: Oxford University Press, 149–66.

Heile, Björn. (2004). Darmstadt as Other: British and American Responses to Musical Modernism. *Twentieth-Century Music*, 1, no. 2, 161–78.

Heile, Björn. (n.d.) Mapping Musical Modernism, digital resource. https://musical modernism.arts.gla.ac.uk/, accessed 28 March 2022.

Heile, Björn, ed. (2009). Introduction: New Music and the Modernist Legacy. In Björn Heile, ed., *The Modernist Legacy: Essays on New Music*. Farnham: Ashgate, 1–10.

Helfgott, Isadora. (2015). *Framing the Audience: Art and the Politics of Culture in the United States, 1929–1945*. Philadelphia, PA: Temple University Press.

Herbert, Trevor. (2003). Social History and Music History. In Martin Clayton, Trevor Herbert and Richard Middleton, eds., *The Cultural Study of Music: A Critical Introduction*. Abingdon, UK: Routledge, 146–56.

Hersch, Charles. (2007). *Subversive Sounds: Race and the Birth of Jazz in New Orleans*. Chicago: University of Chicago Press.

Hesmondhalgh, D. (1998). The British Dance Music Industry: A Case Study of Independent Cultural Production. *The British Journal of Sociology*, 49, no. 2, 234–51.

Hesmondhalgh, David. (1999). Indie: The Institutional Politics and Aesthetics of a Popular Music Genre. *Cultural Studies*, 13, no. 1, 34–61.

Higgins, Dick. (2018/1987). Fluxus: Theory and Reception. In Steven Clay and Ken Friedman, eds., *Intermedia, Fluxus and the Something Else Press: Selected Writings by Dick Higgins*. New York: Siglio, 88–114.

Hill, Juniper. (2009). The Influence of Conservatory Folk Music Programmes: The Sibelius Academy in Comparative Context. *Ethnomusicology Forum*, 18, no. 2, 207–41.

Hill, Sarah. (2015). *San Francisco and the Long 60s*. New York and London: Bloomsbury.

Hill Collins, Patricia. (1990). *Black Feminist Thought: Knowledge, Consciousness and the Politics of Empowerment*. New York: Routledge.

Hiller, Paul. (1997). *Arvo Pärt*. Oxford: Oxford University Press.

Hills, Matt. (2002). *Fan Cultures*. London: Routledge.

Hind, Rolf. (2015). Queer Pitch: Is There Such a Thing? *The Guardian*, 12 September. Available at: www.theguardian.com/music/musicblog/2015/sep/

12/queer-pitch-classical-music-gay-composers-by-rolf-hind, accessed 19 October 2020.

Hindley, Clifford. (1995). Britten's Parable Art: A Gay Reading. *History Workshop Journal*, 40, no. 1, 63–90.

Hisama, Ellie. (2006). *Gendering Musical Modernism: The Music of Ruth Crawford, Marion Bauer, and Miriam Gideon*. Cambridge: Cambridge University Press.

Ho, Allan B. and Dmitri Feofanov. (1998). *Shostakovich Reconsidered*. London: Toccata.

Hobsbawm, Eric. (1998). *Behind the Times: The Decline and Fall of the Twentieth-Century Avant Gardes*. London: Thames and Hudson.

Hodeir, André. (2001/1959). Monk or the Misunderstanding. In Rob van der Bliek, ed., *The Thelonious Monk Reader*. New York: Oxford University Press, 118–34.

Hoggart, Richard. (2009/1957). *The Uses of Literacy: Aspects of Working-Class Life*. London: Penguin Classics.

Holliday, Billie. (2018). *Lady Sings the Blues*. London: Penguin Classics.

Hollis, Patricia. (1998). *Jennie Lee: A Life*. Oxford: Oxford University Press.

Holloway, Robin. (1979). *Debussy and Wagner*. London: Eulenburg.

Holmes, Thom. (2020). *Electronic and Experimental Music: Technology, Music and Culture*. 6th edition. New York and London: Routledge.

hooks, bell. (1990). Postmodern Blackness. *Postmodern Culture*, 1, no. 1. Available at: https://muse.jhu.edu/article/27283

Hornby, Nick. (1994). *Fever Pitch: A Fan's Life*. New York: Penguin Books.

Hornby, Nick. (1996). *High Fidelity*. London: Indigo.

Hosokawa, Shuhei. (1999). Salsa no Tiene Frontera: Orquesta de la Luz and the Globalization of Popular Music. *Cultural Studies*, 13, no. 3, 509–34.

Huang, Hao and Rachel Huang. (2013). She Sang as She Spoke: Billie Holiday and Aspects of Speech Intonation and Diction. *Jazz Perspectives*, 7, no.3, 287–302.

Hughes, Langston. (2015/1940). *The Big Sea*. New York: Farrar, Straus and Giroux.

Huron, David and Ann Ommen. (2006). An Empirical Study of Syncopation in American Popular Music, 1890–1939. *Music Theory Spectrum*, 28, no. 2, 211–32.

Hutcheon, Linda. (1988). *A Poetics of Postmodernism: History, Theory, Fiction*. London: Routledge.

Huyssen, Andreas. (1986). *After the Great Divide: Modernism, Mass Culture and Postmodernism*. Bloomington: Indiana University Press.

Iddon, Martin. (2011). Darmstadt Schools: Darmstadt as a Plural Phenomenon. *Tempo*. 65, 2–8.

Iddon, Martin and Philip Thomas. (2020). *John Cage's Concert for Piano and Orchestra*. Oxford: Oxford University Press.

Ivens, Freya-Jarman. (2011). *Queer Voices: Technologies, Vocalities, and the Musical Flaw*. New York: Palgrave Macmillan.

Jameson, Frederic. (1991). *Postmodernism, or, The Cultural Logic of Late Capitalism*. London: Verso.

Janssen, Susanne and Marc Verboord. (2015). Cultural Mediators and Gatekeepers. In J. Wright, ed., *International Encyclopedia of the Social & Behavioral Sciences*, 2nd ed. Oxford: Elsevier, 440–6.

Jenkins, Henry. (2007). *Transmedial Storytelling 101: Confessions of an Aca-Fan* [blog]. Available at http://henryjenkins.org/blog/2007/03/transmedia_storytelling_101.html, accessed 15 September 2019.

Jenkins, Henry. (2006). *Convergence Culture: Where Old and New Media Collide.* New York: New York University Press.

Joe, Jeongwon and Rose Theresa. (2002). *Between Opera and Cinema.* New York: Routledge.

Johnson, Hafiz Shabazz Farel and John Miller Chernoff. (1991). Basic Conga Drum Rhythms in African-American Musical Styles. *Black Music Research Journal*, 11, no. 1, 55–75.

Johnson, James. (1995). *Listening in Paris: A Cultural History.* Berkeley and Los Angeles: University of California Press.

Johnson, Julian. (2002). *Who Needs Classical Music? Cultural Choice and Musical Value.* New York and Oxford: Oxford University Press.

Johnson, Julian. (2020). *After Debussy.* Oxford: Oxford University Press.

Johnston, Ben. (2006). *'Maximum Clarity' and Other Writings on Music.* Ed. Bob Gilmore. Urbana: University of Illinois Press.

Joseph, Brandon. (2002). 'My Mind Split Open': Andy Warhol's Exploding Plastic Inevitable. *Grey Room*, no. 8, 81–107.

Judt, Tony. (2005). *Postwar: A History of Europe since 1945.* London: Vintage.

Judt, Tony. (2008). *Reappraisals: Reflections on the Forgotten Twentieth Century.* New York: Penguin.

Julien, Olivier. (1999). The Diverting of Musical Technology by Rock Musicians: The Example of Double-Tracking. *Popular Music*, 18, no. 3, 357–65.

Julien, Oliver. (2008). 'A Lucky Man Who Made the Grade': Sgt. Pepper and the Rise of a Phonographic Tradition in Twentieth-Century Popular Music. In Olivier Julien, ed., *Sgt. Pepper and the Beatles: It Was Forty Years Ago Today.* Farnham: Ashgate, 147–70.

Kahn, Douglas. (1990). Track Organology. *October*, 55, 67–78.

Kahn-Harris, Keith. (2006). Roots? The Relationship between the Global and the Local in the Extreme Metal Scene. In Andy Bennett, Barry Shank and Jason Toynbee, eds., *The Popular Music Studies Reader.* New York: Routledge, 128–36.

Kajikawa, Loren. (2009). Eminem's 'My Name Is': Signifying Whiteness, Rearticulating Race. *Journal of the Society for American Music*, 3, no. 3, 341–63.

Kaplan, Abraham. (1972). The Aesthetics of the Popular Arts. In James B. Hall and Barry Ulanov, eds., *Modern Culture and the Arts.* New York: McGraw-Hill.

Kärjä, Antti-Ville. (2006). A Prescribed Alternative Mainstream: Popular Music and Canon Formation. *Popular Music*, 25, no. 1, 3–19.

Kassabian, Anahid. (2001). *Hearing Film: Tracking Identifications in Contemporary Hollywood Film Music.* New York: Routledge.

Kassabian, Anahid. (2010). Have Canons Outlived Their Usefulness? *Journal of Popular Music Studies*, 22, no. 1, 74–8.

Kassabian, Anahid. (2013a). The End of Diegesis As We Know It. In C. Gorbman, J. Richardson and C. Vernallis, eds., *The Oxford Handbook of New Audiovisual Aesthetics*. New York: Oxford University Press, 89–106.

Kassabian, Anahid. (2013b). *Ubiquitous Listening: Affect, Attention, and Distributed Subjectivity*. Berkeley and Los Angeles: University of California Press.

Kater, Michael H. (1989). Forbidden Fruit? Jazz in the Third Reich. *The American Historical Review*, 94, no. 1, 11–43.

Katz, David. (2000). *People Funny Boy: The Genius of Lee 'Scratch' Perry*. Edinburgh: Payback Press.

Katz, Mark. (2010). *Capturing Sound: How Technology has Changed Music*. Berkeley and Los Angeles: University of California Press.

Katz, Mark. (2012). *Groove Music: The Art and Culture of the Hip-Hop DJ*. Oxford: Oxford University Press.

Keightley, Keir. (1996). 'Turn It Down!' She Shrieked: Gender, Domestic Space, and High Fidelity, 1948–59. *Popular Music*, 15, no. 2, 149–77.

Keightley, Keir. (2001). Reconsidering Rock. In Simon Frith, Will Straw and John Street, eds., *The Cambridge Companion to Pop and Rock*. Cambridge: Cambridge University Press. 109–42.

Keightley, Keir. (2004). Long Play: Adult-Oriented Popular Music and the Temporal Logics of the Post-War Sound Recording Industry in the USA. *Media, Culture & Society*, 26, no. 3, 375–91.

Keightley, Keir. (2010). Taking Popular Music (and Tin Pan Alley and Jazz) Seriously. *Journal of Popular Music Studies*, 22, no. 1, 90–7.

Keightley, Keir. (2013). Tin Pan Allegory. *Modernism/Modernity*, 19, no. 4, 717–36.

Keil, Charles and Stephen Feld. (1994). *Music Grooves*. Chicago: University of Chicago Press.

Kelley, Robin D. G. (2000). A Sole Response. *American Quarterly*, 52, no. 3, 533–45.

Kelley, Robin D. G. (2009). *Thelonious Monk: The Life and Times of an American Original*. New York: Free Press.

Kenney, William Howland. (1993). *Chicago Jazz: A Cultural History 1904–1930*. New York: Oxford University Press.

Kenyon, Nicholas, ed. (1988). *Authenticity and Early Music*. Oxford: Oxford University Press.

Kerman, Joseph. (1983). A Few Canonic Variations. *Critical Inquiry*, 10, no. 1, 107–25.

Kerman, Joseph. (1985). *Contemplating Music: Challenges to Musicology*. Cambridge, MA: Harvard University Press.

Kerman, Joseph. (2005/1956). *Opera as Drama*, 50th anniversary ed. Berkeley and Los Angeles: University of California Press.

Kernodle, Tammy. (2008). 'I Wish I Knew How It Would Feel to Be Free': Nina Simone and the Redefining of the Freedom Song of the 1960s. *Journal of the Society for American Music*, 2, no. 3, 295–317.

Keyes, Cheryl L. (2004). *Rap Music and Street Consciousness*. Urbana and Chicago: University of Chicago Press.

Kimsey, John. (2008). The Whatchamacallit in the Garden: Sgt. Pepper and Fables of Interference. In Olivier Julien, ed., *Sgt. Pepper and the Beatles: It Was Forty Years Ago Today*. Aldershot: Ashgate Publishing, 121–38.

King, Jason. (2013). The Time Is Out of Joint: Behind the Scenes on D'Angelo's *Voodoo*. *Slate*, February 15. Available at: www.slate.com/articles/arts/music_box/2013/02/ behind_the_scenes_with_questlove_and_d_angelo_on_voodoo .html (accessed 15 October 2019).

Kinsey, Alfred, Wardell Pomeroy and Clyde Martin. (1948). *Sexual Behavior in the Human Male*. Philadelphia, PA: Saunders.

Kinsey, Alfred, Wardell Pomeroy, Clyde Martin and Paul Gebhard. (1953). *Sexual Behavior in the Human Female*. Philadelphia, PA: Saunders.

Kittler, Friedrich. (1999). *Gramophone, Film, Typewriter*. Stanford, CA: Stanford University Press.

Kleppinger, Stanley V. (2003). On the Influence of Jazz Rhythm in the Music of Aaron Copland. *American Music*, 21, no.1, 74–111.

Koestenbaum, Wayne. (1993). *The Queen's Throat: Opera, Homosexuality, and the Mystery of Desire*. New York: Da Capo.

Koozin, Timothy. (2011). Guitar Voicing in Pop-Rock Music: A Performance-Based Analytical Approach. *Music Theory Online*, 17, no. 3, www.mtosmt.org/issues/ mto.11.17.3/mto.11.17.3.koozin.html

Korsgaard, Mathias Bonde. (2013). Music Video Transformed. In Claudia Gorbman, John Richardson and Carol Vernallis, eds., *The Oxford Handbook of New Audiovisual Aesthetics*. New York: Oxford University Press, 501–24.

Korsgaard, Mathias Bonde. (2017). *Music Video After MTV: Audiovisual Studies, New Media, and Popular Music*. New York: Routledge.

Kramer, Jonathan D. (1988). *The Time of Music*. New York and London: Schirmer Books.

Kramer, Lawrence. (1990). *Music as Cultural Practice, 1800–1900*. Berkeley and Los Angeles: University of California Press.

Kramer, Lawrence. (1994). Charging the Canons. In Katherine Bergeron and Philip V. Bohlman, eds., *Disciplining Music Musicology and Its Canons*. Chicago: The University of Chicago Press.

Kramer, Lawrence. (1995). *Classical Music and Postmodern Knowledge*. Berkeley and Los Angeles: University of California Press.

Kramer, Lawrence. (1996). Powers of Blackness: Africanist Discourse in Modern Concert Music. *Black Music Research Journal*, 16, no. 1, 53–70.

Kramer, Lawrence. (1998). *Franz Schubert: Sexuality, Subjectivity, Song*. Cambridge: Cambridge University Press.

Kramer, Lawrence. (2015). Opera as Case History: Freud's Dora, Strauss's Salome, and the Perversity of Modern Life. *The Opera Quarterly*, 31, nos. 1–2, 110–15.

Kristeva, Julia. (1980/1966). Word, Dialogue, and Novel. In Julia Kristeva, *Desire in Language: A Semiotic Approach to Literature and Art*, ed. Leon S. Roudiez, trans. Thomas Gora et al. New York: Columbia University Press, 64-91.

Kronfeld, Maya. (2019). The Philosopher's Bass Drum: Adorno's Jazz and the Politics of Rhythm. *Radical Philosophy*, 2, no. 5, 34–47.

Kruse, Holly. (2003). *Site and Sound: Understanding Independent Music Scenes.* New York: Peter Lang.

Kubik, Gerhard. (1994). *Theory of African Music, Vol. II.* Chicago: University of Chicago Press.

Kurabayashi, Y. and Takahashi Ito. (1992). Socio-Economic Characteristic of Audiences for Western Classical Music in Japan: A Statistical Analysis. In Ruth Towse and Abdul Khakee, eds., *Cultural Economics.* Berlin: Springer-Verlag, 257–87.

Lacan, Jacques. (1998/1973). *The Four Fundamental Concepts of Psychoanalysis*, ed. Jacques-Alain Miller, trans. Alan Sheridan. New York: W. W. Norton.

Lacasse, Serge. (2001). Interpretation of Vocal Staging by Popular Music Listeners: A Reception Test. *Psychomusicology: A Journal of Research in Music Cognition*, 17, nos. 1–2, 56–76.

Lachenmann, Helmut and Richard Toop (trans.). (2004). Composing in the Shadow of Darmstadt. *Contemporary Music Review*, 23, nos. 3–4, 43–53.

Laing, Dave. (2004). Copyright, Politics and the International Music Industry. In Simon Frith and Lee Marshall, eds., *Music and Copyright*, 2nd edition. Edinburgh: Edinburgh University Press, 70–86.

Lambert, Constant. (1934). *Music Ho! A Study of Music in Decline.* New York: Charles Scribner's Sons.

Lambert, Philip. (2008). Brian Wilson's Pet Sounds. *Twentieth-Century Music*, 5, no. 1, 109–33.

Lambert, Philip. (1996). Ives and Berg: 'Normative' Procedures and Post-Tonal Alternatives. In Geoffrey Block and J. Peter Burkholder, eds., *Charles Ives and the Classical Tradition.* New Haven, CT: Yale University Press, 105–30.

Lambert, Philip. (1997). *The Music of Charles Ives.* New Haven, CT: Yale University Press.

Langer, Suzanne. (1953). *Feeling and Form: A Theory of Art.* New York: Charles Scribner's Sons.

Larson, Kay. (2012). *Where the Heart Beats: John Cage, Zen Buddhism and the Inner Life of Artists.* New York: Penguin.

Latartara, John. (2007). Cage and Time: Temporality in Early and Late Works. *College Music Symposium*, 47, 100–16.

Latour, Bruno. (1987). *Science in Action.* Cambridge, MA: Harvard University Press.

Lawrence, Tim. (2009). *Hold On to Your Dreams: Arthur Russell and the Downtown Music Scene, 1973–1992*. Durham, NC and London: Duke University Press.

Lawson, Colin and Robin Stowell. (1999). *The Historical Performance of Music: An Introduction*. Cambridge: Cambridge University Press.

Leavis, F. R. (1930). *Mass Civilization and Minority Culture*, Minority Pamphlet No. 1. Cambridge: The Minority Press. https://is.cuni.cz/studium/predmety/index.php?do=download&did=41298&kod=JJM117, accessed 27 October 2020.

Lebrecht, Norman. (2017). The Chinese Are Coming. *The Spectator*, 25 November. www.spectator.co.uk/article/the-chinese-are-coming, accessed 6 November 2020.

Lee, Kayoung. (2013). The Reception of Bach's Music in Korea from 1900 to 1945. *Bach*, 44, no. 2, 25–51.

Leech-Wilkinson, Daniel. (1984). What We Are Doing With Early Music Is Genuinely Authentic to Such a Small Degree That the Word Loses Most of Its Intended Meaning. *Early Music*, 12, no. 1, 13–16.

Lely, John and James Saunders. (2012). *Word Events*. London: Bloomsbury.

Leppert, Richard. (1988). *Music and Image: Domesticity, Ideology and Socio-Cultural Formation in Eighteenth-Century England*. Cambridge: Cambridge University Press.

Lendvai, Ernő. (1979). *Béla Bartók: An Analysis of His Music*. London: Kahn and Averill.

Leonard, Marion. (2007a). Constructing Histories through Material Culture: Popular Music, Museums and Collecting. *Popular Music History*, 2, no. 2, 147–67.

Leonard, Marion. (2007b). *Gender in the Music Industry: Rock, Discourse and Girl Power*. Farnham: Ashgate.

Leonard, Marion and Robert Knifton. (2015). Introduction: Special Issue on Popular Music and Heritage. *Popular Music History*, 10, no. 2, 107–12.

Leong, Daphne. (2004). Bartók's Studies of Folk Rhythm: A Window into His Own Practice. *Acta Musicologica*, 76, no. 2, 253–77.

Lessig, Lawrence. (2004). *Free Culture: How Big Media Uses Technology and the Law to Lock Down Culture and Control Creativity*. New York: Penguin.

Lessig, Lawrence. (2008). *Remix: Making Art and Commerce Thrive in the Hybrid Economy*. London: Bloomsbury.

Levi, Erik. (1994). *Music in the Third Reich*. London: Macmillan.

Lévi-Strauss, Claude. (1974/1958). *Structural Anthropology*. New York: Basic Books.

Levine, Lawrence. (1988). *Highbrow Lowbrow: The Emergence of Cultural Hierarchy in America*. Cambridge, MA: Harvard University Press.

Levinson, Jerrold. (1996). Film Music and Narrative Agency. In David Bordwell and Noël Carroll, eds., *Post-Theory: Reconstructing Film Studies*. Madison: The University of Winconsin Press, 248–82.

Leyshon, Andrew, David Matless and George Revill, eds. (1998). *The Place of Music*. NYC and London: The Guildford Press.

Lindberg, Ulf. (2003). Popular Modernism? The 'Urban' Style of Interwar Tin Pan Alley. *Popular Music*, 22, no. 3, 283–98.

Ling, Jan. (2003). Is 'World Music' the 'Classical Music' of Our Time? *Popular Music*, 22, no. 2, 235–40.

Lipsitz, George. (2011). New Orleans in the World and the World in New Orleans. *Black Music Research Journal*, 31, no. 2, 261–90.

Liptrot, Michelle. (2014). 'Punk Belongs to the Punx, Not Business Men!' British DIY Punk as a Form of Cultural Resistance. In The Subcultures Network, ed., *Fight Back: Punk, Politics and Resistance*. Manchester: Manchester University Press.

Litwack, Leon. (1998). *Trouble in Mind: Black Southerners in the Age of Jim Crow*. New York: First Vintage Books.

Lochhead, Judy and Joseph Auner, eds. (2002). *Postmodern Music/Postmodern Thought*. New York: Routledge.

Locke, Ralph P. (2009). *Musical Exoticism: Images and Reflections*. Cambridge: Cambridge University Press.

Lomax, Alan. (1972). An Appeal for Cultural Equity. www.culturalequity.org/alan-lomax/appeal. Accessed 15 October 2019

London, Justin. (2004). *Hearing in Time: Psychological Aspects of Musical Meter*. New York: Oxford University Press.

Loosely, David. (1995). *The Politics of Fun: Cultural Policy and Debate in Contemporary France*. Oxford: Berg.

Lopes, Paul. (2002). *The Rise of a Jazz Art World*. Cambridge: Cambridge University Press.

Lorde, Audre. (1984). The Master's Tools Will Never Dismantle the Master's House. In Audre Lorde, *Sister Outsider: Essays and Speeches*. Berkeley, CA: Crossing Press. 110–14.

Losada, C. Catherine. (2009). Between Modernism and Postmodernism: Strands of Continuity in Collage Compositions by Rochberg, Berio, and Zimmermann. *Music Theory Spectrum*, 31, no. 1, 57–100.

Lott, Eric. (1988). Double V, Double-Time: Bebop's Politics of Style. *Callaloo*, 36, 597–605.

Lowy, Adrienne. (2010). Ready Steady Go! Televisual Pop Style and the Careers of Dusty Springfield, Cilla Black, Sandie Shaw and Lulu. In Ian Inglis, ed., *Popular Music and Television in Britain*. Farnham: Ashgate.

Lyotard, Jean-François. (1984/1979). *The Postmodern Condition: A Report on Knowledge*. Minneapolis: University of Minnesota Press.

Macan, Edward. (1992). The Spirit of Albion in Twentieth-Century English Popular Song: Vaughan Williams, Holst, and the Progressive Rock Movement. *The Music Review*, 53, no. 2, 100–25.

Macan, Edward. (1997). *Rocking the Classics: English Progressive Rock and the Counterculture*. Oxford: Oxford University Press.

MacDonald, Ian. (2008). *Revolution in the Head: The Beatles' Records and the Sixties*, 2nd ed. London: Vintage.

MacDonald, Ian. (2003). Pulse of the Machine. In Ian MacDonald, *The People's Music*. London: Random House, 148–53.

Maconie, Robin. (1976). *The Works of Karlheinz Stockhausen*. Oxford: Oxford University Press.

Maconie, Robin. (1989). *Stockhausen on Music: Lectures and Interviews*. New York: Marion Boyars.

Maffesoli, Michel. (1996). *The Time of the Tribes: The Decline of Individualism in Mass Society*. London: SAGE.

Magee, Gayle Sherwood. (2008). *Charles Ives Reconsidered*. Urbana: University of Illinois Press.

Maguire, Jennifer Smith and Julian Matthews. (2010). Cultural Intermediaries and the Media. *Sociology Compass*, 4, no. 7, 405–16.

Maira, Sunaina. (1999). Identity Dub: The Paradoxes of an Indian American Youth Subculture. *Cultural Anthropology*, 14, no. 1, February, 29–60.

Malone, Bill. (1968). *Country Music USA*. Austin: University of Texas Press.

Mann, William. (1963). What Songs the Beatles Sang. *The Times*, 27 December. S 4.

Maraš, Svetlana. (2017). Thingification of Compositional Process: The Emergence and Autonomy of Extramusical Objects in Western Art Music. In Kathleen Coessens, ed., *Experimental Encounters in Music and Beyond*. Leuven: Leuven University Press, 43–56.

Marcus, Greil. (1989). *Lipstick Traces*. Cambridge, MA: Harvard University Press.

Marshall, Wayne. (2006). Giving Up Hip-hop's Firstborn: A Quest for the Real after the Death of Sampling. *Callaloo* 29, no. 3, 868–92.

Marshall, Wayne and Peter Manuel. (2006). The Riddim Method: Aesthetics, Practice, and Ownership in Jamaican Dancehall. *Popular Music*, 25, no. 3, 447–70.

Martin, Henry. (2012–13). Expanding Jazz Tonality: The Compositions of John Coltrane. *Theory and Practice*, 37–8, 185–219.

Marx, Karl. (1867–1894). *Das Kapital*. 4 vols. Hamburg: Otto Meissner.

Marx, Karl and Friedrich Engels. (1848). *Das Kommunistische Manifest*. London: Workers' Educational Association.

Marx, Leo. (1964). *The Machine in the Garden: Technology and the Pastoral Ideal in America*. Oxford: Oxford University Press.

Masters, Marc. (2008). *No Wave*. Black Dog Publishing.

Masters, William and Virginia Johnson. (1966). *Human Sexual Response*. Toronto and New York: Bantam Books.

Mathias, Rhiannon. (2012). *Lutyens, Maconchy, Williams and Twentieth-Century British Music: A Blest Trio of Sirens*. Farnham: Ashgate.

Matsumoto, Naomi. (2020). The 'Other' Reversed? Japan's Assimilation of Carmen between 1885–1945. In Richard Langham Smith and Clair Rowden, eds., *Carmen Abroad: Bizet's Opera on the Global Stage*. Cambridge: Cambridge University Press, 284–303.

Maultsby, Portia K. (2005). Africanisms in African American Music. In Joseph E. Holloway, *Africanisms in American Culture*, 2nd ed. Bloomington: Indiana University Press, 326–55.

Maus, Fred. E. (2001). Glamour and Evasion: The Fabulous Ambivalence of the Pet Shop Boys. *Popular Music*, 20, no. 3, 379–93.

Mayhew, Emma. (2004). Positioning the Producer: Gender Divisions in Creative Labour and Value. In Sheila Whiteley, Andy Bennett and Stan Hawkins, eds., *Music, Space and Place: Popular Music and Cultural Identity*. Aldershot: Ashgate Publishing Limited, 149–62.

McAlpine, Kenneth, Matthew Bett and James Scanlan. (2009). Approaches to Creating Real-Time Adaptive Music in Interactive Entertainment: a Musical Perspective. 35th Audio Engineering Society International Conference 2009, London, 1 February. Abertay University. https://rke.abertay.ac.uk/en/publications/ approaches-to-creating-real-time-adaptive-music-in-interactive-en, accessed 17 September 2019.

McClary, Susan. (1989). Terminal Prestige: The Case of Avant Garde Music Composition. *Cultural Critique*, 12, 57–81.

McClary, Susan. (1991). *Feminine Endings*. Minneapolis: University of Minnesota Press.

McClary, Susan. (1992). *Georges Bizet: Carmen*. Cambridge: Cambridge University Press.

McClary, Susan. (2000). *Conventional Wisdom: The Content of Musical Form*. Berkeley and Los Angeles: University of California Press.

McClary, Susan. (2002). This Is Not a Story My People Tell: Musical Time and Space According to Laurie Anderson. In Susan McClary, *Feminine Endings: Music, Gender, and Sexuality*, 2nd ed. Minneapolis: University of Minnesota Press.

McClary, Susan. (2004). Rap, Minimalism and Structures of Time in Late Twentieth-Century Culture. In Daniel Warner, ed., *Audio Culture*. London: Continuum, 289–98.

McClary, Susan. (2006). Constructions of Subjectivity in Schubert's Music. In Philip Brett, Elizabeth Wood and Gary C. Thomas, eds., *Queering the Pitch*, 2nd ed. New York: Routledge, 205–34.

McClatchie, Stephen. (1996). Benjamin Britten, 'Owen Wingrave' and the Politics of the Closet; Or, 'He Shall Be Straightened Out at Paramore'. *Cambridge Opera Journal*, 8, no. 1, 59–75.

McDonald, Matthew. (2010). 'Jeux de Nombres': Automated Rhythm in The Rite of Spring. *Journal of the American Musicological Society*, 63, no. 3, 499–551.

McGee, Kristin. (2008). The Feminization of Mass Culture and the Novelty of All-Girl Bands: The Case of Ingenues. *Popular Music and Society*, 31, no. 5, 629–62.

McKee, Abaigh. (n.d.) Art and Music under the Third Reich: Entartete Kunst and Entartete Musik Exhibitions. Music and the Holocaust. http://holocaustmusic .ort.org/politics-and-propaganda/third-reich/entartete-musik/, accessed 9 April 2022.

McLeod, Kembrew and Peter DiCola. (2011). *Creative License: The Law and Culture of Digital Sampling*. Durham, NC: Duke University Press.

McLeod, Kembrew and Rudolf Kuenzil, eds. (2011). *Cutting Across Media: Appropriation Art, Interventionist Collage, and Copyright Law*. Durham, NC: Duke University Press.

McLuhan, Marshall. (2001/1964). *Understanding Media: The Extensions of Man*. London and New York: Routledge.

McMillin, Scott. (2006). *The Musical as Drama*. Princeton, NJ: Princeton University Press.

McRobbie, Angela. (2000). Settling Accounts with Subculture: A Feminist Critique. In Angela McRobbie, *Feminism and Youth Culture*. New York: Routledge, 26–43.

Mead, Andrew. (2011). Parallel Processes: Milton Babbitt and Total Serialism. In Marc Delaere, ed., *Rewriting Recent Music History: The Development of Early Serialism 1947–1957*. Leuven: Peeters.

Meintjes, Louise. (1990). Paul Simon's *Graceland*, South Africa, and the Mediation of Musical Meaning. *Ethnomusicology*, 34, no. 1, 37–73.

Melfi, Daniel. (2018). The Design Collective Defining the Look of Berlin Techno. *Format*. Available at: www.format.com/magazine/features/.design/pfadfinderei-design-berlin-electronic-music-moderat, accessed 17 September 2019.

Melvin, Sheila and Jindong Cai. (2004). *Rhapsody in Red: How Western Classical Music Became Chinese*. New York: Algora Publishing.

Messiaen, Olivier. (1944). *Technique du mon langage musicale*. Paris: Alphonse Leduc.

Messiaen, Olivier. (1949–1992).*Traité de rythme, de couleurs, et d'ornithologie*. Paris: Alphonse Leduc.

Metzer, David. (2003). *Quotation and Cultural Meaning in Twentieth-Century Music*. Cambridge: Cambridge University Press.

Meyer, Leonard B. (1967). *Music, the Arts and Ideas: Patterns and Predictions in Twentieth-Century Culture*. Chicago: University of Chicago Press.

Middleton, Jason and Roger Beebe. (2002). The Racial Politics of Hybridity and 'Neo-Eclecticism' in Contemporary Music. *Popular Music*, 21, no. 2, 159–72.

Middleton, Richard. (1990). *Studying Popular Music*. Buckingham: Open University Press.

Middleton, Richard. (2000a). Work-in(g)-Practice: Configurations of the Popular Music Intertext. In Michael, Talbot, ed., *The Musical Work: Reality or Invention?* Liverpool: Liverpool University Press, 59–87.

Middleton, Richard. (2000b). Musical Belongings: Western Music and Its Low-Other. In Georgina Born and David Hesmondhalgh, eds.,*Western Music and Its Others: Difference, Representation, and Appropriation in Music*. Berkeley and Los Angeles: University of California Press, 59–85.

Middleton, Richard, ed. (1990). *Reading Pop*. Oxford: Oxford University Press.

Mikkonen, Simo. (2010). 'Muddle Instead of Music' in 1936: Cataclysm of Musical Administration. In Pauline Fairclough, ed., *Shostakovich Studies 2*. Cambridge: Cambridge University Press, 231–48.

Millea, James. (2019). Hip Hop Music and (Reading) the Narrative Soundtracks of New Black Realist Cinema. In Justin D. Burton and Jason Lee Oakes, eds., *The Oxford Handbook of Hip Hop Music*. Oxford: Oxford University Press.

Miller, Kiri. (2012). *Playing Along: Digital Games, YouTube and Virtual Performance*. New York: Oxford University Press.

Miller, Kiri. (2013). Virtual and Visceral Experience in Music- Oriented Video Games. In Amy Herzog, John Richardson and Carol Vernallis, eds., *The Oxford Handbook of Sound and Image in Digital Media*. New York: Oxford University Press, 517–35.

Miller, Kiri. (2017). *Playable Bodies: Dance Games and Intimate Media*. New York: Oxford University Press.

Miller, Paul D. (2008). *Sound Unbound*. Cambridge, MA: The MIT Press.

Milner, Greg. (2009). *Perfecting Sound Forever: The Story of Recorded Music*. London: Granta Publications.

Milstein, Silvina. (1992). *Arnold Schoenberg: Notes, Sets, Forms*. Cambridge: Cambridge University Press.

Mitchell, Tony, ed. (2001). *Global Noise: Rap and Hip-Hop Outside the USA*. Middletown, CT: Wesleyan University Press.

Monsaingeon, Bruno. (2001). *Sviatoslav Richter: Notebooks and Conversations*. Trans. Stewart Spencer. London: Faber and Faber.

Monson, Ingrid. (1994). Doubleness and Jazz Improvisation: Irony, Parody, and Ethnomusicology. *Critical Inquiry*, 20, no. 2, 283–313.

Moore, Allan. (1992). Patterns of Harmony. *Popular Music*, 11, no. 1, 73–106.

Moore, Allan. (2001). *Rock: The Primary Text. Developing a Musicology of Rock*. Aldershot: Ashgate.

Moore, Allan. (2002). Authenticity as Authentication. *Popular Music*, 21, no. 2, 209–23.

Moorefield, Virgil. (2005). *The Producer as Composer: Shaping the Sounds of Popular Music*. Cambridge, MA and London: The MIT Press.

Morgan, Robert P. (1991). *Twentieth-Century Music*. New York and London: W. W. Norton & Co.

Mosch, Ulrich. (2017). Foundation or Mere Quotation? Conditions for Applying the Tonality Concept to Music after 1950. In Felix Wörner, Ullrich Schneider and Philip Rupprecht, eds., *Tonality since 1950*. Stuttgart: Frank Steiner Verlag, 27–49.

Motter, Paul and Peter Schu. (2015). A History of Marshall Amps: The Early Years. *Reverb*. (8 May). https://reverb.com/uk/news/a-history-of-marshall-amps-the-early-years

Mulvey, Laura. (1975). Visual Pleasure and Narrative Cinema. *Screen*, 16, no. 3, 6–18.

Murch, Walter. (2000). Stretching Sound to Help the Mind See. *New York Times*. Available at: http://filmsound.org/murch/stretching.htm, accessed 20 December 2018.

Nattiez, Jean-Jacques. (1990/1987). *Music and Discourse: Towards a Semiology of Music*. Princeton, NJ: Princeton University Press.

Negus, Keith. (1992). *Producing Pop: Culture and Conflict in the Popular Music Industry*. London: E. Arnold.

Negus, Keith. (1996). *Popular Music in Theory: An Introduction*. Cambridge: Polity Press.

Negus, Keith. (1999). *Music Genres and Corporate Cultures*. London: Routledge.

Negus, Keith. (2002). The Work of Cultural Intermediaries and the Enduring Distance Between Production and Consumption. *Cultural Studies*, 16, no. 4, 501–15.

Negus, Keith. (2010). Bob Dylan's Phonographic Imagination. *Popular Music*, 29, no. 2, 213–27.

Neidhöfer, Christoph. (2005). A Theory of Harmony and Voice Leading for the Music of Olivier Messiaen. *Music Theory Spectrum* 27, no. 1, 1–34.

Nelson, Alondra. (2000). AfroFuturism: Past-Future Vision. *Colorlines*, 3, no. 1, 34–7.

Nettl, Bruno. (2005). *The Study of Ethnomusicology*. Chicago: University of Illinois Press.

Niebur, Louis. (2010). *Special Sound: The Creation and Legacy of the BBC Radiophonic Workshop*. Oxford: Oxford University Press.

Novak, David. (2013). *Japanoise: Music at the Edge of Circulation*. Durham, NC: Duke University Press.

Novitz, David. (1992). *The Boundaries of Art*. Philadelphia: Temple University Press.

Nyman, Michael. (1999/1974). *Experimental Music: Cage and Beyond*. Cambridge: Cambridge University Press.

O'Brien, Lucy. (2007). *Madonna: Like an Icon*. London: Bantam Press.

O'Hara, Patricia. (1997). 'The Woman of To-day': The *Fin de Siècle* Women of *The Music Hall and Theatre Review*. *Victorian Periodicals Review*, 30, no. 2, 141–56.

Oldcorn Reid, Caroline. (1976). Middle Class Values and Working Class Culture in Nineteenth Century Sheffield. (PhD, University of Sheffield)

Oliver, Paul. (1960). *Blues Fell This Morning*. London: Cassell.

Oliveros, Pauline. (2005). *Deep Listening: A Composer's Sound Practice*. New York: iUniverse.

Orbach, Susie. (1978–1982). *Fat Is a Feminist Issue*. Volume I, New York: Paddington Press; Volume II, New York: Berkley Books.

Osborne, William. (2000). Pauline Oliveros' Deep Listening and the *Sonic Meditations*. In Deborah Johnson and Wendy Oliver, eds, *Women Making Art*, New York: Peter Lang, 65–86.

Osmond-Smith, David. (1985). *Playing on Words: A Guide to Luciano Berio's Sinfonia*. Royal Musical Association Monographs. New York: Routledge.

Oswald, John. (1999). Plunderstanding Ecophonomics. In John Zorn, ed., *Arcana: Musicians on Music*. New York: Granary, 9–17.

Owens, Thomas. (1995). *Bebop: The Music and Its Players*. New York: Oxford University Press.

Packer, Renée Levine and Mary Jane Leach, eds. (2015). *Gay Guerrilla: Julius Eastman and His Music*. Rochester, NY: University of Rochester Press.

Page, Tim. (1986). Steve Reich, a Former Young Turk, Approaches 50. *New York Times*, June 1. Section 2, p. 23. Available at: www.nytimes.com/1986,06/01/arts/steve-reich-a-former-young-turk-approaches-50.html

Panassié, Hugues. (1936/1934). *Hot Jazz: The Guide to Swing Music*. Trans. Lyle Dowling and Eleanor Dowling. London: Cassell.

Paris, Jeffrey and Michael Ault. (2004). Subcultures and Political Resistance. *Peace Review*, 16, no. 4 (December), 403–7.

Parrott, Andrew. (2000). *The Essential Bach Choir*. Woodbridge: Boydell Press.

Parsons Smith, Catherine. (1994). 'A Distinguishing Virility': Feminism and Modernism in American Art Music. In Susan C. Cook and Judy S. Tsou, eds., *Cecilia Reclaimed: Feminist Perspectives on Gender and Music*. Urbana: University of Illinois Press, 90–106.

Partch, Harry. (1979). *Genesis of a Music*, 2nd ed. New York: Da Capo.

Partridge, Christopher. (2007). King Tubby Meets the Upsetter at the Grass Roots of Dub: Some Thoughts on the Early History and Influence of Dub Reggae. *Popular Music History*, 2, no. 3, 309–31.

Patteson, Thomas. (2016). *Instruments for New Music: Sound, Technology and Modernism*. Oakland, CA: University of California Press.

Paulin, S. (2000). Richard Wagner and the Fantasy of Cinematic Unity: The Idea of the *Gesamtkunstwerk* in the History and Theory of Film Music. In J. Buhler, C. Flinn and D. Neumeyer, eds., *Music and Cinema*. Hanover, NH: Wesleyan University Press, 58–84.

Peles, Stephen. (1998). Serialism and Complexity. In David Nicholls, ed., *The Cambridge History of American Music*. Cambridge: Cambridge University Press, 496–516.

Penman, Ian. (2013). Even If You Have to Starve. *London Review of Books*. www.lrb.co.uk/v35/n16/.ian-penman/even-if-you-have-to-starve, accessed 16 November 2018.

Penman, Ian. (2015). Swoonatra. *London Review of Books*. www.lrb.co.uk/the-paper/v37/n13/ian-penman/swoonatra, accessed 8 March 2022.

Perchard, Tom. (2011). Hip Hop Samples Jazz: Dynamics of Cultural Memory and Musical Tradition in the African American 1990s. *American Music*, 29, no. 3, 277–307.

Perchard, Tom. (2006). *Lee Morgan: His Life, Music and Culture*. London: Equinox.

Perchard, Tom. (2015a). *After Django: Making Jazz in Postwar France*. Ann Arbor: University of Michigan Press.

Perchard, Tom. (2015b). New Riffs on the Old Mind-Body Blues: 'Black Rhythm', 'White Logic', and Music Theory in the Twenty-First Century. *Journal of the Society for American Music*, 9, no. 3, 321–48.

Peterson, Richard A. (1990). Why 1955? Explaining the Advent of Rock Music. *Popular Music*, 9, no. 1, 97–116.

Peterson, Richard and Roger Kern. (1996). Changing Highbrow Taste: From Snob to Omnivore. *American Sociological Review*, 61, no. 5 (Oct.), 900–7.

Phelan, Gary. (1993). Image Banks. *Circa*, no. 66, 18–21.

Phillips, Trevor. (2003). The State of London. In Joe Kerr and Andrew Gibson, eds., *London from Punk to Blair*. London: Reaktion.

Piekut, Ben. (2014). Indeterminacy, Free Improvisation, and the Mixed Avant-Garde: Experimental Music in London, 1965–75. *Journal of the American Musicological Society*, 67, no. 3 (Fall), 769–824.

Pinch, Trevor and Nellie Oudshoorn. (2005). *How Users Matter: The Co-Construction of Users and Technology*. Cambridge, MA: The MIT Press.

Pinch, Trevor and Frank Trocco. (2002). *Analog Days: The Invention and Impact of the Moog Synthesizer*. Cambridge, MA: Harvard University Press.

Pitts, Stephanie. (2005). What Makes an Audience? Investigating the Roles and Experiences of Listeners at a Chamber Music Festival. *Music and Letters*, 86, no. 2, 257–69.

Pollock, Griselda. (1999). *Differencing the Canon: Feminism and the Writing of Art's Histories*. London and New York: Routledge.

Pomeroy, Boyd. (2003). Debussy's Tonality: A Formal Perspective. In Simon Trezise, ed., *The Cambridge Companion to Debussy*. Cambridge: Cambridge University Press, 155–78.

Pople, Anthony. (1994). Messiaen's Musical Language: An Introduction. In Peter Hill, ed., *The Messiaen Companion*. London: Faber and Faber, 15–50.

Porcello, Thomas. (1991). The Ethics of Digital Audio-Sampling: Engineers Discourse. *Popular Music* 10, no. 1, 69–84.

Porter, Dennis. (1994). Orientalism and Its Problems. In Patrick Williams and Laura Chrisman, eds., *Colonial Discourse and Post-Colonial Theory*. New York: Columbia University Press, 150–61.

Porter, Lewis. (1999). *John Coltrane: His Life and Music*. Ann Arbor: University of Michigan Press.

Potash, Chris. (1997). *Reggae, Rasta, Revolution: Jamaican Music from Ska to Dub*. New York: Schirmer Books.

Potter, Keith. (2000). *Four Musical Minimalists*. Cambridge: Cambridge University Press.

Potter, Keith. (2016). 1976 and All That: Minimalism and Post-Minimalism, Analysis and Listening Strategies. (Keynote address at the First International Conference on Minimalist Music, September 2007, University of Bangor, Wales.) Available at http://minimalismsociety.org/wp-content/uploads/2016/.01/Keith-Potter.pdf, accessed 15 July 2019.

Potter, Russell A. (1995). *Spectacular Vernaculars: Hip-Hop and the Politics of Postmodernism*. Stony Brook, NY: State University of New York Press.

Potts, Adam. (2015). The Internal Death of Japanoise. *Journal for Cultural Research*, 19, no. 4, 379–92.

Pough, Gwendolyn. (2004). *Check It While I Wreck It: Black Womanhood, Hip-Hop Culture, and the Public Sphere*. Lebanon, NH: Northeastern University Press.

Prévost, Edwin. (1995). *No Sound Is Innocent*. Harlow: Copula.

Prieto-Rodríguez, Juan and Victor Fernández-Blanco. (2000). Are Popular and Classical Music Listeners the Same People? *Journal of Cultural Economics*, 24, no. 2 (May), 147–64.

Příhodová, Barbora. (2011). The Power of Images in Performance: Josef Svoboda's Scenography for Intolleranza 1960 at Boston Opera Company. In Celia Morgan and Filipa Malva, eds., *Activating the Inanimate: Visual Vocabularies of Performance Practice*. Leiden: Brill, 31–40. www.inter-disciplinary.net/wp-content/uploads/2011/10/prihodovappaper.pdf, accessed 23 April 2017.

Purcell, Natalie. (2003). *Death Metal Music: The Passion and Politics of a Subculture*. Jefferson, NC: MacFarland.

Quinn, Eithne. (2005). *Nuthin' But a 'G' Thang: The Culture and Commerce of Gangsta Rap*. New York: Columbia University Press.

Radano, Ronald. (2000). Hot Fantasies: American Modernism and the Idea of Black Rhythm. In Ronald Radano and Philip Bohlman, eds., *Music and the Racial Imagination*. University of Chicago Press, 459–80.

Radano, Ronald. (2003). *Lying up a Nation: Race and Black Music*. Chicago: University of Chicago Press.

Raeburn, Bruce Boyd. (2009). Stars of David and Sons of Sicily: Constellations Beyond the Canon in Early New Orleans Jazz. *Jazz Perspectives*, 3, no. 2, 123–52.

Ramsey, Guthrie. (2004). *Race Music: Black Cultures from Bebop to Hip-Hop*. Berkeley and Los Angeles: University of California Press.

Ramsey, Guthrie. (2007). Secrets, Lies and Transcriptions: Revisions on Race, Black Music and Culture. In Julie Brown, ed.,*Western Music and Race*. Cambridge: Cambridge University Press, 24–36.

Rasch, Ronald. (2013). A Word or Two on the Tuning of Harry Partch. In D. Dunn, ed., *Harry Partch: An Anthology of Critical Perspectives*. New York: Routledge, 25–40.

Regev, Motti. (2006). Introduction. *Popular Music*, 25, no. 1, 1–2.

Regev, Motti. (2013). *Pop-Rock Music: Aesthetic Cosmopolitanism in Late Modernity*. Cambridge: Polity Press.

Rehding, Alexander. (2014). Of Sirens Old and New. In Sumanth Gopinath and Jason Stanyek, eds., *The Oxford Handbook of Mobile Music Studies*, Vol. 2. New York: Oxford University Press, 77–106.

Reich, Steve. (2002). *Writings on Music, 1965–2000*. Oxford: Oxford University Press.

Reich, Steve. (2002/1968). Music as a Gradual Process. In Steve Reich, *Writings on Music, 1965–2000*. New York: Oxford University Press, 34–5.

Reich, Willi. (1971). *Schoenberg: A Critical Biography*. Trans. Leo Black. London: Longman.

Relph, Edward. (2008/1976). *Place and Placelessness*, new ed. London: Pion.

Reynolds, Simon. (1998). *Energy Flash: A Journey Through Rave Music and Dance Culture*. London: Picador.

Reynolds, Simon. (2005). *Rip It Up and Start Again: Post-Punk 1978–84*. London: Faber and Faber, Ltd.

Reynolds, Simon. (2006). Haunted Audio. *The Wire*, 273, 26.

Reynolds, Simon. (2012a). HAUNTED AUDIO a/k/a SOCIETY OF THE SPECTRAL: Ghost Box, Mordant Music and Hauntology. *ReynoldsRetro*. Originally published in *The Wire* (2006). Available at: http://reynoldsretro .blogspot.com/2012/05/, accessed 28 July 2019.

Reynolds, Simon. (2012b). *Retromania: Pop Culture's Addiction to Its Own Past*. London: Faber and Faber Ltd.

Reynolds, Simon. (2016). How Prince's Androgynous Genius Changed the Way We Think About Music and Gender. *Pitchfork*, April 22, https://pitchfork.com/ features/.article/9882-how-princes-androgynous-genius-changed-the-way-we-think-about-music-and-gender/, accessed 19 October 2020.

Reynolds, Simon. (2018). How Auto-Tune Revolutionized the Sound of Popular Music/Online Article). *Pitchfork*. Uploaded 17 September (2018). Available at: https://pitchfork.com/features/article/how-auto-tune-revolutionized-the-sound-of-popular-music/#, accessed 19 December 2019.

Rhee, Jieun. (2005). Performing the Other: Yoko Ono's *Cut Piece*. *Art History* 28, no.1, 96–118.

Richardson John, Claudia Gorbman and Carol Vernallis, eds., *The Oxford Handbook of New Audiovisual Aesthetics*. New York: Oxford University Press.

Rietveld, Hillegonda C. (1998). *This Is Our House: House Music, Cultural Spaces and Technologies*. Aldershot: Ashgate.

Rigby, Brian. (1991). *Popular Culture in Modern France: A Study of Cultural Discourse*. London: Routledge.

Robin, William. (2021). *Industry: Bang on a Can and New Music in the Marketplace*. Oxford: Oxford University Press.

Robinson, Lillian. (1983). Treason Our Text: Feminist Challenges to the Literary Canon. *Tulsa Studies in Women's Literature*, 2, no. 1, 83–98.

Rodgers, Tara. (2010). *Pink Noises: Women on Electronic Music and Sound*. Durham, NC and London: Duke University Press.

Rodman, Gilbert. (1999). Histories. In B. Horner and T. Swiss, eds., *Key Terms in Popular Music and Culture*. Malden: Blackwell Publishers Inc., 35–45.

Rogers, Holly. (2013). *Sounding the Gallery: Video and the Rise of Art-Music*. Oxford: Oxford University Press.

Rogers, Holly. (2014a). *Music and Sound in Documentary Film*. London: Routledge.

Rogers, Holly. (2014b). The Musical Script: Norman McLaren, Animated Sound and Audiovisuality. *Animation Journal*, 22: 68–84.

Rogers, Holly. (2019). Audio-Visual Collisions: Moving Image Technology and the Laterna Magika Aesthetic in New Music Theatre. In R. Adlington, ed., *New Music Theatre in Europe: Transformations Between 1955–1975*. Abingdon: Routledge, 79–100.

Rogers, Holly. (2020). The Audiovisual Eerie: Transmediating Thresholds in the Work of David Lynch. In C. Vernallis, H. Rogers and L. Perrott, eds., *Transmedia Directors: Artistry, Industry and New Audiovisual Aesthetics*. New York: Bloomsbury Academic, 241–70.

Rogers, Holly and Jeremy Barham. (2017). *The Music and Sound of Experimental Film*. Oxford: Oxford University Press.

Ronson, M. (2014). How Sampling Transformed Music.[Online Video]. *TED Talks*. Available at www.ted.com/talks/mark_ronson_how_sampling_transformed_music?language=en, accessed 19 December 2019.

Roquer González, J. (2018). Sound Hyperreality in Popular Music: On the Influence of Audio Production in Our Sound Expectations. In E. Encabo, ed., *Sound in Motion: Cinema, Videogames, Technology and Audiences*. Newcastle upon Tyne: Cambridge Scholars Publishing, 16–39.

Rose, Tricia. (1994). *Black Noise: Rap Music and Black Culture in Contemporary America*. Middletown, CT: Wesleyan University Press.

Rosen, Charles. (1971). *The Classical Style*. London: Faber.

Rosen, Charles. (2000). The New Musicology. In Charles Rosen, *Critical Entertainments: Music Old and New*. Cambridge, MA: Harvard University Press, 255–72.

Rosen, Charles. (2012). Western Music: The View From California. In Charles Rosen, *Freedom and the Arts: Essays on Music and Literature*. Cambridge, MA and London: Harvard University Press, 210–39.

Rosenberg, Emily S. (2012). *A World Connecting: 1870–1945*. Cambridge, MA: Harvard University Press.

Ross, Alex. (2008). *The Rest Is Noise: Listening to the Twentieth Century*. London: Fourth Estate.

Ross, Kristin. (1995). *Fast Cars, Clean Bodies: Decolonization and the Reordering of French Culture*. Cambridge, MA: The MIT Press.

Rowland, David and Jonathan Cross. (1998). *The Cambridge Companion to the Piano*, 1st ed. Cambridge: Cambridge University Press.

Rupprecht, Philip. (2012). Among the Ruined Languages: Britten's Triadic Modernism, 1930–1940. In Felix Wörner, Ulrich Schneider and Philip Rupprecht, eds., *Tonality 1900–1950*. Stuttgart: Steiner Verlag, 223–45.

Russell, George. (1953). *The Lydian Chromatic Concept of Tonal Organization*. New York: Concept.

Russolo, Luigi. (1967/1913). *The Art of Noises*. Trans. Robert Filliou. New York: Something Else Press.

Rutherford-Johnson, Tim. (2017). *Music After the Fall: Modern Composition and Culture Since 1989*. Berkeley and Los Angeles: University of California Press.

Ryan, Jack. (2012). *Recollections. The Detroit Years: The Motown Sound by the People Who Made It*. Toronto: Glendower Media.

Ryan, John. (1985). *The Production of Culture in the Music Industry: The ASCAP–BMI Controversy*. Lanham, MD: University Press of America.

Said, Edward. (1978). *Orientalism: Western Conceptions of the Orient*. London: Penguin.

Salzman, Eric. (2001/1967). *Twentieth-Century Music: An Introduction*. London: Pearson.

Sanjek, Russell. (1996). *Pennies from Heaven: The American Popular Music Business in the Twentieth Century*. New York: Da Capo.

Sartre, Jean-Paul. (1969/1943). *Being and Nothingness*. Trans. Hazel Barnes. London: Routledge.

Saunders, Frances Stonor. (1999). *Who Paid the Piper? The CIA and the Cultural Cold War*. London: Granta.

Sawyers, June Skinner Sawyers. (2006). *Read the Beatles: Classic and New Writings on the Beatles, Their Legacy, and Why They Still Matter*. New York: Penguin Books.

Saylor, Eric. (2008). 'It's Not Lambkins Frisking at All': English Pastoral Music and the Great War. *The Musical Quarterly*, 91, nos. 1–2, 38–59.

Schaeffer, Pierre. (2017/1966). 'What Can Be Heard'. In Pierre Schaeffer, *Treatise on Musical Objects: An Essay Across Disciplines*, trans. Christine North and John Dack. Los Angeles and Berkeley: University of California Press, 73–9.

Schafer, R. Murray. (1977). *The Soundscape: Our Sonic Environment and the Tuning of the World*. Rochester, VT: Destiny Books.

Scherer, Frederic M. (2004). *Quarter Notes and Bank Notes: The Economics of Music Composition in the Eighteenth and Nineteenth Centuries*. Princeton, NJ: Princeton University Press.

Schleifer, Ronald. (2011). *Modernism and Popular Music*. Cambridge: Cambridge University Press.

Schloss, Joseph. (2004). *Making Beats: The Art of Sample-Based Hip Hop*. Middletown, CT: Wesleyan University Press.

Schnittke, Alfred. (2002/1971). Polystylistic Tendencies in Modern Music. In Alfred Schnittke, *A Schnittke Reader*, ed. Alexander Ivashkin. Bloomington: Indiana University Press, 87–90.

Schoenberg, Arnold. (1954). *Structural Functions of Harmony*. New York: W. W. Norton.

Schoenberg, Arnold. (1963). *Preliminary Exercises in Counterpoint*. London: Faber.

Schoenberg, Arnold. (1967). *Fundamentals of Musical Composition*. London: Faber.

Schoenberg, Arnold. (1983/1911). *Theory of Harmony/Harmonielehre*. Trans. Roy E. Carter. Berkeley and Los Angeles: University of California Press.

Schoenberg, Arnold. (1984/1941). Composition with Twelve Tones, no. 1. In Leonard Stein, ed., *Style and Idea*. London: Faber, 214–45.

Schumacher, Thomas. (1995). 'This Is a Sampling Sport': Digital Sampling, Rap Music and the Law in Cultural Production. In Simon Frith, ed., *Popular Music: Critical Concepts in Media and Cultural Studies: The Rock Era*, Vol. 2. London: Routledge, 169–90.

Schumacher, Thomas G. (2004). 'This Is a Sampling Sport': Digital Sampling, Rap Music and the Law in Cultural Production. In Murray Forman and Mark Anthony Neal, eds., *That's the Joint: The Hip-Hop Studies Reader*. New York and London: Routledge, 443–58.

Schur, Richard L. (2009). *Parodies of Ownership: Hip-Hop Aesthetics and Intellectual Property Law*. Ann Arbor: University of Michigan Press.

Schwartz, Elliott and Godfrey, Daniel. (1993). *Music Since 1945: Issues, Materials, and Literature*. New York City: Schirmer Books.

Schwichtenberg, Cathy. (1993). Madonna's Postmodern Feminism: Bringing the Margins to the Center. In Cathy Schwichtenberg, ed., *The Madonna Connection: Representational Politics, Subcultural Identities, and Cultural Theory*. New York: Routledge, 129–45.

Scott, Derek B. (2008). *Sounds of the Metropolis: The 19th-Century Popular Music Revolution in London, New York, Paris, and Vienna*. New York: Oxford University Press.

Scruton, Roger. (1999). *The Aesthetics of Music*. Oxford: Oxford University Press.

Shank, Barry. (1994). *Dissonant Identities: The Rock 'n' Roll Scene in Austin, Texas*. London: Wesleyan University Press.

Shepherd, John. (1991). *Music as a Social Text*. Cambridge: Polity Press.

Shepherd, John. (2003). Music and Social Categories. In Martin Clayton, Trevor Herbert and Richard Middleton, eds., *The Cultural Study of Music: A Critical Introduction*. Abingdon: Routledge, 69–79.

Shipton, Alyn. (2008). *A New History of Jazz*, 2nd ed. London: Bloomsbury.

Shreffler, Anne. C. (2013). Musikalische Kanonisierung und Dekanonisierung im 20. Jahrhundert. Trans. Fabian Kolb. In K. Pietschmann, and M. Wald-Fuhrmann, eds., *Der Kanon der Musik: Theorie und Geschichte: Ein Handbuch*. Munich: edition text + kritik. English original available at www.academia.edu/241625/Musical_Canonization_and_Decanonization_in_the_Twentieth_Century_original_English_version, accessed 2 March 2020.

Shuker, Roy. (2010). *Wax Trash and Vinyl Treasures: Record Collecting as a Social Practice*. Aldershot: Ashgate.

Simonelli, David. (2007). BBC Rock Music Programming on Radio and Television and the Progressive Rock Audience, 1967–1973. *Popular Music History* 2, no. 1, 95–112.

Simpson-Litke, Rebecca and Stover, Chris. (2019). Theorizing Fundamental Music/Dance Interactions in Salsa. *Music Theory Spectrum*, 41, no. 1, 74–103.

Sinclair, Andrew. (1995). *Arts and Cultures: The History of the 50 Years of the Arts Council of Great Britain*. London: Sinclair-Stevenson.

Skinner Sawyers, June. (2006) 'Must Be Born Again': Resurrecting the Anthology of American Folk Music. *Popular Music*, 25, no. 1, 57–75.

Slobin, Mark, ed. (2002). *American Klezmer: Its Roots and Offshoots*. Berkeley and Los Angeles: University of California Press.

Small, Christopher. (1998). *Musicking: The Meanings of Performing and Listening*. Middletown, CT: Wesleyan University Press.

Smith, Giles. (1995). *Lost in Music: A Pop Odyssey*. London: Picador.

Smith, Jeff. (1998). *The Sounds of Commerce: Marketing Popular Film Music*. New York: Columbia University Press.

Smith, Jeff. (2003). Banking on Film Music: Structural Interactions of the Film and Record Industries. In Kay Dickenson, ed., *Movie Music, The Film Reader*. London and New York: Routledge, 63–82.

Smith, Jeff. (2013). The Sound of Intensified Continuity. In John Richardson, Claudia Gorbman and Carol Vernallis, eds., *The Oxford Handbook of New Audiovisual Aesthetics*. Oxford: Oxford University Press, 331–56.

Smith, Patti. (2010). *Just Kids*. London: Bloomsbury.

Smith, Sophy. (2013). *Hip-Hop Turntablism, Creativity and Collaboration*. Farnham: Ashgate.

Smith, Suzanne E. (1999). *Dancing in the Street: Motown and the Cultural Politics of Detroit*. Cambridge, MA: Harvard University Press.

Smith, Terry, ed. (1998). *In Visible Touch: Modernism and Masculinity*. Chicago: Chicago University Press.

Smyth, Ethel. (1996/1933). Female Pipings in Eden. In C. Neuls-Bates, ed., *Women in Music: An Anthology of Source Readings from the Middle Ages to the Present*. Boston, MA: Northeast University Press, 278–96.

Snead, James A. (1984). Repetition as a Figure of Black Culture. In *Black Literature and Black Literary Theory*, ed. Henry Louis Gates, Jr. New York and London: Routledge, 59–79.

Solie, Ruth. (1980). The Living Work: Organicism and Musical Analysis. *19th-Century Music*, 4, no. 2. 147–56.

Sontag, Susan. (2009/1966). Against Interpretation. In Susan Sontag, *Against Interpretation and Other Essays*. London: Penguin Classics, 3–14.

Soocher, Stan. (1999). *They Fought the Law: Rock Music Goes to Court*. New York: Schirmer.

Southern, Eileen. (1971). *The Music of Black Americans: A History*. New York: W. W. Norton and Company.

Spellman, A. B. (1967). *Four Lives in the Bebop Business*. London: MacGibbon & Kee.

Spicer, Mark. (2004). (Ac)cumulative Form in Pop-Rock Music. *Twentieth-Century Music*, 1, no. 1, 29–64.

Spielmann, Yvonne. (2008). *Video: The Reflexive Medium*. Cambridge, MA: MIT Press.

Spivak, Gayatri Chakravorty. (1990). Practical Politics of the Open End. In Sarah Harasym, ed., *The Post-colonial Critic: Interviews, Strategies, Dialogues*. London: Routledge, 95–112.

Stanbridge, Alan. (2004). A Question of Standards: 'My Funny Valentine' and Musical Intertextuality. *Popular Music History*, 1, no. 1. 83–108.

Steinskog, Erik. (2018). *Afrofuturism and Black Sound Studies*. London: Palgrave Macmillan.

Sterne, Jonathan. (2003). *The Audible Past: Cultural Origins of Sound Reproduction*. Durham, NC: Duke University Press.

Sterne, Jonathan. (2007). Media or Instruments? Yes. *Offscreen* 11 (8–9), September. Available at https://offscreen.com/view/sterne_instruments, accessed 13 July 2019.

Sterne, Jonathan. (2012). *MP3: The Meaning of a Format*. Durham, NC and London: Duke University Press.

Stewart, Alexander. (2000). 'Funky Drummer': New Orleans, James Brown and the Rhythmic Transformation of American Popular Music. *Popular Music*. 19, no. 3. 293–318.

Stewart, James T. (1968). The Development of the Black Revolutionary Artist. In LeRoi Jones and Larry Neal, eds., *Black Fire: An Anthology of Afro-American Writing*. New York: Morrow Paperbacks, 3–10.

Stewart, Jesse. (2011). No Boundary Line to Art: 'Bebop' as Afro-Modernist Discourse. *American Music*, 29, no. 3, 332–52.

Stiglitz, Joseph. (2002). *Globalization and Its Discontents*. London: Allen Lane.

Stilwell, Robynn J. (2007). The Fantastical Gap between Diegetic and Nondiegetic. In Daniel Goldmark, Lawrence Kramer and Richard D. Leppert, eds., *Beyond the Soundtrack: Representing Music in Cinema*. Berkeley and Los Angeles: University of California Press, 108–204.

Stimeling, Travis D. (2011). 'Phases and Stages, Circles and Cycles': Willie Nelson and the Concept Album. *Popular Music* 30, no. 3, 389–408.

Stockhausen, Karlheinz. (1959). Musik und Graphik. In Wolfgang Steinecke, ed., *Darmstädter Beiträge zur neuen Musik 3*. Mainz: Schott.

Stockhausen, Karlheinz. (1963–2017). *Texte zur Musik*, 17 volumes. Cologne: DuMont Buchverlag.

Stockhausen, Karlheinz. (1989). *Towards a Cosmic Music*. Ed. Tim Nevill. Shaftesbury: Element Books.

Stokes, Martin. (1994). Introduction: Ethnicity, Identity and Music. In Martin Stokes, ed., *Ethnicity, Identity and Music: The Musical Construction of Place*. Oxford and New York: Berg, 1–28.

Stokes, Martin. (2007). On Musical Cosmopolitanism. The Macalester International Roundtable 2007. St. Paul, MN. Available at https://digitalcommons.macalester.edu/intlrdtable/3, accessed 9 April 2022.

Storch, Robert. (1982). *Popular Culture and Custom in Nineteenth-Century England*. London: Croom Helm.

Stras, Laurie. (2010). Voice of the Beehive: Vocal Technique at the Turn of the 1960s. In Laurie Stras, ed., *She's So Fine: Reflections on Whiteness, Femininity, Adolescence and Class in 1960s Music*. Aldershot: Ashgate Publishing, 33–55.

Stratton, Jeff. (2005). Dub from the Roots. *Miami New Times*. Available at www .miaminewtimes.com/music/dub-from-the-roots-6341622, accessed 17 December 2019.

Straus, Joseph N. (1995). *The Music of Ruth Crawford Seeger*. Cambridge: Cambridge University Press.

Street, John. (1993). Musicologists, Sociologists and Madonna. *Innovation*, 6, no. 3, 277–89.

Street, John. (2011). *Music and Politics*. Cambridge: Polity Press.

Strickland, Edward. (1993). *Minimalism: Origins*. Bloomington: Indiana University Press.

Strunk, Steven. (1988). Harmony. In Barry Kernfeld, *The New Grove Dictionary of Jazz*. London: Macmillan, 485–96.

Sturrock, John. (2003). *Structuralism*, 2nd ed. Malden, MA: Blackwell.

Subotnik, Rose Rosengard. (1996). Toward a Deconstruction of Structural Listening: A Critique of Schoenberg, Adorno, and Stravinsky. In Rose Rosengard Subotnik, ed., *Deconstructive Variations: Music and Reason in Western Society*. Minneapolis: University of Minnesota Press, 148–76.

Sutcliffe, Anthony. (1984). Introduction: Urbanization, Planning and the Giant City. In Anthony Sutcliffe, ed., Metropolis 1890–1940. London: Mansell, 1–18.

Swafford, J. (1992). *The Vintage Guide to Classical Music*. London: Vintage Books.

Tagg, Philip. (1991). *Fernando the Flute: Analysis of Musical Meaning in an ABBA Mega-Hit*. Liverpool: University of Liverpool.

Tagg, Philip. (2000). 'The Work': An Evaluative Charge. In Michael Talbot, ed., *The Musical Work: Reality or Invention?* Liverpool: Liverpool University Press, 153–67.

Tagg, Philip. (1982). Analysing Popular Music: Theory, Method and Practice. *Popular Music*, 2, 37–67.

Talbot, Michael, ed. (2000). *The Musical Work: Reality or Invention?* Liverpool: Liverpool University Press.

Taruskin, Richard. (1980). Russian Folk Melodies in *The Rite of Spring*. *Journal of the American Musicological Society*, 33, no.3, 501–43.

Taruskin, Richard. (1995). *Text and Act: Essays on Music and Performance*. New York: Oxford University Press.

Taruskin, Richard. (1997). *Defining Russia Musically: Historical and Hermeneutical Essays*. Princeton, NJ: Princeton University Press.

Taruskin, Richard. (2001). Nationalism. *Grove Music Online*. https://doi.org/10 .1093/gmo/9781561592630.article.50846, accessed 22 March 2022.

Taruskin, Richard. (2005). *The Oxford History of Western Music, Volume 3: The Nineteenth Century*. New York and Oxford: Oxford University Press, 665–6.

Taruskin, Richard. (2007). The Musical Mystique: Defending Classical Music Against Its Devotees. In Richard Taruskin, *The Danger of Music, and Other Anti-Utopian Essays*. Berkeley and Los Angeles: University of California Press, 330–53.

Taruskin, Richard. (2010a). *Music in the Early Twentieth Century*. New York and Oxford: Oxford University Press.

Taruskin, Richard. (2010b). *Music in the Late Twentieth Century*. New York and Oxford: Oxford University Press.

Taylor, Leila. (2019). *Darkly: Blackness and America's Gothic Soul*. London: Repeater.

Taylor, Timothy D. (2007). *Beyond Exoticism: Western Music and the World*. Durham, NC: Duke University Press.

Taylor-Jay, Claire. (2009). 'I Am Blessed With Fruit': Masculinity, Androgyny and Creativity in Early Twentieth-Century German Music. In Ian Biddle and Kirsten Gibson, eds., *Masculinity and Western Musical Practice*. Farnham: Ashgate, 183–208.

Tenney, James. (1964). *META (+) HODOS: A Phenomenology of Twentieth-Century Musical Materials and an Approach to the Study of Form*. New Orleans: Tulane University Press.

Tetzlaff, David. (1993). Metatextual Girl: → Patriarchy → Postmodernism → Power → Money → Madonna. In Cathy Schwichtenberg, ed., *The Madonna Connection: Representational Politics, Subcultural Identities, and Cultural Theory*. New York: Routledge, 239–64.

Théberge, Paul. (1989). The 'Sound' of Music: Technological Rationalization and the Production of Popular Music. *New Formations*, 8, 99–111.

Théberge, Paul. (1997). *Any Sound You Can Imagine: Making Music/Consuming Technology (Music Culture)*. Hanover, NH: Wesleyan University Press.

Théberge, Paul. (2004). The Network Studio: Historical and Technological Paths to a New Ideal in Music Making. *Social Studies of Science*, 34, no.5, 759–81.

Thomas, Philip. (2007). Determining the Indeterminate. *Contemporary Music Review* 26, no. 2, 129–40.

Thompson, Emily. (2002). *The Soundscape of Modernity: Architectural Acoustics and the. Culture of Listening in America, 1900–1933*. Cambridge, MA: MIT Press.

Thompson, Hunter S. (1998). *Fear and Loathing in Las Vegas*. New York: Vintage Books.

Thorau, Christian and Hansjakob Ziemer. (2019). The Art of Listening and Its Histories: An Introduction. In Christian Thorau and Hansjakob Ziemer, eds., *The Oxford Handbook of Music Listening in the 19th and 20th Centuries*. Oxford: Oxford University Press, 1–36.

Thornton, Sarah. (1990). Strategies for Reconstructing the Popular Past. *Popular Music*, 9, no. 1, 87–95.

Thornton, Sarah. (1996). *Club Cultures: Music, Media and Subcultural Capital*. Middletown, CT: Wesleyan University Press.

Tick, Judith. (1997). *Ruth Crawford Seeger: A Composer's Search for American Music*. New York and Oxford: Oxford University Press.

Tingen, Paul. (2001). *Miles Beyond: The Electric Explorations of Miles Davis, 1967–1991*. New York: Billboard Books.

Tomlinson, Gary. (1992). Cultural Dialogics and Jazz: A White Historian Signifies. In K. Bergeron and P. Bohlman, eds., *Disciplining Music: Musicology and Its Canons*. Chicago and London: University of Chicago Press, 64–94.

Tomlinson, Gary. (1984). The Web of Culture: A Context for Musicology. *19th-Century Music*, 7, no. 3, 350–62.

Tomlinson, Gary. (2003). Musicology, Anthropology, History. In Martin Clayton, Trevor Herbert, and Richard Middleton, eds., *The Cultural Study of Music: A critical Introduction*. Abingdon: Routledge, 31–44.

Tompkins, Dave. (2010). *How to Wreck a Nice Beach: The Vocoder from World War II to Hip-Hop, the Machine Speaks*. Chicago: Stop Smiling Media.

Toop, David. (1995). *Ocean of Sound: Ambient Sound and Radical Listening in the Age of Communication*. London: Serpent's Tail.

Toop, David. (2011). *Sinister Resonance: The Mediumship of the Listener*. London: Bloomsbury.

Toop, David. (1984a). Electro: The Beatbox Bites Back. *The Face* 49 (May), 45–9.

Toop, David. (1984b). *Rap Attack*. London: Pluto Press.

Toynbee, Jason. (2000). *Making Popular Music: Musicians, Creativity and Institutions*. London: Hodder Arnold.

Toynbee, Jason. (2002). Mainstreaming: From Hegemonic Centre to Global Networks. In David Hesmondhalgh and Keith Negus, eds., *Popular Music Studies*. London: Hodder Arnold, 149–63.

Trumpener, Katie. (2000). Béla Bartók and the Rise of Comparative Ethnomusicology: Nationalism, Race Purity, and the Legacy of the Austro-Hungarian Empire. In Ronald M. Radano and Philip V. Bohlman, eds., *Music and the Racial Imagination*. University of Chicago Press, 403–34.

Tucker, Sherrie. (2002). Big Ears: Listening for Gender in Jazz. *Current Musicology*, nos. 71–3, 375–408.

Tucker, Sherrie. (2004). A Feminist Perspective on New Orleans Jazzwomen. A New Orleans Jazz National Historical Park Research Study. Available at www .nps.gov/jazz/learn/historyculture/.upload/New_Orleans_Jazzwomen_RS-2.pdf, accessed 9 April 2022.

Upchurch, Anna Rosser. (2016). *The Origins of the Arts Council Movement: Philanthropy and Policy*. London: Palgrave.

Urry, John. (2007). *Mobilities*. Cambridge: Polity Press.

Uy, Michael Sy. (2020). *Ask the Experts: How Ford, Rockefeller, and the NEA Changed American Music*. Oxford: Oxford University Press.

Vaidhyanathan, Siva. (2001). *Copyrights and Copywrongs: The Rise of Intellectual Property and How It Threatens Creativity*. New York: New York University Press.

van Emmerik, Paul. (2002). An Imaginary Grid: Rhythmic Structure in Cage's Music Up to Circa 1950. In David Patterson, ed., *John Cage: Music, Philosophy, and Intention, 1933–1950*. New York: Routledge, 217–37.

Varèse, Edgard. (1971). The Liberation of Sound. In Benjamin Boretz and Edward T. Cone, eds., *Perspectives on American Composers*. New York: Norton, 32.

Vasulka, Steina. Violin Power, the Performance 1992 to Present: An Interactive Performance by Steina. *Vasulka.org.* Available at www.vasulka.org/Steina/Steina_ViolinPower/ViolinPower.html, accessed 20 December 2018.

Veal, Michael. (2007). *Dub: Soundscapes and Shattered Songs in Jamaican Reggae.* Middletown, CT: Wesleyan University Press.

Vernallis, Carol. (1998). The Aesthetics of Music Video: An Analysis of Madonna's 'Cherish'. *Popular Music,* 17, no. 2, 153–85.

Vernallis, Carol. (2004). *Experiencing Music Video: Aesthetics and Cultural Context.* New York: Columbia University Press.

Vernallis, Carol. (2013). *Unruly Media: YouTube, Music Video, and the New Digital Cinema.* Oxford: Oxford University Press.

Vernallis, Carol, Holly Rogers and Lisa Perrott, eds. (2020). *Transmedia Directors: Artistry, Industry and New Audiovisual Aesthetics.* New York: Bloomsbury.

Volkov, Solomon. (1979). *Testimony: The Memoirs of Dmitri Shostakovich.* Trans. Antonina W. Bouis. New York: Harper & Row.

Volmar, Axel. (2019). Experiencing High Fidelity: Sound Reproduction and the Politics of Music Listening in the Twentieth Century. In Christian Thorau and Hansjakob Ziemer, eds., *The Oxford Handbook of Music Listening in the 19th and 20th Centuries.* Oxford: Oxford University Press, 395–420.

Von Eschen, Peggy. (2004). *Satchmo Blows Up the World: Jazz Ambassadors Play the Cold War.* Cambridge, MA: Harvard University Press.

Wagner, Richard. (2014/1870). Beethoven. In R. Allen, trans., *Richard Wagner's Beethoven (1870): A New Translation.* Woodbridge: Boydell and Brewer. Available at www.jstor.org/stable/10.7722/j.ctt6wp854, accessed 19 December 2019.

Waksman, Steve. (1999a). Black Sound, Black Body: Jimi Hendrix, the Electric Guitar, and the Meanings of Blackness. *Popular Music & Society,* 23, no. 1, 75–113.

Waksman, Steve. (1999b). *Instruments of Desire: The Electric Guitar and the Shaping of Musical Experience.* Cambridge, MA: Harvard University Press, 12.

Waksman, Steve. (2003). Reading the Instrument: An Introduction. *Popular Music and Society,* 26, no. 3, 251–61.

Waksman, Steve. (2010). Imagining an Interdisciplinary Canon. *Journal of Popular Music Studies,* 22, no. 1, 68–73.

Walker, Robert. (1992). Eruptions: Heavy Metal Appropriations of Classical Virtuosity. *Popular Music,* 11, no. 3, 263–308.

Walser, Robert. (1993). *Running With the Devil: Power, Gender, and Madness in Heavy Metal.* Middletown, CT: Wesleyan University Press.

Walser, Robert. (2003). Popular Music Analysis: Ten Apothegms And Four Instances. In Allan Moore, ed., *Analyzing Popular Music.* Cambridge: Cambridge University Press, 16–38.

Walsh, Stephen. (2006). *Stravinsky: The Second Exile: France and America, 1934–1971.* Berkeley and Los Angeles: University of California Press.

Ward, Brian. (1998). *Just My Soul Responding: Rhythm and Blues, Black Consciousness and Race Relations.* London: University College London Press.

Ward-Griffin, D. (2018). As Seen on TV: Putting the NBC Opera on Stage. *Journal of the American Musicological Society*, 71, no. 3, 595–654.

Warwick, Jacqueline. (2007). *Girl Groups, Girl Culture: Popular Music and Identity in the 1960s.* New York: Routledge.

Waters, Keith. (2016). Chick Corea and Postbop Harmony. *Music Theory Spectrum*, 38, no. 1, 37–57.

Watkins, Holly. (2008). Schoenberg's Interior Designs. *Journal of the American Musicological Society*, 61, no. 1, 123–206.

Watson, Allan. (2015). *Cultural Production in and Beyond the Recording Studio.* New York: Routledge.

Watson, Mary R. and N. Anand. (2006). Award Ceremony as an Arbiter of Commerce and Canon in the Popular Music Industry. *Popular Music*, 25, no. 1, 41–56.

Waxer, Lise. (2002). Llegó La Salsa. In Lise Waxer, ed., *Situating Salsa: Global Markets and Local Meanings in Latin Popular Music.* New York and London: Routledge, 219–46.

Weber, William. (1994). The Intellectual Origins of Musical Canon in Eighteenth-Century England. *Journal of the American Musicological Society*, 47, no. 3, 488–520.

Weberman, A. J. (1969). *Dylanology.* Hong Kong: Whitepress Corp.

Webern, Anton. (1963). The Path to Composition with Twelve Tones. *The Path to the New Music.* Trans. Leo Black. Bryn Mawr: Theodor Presser.

Wehileye, Alexander G. (2002). 'Feenin': Posthuman Voices in Contemporary Black Popular Music. *Social Text*, 20, no. 2. 21–47.

Weisbard, Eric. (2005). These Magic Moments. *Popular Music*, 24, no. 3, 339–56.

Wellburn [sic], Ron. (1971). The Black Aesthetic Imperative. In Addison Gayle, ed., *The Black Aesthetic.* Garden City, NY: Doubleday, 132–49.

Wellens, Ian. (2002). *Music on the Frontline: Nicolas Nabokov's Struggle against Communism and Middlebrow Culture.* Aldershot: Ashgate.

West, Cornell. (1993/1989). Black Culture and Postmodernism. In Joseph Natoli and Linda Hutcheon, eds., *A Postmodern Reader.* Albany: State University of New York Press, 390–7.

White, Harry. (1998). *The Keeper's Recital: Music and Cultural History in Ireland.* Cork: Cork University Press.

White, Hayden. (1978). *Tropics of Discourse: Essays in Cultural Criticism.* Baltimore, MD and London: The Johns Hopkins University Press.

Whiteley, Sheila. (2000). *Women and Popular Music: Sexuality, Identity and Subjectivity.* London: Routledge.

Whiting, Steven Moore. (1999). *Satie the Bohemian: From Cabaret to Concert Hall.* Oxford: Oxford University Press.

Whitmore, Aleysia. (2016). The Art of Representing the Other: Industry Personnel in the World Music Industry. *Ethnomusicology*, 60, no. 2, 329–55.

Whittall, Arnold. (1975). Tonality and the Whole-Tone Scale in the Music of Debussy. *Music Review*, 36, 261–71.

Whittall, Arnold. (1999). *Musical Composition in the Twentieth Century*. Oxford: Oxford University Press.

Whittall, Arnold. (2008). *Serialism*. Cambridge: Cambridge University Press.

Whittington, William. (2014). Lost in Sensation: Re-Evaluating the Role of Cinematic Sound in the Digital Age. In Amy Herzog, John Richardson and Carol Vernallis, eds., *The Oxford Handbook of Music and Sound in Digital Media*. New York: Oxford University Press, 61–76.

Wierzbicki, James. (2016). Sound Effects/Sound Affects: 'Meaningful' Noise in the Cinema. In Liz Greene and Danijela Kulezic-Wilson, eds., *The Palgrave Handbook of Sound Design and Music in Screen Media: Integrated Soundtracks*. London: Palgrave, 153–68.

Willemsen, Steven and Miklós Kiss. (2015). Unsettling Melodies: A Cognitive Approach to Incongruent Film Music. In Á. Pethő, ed., *The Cinema of Sensations*. Cambridge: Cambridge Scholars Publishing, 103–20.

Williams, Alan. (2006). Phantom Power: Recording Studio History, Practice and Myth. (PhD dissertation, Brown University)

Williams, Alastair. (2002). Cage and Postmodernism. In David Nicholls, ed., *The Cambridge Companion to John Cage*. Cambridge: Cambridge University Press, 227–41.

Williams, Alastair. (2013). *Music in Germany since 1968*. Cambridge: Cambridge University Press.

Williams, Paul. (1990). *Bob Dylan: Performing Artist Volume 1*. San Francisco: Underwood-Miller.

Williams, Paul. (1994). *Bob Dylan: Performing Artist Volume 2*. London: Omnibus.

Williams, Paul. (2004). *Bob Dylan: Performing Artist 1986–1990 & Beyond: Mind Out of Time*. London: Omnibus.

Williamson, Clive. (1990). Bob Moog – SoundArchives. *SoundArchives*. Available at: www.soundarchives.co.uk/.bob-moog/, accessed 27 July 2019.

Williamson, John and Martin Cloonan. (2007). Rethinking the Music Industry. *Popular Music*, 26, no. 2, 305–22.

Wilmer, Valerie. (1999). *As Serious As Your Life: John Coltrane and Beyond*, 2nd ed. London: Serpent's Tail.

Wilson, Carl. (2014). *Let's Talk About Love*. Continuum: London.

Wilson, Elizabeth. (2006). *Shostakovich: A Life Remembered*, 2nd ed. London: Faber.

Winters, Ben. (2010). The Non-Diegetic Fallacy: Film, Music, and Narrative Space. *Music and Letters*, 91, no. 2, 224–44.

Wolfe, Cary. (2009). *What Is Posthumanism?* Minneapolis: University of Minnesota Press.

Wolfe, Paula. (2012). A Studio of One's Own: Music Production, Technology and Gender. Journal on the Art of Record Production, 7. Available at: www .arpjournal.com/asarpwp/a-studio-of-one's-own-music-production-technology-and-gender/, accessed 17 December 2019.

Wolff, Janet. (1981). *The Social Production of Art*. New York: St. Martin's Press.

Wolfreys, Julian. (1998). *Deconstruction • Derrida*. New York: St. Martin's Press.

Wörner, Felix, Ullrich Schneider and Philip Rupprecht, eds. (2012). *Tonality 1900–50*. Stuttgart: Frank Steiner Verlag.

Wörner, Felix, Ullrich Schneider and Philip Rupprecht, eds. (2017). *Tonality since 1950*. Stuttgart: Frank Steiner Verlag.

Wyn Jones, Carys. (2008). *The Rock Canon: Canonical Values in the Reception of Rock Albums*. Aldershot: Ashgate.

Yang, Mina. (2007). East Meets West in the Concert Hall: Asians and Classical Music in the Century of Imperialism, Post-Colonialism, and Multiculturalism. *Asian Music* 38, no. 1 (Winter/Spring), 1–30.

Yllö, Kersti and Michele Louise Bograd. (1988). *Feminist Perspectives on Wife Abuse*. Newbury Park, CA: SAGE.

Young, Miriama. (2019). Proximity/Infinity: The Mediated Voice in Mobile Music. In Nina Sun Eidsheim and Katherine Meizel, ed., *The Oxford Handbook of Voice Studies*. Oxford: Oxford University Press, 403–18.

Zagorski-Thomas, Simon. (2014). *The Musicology of Record Production*. Cambridge: Cambridge University Press.

Zak III, Albin. (2012). No-Fi: Crafting a Language of Recorded Music in 1950s Pop. In Simon Frith and Simon Zagorski-Thomas, eds., *The Art of Record Production: An Introductory Reader for a New Academic Field*, 2nd ed. London: Routledge, 43–56.

Zimmermann, Bernd Alois. (2014/1960). Lenz and Aspects of New Opera. *The Opera Quarterly*, 30, no. 1, 135–9.

Zorn, John, ed. (2000–2012). *Arcana*, 6 vols. New York: Granary Books.

Zuckerman, Bruce, Josh Kun and Lisa Ansell, eds. (2011). *The Song Is Not the Same: Jews and American Popular* Music. West Lafayette, IN: Purdue University Press.

Index

Massy, Sylvia
  Undertow (Tool), 247
Master P, 31
Masters, William, 19
Matmos
  A Chance to Cut is a Chance to Cure, 216
Matsumoto, Naomi, 376
Matthias Hauser, Josef, 60
Maus, Fred, 329, 330, 331
Mayakovsky, 93
Mayer, Emilie, 121
Maytals, Toots and the, 236
  'Pressure Drop', 44
McCartney, Paul, 149, 150, 238
McClary, Susan, 60, 75, 76, 89, 97, 177, 178,
    199, 200, 225, 326, 330, 331
  Feminine Endings, 199
McDonald, Matthew, 156
McGuire, William
  Show Girl (musical), 186
McLaren, Norman
  synthetic sound techniques, 302
McLean, Jackie, 389
McLuhan, Marshall, 96
McMillin, Scott, 183
McMurray, Lillian, 248
McRobbie, Angela, 246, 368
media theory, 96
Meek, Joe, 217, 232
Mehring, Walter, 382
Melvin, Sheila, 378
Mendelssohn, Fanny, 124
Mendelssohn, Felix, 105, 124
Mercury, Freddie, 334
Merzbow, 392, 394, 395
  Venereology, 394
Messiaen, Olivier, 63, 64, 74, 111, 168, 172, 183,
    190, 191, 209
  additive rhythm, 168–9
  harmonic practice, 188, 189
  'Mode de valeurs et d'intensités', 63
  ondes martenot, 216
  'Prière du Christ montant vers son Père', 190
  Quatuor pour la fin du temps, 169
  Turangalila-Symphonie, 216
metal, 110
Metallica (group), 269
Meters, the (group), 31
Metzer, David, 89, 91
Meyer, Leonard B., 199, 200, 201
Meyer-Eppler, Werner, 75
Michael, George, 334
Middleton, Richard, 87, 212, 221, 222

migration. *See* globalisation
Milhaud, Darius, 55, 57, 85
  La Création du monde, 55
Miller, Glenn and His Orchestra
  'Danny Boy', 164
Mills Brothers, the
  'Sweet Adeline', 180
Mills College, 1
Milton Keynes, 36
Mingus, Charles
  Black Saint and the Sinner Lady, 148
minimalism, 2, 155, 170, 177, 192
  cultural practice, as, 172
  compositional techniques, 90, 171–2
  female sexuality, 328
  found sounds, 171
  magnetic tape, 171
  phenomenology, 172
  rhythm, repetition, 170–3
  subjective experience, 90, 173
Minogue, Kylie, 312
Mississippi Delta, 31, 118
Mitchell, Joni
  'Harry's House / Centerpiece', 93
  'The Jungle Line', 93
  Ladies of the Canyon, 150
Mitchell, Tony, 41
Mitterand, François, 286
mod culture, 368
modernism, 46–76
  automatic writing, 55
  avant-gardes, 52–4
  cult of progress, the, 48, 79
  Futurism, 68
  gender, 56
  high/low art, 47
  institutionalisation of, 74–6
  modern architecture, 75
  Paris, 49
  psychoanalysis, influences on music, 55–6
  serial and twelve-tone techniques, 60–7, 168
  subjectivity, 54–6
  Vienna, 49
modernity, 46
  Fordism, 363
Mojo (magazine), 116
Monde Bruits, 395
Monk, Meredith, 123, 220
  post-minimalism, 173
  'Tablet', 173
Monk, Thelonious, 70, 74, 212
  'Evidence', 74
Monkees, the